CUBAN STUDIES 52

CUBAN STUDIES 52

ALEJANDRO DE LA FUENTE, *Editor*
LILLIAN GUERRA, *Book Review Editor*
LAUREN KREBS, *Managing Editor*

UNIVERSITY OF PITTSBURGH PRESS

CUBAN STUDIES

Alejandro de la Fuente, Editor
Lauren Krebs, Managing Editor

Manuscripts in English and Spanish may be submitted to Alejandro de la Fuente, Editor, by email at cubanstudies@fas.harvard.edu. Maximum length is 10,000 words, including notes and illustrations. Please include an abstract of the article both in English and Spanish of no more than 200 words. Also include a short biographical paragraph of no more than 3 sentences. We prefer Chicago style (17th edition), but MLA style is also acceptable. Cuban Studies takes no responsibility for views or information presented in signed articles. For additional editorial inquiries, contact us at the email address above.
Review copies of books should be sent to: Lillian Guerra, University of Florida, Department of History, 025 Keene-Flint Hall, Gainesville, FL, 32611-7320, USA. For additional inquiries about book reviews, send an email to lillian.guerra@ufl.edu.

Orders for volumes 16–51 of Cuban Studies and standing orders for future volumes should be sent to the University of Pittsburgh Press, Chicago Distribution Center, 11030 South Langley, Chicago, IL, 60628-3893, USA; telephone 800-621-2736; fax 800-621-8476.

Back issues of volumes 1–15 of Cuban Studies, when available, may be obtained from the Center for Latin American Studies, University Center for International Studies, 230 South Bouquet Street, 4200 Wesley W. Posvar Hall, Pittsburgh, PA, 15260.

Published by the University of Pittsburgh Press, Pittsburgh, PA, 15260
Copyright © 2022, University of Pittsburgh Press
All rights reserved
Manufactured in the United States of America
Printed on acid-free paper

Library of Congress Card Number
ISBN 13: 978-0-8229-4746-2
ISBN 10: 0-8229-4746-3
US ISSN 0361-4441
10 9 8 7 6 5 4 3 2 1

Contents

vi : *Contents*

Nota del editor

Alejandro de la Fuente

Seguramente no es casualidad que este número de *Cuban Studies* incluya dos dosieres destinados a estudios urbanos. Los temas de urbanización, conservación, capacidad constructiva, sostenibilidad y desarrollo urbano adquieren visibilidad e importancia en el campo de los estudios cubanos, en la misma medida en que las ciudades de la isla experimentan un profundo e inexorable deterioro material, agudizando viejos problemas (como el déficit habitacional) y generando nuevos desafíos en áreas como la sanidad y seguridad ciudadanas. La muerte, a inicios del 2020, de tres niñas que transitaban por el barrio Jesús María, en la Habana Vieja, producto del derrumbe del balcón de un edificio en demolición, volvió a poner estos temas sobre la mesa con singular intensidad y urgencia. El deterioro urbano de la Habana y otras ciudades cubanas es conocido: las cifras oficiales aseguran que casi un 40 por ciento de unidades habitacionales se encuentra "entre regular y mal estado técnico" y que el déficit habitacional alcanza casi el millón de unidades, un cuarto del fondo habitacional existente, que asciende a unos cuatro millones.[1] El escritor Antonio José Ponte capturó este proceso con singular maestría en su cuento "Un arte de hacer ruinas" (2000), donde una Habana superpoblada y derruida se transforma en "Tuguria, la ciudad hundida, donde todo se conserva como en la memoria," que sirvió de inspiración al documental alemán Arte nuevo de hacer ruinas (2006), de Florian Borchmeyer y Matthias Hentschler.

La Tuguria de Ponte sigue más o menos en pie, desafiando la gravedad y el mal gobierno, pero ha evolucionado durante las últimas décadas. El "mal estado técnico" de las viviendas existentes, el déficit habitacional y los derrumbes constantes coexisten en tensión con los nuevos hoteles de lujo que se construyen a lo largo de la isla para el mercado turístico. Hay una Habana histórica que se desmorona y otra que se levanta —de la mano de inversionistas extranjeros— de los conglomerados empresariales militares que ahora controlan la economía del país y de trabajadores importados bajo condiciones opacas y de dudosa legalidad. Como afirman los coordinadores del dosier "La Habana en el siglo XXI," las promesas socialistas del programa de vivienda popular cohabitan con procesos de gentrificación capitalista apuntalados por una incipiente liberalización del mercado inmobiliario. Estos palimpsestos urbanos, en los que lo nuevo intenta borrar, con éxito limitado, trazos anteriores, son típicos de las ciudades coloniales iberoamericanas, como demuestran los trabajos incluidos en otro dosier del número "Havana: New Research and Critical Reflections on an Urban Palimpsest after Five Centuries," que rastrea la historia de la ciudad en sus primeros quinientos años.

La relación entre ruinas, derrumbes, palimpsestos y turismo es complicada. Son los hoteles de lujo los que hacen de las ruinas una atracción turística, destacando de paso trazos de la antigua ciudad puerto, de la otrora Llave del Nuevo Mundo, de la ciudad que fue. La vieja Habana, con sus cabildos de nación, sus fortalezas imponentes, sus modestas iglesias. Una Habana de fosos formidables y de retablos mediocres. La revolución añadió sabores y expectativas. La modalidad de "viaje revolucionario" permitió a intelectuales y activistas de todo el mundo acercarse a la Cuba de los sesenta para vislumbrar futuros de igualdad y justicia. Estas miradas, objeto del otro dosier del número, "Visiones, entusiasmos y disidencias de la Revolución cubana en la escena intelectual latinoamericana de los años sesenta," estaban centradas en el porvenir, en futuros en construcción. Los visitantes del parque jurásico cubano contemporáneo llegan a ver lo que queda, antes de que desaparezca. *Before it is too late*, como dicen muchos visitantes norteamericanos, que viajan a Cuba en busca de absolución por culpas imperiales, propias y ajenas. Los viajeros revolucionarios de los sesenta venían a Cuba para ver el futuro. Los de hoy visitan las ruinas que produjo ese proyecto.

Estos viajes son, esencialmente, viajes hacia adentro: actos de introspección. Los habitantes del parque y sus ruinas no importan. Pero esas cubanas y cubanos están ahí, intentando hacer país, más allá de los escombros y la basura. Los residentes de San Isidro lo han dicho claramente. Ese barrio habanero no aparecía en los itinerarios turísticos de Tuguria, pero ahora mismo está al centro de nuevos imaginarios y posibilidades. "Donde todo se conserva como en la memoria."

NOTA

1. Las cifras son mencionadas por Vivian Bustamante Molina, "La política de la vivienda proyecta solución integral a problema sensible y priorizado por el gobierno," *Granma*, 19 de diciembre de 2018.

CUBAN STUDIES 51

DOSSIER: HAVANA: NEW RESEARCH AND CRITICAL REFLECTIONS ON AN URBAN PALIMPSEST AFTER FIVE CENTURIES

RAY HERNÁNDEZ-DURÁN

Prolegomenon: Havana, Body and Soul: From Urban Theory to Social Practice, and Back Again

ABSTRACT

Latin American cities can be seen as peculiar expressions of European forms of urbanism, given such factors as the colonial context of their foundation and their subsequent instrumentalization in the formation and maintenance of empire, the usual (often violent) repurposing of preexisting indigenous settlement sites, the diverse range of populations that moved through those spaces and adapted the built environment to their expectations and needs, and the various historical and political developments of the Spanish colonial world. Any serious examination of the Latin American city must thus consider the foundation of the urban environment and its reinscription by the heteroglot inhabitants that brought such spaces to life. What we find today are cities constituted both materially and symbolically by sedimented layers of time, memories, and stories that not only embody a history or social biography but also reflect and shape human movement and human consciousness. Thinking of the city in such terms, I ask, How can we approach the study of the Spanish colonial city, generally, and of Havana, specifically, in such a way that reveals these complex, protean dynamics and presents a more nuanced understanding of the material and social life of the American built environment?

RESUMEN

Las ciudades latinoamericanas pueden considerarse variaciones peculiares de formas urbanísticas europeas, dados factores como el contexto colonial de su fundación y su instrumentalización subsecuente en la formación y mantenimiento del Imperio, la usual —y en ocasiones violenta— adaptación de asentamientos indígenas preexistentes, el rango diverso de los pueblos quienes pasaron por esos espacios y adaptaron el ambiente construido de acuerdo a sus expectativas y necesidades, y los acontecimientos históricos y políticos únicos al mundo colonial español. Cualquiera examinación de la ciudad latinoamericana, consecuentemente, debe tomar en cuenta la fundación del ambiente urbano y su reinscripción por los habitantes heteroglotos quienes animaron esos espacios. Lo que vemos hoy son ciudades constituidas, físicamente y simbólicamente, por capas temporales de memoria y de narraciones sedimentadas que no solo encarnan una historia o biografía social pero que igual reflejan y dirigen el movimiento humano y dan forma a una conciencia humana. Aproximando la ciudad en tales términos, pregunto, ¿cómo podremos conformar un estudio de la urbe colonial española, generalmente, y

3

el de la Habana, específicamente, en tal manera que revele estas dinámicas complejas y proteicas, y que presente un acercamiento más profundo y matizado de la vida material y social del ambiente americano construido?

In this sense, nothing said of Aglaura is true, and yet these accounts create a solid and compact image of a city, whereas the haphazard opinions which might be inferred from living there have less substance. This is the result: the city that they speak of has much of what is needed to exist, whereas the city that exists on its site, exists less.
—Italo Calvino, *Invisible Cities*

Cities are dynamic organic entities, at once physical as well as ideational, and always in motion. Latin American cities are peculiar expressions of European forms of urbanism, given such factors as the colonial context of their foundation and their subsequent instrumentalization in the formation and maintenance of empire, the usual (often violent) repurposing of preexisting indigenous settlement sites, the diverse range of populations that moved through those city spaces and adapted the built environment to their expectations and needs, and the various historical and political developments of the Spanish colonial world that had an undeniable impact on the form and life of cities throughout the early modern Americas. Any serious examination of the Latin American city must thus consider the reshaping of the colonial urban environment both materially and symbolically and its reinscription by the heteroglot inhabitants that brought such spaces to life, from imperial officials and social elites to commoners and slaves. The accumulation and negotiated blending of spatial and built, including performative, idioms across time yielded urban environments that continue to bear the marks of the social and political peculiarities of the Spanish colonial matrixes that gave birth to them. With these ideas in mind, I ask, how can we approach the study of the Spanish colonial city in such a way that reveals these complex, protean dynamics and presents a more nuanced understanding of the material and social life of those built environments?

As has been noted by scholars of urbanism in the Spanish Americas, such as Richard Kagan, George Kubler, and Martín Soria, the idea of the city comprises two elements—*urbs*, the physical space itself, including architectural construction, avenues, plazas, and monuments, and *civitas*, the human element inhabiting, employing, and/or moving through the built environment—that can be traced back to ancient classical sources and its development to various thinkers from the early modern period through the twentieth century, including Vitruvius, Alberti, Palladio, Ruskin, and Viollet-le-Duc.[1] More recent theoretical considerations of space, such as those proposed by Henri Lefebvre in the past century, can be seen as critically engaging, rearticulating, or refining these older paradigms. For instance, Lefebvre distinguishes "representations of space" and "representational" or "perceived space." On the one hand, landscape painting, urban views, and cartography, that is, images that operate within a larger network of conventional signs, and on the other, architecture and other planned spaces that frame spatiotemporal movement and phenomenologically structure human experience.[2] From this perspective, colonial urban spaces can be seen as encoded with a network of signs whose significance was externalized by a range of public performances that functioned as a tool for communication and a catalyst for subject formation.[3] The postulate that the city can be understood as a text or index, as a physical-spatial translation of ideas, blurs the traditional distinction between *urbs* and *civitas*, since it frames the built environment as an ideologically determined cultural construct that also operates within the semiotic field and is thus contingent on human action and interpretation for its signification and reception. This approach inevitably imbricates verbal, pictorial, and written forms along with the built environment in generating ideas, perceptions, and representations of urban space and in constructing memory, meaning, and subjectivity.[4]

The introduction of European cities in the Americas, first in the Caribbean and shortly after on the Indigenous American mainland, had a particularly targeted function, given the colonial context of their foundation and the intent to reconfigure indigenous urban and natural landscapes, to visibly manifest Christian Iberian society, and to impose a new sociospatial order. Richard Kagan proposed that, unlike other European nations, Spain employed cities as a tool of imperial legitimation, creating what he termed an "empire of cities."[5] Similarly, the colonial Latin American art historian Tom Cummins noted that a feature of Spanish colonialism that distinguished it from British or French colonialism was the ubiquitous presence of large urban centers across Spain's vast imperial territories and the salient role of those cities in the organization and administration of the global Spanish Catholic empire.[6] It is clear that Spanish colonial cities weren't simply intended to serve as habitats and work spaces for imperial officials or Iberian settlers; they were also meant to be seen and experienced by Natives and later by other subjected non-European populations, namely, enslaved Africans and free Blacks (most of whom would serve as a labor source or tribute-paying class in the Iberian feudal system). To these communities, the Iberian "ideal city" would function as a mechanism of reeducation, reorganization, and disciplining.[7] It is that potentiality of the built environment to surveil and control bodies, to organize individuals into communities and reify hierarchies, to regulate movement and productivity, and to shape individual and communal consciousness that has historically rendered it an effective tool to all manner of political states throughout history; in this case, colonial Iberian urban practices can be traced back to the ancient classical world after which early modern Spain was modeling itself as the presumed heir to the Roman Empire as its political power spread across the globe.[8]

If urban planning and official architectural vernaculars are indexes of dominant worldviews and institutional politics at any given time and place, what does it mean, then, when cities or portions of cities are redesigned or rebuilt over time as the circumstances, needs, and objectives of governments and urban populations change? Similarly, how are we to read the urban landscape when older, historical forms are retained, re-created, or referenced in the present? Thinking of the urban environment as a palimpsest provides a useful conceptual model when considering such questions since a fundamental characteristic of cities, and Latin American cities, in particular, such as Mexico City, Cuzco, or in this case, Havana, is the gradual accumulation in a usually condensed urban center of varying architectural idioms, including attempts at implementing different urban models at various times in those same spaces.[9] The result is a pastiche, a layering, or an accumulation of different moments that evinces the city's historical organic evolution while simultaneously collapsing that history within the boundaries of a delimited urban space. Different periods and styles coexist in the city in an anachronistic fashion, yielding heterotopic spaces that may be repurposed and reinscribed with new meaning but that continue, as a condition of their original function, to reference earlier iterations, thus remaining haunted by their previous lives.[10] The colonial art historian Barbara Mundy, in the introduction to her book *The Death of Aztec Tenochtitlan, the Life of Mexico City* (2015), refers to the work of Henri Lefebvre and recognizes this transhistorical dimension of the city space when she states, "While I have treated the three intersecting spheres, representations of space, lived spaces, and spatial practices, in a largely synchronic fashion, it is worth underscoring their diachronic nature, and what a conservative force a relationship to past representations and practices can be."[11] The coexistence of disparate temporalities yields a heterotopic urban environment that preserves some semblance of the dynamics and tensions of different social groups that have occupied that space, from institutional authorities to social elites to laborers. The city, as palimpsest, can thus be read as a visual and material index or biography of its inhabitants and their actions across time.

In terms of the lived experience in/of the urban environment, the reality of the city exists simultaneously on various levels. It exists as man-made physical and spatial constructions; as images in the form of prints, paintings, and photographs, or as maps, city views, and urban landscapes.[12] It exists as text in stories that are written about it or in anecdotes that are shared orally, and it exists symbolically, in our memory, and as impressions each individual experiences moment by moment, walking down a street, sitting on a park bench, enjoying coffee at a favorite café, or riding a subway to work. Here I'm reminded of the work of such figures as Roland Barthes, Ángel Rama, and Italo Calvino.[13] An underlying assumption in the work of these writers and others is that the meaning of a city space, if not the space itself, is fluid, unfixed, and subjective, as urban inhabitants move in and through the city in tune with their circadian rhythms, movements that are regulated by mundane routine, by the physical structure of the city, and by intermittent disruptions of daily patterns occasioned by such things, as public events, annual festivals, recreational activities, and other random happenings.

This observation points to the subjective complexity of reception by recognizing that the diverse inhabitants of a city experience, perceive, employ, and/or remember, maybe even feel, the urban environment in very different ways, according to such historically and culturally determined conditions, as social rank, profession, gender, and race, all variables constituting a protean web of consciousnesses and sociospatial relationships that are instantiated by the physical environment.[14] Implied in these statements is the temporal nature of human awareness and experience, and the dynamic (re)formulation of space by all members of society, not just governments or institutional entities. Official monologic articulations have generally been aimed at reasserting authority, maintaining a utopic social order, and reifying the urban inhabitant's imagined and/or spatial location within that order; but when speaking of subjective experience, we must also consider individual agency. A government can construct or reconfigure a structure or space with specific aims in mind; however, ultimately, it is up to the individual, whether an inhabitant or a visitor, who will respond to such a programatized spatial construction on their own terms and from their unique subjective position. Typical responses may follow a predetermined schema, whereas others may be novel and unexpected, as when individuals or communities take over a space and repurpose it to a use that was unintended, or when different communities respond to the multivalent symbolism of an official historical monument and read its meaning or significance in alternate, unofficial, or even contradictory ways.[15] This reading of space suggests that subjectivity, individual and corporate, may not only shape the meaning of space but that identity may, too, be constructed or reified by it in turn, leading us also to understanding the potential racialization and gendering of space.

Havana presents an ideal case study for the critical approximation of the early modern Ibero-American city from this perspective, given its early foundation, its significance throughout the colonial period, and the transformations the city experienced in response to the changing politics in Spain and its territories throughout what was for Cuba a long Spanish colonial era that began in the early sixteenth century and extended through 1898.[16] Havana, originally founded on the south coast of the island in 1514–1515, was relocated to the north coast at Puerto Carenas in 1519. Originally named San Cristóbal de la Habana, the city served as the launching point for expeditions into the American mainland in the sixteenth century and as the main port in the Caribbean, where its primary value lay early on. It wasn't until 1592 that King Philip II of Spain granted Havana the title of *ciudad*, guaranteeing its status among the capital cities of the nascent but growing empire and setting in motion a series of events that would guide the development of the settlement, as well as the rest of the island. Throughout the colonial period, Havana functioned as the Atlantic gateway to and from the Americas, and eventually, it was fortified to guard against attacks by pirates and other seafaring raiders. Havana's strategic location made it useful to the Spanish military, and over time, it became an important commercial center where goods from around the world were traded, shipped to Spain, and distributed throughout the American territories claimed by the Spanish Crown. Throughout the seventeenth century, the city was expanded, becoming the third-largest city in the Spanish Americas by the mid-eighteenth century, a period marked by significant change on the island.

The British occupation of Havana from 1762–1763 was a pivotal moment that permanently altered the cultural, political, and economic terrain of Cuba, in part, by motivating the growth of the sugar industry and the plantation system, which established a demand for labor and spurred the growth and continuation of the African slave trade well into the nineteenth century. With commercial relationships established between the Caribbean and the rest of North America, Cuba and Havana, in particular, accumulated great wealth and achieved a high level of prosperity. It was during this period, that is, the early nineteenth century, that the Bourbon Spanish monarchy initiated a major reconstruction program in Havana with the intention of modernizing the urban landscape in line with both the dominant Enlightenment principles of the time and the affluence and taste of Cuba's aristocratic landowners. Throughout the rest of the nineteenth century and into the twentieth, Cuba flourished and attracted immigrants and the attention of elites in Europe and the United States, until the Revolution of 1959, when the implementation of a communist political and economic system resulted in the expropriation of private properties and the US imposition of an embargo. Throughout Cuba's long, complex history, Havana experienced significant changes in line with the changing political ideas and priorities of its leadership, the exigencies of the island's economic productivity and status, and the varied, sometimes conflicting, intentions and needs of its diverse inhabitants. What all this suggests is that anyone who wishes to examine Havana's development over the past five hundred years must take into account the city's shifting material, spatial, and symbolic order as a condition of the intersections between its intended, ideal form and function and the daily life and agency of the communities that inhabited and personalized its spaces.

The papers presented in this issue query these processes through an examination of the fabric of the city itself and its constructions, the ideal objectives of institutional authorities, some more successful than others, and the actions or responses of its multiform, diverse inhabitants.[17] They touch on some of these ideas in different ways and by looking at different moments in the life of Havana, starting in the early nineteenth century through the mid-twentieth.

Education (responding to Enlightenment principles), social identity, race, class, social regulation, economic productivity, modernization, history, politics, and nationalism are all themes that play a part in the urban developments and practices here explored.

Paul Niell starts by looking at the public processions in Havana, which were organized and carried out every year on January 6 in celebration of the Epiphany by the *cabildos de naciones,* societies composed of both free Blacks and enslaved Africans. Although Niell primarily focuses on the early nineteenth century, such public festivities clearly originated much earlier as the importation of enslaved Africans increased and the local Black population grew and adapted to the Cuban physical and social environment. As Niell describes, the loud dynamic performances that took place in the streets of the city leading up to the main plaza inverted the racialized conventions that normally dictated life in the colonial city but they were allowed as long as the established social hierarchy returned to normal afterward and the social order was maintained. As such, these public festivities existed between freedom and control. An underlying thread in this discussion is the degree of agency various social and racial groups in the city, such as the Afro-Cuban population, had and how these communities' actions help us understand the fuller complexity of the push and pull of Havana's social fabric in terms of the negotiation of power. Paul examines different spaces in the city, including, the *barrios extramuros*, the *plaza*, the *paseo*, and the streets, along with various monuments found throughout the city, in terms of how performances of surveillance and visibility at those sites embodied the intersections of class, race, and gender, giving form to social meaning and identity. Additionally, he brings in images and texts in the form of history painting and the novel as extensions of such practices, which served to reify memory, subjectivity, and the spatial dynamics of Havana. In the end, he notes how the changing nature of the city, in its asynchronous complexity, invites us to consider new models or approaches in the study of the urban environment, thus supporting the use of the palimpsest as a viable lens through which to examine the Cuban capital.

Emily Sessions shifts the conversation from the wider city or colonial center to the Botanical Garden of Havana.[18] She expresses an interest in looking at how garden designs change over time and how those shifts correspond to the changing priorities of Havana's white elites. She notes that typical scholarship on the subject has failed to address how the garden designs reflected and shaped the sociopolitical function of those spaces; consequently, she treats the proposed remodeling projects as case studies to consider how the garden was utilized as a social and political tool by institutional authorities over time. She begins with French engineer, Frederick Lemaur's proposed design of 1821, which was intended to reaffirm Cuba's loyalty to the Spanish Crown and highlight the biodiversity of the island. Added elements of the new plan included emphasizing Cuban elites' cosmopolitan taste in contrast to the supposed more provincial, unlettered taste of artists of color and reifying the racial hierarchy structuring larger Cuban society. The layout and physical design of the garden, in terms of how traffic was directed and where the slaves' work spaces and quarters were located both reflected and spatially reinforced the racially segregated social structure in Cuba while underlining the labor that undergirded sugar production. The second case study, based on Ramón de la Sagra's plan of 1828, similarly, expressed Cuba's loyalty to Spain but it shifted the focus on local flora from a strictly scientific interest in botany to agricultural production, and was intended to inspire an interest in botany among Cuban youths. Interestingly, although de la Sagra appears to have been conflicted about slavery, he saw its abolition as disastrous, socially and economically, for Cuba. His plan was thus partially motivated by a desire to attract immigrants from Europe to increase the white population, in response to the perceived threat of an increasing African presence on the island. The third and final case study examines a period of neglect of the garden and a proposal to relocate it outside of the city at a site known as El Molino del Rey, to which there was some opposition. As Sessions points out, once the garden was moved, it no longer functioned as a site of scientific and/or agricultural investigation or instruction but became purely recreational. The identification and analysis of these three periods in the garden's history successfully illustrates how the various plans implemented throughout the nineteenth century corresponded to changing ideas of empire and race.

Joseph Hartman approaches the palimpsest question from a completely different angle and considers the effects of a hurricane that hit Cuba in 1926 that laid waste to Havana and other parts of the island.[19] An interesting take on the palimpsest concept, Joseph considers the role of destruction as an act of erasure that provides a clean surface ready for new inscriptions. He places this climatic catastrophe in relationship to a longer history of violent encounters in the Caribbean, beginning with the clash between indigenous communities and the Spanish, rebellions during the colonial period, the wars for independence, and the revolution. To this genealogy, Joseph adds natural catastrophes as a constant threat in the history of the island, one that has shaped the Cuban landscape, its culture, and society. The obliteration of much of the island caused by the hurricane in 1926, which occurred during the Gerardo Machado dictatorship, was documented by a photographer that Machado commissioned to capture the state of the city and its surroundings. The resulting images of devastation were aimed at both Cuban citizens and potential US investors, and the disaster was leveraged by the Machado administration to promote the idea that Machado's government would restore Cuba and its people, a strategy that motivated an increase in tourism to the island and foreign investments. The focus on the photos of the ruins and, in certain cases, their aesthetic qualities underlines their propagandistic potential, in terms of representing a population that was, both, resilient and productive, and suggesting, furthermore, a society in the process of rebuilding and modernizing. Interestingly, he points out how the storms that naturally occur in the Caribbean brought together neighboring countries in the region to share their experiences and explore responses or solutions. As Joseph notes in the conclusion, the hurricane opened opportunities for new construction and the formation of new international relationships, all of which, led to the production of an "aesthetics of disaster" as part of the modernity promoted by the Machado regime.

The final essay in this section by Fredo Rivera questions the claim of Cuba's "Soviet" approach to architectural production by examining how the revolutionary vanguard and its socialist projects were in actuality informed by a Cuban nationalism and coloniality.[20] Similar to Sessions's approach, they look not at the city itself but at one monumental construction, the brutalist Pabellón from 1963 and its exhibitions, which was constructed for and presented at the 1957 World Congress of Architecture held in Havana. They note how local landscape and historical architectural elements were integrated and accommodated into a brutalist idiom, which presented a modernized image of Cuba while maintaining ties to the island's indigenous past, colonialism, and the distinct architectural vernaculars that developed on the island. The exhibitions reinforced this chronological, cultural reading. The result presented an evocative tension between modernity and tradition, which was rife with political implications. Here, Rivera sees the palimpsest as appropriately emblematic of the socialist modernity that took form in Cuba during this time. An overall narrative emerges from the work as a whole, one that traces the Cuban people's struggle for liberation leading up to the Revolution and the reading of a Third World Modern. They conclude by stating that the palimpsest is useful to understand the construction of utopia and late modernity in Cuba, one through which the island is presented as a model for postcolonial modernism. In the Pabellón, Cuba's history, its architectural or urban landscape, and its imagined and/or idealized future are condensed or collapsed into one monumental signifier. As Rivera notes, the World Congress of Architecture allowed Cuba to highlight its contributions to contemporary architecture and museography.

Each of these essays deftly applies the idea of the palimpsest to analyze and interpret different types of urban programs and performances in Havana from the late colonial period through the time of revolution in the mid-twentieth century. The research and the propositions presented suggest new ways of thinking about spatial and architectural constructions and their visual corollaries, as well as the site-specific nature of such projects. The application of the palimpsest model not only reveals the ideals or motives behind these proposed plans but also opens up new avenues of inquiry that recognize the shifting nature of Cuban governments and the polyvalent reception among the city's pluralistic inhabitants, including, foreign audiences, in certain cases. Recognizing the multiple intersections between official programs, built spaces, and local communities provides a plethora of different readings of the city, its history, its uses, and its meanings that are not only complex and interpolated but also in constant flux. From this perspective, the city resembles a living organism whereby the fusion of *urbs* and *civitas,* like body and soul, engenders and fuels its unique, dynamic life over time. Thinking of the accumulated physical deposits that give Havana form and the sedimented layers of history and humanity that shape life on the island, I would like to conclude with the following quote by author, Brin-Jonathan Butler, who, writing about his time in Cuba during Castro's last days, captures a central current of thought in the essays that follow: "While guidebooks might tell you that time collapsed here, another theory says that in Latin America, all of history coexists at once."[21]

NOTES

1. See Hanno-Walter Kruft, *A History of Architectural Theory from Vitruvius to the Present* (New York: Princeton Architectural Press, 1994); Richard Kagan and Fernando Mariás, *Urban Images of the Hispanic World, 1493–1793* (New Haven, CT: Yale University Press, 2000); and George Kubler and Martín Soria, *Art and Architecture in Spain and Portugal and Their American Dominion: 1500–1800* (Baltimore: Penguin Books, 1959).

2. Henri Lefebvre, *The Production of Space,* trans. Donald Nicholson-Smith (Oxford: Blackwell Publishers, 1991), 36–46. For a discussion of phenomenology, see Maurice Merleau-Ponty, *Phenomenology of Perception* (Abingdon, UK: Routledge; New York: Taylor and Francis, 2011); and Peter Reynaert, "Embodiment and Existence: Merleau-Ponty and the Limits of Naturalism," *Analecta Husserliana: Phenomenology and Existentialism in the Twentieth Century* 104 (2009): 93–104.

3. Alan Blum, *The Imaginative Structure of the City* (Montreal: McGill-Queen's University Press, 2003), 24–49; Irving Leonard, *Baroque Times in Old Mexico* (Ann Arbor: University of Michigan Press, 1959); Linda Curcio-Nagy, *The Great Festivals of Colonial Mexico City: Performing Power and Identity* (Albuquerque: University of New Mexico Press, 2004); and Alejandro Cañeque, *The King's Living Image: The Culture and Politics of Viceregal Power in Colonial Mexico* (New York: Routledge, 2013).

4. Tom Cummins and Joanne Rappaport, "The Reconfiguration of Civic and Sacred Space: Architecture, Image, and Writing in the Colonial Northern Andes," *Latin American Literary Review* 26, no. 52 (July–December 1998): 174–200.

5. Kagan and Mariás, *Urban Images.*

6. This observation was taken from a lecture that Tom Cummins (pre-Hispanic and colonial Latin American art historian at Harvard University) gave in a course on the colonial Latin American city at the University of Chicago in winter 1997.

7. For discussions of the ideal city, see Caspar Pearson, *Humanism and the Urban World: Leon Battista Alberti and the Renaissance City* (University Park, PA: Penn State University Press, 2011); Ruth Eaton, *Ideal Cities: Utopianism and the (Un)Built Environment* (London: Thames and Hudson, 2001); and Alfonso Ortiz Crespo, "The Spanish American Colonial City: Its Origins, Development, and Functions," in *The Arts in Latin America, 1492–1820,* ed. Joseph J. Rishel and Suzanne Stratton-Pruitt (New Haven, CT: Yale University Press, 2006), 23–37.

8. Ray Hernández-Durán, "Aztec Art after the Conquest and in Museums Abroad," in *The*

Oxford Handbook of the Aztecs (London: Oxford University Press, 2013), 689–705; Jonathan Edmondson, "Monuments of Empire in Roman Spain and Beyond: August Emerita (Mérida), the 'Spanish Rome,'" *Altera Roma: Art and Empire from Mérida to Mexico,* ed. John M. D. Pohl and Claire L. Lyons (Los Angeles: UCLA and Cotsen Institute of Archaeology Press, 2016), 69–107; Thomas B. F. Cummins, "Toward a New World's Laocoön: Thoughts on Seeing Aztec Sculpture through Spanish Eyes," *Altera Roma: Art and Empire from Mérida to Mexico,* ed. John M. D. Pohl and Claire L. Lyons (Los Angeles: UCLA and Cotsen Institute of Archaeology Press, 2016), 215–255; and Alejandro Cañeque, "Imaging the Spanish Empire: The Visual Construction of Imperial Authority in Hapsburg New Spain," *Colonial Latin American Review* 19, no. 1: 29–68.

9. The term *palimpsest* as employed here derives from manuscript studies and refers to the act of reusing or recycling pages by erasing or overwriting text. This process results in a written page or folio where the earlier script continues to be visible, if not legible, producing a surface consisting of accumulated, layered marks. For more on the palimpsest as it pertains to manuscripts, see Geoff Bailey, "Time Perspectives, Palimpsests, and the Archaeology of Time," *Journal of Anthropological Archaeology* 26, no. 2 (June 2007): 198–223; Sarah Dillon, "Reinscribing De Quincey's Palimpsest: The Significance of the Palimpsest in Contemporary Literary and Cultural Studies," *Textual Practice* 19, no. 3 (Fall 2005): 243–263; and Erica A. Powell, "Recovering Hidden Texts," *Archaeology: A Publication of the Archaeological Institute of America* (March–April 2016), 1–4. For the application of the palimpsest model in relation to urban space, see Michel de Certeau, "The Practice of Everyday Life," in *The Blackwell City Reader,* 2nd ed., ed. Gary Bridge and Sophie Watson (Malden, MA: Blackwell Publishers, 2002), 111–118; Andreas Huyssen, *Present Pasts: Urban Palimpsests and the Politics of Memory* (Stanford, CA: Stanford University Press, 2003); and Kimberly A. Powell, "ReMapping the City: Palimpsest, Place, and Identity in Art Education Research," *Studies in Art Education: A Journal of Issues and Research* 50, no. 1 (Fall 2008): 6–21.

10. For more on the concepts of heterotopia and utopia, as reinscriptions of heterotopic spaces, see Michel Foucault, "Of Other Spaces," *Diacritics* 16, no. 1 (Spring 1986): 17–22; Louis Marin, *Utopics: Spatial Play,* trans. Robert A. Vollrath (London: Macmillan, 1984); and Kevin Heatherington, "The Utopics of Social Ordering: Stonehenge as a Museum without Walls," in *Theorizing Museum: Representing Identity and Diversity in a Changing World,* ed. Sharon Macdonald and Gordon Fyfe (Oxford: Blackwell Publishers and Sociological Review, 1996), 198–217.

11. Barbara E. Mundy, *The Death of Aztec Tenochtitlan, the Life of Mexico City* (Austin: University of Texas at Austin Press, 2015), 14.

12. Kagan and Mariás, *Urban Images.*

13. See Roland Barthes, *Empire of Signs,* trans. Richard Howard (New York: Hill and Wang and Farrar, Straus & Giroux, 1982); Ángel Rama, *The Lettered City,* trans. and ed. John Charles Chasteen (Durham, NC: Duke University Press, 1996); and Calvino, *Invisible Cities.*

14. Michael Holquist, *Dialogism,* 2nd ed. (New York: Routledge, 2002), 14–25.

15. The latter is illustrated by the recent and ongoing removal of confederate monuments across the US South, of monuments to Columbus across the nation, and of monuments to Spanish colonial historical figures, such as, the conquistador, Juan de Oñate and the missionary, Junípero Serra in New Mexico and California, respectively. See Alisha Ebrahimji, Artemis Moshtaghian, and Lauren M. Johnson, "Confederate Statues Are Coming Down Following George Floyd's Death: Here's What We Know," CNN, July 1, 2020; Jackie Salo, "Christopher Columbus Statue Removed outside Columbus City Hall," *New York Post,* July 1, 2020; Erin Vanderhoof, "New Mexico Rethinks Its Conquistador Iconography, One Monument at a Time," *Vanity Fair,* June 18, 2020; and Carolina A. Miranda, "At Los Angeles Toppling of Junipero Serra Statue, Activists Want Full History Told," *Los Angeles Times,* June 20, 2020.

16. For Cuban history, see Gustavo Eguren, *La fidelisíma Habana* (Havana: Editorial Letras Cubanas, 1986); María Luisa Lobo Montalvo, *Havana: History and Architecture of a Romantic*

City (New York: Monacelli Press, 2000); and Alejo Carpentier, *La ciudad de las columnas* (Madrid: Pozuelo de Alarcón, 2004).

17. Three of the following chapters, including this introduction, were originally delivered at the session "Havana: New Research and Critical Reflections on an Urban Palimpsest after Five Centuries," held at the College Art Association Conference in Chicago on February 13, 2020, and chaired by Paul Niell, associate professor of art history at Florida State University.

18. This article was originally presented as the paper "'In Order to Dominate It': Empire, Race, and Power in the Botanical Garden of Havana in the Nineteenth Century" for the panel "Havana: New Research and Critical Reflections on an Urban Palimpsest after Five Centuries," held at the College Art Association Conference in Chicago on February 13, 2020.

19. This article was originally presented as the paper "Hurricanes in Havana: A Visual History of Catastrophe and Capitalism in Machado's Cuba" for the panel "Havana: New Research and Critical Reflections on an Urban Palimpsest after Five Centuries," held at the College Art Association Conference in Chicago on February 13, 2020.

20. This article was originally presented as the paper "From Vanguard to Revolution: Visualizing the 1963 World Congress of Architecture and the 1968 Cultural Congress of Havana" for the panel "Havana: New Research and Critical Reflections on an Urban Palimpsest after Five Centuries," held at the College Art Association Conference in Chicago on February 13, 2020.

21. Brin-Jonathan Butler, *The Domino Diaries: My Decade Boxing with Olympic Champions and Chasing Hemingway's Ghost in the Last Days of Castro's Cuba* (London: Picador, 2015).

PAUL NIELL

Plaza, Paseo, and Street: Urban
Palimpsests of Nineteenth-Century Havana

ABSTRACT

This article considers three disparate but interrelated and complementary urban spaces
in nineteenth-century Havana, Cuba: the plaza, the paseo, and the street. In so doing,
I explore the notion of an urban palimpsest as a productive way we can reconsider
relationships between the physical, mental, and social aspects of the colonial city. To
this end, I examine the colonial development of signifying practices in Havana's urban
spaces and how urban signification was inscribed, performed, lived, interpreted, erased,
and "rewritten" through myriad forms by multiple actors and audiences. Rather than
limiting my attention to only the most permanent forms of spatial annotation, such as
architecture, statues, and other physical elements of the city, I consider the interrelationships between such forms and the social performance of the city. In this way, I use the
idea of the palimpsest as spatial metaphor to approach Havana as a complex and ongoing process of inscription, erasure, and reinterpretation.

RESUMEN

Este ensayo considera tres espacios urbanos dispares pero interrelacionados y comple-
mentarios en la Habana, Cuba: la plaza, el paseo y la calle del siglo XIX. Al hacerlo,
exploro la noción de un palimpsesto urbano como una forma productiva en la que podemos reconsiderar las relaciones entre los aspectos físicos, mentales y sociales de la
ciudad colonial. Para ello, examino el desarrollo colonial de las prácticas significantes
en los espacios urbanos de La Habana y cómo la significación urbana fue inscrita, representada, vivida, interpretada, borrada y "reescrita" a través de innumerables formas
por parte de múltiples actores y públicos. En lugar de limitar mi atención solo a las
formas más permanentes de anotación espacial, como la arquitectura, las estatuas y
otros elementos físicos de la ciudad, considero las interrelaciones entre tales formas y
el desempeño social de la ciudad. De esta manera, utilizo la idea palimpsesto como metáfora espacial para acercarme a La Habana como un proceso complejo e interminable
de inscripción, borrado y reinterpretación.

In 1843, a writer by the name of P. Riesgo, recorded a spectacle that he observed in the streets and plazas of Havana, Cuba: "Numerous groups of negro
men and women cross this big city in all directions, to the beat of the bass
drum. They are ludicrously dressed, with a profusion of ribbons, glass beads,

15

mirrors, old feathers and multicolored strips of cloth. In the middle of each of these groups, there is one of colossal stature whose face is covered with a kerchief, or painted white and flesh-color, making it laughable and ridiculous in the extreme."[1] Though racist and condescending, Riesgo's words allow us to glean some insight into the material and spatial dimensions of the *cabildos de nación* (councils of nations) processions that brought Havana's populations of African descent, enslaved and free, together on the day of the Epiphany, January 6, the Day of Kings. On this occasion, the *cabildos* would perform and process through the streets and urban spaces of Havana.[2]

Processions such as those of the Day of Kings transformed Havana, overturning the daily norms of its streets and public spaces (Figure 1). These conventions of space had been produced over the centuries through a matrix of Spanish law, local social customs, spatial designs, buildings, public performances, and the habitus of everyday life. The *cabildos de nación* unsettled a normative sense of place in the city by reconfiguring and subverting the signs of imperial and colonial power for all to see and experience. Relegated to the *barrios extramuros* (the neighborhoods beyond the city walls) by the 1790s, *cabildo* members would proceed into the walled city of Havana. Other participants included those of the enslaved population released by their masters from

FIGURE 1. Pierre Toussaint Frédéric Mialhe, *El Día de Reyes* (Day of Kings), 1838, lithograph.

outlying haciendas. Arriving from the countryside, these people came on foot or by wagons to Havana, as their domestic counterparts in the city sought leave from urban residences to join their respective *cabildos* in procession.

Composed of a royal court, including a queen and king, *cabildos* displayed their internal hierarchies through dress and behavior, the courtly members adopting the comportment and attire of white elites in Havana. Members of lower social standing wore the clothing of commoners or/and transcultural regalia recombining forms of Amerindian, African, and European descent, in sharp contrast to the comportment associated with Spanish and Creole elites. Dancing and moving dynamically through space were encompassed by the thunderous and ubiquitous drumming that reverberated through bodies and spaces. Performances were processual in that they traversed streets and public spaces before converging on the city's central plaza and the palace of the Spanish governor along its western expanse.[3] In 1891, Ramón Meza recorded an aspect of the Day of Kings processions, a passage worth quoting at length (Figure 2):

From daybreak, all over can be heard the monotonous beat of those big drums made out of hollowed tree trunk and covered on one end by a patch of ox-hide tempered by fire . . . All around, circles would be formed. The enormous drums would be placed to one side as the battery; astraddle, the drummers, tirelessly beating the taut ox-hide with their callused hands . . . Two or three couples would dance in the middle, going into the extravagant contortions, jumping and whirling, their steps in tune to the wild drum beat.

At midday, the merriment was at its height. On Mercaderes, Obispo and O'Reilly Streets, there was a continuous procession of *diablitos* [little devils], all making their way to the Plaza de Armas. The place was soon crowded and it was hardly possible to pass by Government Palace. Onlookers packed the balconies and the sidewalks and climbed the bases of columns, windows and stone balconies surrounding the square . . . In turn, cabildos would come into the Palace courtyard. There the vaults resounded for many hours with the thunderous drumbeat, wild chant and enthusiastic cheers of the Africans. And while below the dancers demonstrated the best of their skills, the captain of each cabildo, pointed hat tucked under his arm, sack across his chest; the standard-bearer, his standard resting against his shoulder; and the teller with his tin box all went up the Palace stairs in the most orderly fashion and, vociferously professing their loyalty, received at least half an ounce in gold for the collection.[4]

As eyewitness accounts suggest, the *cabildos de nación* enacted their performances in Havana on the Day of Kings within a spectrum of freedom and control and through a network of spatial appropriations. As members embraced and celebrated their difference in colonial society through visual and auditory means, they navigated the city's dominant codes in formal ceremonies of deference to the power of the Spanish state. Within a layered matrix of colonial

FIGURE 2. Víctor Patricio de Landaluze, *El Ñáñigo*, lithograph, in *Tipos y costumbres de la Isla de Cuba* (Havana: Miguel de Villa, 1881), 140.

meaning making, the state tolerated such inversions of its civic norms, its *policía* (order in all things), so long as distinctions between inclusion and exclusion, enslaved and free, could be reestablished when the processions ended and the police cleared the streets and plazas (Figure 3). These events exemplify how power and structures of exclusivity in colonial Havana, as in so many other cities of the Spanish world, were constituted spatially.[5] *Cabildo* performances served as spatial metaphors of civic belonging and political aspiration, opportunities to be symbolically recognized in the streets of the walled city and to receive the city's donations. They opened up spaces for the subaltern to be seen and heard on the main plaza and within the patio of the Spanish governor's palace, where the most generous donation would be conferred by the colonial state. Here the various *cabildo* kings could face the colonial governor in Cuba, the chief representative and embodiment of the Spanish monarch on the island.[6] A spatial setting of symbolic power exchange such as this one conferred legitimacy on the *cabildos* as it allowed Spanish authorities a means to keep these populations loyal.

The *cabildos de nación* processions in nineteenth-century Havana speak to the ways subaltern communities in a Spanish Caribbean port manipulated a colonial spatial order composed through architecture, verbal and written language, images, and bodies in motion. Individuals and groups of the African diaspora had no Indigenous claim to land or cultural imprint of place that preceded the Spanish Conquest. Spanish Caribbean cities like Havana

FIGURE 3. Pierre Toussaint Frédéric Mialhe, *Plaza de Armas (Habana)*, 1838, lithograph, in *Isla de Cuba pintoresca* (Havana: Lit. de la Rl. Sociedad Patriótica, 1839).

subalternized populations through racism and patriarchy to extract their labor, thereby producing contested and negotiated environments of complex cultural interchange that were different from colonial cities and territories born of pre-Conquest Indigenous capitals and landscapes of Aztec, Inka, and other Amerindian groups. All the ways in which these types of colonial cities were distinct is beyond the scope of this essay—what I discuss are some of the ways to characterize a city like Havana as a product of spatial juxtapositions between contrasting groups in the process of constituting and negotiating colonial power by attending to various cases of how the city has evolved spatially, in terms of the layers of signifying practices and the political and social actions and actors guiding that process. This approach to the city must be a spatial one, accounting for the intersections of the social, verbal, written, architectural, visual, and multisensory, akin to the concerns raised by Henri Lefebvre.[7] Such an approach must consider processes of urban history and transformation as they pertain to the city's lived environment, its social negotiation of accumulated meanings, materiality, and practices that do not periodize in the same ways as historical, economic, or artistic developments.

These issues of space and meaning in the Spanish colonial city in the Caribbean lend themselves well to the theme of this set of essays on Havana, a focus on the idea of an urban palimpsest. A notion taken from manuscript studies, the palimpsest is a process of inscription, erasure, and reinscription of the written page with something that is then newly interpreted.[8] By analogy, a city is physically and socially built; parts are destroyed; populations remain in one area, sometimes find themselves forced out or decide to move on if they can; and buildings are demolished or covered up with new construction. Rebuilding can incorporate and/or erase the material past. Finally, a population lives and interprets the city, perceiving and orienting itself to the layers of urban signification with which it is confronted, reading and experiencing these juxtapositions in the daily use of the city. The notion of the palimpsest is an approach to consider in attempting to understand the development of Havana in its art and architectural forms, its urbanism, its fine arts, and its social history.

The ebb and flow of urban palimpsestic activity is an overlooked form of meaning making, reception, material creation, and historical development in Havana, as in cities across the world. In this essay, I examine streets, plazas, and *paseos*, three interrelated urban spaces in the city that were inscribed, performed, lived, erased, interpreted, and reinscribed in the nineteenth century in the struggle to maintain, subvert, survive, and transform imperial or colonial power. Such urban spaces played important roles in shaping the experience and understanding of Havana by its many constituencies through time. Acted upon by all their users (who were also in essence their makers) plazas, *paseos*, and streets were shaped by people who held unequal relationships to power based on the intersectionality of their identity. Women, people of African descent and mixed race, and the enslaved were makers of these spaces, even if some had significant limitations placed on their capacities to compose the city in the way of buildings, statues, monuments, and other physical features. Such elements made for long-lasting and hegemonic inscriptions for activation by the church, the colonial state, and dominant individuals and groups in colonial society, who were often the forces behind the physical shaping of the city. What the actual process of meaning making was in nineteenth-century Havana, through the consideration of palimpsest, is an especially important question to consider as the city remembers and reconsiders its history at the five hundredth anniversary of its founding.

Trouble and Agency in the Streets

The paintings and lithographs of the Spanish illustrator Víctor Patricio de Landaluze (1828–1889), who arrived in Havana in 1863, often depict the appropriation of the city's streets by all classes of people in the nineteenth century through a lens of Atlantic racism and patriarchy. Art historians have addressed the rhetorical construction of race, gender, and class through these images and how they encode the dominant values of the social and political elite, including racial entitlement to wealth and social spaces.[9] The images, as with other representational genres of nineteenth-century Havana classified and exploited the *mulata*, the woman of mixed Spanish and African ancestry (Figure 4). Landaluze's emphasis on the types and customs of Havana often focus on the interrelationships of social actor and physical infrastructure. Streets in these images confer identity on their users. The audiences of such prints in Havana may have known something of the urban dynamics depicted, the role of streets as walkways and arteries for the flow of commerce. Streets also served as stages for the constitution and decipherment of personhood, often through a physical encounter with one's colonial "other." In this way, streets furnished space for the cultivation of solidarity among friends and allies within society. They were dense, often noisy places where urban life unfolded and where the elite could scarcely avoid the reality of the city's heterogeneous population.

The experience of the streets of Havana *intramuros* powerfully shaped the city's social imaginary, as expressed in Landaluze's images. Townhouses typically came flush to the street or sidewalks, forming an important barrier for the elite in a racialized landscape where the upper classes generally frowned upon racial mixing (Figure 5). Moving from the shelter of the domicile implied immersion in colonial social networks. White men of the upper classes could venture beyond that threshold into the streets with relative ease where they might encounter and pursuethe apparently ubiquitous *mulata* with whom white men often had sexual liaisons. White women, on the other hand, maintained awkward and disjointed relationships with the streets. Fathers, brothers, and

FIGURE 4. Víctor Patricio de Landaluze, "La mulata de rumbo," lithograph, in *Tipos y costumbres de la Isla de Cuba* (Havana: Miguel de Villa, 1881), 33.

FIGURE 5. Casa at 12 Calle de Oficios, Havana, seventeenth century.

husbands cloistered the women of their households to protect family honor from racial contamination, especially as Havana became a slave society toward the mid-nineteenth century. It was possible for a young white woman of the elite to go out in nineteenth-century Havana and engage the streets, but only in the carriage under the watchful eye of a female chaperone and tended by a coach driver. The foot of a young *blanca* in the walled city would scarcely touch the streets in the nineteenth century, as the carriage could be a platform for shopping and socializing.[10] Streets, therefore, possessed this element of trouble for the white social body while allowing white males to take in the city of Havana as though a Caribbean flaneur.[11]

The driver of the carriage, typically an enslaved man of African descent known as a *calesero*, wore distinctive jackboots, dress coat, and top hat (Figure 6). The frequency with which this figure is described by travel writers and novelists, and portrayed by artists, suggests his ever presence in the streets and public spaces of nineteenth-century Havana in daylight hours (Figures 6–8). Through the material and performative ways the *calesero* projected himself into urban life as a "privileged" figure among the enslaved, he commanded a certain prestige for himself and for his master's family. In the novel *Cecilia Valdés* by Cirilo Villaverde, a story about the social conditions of nineteenth-century Havana illustrated by an illicit affair between a white Creole man and a *mulata* woman, the *calesero* appears with frequency as a key actor in the life of Havana's streets:

On the afternoon of which we are speaking now, one of those frequent collisions occurred between a gig [carriage] occupied by three young ladies that was going down the Calle de la Muralla, and a cart loaded with vehicles heading in opposite directions collided violently, and as a result the hubcap of the second raised the wheel of the first and penetrated its spokes, breaking one of them. The two vehicles were left almost athwart the street after the collision, the gig with its rear facing the door of Uribe's tailor shop, where the mule drawing the cart had now thrust its head. The driver of the cart, seated sideways on top of one of the chests of sugar, with a whip in his right hand, lost his balance and landed in the mud and on the cobblestones of the street with a terrible thud.

And this man, an African by birth, and the other, a mulatto from Havana, instead of hurrying back to their respective vehicles in order to disentangle them and let other conveyances by, hurled awful curses and insults at each other with savage, blind fury. It wasn't that they knew each other, had had fights before, or had previous affronts to avenge; but rather, since they were both slaves, constantly oppressed and mistreated by their masters, without ever having the time or the means to satisfy their passions, they had an instinctive mortal hatred for each other and were merely giving vent to the anger that permanently possessed them the first time a chance had come their way.[12]

In the lower socioeconomic parishes and *barrios* (neighborhoods) of Havana, some of them outside the city walls in the nineteenth century, free people

FIGURE 6. Víctor Patricio de Landaluze, *El calesero*, lithograph, *Tipos y costumbres de la Isla de Cuba* (Havana: Miguel de Villa, 1881), 104.

FIGURE 7. Víctor Patricio de Landaluze, *El puesto de frutas*, lithograph, in *Tipos y costumbres de la Isla de Cuba* (Havana: Miguel de Villa, 1881), 116.

of African descent generated their own society. Nicknamed by the city as *los negros curros*, "the showy blacks," certain flamboyant members of this society worked against the grain of marginalization by making themselves hypervisible, wearing fancy clothing and practicing conspicuous consumption in the streets (Figure 9).[13] In the work of the art historian Krista Thompson's work on the role of light in African-diaspora aesthetic practices, the author identifies the state of being rendered "unvisible" in the Americas among people of African descent as a condition that gives rise to ornate forms of conspicuous consumption.[14] Even when these subjects are/were found in plain sight, as they so often could be on the streets of Havana, some were actively not seen by the dominant classes because of white racism, denying them a sense of full participation and agency in colonial society. To counter this state of "unvisibility," experienced differently from one imperial or national context to the next, various subjects of African descent in Havana responded with hypervisibility, co-opting the means necessary, including jewelry, elaborate clothing, and reflective metals, to counter the dynamics of their being consigned to liminal existence.

The nineteenth-century streets of Havana—in the case of the *cabildos de nación*, the *calesero*, the *curros*, and other individuals and groups of African

FIGURE 8. Víctor Patricio de Landaluze, *El amante de ventana*, lithograph, in *Tipos y costumbres de la Isla de Cuba* (Havana: Miguel de Villa, 1881), 176.

FIGURE 9. Víctor Patricio de Landaluze, *Los curros*, color lithograph, in *Tipos y costumbres de la Isla de Cuba* (Havana: Miguel de Villa, 1881), 128.

descent—furnished space for various types of people to negotiate their own social typologies and to enter into and shape the meaning of spaces. As such, the nineteenth-century streets of Havana were more than physical containers of society. They were dense mediums of layered significance that comprised liminalities between social groups. Streets allowed for the social to be made legible within colonial identity structures through dynamics of self-creation negotiated in different ways by myriad subjects.

Heritage and Memory on the Plaza

Certain pathways provided by the streets of Havana led to the plazas or *plazuelas* (half or third plazas) of the walled city. The *intramuros* contained no fewer than five plazas by the late eighteenth century, including before the western gate of San Cristóbal, the plaza in front of the cathedral, the Plaza de Armas, the plaza alongside the Franciscan mission church, and the Plaza Vieja (used for the public market in the nineteenth century; Figure 10).[15] Different functions of the plaza could elicit disparate behaviors from users. While the Plaza de Armas, by all accounts, routinely established a sense of urban order, refinement,

FIGURE 10. Hippolyte Garneray, *Vista de la Plaza Vieja*, c. 1830, Antique Collection Palau, Antiguitats, Barcelona.

and civic life through daily use and prescriptions for appropriate behavior, the Plaza Vieja may have provoked a different response. The anthropologist Miles Richardson has addressed the phenomenology of the plaza to include the uses and behaviors typical of its space. Richardson notes a restrained sense of subjectivity, a "being-in-the-plaza," which he contrasts with the quick and ready behavior associated with "being-in-the-market."[16] Plazas conditioned behavioral norms and did so through the totality of their experience. People oriented themselves, in part, to the spatial expectations of the plaza on the bases of codes, such as architectural signs, statues, and monuments. But the plaza also functioned as a unitary, if sometimes discordant, spatial system, designed, built, and lived as the essence of the city, its highest expression of civic life. The "defense of the plaza" was often invoked by civil authorities to mean a defense of the city as a whole. In comparison to the street, the plaza embodied spatial expansiveness, a phenomenal feeling of uplift as one entered from the street's narrow confines. The openness of the plaza could constitute a field of surveillance and thereby heighten one's sense of self consciousness, as the rhythms of life in this space conveyed a sense of order.

On the Plaza de Armas in the mid-eighteenth and early nineteenth century, the city installed a series of monuments to commemorate the site of Havana's founding in the year 1519. A vertical pillar ornamented with volutes and crowned by a statue of the Virgin and Child was erected in 1754, and a classical revival structure housing three history paintings known as El Templete followed in 1828, incorporating the earlier pillar (Figures 11–12). The paintings, executed by the French expatriate artist Jean Baptiste Vermay (1786–1832), depicted the first mass and *cabildo* (town council) meeting of the city held by the Spanish conquistadores, a priest, and a group of Amerindians under the ceiba tree where the city was allegedly founded, on the east side of what would become the plaza (Figures 13–14). These two paintings were joined by a third, a representation of the inauguration ceremony of the monument itself in 1828 (Figure 15). I have written about these monuments at length, but here I consider them in light of this notion of urban palimpsest.[17] I am interested in how the accumulated meanings of a city, its urban discourse as in Roland Barthes's conception, condition urban expressions such as these monuments, the sources for which we often confine to art and architecture with genealogies originating in Europe.[18] The erection of El Templete in 1828 and the sponsorship of its paintings served the political agendas of the Spanish state and liberal elite of Havana based on earlier associations and commemorations of the foundational site. Briefly, while members of the "enlightened" public, including clergy, Spanish administrators and merchants, and the Creole (island-born) elite aimed to advance the civic priorities of the Hispanic Enlightenment through this work to educate the population about local history, its formal and iconographic complexities speak to a dissonance of heritage, a lack of agree-

FIGURE 11. Antonio María de la Torre et al., El Templete, 1827–1828, Plaza de Armas, Havana, Cuba. The templelike structure, approximately thirty feet tall from base to the pediment key. Photo by Paul Niell.

ment as the significance of the past conditioned by the concerns of the present.[19] The foundational events of the first mass and *cabildo*, which allegedly occurred beneath a ceiba tree, were represented by Vermay in a naturalistic style through two grand-scale history paintings (Figure 16). Spanish conquistadores, including Diego Velázquez de Culler, who led the conquest of Cuba, gather round the tree with a priest and a group of Indigenous people to install the city as a Christian and civil institution.

While El Templete represents a Spanish imperial projection of power in how it elevates academic neoclassicism and narrates Spaniards as the civilizers of the pictorial narrative, its myriad references to things local, including events, Indians, tropical plants, and most importantly, its deployment in local spaces, speak to the disagreements over the structure of meaning at work in the monument. Signifieds, as Barthes noted, are always transient in the city. First, the 1828 co-opting of the earlier monument from 1754 is an additive process of meaning whereby nothing necessarily seems to have been erased. The ceiba tree is only amplified, as the sense of place in the plaza is inflected with authenticity as, in fact, the site of the city's founding (Figure 17). Second, this amplification

FIGURE 12. Antonio María de la Torre et al., portico, detail of El Templete, 1827–1828, Plaza de Armas, Havana. Photo by Paul Niell.

FIGURE 13. Jean Baptiste-Vermay, *The First Cabildo*, c. 1827–1828, oil on canvas, El Templete, Plaza de Armas, Havana.

FIGURE 14. Jean Baptiste-Vermay, *The First Mass*, c. 1827–1828, oil on canvas, El Templete, Plaza de Armas, Havana.

FIGURE 15. Jean Baptiste-Vermay, *The Inauguration of El Templete*, c. 1827–1828, oil on canvas, El Templete, Plaza de Armas, Havana.

FIGURE 16. Interior of El Templete with views of *The First Mass* and *The Inauguration of El Templete* by Jean Baptiste Vermay. Photo by Paul Niell.

FIGURE 17. Secretaría de Obras Públicas, "Tree of Brotherhood," dedicated February 24, 1928.

of foundational authenticity was done only after social transformations of late eighteenth-century Cuba, which saw a sharp rise in the enslaved population as Spain adjusted its policies toward the transatlantic slave trade to favor Cuban planters. The ceiba tree has long been studied in the Americas as an important element of the African diaspora, sometimes a totemic vortex of spiritual power for populations of Yoruba descent, known as *aché*.[20] Whether audiences of African descent may have venerated the ceiba tree as such in the nineteenth century and whether this was known to the Havana elite remains an open question while all the signifying layers in this monument are not immediately visible. That is, we must consider the monument's formation as embedded in the Cuban landscape as much as the fact that its elements may have been informed by European and international stylistic and visual trends. El Templete was also shaped by its plaza setting and the ways that space had evolved through daily use, ordered ceremonies, and (less frequently) performances such as the January 6 *cabildo de naciones* processions. Through its neoclassical forms, the monument imposed a sense of the correct use and experience of the plaza in the terms of the liberal elite of the 1820s, for its diverse audiences. This combination of symbolic urban site, structure, city planning, and arboreal elements resonates with later examples in Havana as noted by the anthropologist Ivor Miller of the ceiba tree in the Parque de la Fraternidad. Here, he argues, President Gerardo Machado planted the tree as the centerpiece of a new park and adjacent to the recently completed Capitolio to send a political message to populations of African descent. As Miller states, "Coded performances in the Caribbean political arena often have dual implications." [21]

In addition to concerns for the production of meaning through imperial or local dialectics, El Templete offers an exemplary case of the multivocality of urban monuments in Havana. The assertion of Spanish power in the monument, the dominion of Europe it expresses over all things local in Cuba, is complicated by an evident disagreement or alternative reading of signs. While the work affirms an order of empire in which Cuba is to find its natural place, it also articulates and ennobles a sense of place as understood from an American perspective. In the work, multiple combinations of meaning can be made out of the same signs, depending on one's subject position, politics, and worldview in nineteenth-century Havana. If read as a sign of Creole pride of place, references to local history suggest El Templete as a counterhegemonic, Creole monument on the main plaza.[22] Finally, the framing of Havana's foundations as rooted in a narrative of Indians and Spaniards in the monument effectively erased Africans from Cuba's early history, even though people of African descent were likely involved in the colony from the very start. The inauguration painting even contains vignettes among the figures that display Black figures as dependent on whites for their sense of reason and civility. These complex layers of meaning in the monument on a symbolically reinscribed site of the city's foundation and located on the semantic complex of the central plaza are an instructive example of an urban palimpsest and offer a model for its use as a concept.

Refinement and Indigenism on the *Paseo*

The emergence of the eighteenth-century *paseo* (urban promenade) in Madrid materialized the Enlightenment's call for public sociability and well-ventilated urban spaces to produce healthful stages upon which to perform nascent bourgeois identities. Havana, the wealthiest and most heavily trafficked city in the Spanish Caribbean at that moment, saw the creation of *paseos* in the 1790s with the Alameda de Paula between the theater and the San Francisco de Paula hospital, adjacent to the harbor (Figure 18). This space was roughly contemporary to the Paseo de Extramuros, established in an oblong area just beyond the western wall of the city.[23] *Paseos* tended to be established at the flanks of cities in the Spanish Americas, where users could escape urban congestion and, in some cases, the walled enclosure, by engaging with large expanses

FIGURE 18. Pierre Toussaint Frédéric Mialhe, *Alameda de Paula*, 1838, lithograph, in *Isla de Cuba pintoresca* (Havana: Lit. de la Rl. Sociedad Patriótica, 1839).

of space punctuated by fountains and sculpture. Such promenades in Havana were often the site of elite reverie, courting, and socialization at dusk. Alexander von Humboldt described the extramural *paseo* as "delightfully cool resort, and generally after sunset [it] is filled with carriages."[24]

In the Caribbean, such promenades elevated the elite at the expense of other populations, even serving as forms of symbolic erasure, particularly of populations of African descent. The elite resort set space aside to counter the image of the Black city, typified by the life of the streets *intramuros* and the evolving barrios *extramuros*. In contrast, the elite performances in the *paseo* wrote white hegemony into space as a matter of casual urban routine. Meanwhile, in the central plaza of Havana, the Spanish state arranged an evening musical event, generally known as *la retreta*, near dusk when the Caribbean heat began to subside. The attendees of such musical evenings might vary, but these also inscribed space with social meaning through repetition, affirming the loyal city and a population compliant with the colonial social order. By the nineteenth century, Havana developed spaces of increasing racial and gender exclusivity in which the possession of an expensive horse or carriage facilitated access. Cirilo Villaverde wrote:

Cuban or Creole young people considered it beneath their dignity to go to El Prado on foot, and above all to mingle with Spaniards in the lines of Sunday gawkers. As a result only the elite took an active part in the day's promenade: the women invariably in light gigs, a number of elderly individuals in volantes and certain young people from rich families on horseback. . . . The entertainment was limited to riding around the statue of Charles III and the Neptune Fountain when the crowd was small; when it was large the promenade stretched to the Lion Fountain or to some point between the two, where the sergeant of the detachment of dragoons calculated that he ought to station one of his men so as to maintain order and see that the carriages kept their proper distance from each other.[25]

According to Villaverde's novel, fountains marked the social and performative boundaries of the *paseo* and became part of Havana's new spirit of modernity, while the enslaved carriage driver became an active part of that performance, contesting his classification as an inert commodity. Villaverde continues:

The promenade of carriages and men on horseback along the new Prado of Havana then became, in all truth, a spectacle worth contemplating, still partially illuminated by the last golden rays of the setting sun, which on autumn and winter afternoons tone down to handfuls of silver before blending into the perfect, pure blue of heaven's vault. The expert carriage drivers eagerly took advantage of the change offered them to show off their skill and dexterity, not only in controlling the horses, in making their gigs wheel about violently and capriciously, but also their expertise in guiding them through all the tight spots and all the confusion, and getting them out without a single collision or so much as one wheel grazing another. Even timid young ladies, at a peak of excitement from the whirlwind of horses and carriages racing and turning at breakneck speed, enraptured in their airborne shells by the horsemen's actions and at times their words, urged them on: *hence both carriage drivers and horsemen did their utmost to contribute to the danger and the magnificence of the spectacle.*[26]

Numerous images or portraits of the *paseos* of nineteenth-century Havana convey these urban retreats as places where the liberal elite dressed in the latest fashions, flirted, and performed their white entitlement in public space. *Caleseros* usually populate these images as an important part of the spectacle of whiteness in nineteenth-century Havana, which valorized having the financial means and refinement required to own a horse, carriage, and well-dressed enslaved coachman. Indeed, the commodity culture of enslaved bodies shows itself through the ubiquity of the *calesero* in proximity to his white owners in spaces such as the *paseo*. As the street represented social heterogeneity and unpredictable encounters, the *paseo* came to be associated with whiteness and annotated Blackness, especially during the peak hours of use, near sunset. This practice of becoming modern in racialized terms of white and Black through the active use of fashionable spaces for social display in Havana rewrote earlier patterns of elite performance in the plazas of the walled city. Such spaces became among Havana's highest expressions of modernity, offering a reprieve from congestion, access to theaters, and elite solidarity in habitually white spaces, even as they bordered the city's Black world.

As illustrated by Villaverde's novel, members of the elite patronized sculpture along the expanse of the *paseo* to mark the center line between carriage lanes and pedestrian traffic. By the early nineteenth century, a statue of King Charles III stood in the space, along with one of Neptune, Greco-Roman god of the sea, sponsored by the Spanish governor Luis de las Casas in the 1790s (Figure 19). These male sculptural figures stand in contrapposto, characteristic of Greco-Roman statues, with drapery and items signifying their identities. The use of Neptune invoked a figure long associated with colonial entry, across the ocean over which the sea god held sway, and European and viceregal dominion in the Americas.

By the 1830s, a new statue appeared in the *paseo*, that of an Indigenous female figure with feathered skirt and headdress, seated and supporting insignia of Havana, such as a shield with the motif of three castles and key on the city's arms (Figure 20). The Indian figure in the statue holds a cornucopia of harvest abundance in her other arm. In a register below, four dolphins face in disparate directions, spouting water from their mouths into the fountain basin below (Figure 21). Made from Carrara marble and sculpted by the Italian academic artist Giuseppe Gaggini, the Indian Fountain, or Noble Havana, reconfigured the Indigenous trope seen earlier in El Templete at the Plaza de Armas (Figure 22). Its patron, the Conde de Villanueva, was an island-born intendant in the city with ties to the local plantocracy, whose economic interests he worked to advance. What could the installation of an Indigenous figure on the premier *paseo* of nineteenth-century Havana suggest? I have argued previously that this sculpture existed in dialogue with a fountain of Neptune commissioned by a rival of Villanueva, the Spanish governor Miguel Tacón, whose restrictive policies interfered with the goals of the plantocracy.[27] Tacón's sculpture of Neptune, also by Gaggini, was erected near the harbor. This dialogue between sculptures would suggest contrasting inscriptions of urban space in Havana by powerful patrons to serve different constituencies, as with El Templete: the Spanish administration and merchant sector versus the Creole planter class.

In my previous writing on these fountains, I left one element only briefly addressed: the meanings that users of the Paseo de Extramuros, or Isabella II, would have contributed and made of the Fountain of the Indian if such urban monuments and sculptures arise in part from palimpsestic processes in urban terms. An evolving narrative of civic foundations, of Spaniards directing Indians to the light of Christianity and urban civilization, informed El Templete in 1828. Likewise, the Indian Fountain alludes to a city rooted in this early chapter of Spanish colonial history. However, in the fountain, Spain is conspicuously absent, even though academic classicism would seem to have reified

FIGURE 19. Statue of Neptune from the Fountain of Neptune, Havana, ca. 1797, marble, City Museum of Havana. Photo by Paul Niell.

FIGURE 20. Giuseppe Gaggini, Fountain of the Indian, Havana, ca. 1835–36, marble. Photo by Paul Niell.

FIGURE 21. Gaggini, Fountain of the Indian, or Noble Havana, detail showing base and pedestal. Photo by Paul Niell.

FIGURE 22. Fountain of Neptune, Havana, ca. 1837–38, marble. Photo by Paul Niell.

the European claim to the island. The Indian figure, by contrast, suggests that Havana stands on American foundations, as the dolphin figures—symbols of motion in early modern oceanic maps—face in four different directions to suggest the city as a center, with panoramic agency in the Atlantic. Yet the fountain says something else, by virtue of its Indianness. In an urban discursive interplay with El Templete, the fountain suggests that Havana's origins involved a mixed heritage of Spaniard and Indian, to the exclusion of Africans and people of African descent. As Creole elites promenaded in the *paseo*, pulled in their carriages by horses driven by Black *caleseros*, they might have felt it affirmed that their white identities were assured by their sensorial absorption in neoclassicism while their Americanness was affirmed by Indians. Simultaneously, the fountain furnished a stage for addressing the "other" in relational terms, elevating the Indian to normalize the suppression of the Black in the very spaces of daily subordination. As the Indian was drawn closer to whiteness, the Black was further isolated, in new mental and aesthetic structures of colonial exclusion and in a wide-open space of elite sociability.[28] If we consider the city as a matter of space, experienced and discursively composed, then its myriad signs signify to the fullest degree only in the local terms that have developed in spaces through use and experience. As such, considering the signifying potential of the Indian Fountain in its site of nineteenth-century display in tandem with its appearance in other media, such as prints, calls to mind the particular type of engagement that historical subjects have had with the *paseo* and the complex layers of mixed, contrasting, and even incoherent meanings produced by daily life in late colonial society (Figures 23–27).

In the study of Havana's dense array of urban sculptures, monuments, streets, plazas, and *paseos*, we can learn much by attending to the development of artistic styles, forms of urban planning, and of course patrons and artists. Yet our work is incomplete without due consideration of the larger urban environment in which these forms made meaning and the social actors and situations that conditioned those meanings of artistic and architectural forms. A city as old as Havana accumulates many layers of signifying material and practices for navigating the city. Aesthetic life is social life, and transitions between visual regimes are often rough, leading to juxtapositions of old and new that a living population must make sense of in its own terms. In the nineteenth century, people in Havana negotiated a landscape of semantic layers, coexisting artistic styles, and complexities of meaning within which colonial genres of art, archi-

FIGURE 23. Pierre Toussaint Frédéric Mialhe, *Teatro de Tacón (Habana)*, 1838, lithograph, in *Isla de Cuba pintoresca* (Havana: Lit. de la Rl. Sociedad Patriótica, 1839).

FIGURE 24. Pierre Toussaint Frédéric Mialhe, *Puerta de Monserrate (Habana)*, 1838, lithograph, in *Isla de Cuba pintoresca* (Havana: Lit. de la Rl. Sociedad Patriótica, 1839).

FIGURE 25. After Frédéric Mialhe, *General View of the Paseo de Isabel II*, ca. 1853, chromolithograph.

FIGURE 26. Pierre Toussaint Frédéric Mialhe, *El Quitrin (Habana),* 1838, lithograph, in *Isla de Cuba pintoresca* (Havana: Lit. de la Rl. Sociedad Patriótica, 1839).

FIGURE 27. Leading vignette, detail, *Diario de La Habana*, February 18, 1834. Artwork in the public domain.

tecture, text, and bodily performance operated. Signifying practices could rise and fade in the urban discourse, sometimes swept away by shifts in the ritualized calendar and/or major urban changes in the locations of physical things and people. Embracing the challenge of understanding such complexities only enriches our historical knowledge of Havana and invites us to consider new models for the city's interpretation.

NOTES

The author would like to thank Asiel Sepúlveda for his generous assistance in securing images for this article and the College Art Association for sponsoring the panel "Havana: New Research and Critical Reflections on an Urban Palimpsest after Five Centuries," held February 13, 2020, in Chicago that informed several of the articles in this issue of *Cuban Studies* on Havana.

1. Observation of P. Riesgo taken from the essay by Fernando Ortiz, "The Afro-Cuban Festival 'Day of the Kings,'" in *Cuban Festivals: A Century of Afro-Cuban Culture*, ed. Judith Bettelheim (Kingston, Jamaica: Ian Randle Publishers; Princeton, NJ: Markus Wiener Publishers, 2001), 8.

2. As mutual-aid societies and institutional niches for the emergence of new ethno-identity formations, *cabildos* provided solidarity and agency to the African-descended people of colonial Cuba. They belonged to what colonial society inscribed as the *naciones* of Africa from whence the enslaved and free Black population at least in theory came, including Lucumí, Congo, and Arará. By the nineteenth century, with the immense expansion of the enslaved population to support the industrialization of agriculture, *cabildos* had grown significantly in size, number, and importance to their members. For background on the *cabildos de nación* in Havana, see Philip A. Howard, *Changing History: Afro-Cuban Cabildos and Societies of Color in the Nineteenth Century* (Baton Rouge: Louisiana State University Press, 1998); Matt D. Childs, *The 1812 Aponte Rebellion in Cuba and the Struggle against Atlantic Slavery* (Chapel Hill: University of North Carolina Press, 2009). For the procession of the Day of Kings, see Judith Bettelheim, ed., *Cuban Festivals: A Century of Afro-Cuban Culture* (Kingston, Jamaica: Ian Randle Publishers; Princeton, NJ: Markus Wiener Publishers, 2001); Fernando Ortiz, *Los cabildos y la fiesta afrocubanos del Día de Reyes* (Havana: Editorial de Ciencias Sociales, 1992); David H. Brown, *Santería Enthroned: Art, Ritual, and Innovation in an Afro-Cuban Religion* (Chicago: University of Chicago Press, 2003). Brown deserves credit for the notion of *cabildos de nación* as institutional niches for the emergence of new ethno-identity formations.

3. For the discussion of the processual patterns of ritual, see Victor Turner, *The Ritual Process: Structure and Anti-Structure* (New York: Aldine de Gruyter, 1969).

4. For this passage by Ramón Meza, see Ortiz, "Afro-Cuban Festival," 2–4.

5. These thoughts on the spatial constitution of colonial society in Havana are informed by such sources as Pierre Bourdieu, *Outline of a Theory of Practice* (Cambridge: Cambridge University Press, 1977); Anthony Giddens, *The Constitution of Society: Outline of a Theory of Structuration* (Berkeley and Los Angeles: University of California Press, 1984); Henri Lefebvre, *The Production of Space*, trans. Donald Nicholson-Smith (Hoboken, NJ: Wiley-Blackwell, 1992); Bruno Latour, *Reassembling the Social: An Introduction to Actor-Network-Theory* (Oxford: Oxford University Press, 2007). However, the study of colonial urban societies in the Americas and worldwide present scenarios that colonial studies should address, as the aforementioned authors' work pertains largely to Europe. The work of the architectural historian Swati Chattopadhyay has advanced our understanding of the urban spatial dynamics of the colonial city in India. See

"Blurring Boundaries: The Limits of the 'White Town' in Colonial Calcutta," *Journal of the Society of Architectural Historians* 59, no. 2 (2000): 154–179.

6. Alejandro Cañeque, *The King's Living Image: The Culture and Politics of Viceregal Power in Colonial Mexico* (New York: Routledge, 2004).

7. See Lefebvre, *Production of Space*; Thomas B. F. Cummins and Joanne Rappaport, "The Reconfiguration of Civic and Sacred Space: Architecture, Image and Writing in the Colonial Northern Andes," *Latin American Literary Review* 26, no. 52 (1998): 174–200.

8. For the use of the palimpsest to examine processes in European medieval architectural and urban development, see N. C. Aksamija, C. Maines, and P. Wagoner, eds., *Palimpsests: Buildings, Sites, Time* (Turnhout, Belgium: Brepols, 2017).

9. For Landaluze's politics and how they informed his art, see E. Carmen Ramos, "A Painter of Cuban Life: Víctor Patricio de Landaluze and Nineteenth-Century Cuban Politics (1850–1889)," (PhD diss., University of Chicago, 2011). See also Asiel Sepúlveda, "Humor and Social Hygiene in Havana's Nineteenth-Century Cigarette Marquillas," *Nineteenth-Century Art Worldwide* 14, no. 3 (Autumn 2015), http://www.19thc-artworldwide.org/autumn15/sepulveda-on-havana-19th-century-cigarette-marquillas. Various images of the social actors in nineteenth-century Havana produced by the artist can be found in Víctor Patricio de Landaluze, *Tipos y costumbres de la Isla de Cuba* (Havana: Miguel de Villa, 1881).

10. For these social aspects of nineteenth-century urban life in Havana, see Levi Marrero, *Cuba: Economía y sociedad: Azúcar, ilustración y conciencia (1763–1868)* (Río Piedras, PR: Editorial San Juan, 1986), vol. 13; Verena Martínez-Alier, *Marriage, Class and Colour in Nineteenth-Century Cuba: A Study of Racial Attitudes and Sexual Values in a Slave Society*, 2nd ed. (Ann Arbor: University of Michigan Press, 1989); Luis Martínez-Fernández, *Fighting Slavery in the Caribbean: The Life and Times of a British Family in Nineteenth-Century Havana* (Armonk, NY: M. E. Sharpe, 1998).

11. For the social experience of nineteenth-century Paris, see Walter Benjamin, *The Arcades Project*, trans. By Howard Eiland and Kevin McLaughlin (Cambridge, MA: Belknap Press of Harvard University Press, 2002). Much work remains to be done on Havana as a center of nineteenth-century modernity on its own terms.

12. Cirilo Villaverde, *Cecilia Valdés or Angel Hill* (Oxford: Oxford University Press, 2005), 117.

13. Brown, *Santería Enthroned*, 32–34.

14. Krista Thompson, *Shine: The Visual Economy of Light in African Diasporic Aesthetic Practice* (Durham, NC: Duke University Press, 2015).

15. For the streets and plazas of Havana *intramuros*, see Manuel Fernández Santalices, *Las calles de la Habana intramuros: Arte, historia y tradiciones en las calles y plazas de la Habana Vieja* (Havana: Saeta Ediciones, 1989).

16. Miles Richardson, "Being-in-the-Market versus Being-in-the-Plaza: Material Culture and the Construction of Social Reality in Spanish America," in *The Anthropology of Space and Place: Locating Culture*, ed. Setha M. Low and Denise Lawrence-Zúñiga (Malden, MA: Blackwell, 2003), 74–92. For another anthropological view on the plaza, see Setha Low, *On the Plaza: The Politics of Public Space and Culture* (Austin: University of Texas Press, 2000).

17. Paul Niell, "El Templete and Cuban Neoclassicism: A Multivalent Signifier as Site of Memory," *Bulletin of Latin American Research* 30, no. 3 (2011): 344–365; Niell, *Urban Space as Heritage in Late Colonial Cuba: Classicism and Dissonance on the Plaza de Armas of Havana, 1754–1828* (Austin: University of Texas Press, 2015).

18. Roland Barthes writes, "The city is a discourse, and this discourse is truly a language." He considers the city to be composed of countless signifiers, but the signifieds (the meanings produced in the mind of the reader or viewer) are always "transient, mythical creatures." See Barthes,

"Semiology and the Urban," in *Rethinking Architecture: A Reader in Cultural Theory*, ed. Neil Leach, 166–172 (London: Routledge, 1997), quote at 168.

19. For heritage so defined, see Laurajane Smith, *Uses of Heritage* (New York: Routledge, 2006); G. J. Ashworth, Brian Graham, and J. E. Tunbridge, *Pluralising Pasts: Heritage, Identity, and Place in Multicultural Societies* (London: Pluto Press, 2007).

20. For African diasporic religion in Cuba, see Rómulo Lachatañeré, *El sistema religioso de los afrocubanos* (1942; Havana: Editorial de Ciencias Sociales, 2004); Lydia Cabrera, *El Monte: Igbo—Finda, Ewe Orisha—Vititi Nfinda: Notas sobre las religions, la magia, las supersticiones y el folklore de los negros criollos y el pueblo de Cuba*, Colección del Chicherekú en el Exilio (1954; Miami: Ediciones Universal, 1983); Miguel Barnet, *Afro-Cuban Religions*, trans. Christine Renata Ayorinde (Princeton, NJ: Markus Wiener, 2001); Michele Reid, "The Yoruba in Cuba: Origins, Identities, and Transformations," in *The Yoruba Diaspora in the Atlantic World*, ed. Toyin Falola and Matt D. Childs (Bloomington: Indiana University Press, 2004), 111–129. See also Stephan Palmié, *Wizards and Scientists: Explorations of Afro-Cuban Modernity and Tradition* (Chapel Hill, NC: Duke University Press, 2002).

21. Ivor L. Miller, "Religious Symbolism in Cuban Political Performance," *Drama Review* 44, no. 2 (Summer 2000): 30.

22. This counterhegemonic message may have been facilitated by one of the monument's patrons, Bishop Juan José Díaz de Espada y Landa, a man of the Hispanic Enlightenment suspected by the Vatican of Freemasonry. See Fernando Ortiz, *La hija cubana del iluminismo* (Havana: Molina y Compañía, 1943); Eduardo Torres-Cuevas, *Obispo Espada: Ilustración, reforma y antiesclavismo* (Havana: Editorial de Ciencias Sociales, 1990).

23. See Abel Fernández y Simón, "Las fuentes de las plazas, parques y paseos públicos de la Habana colonial," in *Cuba: Arquitectura y urbanismo*, ed. Felipe J. Préstamo y Hernández (Miami: Ediciones Universal, 1995), 337–51; Joaquín E. Weiss, *La arquitectura colonial cubana: Siglos XVI al XIX* (Havana: Instituto Cubano del Libro, Agencia Española de Cooperación International, and Consejería de Obras Públicas y Transportes Junta de Andalucía, 1996), 361–66.

24. This observation was made during Humboldt's time in Cuba on two visits between 1800 and 1804. His *Political Essay* from these travels was first published in Paris in 1826, with an English translation appearing in New York in 1856. See Alexander von Humboldt, *The Island of Cuba: A Political Essay* (Kingston, Jamaica: Ian Randle Publishers, 2001), 80.

25. Villaverde, *Cecilia Valdés*, 130.

26. Villaverde, 131 (my italics).

27. For discussion of the imperial-local tensions in nineteenth-century fountain sculpture in Havana, see Paul B. Niell, "Rhetorics of Place and Empire in the Fountain Sculpture of 1830s Havana," *Art Bulletin* 95, no. 3 (September 2013): 440–464. These fountains are also discussed in the following sources: Eugenio Sánchez de Fuentes y Peláez, *Cuba monumental: Estatuaria y epigráfica* (Havana: Solana Compañía, 1916), 47–68, 139–171; Emilio Roig de Leuchsenring, *La Habana, apuntes históricos* (Havana: Editora del Consejo Nacional de Cultura, 1963), 3:18–21.

28. The idea that the spatial modernity of the *paseo* in a colonial city like Havana might daily perform the work of coloniality in the social performance of racial and gender difference is informed by my reading of decolonial theory, especially the work of Aníbal Quijano and Walter D. Mignolo. See, for example, Aníbal Quijano and Michael Ennis, "Coloniality of Power, Eurocentrism, and Latin America," *Nepantla: Views from the South* 1, no. 3 (2000): 533–580; Walter D. Mignolo, *The Darker Side of Western Modernity: Global Futures, Decolonial Options* (Durham, NC: Duke University Press, 2011).

LEE SESSIONS

"In Order to Dominate It": Empire, Race, and Power in the Botanical Garden of Havana in the Nineteenth Century

ABSTRACT

Havana's botanical garden during the first half of the nineteenth century served at different moments as a site of spiritual contemplation and of medical utility, of increased sugar production and of direct opposition to big sugar. In fact, the very future of Cuban slave society was spatialized on the grounds of the botanical garden. This was especially true in the 1830s when agricultural experimentation that looked toward the end of the system of racialized slavery were being carried out by enslaved workers who shared a bedroom wall with the garden's head botanist. Despite increasing attention paid to the underlying political valence of botanical gardens, there has been little scholarship on how different garden designs themselves reflected the sociopolitical roles these spaces played. In this article, I apply the formal analysis methodology of art history to several surviving nineteenth-century plans for the layout of Havana's botanical garden. I argue that these designs reveal the focus of the space shifting from Cuban biodiversity to cash crop agriculture and, finally, to elite leisure. Furthermore, I argue that these shifting foci, revealed and enabled by these different garden plans, were motivated by shifting views of empire and loyalty held by Havana's white elite.

RESUMEN

El Jardín Botánico de La Habana durante la primera mitad del siglo XIX sirvió en diferentes momentos como lugar de contemplación espiritual y de utilidad médica, de aumento de la producción de azúcar y de oposición directa al gran azúcar. De hecho, el futuro mismo de esclavitud cubana se espacializó en los terrenos del jardín botánico. Esto fue especialmente cierto en la década de 1830s, cuando trabajadores esclavizados que compartían una pared de dormitorio con el botánico jefe del jardín llevaban a cabo experimentos agrícolas que miraban hacia el final del sistema de esclavitud racializada. A pesar de la creciente atención prestada a la valencia política subyacente de los jardines botánicos, ha habido pocos estudios sobre cómo los diferentes diseños de jardines reflejaban los roles sociopolíticos que desempeñaban estos espacios. En este artículo, aplico la metodología de análisis formal de la historia del arte a varios planes sobrevivientes del siglo XIX para la distribución del jardín botánico de La Habana. Sostengo que estos diseños revelan que el enfoque del espacio pasa de la biodiversidad cubana a la agricultura de cultivos comerciales y, finalmente, al ocio de élite. Además, sostengo que estos focos cambiantes, revelados y habilitados por estos diferentes planes de jardín, fueron motivados por puntos de vista cambiantes del imperio y la lealtad de la élite blanca de La Habana.

In 1818, an article on botanical gardens reprinted in a periodical in Havana stated that such gardens served "as a place to study nature in all of its productions in order to dominate it."[1] Study and domination indeed would remain the dominant motives of the group of white elite men who oversaw the botanical garden of Havana for the next forty years.

In this article I place scholarship tracing the history of Havana's botanical garden in conversation, for the first time, with discussion in the history of science about how botanical gardens around the world served as nodes in exchange networks and as tools to extend imperial power.[2] Despite increasing attention paid to this underlying political valence of botanical gardens, and despite a long history of the study of garden designs around the world, there has been little scholarship on how different garden designs themselves reflected the sociopolitical roles these spaces played. I discuss this process in the case of Havana's botanical garden, showing how the space reflected the complex interplay of race and imperial loyalty that defined Cuba's nineteenth century.[3]

I apply the formal analysis methodology of art history to several surviving nineteenth-century plans for the layout of Havana's botanical garden. I argue that these designs reveal the focus of the space shifting from Cuban biodiversity to cash crop agriculture and, finally, to elite leisure. Furthermore, I argue that these shifting foci, revealed and enabled by these different garden plans, were motivated by shifting views of empire and loyalty held by Havana's white elite.

I also argue that, during growing racial unrest, the botanical garden of Havana was used explicitly to drive white emigration, imagined by white elites to quell this unrest. At the same time, throughout the nineteenth century, the botanical garden of Havana depended on the labor and expertise of enslaved black Cubans, and the plans of the garden as well as the written archives hint at the lived experiences of these workers in the space.

1821 Plan for Havana's Botanical Garden

Garden as Demonstration of Imperial Loyalty

Agustín Argüelles, an official in the Ministerio de la Gobernación de la Peninsula, Sección de Fomento, in coordination with the Secretario de Despacho de la Gobernador de la Península, proposed a set of improvements of the "acclimatization garden" of Havana in 1821. The officials hoped in particular that Havana's central location would enable the garden to serve as a key node in a global botanical exchange network. In their proposal, plants were to be transferred from Spanish overseas territories to the botanical garden of Havana for cultivation and propagation, and from there sent on to Real Jardín Botánico of Madrid.[4] If some of these new species became sources of profit for the crown, all the better.

This was a moment, of course, when the Spanish Empire was undergoing massive changes across the globe. Many of their previous colonies were being lost to the wars of independence raging across North and South America, and new sources of funds were urgently required. It was also considered crucial to strongly assert control over Cuba so that the island did not follow its neighbors in calling for independence. This proposal was intended to address each of these requirements.

José Antonio de la Ossa, the garden's director at the time, responded to the crown's request by submitting a report on the state of Havana's botanical garden on December 28, 1821. This report focused largely on the challenges that Ossa had faced, including the poor soil of the location which had been chosen for the garden and his lack of funds. He expressed hope that additional financing would be provided by the crown. More funds, he argued, would in turn improve the garden, allowing for "effective and continuous communication" between Havana and Madrid.[5] In this report, then, Ossa, pledged loyalty to the Spanish crown and seemingly agreed to a new proposal to position Havana as a hub of global specimen exchange to profit the Spanish empire.

This pledge of loyalty was rendered visible in the plan that accompanied Ossa's report, painted by the French engineer Francisco Lemaur. This plan, accompanied by a detailed key, shows the entrance to the garden at the bottom of the page and a wide central path leading away from this entrance (Figure 1). On either side of this central corridor, and a series of straight paths lead away from this entrance. These paths fork and intersect, dividing the rectangle of the garden in half vertically, horizontally into squares, and then into cross and star shapes.

This careful symmetry would have immediately called to many visitors' minds the Real Jardín Botánico of Madrid, which had been redesigned by Francisco Sabanini in 1781 (Figure 2).[6] Sabanini's garden included a prominent central axis with symmetrical spaces on each side that were divided by additional diagonal paths, just like Lemaur's plan for Havana's botanical garden. Furthermore, in both the Madrid garden and the Havana garden, the plants that filled these beds to either side of the central path generally increased in height toward the back of the garden.[7] (Lemaur's plan shows trees near the back of the garden with low-lying plants at the front.) Both botanical gardens, then, seem to have been designed to provide visual access to as much of the space as possible as a visitor enters. This visitor's eye was meant to move straight back into

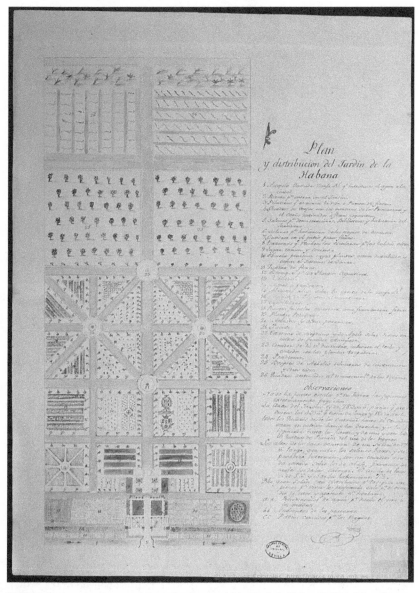

FIGURE 1. Francisco Lemaur, *Plan y distribución del jardín de la Habana*," 1821, ink and watercolor. Archivo General de Indias, Seville, MP-SANTO_DOMINGO, 736.

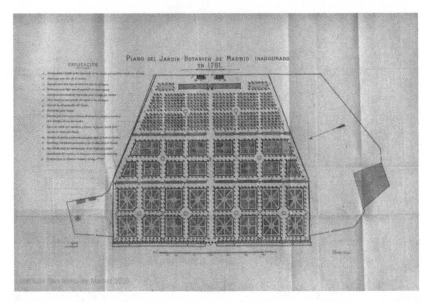

FIGURE 2. Madrid de Migas Calientes, *Plano del Jardín Botánico de Madrid en 1781*, 1875, engraving. Page 445 of *Anales de la Sociedad Española de Historia Natural* (Madrid, 1875). Real Jardín Botánico, Madrid.

the space upon entry, with orderly symmetric beds stretching to either side, proceeding from low-lying plants to tall trees.

The long, wide central path of Lemaur's design was not unique to the Real Jardín Botánico of Madrid, of course. Such central axes had been present in European garden designs since at least the Renaissance period in spaces such as Kensington Gardens and Vaux le Vicomte (Figures 3–4). Each of these, however, lacked the strong diagonal lines intersecting at regular intervals that defined the botanical garden of Havana and the Real Jardín Botánico of Madrid. Lemaur's plan, then, appears to have deliberately echoed the relatively recently built botanical garden at the center of the Spanish empire. This design should, I argue, be understood as a visual pledge of Cuban loyalty at a time when independence movements raged across many former Spanish territories.

Garden as celebration of scientific botany

Lemaur's plan for Havana's botanical garden did not just accede to the crown proposal in its overall design, however, but also in the contents of the garden. The garden under Ossa contained a wide variety of plant specimens, which were arranged on Lemaur's plan to draw attention to their diversity and to reference contemporary botanical practices and research around the world. The garden sections presented by Lemaur included everything from grass, planted

FIGURE 3. Henry Overton and J. Hoole, "Kensington Gardens, London," c. 1720, etching and engraving. Royal Collections Trust, United Kingdom, RCIN 702920.

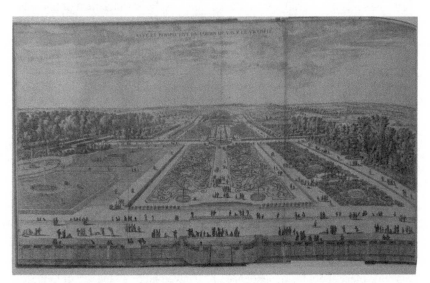

FIGURE 4. Israel Silvestre, *Vue et perspective de Vaux le Vicomte du cote jardin*, seventeenth century, engraving. Bibliothèque Nationale, Paris, France.

beds, vineyards, aquatic plans, shrubs, and beds of fruit plants. Ossa in fact made several lists of the plants that he had successfully cultivated in the garden, together totaling nearly one hundred species.[8] This would not have been an especially impressive selection for a botanical garden of the early nineteenth century but was still respectable, especially considering the garden had been founded only in 1817. Argüelles's proposal, recall, was that Havana's garden collect and acclimatize plant specimens from around the world to eventually send these specimens on to Spain.

Especially noteworthy is the place of pride that Lemaur gave to the Linnaean garden, immediately to the right of the main entrance. This would have been the section of the garden where closely related plants were arranged next to each other and labeled to teach visitors about the Linnaean classification system. This section was not unique to Havana's garden. Carl Linnaeus had developed his system of taxonomy based on binomial nomenclature in his book *Systema Naturae* in 1735 and refined it in subsequent publications. The system spread quickly throughout European scientific establishments of the period and then was carried around the world through publications and botanical expeditions.[9] Including a Linnaean garden in his plan, though, and specifically labeling it as such, should still be understood as a deliberate choice on the part of Lemaur.[10] This emphasis on Linnaean botany in a highly visible location reaffirmed that the overall goal of the garden was the advancement of botanical research and scientific knowledge.

A celebration of local and global biodiversity had, in fact, long been acknowledged as one of the primary goals of the garden. One of the first published articles that had called for a botanical garden in Havana imagined a garden focused on indigenous flora ("the most precious plants that are produced in Cuba") which could be used for botanical study.[11] This emphasis also followed the proposal developed by Agustín Argüelles, that Havana's garden be a site where plants from across the globe would be gathered, acclimatized, and propagated before they were sent to the Real Jardín Botánico of Madrid. As I will discuss, however, the garden would shift in focus over the next several decades away from this focus on Linnaean comparison of plants from around the world toward economic botany and then toward elite leisure.

Garden as Reification of Cuban Slavery

The neatly ordered paths and Linnaean garden of Lemaur's plan were all, of course, maintained almost entirely by enslaved black workers. Ossa himself was quite clear about his dependence on enslaved labor. In the report Lemaur's plan accompanied, he requested funds to purchase and maintain twelve enslaved laborers in total as well as two porters, a gardener, and a botanical assistant to maintain the garden.[12] These men and, possibly, women, were needed not just for digging and weeding, but also planting, planning, pruning, and

harvesting—specialized skills that mobilized each individual's natural historical knowledge.

While many botanical gardens throughout the Caribbean and the Americas depended on the labor and knowledge of enslaved people, these individuals were almost never acknowledged in surviving visual documentation. On
Lemaur's plan for the space, somewhat surprisingly, their presence is quite
apparent. Immediately beyond the fruit trees and Linnaean garden that a visitor would first encounter upon entering, Lemaur depicted a symmetrical set
of living quarters for enslaved black workers and a pair of kitchens (6, 9).
Furthermore, past the geometric beds, fountains, and statues, and past a "forest
of native trees for construction and other uses," lay a set of provision gardens,
labeled by Lemaur as being "for the maintenance of blacks" (26). This would
have been where the garden's enslaved workers grew food to supplement the
rations that were provided. While much of the scholarship on the experience of
visitors to botanical gardens has focused on the experience of elite white visitors, these inclusions in Lemaur's plan help us to imagine and call attention to
another set of experiential landscapes—that of the enslaved black worker.

The wide central path of Havana's botanical garden led the white elite
visitors to the space straight back through the gardens, with symmetrical beds,
fountains, and building unfolding on either side. Ana Amigo notes the perfor-
mativity and political possibility of this movement through space for white
elite visitors, especially for criollo women, calling it a space of "rehabilitation
and leisure within an urban space that was restricted in terms of public life and
socialization."[13] This same path, however, would have led the enslaved black
workers of the garden from their quarters back to the provision gardens behind
the forest, making their way along the darkening path to grow and gather food
at the end of a long day of pruning, planting, and propagating.

Dell Upton discusses the embodied experience that a similarly wide path
leading up to the main house was meant to evoke to visitors to plantations in
Virginia, and how this differed from the way that enslaved people who lived on
the plantation themselves moved through the space. Upton describes the routes
to plantations in eighteenth-century Virginia as "microlandscapes" in which
"the visitor's route to the house involved passing a series of physical barriers
that were also social barriers."[14] White visitors had to pass through these social
barriers to be granted admittance to the great house, and the microlandscape of
the plantation was designed to emphasize these barriers and create a sense of
awe in the visitor. Black visitors to the plantation, however, took an entirely different route to the house, one unstructured by these processional social barriers
but instead by the single elemental social barrier between enslaved and free

In fact, it is possible that Lemaur took the pleasure gardens around the
main residences of some Cuban plantation owners as another model for the
central axis in his garden design. See, for instance, a print from *Los Ingenios*,

FIGURE 5. Detail, Eduard Laplante, *Ingenio San José de la Angosta*, 1855–1857, lithograph, in J. G. Cantero, *Los ingenios: Colección de vistas de los principales ingenios de azúcar de la isla de Cuba* (Havana: Impreso en la litografía de Luis Marquier, 1857), plate 24. Beinecke Library, Yale University.

published in 1857, which shows a garden surrounding the primary residence of Ingenio San José de la Angosta (Figure 5). This garden bears a striking resemblance to Lemaur's plan, with a wide central path leading to a large fountain or statue, intersected by a series of diagonal paths. Much of the funding for Havana's botanical garden came from the expanding sugar industry—the Sociedad Patriótica oversaw the space, and most of the membership of this organization at the time was made up of *ingenieros*.

Lemaur's inclusion of a provision garden, though, also serves as a pointed reminder of the realities of enslaved life. This inclusion was especially surprising as race was increasingly a subject of intense anxiety on the part of white elite Cubans, *criollo* and *peninsulares* alike. The black population of Cuba was increasing rapidly, driven by demand for workers for the exponentially expanding sugar industry. Even the end of the legal slave trade in 1817 through treaty with England barely slowed this process, in part because the illegal shipments of enslaved people continued at a great pace. White racial paranoia was also driven by memory of the Haitian Revolution and continuing rumors of imagined and actual uprisings of enslaved people on Cuba itself, most notably the 1812 Aponte Rebellion.[15] These racial tensions, as I will discuss, only increased in the years to come, and continued to shape the very space of the botanical garden itself.

1828 Plan for Havana's Botanical Garden

Seven years after Lemaur produced his ambitious plan for Havana's botanical garden under Ossa, a new peninsular director, Ramón de la Sagra, entirely reimagined the space. Under Sagra, the garden shifted from focusing on scientific botany and Linnaean study of indigenous flora to a near-total dedication to economic botany and profit extracted from a small set of imported cash crops. This shift was driven in large part by the increasingly popular idea that Cuba needed more white immigrants and that immigrants would in turn be attracted to better agricultural opportunities. Sagra published his plan for the botanical garden in his own magazine, *Anales de Ciencias, Agricultura, Comercio y Artes*, in 1828 (Figure 6).[16]

The page in *Anales* is divided in half. On the left of the page is a plan labeled "Garden in 1827" and on the right "Garden in 1828." The page viewed as a whole, then, functions as a powerful piece of self-promotional propaganda for Sagra, presenting the reader with a vision of stark contrasts and improvements under even the first few months of his directorship of the garden.

The "Garden in 1827" side of the illustration represents the botanical garden, and by extension the state of Cuban science, upon Sagra's appointment as empty and overlooked. The diagram shows the rectangular plot of the garden bisected with a grid of paths, just as in the plan from Lemaur's diagram. However, where each section of this bisected grid had been filled with actual

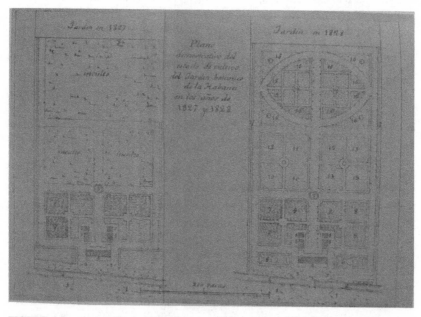

FIGURE 6. Ramon de la Sagra, *Plano demostrativo del estado de cultivo del Jardín Botánico de la Havana en los años de 1827 y 1828*, 1828, engraving, from *Anales de Ciencias, Agricultura, Comercio y Artes*, vol. 2 (Havana: Oficina del Gobierno y Capitanía General, por S.M., 1828). New York Historical Society.

and planned plants from around Cuba and the world in the 1821 plan, Sagra represented nearly the entire garden as bare, "more of an abandoned field than a garden," as he wrote in a report to Spanish officials.[17]

This representation of Havana's botanical garden in 1827 was in direct contradiction to the plan that Lemaur had produced six years earlier, which shows the entire space filled with a wide variety of plants and carefully designed intersecting paths. The truth of the garden's state in 1827 was likely somewhere between these two representations. The 1821 plan was certainly aspirational, as mentioned. Ossa himself noted on in the report from the same time that he did not have access to enough enslaved laborers for the conservation and improvement of the garden and that the plan represented the "continuous tasks" he had planned.[18] However, it is also clear that the botanical garden before Sagra's arrival was not really the abandoned field that Sagra portrayed it as in his illustration.

José Antonio de la Ossa's report to Spanish officials had contained numerous clear requests for the resources he would need to enable Havana's garden to serve as a major node for a transatlantic botanical exchange among Spain and her colonies. Rather than grant Ossa his requests, however, the Ministerio de Ultramar had replaced him with Ramón de la Sagra. Born in Galicia, Spain, Sagra leveraged personal connections as well as his studies of medicine and anatomy at the University of Madrid to secure an appointment in November 1822 as professor of natural history with an appointment to Cuba.[19] Sagra wrote an effusive letter in acknowledgment of this appointment, stating that "the Island of Cuba, located under the fortunate sky of the tropics, where the plant nature is so much its strength and magnificence, can be one of the very rich theaters of scientific research, all the more so as its productions have barely been recognized." He went on to promise to grant access "to the Peninsula of the productions of this rich land."[20] This promise would have been extremely welcome to Spanish officials in 1822.

Garden as Celebration of Agricultural Botany

Sagra's plan for the garden differed from Lemaur's previous plan in several key respects. In Sagra's plan, the educational center was expanded from two neighboring buildings to one large building. The northern section of the garden was changed by Sagra from diagonal intersecting lines to a complex symmetric arrangement of curved and straight lines forming an ovoid shape. Most important, the central section of the garden in Sagra's diagram had been divided into four sets of four quadrants. Four of these are filled with indigo, tobacco, and cotton; two with medicinal plants; one with fruit trees; one with cacao, coffee, and vanilla; and one with sugarcane. The section also includes plots for germinating seeds and for additional botanical teaching. This section showcasing imported cash crops was entirely absent from Lemaur's plan, and shows Sagra's new focus on economic botany.

Furthermore, we can interpret these grids as visual representations of the idea that the imported crops that Sagra was growing in the botanical garden could have interchangeably substituted for each other and, more importantly, that they could have replaced sugar in Cuba's economy. This "interchangeability" was echoed in a Spanish report from this same period in which a Spanish official praised Sagra's proposal for the garden. The letter celebrated in particular the benefits that this garden would offer to "peninsular industry." "There are few countries that, like Cuba, can base their industrial prosperity on a great number of products, vary them, and *substitute them with each other*," the Spanish official wrote. "The acclimatization of these various plants may give Cuba new branches of production, thus multiplying the sources of public prosperity."[21]

Under Sagra, then, the main section of the garden, directly behind the educational building, was given entirely over to agricultural experimentation with cash crops, instead of to showcasing botanical diversity as it had been just a few years ago under Ossa. This might seem a minor change, but it actually represented a major shift in how white Cuban elites understood the connection between botany, imperial loyalty, and race.

In an October 1824 speech for the public opening of a school of public botany, Sagra explained his changes to the garden's design. He stated that his proposed plan for the garden would make visible the relationships between plants of related and different families (a nod toward Linnaean scientific botany) but that the most important part of the garden (the central section) would be the section dedicated to cultivation and acclimatization. The positive results of these studies, he promised, would be visible to the public there.[22]

This shift toward agricultural experimentation on its own is, again, notable, and somewhat surprising given both Cuban and Spanish officials dedication just a few years earlier to the garden serving as the central node to a global specimen exchange network. Sagra's speech, however, also explained his interest in agricultural experimentation beyond sugar. "The only thing that will assure the prosperity of the island of Cuba," he wrote, "is the establishment of small crops, crops that are not gown in anticipation of exorbitant capital." More importantly, he went on to say that such diversified agricultural botany will "increase the necessary population of the country."[23] This phrase, "necessary population," would have been understood by Sagra's audience at the time to specifically mean the white population of Cuba.

White immigration was increasingly thought by white Cubans to be necessary to reduce the possibility of slave revolt as well as to counteract the political, social, and economic power of free Cubans of color. A number of laws were passed to encourage this immigration. In October of 1817, for example, Spain issued a royal cedula calling for an "augmentation" of the white population of Cuba.[24] There were also social and political organizations formed to encourage white immigration, such as the *Junta de Población Blanca*. This council formed in 1817 as a subcommittee of the Sociedad Patriótica, the economic improvement society that was also responsible for maintaining the botanical garden.

Cuba was, of course, not the only Latin American site with white immigration schemes in the mid-nineteenth century. The 1820s and 1830s also saw white artists and politicians in Jamaica seeking to, as Kay Dian Kriz puts it, refine "the rude and toxic West Indian landscape into a space capable of attracting and maintaining a healthy, virtuous, and polite white population."[25] Ernesto Bassi has written on similar schemes in Columbia in the 1820s, and Erika Edwards has recently drawn attention to racial self-fashioning in the whitening rhetoric of nineteenth-century Argentina.[26] What is unique about Cuba, however, is not just that these schemes took place under continuing imperial control rather than new nationhood, but also that these schemes intersected with a rise in interest on the part of white elites in botany and natural history. Sagra stood at this intersection, and reimagined the botanical garden of Havana as a site leading the way in the massive population shift that seemed to many to be the most urgent political issue of their time.

Sagra did, in fact, have some success with his agricultural experiments. In 1830, he was given an order to continue studying the possibility of growing indigo on Cuba, and in 1833 he was commended by the *intendente* of Havana for his success in doing so.[27] In 1834 the Intendente of Havana sent another laudatory report on Sagra's work to Madrid, mentioning his success in creating and introducing agricultural improvements for rural areas, his successful production of indigo and mulberry trees (necessary for silk production), as well as other plants including types of gum and textiles.[28] However, the fact that none of the cash crops listed in Sagra's diagram ever made up a significant portion of Cuban exports, and the fact that sugar exports continued growing each year, should remind us that any success he did have was never replicated on a large scale. In the end, it turned out that the crops that Sagra celebrated in his grids were neither as easy to grow nor as interchangeable as he had represented them.

Garden as Entertainment Space

Under Sagra, then, the botanical garden of Havana was reimagined as a site of agricultural experimentation and a showcase of potentially profitable crops that could be grown on a small white-owned family farm. This potential profit would both encourage white immigration and also curry favor with an increasingly cash-poor Spanish empire. For this system to function, though, the number of white visitors to the garden had to increase.

It was likely partly to showcase Sagra's agricultural experimentation, then, that the white elite entertainment complexes that Ana Amigo discusses were established next to the garden. One of these was a theater called the Diorama, installed in the garden in 1827, which hosted dances and plays. These included a masked dance during the Havana carnival in 1831 and the dance in honor of the *jura* of the infanta Maria Isabel Luisa in October 1833.[29] In part because of these events, Amigo argues that the botanical garden of Havana became during the 1830s a site of white elite leisure and sociality. She adds that this was particularly important in a city with limited public leisure spaces.

This interest in space for white elite leisure can even be seen in Sagra's plans for the garden, which included fountains and statues along the main corridor, where visitors would promenade up and down. In fact, even during Ossa and Lemaur's time at the garden, its design had included decorative elements such as this fountain and statues of "Neptune and Apollo." It remains unclear how many of these statues and fountains were ever actually installed, but their presence on the plans speaks to a rising interest on the part of white elites in Havana to demarcate public space through sculpture with classical references.

Some ten years after Lemaur had created his garden plan, the members of the Sociedad and other white Havana elites commissioned a series of massive classicizing fountains with similar themes around the city, one of which also featured Neptune. Paul Niell reads this set of commissions as representative of a new sense of *buen gusto*, or good taste. White elite Cubans used that term to create a narrative of cultural superiority and to distance themselves from the artistic production of free Cubans artisans of color.[30] Sagra would have been highly aware of the racializing role of public art and, by including a fountain in his plan, seems to have used it to further mark his garden as a space for white leisure in the service of white agriculture and white immigration.

Shifting Role of Enslaved Labor and Black Experience under Sagra

Just as Ossa had, Sagra, though, depended on enslaved workers to build and maintain the garden that he imagined in his plan. In fact, the *Memorias de la Real Sociedad Económica* from the period include several mentions of extended negotiations between Sagra and the Sociedad regarding the number of enslaved workers that would be necessary to execute and maintain his plan for the garden (which Sagra insisted was at least ten enslaved workers).[31] The matter was finally resolved when a member of the Sociedad "donated" an unspecified number of "negros bozales" to the garden.[32]

Just as Lemaur's plan for the garden did, Sagra's plan also shows the quarters for enslaved laborers located immediately behind this building that served as educational center and home for the garden's head professor (Sagra himself). Unlike in Lemaur's plan, however, Sagra did not include the provision garden that these enslaved people would have used for their personal sustenance in his overall design for the garden. The provision grounds almost certainly still would have existed, but they had been excised from this celebratory public rendition of the space.

There are only a few other hints in the written archives about the experience of the enslaved people who lived next door to Sagra, or about the experiences of any non-white, non-elite visitors to the garden under his leadership. One document outlining the reorganization of garden staffing under Sagra noted that he "will be in charge of all of the slaves and field hands of the garden and will treat them with moderation and good order, he will take care to watch for any faults to avoid punishment. . . . The religious acts of the slaves of the garden are the charge of the gardener, they should take mass each Sunday and name one of themselves to go to the church"[33] It is impossible to know if this intentional outlining of proper treatment of enslaved workers was due to conflicts and excessive punishment under Ossa or due to increasing debates over treatment of enslaved labor forces that was taking place across Cuba at this moment.[34]

Overall, however it seems likely that in many ways, the experience of an enslaved laborer living and working at Havana's botanical garden changed little between 1821 and 1828. The laborer still would have worked in the garden, planting, propagating, and pruning throughout the day, would have walked the long path back to the provision grounds at the end of the day and slept in a building behind the educational complex. The laborer would have taken mass on Sunday and may have attended a church in town. While the neat squares of crops on Sagra's plan were meant to attract white immigrants to Cuba, these plots would still have been maintained almost entirely by enslaved black workers.

Botanical Garden's Move to Molinos, 1839–1840

Sagra left Cuba in 1835 to pursue personal natural history projects in France and the United States, and by the end of the 1830s the gardens were in some disarray. Furthermore, the leadership of the garden was being pressured to move, as the space was needed to expand a new railway station and storage depot. The proposed new location for the botanical garden, the Quinta de los Molinos, was the summer home of the Captain General, and lay outside of the walled city of Havana. The move was somewhat controversial—a letter in *El Diario de la Havana* from 1839 discussed the plan indignantly:

That the botanical garden, transferred to El Molinos, would produce the same advantages as it does at its current location seems impossible to me, because who will be the poor man who, in the force of the heat and despite his laziness, has to go to look for the medicinal plants that help his ailments and that are currently two steps from his door; [who are] those who are convalescing who go there to recover their strength; [who are] those Botany students who come to hear the lessons of their professor; who are the farmers who busily ask about their crops, visit the establishment, examine their wealth and acquire inspiration and knowledge to guide them in the new branches of rural industry? . . . Where would the owners of plantations get the products they need? For example, the bread tree, without which I would have had to spend a lot of money last year on the maintenance of my blacks.[35]

This quote neatly summarizes the shifting goals of Havana's botanical garden in the previous decades—to be a source of medicinal plants, information on crops, and botanical knowledge. Furthermore, as the letter hinted, none of these functions would happen as effectively if the garden were moved to the outskirts of the city. This, in fact, proved prophetic. While the gardens under Ossa had been a site for celebrating biodiversity and under Sagra a site for imagining agricultural alternatives to the sugar industry, in its new location the botanical garden functioned almost exclusively as pleasure garden for Havana's elite. Joseph John Gurney in 1840 called it "a place of constant public resort."[36]

Elite Leisure at the Captain General's Doorstep

This shift in focus was made evident and was reinforced by the new layout for the garden, which James Philippo calls "gardens laid out in the style of Versailles."[37] One visitor in 1845 described the experience of the gardens at Quinta de los Molinos in detail:

We'll follow the crowd to the Tacon Garden, some very prettily laid-out grounds enclosing the summer residence of the captain governor . . . a beautiful moonlight, we sauntered down an allée, that looked too inviting to resist; we pursued it till we found ourselves in a sweet garden, where we wandered wondering and delighted. At every turn a new and agreeable surprise; a jet d'eau; a gurgling waterfall, with its moss and grottos; we ascended terraces, sat down in arbors, wound through thick-leaved groves . . . I had no idea where we were, whether on public or private property. . . . I thought of the magical gardens in the Arabian Night.[38]

Similarly, Samuel Hazard wrote in 1873 that the gardens "are open day and night, and any one is allowed to enter and stroll through the beautiful walks, shaded and surrounded by most exquisite tropical flowers, shrubs, and trees."[39]

The earliest plan that survives from the Quinta de los Molinos location is from 1864. This plan shows the irregular shape of the space divided by a long central path, with a series of paths intersecting it at perpendicular angles (Figure 7). This design, then, seems to reference the earlier layout of the garden in its previous location, with its wide central axis and symmetric paths. However,

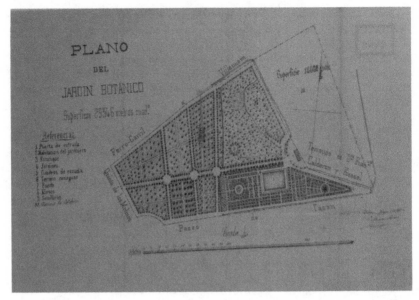

FIGURE 7. Plano del Jardín Botánico de la Habana, 1871. Archivo Histórico Nacional, Madrid, ULTRAMAR, MPD.2948.

the description of the garden seems to specifically refer to the upper right quadrant, in which the orderly beds of Ossa and Sagra's gardens have been replaced by a "ramble" with sinuous paths snaking through the space.

What is apparent from the descriptions above is that the garden had been stripped of nearly all its scientific associations in the minds of visitors, and had become primarily a site of leisure and retreat. The travelers that Ana Amigo quotes describe wandering the grounds, enjoying the atmosphere, and appreciating the flora for its aesthetic qualities, but never mention any kind of intellectual engagement with the botany of the site. Notably, both the Linnaean garden and the agricultural experimentation zones had been excised in the plan for the garden at its Quinta de los Molinos location.

What is also apparent from the quoted description of visiting the garden is that the space had become inextricably linked in the minds of visitors to the *capitán general* himself. This account calls it the "Tacón Garden," after Miguel Tacón y Rosique, the *capitán general* of the time. The *capitán general* was the highest-ranking officer in Cuba and Tacón, even more than others who occupied the position, consolidated the power he held and used it to reshape Havana. Many of the architectural features that define the city today, including the paseos that pass through it, came out of this moment. When the gardens were moved to Quinta de los Molinos, they were understood no longer as a public botanical garden but as a private garden belonging to the *capitán general.*

Thus, the garden that white elite criollos and peninsulares alike had used for several decades to assert loyalty to Spain but also to imagine different forms of local nature, in its new location was entirely subsumed under the assumed ownership of a Spanish official. Although Amigo makes a convincing argument that the botanical garden served as a space to imagine alternative modes of citizenship and sociability beyond the strictures of the colonial agenda, in the end, this space of possibility was claimed by the empire itself.

Emancipation at Molinos?

None of the designs that survive of the gardens in their Quinta de los Molinos location include living quarters or provision grounds for the use of the workers who maintained the grounds. The visual record that would teach us about the experience of these workers, therefore, is nonexistent. The only hint in the archives we have about the experience of enslaved black men and women who worked at the new location of the botanical garden is in a set of letters from 1864 and 1865 which refer to eight freed black workers at the garden and requests for funds to hire an additional eight freed black workers.[40] There is no indication of why emancipated black laborers specifically were desired, given that slavery was still legal in Cuba through 1886. It is possible that some of these workers at the garden were the same individuals who had been enslaved by the Sociedad in the decades prior, who had purchased their freedom or had it purchased for them, but that the Sociedad wished to continue employing in the garden due to their expertise and familiarity with the plants.

These archival punctum, then, raise more questions than they answer. Regardless, these mentions of black workers should remind us that throughout its history the botanical garden of Havana depended not just on the labor but also the natural historical knowledge of the black workers, free and enslaved, who worked there. These individuals maintained the grounds as the focus and the layout of these grounds shifted significantly and laboriously dug up each of the plants and helped move them across town, to the grounds next to the *capitán general*'s house.

Conclusion

Throughout the nineteenth century, the way that the botanical garden of Havana represented Cuban nature to the various audiences who visited the space changed significantly. These changes, from a focus on Cuban biodiversity to a focus on imported crops for small white-owned family farms to a focus on white elite leisure, are reflected in the shifting designs for the gardens grounds.

These changes also show a shifting understanding of the relationship between natural history and Cuban imperial loyalty. Finally, little archival evidence remains of the experiences of the enslaved black workers whose labor and expertise built and maintained the garden, but a few hints of those experiences do allow us to imagine the different experiential landscapes that make up the diagrams and plots that we see today.

This study of the racial and political valences of this space could be productively expanded to include the complicated relationship of the garden to the changing layout of Havana itself, especially to the paseos and the other public gardens that were constructed over the course of the mid-nineteenth century. Furthermore, it would be instructive to learn even more about who visited the botanical garden of Havana at different times and how different groups used and understood the space differently. In particular, it would be extremely interesting to study how the free people of color of Havana and its surroundings used and understood the gardens of the city as their political and economic power grew in the period before the Year of the Lash. My study could also be extended to examine how women from Cuba and abroad located themselves within shifting discourses of gardens and tropical natural history. Karen Robert, for instance, discusses how Mary Gardner Lowell's accounts of Cuba are gendered, with her attention to flora and her use of language referring to beauty and affect.[41] It would be productive to examine other accounts of Cuba written at the time for similarly gendered language and to map such language onto other contemporaneous descriptions of Cuban nature and garden spaces.

My hope is that this study of the intersecting layers of race, empire, and natural history points toward a blueprint for continuing to examine these intersections in other sites and at other moments. Today, citizens from all places and all walks of life are facing challenges not unlike the members of the Havana intelligentsia. Our world, like theirs, is being transformed by ecological crisis, global migrations, and political turmoil. A better understanding how visual culture and the built environment made and makes sense of these transformations will become increasingly crucial in the years to come.

NOTES

1. Real Sociedad Económica de la Habana, *Memorias de La Real Sociedad Económica de La Habana* (Havana: Oficina del Gobierno y de la Real Sociedad Patriótica P. S. M., 1818), 2:187.

2. On the Botanical Garden of Havana, see especially José González de la Peña Puerta, Antonio Ramos Carrillo, and Estaban Moreno Toral, "El Jardín Botánica y la botánica farmacéutica en La Habana del siglo XIX," *Ars Pharmaceutica* 53, no. 3 (2012): 34–39; and Miguel Ángel Puig-Samper and Mercedes Valero, *Historia del Jardín Botánico de La Habana* (Aranjuez: Ediciones Doce Calles and Consejo Superior de Investigaciones Científicas, 2000). On botanical gardens across the world, see Lucile Brockway, *Science and Colonial Expansion: The Role of the British Royal Botanic Gardens* (New Haven, CT: Yale University Press, 2002); Donal McCracken, *Gar-*

dens of Empire: Botanical Institutions of the Victorian British Empire (London: Leicester University Press, 1997); Londa Schiebinger, *Plants and Empire: Colonial Bioprospecting in the Atlantic World* (Cambridge, MA: Harvard University Press, 2004), among others.

3. David A. Sartorius, *Ever Faithful: Race, Loyalty, and the Ends of Empire in Spanish Cuba* (Durham, NC: Duke University Press, 2013); Michele Reid-Vazquez, *The Year of the Lash: Free People of Color in Cuba and the Nineteenth-Century Atlantic World* (Athens: University of Georgia Press, 2011); Aisha K. Finch, *Rethinking Slave Rebellion in Cuba: La Escalera and the Insurgencies of 1841–1844*, Envisioning Cuba (Chapel Hill: University of North Carolina Press, 2015); Ann Twinam, *Purchasing Whiteness Pardos, Mulattos, and the Quest for Social Mobility in the Spanish Indies* (Stanford, CA: Stanford University Press, 2015).

4. Archivo General de Indias, Ultramar, *leg.* 107, no. 35.

5. Archivo General de Indias, Ultramar, *leg.* 108, December 29, 1821, letter.

6. "Jardín Botánico Madrid de Migas Calientes 1781," *Anales de la Sociedad Española de Historia Natural* (Madrid: Don S. de Uhagon, tesorero, 1875), 4:445.

7. For more, see especially Ricardo R. Austrich, "El Real Jardín Botánico de Madrid and the Glorious History of Botany in Spain," *Arnoldia* 47, no. 3 (1987): 1–19.

8. These lists are reproduced in full in Paloma Blanco et al., "Plantas cubanas y documentos de la Ossa en el Real Jardín Botánico de Madrid," *Fontqueria* 36 (1993): 117–46.

9. For more on this process, see, for instance, Staffan Muller-Wille, "Collection and Collation: Theory and Practice of Linnean Botany," *Studies in History and Philosophy of Biological and Biomedical Sciences* 38 (2007): 541–62.

10. For more on the political implications of a Linnaean garden in the space of a colonial botanical garden, see especially Antonio Lafuente and Nuria Valverde's essays in Londa L. Schiebinger and Claudia Swan, eds., *Colonial Botany: Science, Commerce, and Politics in the Early Modern World* (Philadelphia: University of Pennsylvania Press, 2005); and Antonio Lafuente, "Enlightenment in an Imperial Context: Local Science in the Late-Eighteenth-Century Hispanic World," *Osiris* 15 (2000): 155–73.

11. *Memorias de La Real Sociedad Económica de La Habana* (Havana: Oficina del Gobierno y de la Real Sociedad Patriótica P.S.M., 1818), 5:294–302, cited in Puig-Samper and Valero, *Historia del Jardín Botánico de La Habana*, 78.

12. Archivo General de Indias, Ultramar, *leg.* 108, no. 10. Also mentioned in Archivo Nacional de Cuba, Intendencia de Hacienda, *leg.* 318, no. 33, cited in Puig-Samper and Valero, *Historia del Jardín Botánico de La Habana*, 82.

13. Ana Amigo, "Identidad, modernidad, ocio: Jardines urbanos de La Habana en el siglo XIX," *Cuban Studies* 46 (2018): 98.

14. Dell Upton, "White and Black Landscapes in Eighteenth-Century Virginia," *Places* 2, no. 2 (1984): 66.

15. For more, see especially Matt D. Childs, *The 1812 Aponte Rebellion in Cuba and the Struggle against Atlantic Slavery*, Envisioning Cuba (Chapel Hill: University of North Carolina Press, 2006); Sibylle Fischer, *Modernity Disavowed: Haiti and the Cultures of Slavery in the Age of Revolution* (Durham, NC: Duke University Press, 2004).

16. *Anales de ciencias, agricultura, comercio y artes*, vol. 1 (Havana: Oficina del Gobierno y Capitania general, por S.M., 1827).

17. Archivo Nacional de Cuba, *leg.* 1124, no. 72, March 17, 1828, letter from Sagra.

18. Archivo General de Indias, Ultramar, *leg.* 108, no. 8.

19. Camilla Townsend, "'The More I See, the More Surprised I Am': Ramón de La Sagra, Baltimore, and the Concepts of Race of Poverty," in *Strange Pilgrimages: Exile, Travel, and National Identity in Latin America, 1800–1990's*, ed. Ingrid Elizabeth Fey and Karen Racine, Jaguar Books on Latin America 22 (Wilmington, DE: Scholarly Resources, 2000), 44.

20. Archivos Fondos Real Jardín Botánico, I.32.5.4.

21. Archivo General de Indias, Ultramar, *leg.* 149.II, December 3, 1827, letter from Don Jacobo María de Parga. Emphasis added.

22. Real Sociedad Económica de la Habana, *Memorias de La Real Sociedad Económica de La Habana* (Havana: Oficina del Gobierno y de la Real Sociedad Patriótica, 1825), 5:790.

23. Real Sociedad Económica de la Habana, 5:785, 788.

24. This cedula specified that "white" in this context meant white Spaniards from the Peninsula or the Canary Islands, or Catholics from European countries who were allies of Spain and granted Spanish nationality to any such settlers who remained in Cuba for five or more years. In practice, most white immigrants in this policy were French, many of them sugar mill owners from former Saint-Domingue.

25. Kay Dian Kriz, *Slavery, Sugar, and the Culture of Refinement: Picturing the British West Indies, 1700–1840* (New Haven, CT: Yale University Press, 2008), 158.

26. Ernesto Bassi, "The 'Franklins of Colombia': Immigration Schemes and Hemispheric Solidarity in the Making of a Civilised Colombian Nation—ProQuest," *Journal of Latin American Studies* 50, no. 3 (August 2018): 673–701; Erika Denise Edwards, *Hiding in Plain Sight: Black Women, the Law, and the Making of a White Argentine Republic* (Tuscaloosa: University of Alabama Press, 2020).

27. Archivo General de Indias, Ultramar, leg. 149.II, Sept. 28, 1830, letter from palace; September 27, 1833, letter from Intendente of Havana.

28. Archivo Histórico Nacional de España, Ultramar, *leg.* 2, no. 25.

29. Amigo, "Identidad, modernidad, ocio."

30. Paul B. Niell, *Urban Space as Heritage in Late Colonial Cuba: Classicism and Dissonance on the Plaza de Armas of Havana, 1754–1828* (Austin: University of Texas Press, 2015); Paul B. Niell, "Rhetorics of Place and Empire in the Fountain Sculpture of 1830s Havana," *Art Bulletin* 95, no. 3 (2013): 440–64.

31. See, for instance, *Memorias de La Real Sociedad Económica de La Habana.* Vol. 5. (1825), 597 and 770.

32. Real Sociedad Económica de la Habana, *Memorias,* "Esposicion de las tareas que han ocupado a la Real Sociedad Patriotica durante los anos de 1825 y 1826, leida en junta general de 15 de diciembre," D. Joaquin Santos Suarez, 5:30.

33. Real Sociedad Económica de la Habana, 5:607.

34. For more on these debates, see especially Gloria García Rodríguez, Nancy L. Westrate, and Ada Ferrer, *Voices of the Enslaved in Nineteenth-Century Cuba: A Documentary History,* Latin America in Translation/En Traducción/Em Tradução (Chapel Hill: University of North Carolina Press, 2011).

35. *Diario de la Habana* (Havana), May 3, 1839, 1–2.

36. Joseph John Gurney, *A Winter in the West Indies Described in Familiar Letters to Henry Clay, of Kentucky,* electronic resource (London: J. Murray, 1840), 210.

37. James M. Philippo, *The United States and Cuba* (London: Pewtress & Co.; New York: Sheldon, Blakeman, & Co., 1857), 563.

38. Fanny Elssler, *The Letters and Journal of Fanny Elssler: Written before and after Her Operatic Campaign in the United States. Including Her Letters from New York, London, Paris, Havana* (New York: H. G. Daggers, 1845), 44.

39. Samuel Hazard, *Cuba with Pen and Pencil* (London: Sampson, Low, Marston, Low & Searle, 1873), 139.

40. Archivo Histórico Nacional de España, Ultramar, *leg.* 226, exp. 7, letters from August 27, 1865, and December 18, 1865.

41. Mary Gardner Lowell, *New Year in Cuba: Mary Gardner Lowell's Travel Diary, 1831–1832,* ed. Karen Robert, New England Women's Diaries Series (Boston: Massachusetts Historical Society and Northeastern University Press, 2003), introduction.

JOSEPH R. HARTMAN

Hurricanes in Havana: El Ciclón de '26 as Cultural Agent in Machado's Cuba

ABSTRACT

Hurricanes are much more than devastating meteorological events in Havana's history. They *made* the modern city. Like scrapes on the surface of an ancient palimpsest, those annual storms exposed older layers of history while clearing space for new inscriptions. This article reassesses hurricanes' material and visual role in Havana's modernization in the early twentieth century. A devastating storm known as the Ciclón del '26 made ruins of central Havana on October 20, 1926. The storm's destruction spurred creative responses, including photography, poetry, and architectural monuments. Those visual, spatial, and literary objects demonstrated how natural disasters—hurricanes especially—were also cultural artifacts in Havana's urban history. This was especially so in the case of the hurricane of 1926, which catalyzed new public works and visual culture in Havana under the leadership of Cuba's president, then years later dictator, Gerardo Machado y Morales (in power 1925–1933). The regime leveraged the storm to its advantage. They pointed to reconstruction efforts and international collaborations as proof of political goodwill. The architecture and visual cultures that accompanied the Machado era thus culturally constructed the "natural disaster" of 1926. In so doing, the hurricane transformed modern Havana.

RESUMEN

Los huracanes no solo fueron eventos meteorológicos devastadores en la historia de La Habana. También hicieron la ciudad moderna. Como raspaduras en la superficie de un palimpsesto, esas tormentas anuales expusieron capas más antiguas de la historia mientras despejaban espacio para nuevas inscripciones. Este ensayo reevalúa el papel material y visual de los huracanes en el proceso de modernización de La Habana a principios del siglo XX. Una tormenta conocida como el Ciclón del '26 arruinó La Habana el 20 de octubre de 1926. La destrucción provocó respuestas creativas, que incluyeron fotografías, poesía y monumentos arquitectónicos. Esos objetos creativos demostraron cómo los desastres naturales, especialmente los huracanes, también eran artefactos culturales en la historia de La Habana. Esto fue el caso del huracán de 1926, que sirvió como evento catalizador de nuevas obras públicas en La Habana durante el reino del presidente, y después dictador, Gerardo Machado y Morales (en el poder entre 1925 y 1933). El régimen aprovechó la tormenta a su favor, y reconstruyó la ciudad como prueba de buena voluntad política. La arquitectura y las culturas visuales del machadato construyeron así culturalmente el "desastre natural" de 1926. Al hacerlo, el huracán transformó la Habana moderna.

71

It took every metaphor of art, music, dance, and poetry to describe the sublime and terrifying experience of October 20, 1926, when one of the worst hurricanes in Havana's history (El Ciclón de 26) held the city captive:

That Dantesque vision was yet seared into the retinas of Havana's citizens, of their city turned into a tragic dancer by the demented winds of Aquilon. The fury of the elements forced her to endure cruel hours of horrendous nightmare, an unbelievable Zarabanda; the implacable scourge gave the chaotic and disconcerting impression of a Futurist painting. The entire city was, in fact, dislocated, powerless to free herself from the onslaught of the monster, she surrendered to him and, in the beat of the rain and wind—a demonic orchestra in a witch's coven—she twirled in a wild dance, an infernal Charleston, for twelve hours haunted by angst and uncertainty.[1]

This passage comes from a government-sponsored photobook, *El ciclón de 26 sobre la Habana*, published in 1927. The book featured an artful assemblage of hundreds of photographs taken by Cuba's Office of Public Works. The photographs and accompanying prose documented the storm's destruction, and ultimately the Cuban government's swift restoration efforts during the Presidency (later dictatorship) of Gerardo Machado y Morales (in power 1925–1933). From classical literature to avant-garde painting, Latin dance, and Jazz Age referents: The 1920s text demonstrated how natural disasters—hurricanes especially—were also cultural artifacts in Havana's urban history. This was especially so in the case of the hurricane of 1926, which played a pivotal role in the later development of public works and visual culture in Havana during the Machado era. Hurricanes have long intervened in the city's urban development, and they continue to act as a natural force in the cultural life of Havana today.

Hurricanes were not only devastating meteorological events. They also effectively made modern Havana and Cuba. Like fresh scrapes on the surface of an ancient palimpsest, those annual storms exposed older layers of history as they simultaneously cleared space for new inscriptions. Across multiple literatures, we may observe that the city, Havana particularly, is a dialogic space not only inscribed by its users but also constantly abraded, reused, and reinscribed by human and natural actors.[2] Havana thus embodies an urban palimpsest— a surface of layered writings and histories placed on top of one another. A powerful, if sometimes overlooked, fact of that palimpsest metaphor is its relationship with destruction. To create a fresh surface for inscriptions calls for the erasure and attempted abolition of previous texts. In the case of the Cuban city, those moments of effacement and inscription took on multiple forms. Fidel Castro and the Cuban Revolution of 1959 loom large in discourse on Cuba, but we may think of earlier events, such as the violent encounter of the Taíno, Siboney, and Arawak peoples with the Spanish that culminated in the foundation of Havana beneath a native ceiba tree in 1519. Or the mass influx of enslaved Africans in the nineteenth century, which redefined the demography and plantation economy of Cuba. Then there were particular flash points—the Aponte Rebellion of 1812, the Cuban Wars of Independence of 1868 and 1895, and the Cuban Revolution of 1933 that eventually led to Machado and his regime (*el machadato*) being sent into exile.

Historical writings logically have privileged the role of human actors in retelling those moments of destruction and reconstruction in Havana and the wider Cuban nation. Catastrophe, however, was not always a human product. Change sometimes came through the indifference of nature. The Atlantic hurricane season was an especially intense force in Havana, as for the broader geological and cultural history of the greater Caribbean. Huracán was the name of a deity of destruction across multiple Indigenous Caribbean cultures, including the Taíno, Carib, and Maya peoples. Indigenous representations of the same god from southeastern Cuba included counterclockwise spirals around an ambiguously gendered head. Indigenous artworks demonstrated a remarkable visual knowledge of the cyclonic nature of Caribbean storms, hundreds of years before the development of meteorology in Europe (Figure 1).[3] Early modern European colonialists first unwittingly built their cities in vulnerable coastal regions in the Caribbean. They soon joined Indigenous populations in believing that annual hurricanes represented divine (or better, diabolic) interventions.[4] The 750-mile-long Cuban mainland, moreover, lay precisely at the latitudinal point most susceptible to hurricanes in the Caribbean region. The sublime and ancient powers of Huracán often visited the island—and no less its bayside capital—after 1519.

Over its five hundred years of existence, Havana experienced multiple

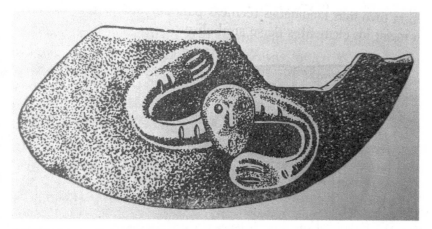

FIGURE 1. *Taíno Storm God (Huracán),* clay vessel shard, date unknown, reproduction from Ortiz, *El Huracán,* 23.

FIGURE 2. Federico Mialhe, *Huracán de 1846*, lithograph, 1846. Courtesy of Museo de Bellas Artes, Havana.

traumas and transformations due to hurricanes. Before official meteorological records, the colonial city of La Habana was perhaps most notoriously devastated in 1846. The "Great Havana Hurricane," likely a Category 5 storm by today's standards, destroyed much of Havana's port, sinking hundreds of boats. The French lithographer Federico Mialhe, famed for his many depictions of colonial Havana, captured that horrifying scene the same year (Figure 2). In the background of Mialhe's print, viewers make out Old Havana and the distinctive tower of the Basílica Menor de San Francisco de Asís, which stands in contrast with the chaotic scene of Havana's harbor in the foreground. The artist likely drew on eyewitness accounts. "Planks and fragments of a thousand ships adrift in shifting winds," one resident described. "Everything tangled, wrecked, ruined."[5] Aside from stocks of sugar, tobacco, and hemp lost in the harbor, the storm threatened the physical city as well. The hurricane produced waves high enough to reach the lanterns on the lighthouse of Havana's iconic El Morro castle. It had winds that took the roofs off most of the city's housing, including architectural monuments like the baroque Catedral de San Cristobal de La Habana. According to official reports, "half the cathedral's sacristy fell to [the] ground, and the windows on its upper floors completely blew out."[6] Perhaps even more important, the hurricane, alongside those of 1844 and 1848, destroyed much of the surrounding farmland, precipitating (while not alone causing) a dramatic shift from coffee growing to sugar plantations.[7]

The existential threat of hurricanes led Havana to become a leader in the emerging field of modern meteorology. Founded by the royal charter of Spanish Queen Isabelle II, the Jesuit Colegio de Belén of Havana created the first major meteorological observatory on the island in 1857. The Observatorio de Belén offered the first hurricane-related forecasts in the world. The trained physicist and priest Benito Viñes served as its director in 1870. Viñes left his mark in the field of meteorology when he argued that hurricanes extended for miles upward, given the large amounts of cirrus clouds produced during storms—an assertion that remained unproved until corroborated by flight technologies in the 1930s.[8] Operating initially out of the northwest tower of the former Belén convent and convalescent hospital in Old Havana, the Belén observatory later moved into a newly built panopticon-inspired campus in Marianao in 1925.[9] By then, the Observatorio Nacional, established during the first US occupation of Cuba (1898–1902), had also begun providing meteorological services. During the second US occupation of Cuba (1906–1909), a distinctive neoclassical and silver-domed building appeared on Casablanca hill in eastern Havana to house the National Observatory.[10] Since its inauguration, the US-founded Cuban institution has worked closely with the Belén Observatory alongside the Weather Bureau in Washington, DC. Together, Havana's meteorological services went on to record several devastating storms throughout the twentieth century. El Ciclón de '26 was among the worst to strike Havana, equaled possibly only by that of 1944 and Hurricane George in 1998.

El Ciclón de '26 was a shocking natural disaster with long-lasting cultural consequences for the urban history of Havana. The human creations that preceded and followed the hurricane transformed it into a cultural agent. A year before the storm, the government of Cuba's infamous president-cum-dictator Gerardo Machado spearheaded an ambitious campaign of public works to transform and modernize Havana and the Cuban nation. Machado's government enacted the Ley de Obras Públicas (Law of Public Works) early in his first term, on July 15, 1925. The public works were to serve as physical manifestations of Machado's campaign slogan: ¡*Agua, caminos, escuelas!*, or "Water, roads, schools!"[11]

In his stump speech, the dark-horse candidate Machado vowed never to contribute to the public debt in his popular ten-part platform. With the Law of Public Works, however, his government soon broke that promise, securing loans of over US$100 million from JP Morgan and Chase National Bank.[12] Flush with money from deep-pocketed US banks, el *machadato* succeeded in constructing a seven-hundred-mile highway through central Cuba that connected via ferry to US Highway 1.[13] The government commissioned the renowned designer and conservator of promenades in Paris, Jean-Claude Nicolas Forestier, to create a new urban plan for Havana based on French Beaux Arts and US City Beautiful and Garden City designs.[14] The regime hired the US firm Purdy & Henderson, as well as the Cuban architects Raúl Otero, Eugenio Rayneri y Piedra, and other professionals, to place El Capitolio at the center of that urban scene (Figure 3).[15] As a colonnaded and domed neoclassic capitol building, El Capitolio looked deceptively similar to that of Washington, DC,

FIGURE 3. Cuba's Office of Public Works, *Palacio del Congreso, March 9, 1929,* photograph. Courtesy of Oficina de la Historiador de la Ciudad de la Habana, Centro de Documentación de la Empresa de Proyectos de Arquitectura y Urbanismo, RESTAURA (OHC Restaura).

also inspired by St. Peter's Basilica and the Panthéon of Paris. More insidious, the regime supplied those projects, in part, with resources extracted by captive laborers, including political prisoners at the recently built Presidio Modelo (model prison) (Figure 4).[16] The prison's five galleys strongly evoked a Benthamite panopticon in design. They were situated on Isla de Pinos (today Isla de la Juventud), south of Cuba's mainland. The regime's construction efforts lasted eight years, until August 12, 1933. At that point, Machado and prominent cabinet members fled Cuba amid labor unrest, street bombs, and gunfire. After extending his second term illegally in 1928, using a heavy hand to squash labor unions, his regime ultimately collapsed under the weight of corruption, police violence, and public disillusionment.

Palm-lined highways throughout the country. Ceibas and royal palm trees in Havana's parks and boulevards. An island of panopticons amid marble-laden mountains and pine forests. The Machado government's public works effectively blurred distinctions between nature and culture, city and country. In so

FIGURE 4. Cuba's Office of Public Works, *Visit of Delegates to Presidio Modelo*, 1928, photograph. Courtesy of OHC RESTAURA.

doing, the regime attempted to render modernization sustainable in Havana and the nation beyond. Detractors pointed to Machado's building campaign as evidence of hubris and corruption. Supporters saw the public works as a recognizable benefit to Havana and the nation. Many still debate the crimes, merits, and failings of Machado's government. Few note how the Atlantic hurricane season nearly destroyed it all. Nor how the regime used the tragedy of one particular storm in 1926 to reinscribe a new architectural landscape on the cultural palimpsest of Havana. That is to say, the public works of the *machadato*, and the marks they left on the urban landscape of Havana, began and ended with two moments of destruction: a hurricane and a revolution.

"Thou Bidest Wall nor Floor, Lord": Resilience and Representation during El Ciclón de '26

Our story begins on a dark and stormy night, followed by a day of nightmares, October 20, 1926. It was then that a massive and traumatic hurricane wiped down much of the urban center of Havana. The storm etched terrifying images deeply into the popular memory of Havana's residents. Survivors later recounted its horror. Gracia Rivera, a young girl at the time, recalled how her grandfather lost his life as he went looking for asthma medicine for his wife during the height of the hurricane: "His raincoat was found later, hanging from a branch." His horse had apparently slipped while crossing the flooded Almendares River that divided the urban neighborhoods of Miramar and Vedado.

There were at least fifty-eight fatalities in Havana that night. Inocencia Acosta Felipe noted the long-lasting psychological effects of the storm. "I wasn't afraid of big cyclones, only of the little 'banana-tree flatteners,' as we call the whirlwinds. Those used to terrify me. Now I'm terrified of thunder and lightning. My face turns green and yellow and becomes so disfigured with fear that I look like someone else."[17]

The Ciclón de '26 was the sixth major hurricane of that year—average in terms of activity but abnormal in the intensity of the storms and their effects on major cities in the wider Caribbean.[18] "The Great Miami Hurricane," one of the most costly and deadly in US history, had struck that city only three weeks earlier.[19] Miami's so-called Big Blow had devastated South Florida's already-deflated real estate market, eventually opening space for new investments in Havana during the Machado era. Before Miami's loss could become Havana's gain, however, Cubans had to weather their own storm. The hurricane started late in the night on October 19. It struck the mainland in the early hours of the morning the next day, culminating in an estimated Category 4 storm by Saffir-Simpson measurements of the late twentieth century. The deadly cyclone had formed from a tropical depression off the coast of Panama and Nicaragua days before (Figure 5). The Ciclón de '26 struck southwest to northeast, opposite the path many hurricanes take. It was a relatively common route, though, for those October storms that presented a special threat to Cuba. Thankfully, the National Observatory, then run by Dr. José Carlos Millás, and the Observatory of Belén, under the direction of Mariano Gutiérrez Lanza, had kept close tabs on the storm as it developed. As a result, Cuba's top-rate meteorological services were able to warn citizens of the impending dangers well ahead of time. The US National Weather Service, in contrast, had just failed to predict Miami's Big Blow until too late.

Cuba's citizens were prepared, but the effects of the hurricane were no less devastating. It first landed on the Isla de Pinos. At the time, Machado's government was in the midst of planning and constructing a massive prison complex near the island's largest city of Nueva Gerona. There, the hurricane wreaked havoc on farmland and nearby villages, including the residences and property of US citizens living on the little island as a remnant of the Cuban-Spanish-American-Philippine War of 1898.[20] When the storm struck, US investors owned nearly 90 percent of the island's land, despite US residents accounting for less than 10 percent of the total population. Postcards of the era attest to the storm's devastating effects on US property, including farms, schools, and residences around the US town of Santa Fe (Figure 6).

Among those estates owned by largely absentee US proprietors was Villa Casas, the fruit plantation of poet Hart Crane's maternal grandfather. It happened that Hart Crane was living on the estate when the storm made landfall. The experience shaped many of his later poetic works. Crane spent six months

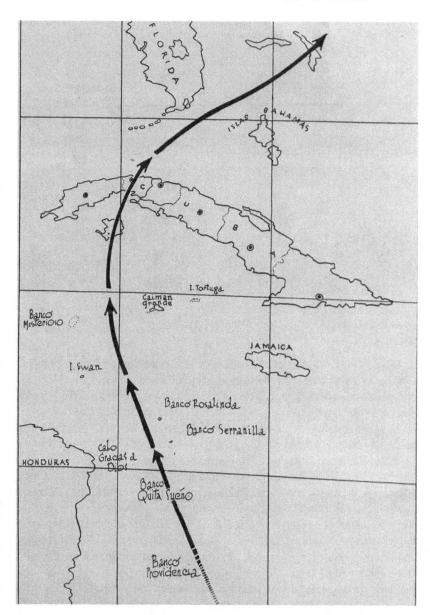

FIGURE 5. *Graphic Showing the Course of the Atmospheric Phenomenon,* reproduction from Aragón and Bau, *Ciclón de 26,* 4.

FIGURE 6. *Postcards of Destruction after Ciclón de 26 (with texts by US residents).* Courtesy of the Archivo Pinero.

on Isla de Pinos aiding his family in repairing the old farm, between May and October of 1926. Although the storm forced the family to sell their ruined estate, it was nevertheless generative for Crane. In "The Hurricane," the US poet described the hurricane of 1926 as a deific power, not unlike that envisioned by Indigenous and later European observers centuries before. "Whip sea-kelp screaming on blond // Sky-seethe, high heaven dashing— // Thou ridest to the door, Lord! // Thou bidest wall nor floor, Lord!"[21]

That Lord of Storm laid waste to old plantation homes on Isla de Pinos. Afterward, it crossed the bay to Batabanó, a sizable town on Cuba's southern coast, just a few hours' drive from Havana. Ocean waters there reached nine feet with winds at hundreds of miles per hour. The Cuban government, under the direction of photographer Manuel Martínez Illa, extensively photographed and filmed the storm's aftershock there and in Havana.[22] Official photographs show entire houses swept into the streets, domiciles turned to driftwood.

One striking image from Batabanó became an icon of the storm's surreal power (Figure 7). The image was that of a leafless royal palm tree skewered by a 4 × 5 beam. The offsetting, and artfully framed, image of a familiar royal palm tree turned strange by the winds reflected the cinematographic training of the photographer as well as the wrath of the storm. Years before, Martínez Illa had studied cinema in the United States and had filmed various documentaries in Brazil and Venezuela for the British Pathé film company before returning

FIGURE 7. *Cover page of El Álbum del Ciclón,* 1927. Courtesy of the Cuban Heritage Collection (CHC).

to Cuba. There, he formed a cinematography shop in Havana's middle-class El Vedado neighborhood. He worked with several popular Cuban magazines, including *El Fígaro, Bohemia,* and *Carteles.* At the start of Machado's first term, Martínez Illa took a position as the head of a newly formed Film and Photography branch of the Office of Public Works. In that capacity, he led a team of photographers in documenting many of the regime's greatest works: the Central Highway and El Capitolio, among others. The team also produced film footage and photographs of the 1926 hurricane, garnering support for aid and relief.

Two bilingual 1927 photobooks, *El álbum del ciclón: 20 de octubre 1926* and the aforementioned *El ciclón de 26 sobre la Habana, historial gráfico-descriptivo del meteoro y sus efectos,* featured Martínez Illa and his team's uncanny image of the skewered palm on their cover pages. Within those books, viewers consume no-less-striking images of flooded streets, overturned trees, leveled parks, and ruined monuments in Havana. Most poignantly, several images depicted the decimation of the neoclassic columns and bronze statuary of the Maine Memorial, a monument created to honor the sinking of the battleship *USS Maine* in Havana's harbor that led to the United States intervention in Cuba's War of Independence in 1898. Surrounded by Cuban day laborers, the bald eagle that rested upon the columns' highest point lay symbolically decapitated on the Malecón—Havana's bayside drive. Later illustrations around the same government photographs even suggested that the Maine Monument had fallen victim to a Greco-Roman god of wind, a personified Aquilon (Figure 8).[23]

If the Ciclón de '26 was a god of destructive force in government illustrations and photographs, then the *machadato* was a mythic hero. Beneath a bust of President Machado in his iconic round glasses, the photobook *El Ciclón de 26 sobre la Habana* described his regime's exceptional leadership with unblushing praise. From one small town to another, Machado himself visited the wreckage and reassured citizens. According to the text, from Havana to the Isla de Pinos, Machado's "exceptional leadership" served as a "mirror" for all self-sacrificing Cuban citizens.[24] The head of state claimed to reflect the finest qualities of Cuba's citizenry. The photographs that followed worked hard to make that case.

Many, in fact, featured physical labor. They were pictures of a productive society. Man and machine civilizing a landscape turned wild. The first images showed groups of young, strong men lifting heavy branches as they cleared the traffic ways of Cuba, especially the Central Highway, then still under construction. The leading man here was El Dinámico (Mr. Dynamic): Carlos Miguel de Céspedes, then Cuba's secretary of works. Multiple photographs showed Céspedes in his Ford automobile, surveying recently cleared roadways. He posed next to a horse in another scene, displaying his knightly efforts. A portrait of the photographer, Martínez Illa, appeared in a roundel next to El Dinámico and his steed, embodying the visualist and materialist arms of the regime (Figure 9). The compassionate face of *el machadato*, meanwhile, took shape in staged photographs of Machado's daughter, Ángela Elvira, handing out clothes to the destitute (Figure 10). Other photographs depicted industrial machines as the path to salvation. Great mechanical cranes lifted trees into place in Havana's city center, especially along El Prado Boulevard and El Parque Central (Figure 11). Captions read: "It may seem in theory that it was an easy job, but everything seems easy . . . after it is done. All the engineering firms put their cranes at the Government's disposal and the latter made good use of them."[25]

Complementing government photographs were those taken by other professional photographers in Cuba. In particular, Enrique "Kiko" Figarola Gómez produced several iconic images for local media outlets, including the prominent newspaper *Diario de la Marina*.[26] One of the most arresting images was that of the equestrian monument of Maximo Gómez, the famed Cuban general who fought alongside Antonio Maceo in the War of Independence of 1895 (see Figure 12). Precariously placed between the rushing waters of Havana's bay and the grounds of Cuba's Presidential Palace (where the photographer stood), the statue transformed into a beacon, a symbol of local culture

FIGURE 8. *Photographs of Maine Monument after 1926 Hurricane*, reproduction from Santovenia, *Libro conmemorativo*, 149.

Manuel Martínez Illa, el Jefe de los Talleres fotográficos de Obras Públicas, filmó una gran película el producto de cuyas exhibiciones queda destinado a engrosar el fondo para socorrer a los damnificados por el ciclón.

Manuel Martínez Illa, Chief Photographer of the Public Works Department, filmed a moving picture which returns are to help the cyclone victims.

FIGURE 9. *Photomontage featuring Carlos Miguel de Céspedes with Horse and Manuel Martínez Illa,* reproduction from Aragón and Bau, *Ciclón de 26,* 70.

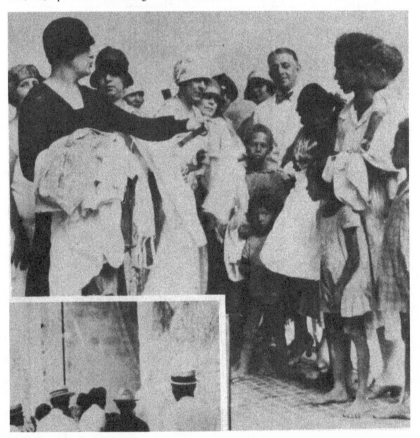

FIGURE 10. *Angela Elvira Handing Clothes to Displaced,* reproduction from Aragón and Bau, *Ciclón de 26,* 74.

FIGURE 11. *Crane at Work Repairing Damages along Paseo de Prado*, reproduction from Aragón and Bau, *Ciclón de 26*, 72.

FIGURE 12. Enrique Figarola Gómez (Kiko), *Monument to Maximo Gomez after Ciclón de 26*, photograph, 1926. Courtesy of the Biblioteca Nacional José Martí.

FIGURE 13. Enrique Figarola Gómez (Kiko), *Flooded Havana Street after Ciclón de 26*, photograph, 1926. Courtesy of the Biblioteca Nacional José Martí.

and survival, surrounded by floodwaters against a mottled sky. In another photograph, the viewer confronts a flooded Havana street (Figure 13). A man in a soaked, unbuttoned shirt stands knee-deep in floodwaters next to his Model T and a sign advertising Ford motor services. A group of men, presumably the service workers at the shop, turn with awareness to the camera's distant lens. Kiko's photographs, like those made by the Cuban government and corporate sponsors, presented an image of Havana at a moment of destruction but also hinted at cultural resilience. Citizens and national monuments, though drowned, remained unbroken.

After the Storm: Water, Roads, Schools . . . and Perturbations

Photographic images of a decimated and then renewed Havana after the storm spoke to the cultural force of that natural disaster. Machado's regime chronicled its efforts in an official 1927 report, *Memoria de los trabajos efectuados con motivo del último ciclón que azotó la isla el 20 de octubre de 1926*. Two thousand copies circulated. The 154-page report included extensive description of damages sustained by the hurricane, the government's response, costs, and statistics. At the end of the book was a republication of an essay on the history of hurricanes in Cuba from 1865 until 1926, written by then director of the Belén Observatory Mariano Gutiérrez Lanza. Of import to the art and architectural history of Havana and Cuba, the report also included an extensive archive of photographs produced by Martínez Illa and his team.

Special attention went to the government's bold response, particularly its appropriation of funds, materials, and labor to preserve and repair patrimony and urban space in Havana. The book reproduced several official decrees published in *Gaceta Oficial de la República de Cuba*. For example, Decree No. 1643, which passed on October 26, 1926, detailed emergency spending. In Havana alone, the government earmarked CP 1,800,000 (roughly equivalent to US dollars) and drew from a reserve of CP 3,600,000, originally slated for roads and infrastructure across Cuba's six provinces. Most of the costs went to material. Foremen (*capataces*) were paid only CP 2.50 a day, and grunt labor (*peones*) received CP 1.76.[27] The Cuban government would not bear the costs alone. The private sector and international relief agencies donated a considerable amount. The Comisión de Donativos received around CP 1.5 million in aid. The largest donations came from Spain and the United States, especially the Comité de Auxilios de Madrid, the Red Cross, Electric Bond and Share Company, JP Morgan, and Chase Bank.[28] The money received and spent was a mere fraction of the loans Machado's government soon borrowed from US banks to finance the larger public works program.

Machado's campaign ran on the promise of *agua, caminos, escuelas* (water, roads, schools). The storm of 1926 presented an early opportunity to make good on those commitments. Foremost, working from early in the morning until late at night, the secretary of public works directed laborers to clear and repair Cuba's highway system after the storm. The monumental task took nearly three weeks to complete. Considerably less time went to repairing Havana's Universidad Nacional, although the symbolism of the act was equally important. Damages caused by the storm had delayed the start of classes. The government quickly set about clearing debris, replanting trees, and restoring damaged property, allowing the school to resume within a matter of days.[29]

Aside from roads and schools, the storm also threatened Havana's waterways. During the height of the hurricane, the Canal de Albear (Albear Aqueduct) suffered damages to a thirty-five-meter stretch along its side. Begun in 1858, the aqueduct was one of the principal suppliers of clean water to the city of Havana. The damages came from internal flooding as well as an external influx of thousands of tons of rushing water caused by a breached embankment where the Western Railroad crossed the Arroyo Orrengo. It was the worst damage the Albear had ever experienced.

Lieutenant Colonel José M. Iglesias took charge of repairs. His team of a hundred workers first built a large temporary canal out of wood, then set about filling in cracks with two hundred sacks of cement. Within five days,

FIGURE 14. *Men at Work Repairing Albear Canal*, reproduction of figure 67 from *Memoria de los trabajos*.

the Albear again pumped seventy million gallons of water to Havana.[30] Photographs showed workers in triumphant poses, repairing the canal. One arresting image depicted a team of workers operating heavy machinery and moving water with gallon buckets. In it, a worker stares determinedly at the camera, eyes shadowed by the brim of his round straw hat (Figure 14). As did Depression-era photographers of the United States, Martínez Illa and his studio pictured the Cuban day laborer as a symbol of hope and modernity triumphant after the storm.[31] The image offered a propagandistic metaphor for the Cuban government itself: hardworking, competent, and noble.

Remarkably, restorations of Havana also included new housing for workers in Marianao who were displaced (*damnificados*) by the storm. One photograph from the *Memoria* shows small, identical concrete homes—each supplied with its own veranda—on a recently cleared street, set against distant palms (Figure 15).[32] The contractor Fernando Roberts built the homes around a newly zoned park at the corner of the streets General Lee, Panorama, General Maceo, and Castillo in the Barrio de Quemados. Such public housing was a unique aspect of the machadato. Machado's government was one of the few

FIGURE 15. *Housing for Displaced Workers in Marianao*, reproduction of figure 69 from *Memoria de los trabajos*.

administrations to create public housing for Cuban laborers before 1959. In addition to homes for hurricane victims in Marianao, Machado's regime later created a small town near the newly built Rancho Boyeros airport outside Havana. They named it Lutgardita after Machado's recently deceased mother. Along with factories, identical neoclassical homes for blue- and white-collar workers, a remarkable Maya-revival theater, a church, and parks, the town also contained La Escuela Técnica "Gerardo Machado."[33] It was a center for decorative arts, where artists worked on paintings and sculptural pieces to adorn the architecture of the Machado regime, including numerous busts of Machado himself. The storm of 1926, in that sense, began a tradition of both intentional housing and luxurious décor in public works, which defined Havana and its suburbs during the Machado era.

Just as the regime memorialized its restoration efforts in photo documentation, it also built panegyrics in stone. A striking image from the government's *Memoria* book included a photograph of a Copa de Carlos Miguel de Céspedes—a marble urn dedicated to Machado's secretary of public works (Figure 16). The Cuban artist Cirilo José Oliva Michelena sculpted the massive *copa* in 1926. It included bas-relief carvings of classicized figures dancing around its circumference and a decorative top. According to captions on two different photographs, the *copa* was located in a park and street named eponymously after Carlos Miguel de Céspedes in Havana's upscale Miramar neighborhood (today the intersection of Quinta Avenida and Calle 42).

The Miguel de Céspedes *copa* and park were among the first of several

FIGURE: 16. *Copa de Carlos Miguel de Céspedes*, reproduction of figure 74 from *Memoria de los trabajos.*

self-indulgent monuments built after the storm. The sybaritic nature of Cuba's secretary of public works provided ample fodder for satire in coming years. The cover page of one 1927 edition of the Cuban satirical magazine *Política Cómica* featured a cartoon rendering of the 1926 hurricane's destruction along the Paseo del Prado, the main thoroughfare of Central Havana (Figure 17). Similar to the regime's propaganda, the image depicts trees bent along the paseo as booming cranes work in the background. In the foreground, two women stylishly dressed stand observing the reconstruction efforts. Their skirts have been blown (presumably by the storm's winds) to reveal their bloomers. The caption reads: "fotografía de los efectos causados en el paseo del prado por la perturbación ciclónica de Carlos Miguel. Photograph of the effects caused along the Paseo de Prado by the cyclonic perturbation of Carlos Miguel." The salacious caption elicited multiple readings. Perhaps Carlos Miguel de Céspedes, Cuba's secretary of public works, took the imagined photograph. Alternatively, Miguel de Céspedes caused the "perturbación" of the women's skirts. Either way, the cartoon effectively indicted the regime's public works agenda and especially its director, with a leering wink and nod.

Storm Chasers: Hurricanes and International Relations in Machado's Cuba

Following Cuba's satirists, we might say that the epicurean architecture of the regime eventually reached its zenith with the suggestively shaped dome of El

FIGURE 17. *Perturbación ciclónica de Carlos Miguel*, cover of *Política cómica*, 1927. Courtesy of Carlos Alberto Fleitas Collection.

Capitolio in 1929. At the time of the storm, however, El Capitolio was but a concrete foundation. By the government's accounts, the building's construction site suffered few damages. The Machado government even pulled money and material resources from the unfinished site to complete necessary repairs in Havana after the storm. Much of that restoration effort focused on replanting trees along Havana's parks and parkways, most notably the Paseo del Prado (or Paseo de Martí), the so-called Caribbean *ramblas* that ran in front of the façade of El Capitolio. Importantly, the storm had miraculously spared the nursery of Aldecoa, where plants and trees had been stored for the regime's larger public works campaign. The preservation of that nursery was a huge boon. As the Office of Public Works put it: "Thanks to the efficiency and speed with which we saved and protected the plants against the ravages of the tempest, the losses were, in reality, insignificant."[34]

The Parque Marté, a colonial-era military camp built in the nineteenth century at the southern foot of the Prado, served as the primary site for replanting and rebuilding efforts. Machado's government would transform that same park in the coming years into El Parque de la Fraternidad Pan-Americana. There, they planted a massive ceiba tree, symbolic of Pan-American fraternity, as well as the Cuban nation and the very foundation of the city of Havana, on February 24, 1928 (Figure 18). The tree was to commemorate the Sixth Annual Pan-American conference held in the city that same year. The ceiba tree had special significance as an indigenous symbol and a spiritual icon for religions of the African diaspora.[35] The large-buttressed tree was also the sort to withstand the strongest headwinds, cultural or natural. Surrounded by an iron fence and adorned with the words of Cuban poet and national hero José Martí, the tree marked one of the most notable new inscriptions produced by the machadato in Havana. It was a symbol imbued with colonial memories, as well—unerasable stains exposed by the storm. Ceiba trees often served as whipping trees on Cuban plantations. The same tree in the Plaza de Armas, under which the Spanish allegedly founded Havana in 1519, likely served a similar judiciary function. It was a site of punishment for criminals and, more often, enslaved Africans.[36] Resonances of colonial-era punishments echoed in the materials of the site, too. The marble plinth that served as the foundation for the tree's iron grille came from quarries mined, in some cases, by men imprisoned by the regime at the Presidio Modelo on Isla de Pinos. It was a symbolic coincidence that the same architect, César Guerra y Massaguer, designed both the iron grille that encased Havana's Tree of Fraternity and the iron galleys of the Presidio that confined dissidents of *el machadato*.[37]

A steady supply of cheap material and forced labor no doubt served as motivation for the regime as it set about restoring damages outside Havana, particularly on the Isla de Pinos. As a special municipality, the isle fell under the purview of Havana's governance. Machado's government took considerable

FIGURE 18. *Tree of American Fraternity, Innauguration, February 24, 1928*, photograph. OHC RESTAURA.

care in rebuilding infrastructure there. Already in 1925, Machado's secretary of the interior, Rogerio Zayas Bazán, had recommended the isle as the site of the regime's model penitentiary. Machado's administration used the storm as an opportunity to purchase more property to achieve the vision of a plantation-style prison. Current landowners, largely US investors like Hart Crane's family, were eager to sell their now-dilapidated landholdings.[38]

Other US residents stuck around, though, and used their financial status to sway government action in the isle's favor for years after the hurricane. Elizabeth Bullock, president of the isle's US-led Hibiscus Club, penned a letter in competent Spanish to Machado on May 13, 1931. She praised Machado for his personal efforts in renewing the island's infrastructure after the storm. Yet Bullock, and the isle's US Chamber of Commerce, hoped that the government would do more to undo the longer-lasting effects of the storm, especially to the island's eponymous pines:

The biggest damage the 1926 cyclone did was not to houses but to pines. The island's prosperity is now at stake. Many families would starve if the Presidio Modelo did not provide them with leftovers. Until the pines return, the island needs another way of living (the fruit business only provides work for two months of the year). Why did tourists once come to the Isle of Pines, with its healthy and tasty springs, beautiful unspoiled beaches, and mountains? We have to use the natural resources of the island—if not, we die.[39]

US landowners requested new trees, a clean water aqueduct, and a general reduction in the cost of driver's licenses. In multiple letters, Bullock even suggested that Machado use prison labor to accomplish those demands. A close relationship between foreign landowners and the Cuban government (often at the cost of Cuban workers and citizens) thus emerged pointedly after the storm of 1926 and continued for decades.[40]

The storm of 1926 created a cocktail of economic and political relationships for the Machado regime and vested US parties. This included the international tourism industry and the US-led project of Pan-Americanism (a program of cultural diplomacy to foster commercial and diplomatic relations among the nations of Americas). The existential threat of hurricanes drove Machado's government toward envisioning broader international coalitions within the Caribbean region, too. The archives of Cuba's secretary of state, for example, revealed an ambitious proposal to create an international congress for combating hurricanes, begun just before Machado's second term in 1929. The conference was to occur in Havana in January 1930. To the author's awareness, it never happened. Nonetheless, correspondence between Cuba's secretary of state and other world powers demonstrated how the Ciclón de '26 effectively hastened political relationships in the region.

Then secretary of state Dr. Rafael Martínez Ortiz drafted a formal proposal in February 1929. It began by citing the "painful experience" of the 1926 hurricane. The traumas caused by the storm led the Cuban government to seek out the cooperation of other nations similarly affected by the ravages of "atmospheric phenomena." The goal of the conference was fourfold: to share information; to implement precautionary measures; to create an international network for aid, police, and other resources to lessen the effects of meteorological events; and most optimistically, to establish a permanent international organization to combat tropical storms.[41]

Hurricanes, after all, threatened not just Cuba but also the entire region in the 1920s. Miami had its Big Blow just a month before the Ciclón de '26 traumatized Havana. Then in 1928, Hurricane San Felipe II devastated San Juan after ruining the French island of Guadeloupe.[42] The same storm system later caused massive flooding and death around Lake Okeechobee in Florida. In 1930, just when Cuba hoped to hold the international conference, the hurricane of San Zenón destroyed much of Santo Domingo in the Dominican Republic. Dramatic urban renewals in Santo Domingo followed during the dictatorship of Rafael Trujillo, which in many ways paralleled the City Beautiful and Beaux Arts plans enacted during *el machadato*. Due to major shifts in climate caused by El Niño–Southern Oscillation weather effects, the decade of the 1920s and into the 1930s, in fact, witnessed the most hurricane activity known in the Caribbean during the past five hundred years.[43]

The unprecedented threat posed by hurricanes demanded unilateral action. Cuba's sub-secretary of state Miguel Ángel Campa received, for the most part, affirmative letters from those who responded. Caribbean and Latin American nations, including the Bahamas, Costa Rica, Haiti, Honduras, Mexico, and Nicaragua all generally agreed the conference should occur and include as many participants as possible. A representative of France, Monsieur L. Rais, likewise wrote at great length about the merit of the project. He cited the recent hurricane of 1928, which not only struck Puerto Rico and the United States but also devastated much of the French colony of Guadeloupe, resulting in close to 1,200 deaths. The French representative made two requests. One, that the congress consider expanding to a global scale (*une extensión mondiale*). He suggested that conference organizers should invite those affected by tropical cyclones in the Pacific and Indian Oceans as well. Two, that the date of the conference be postponed so that French colonial administrators could better coordinate with their counterparts in the colonies (namely Guadeloupe and Martinique).

The US response was more ambiguous, though no less concerned with the state's broader colonial agenda. After two months of delay, then US ambassador Noble Brandon Judah wrote back requesting clarification:

I am directed to enquire of Your Excellency whether or not the Government of the Republic of Cuba has in mind the organization of an International Commission such as the International Relief Union established at Geneva, which would be charged with the control of relief measures in cyclonic and devastated areas. The International Meteorological Committee founded in 1872 has since that time functioned continuously and is at the present more actively engaged than ever before in the assimilation of ships' reports on weather conditions from all quarters of the globe. The Weather Bureau of the United States Department of Agriculture is of the opinion that this activity in itself largely provides for the collection of that information which is so vital a factor in the study of tropical cyclones, hurricanes, and other atmospheric disturbances.[44]

The ambassador thus dismissed the Cuban proposal in polite bureaucratese. The skepticism of the United States toward a Cuban-led initiative at a moment when the US controlled much of the Cuban market while also maintaining a heavy hand in Cuban affairs of state spoke to larger cultural conditions. Cuba was still operating under the provisions of the Platt Amendment up until its abrogation in 1934, which gave the US unparalleled legal control over the island's governance, including the right to intervene militarily. That special relationship affected the US response. Judah's letter, moreover, pointed to a long pattern of the US deployment of "soft power" to advance strategic and economic agendas. While the terrible hurricane season of the 1920s obviously demanded an exceptional international response, in this instance, the hurricane itself did little to break older patterns of colonialism.

Conclusion: Vortices of Stone and Steel

The hurricane of 1926 was an unwitting collaborator with Machado's government. It wiped down the surface of Havana, and the surrounding region, offering fresh space for new modernist inscriptions. At the same time, it revealed older ellipses of colonialism. The storm's destruction offered political opportunities. It was an impetus for new construction and modernization. With debris cleared in a matter of days and parks remade with freshly planted trees, the Cuban government sent a powerful message to international and local constituencies. The storm offered a chance to maintain a foothold in US circuits of trade. It also helped position Cuba as a leader in the science of hurricanes and relief efforts. In their own photographic and written documentation, Machado and his administration appeared battle-ready, compassionate, and full of grit. Like the legend of the Phoenix, a newer and more modern Havana (actually already planned under Machado's Law of Public Works) could take shape.

It helped that many works remained in good form. El Capitolio, then still a concrete foundation, was largely intact. The completed parts of the Central Highway, once cleared, were unscathed. The steel-framed Presidio Modelo held strong—its circular galleys later memorialized, in a way, the swirling and diabolic winds of 1926. The parks and parkways of Havana suffered the most. By then, however, the government had already hired a team of French and Cuban architects to redesign Havana's boulevards and green spaces. The hurricane, if anything, made that new urban plan easier to implement.

The Ciclón de '26 set the stage for a monumental vision. Machado's public works arose from a shared sense of catastrophe in 1926, not unlike that caused by our present-day climate crisis.[45] The storm was one of many cultural agents threaded through an irreducible assemblage of aesthetics, politics, geography, and climate. A sophisticated form of colonialism took shape in capitalist ventures and reconstruction efforts after the hurricane of 1926, too. US banks were all too happy to lend their money to the Cuban government as US investors bought up prime real estate. One cautionary cartoon even depicted the rising threat of US-style consumerism during the era as a massive *tromba*—a cyclone of foreign products sucking bags of money out of the Cuban economy (Figure 19).

A variety of factors, some natural and others cultural, created the perfect storm that defined the public works of *el machadato*. Miami's Big Blow

FIGURE 19. *La Tromba!*, advertisement in *Bohemia* 22, no. 8 (1929): 71. Courtesy of the Instituto de Historia de Cuba.

destroyed a major rival in tourism and cruise circuits. Historical inequities between Cuba and the United States, cemented into law by the Platt Amendment,
made Havana a unique investment opportunity. The US prohibition of alcohol
played a part, encouraging Americans to look for less regulated gambling and
leisure spots. Candidate Machado's own promise to expand the economy beyond the volatile sugar market helped spur investment in tourism. While the
powerful cult of personality that the regime cultivated enabled officials to ag-
grandize themselves through public works and infrastructure.

The architecture and visual cultures that accompanied the Machado era, in
a sense, constructed the "natural disaster" that was the hurricane of 1926. The
storm revealed an aesthetics of disaster, which transformed cultural boundaries
and urban spaces within Havana. El Capitolio, a building that Cuban poet Alejo
Carpentier later called the "apotheosis" of Machado's Cuba, may be among the
most important reminders of those transformations that occurred after 1926.[46]
As it was for Machado, the then newly restored neoclassic Capitol stands today
as a resonant symbol of Cuba's aspirations, uncertain future, and troubled past.
It is a vortex of stone and steel around which swirl cultural winds of change.
Like the ceibas that withstood hurricanes, or the royal palms that held strong
despite impaling winds, El Capitolio has both witnessed and represented destruction, change, and rebirth in Havana. What more will the building withstand, as new dangers threaten the city—whether pandemic, climate change, or
cultural politics? Infused in that question is the constancy of adaptation that the
metaphor of the palimpsest represents. Ruin and revolution are as dependable
as the annual hurricane for Havana.

NOTES

1. Luis Aragón and G. A. Calafell Bau, *El ciclón de 1926: Sobre la Habana; historial
gráfico-descriptivo del meteoro y sus efectos* (Havana: Compañía Litográfica de la Habana,
1926), 4. All translations are author's own. For period reports, see also José Carlos Millás,
"El ciclón del día 20 de octubre," *Boletín del Observatorio Nacional*, no. 1 (October 1926):
312–325; and Millás, "El huracán de octubre de 1926," *Boletín del Observatorio Nacional* 22
(October 1926): 185–225; Mariano Gutiérrez Lanza, *Ciclones que han pasada por la isla de
Cuba: O tan cerca que hayan hecho sentir en ella sus efectos con alguna fuerza desde 1865 a
1933* (Havana: Cultural, 1934).

2. For dialogics, see Mikhail Bakhtin, *Problems of Dostoevsky's Poetics*, trans. Caryl Emer-
son (Manchester, UK: Manchester University Press, 1984), 293. For the palimpsest as metaphor,
see André Corboz, "The Land as Palimpsest," *Diogenes* 31, no. 121 (March 1983): 13.

3. Fernando Ortiz, *El huracán: Su mitología y sus símbolos* (Mexico City: Fondo de Cultura
Económica, 1947), 15–65. See also Kerry Emanuel, *Divine Wind: The History and Science of Hurricanes* (New York: Oxford University Press, 2005), 18–23.

4. Stuart Schwartz, *Sea of Storms: A History of Hurricanes in the Greater Caribbean from
Columbus to Katrina* (Princeton, NJ: Princeton University Press, 2016), 1–70.

5. *Huracán de 1846: Reseña de sus estragos en la isla de Cuba: y relacion ordenada de las*

perdidas y desgracias sufridas en las poblaciones y puertos que visitó, el memorable dia 11 de octubre (Havana: Oficina del Faro Industrial, 1846), 10–11.

6. *Huracán de 1846*, 15.

7. This is the thesis of Louis A. Pérez Jr., *Winds of Change: Hurricanes and the Transformation of Nineteenth-Century Cuba* (Chapel Hill: University of North Carolina Press, 2001). See also Sherry Johnson, *Climate and Catastrophe in Cuba and the Atlantic World in the Age of Revolution* (Chapel Hill: University of North Carolina Press, 2014), 193.

8. Luis Enrique Ramos Guadalupe and Oswaldo Garcia, *Father Benito Viñes: The 19th-Century Life and Contributions of a Cuban Hurricane Observer and Scientist* (Boston: American Meteorological Society, 2014).

9. Eduardo Luis Rodríguez and Pepe Navarro, *La Habana: Arquitectura del siglo XX* (Barcelona: Blume, 1998), 144–247; María Elena Martín Zequeira and Eduardo Luis Rodríguez Fernández, *La Habana: Guía de arquitectura* (Havana: Ciudad de la Habana, 1998), 272.

10. "Inauguración del edificio de astronomía del observatorio nacional," *Revista de la Sociedad Cubana de Ingenieros* 13, no. 6 (1921); and José Carlos Millás, "Defensa de Observatorio Nacional," *Revista de la Sociedad Cubana de Ingenieros* 46, no. 10 (1948): 596–602.

11. Gerardo Machado y Morales, "Mensaje al congreso relación con la Ley de Obras Publicas del 15 de julio de 1925" (Havana, 1925), Biblioteca Nacional de Cuba, José Martí.

12. On the regime's financings, see Chase National Bank of the City of New York, *Cuban Public Works Financing Reply to the Report of the Special Commission Created by Decree-Law No. 140 of April 16, 1934* (New York: Chase National Bank of the City of New York, 1935). See also Luis E. Aguilar, *Cuba 1933: Prologue to Revolution* (Ithaca, NY: Cornell University Press, 1972); Louis A. Pérez Jr., *Cuba: Between Reform and Revolution* (New York: Oxford University Press, 1988), 97–237; and Rolando Rodríguez, *Rebelión en la república: Auge y caída de Gerardo Machado*, 3 vols. (Havana: Editorial de Ciencias Sociales, 2013).

13. Cuba's Office of Public Works, *Memoria administrativa y descriptiva de las obras de la Carretera Central*, 4 vols. (Havana, 1930).

14. Plans for this project reside in the Parisian archives of the SIAF/Cité de l'architecture et du patrimoine/Archives d'architecture du XXe siècle in "Fonds Jean-Claude-Nicolas Forestier" and "Fonds Théodore Leveau."

15. For plans, see Archivo de la Oficina del Historiador de la Ciudad, RESTAURA, Havana, Cuba. For Eugenio Rayneri y Piedra and his father Rayneri y Sorrentino, see Notre Dame Archives of the University of Notre Dame, Notre Dame, Indiana (NDA), GSBB box 1, no. 02; NDA UPEL box 89, no. 1 and 3; NDA UPEL box 105, nos. 5 and 7; NDA UPEL box 100, nos. 15 and 16. For original contracts and descriptions, see Carlos Miguel de Céspedes, *Libro del Capitolio* (Havana: Talleres Tip. de P. Fernández y Cía, 1933).

16. Archivo Nacional de Cuba, Havana, Cuba (ANC), Secretaría de la Presidencia Fondo, 45, no. 4. See also Rogerio Zayas Bazán, *El Presidio Modelo* (Havana: N.p., 1928); and Julio César González Laureiro and Francisco García González, *Presidio Modelo: Temas escondidos* (Havana: Centro Cultural Pablo de la Torriente Brau, 2001).

17. Oscar Lewis, Ruth M. Lewis, and Susan M. Rigdon, *Four Women: Living the Revolution, an Oral History of Contemporary Cuba* (Urbana: University of Illinois Press, 1977), 142 and 349. See also the firsthand accounts of the American diplomat Carlton Bailey Hurst, *The Arms above the Door* (New York: Dodd, Mead & Co., 1932), 324–329.

18. Christopher W. Landsea et al., "A Reanalysis of the 1921–30 Atlantic Hurricane Database," *Journal of Climate* (February 2011): 865–885.

19. See Roger A. Pielke Jr. et al., "Normalized Hurricane Damage in the United States: 1900–2005," *Natural Hazards Review* (February 2008): 29–42; and *A Pictorial History of the Florida Hurricane, September 18, 1926* (Miami: Tyler Pub., 1926).

20. Gonzalo de Quesada, *Los derechos de Cuba a la Isla de Pinos* (Havana: Impr. de Rambla

y Bouza, 1909); see also Joseph R. Hartman, ed., *Imperial Islands: Art, Architecture, and Visual Experience in the US Insular Empire after 1898* (Honolulu: University of Hawaiʻi Press, 2022).

21. Richard Warrington Baldwin Lewis, *The Poetry of Hart Crane* (Princeton, NJ: Princeton University Press, 2015), 382–421.

22. "Los nuevos talleres cine-fotográficas de la Secretaría de Obras Públicas," *Boletín de Obras Publicas* 8, no. 1 (January 1931): 27.

23. Emeterio S. Santovenia, *Libro conmemorativo de la inauguración de la Plaza del Maine en la Habana* (Havana: Talleres del Sindicato de Artes Gráficas, 1928), 148.

24. Aragón and Bau, *El Ciclón del 26*, 59.

25. Aragón and Bau, 72–73.

26. For more on Kiko and other notable photographers of the era, see Juan Manuel Díaz Burgos, Mario Díaz Leyva, and Pace Salina, *Cuba, 100 años de fotografía: Antología de la fotografía cubana, 1898–1998* (Murcia, España: Mestizo, 2000), 9–25. I also thank the Cuban photo historians Jorge Oller Oller and Mabiel Hidalgo for their insights into the biography of these sparsely documented photographers.

27. See also Decreto No. 160, reproduced in Cuba's Secretary of Public Works, *Memoria de los trabajos efectuados con motivo del ultimo ciclón que azotó la isla el 20 de octubre de 1926* (Havana: Imprenta "La revoltosa" de B. Alvarez, 1927), 51–53.

28. ANC, Fondo de Donativos y Remisiones, *legajo* 576, no. 13.

29. Secretary of Public Works, *Memoria de los trabajos*, 85–86.

30. Secretary of Public Works, 79–84.

31. Sharon Corwin, Jessica May, and Terri Weissman, *American Modern: Documentary Photography by Abbott, Evans, and Bourke-White* (Berkeley: University of California Press, 2010).

32. Secretary of Public Works, *Memoria de los trabajos*, 89–90.

33. Secretary of Public Works, *Escuela Técnica Industrial "Presidente Machado"* (Havana: Sindicato de Artes Gráficas de la Habana, 1929).

34. Secretary of Public Works, *Memoria de los trabajos*, 6–7.

35. Secretary of Public Works, *Copia de la escritura no. 28 de acta relativa a la plantación del árbol de la fraternidad americana, verificada en la Ciudad de La Habana República de Cuba* (Havana: Sr. Belisario Álvarez y Suarez, 1928); and Lydia Cabrera, *El Monte: Igbo, Finda, Ewe Orisha, Vititi Nfinda: Notas sobre las religiones, la magia, las supersticiones y el folklore de los negros criollos y el pueblo de Cuba* (Miami: Ediciones Universal, 1975), 192–193.

36. Constancio Bernaldo de Quirós, *La picota en América: Contribución al studio del derecho penal indiano* (Havana: Jesús Montero, 1948), 37–38.

37. Luis Bay Sevilla, "César Guerra, proyectista y constructor de dos edificios modelos: El Presidio de Isla de Pinos y el Balneario Infantil," *Arquitectura* 9, no. 114 (January 1943): 31.

38. Zayas Bazán, *Presidio Modelo*, 24.

39. ANC, Secretaría de Presidencia, Fondo 39, no. 20.

40. Archivo Pinero, Nueva Gerona, Isla de la Juventud, Cuba, *legajo* 11, no. 2. US and British holdings in grapefruit alone more than doubled that of Cuban farmers after the hurricane of 1944.

41. ANC, Secretaría de Estado, Fondo 472, no. 010621.

42. On aid sent to Puerto Rico after the storm of 1928, see ANC, Secretaría de la Presidencia, Fondo C2, no. 72.

43. For more discussion on this period, see Schwartz, *Sea of Storms*, 226–272.

44. ANC, Secretaría de Estado, Fondo 472, no. 010621.

45. Dipesh Chakrabarty "The Climate of History: Four Theses," *Critical Inquiry* 35, no. 2 (2009): 222.

46. Alejo Carpentier, *El recurso del método: Novela* (Mexico City: Siglo Veintiuno Editores, 1974), 203.

FREDO RIVERA

Socialist Modernities in Concrete: Pabellón Cuba as Palimpsest and Stage

ABSTRACT

Built in just three months for the 1963 World Congress of Architects, Pabellón Cuba became a centerpiece for future cultural congresses and conferences in Havana. The edifice presents a brutalist stage, one which embodies modernist ambitions of the era. This article analyzes the layered meanings of Pabellón Cuba, exploring the building as a palimpsest of architectural modernity, a stage for the World Congress of Architects, and a sign for Cuba's global ambitions. It focuses on the design of Pabellón Cuba as well as its inaugural exhibition, *The History of Architecture in Cuba*. While the pavilion presents a utopic, modernist vision in concrete, its inaugural exhibition engaged the visitor in a meandering, media-rich spectacle. As stage and palimpsest, Pabellón Cuba symbolizes the ambitions and contradictions inherent in architecture of 1960s Cuba.

RESUMEN

Construido en menos de tres meses para el Congreso Mundial de Arquitectos de 1963, el Pabellón Cuba fue un lugar central para futuros congresos y conferencias culturales en La Habana. El edificio presenta un escenario brutalista, que representa las ambiciones modernistas de la época. Este artículo explora los múltiples significados del Pabellón Cuba, revelando la función del edificio como un palimpsesto de la modernidad arquitectónica, el escenario del Congreso Mundial de Arquitectos y un signo de las ambiciones globales de Cuba, y centra su análisis en el diseño del Pabellón Cuba y su exposición inaugural, *La historia de la arquitectura en Cuba*. Aunque la arquitectura del Pabellón presenta una visión utópica y modernista en concreto, su exposición inaugural inmergió a los presentes en un rico espectáculo multiforme y multimediático. Como escenario y palimpsesto, Pabellón Cuba simboliza las ambiciones y contradicciones inherentes en la arquitectura cubana de los años sesenta.

In January 1968, the building Pabellón Cuba hosted *Del tercer mundo*, an immersive, graphic exhibition that visually evoked the concept of the "Third World." Visitors encountered a vibrant array of images: a large-scale reproduction of Michelangelo's *The Creation of Adam* from the Sistine Chapel, light-boxes featuring image or text, photographic images of everyday life and struggles in the developing world, bright neon lights. The cacophony of thoughtfully curated images was coordinated with both cinematic presentations and sound

101

installations. Beyond portraying the plight and promise of the Third World, the exhibition presented an alluring aural and visual proclamation for a decolonizing world. The exhibition accompanied the Cultural Congress of Havana, a major convening of nearly five hundred leftist figures from around the world. As Rachel Weiss suggests, "The island nation became ground zero for the imagining of what a new, liberated culture might be."[1] Cuba placed itself as a center of debates regarding cultural production and postcolonial nationalisms. And the exhibition would become an important venue for expressing the Cuban Revolution's aims and ambitions.

At the height of the Cold War, Havana's 1963 Pabellón Cuba became an important vestibule for cultural diplomacy and an architectural model for the new government's more utopian visions (Figure 1). Built in a mere seventy-two days and located on La Rampa in the commercial center of Havana's Vedado neighborhood, the concrete pavilion became an important precedent for the design and curation of Cuba's World Expo pavilions in Montreal (1967) and Osaka (1971). Further, the edifice provided a brutalist framework for exhibitions such as the *Primera muestra de la cultura cubana* (1966), the *Salón de Mayo* (1967), and *Del tercer mundo* (1968). Major exhibitions and related events often provided teleological narratives of revolutionary progress. Such metanarratives were reinforced by the modern yet seemingly neoclassical pavilion. The large, portico-like structures of Pabellón Cuba emerge as a hypermodernist concrete icon, open to and peering over La Rampa. This article discusses the design and programming of Pabellón Cuba, with a focus on its opening in 1963. Inherent in the pavilion's design is a spatial grandiosity with references to Cuba's architectural past and socialist future. As both palimpsest and stage, Pabellón is a sign of Cuba's socialist modernity.

Pabellón as Modernity

The Pabellón Cuba was born in a moment of fervent architectural experimentalism leading up to the World Congress of Architecture, hosted by Havana in November 1963. The congress provided Cuba an opportunity to advertise its diverse building projects, and frame new architectures within ongoing social, economic, and political debates regarding development. Cuba, for some outsiders, became perceived as a socialist utopia. Prominent figures from the international left, including writers such as C. L. R. James and Jean-Paul Sartre, characterized the island nation's 1959 revolution as a new model of governance, counter to the auspices of imperialism and profit.[2] The historian Lillian Guerra explores the role of images in relaying "the 'hyper-reality' of the Revolution, that is, a utopia caught in the process of becoming."[3] Such an illusory hyperreality became the function of utopia in Pabellón Cuba and its inaugural exhibition. Both the structure and its contents promoted triumphal metanarratives regarding a revolutionary modernity. However, a close analysis reveals contradictory elements within the project of a utopic modernism, ones that relate to Guerra's critical analysis of identity and the public sphere: that "the process of revolution itself can be understood as a political production of palimpsests."[4]

Architecture can be understood as a significant venue for the development of utopia. The philosopher Henri Lefebvre, drawing from the writing of Ernst Bloch, explicates the meaning of abstract and concrete utopia in relation to architectural production.[5] Abstract utopia is associated with the technocratic and created by officials "who want to build the perfect city."[6] Lefebvre is specifically concerned with the mediatic nature of architecture as "a form of communication."[7] More simply, the practice of architecture becomes a sign of state desire, its utopia abstracted, or in other words transmitted as a message. However, Lefebvre suggests the political imperative of the state does not determine the efficacy of spatial and architectural forms, as such forms can be transfigured as a means of communication (abstract) and as a vessel for human desire and enjoyment (concrete). In the case of Pabellón Cuba, we can understand the building as a sign of technological prowess and grandiosity, a concrete representation of an abstract utopia. The building's utility, most specifically its meandering program and curated exhibitions, speak to a concrete utopia, where the ideology of the Cuban Revolution is subsumed by visual pleasure and spectacle.

This dichotomy of abstract and concrete utopias translates to tensions inherent throughout modern architecture in Cuba. Architects often negotiated the use of new, more universal methods of construction alongside formal and spatial referents to local traditions or national culture. The tension between past inspirations and new modes of building hints at the palimpsestic nature of modernity itself. Modernity as a concept differs from its sibling terms modernism and modern in that it implies less of a movement (as in the case of modernism) and rather a sense of being modern—a means to describe a sense of being in the wake of modernization and cosmopolitanism. The curator and art critic Dannys Montes de Oca Moreda suggests the development a revolutionary ethos that dually embraces cosmopolitanism and decolonization during the 1960s decade. She identifies social transformation and cultural promotion as "represent[ing] an emerging alternate modernity in the emancipatory debate."[8] Architecture became a technology for expressing this "alternate" or socialist modernity, as the field became oriented toward solutions in housing, education, health care, and industry.

The context of the Cold War, and Cuba's position vis-à-vis Washington, DC, and Moscow, is fundamental to the discourses of modernity in socialist Cuba. In the early 1960s, tensions with the United States heightened, with events such as the Bay of Pigs invasion in 1961 and the Cuban Missile Crisis in

FIGURE 1. Photograph of Pabellón de Cuba along La Rampa, 2009. Photograph by author.

1962. During this period Fidel Castro solidified power and created significant economic and political ties with the Soviet Union. Cuba also solidified ties with nations throughout the Global South. Cuba became an active member of the Non-Aligned Movement (NAM) beginning in 1961 and founded the Organization of Solidarity with the People of Asia, Africa and Latin America (OSPAAAL) in 1966. Pabellón Cuba is a pivotal structure for considering the formation of a revolutionary aesthetic for a global audience. Exhibitions throughout the 1960s reveal a fascinating relationship between design and propaganda, and the pavilion became an important meeting space for local citizens and foreign dignitaries to experience and visualize a projected vision of Cuba. The building is a concrete vessel providing a monumental exhibition space for formidable expressions of a "Third World" modernity.

Modernity in Cuba, architectural or otherwise, is often portrayed as contested or exceptional. Indeed, the historical context of the 1959 Cuban Revolution created an ever-changing space of negotiation for the country, both with its citizens and foreign powers.[9] Nonetheless, Cuba's modernity falls in line with many of its Latin American counterparts, embracing new forms of globalization while drawing from colonial constructs. Scholars such as Antoni Kapcia, Joseph L. Scapaci, Mario Coyula, and Paul Niell have traced the history of Havana's built environment, echoing Walter Mignolo's emphasis on the direct relationship between coloniality and modernity.[10] The vestiges of coloniality carried from Cuba's Republican era into the artistic and architectural production of the revolutionary period. Historian Nicola Miller analyzes the teleological narratives that contribute to a "revolutionary modernity," highlighting that "the government did not so much try to found a wholly new culture as seek to connect the radical elements of Cuba's existing cultural traditions to the revolutionary project of decolonization."[11] Miller argues that Cuba was able to trace nationalist and vanguardist aspects of the past to contribute to a revolutionary project that emphasized cultural production and fervently supported the arts. Cuba's socialist modernity, hence, was drawing from its own colonial and modern past as much as it was employing new, reactionary discourses.

Havana, in the years following the Cuban Revolution in 1959, was the cultural, urban center for a largely agrarian revolution. Pabellón Cuba, as one of the few new buildings built in the core of the city during the 1960s, represents the symbolic function of the city within a new social order. Exhibition sites, architecture, public displays of art and propaganda, mass gatherings, new movies, cultural congresses—Havana became a newly curated site. This new capital of socialist modernity was nonetheless built upon former iterations of the lettered city, appropriating symbols and spaces of former regimes. In many ways Havana's new designs can be understood through Mary Louise Pratt's notion of alternative or "peripheral" modernities, "described in relations of contradiction, complementarity, and differentiation, with respect to those of the center."[12] The Cuban Revolution, with its ideals and contradictions, becomes a means for different deployments of modernity, both concrete and abstract. In this article I explore Pabellón Cuba as a palimpsest of architectural modernity, a stage for the World Congress of Architecture, and a sign for Cuba's global ambitions. The building was a powerful experiment in design, emblematic of the multifarious nature of Cuba's socialist modernity.

Pabellón as Palimpsest

Pabellón Cuba infused Brutalist architecture with sensual, tropical landscaping. Designed by the Cuban architect Juan Campos Almanza, Pabellón Cuba utilized existing urban infrastructure and took advantage of open, urban space for its exterior porticos (Figure 2). Located at the center of La Rampa, the massive structure, predominantly comprised of a terraced exterior, encourages

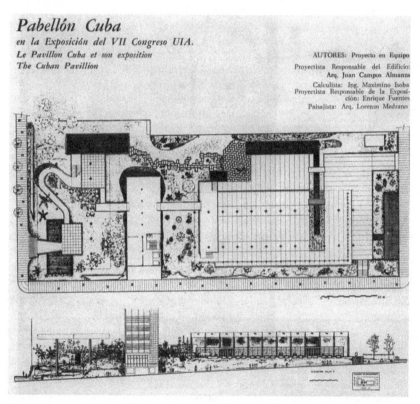

Pabellón Cuba
en la Exposición del VII Congreso UIA.
Le Pavillon Cuba et son exposition
The Cuban Pavillion

AUTORES: Proyecto en Equipo
Proyectista Responsable del Edificio:
Arq. Juan Campos Almanza
Calculista: Ing. Maximino Isoba
Proyectista Responsable de la Exposición: Enrique Fuentes
Paisajista: Arq. Lorenzo Medrano

FIGURE 2. Floor plan and section of Pabellón Cuba, from *Arquitectura Cuba* 64 (November 1963): 6.

a more public form of exhibition. Nonetheless its massive prefabricated concrete grid ceiling, upheld by repeating concrete columns or pilotis, provide a
sculptural, monumental appearance. With the concrete casts poured on site, the
cross-shaped pilotis extend upward toward the impression of a coffered ceiling.
The building aligns with an upward slope along Calle N toward Calle 21, providing a dramatic height for the portico along La Rampa, or Calle 23. In form
and urban context, Pabellón Cuba showcases a concrete palimpsest within the
historic, layered city.

In his essay "Tropical Minimalism: Excellences and ambivalences of an
exhibition pavilion," the architectural historian Eduardo Luis Rodríguez identifies two clear referents for the architecture of Pabellón Cuba. First, he cites the
integration of tradition and modernity spatially through its referents to Cuba's
colonial architecture and the local area's modern architectures. Rodríguez suggests the two massive terraces form porticoes that echo the great mansions of
the Havana's Vedado neighborhood. Further, new technology is used to recall
the spatial grandiosity of a previous era, as Rodríguez writes:

In this way, Pabellón Cuba—at one and the same time building, portico and courtyard—incorporates strategies and elements that clearly refer to that tradition, such as
the achievement of maximum interrelation between interior and exterior, crossed ven-
tilation, noble proportions, large ceilings simultaneously covering ample salons, wide
eaves, the orthogonal framework of beams that bring to mind the coffering typical of
some colonial buildings, the constant repetitive rhythm established by the columns, as
well as the air of monumentality offered by the main façade, opposite 23 Avenue (La
Rampa).[13]

This sense of tradition, however, is counteracted with the building's radical
gesture toward modernity—particularly in its use of material. Rodríguez highlights both architectural referents and siting to reference the role of tradition.

After citing colonial precedents, Rodríguez claims architect Ludwig Mies
van der Rohe as the second major referent for Pabellón Cuba, particularly his
never-built design for Bacardí offices in Santiago de Cuba. By the time of his
design for Bacardí, the German émigré and former director of the Bauhaus
became one of the most important proponents of international modernism in
the United States. Van der Rohe was most known for his elegant, seemingly
minimalist designs, including high rises and prominent civic structures comprised of steel I-beams and glass curtain walls. Taking into account Cuba's
tropical climate, Mies van der Rohe replaced his emblematic use of steel with
reinforced concrete. The structure is simple, with eight cross-shaped columns
holding up a grid-based roof plate. The ground level is an aquarium-like
workspace lobby, with views of the surrounding mountainous terrain. Van der
Rohe's design for the company headquarters echoes Pabellón Cuba's grid-like
rationality and open, exploratory program. The renderings of the building,

however, suggest a less urban, integrative setting. Mies van der Rohe presents a hypermodern aesthetic, using new technologies and materials to form a sleek, universalist aesthetic.

The Pabellón, in many ways, encapsulates trends of high modern architecture that began to develop in late Republican-era Cuba. Prominent architects such as Manuel Copado, Mario Romañach, and Max Borges drew from global trends in modern architecture, experimenting with form and expression. The imprint of modernist architecture in the late Republican era is also evident in a myriad of projects from the early to mid-1960s, including the Parque Deportivo José Marti, CUJAE (or the Ciudad Universitaria José Antonio Echeverría), as well as new plans for Habana del Este, which was featured in the catalog published for the UIA congress. Another important parallel is the 1955–1958 plan for the Palacio de las Palmas by Josep Lluís Sert and Town Planning Associates. The never-built presidential palace utilized a grid-based plan and palm-like concrete columns. As Timothy Hyde writes: "The tension between modernist tenets of abstraction and the symbolic potency of figuration produced a representational equivocation comparable to the ambiguity of the political implications."[14] The Pabellón Cuba is a model of the continued tensions of Cuba's architectural modernity into the revolutionary era.

In many ways, Rodríguez's discussion of the Pabellón Cuba's integration of modernity and tradition is emblematic of the palimpsestic nature of socialist modernity. That is, while the Pabellón may be understand as a radical gesture embodied in concrete, remnants of architectural heritages—both colonial and modern—persist. Further, the pavilion's siting along La Rampa contributes to its prominence, as new architectures corresponded to existing urban hierarchies. The Revolution's attempt to erase bourgeois affects was in no way totalizing, as architects and designers rewrite the socialist city with an attention to past, if even faded, markings. Further, the appropriation and expropriation of buildings in the immediate vicinities of La Rampa and Vedado further emphasizes a palimpsestic rewriting of the city.

Many examples indicate Havana's revolutionary siege, a sign of the city's hybrid and layered architectural modernity. Most prominent is the Habana Hilton hotel, a 1958 high-rise in close proximity to Pabellón Cuba. The hotel served as de facto headquarters for the revolution in its first year, and by 1960 it would be expropriated and renamed the Hotel Habana Libre.[15] The Cuban Revolution rewrote the hotel as a symbol of socialist modernity and revolutionary takeover. On the other hand, the National Bank of Cuba, a high-rise in a prominent location of Centro Habana, was near completion upon the revolution. However, the building was abandoned for over two decades while the revolution prioritized other buildings in the area.[16] The government later completed the unfinished building in 1982, adding eight floors and opening the most prominent hospital in the island. From its abandonment to its conversion, the unbuilt National

Bank and present-day Hospital Ameijeiras is an edifice representative of the layered complexity of appropriation. The abandonment and decay of buildings in Havana over time further presents a tactile appropriation, presenting a shift in values with regard to the revolution's inherited built environment.

The repurposing of buildings went beyond thinking about the need of housing—a concern among much of the socialist Soviet bloc in this era. Appropriation was a fundamental part of the cultural politics of the Cuban Revolution. By reorienting the usage and purpose of buildings constructed during the previous era of notable real estate speculation, the new government remade social and political relations in Havana. Occupying and reorienting landmarks and prominent buildings from the previous political regime and private interests helped maintain the former urban hierarchy but toward an entirely new means. While some mansions and prominent edifices became neighborhood party headquarters, others became schools, polyclinics, pharmacies, embassies, and cultural centers. The appropriation of space became a form of cultural diplomacy, showing the humanistic sensibilities of the new government—both to its public and to international spectators. Utilizing former hierarchies of space also became a means to police and surveil the city.

Likewise, Pabellón Cuba presents a repurposing of space, the pavilion extending from an existing office space. Pabellón Cuba capitalized on its location within a major commercial thoroughfare of Havana.[17] What had been considered the "Broadway of Havana" was redesigned prior to and during the 1963 World Congress of Architecture. Most prominently, new terrazzo tiles featuring the work of Cuban modern artists were placed approximately five feet from one another on the sidewalks of La Rampa and Calle L near the area's most prominent intersection. Examples by regarded modernist painters such Wifredo Lam and Amelia Peláez display the means in which their painterly aesthetic become part of Havana's everyday urban milieu. The tiles complemented other graphic arts campaigns that drew from the vanguardist aesthetics of modern Cuban art to create more populist, accessible forms of visual communication. Pabellón Cuba was part of a coordinated effort to redefine the aesthetics of the city and the public role of arts and culture. The commercial "Broadway of Havana" would become a new cultural center for socialist modernity.

The Pabellón Cuba, along with local visual campaigns, would rewrite the space of La Rampa, but within the purview of recent and more distant pasts. Both in form and urban context, the Pabellón inherited the visual rhetoric of past architectures and appropriated existing spatial hierarchies. It is in this context that the Pabellón emerged as a modernist symbol for the new socialist regime. In her essay regarding the Pabellón and Cuba's 1960s imaginary, Dannys Monte de Oca Moreda writes that, "with its emblematic name, [the Pabellón Cuba] arose to insert, posit, and empower itself as the mausoleum of the revolutionary polis through which a more collective, more democratic, and interactive socialization was designed." In a civic overture, the Pabellón Cuba opened to the public in 1963, communicating the promise of architecture and socialism to the developing nations as well as the triumphal narrative of Cuba's revolutionary modernity.

Pabellón as Stage

Attendees of the 1963 World Congress of Architecture were treated to a cu-rated spectacle. During the inaugural night, guests were ushered from opening speeches at Palacio de Deportes to La Rampa for an outdoor carnival. Along the brief stretch of La Rampa that extends from the seaside Malecón to the former Habana Hilton was Havana's newest edifice—a monumental, imposing exhibi-tion pavilion. At Pabellón Cuba guests encountered the pavilion's inaugural exhibition, *The History of Architecture in Cuba,* which utilized graphic art, fine art, artifacts, didactic displays, and sculptural photographic installations to pro-vide a triumphal narrative. The opening night included a cabaret recalling the history of Cuba, a parallel narrative to the Pabellón's inaugural exhibition.[18] In-cluding a *comparsa* of construction workers, a fireworks show, and other dance performances, the opening festivities were a spectacle. As Havana's newest building, Pabellón would provide a hyperreal stage, enveloping visitors within mediatic and sensorial expressions of a revolutionary and socialist modernity.

Organized under the aegis of the International Union of Architects, the triennial congress brought together architects from around the world to dis-cuss architecture in the so-called developing or underdeveloped world. The congress provided a unique opportunity for Havana to serve as a stage for de-bates regarding the built environment and development. The meeting became a means for Cuba to portray it utopic aims to an international network of profes-sionals. Planned prior to the Cuban Revolution in 1957, the triennial confer-ence did not arrive in Havana without controversy. Formed after World War II, the International Union of Architects sought a program of cultural diplomacy, attempting to work beyond the ideological chasms of the Cold War as an ad-vocate for the profession.[19] Nonetheless, the selection of Havana as the site for the 1963 congress came into dispute with US officials given growing tensions between the two nations. Adding fuel to the flame, Cuban officials introduced an international competition for a Bay of Pigs monument, celebrating Cuba's victory against the US supported insurgency. The US State Department en-couraged architects to not attend the congress. Compromises with US officials and the UIA resulted in the selection of Mexico City as an alternative assembly site immediately following the Havana congress. Nonetheless, the UIA's prime minister Pierre Vago and then president Sir Robert Matthews continuously de-fended the selection of Havana as a site for the congress despite mounting protest.[20] Aware of the volatile situation, Cuban officials sought to emphasize their hospitality while portraying the island as a utopic model in architectural production for the developing world.

Drawing 1,275 participants from abroad, with delegations from seventy-nine nations, the World Congress of Architecture's theme of architecture in the process of development prompted debates regarding the ethical role of architecture at a global level. With the three previous congresses exploring the themes of housing (Le Havre, 1955), urban construction and reconstruction (Moscow, 1958), and new technologies of architecture (London, 1961), the 1963 congress would focus specifically on the developing world. As UIA's president Robert Matthews emphasized at the opening session, the International Union of Architects was "belonged [to by] architects of almost every nation, both developed and developing."[21] The UIA's goal of outreach to lesser-developed countries was met with the nascent Cuban nation trying to prove its muster to professionals working in the developing world, while trying to build strong alliances with other developing nations. Though not explicitly stated, this congress took in the concerns of a newly postcolonial world, all while attempting to remain apolitical. Such an apolitical disposition would prove difficult in the sultry, socialist tropics of Havana, Cuba.

The opening session started at the bright blue and modernist Ciudad Deportiva, an architectural hallmark of the Batista era. The round stadium or coliseum was converted to an assembly hall, with massive vertical banners dividing the space and marking the congress. Toward the back of the stage was a long-curved table for significant participants, toward the front of the stage the podium rose, elevated from its audience, the speaker framed by the vertical banners behind them. The more formal setting of the large assembly hall would be precedent for a grand welcoming with a spectacular Cuban flair. As a city selected for an international congress of architecture based on an architectural boom of the previous political era, the congress provided a stage for showing the promise and architectural ingenuity of socialist modernities.

Upon departing the Ciudad Deportiva visitors were led to festivities at La Rampa, where grand festivities created a celebratory mood. Rumba dancers, rum and fireworks were welcomed guests as the city's former commercial artery was converted into a large carnival. Encompassing the length of La Rampa (Calle 23) from the Habana Libre Hotel—formerly the Havana Hilton and the official hotel hosting delegates—to the Malecón, Havana's commercial and entertainment core became a vanguardist bacchanalia displaying Cuba's hospitality and joviality. Formerly in the epicenter of Havana's speculative high-rise development, the area was reconceived as a cultural space for the masses. According to architecture writer Diana Rowtree, "The delegates' slightly patronizing recognition that the spirit of the Cuban welcome was something far above any oddities that might occur in organisation changed quickly to an astonished regard for the Cuban architecture achievement, both concrete and organisational."[22] Among those concrete manifestations was a new pavilion at the center of La Rampa, serving as a nationalist stage that expressed Cuba's architectural ambitions.

The content, spatial layout, and thematic narrative of Pabellón Cuba's first exhibition provides a teleological narrative of revolutionary redemption. Curated by designer Enrique Fuentes, *The History of Architecture in Cuba* exhibition guided guests through a nationalist saga oppression, struggle, and liberation. Engaging the topic of architecture and culture throughout Cuban history, the exhibition was divided into three major epochs, beginning with precolonial and colonial Cuba at the pavilion's front entrance. As the pavilion was comprise of two porticos extending from an existing building, the opening galleries of the exhibition served as a dramatic porch-like entrance overlooking the popular commercial boulevard La Rampa (Figure 3). The sloped terrain allows

FIGURE 3. Colonial and precolonial displays in front hall of Pabellón Cuba, *Historia y arquitectura de Cuba* exhibition, 1963, from *arquitectura Cuba* 64 (November 1963): 38.

the front portico to grow in height toward the sidewalk, its front concrete columns reaching fourteen meters and contributing to the pavilion's monumentality. Pabellón's front pavilion used the site's natural features, embellishing them into a concocted tropical landscape comprising a spiraling ramp that brings visitors up to the building's third-floor entrance.[23] The landscaping, completed by Lorenzo Medrano, was thought to evoke the Cuban landscape, to be a primordial expression of *cubanidad* within an inherently modernist edifice. Hanging front at center from the coffered concrete ceiling is a massive stained-glass representation of a colonial ship, its back turned to the viewer. The symbol of colonial invasion welcomes the viewer to an exhibition rich in ephemera yet clear in its historical narrative—that of advancing from an oppressive past into a utopic future.

In one display, renderings and photographs of colonial architecture are placed alongside images of the oppressive sugar economy as well as a marble commemoration for Cuba's recent invasions. In the exhibition, images of past oppression are connected to Cuba's current anti-imperialist struggles. At the same time, visual elements of coloniality were celebrated as objects of ingenuity emanating from of a troubled past. For example, one photograph from the journal *Arquitectura Cuba* features a vitrale, or arched stained-glass window typical of eighteenth- and nineteenth-century Havana, as the centerpiece for a display (Figure 4). Black-and-white photographs accompany the vitrale, associating the architectural remnant with a palimpsestic discourse that builds on an impressive past to write a new future.

2, 3, 4) Cuba coloniale.
Colonial Cuba.

2

FIGURE 4. Colonial display at *Historia y arquitectura de Cuba* exhibition, 1963, from *Arquitectura Cuba* 64 (November 1963): 38.

FIGURE 5. Revolutionary architecture display in back hall of Pabellón Cuba, *Historia y arquitectura de Cuba* exhibition, 1963, from *Arquitectura Cuba* 64 (November 1963): 31.

This linear narrative continues into the third floor and surrounding areas of the Republican-era building that anchors Pabellón Cuba. Focusing on architecture from 1902–1958, the official description in the journal *Arquitectura Cuba* states: "During her [Cuba's period of] foreign intervention, the frustration, the protests, the anguish, the dissatisfaction of her condition, take form in hybrid volumes with cinema, slide projections and photos that resemble reality."[24] Utilizing graphic prints, videos and other forms of media, the exhibition continues its narrative of Cuban ingenuity amid massive oppression. Both the precolonial- and colonial-era pavilion and the Republican-era exhibitions emphasize a metanarrative of struggle for liberation. Photography and graphic displays present hyperreality—a sensorial expression of revolution as concrete utopia. This teleological narrative comes to fruition in the gargantuan back portico, featuring displays on "revolutionary" architecture.

The back pavilion, an extensive and spectacular exploration of Revolutionary approaches to architecture and new construction technologies, inventively combined mass media and architectonic displays to spectacularize the utopic aims of Cuba's nascent socialist regime (Figure 5). While the tropical landscaping primordially transformed the brutalism of the building's façade, the rear of the pavilion relied on massive sculptural and architectonic displays of graphic art, text, large-print photographs and filmic projections enhance the seemingly minimalist space of Pabellón Cuba. Stark black-and-white pictures stand next to colorful graphics, the two-dimensional media art forms transposed onto massive geometric sculptural forms, or held up by a long metal posts complementing the pavilion's columns. The intermedia exhibition pushed beyond traditional boundaries between art, commercial design and architecture, placing the practices in dynamic unison with a proclaimed socialist ethos, and recalling the allure of World Expo pavilions.

Nationalist in orientation, *The History of Architecture in Cuba* implied Cuba's ideal position as a role model for postcolonial modernism, or for the decolonizing world, something corroborated in the official texts of the Congress. In the more elegantly curated catalog for the congress, the history of architecture in Cuba and the imperatives of the new government are expounded upon. Meticulously outlined and encyclopedic in tone, the catalog served as a national portrait of architectural ingenuity in Cuba, drawing from the Cuban experience to suggest broader implications. Divided into four primary sections, the book highlighted the major imperatives of the congress and the Cuban government, especially in discussing the role of housing and new technology. The publication was corollary to the exhibition, providing textual context to the visual spectacle of the pavilion.

Pabellón Cuba's inaugural exhibition became a means to represent Cuba's cultural and political ambitions, using curation as a means to present a concrete utopia. British architectural critic James Maude Richards suggests the design of Pabellón Cuba is up to snuff with contemporary examples, and wrote that "the display was brilliantly handled, with the photographic and other material informally and imaginatively set at different levels, within the space created by the concrete structure."[25] For contemporary visitors, including many from so-called developed or First World nations, Pabellón Cuba and its inaugural exhibition presented Cuba's ties with an international avant-garde, with the latest trends in design. Further, it presented Cuba's unique contribution for considering architecture with ambition, however short-lived. As *Arquitectura Cuba* described the World Congress of Architecture's opening: "The whole effect of mal intentioned propagandistic distortions and ideological digression disappeared to coalesce into a feeling and common language that united all the visitors a heroic public, who now greeted them with the joy of those contributing to building a new world. "[26] The World Congress of Architecture allowed Cuba a stage to present its architectural modernity to the world, allowing the island to portray the political and social imperatives of the new country, and to symbolize its socialist modernity.

Pabellón as Sign

Adjacent to the Pabellón Cuba during the World Congress of Architecture was a large graphic sign of a note personally written by Le Corbusier for attendees of the conference. Located on the sidewalk on Calle N, the large sign was visible from La Rampa as well as several vantage points within the back pavilion. It read "watch, look, observe, discern, invent, create." The sign existed as a

reminder of the international scope of modern architecture, a form of deference to CIAM (International Congress of Modern Architecture) ideals. Visible
from the displays of contemporary Cuban architecture, Le Corbusier's message came into dialogue with Cuba, which would present itself as being at a
historical juncture—the opportunity to create a new society. Pabellón Cuba is
itself a sign of socialist modernity and its concrete and abstract utopias.

The string of six verbs provided by Le Corbusier's note to the congress
asks guests and the Cuban public to both perceive (watch, look, observe, discern) and produce (invent, create). From the purview of the World Congress of
Architecture, the diverse, new designs featured in both exhibitions and publications suggests that architects, artists and graphic designers were at the fore-
front of perceiving and conceiving solutions for an ever-changing, decolonizing world. The pavilion was a direct expression of the importance of the visual
in the revolution, something emphasized by the extensive graphic campaign
coordinated by graphic designer José Lucci for the World Congress of Architecture. The ad campaign featured everything from cigarette and matchboxes
to postage stamps.[27] From the new ceramic tiles placed along La Rampa to
various ephemera, the Pabellón Cuba served as a visual icon within a system
of signs. In many ways the World Congress of Architecture became a model for
future congresses, corresponding exhibitions and ad campaigns, which would
be similarly coordinated.

Future exhibitions in the 1960s show the development of the exhibition
space as an intermedia spectacle for redefining *cubanidad* and as a form of soft
cultural diplomacy. In 1966, Casa de las Américas hosted *Primera muestra
de la cultura cubana* at Pabellón Cuba, a collaborative project among writers,
artists and designers. Graphic cubes dominated the Pabellón, as they floated
along and with the pilotis of the front and back pavilions. Textual and graphic
elements were immediately visible, as was the extensive use of black, white,
and red.

The cube served again as a curatorial and architectonic mechanism of representation in the Cuba pavilion at the 1967 World Expo in Montreal, Quebec.
Featured on the August 1967 cover of *Cuba* magazine, the building took the
form of the cube and extended it into geometric corridors of parallelepiped
forms (Figure 6). Designed by architects Sergio Baroni and Vittorio Gar-
rati, both of Italian descent who worked on the National Arts Schools project
(1961–1964), the building comprised rectangular corridors of prefabricated
aluminum, along with large, darkened round plastic windows. The innovative
material created an economic solution for a financially strapped Cuba while
providing a futuristic skin. Further, as Roberto Segre suggests, the 1967 pavilion not only conceived architecture "merely as the configuration of space,
but about the application of graphic elements afterwards, to establish a com-
municative dialogue with visitors."[28] Like the Pabellón Cuba during the World

FIGURE 6. Front cover, Cuba, August 1967. Image of Expo67 Montreal pavilion.

Congress of Architecture, the innovative pavilion was matched with a massive graphic campaign and performative gestures that engaged visitors. The Montreal pavilion also featured a restaurant, cinematic theaters, and graphic integration that extended from the walls to the ceilings. The Cuba pavilion in Montreal provided an all-encompassing experience of space at a graphic and planar level. The concrete ambitions of the 1963 Pabellón Cuba were reconfigured into new forms of technology and representation, as architecture reflected advancements made within the realm of communication design.

The images presented with the 1967 and 1971 pavilions in Montreal and Osaka expressed ideas of globality—of Cuba's place in the world. The ideas generated by these utopic and immersive visual displays abroad were informed by and influenced major exhibitions and public arts project on the island. This is evident in the example of the exhibition *Del tercer mundo* at the Pabellón Cuba. The ambitious exhibition visualized new ways of thinking and being during the Cultural Congress of January 1968. The exhibition was a collaboration between many parties, including designers Enrique Fuentes (curator of the Pabellón's inaugural exhibition), writer Guillermo Rodríguez Rivera, and director of the exhibition project, a young art historian and filmmaker Rebeca Chávez. With a small, simple, pamphlet-like catalog, the magic of the exhibition resided in the mythological aspirations of its display. Unlike more conventional eye-level textual displays, the *Del tercer mundo* exhibition relied entirely on large superimposed graphics that created immersive experiences of the Third World and its sentiments. Placed within the vestibule of Pabellón Cuba, the exhibition presented a new iteration of Cuba's socialist modernity, written on top of a concrete palimpsest.

Since the 1960s, Pabellón Cuba has swayed between hosting major exhibitions and events and standing empty, like a cavernous concrete shell. At times it has been a key venue during the Bienal de la Habana, a major art event held every three to four years. Recent projects, most especially *4D—4Dimensions 4Decades*, have considered the legacy of La Rampa's concrete edifice both through exhibition and publication. Regardless of its contemporary use, the Pabellón remains a symbol for a previous era, of the contributions of architecture, exhibition, or graphic design in forming socialist modernities. As Rafael Rojas writes: "The photographic images of the Revolution, its leaders young and beautiful and their bearded peasants their 'uniformed masses,' walking the Great Western press (The New York Times, Life, Times, Le Monde) between 1959 and 1968, tells of a socialization of the spectacle, different from the thought by Guy Debord and the Situationists, and that is the staging of a utopia in the Third World or, more specifically, in the Caribbean, a border area where sexual, religious and revolutionary symbols have a capital as attributes of a politically alternative community."[29] In this guise, Pabellón Cuba was a revolutionary gesture of a socialist modernity for both foreign visitors and local citizens. It presents a stage for considering utopia's contradictions and inheritances.

NOTES

1. Weiss, "Some Thoughts," 53.

2. Weiss, 56.

3. Guerra, *Visions of Power in Cuba*, 30.

4. Guerra later remarked in *Visions of Power*: "I conceive of the *history* of the early Revolution . . . as a palimpsest" (31, 34). My research builds upon this notion, looking at art, architecture and visual culture as contributing to a palimpsestic understanding of revolutionary modernities.

5. In his multiple volume book *The Principle of Hope* (1938–1947), Ernst Bloch distinguishes abstract utopia as fantastic and compensatory, versus a concrete utopianism that affects and changes economic and political realities in an aspirational manner. At a basic level, Bloch suggests that concrete utopia is about technology and nature not being defined by material and economic relations, which remove it from the bourgeois thinking of the past. While this differs from Lefebvre's definition, the aspirational nature of Bloch's concrete utopia is transposed onto human experiences of pleasure and enjoyment. Bloch, *Principle of Hope*, 3:666–667.

6. Lefebvre, *Toward an Enjoyment of Architecture*, 148.

7. Lefebvre, 53.

8. Moreda, "Practices and Counterpractices," 187.

9. See Kapcia, *Havana*, 120–125.

10. See Mignolo, "Delinking."

11. Miller, "A Revolutionary Modernity," 685.

12. Pratt, "Modernity and Periphery," 35.

13. Rodríguez, "Tropical Minimalism," in Schmidt-Colinet, *Pabellón Cuba 4D*, 51.

14. Hyde, *Constitutional Modernism*, 256.

15. See Lefever and Huck, "Expropriation of the Havana Hilton," 14–20.

16. De la Osa, "Inauguro Fidel," 1–2.

17. See Arrufat, "A Little about La Rampa," in Schmidt-Colinet, *Pabellón Cuba 4D*, 40–49.

18. *Arquitectura Cuba* 331 (1964): 40.

19. Glendinning, "Cold War Conciliation," 197.

20. Glendinning, "Architect as Cold War Mediator," 32–33.

21. Translated from Spanish: "La importancia de la UIA radica en que es una organización internacional a la que hoy pertenecen arquitectos de casi todos los países, tanto desarrollados como en vías de desarrollo." *Arquitectura Cuba* 331 (1964): 16.

22. Rowtree, "Architects in Cuba."

23. Schmidt-Colinet, *Pabellón 4D*, 55.

24. "En ella la intervención extranjera, la frustración, las protestas, la angustia, la inconformidad de una suerte, toman formas en los volúmenes mezclados con cine, transparencias y fotos que ambietan realidad." *Architectura Cuba* 331 (1964): 40.

25. J M R, "Havana Pavilion."

26. "Todo el efecto de las distorciones de la propaganda malintencionada y de las contracciones ideológicas desaparecieron para aglutinarse en un sentimiento y un lenguaje común que unieron a todos los visitantes con el pueblo heroico, que ahora los recibía con la alegría de quien contribuye a construir un mundo nuevo." *Architectura Cuba* 331 (1964).

27. Bermúdez, *La imagen constante*, 94.

28. Translated from: "La arquitectura no es aquí concebida como pura configuración del espacio, sobre cual luego se aplicarán los elementos gráficos internos, para establecer el diálogo

comunicativo con los visitants. El concepto de integración visual entre forma abstracta e imagenes pictóricas ha sido aplicada brillamente en el pabellón: los elementos cromáticos contrastan con las blancas superficies de alumunio, la gigantesca tipografía y las pantallas cinematográficas colocadas en los extremos de los paralelepídedos, establecen la comunicación en todos los niveles de relación escalar entre los visitantes y el pabellón, representando la intensidad comunicativa del ámbito urbano, de las ciudades de Cuba." *Diez años de arquitectura en Cuba revolucionaria*, 171.

29. Rafael Rojas, "Anatomía del entusiasmo," 4, trans. Susan Lord. Cited in Lord, "Irreversible Havana."

BIBLIOGRAPHY

Arquitectura Cuba 331 (1964). Library, Colegio de Arquitectos, Havana, Cuba.

Bermúdez, Jorge R. *La imagen constante: El cartel cubano del siglo XX*. Havana: Editorial Letras Cubanas, 2000.

Bloch, Ernst. *The Principle of Hope*. Vols. 1–3. Cambridge, MA: MIT Press, 1986.

De la Osa, Jose A. "Inauguro Fidel el Hospital Hermanos Ameijeiras," *Granma*, December 4, 1982.

Glendinning, Miles. "The Architect as Cold War Mediator: The UIA Congress of 1963, Havana." *Docomomo Journal* 37 (January 2008): 30–35.

———. "Cold-War Conciliation: International Architectural Congresses in the Late 1950s and Early 1960s." *Journal of Architecture* 21, no. 4 (2016): 630–650.

Guerra, Lillian. *Visions of Power in Cuba: Revolution, Redemption, and Resistance, 1959–1971*. Chapel Hill: University of North Carolina Press, 2012.

Hyde, Timothy. *Constitutional Modernism: Architecture and Civil Society in Cuba, 1933–1959*. Minneapolis: University of Minnesota Press, 2014.

J M R. "Havana Pavilion: Architecture." *Architectural Review (London)* 135, no. 804 (February 1, 1964): a145.

Kapcia, Antoni. *Havana: the Making of Cuban Culture*. Oxford: Berg, 2005.

Lefebvre, Henri. *Toward an Architecture of Enjoyment*. Minneapolis: University of Minnesota Press, 2014.

Lefever, Michael, and Cathleen Huck. "The Expropriation of the Havana Hilton: A Timely Reminder." *International Journal of Hospitality* 9, no. 1 (1990): 14–20.

Lord, Susan. "Havana: Irreversible." *Public* 26, no. 52 (2015): 159–176.

Mignolo, Walter D. "Delinking: The Rhetoric of Modernity, the Logic of Coloniality and the Grammar of De-Coloniality." *Cultural Studies: Globalization and the De-colonial Option* 21, nos. 2–3 (2007): 449–514.

Miller, Nicola. "A Revolutionary Modernity: The Cultural Policy of the Cuban Revolution," *Journal of Latin American Studies* 40, no. 4 (2008): 675–696.

Moreda, Dannys Montes de Oca. "Practices and Counterpractices: Toward the Reconstruction of the Imaginary of 1960s Cuba." *Public* 26, no. 52 (2015): 187–202.

Pratt, Mary Louis, "Modernity and Periphery." In *Beyond Dichotomies: Histories, Identities, Cultures and the Challenge of Globalization*, edited by Elisabeth Mudimbe-Boyi. Albany, NY: SUNY Press, 2002.

Rojas, Rafael. "Anatomía del entusiasmo: La revolución de las ideas." *Encuentro de la Cultural Cubana* 45–46 (2007): 3–14.

Rowtree, Diana. "Architects in Cuba." *The Guardian*, October 9, 1963, 10A.

Schmidt-Colinet, Lisa, ed. *Pabellón Cuba 4D: 4Dimensions, 4Decades*. Berlin: B-books, 2008.

Weiss, Rachel. "Some Thoughts on the Right Way (for Us) to Love the Cuban Revolution." *Public* 26, no. 52 (2015): 49–58.

DOSSIER: LA HABANA EN EL SIGLO XXI /
HAVANA IN THE TWENTY-FIRST CENTURY

MARÍA A. GUTIÉRREZ BASCÓN Y
ROBERTO ZURBANO TORRES

Pensar La Habana en el siglo XXI: Mapas posibles para una ciudad cambiante

RESUMEN

La Habana del siglo XXI reclama ser leída desde una diversidad crítica que permita arrojar luz sobre los nuevos procesos urbanos que están reconfigurando la ciudad a nivel material y simbólico. Las contribuciones recogidas en el *dossier* dan cuenta de lógicas emergentes de privatización, gentrificación y desarrollo desigual asociadas a nuevos flujos de capital, que se suman a problemas de larga data, tales como el déficit habitacional crónico, el rígido y casi total monopolio del Estado sobre la producción del entorno construido, o el posicionamiento del turismo como una suerte de frágil monocultivo que sitúa a la isla —particularmente en la era post-COVID— en una posición de vulnerabilidad económica y que sigue reproduciendo formas de colonialidad urbana. Ante las lógicas urbanas excluyentes generadas por los entrecruzamientos entre el capital transnacional y el Estado, la variedad de posiciones recogidas en el *dossier* intenta dar respuestas críticas: enfoques decoloniales y de estudios críticos de raza, perspectivas *queer*, abordajes feministas y ópticas que destacan la importancia de la participación de las clases trabajadoras en el diseño y la gestión del espacio se constituyen en mapas posibles que ayudan a dilucidar los procesos urbanos que afectan a la ciudad de La Habana en el presente siglo.

ABSTRACT

Reading twenty-first-century Havana from new critical perspectives will help shed light on the new urban processes currently reconfiguring the city at material and symbolic levels. The contributions compiled in this dossier consider emerging logics of privatization, gentrification and uneven development associated to new flows of capital, which add onto long-term issues such as the chronic housing shortage affecting the city, the rigid and almost complete monopoly of the state over the production of the built environment, or the positioning of tourism as a sort of fragile monoculture that places the island—particularly in the post-COVID era—in an economically vulnerable position and continues to reproduce forms of urban coloniality. Facing the exclusionary logics generated by the entanglements of transnational capital flows and the state, the variety of positions gathered in this dossier attempts to provide some critical answers: decolonial approaches and critical race studies, queer perspectives, feminist approaches, and views that emphasize the importance of participatory design and management of urban space by the working classes all function as possible maps to explicate the complex urban processes impacting Havana in the present century.

> Dicen que la autopista va a atravesar la ciudad de arriba abajo. Lo que queda de la ciudad. Por el día avanzan los bulldozers barriendo parques, edificios, shopping centers. Por las noches yo deambulo en las proximidades del mar, entre los escombros, las maquinarias, los contenedores, tratando de imaginar desde ahí la magnitud de lo que se avecina. No cabe duda de que la autopista será algo monstruoso.
>
> —Jorge Enrique Lage, *La autopista: The Movie*

Situada a mediados del siglo XXI, una novela reciente de Jorge Enrique Lage abre sus páginas con la apocalíptica construcción de una enorme autopista que, sin destino aparente, cruza al tiempo que devasta la ciudad de La Habana —o lo que queda de ella, según sugiere la voz narrativa. El lector pronto descubre la existencia de una "Teoría Unificada" que, en el universo de la novela, explicaría el despliegue de la desoladora carretera, y que "tenía que ver con los flujos del dinero, con los desplazamientos del capital, con las economías de mercado. Tenía que ver con un mapa, si suponemos algo parecido a un mapa del tesoro donde el tesoro está moviéndose por todas partes o donde al final no queda claro qué es el tesoro. Los flujos del dinero son, en ese mapa, como autopistas. Hay intersecciones, rizos, desvíos; pero también velocidades, caídas abruptas, saltos de dimensión" (Lage, 35–36).

En *La autopista*, Lage ficciona, así, una Habana futura atravesada por los flujos de un capital cambiante que produce sus propias zonas de circulación y de excepción. O sus saltos dimensionales, al decir de uno de los personajes. Una década antes, casi para abrir el nuevo siglo, el ensayista Iván de la Nuez situaba ya a la isla en un mapa igualmente complejo que incluía, dentro de sus lindes, áreas aún socialistas, pero también, de manera intercalada, brotes de consumo postsocialista: "El turismo, la apertura al dólar y al euro, la incipiente economía de mercado, han hecho de Cuba un país poliédrico en el cual el socialismo comienza a convivir con zonas capitalistas" (168).[1] Si la ficción de Lage desplaza la llegada del capital global —en forma de una monstruosa carretera— hacia un futuro cercano, de la Nuez la encaja en nuestro presente más inmediato. El siglo XXI en Cuba se vislumbra, así, como un panorama aparentemente contradictorio, en el que perviven configuraciones socialistas con articulaciones capitalistas.

Los relatos que con frecuencia posicionan a Cuba y a su ciudad capital al borde de una transición inminente no consiguen capturar esta cartografía de disonancias socioeconómicas que acontecen en el presente y no en un futuro largamente esperado. En su afán por allanar contradicciones, los marcos transicionales desde los que a menudo se ha observado a la isla parecieran ubicarla en una eterna encrucijada. La semántica de la encrucijada ha dado título, de hecho, a una inagotable nómina de congresos, libros, artículos y reportajes dedicados a Cuba en el nuevo siglo. Enfrentada a esta bifurcación constante de caminos, pareciera que la isla caribeña no puede sino elegir dar un salto, de manera unívoca, hacia uno de ellos. Emparentadas con esquemas bipolares deudores de la Guerra Fría, las metáforas de la encrucijada a veces pierden de vista un rompecabezas complejo que en efecto articula fenómenos disímiles, con sus propias particularidades locales. Así, en la Cuba del siglo XXI, la planificación centralizada de la economía convive con la erupción reciente de colosales hoteles de lujo dedicados al turismo en zonas céntricas de La Habana; la cartelería de consignas fidelistas, que siguen demandando sacrificio en pos de un futuro diferido, subsiste junto a un reguetón que, como banda sonora omnipresente del nuevo siglo, invita al goce de un presente inaplazable; y las promesas socialistas del programa de vivienda popular cohabitan con procesos de gentrificación capitalista apuntalados por una incipiente liberalización del mercado inmobiliario. Si hay algo que el nuevo siglo deja claro es que el futuro ya está aquí, aunque este se materialice en procesos que no siempre son capaces de conjugar formas de democracia y justicia social para todos.

Este *dossier* quiere emplazar La Habana en un mapa de complejidades que reclaman ser leídas bajo coordenadas distintas a las de los paradigmas transicionales, o a las narrativas que insistieron en posicionarla como ciudad nostálgicamente paralizada en el tiempo, en espera sigilosa de un cambio drástico que nunca pareció acontecer —o que al menos no lo hizo de manera tajante. La Habana del siglo XXI demanda ser puesta en relación con otras temporalidades y con contextos transnacionales,[2] y observada desde una diversidad crítica que permita arrojar luz sobre las inversiones globales que han venido sucediéndose en los últimos años y cómo estas reconfiguran materialmente la ciudad; sobre el posicionamiento de la industria turística como el nuevo monocultivo económico que produce sus propias exclusiones y borraduras históricas; sobre la emergencia de nuevas clases medias al tiempo que se acrecientan las diferencias sociales; sobre la eclosión de una práctica privada de la arquitectura que proyecta y construye sus diseños en formas que cuestionan el monopolio exclusivo del estado socialista sobre el entorno construido; sobre los nuevos activismos negros y LGBTQ que han expresado sus demandas en el espacio público habanero y sobre la reciente privatización de la noche *queer*; o sobre el déficit habitacional y cómo este continúa constituyendo uno de los grandes desafíos urbanos en el presente siglo.

El *dossier* aparece pasadas ya dos décadas del inicio del siglo XXI, cuando podemos entrever algunas de sus dinámicas más relevantes y de sus especificidades regionales. Aparece, asimismo, poco después de la sonada celebración del 500 aniversario de la fundación de La Habana, que nos recuerda que la capital cubana se construye en torno a líneas de modernidad colonial que siguen reproduciéndose (y celebrándose) en el presente —y que generan, también, sus propias críticas y resistencias. Entre algunas de las diversas miradas que el conjunto de textos aquí recogidos moviliza, se propone un enfoque decolonial que expone la producción histórica de silencios y que aborda de manera crítica la colonialidad que pervive en el tejido urbano y en sus prácticas asociadas; un abordaje que privilegia las dimensiones materiales de la cultura y la importancia de los objetos y su circulación en la constitución de la vida social y urbana; y una aproximación atenta a las manifestaciones afectivas de las identidades *queer* en el espacio público y sensible a, como diría Sara Ahmed, "the messiness of the experiential" (30). En última instancia, la ciudad es vista como un escenario cuya materialidad revela los rastros históricos del tiempo largo de la colonialidad y del periodo posrevolucionario, pero también las marcas contemporáneas de las más recientes transformaciones socioeconómicas, de la emergencia de nuevas subjetividades y del reposicionamiento de la isla caribeña en la economía global.

Abrimos el *dossier* con la investigación etnográfica de Maile Speakman sobre las propuestas de un grupo de altos ejecutivos de empresas tecnológicas de Silicon Valley para crear un moderno espacio de *coworking* en el barrio de El Vedado en La Habana. De nombre "Jungla", el local parece que conjugará —de acuerdo con los *renderings* arquitectónicos a los que la investigadora ha tenido acceso— una naturaleza voluptuosa típicamente asociada al Caribe con un ambiente de alta tecnología, produciendo un tipo particular de imaginario que Speakman denomina como "tropicalidad virtual". Los usuarios de este espacio en El Vedado, que ofrecerá conectividad rápida a internet y acceso a una comunidad cosmopolita de clientes, son imaginados como sujetos blancos, y en su mayoría masculinos, por las representaciones arquitectónicas. Según se desprende de la entrevista con el fundador sueco-británico de Jungla, el espacio de *coworking* está llamado a convertirse en un lugar exclusivo, en una suerte de club privado de internet, fundamentalmente dirigido a "nómadas digitales", es decir, a aquellos ejecutivos y emprendedores que viajan globalmente esperando encontrar en cualquier lugar del mundo acceso rápido a internet, a espacios de diseño minimalista y a una cierta atmósfera *hip*. La clase emergente de emprendedores locales —en su mayoría también blancos— componen el otro grupo proyectado de clientes para el negocio. Además de los fondos provenientes de inversores de Silicon Valley, Jungla se financiará parcialmente con la venta de una marca noruega de ron, de la que el fundador del espacio de *coworking* es también director de marketing. Utilizando una aproximación de estudios críticos de raza, el análisis de Speakman revela que el exclusivo espacio de *coworking* está íntimamente entrelazado con el ron noruego a través de la producción de un cierto imaginario tropical —y racializado— en torno a la isla caribeña. Con el nombre "Black Tears", en supuesta alusión a la famosa canción "Lágrimas negras", la marca de ron activa inadvertidamente una serie de resonancias a la colonización europea, los modos de la plantación esclavista y el mercado transatlántico del ron y el azúcar. La estrategia de marketing del ron noruego, que por el momento solo se comercializa en Europa, moviliza tanto descripciones verbales cargadas de una fuerte emocionalidad racializada, como imágenes de una exotizada escena urbana habanera para promocionar la bebida, de manera que la imagen de Cuba como escenario de placer, fiesta y consumo se convierte en sí misma en una mercancía inmaterial para los consumidores europeos. Speakman detecta, así, una correspondencia entre la violencia simbólica del nombre de la marca de ron y sus técnicas de marketing, y las dinámicas asimétricas de poder —en ejes de clase, raza, género y nacionalidad— que configuran el espacio de Jungla. Por otra parte, Speakman describe un *tour* por La Habana realizado por inversores extranjeros del sector tecnológico, del que la investigadora pudo formar parte como observadora en mayo de 2019. Como parte de este *tour*, los ejecutivos de una corporación especializada en mercados hostiles o de frontera examinaron potenciales edificios a adquirir en el barrio desfavorecido de San Isidro —de mayoría no blanca—, con el objetivo de crear un segundo espacio de *coworking*. Desplegando unas ciertas formas tropicalizantes y neoliberalizantes de mirar, estos ejecutivos colocan a Cuba como paraíso virgen listo para ser incorporado a las lógicas del capital transnacional e integrado al mapa de franquicias tecnológicas globalmente conectadas desde Silicon Valley.

Las formaciones discursivas en torno al Caribe como escenario paradisíaco disponible para el disfrute y el consumo por parte de lo que hoy llamaríamos el Norte Global son de larga data (Sheller 23). Una de las virtudes del trabajo de Speakman reside en trazar la iteración más reciente de este imaginario, al situarlo en el contexto de un tecno-capitalismo en expansión, que la investigadora define como constelación de plataformas *online*, infraestructuras digitales corporativas y modelos espaciales hegemónicos producidos desde Silicon Valley. Particularmente a partir del *boom* post-Obama, con la llegada de la plataforma Airbnb y de los servidores de Google a la isla, Speakman argumenta que los tecno-capitalistas han proyectado un imaginario de tropicalidad virtual sobre la ciudad de La Habana, reciclando viejos mitos del Caribe para producir nuevos ensamblajes de datos, circulación de capitales y fantasías neoextractivistas en torno a una Cuba imaginada como paraíso virgen listo para ser explotado. La investigación cuidadosa de Speakman en torno a los actores, la producción de imaginarios y las operaciones a menudo invisibles del capital evidencia nuevas prácticas de expansión geográfica del capitalismo computacional. Estas prácticas y sus imaginarios asociados tienen, según el análisis de Speakman, efectos materiales tangibles en la reconfiguración espacial de la ciudad. Siguiendo una lógica del enclave, los nuevos espacios del ocio y el consumo —*rooftops* exclusivos, espacios de diseño, clubes privados de internet— estarían ya generando procesos de gentrificación y homogenización del espacio urbano habanero que se prefigurarían como excluyentes.

El trabajo del crítico cultural Roberto Zurbano Torres coincide con el de Speakman en señalar dinámicas de gentrificación que se han hecho especialmente visibles en el último lustro en La Habana. Tomando como caso de estudio el barrio de El Ángel, situado en La Habana Vieja, Zurbano Torres explica que la rápida transformación del conjunto de calles en los alrededores de la Loma del Ángel ha sido fruto de una segunda oleada gentrificadora a cargo del nuevo capital privado. La primera fase de la gentrificación correspondería en el espacio habanero, de acuerdo con las observaciones del crítico, con la agenda de restauraciones implementada por la Oficina del Historiador en el casco histórico que, a partir de la década del noventa, produjo una serie de desplazamientos de la población local hacia zonas periféricas de la ciudad. En ambos casos, la gentrificación ha significado un proceso de sustitución de poblaciones —en base a divisiones de clase que a menudo se superponen con líneas raciales— y un contraste cada vez más acentuado de la ciudad, en palabras de Zurbano Torres, entre una Habana dolarizada y una Habana sin dólares. Junto a la incipiente gentrificación urbana, Zurbano Torres identifica al turismo como responsable de imponer nuevas formas de colonialidad —entendida como el patrón de dominación originado durante el colonialismo moderno, pero que trasciende sus estrictos límites históricos para hacerse presente en sociedades actuales— en el tejido urbano y social de La Habana del siglo XXI. Basándose en la teoría de la economía de plantación propuesta por Lloyd Best y Kari Polanyi Levitt, el investigador posiciona al turismo como un monocultivo económico de tipo extractivista, o como una iteración invisible de la plantación que sigue reproduciendo jerarquías raciales y situando la negritud como identidad subordinada en el espacio urbano.

El artículo de Zurbano Torres se organiza como una suerte de *tour* antiturístico por La Habana Vieja para revelar las nuevas formas de la colonialidad (turismo y gentrificación), pero también las huellas silenciadas del pasado afrodescendiente. Movilizando una mirada decolonial atenta tanto al pasado como al presente, el *tour* que Zurbano Torres nos propone seguir a través de las calles del casco histórico de La Habana devela la temporalidad palimpséstica de la colonialidad como elemento articulador de los procesos de urbanización de ayer y de hoy. Así, en un mismo espacio descubrimos las marcas del pasado y cómo estas tienen su continuidad en los silencios y las lógicas excluyentes del presente. En la Plaza de la Catedral, Zurbano Torres nos recuerda la sangre derramada por los constructores negros del imponente templo colonial, al tiempo que dirige nuestra atención a la condición de escenario turístico que la actual plaza ha adquirido. En ella se dan cita mujeres afrodescendientes que juegan el rol de floristas o cartománticas, reproduciendo los estereotipos coloniales que la industria turística demanda. El análisis del crítico nos aclara que la población afrodescendiente tiene a menudo dificultades para acceder al mercado del turismo y, cuando lo hace, es para ocupar posiciones subordinadas, en ocasiones a modo de atrezo para completar la escenografía turística.[3]

El *tour* que se despliega en las páginas del trabajo de Zurbano Torres tiene su origen en un itinerario que el investigador diseñó originalmente para estudiantes de universidades norteamericanas, algunos de ellos afrodescendientes. Conocemos, a partir del recuento del crítico, las respuestas de algunos estudiantes afroamericanos al recorrido por La Habana negra. Se iluminan, así, una serie de conexiones hemisféricas de las luchas antirracistas de poblaciones afrodescendientes que desbordan los marcos estrictamente nacionales. A lo largo del *tour*, la visibilización de silencios se convierte en la principal estrategia, de manera similar a la posición efectiva que esta herramienta ha ocupado en el repertorio del activismo antirracista en los últimos años. No en vano Zurbano Torres enmarca su trabajo con una cita del antropólogo haitiano Michel-Rolph Trouillot, que nos incita a desafiar la opacidad del poder, descubriendo y nombrando sus raíces.

Por su parte, David Tenorio aborda las complejidades de la conformación de los espacios públicos/íntimos *queer* en La Habana, en un contexto de institucionalización —por parte del poder estatal— del activismo LGBTQ, al tiempo que se produce el reposicionamiento de la isla en los sistemas del capital global. En el nuevo escenario que se abre con el siglo XXI, la industria turística vuelve a duplicar la imagen del Caribe como paraíso tropical de placer y, más concretamente, de posibilidades sexuales ilimitadas, también para el deseo homoerótico. El artículo de Tenorio da cuenta de la inauguración, en 2016, de una línea de cruceros que, operados por una compañía de viajes griega, estaban dirigidos específicamente a clientes LGBTQ y contaban a bordo con especialistas del Ministerio de Turismo de Cuba que hacían las veces de guías en las ciudades cubanas visitadas durante la travesía. Empresas turísticas internacionales se ponen, así, de acuerdo con instancias del Estado cubano para atraer el dinero rosa proveniente de las comunidades LGBTQ del Norte Global. En La Habana, a través de un recuento autoetnográfico, Tenorio reseña las interioridades del cabaret Las Vegas, un espacio de la noche LGBTQ de propiedad estatal. Entre el público que acude a ver el espectáculo de la noche se encuentran representantes del Centro Nacional de Educación Sexual (CENESEX), institución estatal liderada por Mariela Castro que, desde 2007, ha venido organizando anualmente las Jornadas contra la Homofobia y la Transfobia. En los alrededores del cabaret, según la etnografía del investigador, se congregan *pingueros* que participan de la economía informal del trabajo sexual, en buena parte ligada al turismo internacional. La Habana, como uno de los principales atractivos turísticos del Caribe, y su noche *queer*, quedan así inscritas en las economías globales libidinales como enclaves para el trabajo sexual. A través de su análisis atento a estas economías del trabajo erótico y afectivo, Tenorio detecta procesos de privatización de la noche *queer* y de comercialización de la diversidad sexual por parte del Estado cubano en la era del capitalismo global. La celebración oficialista de la diversidad contrasta, como bien señala el investigador, con la precariedad material que marca las vidas de las mujeres trans que se dedican al trabajo sexual en el espacio público, cuyas voces Tenorio pone al centro en una parte de su trabajo. Aunque la mayoría de las mujeres trans a las que el investigador entrevista reconocen los aciertos de la agencia gubernamental comandada por Mariela Castro en su apoyo al colectivo LGBTQ, algunas de ellas son también explícitas en señalar los límites de un activismo estatalizado y en demandar espacios propios para su autoagenciamiento.

Una instancia rupturista del activismo *queer* con respecto a esta limitante institucionalidad estatal que Tenorio incluye en su análisis es la marcha LGBTQ organizada de manera independiente al CENESEX en mayo de 2019, después de que Mariela Castro anunciara la cancelación de la oficial Conga contra la Homofobia y la Transfobia de ese mismo año. Haciendo uso de las redes sociales, miembros de la comunidad LGBTQ y sus aliados convocaron una marcha pública que, desligada de la esfera estatal, hizo su sorpresiva aparición en el habanero Paseo del Prado, siendo bruscamente interrumpida por efectivos policiales. Tenorio sugiere que la marcha alternativa manifiesta la creciente agencia crítica de un colectivo LGBTQ que es capaz de movilizar prácticas digitales de organización política y articularlas con prácticas del cuerpo desplegadas en el espacio urbano en una forma desvinculada de las instituciones estatales. Para dar cuenta de los complicados y a veces contradictorios ensamblajes y desensamblajes del activismo y las prácticas *queer* con respecto a las instituciones del Estado, Tenorio toma prestado el concepto de la conga como un proceso rítmico de negociación de convergencias y divergencias. La conga es propuesta, entonces, como forma diversa de entender las luchas cotidianas de las comunidades *queer* y trans en La Habana y su relacionalidad estratégica, o danza rítmica, con los espacios estatales para el activismo. Esta conga que Tenorio identifica oscila entre la visibilidad y la invisibilidad de las comunidades LGBTQ locales, entre su celebración legal y la ilegalización de algunas de sus prácticas, entre la sexualidad tropicalizada por el Estado y por la industria turística y la precariedad material efectiva de muchas vidas *queer* y trans.

La investigación de María A. Gutiérrez Bascón converge con el resto de contribuciones del *dossier* en destacar el peso ascendente de los nuevos flujos de capital en la conformación del espacio urbano de La Habana y sus prácticas asociadas. En su artículo sobre la nueva arquitectura cubana y su despliegue creativo y comercial en la capital cubana durante la última década, Gutiérrez Bascón se aproxima, a través de entrevistas en profundidad y análisis de obras y prácticas arquitectónicas, al hasta ahora poco estudiado fenómeno de los estudios de arquitectura que ofrecen sus servicios de diseño de manera independiente al Estado en La Habana y otras ciudades cubanas. La investigadora sitúa la emergencia de estos nuevos estudios de arquitectura en el contexto de las reformas raulistas que permitieron una relativa ampliación del sector privado o cuentapropista, especialmente a partir del año 2011. La eliminación de algunas restricciones relativas a los viajes y las remesas en 2009 y 2011 desde la administración Obama, favoreció, por su parte, la llegada de flujos de inversión hacia la isla, incluyendo capital de la diáspora cubana. Estos elementos apuntalaron un paisaje económico que empezó a dar cabida a un creciente ecosistema de negocios privados en La Habana: nuevos restaurantes, bares, gimnasios, *spas*, heladerías y pastelerías comenzaron a proliferar en la ciudad en manos de una emergente clase media, que se convirtió a su vez en cliente de los nuevos estudios de arquitectura independientes. Resurge, así, una figura clave para la práctica arquitectónica: el cliente privado. Los estudios emergentes funcionan, no obstante, como señala la investigadora, en contradicción con los marcos legales existentes para el trabajo por cuenta propia: a falta de una licencia específica para el diseño arquitectónico, los nuevos estudios han abierto sus puertas con licencias de decoración o de albañilería. A pesar de las limitaciones jurídicas, las firmas jóvenes han conseguido expandir la práctica de la arquitectura más allá de la parálisis y la ortodoxia asociadas a la burocracia estatal y sus empresas de diseño.[4]

El artículo de Gutiérrez Bascón se concentra en seis estudios de arquitectura establecidos en La Habana entre los años 2008 y 2017 para proveer una cartografía de las diversas sensibilidades arquitectónicas que este tipo de prácticas privadas han desplegado en la última década. Así, vemos cómo la oficina H[r]g Arquitectura ha articulado su proyecto en torno a ideas de sostenibilidad y reciclaje, y alrededor de la incorporación de códigos históricos locales. La firma Apropia Estudio, por su parte, ha manifestado la necesidad de construir una "arquitectura propia" que responda tanto a los materiales disponibles localmente como a las demandas contextuales. El equipo de Nivel 4 Estudio coincide en vincular su práctica contemporánea con tradiciones arquitectónicas locales, particularmente con el movimiento moderno de las décadas de 1940 y 1950 y sus reflexiones en torno a la identidad nacional y la importancia del elemento climático en el diseño. La arquitecta al frente de Pino Estudio pone el acento en la relevancia de los espacios menores en la arquitectura y organiza su práctica tomando en consideración la dimensión afectiva del trabajo de diseño. Por su parte, el espacio Órbita XX se piensa como un proyecto hecho por mujeres, para mujeres: la arquitecta fundadora enfatiza el papel de las mujeres en la arquitectura no solo como diseñadoras, sino también como clientas. En redes sociales, el proyecto busca, asimismo, generar un archivo digital que subraye la contribución histórica, a menudo invisibilizada, de las mujeres cubanas en la conformación del entorno construido en la isla. Finalmente, Infraestudio se introduce en el panorama de los nuevos estudios cubanos con una propuesta conceptual, que busca invertir el conocido lema racionalista de "la forma sigue a la función" para proponer que la forma del edificio se libere de las imposiciones funcionales y acompañe a los conceptos que poéticamente guían el diseño. El resultado de las indagaciones estéticas de Infraestudio son casas que adoptan materializaciones formales poco comunes y que disputan las nociones tradicionales del confort doméstico. Gutiérrez Bascón muestra, asimismo, cómo algunos de estos colectivos optan por repensar las fronteras de la propia actividad de diseño —cuestionando, por ejemplo, la asunción de que el edificio construido deba constituir el fin último de la arquitectura, o inclinándose por no llamarse a sí mismos estudios con objeto de flexibilizar la producción artística y técnica del grupo—, como si reconstruir una tradición arquitectónica vista como interrumpida durante los años de parálisis posrevolucionaria implicara también reimaginar los límites de la práctica arquitectónica.

Cerramos el *dossier* con la mirada del sociólogo Carlos García Pleyán sobre los futuros posibles de la vivienda social en La Habana. El investigador se aproxima al déficit habitacional que afecta de manera aguda a la capital cubana —y a otras ciudades de la isla— para proponer que se reevalúen los procedimientos aplicados hasta el momento por las entidades estatales y que se implementen enfoques innovadores que tengan en cuenta la magnitud y la complejidad del problema. Para García Pleyán, se hace necesario asumir que el objetivo debe ser rehabilitar la vivienda ya existente e introducir nuevas unidades habitacionales al interior de la ciudad, en lugar de generar grandes desarrollos periféricos, que ya han demostrado ampliamente su falta de sostenibilidad a nivel global. De esta manera, se plantea la cuestión habitacional como problema interrelacionado con el de la posible pérdida del invaluable patrimonio edilicio de La Habana. Uno de los principales retos urbanos del siglo XXI será, así, el de producir las viviendas necesarias dentro de la trama urbana ya consolidada, de manera atenta tanto a las demandas constructivas que una ciudad con altos valores patrimoniales reclama, como a las necesidades de una población diversa y cambiante. En ese sentido, el investigador deja claro que el catálogo de viviendas "tipo" con el que cuenta el Ministerio de la Construcción (MICONS) —entidad responsable de la política de la vivienda en Cuba— no ofrece soluciones adecuadas al complejo escenario abierto por el déficit habitacional que caracteriza a la capital y por el preocupante estado de conservación en el que se encuentra parte de su patrimonio arquitectónico. La prefabricación como método constructivo y las soluciones "tipo" no podrán constituir la única respuesta al problema de la vivienda en La Habana; por el contrario, el panorama presente requiere que se diseñen proyectos arquitectónicos y urbanísticos específicos para cada parcela en particular, independientemente de que se trate de rehabilitar vivienda ya existente, de ampliarla o de incorporar nuevas inserciones en los vacíos urbanos a menudo dejados por los frecuentes derrumbes.

Examinando de manera cuidadosa los datos disponibles en los documentos publicados por el MICONS y la información de recabación propia, García Pleyán propone algunas soluciones para remediar la falta de vivienda en las ciudades cubanas durante la década que comienza. Según la política de vivienda anunciada por el MICONS en 2018, se prevé la producción de alrededor de un millón de viviendas —incluyendo la rehabilitación y la nueva construcción— en toda la isla antes de 2029. En La Habana, la cifra sería de 185,000 unidades. Puesto que un porcentaje considerable de la construcción y rehabilitación de estas viviendas deberá ser asumido por los propios ciudadanos de manera privada, García Pleyán argumenta que será necesario contar con aquellos profesionales del diseño que desde hace aproximadamente una década han venido estableciendo estudios privados de arquitectura en la isla. Dado el desafío cuantitativo y cualitativo que el escenario habitacional de La Habana y las ciudades cubanas plantea, el investigador argumenta que las soluciones no podrán recaer en las limitadas empresas estatales de diseño arquitectónico, ni tampoco en los esfuerzos dispersos que puedan llevar a cabo los nuevos estudios privados. Se hará necesaria, dice García Pleyán, una articulación público-privada capaz de movilizar a unos 1,700 arquitectos que se dediquen a proyectar vivienda —a razón de unos doce proyectos al año por arquitecto— de manera atenta a las demandas contextuales. Más allá de esta novedosa fórmula organizativa, el sociólogo propone que se replanteen los recursos financieros disponibles —flexibilizando los créditos o reintroduciendo el alquiler social— y las opciones habituales de tenencia y gestión de la vivienda —incluyendo alternativas como la vivienda en gestión o propiedad cooperativa o nuevos modelos de *co-housing*. Por último, el sociólogo enfatiza la necesidad de introducir enfoques participativos en el diseño y la gestión de soluciones urbanas, particularmente en la transformación de los barrios precarios. El trabajo de García Pleyán llama, en suma, a dejar de lado los enfoques rígidos y a contemplar posibles colaboraciones entre las entidades estales y las jóvenes firmas privadas de arquitectura estudiadas por Gutiérrez Bascón en su artículo. En un futuro escenario de posible ampliación de los aún restrictivos marcos legales relativos a la práctica privada de la arquitectura, estos nuevos estudios podrían dedicar parte de la experiencia técnica y creativa adquirida en los últimos años al planeamiento de vivienda social y participar, así, en la producción pública de la arquitectura de la ciudad.

En suma, el presente *dossier* traza una serie de mapas posibles para entender una Habana ya inmersa en procesos de reconfiguración espacial, en un contexto marcado por nuevos desplazamientos del capital. Algunas de las aportaciones aquí recogidas cuestionan, por una parte, el monopolio casi exclusivo del Estado sobre la producción del entorno construido, valorizando la actividad de diseño de grupos de arquitectura constituidos con independencia a las entidades estatales y que podrían aportar soluciones, si los marcos legales lo permiten, al problema del déficit habitacional que afecta gravemente a la ciudad. Otras contribuciones, por su parte, alertan sobre las lógicas de privatización, gentrificación y desarrollo desigual asociadas a los nuevos flujos de capital que, por otra parte, entran en ocasional relación con las agendas del Estado. Un caso claro de esta asociación de los capitales trasnacionales con el estado socialista y sus corporaciones militares son los imponentes hoteles de lujo construidos en la capital a partir de 2017, a los que hacen breve referencia los artículos de Zurbano Torres y Gutiérrez Bascón.[5] Esa Habana del turismo parece seguir en crecimiento constante en el nuevo siglo, constituyéndose en uno de los centros de una suerte de frágil monocultivo que sitúa a la isla, particularmente en la era post-COVID, en una posición de vulnerabilidad económica, y que sigue reproduciendo, al mismo tiempo, formas de colonialidad urbana. Ante las lógicas urbanas excluyentes generadas por los entrecruzamientos entre el capital transnacional y el Estado, una variedad de posiciones intenta dar respuestas críticas: enfoques decoloniales y de estudios críticos de raza, como los que ofrecen los trabajos de Roberto Zurbano Torres y Maile Speakman; perspectivas *queer*, como las que recoge la investigación de David Tenorio; abordajes feministas como los del grupo de arquitectura Órbita XX, citado en el artículo de María A. Gutiérrez Bascón; u ópticas que destacan la importancia de la participación de las clases trabajadoras en el diseño y gestión del espacio, como la articulada por la propuesta de Carlos García Pleyán. Este *dossier* ha querido crear un mapa que haga espacio a esa diversidad crítica en su mirada a los procesos urbanos que afectan a la ciudad de La Habana en el siglo XXI.

NOTAS

1. Se trata de un ensayo de 2003 titulado "Spielberg en La Habana: Un reporte en minoría", recogido en la reciente colección *Cubantropía*, publicada por la editorial Periférica en 2020.

2. En *Making Cities Global: The Transnational Turn in Urban History*, los historiadores urbanos A. K. Sandoval-Strausz y Nancy H. Kwak abogan por una transnacionalización de los estudios urbanos que contribuya a repensar las diferentes escalas, temporalidades y redes de la transformación urbana. El giro transnacional propuesto para estudiar las ciudades contemporáneas pondría en estrecha relación los procesos de la globalización con los propios desarrollos urbanos de diversos contextos.

3. Respecto a la posición de la población cubana afrodescendiente en la industria turística, la investigadora Devyn Spence Benson ha explicado, en una línea similar, que en los últimos años "most new (and higher paying) jobs in the tourist economy have gone to lighter skinned or white Cubans" y que, a pesar de la apariencia de integración racial en la isla, "Afro-Cubans are discretely barred entrance into tourist hotels, or have limited access to good-paying, front-of-the-house jobs in major hotel chains" (n/p).

4. Es preciso anotar que, tras la redacción inicial de esta introducción, se produjo la prohibi-

ción efectiva de la arquitectura independiente en la isla, con la inclusión del diseño arquitectónico en la lista de actividades para las que se prohíbe el trabajo por cuenta propia, publicada por el Ministerio de Trabajo y Seguridad Social de Cuba el 11 de febrero de 2021. La nueva norma sustituye la limitada lista previa de 127 actividades permitidas por una de actividades prohibidas. Aunque el cambio de política puede ser visto como una relativa expansión del sector privado, lo cierto es que hay áreas de interés para el Estado, tales como la arquitectura, que quedan fuera del alcance de los emprendedores de la isla en el nuevo marco legal anunciado.

5. En referencia a la función económica y de captación de inversiones de las Fuerzas Armadas Revolucionarias con relación a la proliferación de hoteles y otros servicios en La Habana, puede consultarse el texto de Alina López Hernández, "Economía militar en Cuba", publicado por *La Joven Cuba.*

REFERENCIAS

Ahmed, Sara. "Happy Objects." *The Affect Theory Reader*, editado por Melissa Gregg y Gregory J. Seigworth, Duke UP, 2010, pp. 29–51.

de la Nuez, Iván. *Cubantropía.* Periférica, 2020.

Lage, Jorge Enrique. *La autopista: The Movie.* Esto No Es Berlín Ediciones, 2015.

López Hernández, Alina. "Economía militar en Cuba." *La Joven Cuba*, 8 de octubre de 2020, https://jovencuba.com/economia-militar/.

Sandoval-Strausz, A. K., y Nancy H. Kwak, eds. *Making Cities Global: The Transnational Turn in Urban History.* U of Pennsylvania P, 2018.

Sheller, Mimi. "Natural Hedonism: The Invention of Caribbean Islands as Tropical Playgrounds." *Tourism in the Caribbean: Trends, Development, Prospects*, editado por David Timothy Duval, Routledge, 2004, pp. 23–38.

Spence Benson, Devyn. "What President Obama's Visit to Cuba Means for Cubans of African Descent." *Huffington Post*, 19 de marzo de 2016, https://www.huffpost.com/entry/obamas -visit-cuba-means-afro-cubans_b_9507154.

MAILE SPEAKMAN

Virtual Tropicality: Technocapitalist Visions of Havana's Urban Future

ABSTRACT

This article traces how the imaginations and ideas of Silicon Valley associates and adjacent investors and founders materialized into blueprints for a coworking space named Jungla in Havana's Vedado neighborhood. Drawing on a year of ethnographic research in Havana and a month of research in Silicon Valley, I use interviews with Jungla's founders and investors alongside participant observation of a US venture capital tour of Havana to consider how Jungla fits into a broader US technocapitalist imaginary of Havana. Havana's lack of incorporation into US corporate technology markets provokes technocapitalists to see the city as a space of promise for future returns, as a space to build out tech franchises that already operate in other global cities, and as a frontier space for new experimental ventures. The Obama boom enabled US and European technocapitalists to imagine Havana as a virtual tropical space, as both a vacant site ripe for capitalist possibility and a site of immense creativity where companies can harness local talent to expand US and European markets. Although it is very difficult to imagine Havana as a high-speed center of technocapitalism, Silicon Valley's virtual tropical imaginaries of Havana have a profound impact on the material life of the city.

RESUMEN

Este artículo sigue la historia de cómo se materializó la idea de un grupo de ejecutivos de tecnología de Silicon Valley y Europa en los planos para un espacio de colaboración llamado Jungla en el barrio de El Vedado en La Habana. Este ensayo se basa en un año de investigación etnográfica en La Habana y un mes en Silicon Valley. Utilizo entrevistas con los fundadores e inversores de Jungla junto con mi observación participante de una gira de inversores estadounidenses por La Habana. La falta de incorporación de La Habana a los mercados tecnológicos corporativos de los EEUU provoca que los tecnocapitalistas vean la ciudad como un espacio prometedor para futuras ganancias, como un espacio para construir franquicias tecnológicas que ya operan en otras ciudades mundiales, y como un espacio fronterizo para nuevas empresas experimentales. Sostengo en este ensayo que el *boom* de Obama permitió a los tecno-capitalistas de Europa y los EEUU imaginar a La Habana como un espacio tropical virtual. Para ellos La Habana es un sitio vacante que está listo para posibilidades capitalistas y a la misma vez es un sitio de inmensa creatividad donde las empresas pueden aprovechar el talento local para expandir los mercados de los EEUU y Europa. Aunque es muy difícil imaginar a La Habana como un centro de tecno-capitalismo, los imaginarios trópico-virtuales de La Habana desde Silicon Valley tienen un profundo impacto en la vida material de la ciudad.

138

Jungla is a white three-story square building with two Corinthian columns and an outdoor metallic staircase that leads patrons to a third-story rooftop bar (Figure 1).¹ It is located in Havana's El Fanguito neighborhood, a few blocks from the Fábrica del Arte, an arts and entertainment space in a repurposed cooking oil factory. Patrons drink espresso and rum in the open air on the rooftop or surf the internet on MacBook Pros on the members-only second floor (Figure 2). This coworking space is enclosed by large industrial windows and is lit by artisanal teardrop filament lightbulbs that hang from the ceiling. The building's walls are covered in ferns and other leafy green plants (Figure 4). Ready for a drink, patrons climb up to the rooftop and order a cocktail at the stylized slate gray bar. They sit in Tolix Model A chairs, galvanized steel French bistro chairs that are displayed in modern art museums as emblems of twentieth-century French industrial design. All the patrons are light-skinned men, except one light-skinned woman who gazes out at the city. She has long braided brunette hair and wears a red shirt (Figure 3).

Jungla does not exist yet. It is an imaged space that architects in Miami and Havana have artistically rendered. The architects on the Cuban side are registered as artists, since Cubans cannot officially be architects for nonstate entities. Hugh, a Swedish Brit who works for a Norwegian rum company, hired these architects to render a rum-themed coworking space, which he is slowly building in the northwestern part of Havana's Vedado district.² The project has many investors, including a Silicon Valley–based Cuban American named Rafael who shared the renderings with me over drinks in South Berkeley in early 2020. What does it mean to envision this space three thousand miles from Havana from the vantage point of Silicon Valley? The Jungla plans illuminate a technocapitalist spatial imaginary of Havana's future. Everything from the lighting scheme to the Tolix chairs that run for €237 to the members-only internet area connect Jungla to an archipelago of global digital nomad spaces and the corporate models of companies like WeWork and Soho House. The world's tech start-up entrepreneurs would surely find a recognizable home in Jungla.

Jungla will not be Havana's only exclusive or tech-oriented space, but it seems to be the first idea for a space in Havana where internet access is based on a members-only model and where a portion of investment funds are coming from a Silicon Valley–based backer. Spaces such as Centro's Copincha, where Habaneros fix computer hardware and share skills in the founder's home, are financed by a very small monthly fee that most Habaneros can afford. Other Cuban entrepreneurs who I talked to in 2019 envisioned coworking spaces that ultimately were thwarted by the extremely high price of internet connection in Cuba and the unlikelihood that a locals-oriented space could turn a profit. These entrepreneurs instead funneled their coworking start-up money into more profitable Airbnb rentals and tour businesses. The capital necessary for a private internet club like Jungla, which would provide a more exclusive

FIGURES 1 AND 2. Jungla Renderings, sent to author by investor.

experience than Havana's Wi-Fi parks and computation centers, must come from outside of the city.

In this essay I trace how the imaginations and ideas of Silicon Valley associates and adjacent investors and founders have materialized into the blueprints for a coworking space in Havana's Vedado neighborhood. First, drawing on a year of ethnographic research in Havana and a month of research in Silicon Valley, I document Jungla founder Hugh's vision of the space as it relates to his location as a rum marketer and European expatriate who arrived in Havana

in search of new ventures after the city's post-Obama tourist and tech boom. Second, I use interviews with Jungla's primary investor Rafael, a Miami-born Cuban American who works in Silicon Valley, alongside participant observation of a US venture capital tour of Havana to consider how Jungla fits into a broader US corporate imaginary of Havana as another site to build globally connected technology franchises for Silicon Valley associates. Havana's lack of incorporation into US corporate technology markets provokes technocapitalists to see the city as space of promise for future returns, a space to build out franchises that already operate in other global cities, and as a frontier space

FIGURES 3 AND 4. Jungla Renderings, sent to author by investor.

for new experimental ventures. I argue that the Obama boom enabled US and European technocapitalists to imagine Havana as a virtual tropical space, as both a vacant site ripe for capitalist possibility and a site of immense creativity where companies can harness local talent to expand US and European markets. Key to this imaginary is the complex interplay between the immaterial, artistic, and emotional labor of Cubans and the influx of US-based cloud services into Havana. Since the US embargo against Cuba does not block cloud services or the sale of art, and because the Cuban government is more permissive

of entrepreneurial and architectural projects that are categorized as "artistic," US companies like Google have legally been able to install servers in Havana while Habanero *cuentapropistas* (private business owners) have legally been able to sell designs, art, and information-based services to foreign buyers. Thus, artistic renderings of buildings like Jungla can be exported internationally. Although it is very difficult to imagine Havana as a high-speed center of technocapitalism, Silicon Valley's virtual tropical imaginaries of Havana have a profound impact on the material life of the city.

Havana is shaped as much by tourist representations and imaginaries as it is shaped by the materiality of everyday life (Bobes 16; Dopico 452). To Velia Cecilia Bobes, "virtual Havana" emerged in the post-Soviet era when an influx of tourists started to pay to see the city's ruins (26). As Ana María Dopico notes, foreign commercial photographers capitalized on what they portrayed as the "the fashionable status and historical exceptionalism of the city as living ruin" during Havana's post-Soviet Special Period (451). The images that these photographers circulated intensified the city's "aesthetic and sensual fetishization" and reified its "tourist apartheid" (Dopico 451, 453). This virtuality that characterizes Havana intensifies what José Quiroga calls the city's *irreality*, a term he uses to highlight the disjuncture between how Habaneros "really live" and how they "imagine themselves living" (275).

In the post-Obama era, Havana is not only scripted by global photography markets and *National Geographic* features but also by social media platforms and US technology markets. The partial integration of US technological infrastructures and platforms within Havana's economy is an intensification of the Cuban state's opening of the city to global capital via joint ventures and tourist development during the Special Period. While the post-Soviet opening connected the Cuban economy to multinational hotel corporations, the Obama boom centered the installation of US digital platforms and infrastructure ("Statement by the President on Cuba Policy Changes"). Habaneros call this influx of US companies, travelers, dollars, and ideas about the future that followed the Obama Administration's renewal of diplomatic relations with Cuba in 2014: *el boom*. The most concrete manifestation of *el boom* was the introduction of Airbnb's platform and Google's servers to Cuba (Robbins; Williams).

El boom continues to impact Havana even during a time of distance, economic downturn, and disconnection. Although the Trump administration severely cut personnel at the US embassy in Havana and implemented harsher sanctions on the movement of goods, money, and visitors between the United States and Cuba, it largely left telecommunications and technology market policies untouched ("Cuba Sanctions"). Google sponsored a Cuban fashion line in 2018, its servers continue to run, and in 2019 the company signed a memorandum of understanding with Cuba's state-run telecommunications company ETECSA (Empresa de Telecomunicaciones de Cuba SA) as a first step toward building a new fiber optic cable to the island (Marsh; Clandestina Team, "Press Release").[3] As for Airbnb, Havana was the most profitable city for Airbnb experiences in the Americas in 2017 (Chase).

I argue that what I call *virtual tropicality* characterizes US and European technocapitalists' vision for Havana in the post-Obama era. Jungla is a virtual tropical space. It is a digitally rendered speculative tech space that investors envision alongside tropicalized imaginaries of Havana's spaces and people. Jungla is one example of a broader pattern in which US technological associates imagine potential ventures in Global South locations where global capitalism is not yet fully hegemonic. I call these potential ventures tropical futures markets. Tropical ways of seeing, as Krista A. Thomson notes in her work on the Anglophone Caribbean, are "the complex visual systems through which the islands were imaged for tourist consumption and the social and political implications of these representations on actual physical space on the islands and their inhabitants" (5). Historically, European colonists and US imperialists have employed this mode of seeing in their travel accounts of journeys in Latin American and the Caribbean (Thompson; Pratt; Redfield; Casid; Driver and Martins; Bender and Lipman). Tropical imaginaries trope both landscapes and people (Aparicio and Chávez-Silverman 8). When technocapitalists tropicalize Havana's residents, they imagined Habaneros as a resource, or—to put it bluntly in the words of some of my interlocutors—"human capital." I advance this scholarship on tropicality by shifting its focus on tourism to technocapitalism, or the constellation of online platforms, corporately owned digital infrastructure, and hegemonic spatial models that Silicon Valley exports throughout the globe. In this circumstance, technocapitalists participate in the "aesthetic and sensual fetishization" of the city while also imagining it as a different kind of virtual city—one that reflects the aesthetics and values of global technocapitalist start-ups, franchises, and coworking spaces such as WeWork, Soho House, Y Combinator, and Airbnb (Dopico 451). This Havana is integrated into what Fernando Coronil calls "the planetary culture" of neoliberal globalization. It is an imagined city that caters to platform tourists, digital nomads, and local elites (354).

"We Can't Be a Norwegian Rum": Race, Class, and Creative Capital in Jungla's Virtual Tropical Space

On a humid October afternoon in Havana's Vedado neighborhood, while the city endured a crippling oil crisis due to US sanctions, or what colloquially was known as *la coyuntura*, I sat for coffee with the founder of Jungla at a Cuban-German café where expats come to buy bread.[4] Hugh, a former Conservative Party campaign manager in the United Kingdom who enjoys Havana's warehouse parties, mentioned that he and a large coterie of foreigners from several countries came to Cuba "just after Obama, when things were booming." He wistfully recounted that since the end of the boom it "has been hard to find work as a foreigner in Havana" and that he was the only one of his expat friend group who found a way to stay. Hugh has maintained his presence in Vedado through his work as a marketing director and Cuba consultant for a Norwegian brand called Black Tears, a joint venture between Norway's Island Rum Company and the Cuban State's Ministry of Sugar rum conglomerate Tecno Azucár. Tecno Azucár has historically produced smaller-scale rums such as Mulata and Santería that have had less global reach than Cuba Ron and Pernod Ricard's Havana Club. Black Tears was born from a recent opening in Cuban rum markets as Pernod Ricard's exclusive contract with Cuban state rum operations recently expired. While I didn't expect to learn about Cuban rum markets while interviewing Hugh about Jungla, it turns out that rum markets and Hugh's technocapitalist vision for Havana's future are deeply intertwined.

Powered by money from both Silicon Valley and Black Tears rum, Jungla will occupy a recently renovated residential building in the El Fanguito neighborhood near Havana's Fábrica del Arte and the Línea tunnel. Hugh was unable to purchase the building himself, as foreigners cannot own property in Cuba. Instead, Hugh took the risk of not having the property in his name and acquired the space through a Cuban buyer. He then changed the licensing of the space from a residential space to a commercial bar. Although there is no legal category in Cuba for a coworking space under the country's private business (*cuentapropismo*) laws, bars and coffee shops are allowed to legally provide Wi-Fi. Black Tears is backing the project because the bar will serve the company's rum. Consider the phrase "the bar will serve Black Tears." While the company defends its namesake as a translation of Trío Matamoros's famous song "Lágrimas negras," the name evokes the violence of hundreds of years of European colonization and the development of the transatlantic slave trade to advance rum and sugar markets.

Through interviews with Hugh, I learned that Jungla will provide a spatial platform for ongoing social media rum marketing campaigns to persuade European consumers to purchase Black Tears rum. Currently, Black Tears employs two Cuban influencers to create social media content at Havana's hippest warehouse parties like Fiesta Hapé, a rotating DJ night sponsored by a Belgian collective. In this content, influencers snap photos of themselves partying with a planted bottle of Black Tears rum, which is available in Europe and cannot yet be purchased in Cuba. Consistent with the many do-it-yourself methods for bringing global commodities into the country, Hugh himself imports bottles of Black Tears rum in his suitcase from the distillery in Europe and gives them to influencers as props. I asked Hugh about this strategy and its relationship to Jungla:

To be honest, it's not really about the money here. It's about the marketing side of things, because when tourists come here and they see that rum, they'll connect with Cuba when they're back in the supermarket. So, for example, Fiesta Hapé, we get it into that party. People go to that party. They then associate it with Havana. We can't be a Norwegian rum—it messes the brand up.

Hugh then remarked that the name "Black Tears" could not be "Lágrimas negras" because it took him months to be able to pronounce the Spanish version and "an Englishman ordering rum in London" might similarly struggle. Both the company's name and its approach toward Havana's urban spaces prioritize legibility within European rum and tourist markets. By using Fiesta Hapé and

Jungla to sell rum, Black Tears instrumentalizes Havana as a marketing stage. This stage is essential to the company's marketing operations because, as Hugh suggests, consumers would not purchase a Norwegian rum. The imaginary of the Caribbean as a site of pleasure, leisure, and rum drinking is essential to the success of Black Tears marketing on social media platforms. Havana's urban culture becomes an Instagram export when influencers pose with bottles of Black Tears rum. However, Jungla would further entrench this dynamic in physical space by giving the rum company a permanent site to stage the city for foreign consumers via digital platforms. These spectacles that simulate the local are key components for integrating Havana's urban space into global capitalist markets. Rum marketers tropicalize Havana as a site of indulgence and consumption, bottling and exporting Havana's immaterial cachet to global consumers. Jungla will not simply be Havana's first coworking space. Its construction signals the global marketing imaginary of Havana becoming a materialized and tangible part of the city's built environment.

Although Black Tears uses Havana to market rum, Jungla may not be a space where all Habaneros are welcome. Asymmetrical power dynamics of race and gender operate in the production of the imagined-and-real Jungla. The majority of the project's founders, investors, and architects are white or light-skinned men, while the only woman involved in the project is an Instagram influencer. In the virtual realm, the digitally rendered people who inhabit the Jungla blueprints are majority male and exclusively white or light-skinned. Whether by choice of the architecture design firm or the founders and investors who contracted the plans, Afro-descendant people are not imagined as patrons of the space. Consistent with the symbolic violence of a Cuban-European joint rum venture being named "Black Tears," Jungla is imagined as an overwhelmingly white space.

Class and nationality are also key factors that limit membership in this space. In fact, during an interview Jungla's Silicon Valley–based Cuban American investor Rafael worried the space would be available only to "rich people and capitalists, which wouldn't look good in Cuba." This concern is largely because the concept for Jungla's coworking floor is modeled after spaces like Soho House, where only a limited set of paying members can access the internet. When I asked Hugh about who the space is for, he answered:

I have had enough conversations with expats and other people to realize that Jungla has been needed. You've got the park down at the other end. You've got these amazing industrial abandoned warehouses. I know it's for everyone's benefit. . . . the creatives of Havana I find live in Vedado, Playa, Miramar. They don't live in Havana Vieja.

Hugh imagines the space to be "for everyone" even as it appears to be premised upon a number of exclusions. Hugh imagines expats or non-Cubans, such as himself, as his primary target clients. He often lamented having to travel from Vedado to Havana Vieja to work, calling the commute a "nightmare" that Jungla's location in Vedado could resolve. As he put it, he is creating the coworking space for himself. He imagined Havana "creatives" as living in—and creativity flourishing—in the historically wealthier and whiter neighborhoods of Vedado, Playa, and Miramar. Here the word *creatives* stands in for Havana's emerging entrepreneurial class, which skews toward white because of the greater access white Cubans have to remittances and foreign start-up capital (Blue; Eckstein). Although these creatives may have businesses in Havana Vieja's tourist district, they often opt to live in renovated houses in the city's more modern neighborhoods. Hugh's construction of the geography of creativity in Havana obscures the creative endeavors of those who live in the poorer, cramped apartments of Havana Vieja or in neighborhoods where tourists and expatriates do not stay. These areas of the city are home to a greater share of the city's black residents. The creativity of Habaneros who live outside of Vedado, Playa, and Miramar is not legible in Hugh's imaginary of Havana because this creativity does not necessarily advance technocapitalist development in the city or the fortunes of or rum markets in Europe.

Hugh understands the abandoned warehouses of El Fanguito, a postindustrial part of Vedado that once housed many factories and continues to house the boats of local fisherman, as potential sites of investment. Jungla's use of a postindustrial aesthetic in a transformed residential property mirrors the renovated aesthetic of La Fábrica del Arte. The movement toward renovation of factories and the production of postindustrial aesthetics in spaces like Jungla puts Havana on the map of cities that have leveraged postindustrial building stock for gentrification (Shaw; Zukin et al.; Stehlin). However, unlike in other global cities undergoing gentrification, this spatial framework exists within the Cuban state's complex economic formation, which blends socialist central planning and capital regulation with highly regulated openings for local private ventures and foreign joint ventures with multinational capitalist firms. La Fábrica in some ways spatially encapsulates these contradictions as its 2 CUC (US$2) entry fee makes it moderately accessible to locals even as its VIP spaces, food offerings, and adjacent upscale restaurant add an exclusive atmosphere to the space. Within these already existing dynamics that characterize development in the neighborhood, Jungla would represent a move toward further exclusivity as only paying members would be granted access to the internet.

Imagined as a space for affluent white customers, Jungla instrumentalizes tropes of blackness, tropicality, and Cuban creativity to entice Cuban entrepreneurs, tourists, and expats to become members of the space. Both the space's name and the luscious tropical plants that will grow on the walls are part of what Hugh calls a "jungle concept." To enhance this concept, Hugh plans to decorate the generic, postindustrial interior with African wax fabric pillows and furniture coverings. Hugh will source the fabric from a company called Wasasa, run by two Euro-descendant Cuban entrepreneurs who make fanny packs and yoga gear from imported wax fabric. In 2019, Wasasa became a sign of class status and hipsterdom within Havana's local entrepreneurial scenes. The company's original marketing slogan, "Afro-Caribbean design," masked the product sourcing and the composition of the company, as no Afro-Caribbean people work on the design team and the founders import West African fabrics to the Caribbean by way of European markets. In Hugh's tropical vision, Wasasa's West African wax fabrics embody local cultural aesthetics and match his jungle theme even though their circulation is limited to Havana's majority-white and affluent entrepreneurial circles. Jungla will entice these creatives and entrepreneurs to buy memberships, but far more Habaneros will face de facto exclusion. As many Habaneros participate in the #BajenLosPreciosdelInternet (Lower the Internet Prices) Twitter campaign to get ETECSA to make the internet more accessible for all Cubans, spaces like Jungla will limit internet access, likely to a paying few ("'Lower Internet Prices,' Cubans Demand").

Throughout our conversation Hugh's vision of Havana was informed by two different iterations of tropicality. The first was his sense that he could bottle what he viewed as the city's unique essence and market it to European rum consumers. The second vision had less to do with his perception of the city's uniqueness or essence and more to do with his imaginary of Havana as an ahistorical space of capitalist possibility. For example, as he described why he left his job in England as a Tory campaign manager to start a coworking space in Havana, he remarked:

Cuba is like a blank canvas. You can bring ideas that have worked in England and just copy them and have them here, which is quite fun to be honest. That's the great thing about here for the young person. As a foreigner you can do a lot of shit and it's all new. I can't do all these projects that I'm doing now elsewhere. I would never in a million years do them in London because they have been done.

Hugh's understanding of Cuba as a "blank canvas" constructs the country as a vacant land without history that solely holds promise for new ventures that originate elsewhere. His vision echoes numerous European colonists and later US annexationists who have gazed at the Caribbean as a virgin site of abundance that invites new market ventures (Pratt; Driver and Martins; Bender and Lipman). Despite the Cuban state's numerous limitations on foreign capital investment in Havana, and the difficulty of establishing oneself as an expatriate due to immigration laws, Hugh imagines himself as an agent of capital or a contemporary pioneer who can develop projects that would be impossible in the United States or Europe. This vision is partially because the overhead for starting a business like Jungla is far lower in Havana than in London or San Francisco. It is also bolstered by the imaginary of Havana as a space of virtual tropicality—a secluded or uninhabited paradise where capitalist markets haven't been fully developed.

Although Hugh premised Jungla's potential on Cuba's tropical vacancy, he also invoked a notion of tropicality though which Cubans are figured as innately creative. When I asked Hugh about his daily routine, he commented: "It's amazing to work with the Cubans, I find them generally such a talented people, much more talented than me. They lack the platform should we say, to fulfill that." As Aparicio and Chávez-Silverman note when defining the term, to tropicalize is "to trope or imbue a particular space, geography, group, or nation with a set of traits, images, and values" (8). Hugh tropicalizes Cubans by imbuing them with talent and creativity. This characterization breaks from negative and overtly racist depictions that European colonists and US imperialists have used to described locals in tropicalized spaces as "savage" or "lazy," but Hugh's celebration of the ostensible natural creativity of Cubans frames their creativity as a lucrative natural resource (Bender and Lipman 21). In his view, Habanero creativity is useful for marketing Black Tears:

I think one of the things that is pretty overlooked and that we originally pitched to Black Tears, is that there is an amazing urban culture from music, skaters, street artists, which is very authentic. I mean you get that anywhere in Cuba, that whatever it is, it is just authentic because it hasn't been messed around or it basically hasn't been commercialized. So, I think there's a rich asset there in terms of the urban culture, which has yet to be—I mean, it has in the last three or four years certainly increased and commercialized—but I think there's a lot more potential to it.

For Hugh the creative urban culture of Havana is a "rich asset" that might advance the market value of Black Tears rum. He hopes to harness this "asset" for foreign markets, or "use all the creatives of Havana," as he said at another moment, to "give something that is needed" to support the city and "do some good." By "using all the creatives of Havana" or hoping to capitalize on the "asset of urban culture" to sell Black Tears, Hugh traffics in the language of neoliberal globalization, which is exemplified in the language of World Bank portfolios that assess a particular country's potential value to global markets. As Fernando Coronil notes, World Bank portfolios valorize people as capital, their value is solely tied to their ability to produce wealth. As he argues, "the definition of people as capital means that they are to be treated as capital—taken into account insofar as they contribute to the expansion of wealth and marginalized if they do not" (365). Jungla is a spatial platform that embodies the logic of the World Bank portfolio and mirrors the repetition of Silicon Valley's global aesthetic. The logic and repetition of global coworking spaces that are members only and predicated on race, gender, and class hierarchies are themselves akin to algorithms that code the city. The portrayal of Jungla, an exclusive coworking space to expand a Cuban-Norwegian rum brand, as a humanitarian endeavor or as a public social good radically obscures its design. By design, Jungla is a space that is shaped by asymmetrical power dynamics and a political economy that was built to exclude.

Black Tears' embrace of Havana's urban scenes has been part of its re-branding campaign from what Hugh called a "vanilla" rum brand to something that is "dark, alternative, creative, and sensual," something that represents Havana's "cool urban characters." The transformation of Habanero urban culture into a marketable trope that will be concretized in Jungla is already under-way on the Black Tears website. Black Tears marketers, based in Norway, use discourses of tropicalization and racialized affect to sell rum to European consumers:

Cuba is a place where people don't hold back, where people express their true emotions. We want to tell the world the whole truth and nothing but the Cuban truth. Down to the seductive spices, the emotional blend and the passionate craftsmanship. Black Tears is all about emotions and it is inspired by the Cuban song Lágrimas Negras that tells the story of a young woman who sobbed into a vat of rum, filling it with her sorrow. This bottle is packed with emotions to celebrate the Cuba of today (The Island Rum Company).

This marketing that frames Black Tears as emblematic of a "Cuban truth" dis-tills the immaterial character of life in Cuba into a consumer good. By drinking Black Tears, the consumer can imbibe Cuban emotionality, passion, sociality, and the very life force and soul of the country. This description tropicalizes an entire nation of people as seductive, creative, and emotional in contrast to the nameless European clients who consume the rum. By consuming Cuban tears in particular, clients are invited to imbibe and enjoy the racialized vio-lence of the transatlantic rum trade. Both Havana—as the primary locale for Black Tears marketing—and the racialized black Cuban body become bottled essences. This affective and tropicalized imaginary of Cubans has the potential to deeply impact the contours of the city as it physically manifests in entrepre-neurial spaces like Jungla. The marketing of tropical *cubanidad*, coupled with investments in majority-white and relatively wealthy Cuban entrepreneurial spaces, promises to code Havana's built environment and social geography to reflect the aesthetics and values of Silicon Valley.

Tropical Futures Markets and Havana's Nonplaces

In his essay "The Generic City," Rem Koolhaas defines the generic city as a homogenous space "without history" where "the only activity is shopping"

(1260). Koolhaas uses technological infrastructure as a metaphor for this kind of city: "The Generic City is fractal, an endless repetition of the same simple structural module; it is possible to reconstruct it from its smallest entity, a desktop computer, maybe even a diskette" (Koolhaas et al. 1251). Using the desktop computer or the disk as the unit that builds the generic city gestures toward the homogenized design and aesthetic that Silicon Valley exports globally. It is impossible to construct the generic city without a particular type of circulation of global technological infrastructure and a standardized aesthetic.

To categorize Havana as a generic city or a nonplace is nearly unthinkable. Intellectuals who theorize the conditions of the city note how the different architectural styles cohabitate and expose the history of the city, layer by layer (Birkenmaier and Whitfield). However, the post-Obama boom catalyzed new visions of the city as a space that could be potentially legible to digital nomads and global technology associates. On a technological investment tour of Havana's San Isidro neighborhood in 2019, US venture capitalists gestured toward a more generic Havana. Jungla's homogeneous design (beyond the African wax pillows for a "local" touch) is one vision that exemplifies this larger imaginary. Technocapitalists view Havana as a future nonplace, or a potential stop on the map of places where start-up founders can seamlessly travel and expect to find high-speed internet, minimalist design, and a certain kind of cortado.

A Silicon Valley–based investor named Rafael invited me on the venture capital tour. Rafael is a Miami-born Cuban American who has taken a keen interest in developing technology markets in Cuba both for their potential profitability and to reconnect with his uncle in Havana and with the city his parents left in the early 1970s. His involvement in multiple technology ventures in Havana including a software outsourcing venture, a local entrepreneurship initiative to take Cuban tech entrepreneurs to Silicon Valley, and an investment in Jungla align closely with President Obama's vision of changing the Cuban economy through technocapitalism.

Although Rafael eventually became an investor in Jungla's Vedado-based project in 2020, in 2019 he was most interested in founding a separate co-working space in San Isidro. He chose San Isidro because of a recent project in which a Cuban movie star and a Cuban American restaurant owner invited international graffiti artists to paint the neighborhood in an attempt to produce Havana's first arts district akin to Miami's Wynwood district or New York's Soho neighborhood (Clandestina Team, "Actually I'm Creating an Art District in Old Havana"). In May 2019, Rafael invited a group of venture capitalists to San Isidro to entice them to develop and finance a future coworking space in Havana. The venture capitalist firm, which I call Imagine Markets, is a US-based international development firm that funds businesses in war-torn countries or in countries that are generally antagonistic toward US markets. As experts in "conflict zones, fourth world economies, and frontier markets," this firm "goes where others won't." Rafael's hope during this investment tour was that they would be interested in going to Havana's San Isidro neighborhood to help him finance and navigate what he and they consider a hostile investment market. Besides securing investors, Rafael was in the process of repatriating to Cuba so that he could legally buy property in Havana.

While touring San Isidro, Rafael, the Imagine Markets investors, and I gazed up at the three-story residential building that Rafael hoped would become a coworking space. A bit later at lunch, at an upscale graffiti-themed restaurant featuring the artwork of commercially successful graffiti artists from New York, Miami, Brazil, and Germany, Steve and Dave from Imagine Markets reflected on how Rafael's coworking space idea could be the next Soho House Havana. Soho House is an exclusive society started by a London entrepreneur; it offers leisure, tourist, and coworking spaces all over the globe that particularly cater to tech start-up founders, venture capitalists, and Silicon Valley incubators (Tiku). A committee selectively chooses members, who pay thousands of dollars of year to access global Soho Houses if selected (Compton). Steve and Dave held Soho House memberships, which they boasted about at the luncheon. To them, on their second day ever in Cuba, it seemed easy to bridge the distance between Soho House's global network of membership clubs and San Isidro, the southern part of Havana's colonial neighborhood that historically has been an underresourced, majority Afro-descendant neighborhood since emancipation (Oficina del Historiador). To Steve and Dave, San Isidro's history and even the political economy of post-Soviet Cuba were afterthoughts. Although the development of a Soho House Havana seems almost impossible given Cuba's foreign ownership laws and its limits on private property (Cubans legally can have one city house and one country house), these visitors found a way to incorporate San Isidro into their imaginative global geography of interconnected elite technology spaces.

As Imagine Market's investors talked about the possibility of a Soho House Havana, they embodied Fernando Coronil's articulation of the ethos of millennial capitalism. Coronil communicates this ethos with a quote from a 1990s Bankers Trust executive named Charles Sanford: "Think of the world as a landscape of opportunity—everything from distressed Japanese real estate to Russian oil futures–marketed and packed by giant banks like BankAmerica or by fund companies like Fidelity Investments and the Vanguard Group" (367). Coronil notes that "Cuban tourism" or "Gabon aroma futures" could easily replace "Russian oil futures" or "distressed Japanese real estate." In this global market imaginary, the entire world becomes a vacant, tropicalized space of opportunity where distinct places are interchangeable and can be measured only by their ability to produce profit. A place's specificity is thus important only if that specificity enables it to produce a niche market. Since the Obama boom, the imagined categories of "Cuban tech futures" and "Havana tech space real estate markets" have started to fill this rotating market space in the minds of technocapitalists. Steve and Dave, who told me that they invest in anything from Yemeni brick futures to start-ups in Gaza to Ghanaian agriculture, are adding Havana to their list of interchangeable markets. Importantly, this vision did not completely align with Rafael's vision of Havana, as he has family in the city and has attachments to it that exceed the desire to turn a profit. At another luncheon during the short trip, conflict broke out between Rafael and the investors after Dave declared, "We couldn't care less about Havana, we just care about the feasibility of your investment project." Although Steve, Dave, and Rafael all come from US corporate technology and investment backgrounds, Rafael's Cuban American identity and his desire to reconnect with Havana set him apart from the others.

Months after I accompanied Rafael and the investors on the May 2019 Imagine Markets tour, Rafael returned to Havana for a short October visit. In a café in Vedado's cinema district, I asked him why he wanted to create a coworking space in Havana. He explained that the idea grew out of an earlier tourist business that his good Cuban American friend Ana had operated during the Obama boom. As huge numbers of US visitors started to arrive in Cuba, Rafael and Ana dreamed of a real estate collaboration:

We were going to buy a building and turn it into a beautiful Airbnb and put it in *Condé Nast Traveler* and all that stuff. The deal was to use her status, you know, use my status to buy a lot of these buildings that are chopped up into three or more titles. In order to do so, like when you take over a big property, you sometimes need three people with the ability to buy and the cash.

As Rafael explains, Cuban Americans who have repatriated are the only foreigners who can legally purchase a property in Cuba because they are legally seen as Cuban citizens and residents. Since the Cuban revolutionary state divided up many larger properties into smaller properties after 1959, it is strategic for prospective large building buyers to team up so they can combine multiple building titles and own the whole property. A single buyer, for example, might end up with only a section of a desired building rather than the whole building. In Rafael's case, his first entrance into trying to buy property in Havana was embedded in emerging US corporate tourist and tech markets in the city. Through integrating a newly purchased building into Airbnb's digital tourist platform and circulating images of it to *Condé Nast Traveler*'s readership, Rafael could transform a residential home into a rental home and market images of it to prospective US clients. Just as photography markets scripted Havana for the consumption of international tourists in the 1990s, Airbnb's platform and the "interactive lifestyle magazine it produces" has the power to script Havana to make it legible to global tourist markets (Dopico; Chayka 6). As Kyle Chayka notes, Airbnb, in its quest to replace the hotel industry, has created a platform that is capable of producing a consistent aesthetic across space and time that globally replicates "the industrial look and the midcentury" or "the neutered Scandinavianism of HGTV." With more than six million listings worldwide, Airbnb lists far more rooms than any global hotel conglomerate. This shift provokes a reevaluation of the hotel as the central symbol of tourism and capitalist joint ventures in Havana. While the hotel is the symbol of post-Soviet Havana in the 1990s, the Airbnb rental, experience, and aesthetic embody a post-Obama Havana.

After the Trump election, the dwindling number of US visitors to Havana made Rafael's *Condé Nast Traveler* venture a bust. Although global visitors continued to book Airbnbs in Havana, Rafael and Ana's main client base were from the United States. However, the election did not end Rafael's dream of owning a building in Havana. In 2017, as a cloud platform marketing specialist who brokered deals between Salesforce and Latin American companies, Rafael got Salesforce to match funds for a Global Aware humanitarian trip to Havana. He used the funds to host a Best Apps of Cuba soiree for CubaEmprende, an entrepreneurship project in Havana sponsored by the Catholic Church. From there he got involved in bringing one of the competition winners to Silicon Valley, hosting a Cuba Pavilion at Tech Crunch, and hosting multiple fundraisers for Havana-based technology projects with high-profile finance and tech executives in New York and San Francisco.

When I met Rafael in 2019, he had decided that two different coworking spaces would be his next Havana-based projects. One space he would own, and the other he would invest in. As we talked about Jungla, the other proposed coworking space in Vedado that he planned to invest in, he expressed reservations about Jungla's future exclusivity:

It's tricky because Jungla is like Soho House and the first thing that comes to my mind when I think of Soho House is exclusive. That's not a word that people like to throw around here. Exclusive is not good. Right? It reeks of elitism. I think it's a great problem. I think they need to sort of push it in the right way where nobody is excluded. With your membership, you get a little better internet access. Even then, you probably still have a Nauta (Cuba's state-run Wi-Fi access account) and you log into your own account. I told him to be careful because you don't want to talk about exclusive or capitalist, rich people coming here. So, I'm not going to get involved in it from a founder perspective. I think it'd be better just to take any small bit of equity in it, just to say: "Oh yeah, I helped you build up a brand. I worked on this project."[5]

In this quote, five months after Steve and Dave dreamed of a Soho House Havana, Rafael worries about the optics of a membership-only coworking space to Cuba's communist government. This type of members-only exclusivity is a social dynamic that has long been part of Havana's hotels and upscale restaurant spaces but has not extended to a private internet club. Although internet access is expensive to many Habaneros—the equivalent of US$1 an hour in a country where the state salary is $32–$44 a month—those who access it do so in the city's many public Wi-Fi hotspots in parks and on the Malecón (Associated Press; Dye et al.). Even Google, which partnered with the Cuban artist KCHO to bring Habaneros Wi-Fi at his studio in 2016, made the connection free and open to the public while the project was up and running (Voon). In other words, Jungla, with its Havana Soho House model, would be the first to make a members-only internet space in the city.

Beyond issues of social exclusion, Rafael's equity in Jungla exists in an informal system of trust. Under current Cuban private business laws, business owners can only have a stake in their own venture (Sulkowski). Thus, Rafael's current investment in Jungla is similar to Hugh's use of a Cuban buyer to hold the property title. Both the equity deal and the real estate deal are risks Hugh and Rafael are willing to take without legal protection through the Cuban state. In contemporary Havana, many stories circulate about informal joint business ventures with foreigners that Cuban citizens eventually take over. For example, the Cuban owner of Havana Vieja's trendy restaurant El Chanchullero allegedly pushed out his joint partner and foreign investor after the place got off the ground. Why are Hugh and Rafael willing to assume risk involved in informal joint entrepreneurial ventures in Havana? They do so because they believe the Cuban model will eventually mirror a US finance structure. Otherwise their ventures would not be profitable. Hugh and Rafael gamble on Havana's future itself as future market returns are possible only if the current structure changes.

Although Rafael knew he was gambling on Cuban economic futures, he also easily integrated US technological start-up investment models into his vision for his own coworking space in San Isidro:

I want to do something more around building capacity of start-ups. It's more of a Y Combinator/WeWork kind of a thing. In the long term, it would be something where I get a percentage of your company and give you housing space. I get 2 percent of the equity. That's a very common model: you pay the really cheap rent plus equity and I build a prestigious brand. People are happy to do it. Anybody who gets into Y Combinator, they're like: Yeah! We became a Y company.

In this quote, the corporate model of Y Combinator, a company that funds young start-ups, and the global spatial model of WeWork, a worldwide coworking franchise, are integrated into Rafael's vision for Havana. Rafael has met with Cuban Ministry of Economy and Planning (MEP) officials and talked over part of his plan, but he doesn't think an above-board investment will be fully possible without the advent of the C Corporation in Cuba. His current idea is to wait and see if the C Corporation comes through as part of the UN group CEPAL's Plan 2030 for the economy (Observatorio Regional de Planificación para el Desarrollo).[6] Here both the spatial and the temporal frame of Rafael's vision is imbued with a technocapitalist optimism for market conditions that do not exist in Havana. What are Imagine Markets investors doing in Havana if it will take ten years for the corporate entity they operate through to even be part of the picture? Though the visions of Imagine Markets and Rafael seem to be visions of "irreality," their projections of Soho House Havana, WeWork Havana, and Y Combinator Havana are spatial imaginaries for remaking the city. These ideas, when combined with formal joint ventures with the Cuban state or informal joint ventures with Cuban citizens who can own property, do have the power to shape the contours of the city. Airbnb is one example of a Silicon Valley platform that already has affected Havana's housing markets and has brought platform tourists into new parts of the city. Other companies like WeWork do not operate in Havana and remain part of the irreality of those who imagine Havana as a technocapitalist city. This vision of Havana's future can clash with its present. For example, while working at Havana's Instituto Juan Marinello, a state-run cultural institution, I frequently spent time in a shared office that was themed around the work of Vladimir Lenin and Antonio Gramsci. When I told Steve, one of the Imagine Markets investors about working in a collective office space, he replied "Oh, so you've rented a WeWork in Havana." This encounter reveals how US technocapitalist imaginaries ahistorically flatten and rationalize local space to fit a global ideal. Not every technocapitalist franchise can operate in contemporary Havana, but the imaginations of technocapitalist expats and visitors are actively shaping the material realities of the city. The possibility of a US corporate technocapitalist Havana became thinkable only after the Obama boom.

Conclusion

The complex interplay of immaterial and material is key to understanding how a Silicon Valley investor, a European expat, a group of Cuban and Cuban American architects, and a joint Cuban Ministry of Sugar and Norwegian rum venture came to contribute to an imagined coworking space in progress in El Fanguito. I call the imaginary that produced this space virtual tropicality, as it reflects both the desires and homogenizing spatial codes of Silicon Valley and the technocapitalist projections of tropicality onto Havana's built environment and its people as a marketing strategy. In October 2019, Hugh and I discussed the role of the immaterial in the relationship between Habaneros and global markets:

H: So, I think the tech community and any part of the creative community has a lot of growth potential. It is just because of the education and the creativity that is based here and the fact that they have nonphysical stuff.

M: What do you mean by nonphysical?

H: As selling a project, exporting a product to a certain code or selling it design or something and the fact that it's not covered by the embargo. I don't know the correct and technical term, but non-physical. Well, IXPs [internet exchange points], which are nonphysical, are not covered by the embargo. So, an architect can still do business with an American architectural firm.

In this exchange, I read the nonphysical as both technocapitalist perceptions of the affects and creativity of Habaneros and also the material conditions of Habanero market exchanges. It is important to note that here "Cuban education" and the long history of the Cuban Revolutionary government's investment in the arts becomes a commodifiable asset. Here a free socialist arts education becomes something that can easily be plugged into a capitalist World Bank portfolio framework. Although this has been the case since the opening of Cuban markets in the 1990s, art, design, and immaterial exchanges have taken on new forms since the Obama boom. Architectural designs and digital creative projects can move more freely between Cuba and global capitalist markets becausee both the Cuban government and the US embargo have more permissive legal categories around the movement of art. Additionally, the Helms-Burton Act of 1996 did not block cloud services, code, or internet exchange points simply because these things were beginning to emerge in the 1990s. Thus, the sectors that have become highly profitable under late capitalism and platform capitalism, namely data, design, services, and affective and immaterial labor, are key in bridging Havana to global technology markets. These markets, which themselves have been developed under the umbrella term *art and technology*, are capable of producing homogeneous, gentrified space worldwide. Havana has played some role in the minds of technocapitalists since the Special Period, but the Obama boom and the arrival of Airbnb executives, Google executives, and others catalyzed and intensified the technocapitalist imaginaries of Havana.

When I asked Hugh about the future of his venture under another potential Trump administration, he answered: "I think we should give Trump two hotels in Havana and then we could go about our business." Hugh's answer suggests that some technocapitalists have a pliant and flexible political standpoint in which issues like the embargo are problems only because they prevent capital flow, not because they harm Cuban people. In fact, the control the US embargo wields over Cuban economic futures allows it to both block many other potential alliances and economic configurations while simultaneously presenting US technocapitalism as the only solution to Cuba's problems upon opening. The strategy of blockade starves and limits alternatives while the strategy of corporate technological development begins to look like Cuba's only option. Havana as an urban space is subject to these rotating strategies as US administrations fluctuate. Fernando Coronil asks: "If colonialism is the dark side of European capitalism, what is the dark side of globalization?" (358). What might be the dark side of US technocapitalism in Havana? The dark side of US technocapitalist imaginaries in Havana might be their ability to foreclose on other urban, social, and spatial possibilities. Havana is a city with many layers and public spaces like the Malecón open to the city's residents. The gentrifying and homogenizing forces of US technological capital promise elite rooftops, members-only internet clubs, and spaces designed for expats, tourists, and others who can pay. Their spatial logics do not engender the democracy of the Malecón or move toward equal access to technology that campaigns such as #BajenLosPreciosdelInternet embody. Virtual tropical visions of Havana see advance technological infrastructures in the city as tied to the extraction of data or profit. Virtual tropicality forecloses on the many Havanas that have been and could be by putting forth a singular and homogenizing imaginary of urban space in a city where multiple visions are possible.

NOTES

1. Many thanks to María A. Gutiérrez Bascón, Roberto Zurbano, Jimena Codina, Brandon Mancilla, the RITM Dissertation Writing Group at Yale, Jacinda Tran, Ana Ramos-Zayas, Rebecca Potts, and Jackson Smith for your engagement with this project.

2. The names of all interlocutors have been changed in this essay.

3. Currently the only such cables are the US government's Guantanamo Bay cable and the Alba-1 military cable from Venezuela.

4. *La coyuntura* (meaning "conjuncture" or "situation" in English) was a moment of crisis and oil shortage in Cuba in September 2019 after US sanctions blocked incoming oil tankers from regular deliveries.

5. A "nauta" refers to the ETECSA Wi-Fi cards that users can access at parks and other hot spots.

6. CEPAL refers to the Economic Commission for Latin America and the Caribbean.

BIBLIOGRAPHY

Aparicio, Frances R., and Susana Chávez-Silverman, eds. *Tropicalizations: Transcultural Representations of Latinidad*. Dartmouth College P, 1997.

Associated Press. "Cuba Announces Increase in Wages as Part of Economic Reform." *NBC News*. https://www.nbcnews.com/news/latino/cuba-announces-increase-wages-part-economic-reform-n1024451.

Bender, Daniel E., and Jana K. Lipman, eds. *Making the Empire Work: Labor and United States Imperialism*. NYU P, 2015.

160 : Maile Speakman

Birkenmaier, Anke, and Esther Whitfield, eds. *Havana beyond the Ruins: Cultural Mappings after 1989*. Duke UP, 2011.

Blue, Sarah A. "The Erosion of Racial Equality in the Context of Cuba's Dual Economy." *Latin American Politics and Society*, vol. 49, no. 3, 2007, pp. 35–68. JSTOR.

Bobes, Velia Cecilia. "Visits to a Non-Place: Havana and Its Representation(s)." *Havana beyond the Ruins: Cultural Mappings after 1989*, edited by Anke Birkenmaier and Esther Whitfield, Duke UP, pp. 15–30.

Casid, Jill H. *Sowing Empire: Landscape and Colonization*. U of Minnesota P, 2004.

Chase, Simons. *How Airbnb's Experience in Cuba Could Impact Mass Tourism Everywhere*. http://cubajournal.co/how-airbnbs-experience-in-cuba-could-impact-mass-tourism-everywhere/.

Chayka, Kyle. "Welcome to Airspace: How Silicon Valley Helps Spread the Same Sterile Aesthetic across the World." *The Verge*, 3 Aug. 2016. https://www.theverge.com/2016/8/3/12325104/airbnb-aesthetic-global-minimalism-startup-gentrification.

Clandestina Team. "Actually I'm Creating an Art District in Old Havana." *Clandestina | Cuba's First Online Clothing Store*. https://clandestina.co/blogs/clandestina-is-something-else/actually-i-m-creating-an-art-district-in-old-havana.

———. "Press Release: Independent Cuban Fashion Label Clandestina and Google Together Launch a New Clothing Collection Inspired by Cuba Coming Online." *Clandestina | Cuba's First Online Clothing Store*. https://clandestina.co/blogs/clandestina-is-something-else/press-release-independent-cuban-fashion-label-clandestina-and-google-together-launch-a-new-clothing-collection-inspired-by-cuba-coming-online.

Compton, Nick. "Member's Market: Soho Home Lets You Take Soho House Furniture Away with You." *Wallpaper**, 12 Sept. 2016. https://www.wallpaper.com/lifestyle/soho-house-launches-soho-home-ecommerce-site.

Coronil, Fernando. "Towards a Critique of Globalcentrism: Speculations on Capitalism's Nature." *Public Culture*, vol. 12, no. 2, May 2000, pp. 351–74. https://doi.org/10.1215/08992363-12-2-351.

"Cuba Sanctions." US Department of State. https://www.state.gov/cuba-sanctions/.

Dopico, Ana Maria. "Picturing Havana: History, Vision, and the Scramble for Cuba." *Nepantla: Views from South*, vol. 3, no. 3, 2002, pp. 451–93.

Driver, Felix, and Luciana Martins, eds. *Tropical Visions in an Age of Empire*. U of Chicago P, 2005.

Dye, Michaelanne, et al. "Locating the Internet in the Parks of Havana." *Proceedings of the 2017 CHI Conference on Human Factors in Computing Systems*, Association for Computing Machinery, 2017, pp. 3867–78. https://doi.org/10.1145/3025453.3025728.

Eckstein, Susan. "Immigration, Remittances, and Transnational Social Capital Formation: A Cuban Case Study." *Ethnic and Racial Studies*, vol. 33, no. 9, 2010, pp. 1648–67. https://doi.org/10.1080/01419871003725410.

Island Rum Company. *Blacktears—Black Tears Original Cuban Spiced*. 2019, https://www.blacktears.com.

Koolhaas, Rem, et al. *S M L XL*. 2nd ed., Monacelli Press, 1997.

"'Lower Internet Prices,' Cubans Demand on Twitter." *OnCubaNews English*, 3 June 2019. https://oncubanews.com/en/cuba/lower-internet-prices-cubans-demand-on-twitter/.

Marsh, Sarah. "Google, Cuba Agree to Work toward Improving Island's Connectivity." *Reuters*, 28 Mar. 2019. https://www.reuters.com/article/us-cuba-usa-google-idUSKCN1R91ZP.

Observatorio Regional de Planificación para el Desarrollo. *Plan nacional de desarrollo económico y social 2030 de Cuba*. https://observatorioplanificacion.cepal.org/es/planes/plan-nacional-de-desarrollo-economico-y-social-2030-de-cuba.

Oficina del Historiador. *Censo de poblacion y viviendas Centro Histórico La Habana Vieja y*

Malecón tradicional. 2001, http://www.planmaestro.ohc.cu/recursos/papel/investigaciones/resultado-sanisidro.pdf.

Pratt, Mary Louise. *Imperial Eyes: Travel Writing and Transculturation*. 2nd ed., Routledge, 2007.

Quiroga, José. "Bitter Daiquiris: A Crystal Chronicle." *Havana beyond the Ruins: Cultural Mappings after 1989*, Duke UP, pp. 270–85.

Redfield, Peter. *Space in the Tropics: From Convicts to Rockets in French Guiana*. U of California P, 2000.

Robbins, Carla Anne. "What Obama's Historic Visit to Cuba Really Means for US Businesses." *Fortune*, 23 Mar. 2016, https://fortune.com/2016/03/23/cuba-obama-castro/.

Shaw, Wendy S. "Sydney's SoHo Syndrome? Loft Living in the Urbane City." *Cultural Geographies: London*, vol. 13, no. 2, 2006, pp. 182–206. http://dx.doi.org/10.1191/1474474006eu356oa.

"Statement by the President on Cuba Policy Changes." 17 Dec. 2014, https://obamawhitehouse.archives.gov/the-press-office/2014/12/17/statement-president-cuba-policy-changes.

Stehlin, John. "The Post-Industrial 'Shop Floor': Emerging Forms of Gentrification in San Francisco's Innovation Economy." *Antipode*, vol. 48, no. 2, 2016, pp. 474–93. https://doi.org/10.1111/anti.12199.

Sulkowski, Adam J. "Rodolfo's Casa Caribe in Cuba: Business, Law, and Ethics of Investing in a Start-up in Havana." *Journal of Legal Studies Education*, vol. 34, 2017, pp. 127–162. https://doi.org/10.1111/jlse.12059.

Thompson, Krista A. *An Eye for the Tropics: Tourism, Photography, and Framing the Caribbean Picturesque*. Duke UP, 2007.

Tiku, Nitasha. "For Soho House, The Tech Set Is the New Clubbable Class." *Observer*, 4 Oct. 2011, https://observer.com/2011/10/for-soho-house-the-tech-set-is-the-new-clubbale-class/.

Voon, Claire. "Artist Invites Havana Locals into His Studio for Free High-Speed Wifi." *Hyperallergic*, 25 Mar. 2016, hyperallergic.com, https://hyperallergic.com/286203/artist-invites-havana-locals-into-his-studio-for-free-high-speed-wifi/.

Williams, Martyn. "Google Becomes First Foreign Internet Company to Launch Service in Cuba." *CIO*, 26 Apr. 2017, https://www.cio.com/article/3192670/google-becomes-first-foreign-internet-company-to-launch-service-in-cuba.html.

Zukin, Sharon, et al. "New Retail Capital and Neighborhood Change: Boutiques and Gentrification in New York City." *City & Community*, vol. 8, no. 1, 2009, pp. 47–64. https://doi.org/10.1111/j.1540-6040.2009.01269.x.

ROBERTO ZURBANO TORRES

La plantación invisible: Un tour por La Habana negra

RESUMEN

La estrategia crítica decolonial que propongo en este ensayo requiere de un esfuerzo epistemológico que aúna reflexión, debate y prácticas culturales a través de las cuales desmontar la razón colonial y sus herramientas de sometimiento. La colonialidad se impone, sutilmente, en buena cantidad de ofertas para el turismo en La Habana de hoy, sin tener en cuenta cómo estas reproducen códigos excluyentes y discriminatorios. El texto es una invitación a un recorrido antiturístico por una Habana negra invisible, revelando nuevas formas de colonialidad que el turismo, la creciente gentrificación y la llegada de nuevos capitales han impuesto sobre el tejido urbano y social de La Habana del siglo XXI. Al tiempo que miramos al momento presente y sus nuevas formas de colonialidad, nuestro caminar por La Habana Vieja se encarga también de develar las huellas de un pasado afrodescendiente convenientemente silenciado. En un itinerario que parte de la Plaza de la Catedral para terminar en la Loma del Ángel, dejamos que hable el silencio colonial y se visualice aquello que no está presente, pero que se intuye.

ABSTRACT

The critical decolonial perspective that I put forth in this essay requires an epistemological effort that combines reflection, debate, and a cultural praxis through which colonial reason and its tools of subjugation might be dismantled. Coloniality is imposed, in subtle ways, through many of the tourism products and services in today's Havana, without taking into consideration the ways these services reproduce excluding and discriminatory codes. This text is an invitation to an antitouristic tour throughout an invisible Black Havana. It reveals new forms of coloniality that tourism, growing gentrification processes and the new influx of foreign capital have imposed over twenty-first-century Havana's urban and social fabric. While we look at the present moment and its new forms of coloniality, our walking throughout Old Havana is also tasked with revealing the traces of an Afro-descendant past that has been conveniently silenced. In an itinerary that departs from the Plaza de la Catedral to finally arrive at the Loma del Ángel, we let the colonial silence speak for itself, and we also allow for that which is not present but can be intuitively perceived to be visualized.

> La mayor característica del poder puede ser su invisibilidad;
> el mayor reto, mostrar sus raíces.
>
> —Michel-Rolph Trouillot

162

Una mirada decolonial para entender La Habana del siglo XXI

Nuevas formas del activismo social superan la dicotomía activista-académico y promueven la intervención de nuevos conceptos y métodos en pos del mejoramiento social desde las contribuciones que cada uno aporta. Es difícil hablar hoy en Cuba de un activismo naif, desentendido de conceptos y análisis críticos y autocríticos en sus prácticas más diversas. Tampoco la academia es la misma. Al menos una parte de ella es cada vez más consciente de cómo las prácticas sociales y culturales, junto a las movilizaciones de ideas y acciones comunitarias, construyen nuevos significados y apropiaciones de líneas teóricas propuestas por académicos preocupados en participar, acompañar y esclarecer el modo en que se introducen o rechazan determinadas teorías en el trabajo social. La colaboración, el intercambio y los proyectos conjuntos comienzan a superar los viejos desencuentros y, así, cada parte ha ganado en claridad, responsabilidad y compromiso social.

A mi juicio, uno de los caminos que aporta mayor interacción entre activistas y académicos es el enfoque decolonial, que piensa el campo social desde varias subjetividades actuantes y ofrece una perspectiva que destierra esa mirada con que la historiografía dominante subalternizó otros grupos sociales, reduciendo su protagonismo histórico a papeles de segunda y tercera clases: "Si en la visión dominante el ente colonizado aparece como problema, el giro decolonial plantea a las personas colonizadas como agentes que plantean problemas" (Maldonado-Torres 562). Es un proceso que exige replanteos historiográficos y políticos a viejos discursos establecidos por el dominio de un grupo social que ha sometido a otros con sus mejores herramientas (por ejemplo, ciencia, ley, religión). El giro decolonial propone un vuelco epistemológico y desacralizador, donde los subalternos descubren las ataduras que les convierten en instrumentos y víctimas de una dominación social tan compleja que apenas pueden rechazar o denunciar.

El activismo que surgió en Cuba a finales del siglo pasado procuró un diálogo e intercambio con instituciones políticas y gubernamentales. De la misma manera, generó demandas y propuestas que no fueron escuchadas ni respetadas, sino más bien temidas, pues las instancias gubernamentales consideraron que las organizaciones antidiscriminatorias, además de exagerar sus denuncias, podrían fragmentar la unidad nacional y ponerse al servicio de los "enemigos de la Revolución". Varias organizaciones de este tipo comenzaron a aparecer en la isla durante los años noventa del siglo pasado, mayoritariamente en La Habana: proyectos, agrupaciones y otras formas asociativas cultural, ideológica y políticamente variadas con respecto al género, las profesiones, las generaciones, las religiosidades, etc., y esencialmente preocupadas por la participación y los derechos de la población negra en la Cuba de hoy.

Aunque tales organizaciones expresan un malestar social muy específico, presidido por las nuevas formas de discriminación racial, su labor e impacto social tiene limitaciones en el trabajo comunitario, en sus niveles de intercambio y en su estatus legal; todo ello en medio de un contexto verticalista, que ofrece poco margen a la participación popular. Aun con el apoyo de varios sitios, blogs y boletines digitales, el activismo antirracista enfrenta varios retos referidos a la comunicación y articulación entre las mismas organizaciones, así como en relación a los diversos modos de definir e interpretar la lucha antirracista dentro de la isla. Aun así, dicho activismo no abandona su labor principal de crítica, reivindicación y mejoramiento de un grupo social discriminado. Tampoco el entorno socioeconómico y político de la ciudad proporciona a dichas organizaciones espacios propios donde realizar sus acciones, a diferencia de otras asociaciones cubanas de origen europeo, asiático, hebreo y árabe que poseen sedes propias y otros inmuebles identificados con sus orígenes étnicos e intereses identitarios. El antecedente más cercano a los espacios negros de la ciudad fueron las desaparecidas Sociedades negras en Cuba, que existieron entre 1878 y 1960 (Montejo 8). Curiosamente, estas fueron oficialmente disueltas, mientras las otras sociedades sobrevivieron en un limbo que, décadas después, les permitió recuperarse legal y económicamente.

La estrategia crítica decolonial que proponemos desde algunos de estos espacios de reflexión y activismo requiere de un esfuerzo epistemológico que aúna reflexión, debate y prácticas culturales a través de las cuales desmontar la razón colonial y las herramientas con que se sometió a tantos sujetos y grupos sociales a la inferiorización, la pobreza y la invisibilidad. Un nuevo activismo antirracista surge en el siglo XXI con presupuestos no solo renovados, sino también diversificados, ante viejas y nuevas formas del racismo. El discurso antirracista reciente se expresa a través de la crítica feminista, de micropolíticas y acciones comerciales, publicistas, comunitarias y pedagógicas que refuerzan el ambiente antidiscriminatorio en una ciudad cuyo espectro económico se polariza entre barrios gentrificados, zonas turísticas y espacios de precariedad material, ubicados no solo en la periferia, sino también en barrios de La Habana Vieja, El Vedado o el desafortunado Centro Habana, donde los esfuerzos de restauración brillan por su abandono. Este texto pretende dar cuenta de uno de esos nuevos modos antirracistas y de lucha contra lo que se ha denominado la *colonialidad del poder* y sus expresiones urbanas en la capital cubana.[2]

En este texto, atravieso La Habana mirándola de cerca, críticamente y por encima de los absurdos límites que alguna vez separaron a cubanos y extranjeros en el disfrute de sus espacios turísticos. A lo largo de estas páginas, invito a un recorrido antiturístico por la capital habanera buscando las huellas de las contribuciones que los negros aportaron a la historia de la ciudad, huellas difíciles de develar si seguimos el rastro que ha dejado la historiografía, el periodismo y las sucesivas restauraciones urbanísticas y arquitectónicas producidas en los siglos XX y XXI. Les pido que observen, pregunten y no hagan *selfies* ni grabaciones, sino que aprendan a mirar lo que es invisible a los ojos, pero no al corazón, ni a la Historia. En el camino iremos incorporando modos de identificar, describir y evaluar cómo la colonialidad, el turismo y el capital extranjero afectan sujetos, paisajes e inmuebles del entorno urbano. Practicaremos algunos ejercicios críticos (visualización, comparación, cuestionamiento y valoración), en colectivo. Para ello, el enfoque decolonial será la brújula que nos guíe por el entramado habanero, colonial y colonizado, junto a una mirada crítica y autocrítica que entrené en el activismo antirracista de finales del siglo pasado. Nos ayudaremos también de mis tres preguntas básicas que suelen corregirme cualquier desviación en el camino: *¿de quiénes estamos hablando?*, *¿dónde están ellos?*, y *¿por qué no están?*

Todo comenzó en el año 2007 como parte del programa académico impartido en Casa de las Américas para estudiantes de universidades estadounidenses (CASA, o Consortium for Advanced Studies). Los profesores de aquel curso tuvimos que refundar el programa en términos de una propuesta más competitiva en el naciente mercado del conocimiento que ya compartíamos con otras instituciones. Propusimos ofrecer una experiencia pedagógica actualizada, lo más cercana posible a las investigaciones y problemáticas que estaban teniendo lugar en la realidad cubana: las nuevas aperturas económicas, el sector privado, el internet, el feminismo y el debate racial fueron incorporados, entre otros temas. Valiosos intelectuales, profesores y artistas, de dentro y fuera de la Casa de las Américas, integraron un claustro muy diverso. Aquella propuesta resultó novedosa y competitiva frente a otros espacios académicos, culturales y socio-religiosos que, en ese momento, también ofrecían temas y enfoques que no eran usuales en las universidades cubanas.

Bajo el título de "Desigualdades en Cuba" fundamos una serie de asignaturas donde me correspondió introducir una variante de estudios de raza, no al estilo estadunidense, ni inglés o brasileño, sino abordando, a partir de teorías diversas, acontecimientos, figuras y tendencias claves en la historia de la población negra cubana. Mi experiencia más cercana al tema era el Curso sobre Historia Social del negro en Cuba que Tomás Fernández Robaina fundara a finales del siglo pasado en la Biblioteca Nacional. Pero mi enfoque era menos histórico y más informado sobre el debate racial cubano de los últimos lustros en Cuba, tratando de insertarlo entre los debates latinoamericanos e intentando subrayar el peso de este debate entre los movimientos sociales de la región. Mis clases no eran neutrales, ni pretendían serlo, y a algunos colegas les resultaba molesto cuando aportaba de mis propias vivencias como activista. Al final, los estudiantes aprendían sobre otros modelos raciales y asumían las diferencias y similitudes entre la situación racial de Cuba y de Estados Unidos.

Desde entonces y hasta el último semestre del 2019 en que fui separado de este curso, mi clase comenzaba con un recorrido por La Habana Vieja, tratando de entender la ciudad como un espacio marcado por una identidad plural que, ante el turismo, era ocultada, quedando solo el rostro hispano. Era mi modo de introducir a los estudiantes en el siglo XIX cubano a través de las calles de La Habana Vieja. En principio, el recorrido estaba dirigido a los estudiantes del consorcio de universidades estadounidenses. Luego se extendió a otros estudiantes y amigos, hasta que más tarde se convirtió en la clase que formalmente inicia el curso que El Club del Espendrú, organización antirracista fundada en 2012 y de la que formo parte, realiza anualmente para iniciar a jóvenes cubanos de diversa formación en el conocimiento de las raíces de su historia negra, ausente en el currículum de la enseñanza cubana. Una agencia de viajes quiso contratarme, pero algunos guías de la zona le dieron las peores recomendaciones sobre mi tour: "es un anti-guía", dijo alguien, y quizás tenga razón.

Turismo, raza y colonialidad en La Habana Vieja

Hacia 2010 comenzó a crecer el turismo negro en La Habana: llegaban visitantes de Jamaica, Trinidad y Tobago, afroamericanos desde Estados Unidos, incluso turistas de países africanos. Sus preguntas sobre la cuestión racial en la ciudad eran insuficientemente respondidas por los guías de turismo. Con frecuencia, las preguntas más explícitas en torno a la esclavitud, el racismo, la representación de negros en el gobierno, los medios y el mundo de los negocios les resultaban incómodas o desconcertantes a los guías oficiales. De hecho, varios de estos profesionales del turismo me confesaron no saber mucho sobre la historia negra de Cuba. A un grupo de ellos los llevé en una ocasión a Triunvirato, el ingenio matancero donde se produjo, en noviembre de 1843, la primera sublevación esclava liderada por mujeres y, sorprendentemente, los guías no conocían el lugar y dudaban del interés que un ingenio como Triunvirato pudiera tener para el turismo internacional. Afortunadamente, muchos de estos espacios entre La Habana y Matanzas, entre los que se encuentra el ingenio Triunvirato, han sido incluidos por la UNESCO en el proyecto "La Ruta del Esclavo" y convertidos en espacio de reconocimiento público. Se trata de una red de ingenios, cafetales, sitios y monumentos que recuperan una memoria insuficientemente promovida por las agencias de turismo. Pocos de estos guías de turismo reconocían que la historia que contaban había sido mutilada, en aras de ofrecer una versión más amable a los visitantes, invisibilizando la contribución de los negros a la cultura y sociedad cubanas.

En las siguientes páginas, llevaré al lector por algunas de las calles del llamado casco histórico de La Habana, dejando que hable el silencio colonial y se visualice aquello que no está presente, pero se intuye. Les invito a colocarnos frente a la catedral habanera y escuchar los sonidos, más bien el murmullo de la plaza, y observar detrás de los colores que la inundan cada mañana, especialmente durante la temporada alta de turismo. Lo que vemos y escuchamos será insuficiente para nuestro ejercicio de reivindicación afro. Se requiere aprender a mirar los vacíos de la historia desde una conciencia crítica que vaya interrogando y esclareciendo cómo y dónde se han invisibilizado sujetos, temas y problemáticas del mundo colonial cubano, sobre los que se ha guardado durante siglos un increíble silencio. Solo una mirada atenta hará visible aquello que ha sido expulsado durante la colonia y la República de las narrativas historiográficas que definen la nación, incluso durante el periodo revolucionario, donde persisten dichos ocultamientos y exclusiones, junto a las recientes restauraciones de la Oficina del Historiador de la Ciudad de La Habana (OHCH). La ruta que tomaremos en estas páginas revelará las nuevas formas de colonialidad que el turismo, la creciente gentrificación y la llegada de nuevos capitales reimponen en el tejido de la ciudad de este siglo XXI.

Huelga recordar que Cuba ha sido en los últimos sesenta años una alternativa social, política y económica en el Caribe y Latinoamérica. La presencia de una revolución tempranamente adscrita al socialismo produjo una relación diferente con el entorno político y económico de la región, basada principalmente en el turismo. Las relaciones comerciales fueron mayoritariamente con los países socialistas y, cuando desaparece el muro de Berlín, la isla pierde sus principales proveedores. El turismo fue una de las pocas opciones que tuvo el país para recuperarse económicamente. La sociedad cubana, marcada por los presupuestos de un socialismo emancipador en términos sociales, en el plano económico estaba devastada y se vio urgida a desarrollar una infraestructura para el turismo con fórmulas de inversión extranjera, empresas mixtas y readecuación de su mercado laboral en este sector de rápido crecimiento económico. Las primeras oleadas turísticas a Cuba se concentran en bondades naturales como sol y playa, y aplazan las ganancias culturales de una sociedad con altos niveles de instrucción, salud y seguridad. La naciente industria turística cubana tuvo que adaptarse a las demandas de inversionistas y empresas mixtas que se instalaron en Cuba con exigentes estándares de calidad y competencia, con grandes ventajas sobre las empresas cubanas, con las cuales explotaron las condiciones naturales y los recursos humanos de la isla al estilo de una plantación esclavista del siglo XIX.

En el Caribe, la matriz de dominación colonial fue la plantación esclavista, modelo económico y político contra el cual la masa esclavizada y los negros libres siempre intentaron diversas formas de resistencia, como el cimarronaje y las sublevaciones en contra de los crueles maltratos de los esclavistas. La economía de plantación fue el modelo de mayor éxito económico, cuyos presupuestos tenían que ver con la mano de obra barata, la exportación hacia la metrópoli de las diversas materias primas (algodón, cacao, tabaco, azúcar, frutas, café y minerales), así como el empobrecimiento de las propias colonias debido al fuerte extractivismo. Como explican los economistas Lloyd Best y Kari Polanyi Levitt en *Teoría de la economía de plantación*, "a pesar de los cambios reales en la economía y del crecimiento significativo en el transcurso del tiempo, las características esenciales de la economía de plantación original aún persisten [en el Caribe]" (11). Es decir, en pleno siglo XX, la economía de plantación se reproduce como fórmula e ideología de producción y explotación. Así, esta configuración económica reaparece en grandes monopolios agrícolas como la United Fruit Company y las empresas mineras, reproduciéndose posteriormente en las compañías petroleras y, al final de los años cincuenta, en las nacientes compañías de turismo.

La industria del turismo contemporáneo (por ejemplo, compañías de aviación, agencias de viaje, cadenas hoteleras) está configurada por las estructuras (no tan invisibles) de la economía de plantación. Más allá de sus sofisticados intercambios de bienes y servicios, las relaciones comerciales entre las islas caribeñas y el Primer Mundo siguen siendo asimétricas y marcadas por las reglas del juego económico, tecnológico y cultural que impone un contexto de economía neoliberal. Cuba no está exenta de las consecuencias materiales y culturales de estos flujos de capitales que no significan solamente pérdidas y ganancias económicas. En otro texto he advertido "del surgimiento de instancias o maquinarias blanqueadoras que rechazan, subordinan, invisibilizan, distorsionan o reducen el protagonismo negro en la sociedad cubana" (Zurbano Torres 32–33). Aunque existen alternativas como el turismo ecológico, histórico, de salud y de eventos, no es difícil advertir la impronta colonial en muchas propuestas turísticas. La colonialidad se impone sutilmente en buena cantidad de ofertas para el turismo, sin tener en cuenta cómo estas menoscaban la diversidad cultural y la riqueza identitaria de la nación, reproduciendo códigos excluyentes y discriminatorios.

Es, en este sentido, que utilizo el término de *economía de plantación,* para identificar en las propuestas turísticas a una serie de acciones discriminatorias y lesivas a la dignidad de grupos llamados minoritarios —como mujeres, negros, asiáticos, árabes, etc.—, a través del uso, abuso o distorsión de sus imágenes, cuerpos, culturas, religiosidades y dignidades. No se trata de una disquisición económica, sino de una definición cultural que permite ver en buena parte del entramado turístico operaciones de inferiorización, deshumanización y depredación de personas, culturas y territorios en función de mercados y actos de irresponsabilidad social.

De la Plaza de la Catedral a la Plaza Vieja: Buscando las huellas del pasado afrodescendiente

En una entrevista al gran historiador cubano Manuel Moreno Fraginals, él recordaba a Wenceslao, un señor negro de noventa años que había sido esclavo, a quien conoció sentado en los escalones de entrada a la catedral y que le enseñó a ver una Habana desde abajo, "desde el punto más bajo de la escala social" (Moreno Fraginals 10). Me propongo empezar el recorrido, justamente, desde ese punto de vista "más bajo de la escala social", no mirando desde los balcones ni desde las cámaras del turista que busca enfocar exotismo y tranquilidad, sino observando La Habana desde la perspectiva de aquellos negros que con sus oficios construyeron cada edificio, pusieron cada piedra de sus calles y sazonaron sus sabores y costumbres, desde el esfuerzo y las aspiraciones de esclavizados, cimarrones urbanos y negros libres. Quién diría que, muchos años después, esta misma Plaza de la Catedral sería el lugar de inicio de la visita oficial a Cuba en 2016 del primer presidente negro de los Estados Unidos.

La plaza alberga una de las catedrales barrocas más bellas de las Américas, de la cual se conoce el nombre de sus arquitectos, escultores y orfebres de origen español e italiano. Sin embargo, no se reconoce el nombre del maestro de obras negro que hizo crecer la imponente y definitiva versión de la catedral, erigida con piedras subidas hasta la altura del campanario por negros que a veces caían, accidentados, al vacío. Aquel maestro de obras se hizo famoso por encontrar una buena manera de disminuir los accidentes, colocando sogas y telas entre los andamios, que funcionaran a modo de red protectora en el caso de que un hombre cayera desde las alturas. Fue de gran beneficio, pues en esa época morían diariamente varios constructores negros a causa de uno u otro percance. Puede decirse, entonces, que la catedral también fue construida con la sangre negra de aquella época.

En esa misma plaza, varios siglos atrás, al filo del amanecer, varias mujeres negras recién paridas esperaban quien comprara la leche de sus senos para amamantar a los niños blancos de las familias criollas ricas. Mientras permanecían escondidas tras las columnas, alguien negociaba un precio para luego llevarlas hasta las casonas donde daban de mamar a otros niños la leche que pertenecía a los propios. Otras ausencias y silencios guardan hoy esta plaza bulliciosa y colorida en la cual los turistas disfrutan la opción de vivir simultáneamente entre el pasado y el presente, sin los conflictos de sendas épocas. El turista no tiene medida del significado retrospectivo de este silencio colonizador, de modo que nunca trato a mis estudiantes como turistas o "yumas" desentendidos de la historia, sino como posibles entes críticos que interroguen tales silencios, tal y como deberían procurar hacer nuestros agentes turísticos.

Al doblar hacia la calle Mercaderes, nos topamos con un hermoso y amplísimo mural, inaugurado en el año 2000, que reúne personalidades importantes del siglo XIX cubano (Figura 1). Se trata de 67 figuras ilustres de las ciencias, la cultura y la política cubanas: aparecen Félix Varela, el Obispo Espada, Cirilo Villaverde, Tomás Romay, Gertrudis Gómez de Avellaneda y Domingo del Monte, entre otras personalidades. Es curioso que no aparezca la figura de José Martí en este mural, donde la política parece ocultarse bajo la sombrilla de las señoras que se muestran de espaldas al espectador. No son pocas las cubanas brillantes del siglo XIX, y en este mural aparecen incluso las que nunca estuvieron en el Liceo Artístico y Literario de La Habana, realmente situado al otro

FIGURA 1. *Mural de las personalidades*, situado en la calle Mercaderes. En la imagen, Roberto Zurbano explica el mural a los asistentes del segundo curso "Lo que nos corresponde: Visibilizando historias afrodescendientes en Cuba." Foto de Amílcar Ortiz.

lado de la calle Mercaderes. Se trata, no está demás señalar aquí, de un mural-espejo que refleja la fisonomía de la fachada del Palacio del Marqués de Arcos, que acogió el mencionado Liceo desde 1844 hasta 1869. La obra pretende ser una representación de las selectas figuras —todas ellas blancas— que asistían al lugar.

Llama la atención la presencia de dos sujetos negros en el extremo inferior derecho del mural: el excelso violinista Claudio Brindis de Salas y el poeta mulato Juan Francisco Manzano, autor de la única autobiografía escrita por un esclavo en la América hispana. Están correctamente vestidos, quizás esperando ser llamados a la velada de esa tarde en el Liceo, donde los negros no tenían acceso a sus salones de la alta sociedad, a no ser en la función que le destinaban sus oficios: cocineros, sirvientes, caleseros y músicos, entre otros pocos. Brindis de Salas fue un violinista excepcional que paseó su arte por las cortes europeas, donde le llamaban el Paganini negro, un modo de subordinar su talento. Manzano escribió su biografía a cambio de su libertad, que sería comprada por los intelectuales blancos del círculo literario presidido por Domingo del Monte. Ellos reescribieron la autobiografía del poeta esclavo, borrando las infamias y maltratos que este recibiera de sus amos y rescribiendo el original. Dichos escritores proclamaban ser abolicionistas, pero su estatus económico provenía de las plantaciones esclavistas de sus familias. Ambos artistas negros de reconocidos talentos en su época fueron apartados, también en un mural del siglo XXI, al lugar del subalterno.

Si este mural coloca en los salones del Liceo a figuras históricas que nunca pisaron el lugar, bien pudieran incluirse otras importantes personalidades decimonónicas como José Martí o Antonio Maceo, las figuras más altas de la política y la guerra durante el siglo XIX en Cuba, de modo que estos grandes acontecimientos que marcan el siglo estuvieran presentes. Se trata, no obstante, de un mural diseñado para el turismo, es decir, para subjetividades ya colonizadas por el consumo de imágenes que no ofrecen conflicto. Podría decirse que la historia del siglo XIX que ofrece este mural pretende ocultar, desde una actualizada vocación colonizada, la poderosa economía de plantación que sostuvo instituciones como este Liceo, construido sobre el dolor y la sangre de quienes producían el azúcar en los ingenios. Si no ejercemos una mirada crítica decolonial sobre el turismo de hoy, no sabremos cómo este recoloniza el presente y ocupa el lugar económico de la vieja plantación esclavista. Me pregunto por qué nuestros artistas no intentan hacer un gran mural, como este, con las grandes figuras negras del siglo XIX. ¡Sorprendería a muchos reconocer las grandes contribuciones que hicieron a la sociedad cubana de entonces!

Asumiendo la perspectiva decolonial, vemos cómo el diseño colonial que rezuma este fresco historicista se repite en la actualidad, como una farsa histórica, en medio de la cercana Plaza de la Catedral. Cuando digo *farsa* no es una metáfora, ni simple retórica, pues en cuanto llegamos a la Plaza de la Catedral lo primero que vemos son pequeños grupos de mujeres negras, jóvenes y viejas, vestidas tal y como solían hacerlo sus ancestros hace dos siglos, es decir, exhibiendo los uniformes coloniales que requiere el mercado laboral del turismo: por ejemplo, floristas, cartománticas, peinadoras, damitas de compañía para retratarse junto a los turistas (Figura 2). Allí ejercen un tráfico de sus identidades que les permite ganar el sustento del mes, luego de pagar los impuestos que exige el despliegue de sus personajes en el espacio público de La Habana Vieja.

Algunas venden artesanías y muñecas que caricaturizan los rostros y cuerpos afrodescendientes y lo hacen desde la amarga conciencia de un mercado que solo sabe trabajar eficientemente con estereotipos: labios gruesos pintados de rojo, nalgas y senos exagerados y el tabaco de ocasión. No es casual que en este mercado predominen mujeres, quienes exhiben, con toda intención, una africanía que las guías de turismo callan. Su rol como objeto de farsa neutraliza la historia real de violaciones y negociaciones sexuales que enfrentaron las mujeres negras esclavizadas. Sus personajes, rezumantes de alegría y colorido entusiasmo, impiden una mirada crítica hacia el pasado colonial y sus horrores. Mirar hacia atrás, como la mujer de Lot, pero de forma más oscura y confundida, anularía su esfuerzo por obtener el sustento familiar, jugando a hacer lo

FIGURA 2. Mujeres cartománticas en la Plaza de la Catedral. Foto de Roberto Zurbano.

que sus antepasados hacían dos siglos atrás. Solo tengo una pregunta que va de la farsa a la realidad: ¿tienen otras opciones?

Abandonamos la plaza tomando San Ignacio e ignorando los ofrecimientos de jóvenes negros y mestizos para comer en los restaurantes privados del callejón del Chorro, de muy buena calidad y con excelentes platos criollos propuestos, ya en el interior de estos espacios, por elegantes camareros blancos. En esta calle hay muchos negocios privados ofreciendo los mismos *souvenirs*: gorras del Che Guevara, copias de viejos autos americanos, fotos de los primeros años de la revolución, junto a una tienda de ropas y objetos espectacularmente caros y hermosos. Frente a la tienda, una cafetería de helados de frutas exhibe un cartel de "anti-racist zone" que rechaza otras discriminaciones, en inglés, pensado, como casi todos los productos de esta calle, para el turismo internacional (Figura 3).

Atravesamos la calle O'Reilly, donde trabajan varios obreros en la restauración de un edificio. Hace unos 175 años un periódico habanero anunciaba que en esta misma calle se vendía una mujer negra esclava recién parida (Figura 4). Doblamos a la derecha bordeando el restaurado Colegio de San Gerónimo, la primera universidad habanera fundada en 1728 y, al volver a Mercaderes, descubrimos tres bustos emplazados alrededor del aniversario 500 de la ciudad,

FIGURA 3. Cartel situado a la entrada de una cafetería privada en la calle San Ignacio. Foto de Roberto Zurbano.

VENTA DE ESCLAVOS.

UNA NEGRA se vende, recien parida, con abundante leche, escelente lavandera y planchadora, con principios de cocina, jóven, sana y sin tachas, y muy humilde: darán razon en la calle de O. Reilly n? 16, el portero. 6 30

UNA NEGRA se vende por no necesitarla su dueño, de nacion conga, como de 20 años, con su cria de 11 meses, sana y sin tachas, muy fiel y humilde, no ha conocido mas amo que el actual, es regular lavandera, planchadora y cocinera: en la calle del Baratillo casa n? 4 informarán. 31

VENTA DE ANIMALES.

SANGUIJUELAS de buen tamaño y sobresaliente calidad, se hallan de venta en la barbería plazuela de S. Juan de Dios, y tambien en la calle del Sol. esquina á la de Compostela frente á la hojalatería, barbería de Reyes Satiesteban á peso doc?, con la satisfaccion que pueden devolver las que no peguen por casualidad, pues con lo que garantizo lo buenas que son, y puesta por el mismo autor con la velocidad de 2 minutos, como lo tiene acreditado con las principales familias de esta capital, por 12 rs. doc. bien sean fuertes ó sencillos. 30-4

VENTA DE LIBROS.

LOS HIJOS DEL TIO TRONERA.

PARODIA DEL TROVADOR. Este chistosísimo sainete picaresco, en verso, original del célebre poeta D. Antonio Garcia Gutierrez, y que fué tan aplaudido en el gran teatro de esta capital, se ha impreso con el mayor esmero, y se halla de venta á 2 rs. senc. en la librería de la Prensa y en la de D. Antonio Charlain, calle del Obispo número 114. 4-2.

FIGURA 4. Anuncio de venta de esclavos en el Diario de la Marina (3 de febrero de 1846).

que rinden homenaje a tres importantes figuras de las antiguas metrópolis europeas: Miguel de Cervantes, William Shakespeare y Luís de Camoens, los llamados padres del idioma español, inglés y portugués, respectivamente.[3] Es curioso que no haya un busto de Alexander Pushkin, también llamado padre del idioma ruso. Ah, pero recuerdo que Pushkin era mulato. ¿Su cabellera rizada se vería bien junto a los otros?

Salimos a la calle del Obispo, de abrumador paso peatonal durante el día. En la esquina del Café París, retomamos San Ignacio. Aquí termina el mundo del turismo, los edificios recién pintados, las cafeterías con cerveza helada y música en vivo. Entramos a una zona deprimida de varias cuadras. Ahora

FIGURA 5. Un hombre observa, sentado, la calle Mercaderes. Al fondo, el Colegio de San Gerónimo y la estatua de Cervantes. Foto de María A. Gutiérrez Bascón.

cambian los olores y comienzan los ruidos, los charcos, los solares de paredes sin pintar que no pueden ocultar rajaduras, ni tendederas, cables y cicatrices del hacinamiento que comparten las familias residentes. No me detengo a invadir sus espacios privados, ni explicar su visible precariedad, evadiendo esa tentación a la porno-miseria que llena miles de páginas, videos y fotos sobre Cuba. Es un dolor que no quiero compartir, ni hacer de la pobreza un circo para turistas.

Es una decisión que resuelvo, en el recorrido, avanzando con rapidez y mostrando, a la altura de la calle Lamparilla, un edificio de apartamentos recién construido para antiguos vecinos de La Habana Vieja que perdieron sus casas por derrumbe. Aunque no se construyó en el tiempo y la calidad con que se erigen los hoteles de la ciudad, este inmueble acoge decenas de familias y significa un homenaje a la resistencia de esos vecinos que nunca abandonaron su barrio, reclamando y esperando varios años, en difíciles condiciones, hasta que fuera restituido su *derecho a la ciudad*, de acuerdo con el pronóstico de Henri Lefebvre. Muchos residentes se convirtieron en constructores de su propio inmueble, haciendo de la autogestión una clave de empoderamiento colectivo frente a ese gesto hipócrita con que la desidia del gobierno local veía derrumbarse cientos de edificaciones coloniales que, meses o años más tarde, entregaba a las constructoras de hoteles. En fin, este edificio multifamiliar,[4] de mediocre diseño para la zona colonial, es una conquista y una respuesta al desplazamiento sufrido por otros.

Más entusiasmado, atravieso olores y sabores de pequeñas cafeterías antes de llegar a la esquina de San Ignacio y Amargura, donde les muestro uno de los hoteles más bellos de la ciudad, el Raquel, nombre bíblico caro a los judíos —llamados polacos en Cuba—, quienes desde principios del siglo XX desplazaron a negros libres, comerciantes y artesanos que desde el siglo XVIII habían convertido la callejuela en una floreciente zona comercial. Luego, los judíos, perseverantes y prósperos, sumaron a viviendas y negocios del barrio sus instituciones religiosas y educacionales. En la misma esquina, transversal al Hotel Raquel, hay un local que fuera tienda de comida orgánica hace unos años y que es hoy una tienda de implementos y alimentos para mascotas. Asomados al cristal, vemos que sus empleados disfrutan el aire acondicionado y no están muy ocupados. ¿Quiénes consumen en La Habana comida orgánica o implementos para mascotas? Una creciente clientela que asume nuevas formas de consumo y quizás, también, una nueva clase media. Eso aprendí leyendo *La nueva frontera urbana*, el clásico libro de Neil Smith sobre la gentrificación. Su mirada de geógrafo radical enseña que este tipo de local de alto consumo es como una aduana donde el transeúnte es sutilmente interrogado sobre su estatus, clase, nacionalidad y pertenencia a la polis (Smith 22). No necesito entrar para saber que esa tienda funciona como una de las fronteras invisibles entre una Habana dolarizada y otra Habana sin dólares. A pesar de no ser una

FIGURA 6. Roberto Zurbano señala la tarja en homenaje al Partido Independiente de Color, situada en la calle Amargura. Foto de Amílcar Ortiz.

ciudad socialmente segregada, tales espacios anuncian una callada gentrificación con varios protagonistas en competencia. En esta zona es visible el esfuerzo restaurador de la OHCH, que satisface demandas vecinales y públicas con algunos edificios de apartamentos, escuelas, asilos de ancianos, hogares maternos y teatros, insertándolos en el tejido urbano entre *boutiques*, hostales y locales privados convertidos en pequeños bares y tiendas de *souvenirs* para el turismo.

En esta calle Amargura se halla una de las pocas tarjas que ofrece alguna historia negra de la ciudad (Figura 6). Se colocó en agosto del 2012 a petición de organizaciones antirracistas para celebrar el centenario de la masacre los miembros del Partido Independiente de Color que, en mayo del 1912, fueron asesinados por orden del presidente de la República, el general José Miguel Gómez. Se cuentan entre mil y tres mil las víctimas que mal armadas se alzaron reclamando su participación en las elecciones de ese mismo año, para las cuales dicho partido fue declarado ilegal. Una enmienda escrita por el congresista negro Martín Morúa Delgado no solo había anulado sus derechos, sino que había criminalizado las demandas de los Independientes de Color, que fueron víctimas de una violenta respuesta gubernamental, a todas luces racista.

El acontecimiento estuvo silenciado durante casi medio siglo, solo intermitentemente abordado por algunos historiadores (Armando Plá, Serafín Portuondo Linares, Rafael Fermoselle, Aline Helg, Jorge Ibarra, Tomás Fernández Robaina, Alejandro de la Fuente) en ediciones de poca circulación y no comienza a estudiarse en nuestras escuelas hasta el siglo XXI. La tarja representa la reivindicación moral de la singular institución política fundada por los negros cubanos, cuyos reclamos, por cierto, no se centraban exclusivamente en la cuestión racial, sino que incluían demandas básicas para una democracia plena, tales como la jornada laboral de ocho horas. En este lugar, estudiantes y turistas preguntan mucho y les recomiendo buscar la extensa bibliografía que se ha publicado, particularmente fuera de Cuba.

Debo agregar que el autor intelectual de la masacre, el general José Miguel Gómez, entonces presidente de la República, tiene el mayor mausoleo que se le haya dedicado en Cuba a una figura pública, emplazado en la Avenida de los Presidentes, en el barrio de El Vedado. La fría evasiva con que la mayoría de los historiadores cubanos tratan este tema fue superada con justicia poética en la reivindicación a sus víctimas que hizo Obsesión, grupo pionero del hip-hop cubano. Su tema "Calle G" (2011), reconocido popularmente como "Túmbenla", conmina a derribar la estatua del presidente asesino y corrupto, entonces recién restaurada por la Oficina del Historiador. Este rap fue considerado "terrorista" por Ana Cairo, prestigiosa intelectual cubana negra, a quien no pude convencer de lo contrario durante el panel "El autor y su obra" dedicado a Tomás Fernández Robaina,[5] donde compartíamos la mesa con el historiador Jorge Ibarra, quien no hacía más que reírse. Finalmente, pregunté a la Dra. Ana Cairo cómo llamaba a la tardanza para colocar en Carlos III y Belascoaín la estatua del luchador negro independentista José Antonio Aponte, líder de la primera rebelión nacional contra el poder español, a quien en 1812 arrancaron la cabeza y la exhibieron durante dos semanas en la esquina referida, exactamente cien años antes de la Masacre de los Independientes de Color. No tuve respuesta.

Creo que el debate sobre la ausencia de estatuas de figuras negras podría ser largo. Propongo, tarareando el tema de Obsesión, salir a la Plaza Vieja, por la esquina de Mercaderes y Teniente Rey, donde hay una tienda Benetton, por más señas. A la sombra de sus colores avistamos una de las plazas más importantes de La Habana colonial, también llamada Plaza del Mercado, por su antigua función comercial, hoy revalidada por el turismo (Figura 7). Hace tres siglos, mientras fue legal la trata de negros traídos de África o de otras islas caribeñas, en esta plaza se vendían de igual manera vegetales, pescado y especias, que negros esclavizados.

Esta explicación es interrumpida por el sonido de una comparsa que intenta, bajo el sol, divertir y sumar a los turistas que disfrutan la plaza o consumen en los cafés, cerveceras y *boutiques* cercanas (Figura 8). Son personas de todas las razas cuyas coloridas vestimentas y máscaras recuerdan el desfile del Día de Reyes, fiesta aprobada por los gobiernos coloniales del siglo XIX en que los esclavos salían a repartir caramelos y pedir en las puertas de las casonas alguna moneda o dulce (Figura 9). Hoy solo buscan las propinas de los turistas. Son los mismos sonidos, los mismos gestos festinados y caritativos que multiplican los estereotipos coloniales y los silencios de esta ruidosa plaza.

FIGURA 7. Plaza Vieja. Foto de María A. Gutiérrez Bascón.

Bajo la sombra, doy una tarea a mis estudiantes: les incito a buscar en toda la plaza una huella, aunque sea pequeña, de la presencia negra. Tienen cinco minutos para llegar a San Ignacio y Muralla, buscar dentro y fuera de la cervecería holandesa, desplazarse a Mercaderes y Muralla, mirar por los cristales de la *boutique* Paul and Shark o disfrutar la fachada catalana del Hotel Cueto, reconstruido en la misma esquina. Sin embargo, sé que ni siquiera podrán descubrir "los entresuelos de las casas-almacén,[6] típicas de la Plaza Vieja, que eran ocupados por los esclavos, pues se restaura[ron] de la misma forma que el resto de los suelos, de manera que el hecho de que estos eran ocupados por personas africanas y esclavizadas queda, de alguna manera, silenciado" (Gutiérrez Bascón 113). Este silencio, junto a otros que nuestro recorrido revela, ha cavado fosas profundas en la memoria histórica, de las cuales no podría culparse solo al turismo, sino a la dimensión epistemológica de un proyecto urbanístico y arquitectónico con pocas bases críticas sobre la historia colonial del espacio cubano (Pérez de la Riva 133). Coincido con la investigadora María A. Gutiérrez Bascón cuando afirma: "En fin, lo que nos enseña el caso de la Plaza Vieja, con los muy diversos proyectos que se propusieron para ordenar el espacio público, es que el patrimonio es socialmente construido en inevitable acuerdo con lógicas de mercado internacionales. Con la Plaza Vieja, la OHCH manufactura un espacio que resulta óptimo para el consumo visual del turista internacional que busca huellas de la antigua grandeza colonial en el trópico— y sin recordatorios evidentemente visibles, podríamos añadir, del sistema de

FIGURA 8. La comparsa desfila por La Habana Vieja. Foto de María A. Gutiérrez Bascón.

plantación que permitió la construcción de las grandes mansiones de la sacarocracia habanera" (114).[7]

Entonces, la infructuosa tarea de búsqueda de mis estudiantes se coinvertía en una breve pausa para tomar fotos, mientras confirmaban mi decepción y el modo excluyente con que arquitectos y restauradores diseñaron la actual vida de esta plaza. Si tales servidores públicos no conocen las contribuciones negras a la ciudad, deberían saberlo; pero si las niegan a sabiendas, su culpa es doble, por compartir tanto desdén colonial y racista. Y poco podrían criticar o exigir al sector privado que integre a la historia habanera aquellos que fueron sus primeros constructores, quienes aportaron oficios y saberes a la dinámica de la sociedad. Por otro lado, tal diseño no solo excluye a los negros, sino a

FIGURA 9. Día de Reyes. Litografía de Federico Mialhe para el *Libro pintoresco de la isla de Cuba* (1855).

todos los cubanos, pues se restaura en función de la industria turística y de los visitantes extranjeros.

En términos prácticos, este diseño se articula dentro de una política de urbanización excluyente o selectiva, a través de la cual no pocos vecinos de La Habana Vieja (negros, mestizos y blancos) fueron desplazados, no siempre con su consentimiento, hacia zonas periféricas de la ciudad. Este es el primer momento de la gentrificación en La Habana, promovida por instancias gubernamentales, particularmente la Oficina del Historiador de la Ciudad de La Habana, apoyada por el financiamiento de organismos internacionales, inversionistas extranjeros e inversores nacionales. Lo cierto es que pocas instancias de gobierno han ejercido en las últimas décadas un manejo e impacto social tan significativo en la geografía económica de la ciudad como esta Oficina, cuya estrategia de restauración muchas veces coincidió con ciertos modelos de gentrificación pública que tienen lugar en otros países de la región (por ejemplo, Colombia, México, Argentina).

El debate sobre la gentrificación habanera ha sido muy discreto, en parte porque la labor de la OHCH es merecedora de los altos elogios de personalidades e instituciones nacionales y extranjeras. En segundo lugar, la OHCH ha sido casi la única instancia cubana que ha podido ejecutar no solo el trabajo de restauración del centro histórico, sino ejercer políticas de urbanización, inversión inmobiliaria y otras estrategias, junto a las inversiones del sector turístico, con menos incidencia social directa. Y la última razón es la resistencia de arquitectos y urbanistas en asumir un término extrapolado de contextos diferentes al Caribe y Latinoamérica.

Sin embargo, estudiosos del entorno urbano latinoamericano como Antoine Casgrain y Michael Janoschka abordan la gentrificación en diferentes ciudades de la región, vinculándolas al capitalismo neoliberal y sus modos de penetración en el mercado inmobiliario de nuestros países. Muchas de sus caracterizaciones se comprueban en Cuba, cuando hablan, por ejemplo, de "la gentrificación simbólica a través de las actividades turísticas y culturales, destacando así la transformación de un barrio como enclave de consumo exclusivo y de producción cultural, en desmedro de la actividad residencial y los servicios de primera necesidad" (Casgrain y Janoschka 25). Esto, para poner un solo ejemplo, sucede exactamente igual en la plaza que acabamos de visitar.

La Loma del Ángel: Gentrificación y nuevos consumos bajo la mirada de Cecilia Valdés

El segundo momento de la gentrificación en la capital cubana está protagonizado por un sector privado que, apoyado en agencias inmobiliarias privadas y testaferros cubanos, representa los nuevos dueños extranjeros y sus capitales, que en pocos años han transformado edificios, calles y barriadas no solo de la zona histórica de la ciudad. En la propia Habana Vieja visitaremos uno de esos barrios, donde tienen lugar escenas claves de *Cecilia Valdés o la Loma del Ángel*, la novela cubana más importante del siglo XIX. Escrita por Cirilo Villaverde, se trata de una descarnada mirada a la sociedad cubana del siglo XIX, en especial la sociedad habanera marcada por la esclavitud, en cuya lectura reconocemos calles, edificios, personajes y, sobre todo, conflictos de una Habana decimonónica que pudiéramos identificar como contemporáneos. Al llegar a la plaza, nos recibe el busto del escritor y la estatua de su mítica Cecilia, cuyo drama quedó sellado en las puertas de la Iglesia del Santo Ángel (Figura 10). Aún se recuerda la seductora belleza de la joven mulata que hoy parece inspirar a los emprendedores de los más de veinte negocios de la zona: hostales, cafeterías, pizzerías, restaurantes, galerías y tiendas de arte, ropas, zapatos y otros bienes y servicios de alta calidad para el consumo de turistas y clientes cubanos de alto estándar.

La Loma del Ángel es otro de los barrios superpoblados de La Habana Vieja, atravesado por economías informales, formas de convivencia colectiva y solidaria, sin distinción de clases, abierto al mestizaje y la religiosidad popular. Aquí confluyen generaciones de oriundos con varias oleadas de migrantes, apiñados en ciudadelas y solares cercanos a los nuevos hoteles, *boutiques* y restaurantes que genera la avalancha turística de las últimas décadas. No obstante, el barrio no parece beneficiado por dicha avalancha, pues sus inmuebles

FIGURA 10. *Loma del Ángel*. En la esquina inferior izquierda, la estatua de Cecilia Valdés observa sigilosamente a los clientes del Café del Ángel que pueblan la plaza. A la derecha, sobre la fachada del edificio, el busto de Cirilo Villaverde. Foto de María A. Gutiérrez Bascón.

muestran un deterioro que los gobiernos locales no pueden solventar y que los proyectos de restauración no abarcan, a pesar de su ubicación cercana al Paseo del Prado, el Museo de la Revolución, el Malecón o el Museo Nacional de Bellas Artes. Es la otra cara de la moneda que revela un joven cronista: "a pocos metros de donde se instaura el glamur del Manzana Kempinski y el Packard, se extiende una ciudad desvencijada, con aguas pútridas en mil y un lugares, desabastecimiento de agua, vertederos…" (Echevarría).

A tres cuadras de allí, en una de las esquinas del parque frente al memorial Granma, debió existir un monumento a la memoria de los jóvenes miembros de la Sociedad Secreta Abakuá que el 27 de noviembre de 1871 fueron masacrados tratando de salvar las vidas de ocho estudiantes de medicina, injustamente acusados por el gobierno español. Tato Quiñones, intelectual y activista, insistió en reivindicarles junto al desfile oficial que año tras año baja por San Lázaro, desde la escalinata de la Universidad de La Habana, hasta llegar a Prado y Malecón, donde en 1890 se erigió un mausoleo dedicado a los estudiantes inocentes. Sin pedir permiso, Tato compulsó a muchos abakuá y luchadores antirracistas a rendir especial homenaje, cada año, en la esquina de Morro y Colón, donde, según la prensa de la época, fueron masacrados los jóvenes abakuá. Desde el año 2006 este sitio fue bautizado como la Esquina de la Descolonización, marcada por dos firmas abakuá en forma de escultura, una tarja explicando el suceso y una frase en lengua efik ("Bonco itá ekue jurakatime akanaran krukoró") que reivindica la acción y a sus jóvenes mártires negros (Figura 11).

FIGURA 11. Esquina de la Descolonización, en la intersección de las calles Morro y Colón. Foto de Gretel Marín.

El Ángel es entonces un barrio que dialoga y convive con otros espacios cercanos en esa misma clave popular, de sobrevida y resistencia. Eso también atrajo a los agentes de la gentrificación (corredores inmobiliarios, testaferros de inversionistas extranjeros y nueva clase media cubana). Ellos proponen un diálogo bajo las reglas de la gentrificación privada, que son las del capital, la distinción social y los nuevos patrones de consumo de bienes y servicios que ostenta una nueva clase media, deseosa por instalarse en la zona a cualquier precio; es decir, a un precio de inversión que multiplique sus capitales (financiero, cultural, de estatus) en breve tiempo.

Pocos vecinos pudieron remodelar sus apartamentos para venderlos a mejor precio, para vivir mejor, para rentar ellos mismos o, simplemente, para negociar su pertenencia al nuevo carácter social del barrio o para poder elegir un buen inmueble en otra zona. El resto de los ocupantes se aconsejó —o los agentes les aconsejaron— vender y moverse a otros barrios más o menos cercanos, donde continúa el deterioro habitacional, pero donde al menos pueden seguir accediendo a productos de consumo básico a un nivel asequible a sus bolsillos. Se trata de una negociación forzosa, donde los agentes de la gentrificación llevan ventajas y las ofrecen a los residentes como atractivas ofertas que, lamentablemente, no podrán rechazar. Luego, una vez que se desplaza a los viejos residentes de sus propiedades, también se trata de desplazar sus prácticas culturales hacia algún lugar donde no sean molestas para las nuevas dinámicas que distinguirán al barrio y sus nuevos residentes.

Los desplazados no suelen reconocer, de inmediato, su condición de víctimas del proceso depredador y de marginalización social que es la gentrificación, filosa palabra que aún no maneja el activismo social en Cuba, pues se desconoce como otra forma de violencia, discriminación y opresión que crece silenciosamente en la ciudad. Gradualmente, la naciente clase media va desplazando las antiguas prácticas culturales del barrio que le resultan incompatibles con su nuevo estilo de vida. Asistimos a la desaparición o estilización de prácticas como los juegos de dominó, los cumpleaños, los toques de santos, las visitas de familiares o amigos y los propios juegos infantiles, hasta llegar a restringir o rechazar acciones cotidianas usuales en el barrio antes de la gentrificación, para ir formalizando (o imponiendo) una serie de estilos de vida y de comportamientos sociales que operan como las nuevas reglas del paisaje urbano.

Solo bastó un lustro para cambiar la precaria condición de algunos inmuebles en el Ángel. Su transformación visual, arquitectónica y funcional tuvo lugar a una increíble velocidad. Surgieron rutilantes fachadas, de sorprendentes diseños interiores, excelente uso de espacios y materiales tradicionales. Será difícil calcular el capital que se ha gastado en la compra de los viejos edificios, en los materiales de construcción, en la mano de obra empleada y en la contratación del personal especializado (arquitectos, diseñadores y otros expertos), que han dado un acabado impecable a cada espacio. Curiosidad aparte, solo trato de poner el énfasis en la alta concentración de capitales que recibe un pequeño espacio de la ciudad en un breve periodo de tiempo, lo cual provoca una fuerte marginación y un veloz desplazamiento de personas y de familias enteras desde este territorio hacia otras zonas de La Habana.

Al recorrer los nuevos espacios raramente encontraremos dueños y empleados negros o mestizos, sino rostros mayoritariamente blancos, siguiendo un patrón que se repite en Cuba en negocios vinculados al turismo internacional. No conozco una estadística que confirme lo que digo, pero a buena parte de la clientela extranjera de estos lugares sorprende la mayoritaria blancura de cajeros, bármanes y meseros. Sin embargo, hay una empleomanía menor (personal de limpieza, estibadores, porteros, vigilantes nocturnos, pequeños proveedores, etc.) de piel más oscura, que son los peores pagados, los más inestables en sus puestos y los menos visibles a los clientes. Aun así, estos trabajadores locales se suman gustosos a los cientos de empleos formales e informales del nuevo mercado laboral que genera el proceso de transformación del barrio en una de las zonas comerciales más chic de la ciudad.

Cuando definitivamente se instala esa clase media empoderada (y medio engreída), esta intenta convertir sus normas en obligaciones que se extiendan a toda la zona gentrificada del barrio, en un ejercicio de conquista territorial. Luego, buscan aceptación social para someter el resto del barrio a sus designios clasistas, a través del estricto cumplimiento de leyes y ordenanzas urbanas que hacen coincidir con sus reglas de convivencia. En este proceso suelen apelar (o involucrar) a autoridades del gobierno, la policía y otras instituciones de la ciudad. Algunas de estas medidas se convertirán en el ejercicio discriminatorio o excluyente de una clase dominante que pretende recolonizar el espacio social, disciplinar los sujetos que no comparten su estatus y, de paso, convertirles en subalternos al servicio de sus intereses.

Es significativo cómo estos espacios de gentrificación privada acogen una mayor cantidad de clientes nacionales, incluyendo familias enteras que podemos ver consumiendo en días de celebración (por ejemplo, graduaciones, cumpleaños), fenómeno menos común en restaurantes y bares estatales. Ello hace que la mirada nacional sobre estos lugares establezca las comparaciones pertinentes entre un antes y un ahora que el turista no alcanza a distinguir. Ocasionalmente, esa mirada cercana de parte de los consumidores cubanos se torna crítica ante los patrones de comportamiento y los requisitos laborales que exige el lugar. Esa posición crítica ocurre independientemente de que estos clientes se sientan o no parte de la atmósfera de exclusividad que generan los nuevos negocios, y es un dato a considerar cuando analizamos el grado de aceptación social o de resistencias que suscita el proceso gentrificador entre la población local.

Para cerrar la clase, el último ejercicio que doy a mis estudiantes es tomar un refrigerio en algún bar o cafetería del barrio y, desde adentro, reconocer marcas de consumo, restricciones, ausencias, ostentación o discriminación. Es la última oportunidad para saber cuáles sujetos están presentes y cómo lo están —¿favorecidos o marginalizados? ¿De quiénes estamos hablando?, ¿dónde están ellos? y ¿por qué no están?, mis tres preguntas básicas parecen replegarse ante el contexto gentrificado que solo habla de posesión o desposesión, sin reparar en aquellos que no tienen inmuebles, ni capital, ni clase social... Esos desclasados: desempleados o mendigos que atraviesan el barrio, registran la basura, piden alguna moneda y siguen. Las ausencias y los silencios son poderosas categorías decoloniales que expresan críticamente subjetividades e intenciones de clase, género, raza y nacionalidad. Este ejercicio final requiere más entrenamiento y agudeza para distinguir cómo el capital oculta, entre el brillo y la basura, sus víctimas de cada día.

Así termina el recorrido, en un tono ligeramente crítico que va acomodando las preguntas y respuestas al aprendizaje vivencial ahora, reflexivo después. Al final, pido una nota crítica de trescientas palabras en dos sentidos: uno negativo y otro positivo. En esas notas suelo encontrar revelaciones, como aquella de una joven afroamericana que dijo reconocer, con pelos y señales, los fantasmas de La Habana colonial y haber aprendido una forma de exorcizarlos. Es un recorrido que me gusta hacer con jóvenes, pues aprenden velozmente cómo descubrir las estructuras invisibles de la dominación, para qué sirve tal descubrimiento y cómo usarlo. Pero esa es otra clase que no se puede impartir

en un solo día y mucho menos en un aula. Terminamos con una foto de grupo, donde ciertos fantasmas aún se burlan de nosotros.
En Centro Habana, octubre de 2020

NOTAS

1. El presente texto nace de dos conferencias ofrecidas en la Casa de las Américas en 2018 y 2019. La primera, "La plantación invisible: Raza, turismo y colonialidad en el siglo XXI", tuvo lugar en el marco del primer curso de verano "Insurgencias afroamericanas", el 13 de julio de 2018. La segunda, "Turismo versus plantación: una propuesta de afro-reparación a la industria del turismo en el Caribe", fue impartida el 21 de junio de 2019 como parte del I Coloquio Internacional de Estudios sobre Afroamérica. Ambos eventos fueron organizados por el Programa de Estudios sobre Afroamérica de la Casa de las Américas. Quiero agradecer a Gretel Marín por su incondicional apoyo durante la escritura de este texto, su mirada de cineasta y su acompañamiento por los lugares que abordo en La Habana Vieja. También a Amílcar Ortiz, cuyas fotos revelan, hace años, mis paseos críticos por la ciudad.

2. La colonialidad del poder es un concepto introducido por el sociólogo peruano Aníbal Quijano en los años noventa para dar cuenta de una configuración específica del poder mundial capitalista, colonial/moderno y eurocentrado. De acuerdo con Quijano, la colonialidad "[s]e funda en la imposición de una clasificación racial/étnica de la población del mundo como piedra angular de dicho patrón de poder, y opera en cada uno de los planos, ámbitos y dimensiones, materiales y subjetivas, de la existencia cotidiana y a escala social" (Quijano "Colonialidad" 93). Quijano señala, además, la pervivencia de la colonialidad como patrón de dominación más allá del periodo histórico colonial: "Tal colonialidad del poder ha probado ser más profunda y duradera que el colonialismo en cuyo seno fue engendrado y al que ayudó a ser mundialmente impuesto" (Quijano "¡Qué tal raza!" 192).

3. Para ser más precisos, la estatua de Luís de Camoens fue inaugurada en el año 2014 y la de Miguel de Cervantes en 2017. Por su parte, aquella que representa a William Shakespeare fue descubierta por el príncipe Carlos de Inglaterra durante su visita a La Habana en marzo de 2019.

4. En la fachada del edificio Lamparilla 68 reza: "El Gobierno de Italia a través de la Organización Internacional Ítalo-Latinoamericana ha contribuido con la Oficina del Historiador de la Ciudad a la construcción de este edificio para la creación de 39 viviendas sociales".

5. El panel tuvo lugar el 15 de julio de 2015 en la Biblioteca Provincial Rubén Martínez Villena, en la Plaza de Armas de La Habana Vieja.

6. Según explican Scarpaci, Segre y Coyula en su libro *Havana: Two Faces of the Antillean Metropolis*, la *casa almacén* contaba con una planta baja donde se guardaba la mercancía, como los sacos de azúcar o café. Los entresuelos, de techos bajos, eran ocupados por los esclavos. El dueño de la casa y su familia vivían en el piso más alto, o *piano nobile* (312).

7. El término *sacarocracia* fue utilizado, entre otros, por el historiador Manuel Moreno Fraginals para nombrar a la aristocracia cañera dueña de las grandes plantaciones esclavistas, que tuvo su gran auge en Cuba en el siglo XIX.

REFERENCIAS

Best, Lloyd A., y Kari Polanyi Levitt. *Teoría de la economía de plantación: Una aproximación histórica e institucional del desarrollo del Caribe*. Casa de las Américas, 2008.
Casgrain, Antoine, y Michael Janoschka. "Gentrificación y resistencia en las ciudades latino-

americanas: El ejemplo de Santiago de Chile." *Andamios: Revista de Investigación Social*, vol. 10, núm. 22, 2013, pp. 19–44.

Echevarría, Ahmel. "Empujar cuesta arriba una enorme bola de mierda." *Hypermedia Magazine*, 23 de junio de 2020, https://www.hypermediamagazine.com/columnistas/por-la-ruta-de-la-seda/empujar-cuesta-arriba-una-enorme-bola-de-mierda/.

Gutiérrez Bascón, María A. "La reconstrucción patrimonial de la Plaza Vieja en La Habana: Monumentalidad colonial y turismo global en una isla (post)socialista." *Pós-Limiar: Revista do Programa de Pós-Graduação em Linguagens, Mídia e Arte [PUC-Campinas]*, vol. 1, núm. 2, julio de 2018, pp. 103–16.

Maldonado-Torres, Nelson. "El Caribe, la colonialidad, y el giro decolonial." *Latin American Research Review*, vol. 55, núm. 3, 2020, pp. 560–73.

Montejo Arrechea, Carmen V. *Sociedades negras en Cuba: 1878–1960*. Editorial Ciencias Sociales, 2004.

Moreno Fraginals, Manuel. Entrevista por Olga Cabrera e Isabel Ibarra. "Fragmentos de una conversación interrumpida." *Revista Encuentro de la cultura cubana* n. 10, 1998, pp. 3–10.

Pérez de la Riva, Juan. *La conquista del espacio cubano*. Fundación Fernando Ortiz, 2004.

Quijano, Aníbal. "Colonialidad del poder y clasificación social." *El giro decolonial: Reflexiones para una diversidad epistémica más allá del capitalismo global*, editado por Santiago Castro-Gómez y Ramón Grosfoguel, Siglo del Hombre Editores, 2007, pp. 93–126.

———. "¡Qué tal raza!" *Revista del CESLA: International Latin American Studies Review*, núm. 1, 2000, pp. 192–200.

Scarpaci, Joseph L., et al. *Havana: Two Faces of the Antillean Metropolis*. University of North Carolina Press, 2002.

Smith, Neil. *La nueva frontera urbana: Ciudad revanchista y gentrificación*. Traficantes de Sueños, 2012.

Trouillot, Michel-Rolph. *Silenciando el pasado: El poder y la producción de la Historia*. Editorial Comares, 2017.

Zurbano Torres, Roberto. "Racismo vs. socialismo en Cuba: Un conflicto fuera de lugar (apuntes sobre/contra el colonialismo interno)." *Meridional: Revista Chilena de Estudios Latinoamericanos*, núm. 4, 2015, pp. 11–40.

DAVID TENORIO

Havana's Last Conga: Trans Engagements and Queer Moves in Twenty-First-Century Cuba

ABSTRACT

As a way of tracing the public encounters shaping queer space, something referred to in here as "queer moving," in this article, I move around media objects—Facebook posts, newspaper articles, Twitter posts, and film—digital stories, and personal interviews related to four distinctly public queer encounters: the 2019 Conga against Homophobia and its counterpart, the Unauthorized Conga (*marcha no autorizada*); the Cenesex-funded trans activist network TransCuba; and the emergence of private spaces in Havana's nightlife for queer/trans intimacy. Through this transversal approach, I situate the concept of conga as a strategic affective engagement, a queer move, that mediates queer/trans political resistance and everyday survival in Cuba. In thinking with trans women's everyday engagements and disengagements with the public, the notion of trans engagements emerge from their stories not only as a trace of queer moving but also as an embodied practice to negotiate and contest a body politics of exposure. Situating the prefix *trans* as a relationality to trans world making allows me to trace a dynamic social choreography between survival and negotiation while unsettling static conceptualizations of Cuban sexual dissidence.

RESUMEN

A modo de trazar los encuentros públicos presentes en la formación del espacio queer, algo a lo que aquí me refiero como un "moverse queer," este artículo transita en torno a objetos mediáticos (publicaciones de Facebook y Twitter, artículos de periódico, películas), historias digitales y entrevistas personales relacionadas con cuatro encuentros públicos queer: la Conga contra la Homofobia de 2019 y su contraparte, la Conga no autorizada (o marcha no autorizada); la red de trans activismo TransCuba, financiada por el Cenesex; y la emergencia de espacios privados para la intimidad queer/trans en la noche habanera. A través de esta aproximación transversal, sitúo el concepto de conga como una estrategia afectiva, un "moverse queer," que media la relación entre la resistencia política queer/trans y su supervivencia cotidiana en Cuba. Pensando con las mujeres trans, entre sus conexiones y desconexiones con lo público, la noción de conexiones trans emerge de sus historias no solo como una huella del "moverse queer," sino también como una práctica acuerpada que participa en la negociación y disrupción de la exhibición de corporalidades disidentes. Situar el prefijo *trans* como una relacionalidad con respecto a las formas trans de hacer mundo, despliega una fuerza dinámica, en una especie de danza entre la supervivencia y la negociación, al mismo tiempo que impugna las conceptualizaciones estáticas de la disidencia sexual cubana.

It's the rhythm of the island, and like the sugar cane so sweet
If you want to do the conga, you've got to listen to the beat
"Conga," Miami Sound Machine

Mi unicornio azul se me ha perdido ayer, se fue.
"Unicornio," Silvio Rodríguez

Pedro Lemebel's pink unicorn plays in public bathrooms and city parks (237–241), where moans of pleasure add to the soundwaves of a queer sensibility that travels far and wide. A pink unicorn appears sublimely as a queer fable felt by queer folk dancing to the exhilarating rhythm of Gloria Estefan's "Conga" at an Orlando queer nightclub, where tears of queer loss evoke Silvio Rodríguez's "Unicornio."[1] Each sound beat condenses a mood, a phantasmatic affectivity, that in turn propels a movement of bodies. But these songs could very much represent the polarities of a Cuban imaginary resting, on the one hand, on a nostalgia for the past, and an uncertain futurity, on the other. These extremes are better described as a dance of different political formations of loss, a sort of queer moving of bodies, floating around the inescapable island. A sense of a queer utopia, as proposed by José Esteban Muñoz, sparks as distant a star of hope oscillating between political continuity and rupture, as fathomed by J. Moufawad-Paul. Public restrooms and city parks, nonetheless, are physical sites in which queer/trans intimacy is openly manifested and erotically embodied. The materiality of queer/trans bodies assembles an affective bridge connecting the public and private, while the queer soundwaves festively arrange bodies to shape a marching crowd, a dance mob, or a collective protest. In this sense, I am alluding to dance and movement as a way of embracing the public exposure of queer/trans bodies, forming public spaces of queer intimacy.[2]

In Cuba, the symbolic, material, and biopolitical struggles for queer space have a strong precedent in the last half of the twentieth century: the Night of the 3Ps (La Noche de las Tres Pés),[3] the UMAPs (Military Units to Aid Production), the Mariel boat lift, the HIV sanatoriums, the creation of Cenesex. These public events modulate different biopolitical tactics handling the exposure of queer/trans intimacy: persecution, internment, expulsion, abjection, and annexation. If the dissolution of Comecon, the Soviet economic bloc, unleashes a series of socioeconomic reforms in the last decade of the twentieth century, known as the Special Period, then the emergence of an erotic economy as an effect of such transformations marks the beginning of sensual encounters with global capitalism, recalibrating notions of public and private space concerning trans/queer conviviality and intimacy in twenty-first-century Cuba. As a way of tracing the public encounters shaping queer space, something referred to in here as "queer moving," in this article I move around media objects—Facebook posts, newspaper articles, Twitter posts, and film—digital stories, and personal interviews related to four distinctly public queer encounters: the 2019 Conga against Homophobia and its counterpart, the Unauthorized Conga (*marcha no autorizada*); the Cenesex-funded trans activist network TransCuba; and the emergence of private spaces in Havana's nightscape for queer/trans intimacy. Through this transversal approach, I situate the concept of conga as a strategic engagement, a queer moving, that mediates queer/trans political resistance and everyday survival in Cuba. In thinking with trans women's everyday engagements and disengagements with the public, the notion of transforming disengagements emerges from their stories not only as a trace of queer moving but also as an embodied practice to negotiate and contest a body politics of exposure. Situating the prefix *trans* as a relationality to trans world making allows me to trace a dynamic social choreography between survival and negotiation while unsettling static conceptualizations of Cuban sexual dissidence.

Track A: Cenesex's Conga

Under the direction of Mariela Castro Espín, Cenesex (National Center for Sexual Education) has been a champion for LGBTQ+ rights in Cuba since 2000. Jon Alpert's HBO documentary *Mariela Castro's March: Cuba's LGBT Revolution* (2015) depicts a triumphant Mariela leading a crusade against homophobia and transphobia across the country. Although the consolidation of Cenesex in the 2000s undoubtedly brought topics of non-heterosexuality and gender nonconformance into public policy since its inception in 1988, the documentary creates a redemptive fiction around the figure of Mariela Castro, highlighting a revolutionary paternalism inherent to Cuban socialism while minimizing the actual everyday struggles for survival facing queer/trans people, particularly trans women.[4] In Alpert's documentary, Cenesex appears as a sanctuary for queer/trans collectives, although the film actually focuses on the evidently distant LGBTQ+ stories taking place beyond the boundaries of Havana's official institutionalism. Portrayed as a protagonist for LGBTQ+ recognition in this film, Mariela Castro, in her quest against sexual discrimination, focuses less on developing antidiscriminatory legislation than on staging a public fight against a distinct culture of machismo still prevalent across the island, especially in rural areas.

One of Cenesex's public stages has been the creation of an annual campaign against homophobia and transphobia. Celebrated since 2007, the Cuban Day against Homophobia and Transphobia (La Jornada Cubana contra la Homofobia y la Transfobia), commemorates the International Day against Homophobia with a series of art exhibits, conferences, debates, and a night gala, including the now-internationally-famous Conga against Homophobia (La Conga contra la Homofobia).[5] Under the slogan of "Homofobia no, socialismo sí," the conga is equivalent to a Cuban gay pride parade in that LGBTQ+ collectives march through the streets of Havana demanding recognition and freedom of expression.[6] The parade route has changed over the years. For instance, in 2016, the parade started at La Piragua Park, at the intersection of Malecón and Línea, and ended in the cultural esplanade at Pabellón Cuba, along Calle 23. In 2018, however, it circulated from Avenida Paseo to Calzada and Calle 12 in Vedado. What remains consistent is that the conga usually stays within the vicinity of Vedado, one of Havana's wealthiest neighborhoods. In the 2014 Conga, Mariela Castro was accompanied by the general secretary of ILGALAC (International Lesbian, Gay, Bisexual, Trans and Intersex Association for Latin America and the Caribbean), as well as by the notable LGBTQ+ activists Gloria Careaga and Víctor Hugo Robles, from Mexico and Chile, respectively.[7] Chilean actress Daniela Vega was photographed with Castro riding a convertible car during the 2018 conga, which had the most participants to date, including the global company Google.[8]

Through Alpert's documentary lens—as if preaching a socialist gospel of equality and emancipation—Mariela Castro appears a savior journeying across the island, hearing the voices of sexual diversity and attempting to address the violent consequences of homophobia and transphobia. Although the film features a total of seven stories, the profiles are overshadowed by Castro's central narrative against machismo in favor of LGBTQ+ visibility and freedom. The prominence given to Mariela Castro's voyage, however, seems to conflate her own understanding of intimacy and belonging with that of the Cenesex's, especially in a scene showing Castro and her husband, the Italian entrepreneur Paolo Titolo, as they embark together on their campaign. From this depiction, the (heterosexual) family emerges not only as a preferred mode of intimate relationality but also as a central axis for Cenesex's LGBTQ+ activist agenda. In resonance with a gesture toward the institutionalization of a culture of heterosexuality, Cenesex, since 2014, also developed an awareness campaign around parenthood, known in Spanish as Jornadas de Maternidad y Paternidad: Iguales en Derechos y Responsabilidades. In its latest iteration, the event was planned around the theme "healthy limits of family education" (*educar con límites saludables*) with a series of workshops related to motherhood, fatherhood, and child development, from February to June 2020. As a framework for "a prosperous and sustainable socialist society," Mariela Castro fathoms authority as a practice of establishing "necessary" limits to ensure family care in contrast to authoritarianism, an arbitrary imposition of boundaries.[9]

A general discomfort around the public figure of Mariela Castro points to her purported view of the family through the eyes of a heterosexual (cis) woman, as well as to her personal ties with the revolution.[10] Nonetheless, she is consistent in her public policies in recognizing and defending the culture of heterosexuality as constitutive of a socialist culture of inclusion. On the topic, Castro explains that one of the conga's main objectives is "to sensitize the population and inform them that the family must be a place of love, inclusion and respect and not a place for discrimination" ("sensibilizar a la población e informarle que la familia debe ser un lugar de amor, de inclusión y de respeto y no un lugar de discriminación").[11] A critical intervention to understanding queer/trans relationality, intimacy, and politics in twenty-first-century Cuba must place Mariela Castro's public remarks within a larger constellation of Cuban acts attending to the public exposure of queer/trans bodies. The exceptionalism defining an emergent nationalist discourse at the turn of the twentieth century placed queer/trans people at the margins (Bejel 8). The discourses maintaining the "healthy limits" of a socialist society in Cuba have remained consistent with a paternalist gesture that places heterosexuality, and more evidently a traditional notion of family as nation, at the center of a politics of emotion around gender development (e.g., love, care, respect, motherhood, fatherhood, childhood) And yet as Bejel further argues, "Cuban nationhood has been defined, in part, by its rejection of gayness and queerness" and transness (xiv).

A distinct feature of Mariela Castro's discursive deployment of a healthy society, a reiteration of a socialist nationalism amid a global LGBTQ+ rights framework, rests on an emotional politics of the family as the basis for (socialist) belonging and intimacy, which prompts a material and affective breakdown between the public and private spheres. That is, the public inclusion of queer/trans relationality and intimacy is contingent upon espousing the heterosexual ideology embedded in Cenesex's socialist vision of the family. In other words, the legal recognition of queer/trans intimacy is tolerated inasmuch it resembles the structures of heterosexual relationality, centered on family reproductive life. Along this vein, if the Cuban political establishment's main concern was to annex queer/trans relationality under the law, same-sex marriage legislation would have been enshrined under the 2019 Cuban Constitution. The public debate around the referendum concerning Article 68 shows otherwise.[12] Yet, upon receiving the Maguey Activista Prize in LGBTQ+ activism at the 2017 International Film Festival in Guadalajara, Mexico, Mariela Castro stated that same-sex legislation is not Cenesex's only concern, but one among many seeking to achieve equality of opportunities for all sexual minorities ("la meta principal es la igualdad de oportunidades"). It was not until recently, after a sweeping referendum in 2022, that Cuba's family law code was amended to include same-sex marriage legislation. Considering her public views on the issue, it becomes clear that Mariela Castro's purported position in support of same-sex marriage is, at most, consistently ambiguous.

I engage in this comparison of Mariela Castro's seemingly incoherent statements to trace the tip of a political iceberg that is floating atop a sea of complexity impacting LGBTQ+ activism in Cuba today. As explicitly stated again and again by director Mariela Castro, Cenesex's public ambiguity is not only consistent with but also an extension of a long trajectory of biopolitical moves to protect the revolution's emancipatory force, one that has, again and again, debilitated queer/trans relationality and intimacy, as well as other strands of non-state-related activism. In the history of the Cuban Revolution, LGBTQ+ matters (e.g., individuals, collectives, practices, discourses, imaginaries) have been branded as ideologically divergent, counterrevolutionary, as having a distinctly queer capitalist ideology. In this sense, queer/trans relationality appears as a form of political dissidence, as if standing against the law, ready to attack the fundamental health of the revolution. But conceptualizing queer/trans relationality and intimacy as threats to the otherwise healthy body politic of socialist unity would undermine the agential vibrancy and political plasticity enacted through queer/trans practices.

Although Alpert's documentary looks to debunk Cold War imaginaries around Cuba that remain well and alive in the United States, I contend that assigning a central role to Mariela Castro's involvement in LGBTQ+ activism not only advances a rampant providentialism inherently present in the revolution's androcentric project but also exhibits Cenesex's consistent response in dealing with the public exposure of queer/trans bodies by means of their manipulated commodification. Simply put, the revolution, and by extension Cenesex, recognizes the rich potentiality of capital value found in LGBTQ+ matters. Alpert's HBO documentary is a case in point. Furthermore, the film underscores a socialist version of identity politics, as sexually transgressive practices and non-heterosexual cultures have often been associated more with a capitalist counterrevolutionary ideology than with alternative modes of intimacy. To a certain degree, Cenesex's programmatic development shows the continuing collapse between the public and private space, as well as the increasing commodification of queer/trans relationality and intimacy in a global stage. In the end, the lyrics of a queer song have already been captured by the Revolution's crumbling utopia; its beat includes the commercialized deployment of sexual diversity.

Track B: The Unauthorized Conga

Days before celebrating its twelfth annual Conga against Homophobia and Transphobia, scheduled to take the streets on May 11, 2019, Cenesex abruptly canceled an event that, according to the *Los Angeles Times*, "became an internationally lauded symbol of Cuba's acceptance of gay and transgender rights."[13] Since its inception in 1988 as an extension of the Cuban Women's Federation (FCM) and later as a dependency of the Ministry of Public Health (MINSAP), Cenesex has functioned as the sole institutional body regulating queer/trans public policy while funding gender confirmation surgeries and training to raise awareness on issues concerning gender and sexuality across the country. The sudden announcement took by surprise some of the closest collaborators within Cenesex's ranks. Journalist and Cenesex activist Francisco Rodríguez, also known as "Paquito el de Cuba," shared that the Conga represented an event of tremendous visibility for LGBTQ+ collectives, adding: "Tengo la tranquilidad de que nada ni nadie nos podrá regresar al closet, ni quiero ni puedo creer que alguien así lo pretenda" (I am at ease knowing that nothing or no one is putting us back in the closet, nor do I want to know or believe that anyone would want to do that). According to an official message about the cancellation on Facebook, Cenesex referred to "new tensions in the international and regional panorama" and their effect on everyday life and public policy in Cuba. The Marxist feminist Yasmín S. Portales-Machado argues that, although Cenesex's cancellation of the 2019 conga was sudden, there existed a series of factors that catalyzed the decision and the subsequent "conga crisis." Among these background elements, downplayed by the media, the author situates Cuba's constitutional referendum, including public debates around Articles 68 and 40—concerning marriage equality and discrimination, respectively—as well as contentions concerning the absence of the word *communist* from the drafts. Portales-Machado also mentions that one of the many tensions propelling the "conga crisis" rests on the increasingly public influence that Evangelical groups have had in issues concerning sexual rights and women's reproductive rights.[14]

Within hours of Cenesex's announcement on May 6, activists, artists, and LGBTQ+ groups circulated the idea of organizing an Alternative Conga through social media under the hashtag #LaMarchVa (Facebook, Twitter, and group chats). Following Cenesex's cancellation, it was a surprise to witness the invasion of the public space by an alternative LGBTQ+ Conga, which claimed the city without any formal support from the revolutionary establishment, which regulates and punishes the organization of massive gatherings, including protests, under the Ministry of Justice's Law No. 54.[15] Amid the echoing chants of "Sí se puede," "Cuba diversa," or "Lo más grande Cuba," around three hundred people marched along Old Havana's iconic Paseo del Prado. On journalist Luz Escobar's Twitter account, a video uploaded on May 11 at 4:18 p.m. shows a diverse group of people, including queer/trans activists and LGBTQ+ allies marching down Paseo del Prado while enthusiastically taking pictures and waving rainbow flags. The mood seems festive, and Escobar highlights the fact that LGBTQ+ people occupied Havana's streets in spite of several attempts by government security forces to intimidate protesters.[16]

Queer waves peacefully inundate El Prado's marbled runway. Flags, bodies, and sounds merge to create a public soundtrack, a remix of unicorns and rainbows. The march's chants bring to life queer fables of lost polychromatic unicorns, and queer music lights up the fire nested within the hearts of protesters. A queer fire sparks a sensual moving of bodies flowing through Malecón. As if chasing after a mythical creature, a police squad welcomes the marching crowd with batons and struggles to stop the parade. Deafening cries for help silence the festive beats of a queer soundtrack, as police sirens erupt the apparent stillness of Old Havana.

Newspaper *El País*'s YouTube channel features a video capturing the concatenation of events. Police forces publicly confronted activists at the intersection of Paseo del Prado and Malecón. At least three people were detained, states a reporter, before showing a police officer scorning protesters because, the policeman claims, they know about the illegality of the event.[17] On the day of the alternative conga, state security operatives harassed activist Jancel Moreno and two of his close relatives and detained activists Isbel Díaz Torres and Jimmy Roque for twenty-four hours. Event organizers Iliana Hernández, Boris González, Ariel Ruiz Urquiola, Óscar Casanella, and Yasmanny Sánchez were beaten and detained. Others were kidnapped days after by state police. In 2020, Iliana Hernández was charged with illegal possession of mobile journalism equipment.[18] The discussion sparked days, weeks, and a year after places less attention on whether the alternative conga had broken the law or not than on condemning the unnecessary display of state violence and police brutality, especially taking into consideration that Cenesex designed and implemented antidiscrimination training for state police forces. Whether or not Cenesex decided to cancel abruptly, the occupation of public space by LGBTQ+ collectives points not only to tangible digital practices for political organizing but also to a strong political sensibility and agency within LGBTQ+ collectives. As such, the exposure of queer/trans bodies at the alternative conga inscribes a series of embodied practices of agency, bringing more significance to the paradoxical relationship between the Cuban political establishment, mainly through Cenesex, and the vitality of LGBTQ+ practices in Havana today.

Alberto Roque Vega, a founding organizer of the Cuban Days against Homophobia and Transphobia, condenses the aftermath of May 11 into four main points: an existing critical mass of LGBTQ+ activists, a close resemblance of both congas to a neoliberal and classist parade, a political pendulum in LGBTQ+ public policy, and a milestone in Cuban LGBTQ+ activism.[19] Whereas Yasmín S. Portales-Machado points out the different entanglements leading to the unauthorized conga and the display of state violence in dealing with the public exposure of queer/trans bodies, Roque Vega outlines the political significance of the event in terms of collective agency. Both coincide in the pivotal role of digital practices in shaping a robust LGBTQ+ cyberactivism.

Thus far, I have traced the multiple media objects describing two detonating events in the recent history of queer/trans exposure in Cuban public space. With no intention to echo a queer heroism or a queer whitewash, I highlight some of the practices that build a queer/trans public sphere in twenty-first-century Cuba following these events: a queer digital network, capacity for spatial mobilization, capital value, and critical agency outside governmental institutions. Before I turn to analyzing the formation of this novel public sphere, I think with TransCuba's trans activists and their strategic (dis)engagements with Cenesex. I briefly conceptualize the notion of conga as queer moving, an embodied practice of everyday survival for queer/trans collectives in Cuba.

Conga as Queer Moving

A complex embodiment of transculturation can be traced in Santiago de Cuba's rich carnival formations. In this scenario, *congas* are neighborhood-based musical ensembles composed of bass drums led by a soloist *corneta china*, a reed instrument introduced in Cuba in the nineteenth century by Chinese immigrants. Conga calls on popular participation not only of neighbors but also of passersby who dance to a specific type of movement: *arrollando* (Milstein 247; Wirtz 62). Conga's *arrollando*, or rolling along, involves a circular movement of the hips, following a side-to-side motion. While conducting ethnographic work in Santiago, the performance practitioner Liani Milstein vividly described a sensorium around *conga*:

A few moments later I saw a wave of people come up over the top of a hill. As they came closer, my friend pulled us into the procession and off we went, carried down the street by the mass of people. Sweaty bodies pressed up against my own, squirming in sync with a music that I had definitely never heard before. I felt like I was being carried through the streets on a conveyor belt, as if there were a great force driving us all as we wiggled in unison to the relentless thumping and clanging of that rhythm. After we pulled ourselves out of the group, I collected myself and asked, "What was that?" "That," my friend answered, "was a conga." (224)

Milstein's account brings forward not only a sense of moving but also a material, tactful effervescence embodied through the collective practice of conga: "a wave of . . . sweaty bodies," "a great force driving us all," or "the relentless thumping and clanging." Conga emerges as a rhythmic assemblage of bodies, sensations, chants, and moves, distributed across a particular time and space, emerging momentarily as a force of vitality. More than inscribing an epistemology, a way of knowing, into the material confines of the body, conga responds to a queer relationality, a way of being and interacting, a queer intimacy oscillating like a pendulum, from side to side, running through the open streets, through the everyday cartographies of "poverty, racism, violence and other forms (old and new) of social inequality" (43), as Roberto Zurbano poignantly phrased it.

In retooling Fernando Ortiz's notion of transculturation as a means to understand the temporal and spatial dimensions of racialization in Santiago's carnival performances, Kristina Wirtz uses the phrase "fractal belonging" to refer the "processes of convergence and differentiation at any spatial or temporal scale" (61) in arguing for racial mobilities as undercurrents shaping Blackness in Cuba. Fractal belonging also incorporates Wirtz's notion of micromobilities, or "people's movements through their immediate lived space" (59). This conceptualization of movement is contingent on various affective trajectories, intersecting at the performance of conga, which is not a "folkloric" rendition of transculturation but a complex process of negotiation, between "convergence and differentiation." This strategic dance also primes struggles of everyday survival for queer/trans collectives in Havana as they move through various affective formations of racial, gendered, or sexual belonging, so as to become (il)legible subjects of Cuban socialism. Nonetheless, this process of negotiation is not one that occurs, as Zurbano notes, in the lettered city or within the hermeneutical cage of political rhetoric; rather, it occurs as ephemeral acts electrifying bodies, spaces, sensations, and matter (44).

By staging an alternative conga, these material entanglements and everyday negotiations become visible practices that can be traced in online news articles, Facebook and Twitter posts, blog posts, and video recordings. The indexicality of the digital, however, is an intrinsic element of these practices that also depends on other trajectories, such as economic, racial, spatial, and gendered ones. In the case of Milstein's vivid description of a Santiago conga, the movement of bodies brings forward a festive pulse guiding the occupation of public space.

On an empty street of the city of Cárdenas, about 116 kilometers east of Havana, a blank wall stands with an inscription: "Da lo mismo ganar que perder, lo importante es el juego" (winning or losing doesn't matter, what is important is the game). A plaque marking the birthplace of the Cuban queer playwright and poet Virgilio Piñera serves as a stark reminder of one of the defining characteristics of queer/trans relationality and intimacy: playfulness and its situatedness in relation to historical processes of racialization, sexualization, politization, and commodification. Even in the lettered archive of queer Cuban literature, playfulness has affected the formation of a queer poetics of play.[20] In the case of the alternative conga, a sense of playfulness also flows out of a queer moving through public space. To invoke the notion of queer moving means to label conga as an embodied practice emerging from LGBTQ+ collectives in response to governmental biopolitical tactics of dealing with the public exposure of queer/trans practices of intimacy.

These festive pulsations playfully drive queer/trans relationality as a mode of intimacy, that is, as a way of connecting with others and with an immediate material environment. The gravitational force of queer/trans play, which also blurs the distinction between private and public, is also a dance between life and death, as the very exposure of certain queer/trans bodies, as seen in the alternative conga, detonate violent acts to contain their public display. As seen in the *El País* video showing a state police response, these alternative queer acts are deemed "illegal," signaling that a festive gathering can be tolerated in public only so long as it is organized and regulated by Cenesex, a branch of the Cuban political establishment. In this sense, a queer moving condensed in conga is a side-to-side public movement, a moving that involves the exposure of queer/trans bodies and mimics the pendular politics of LGBTQ+ policy in Havana. As queer moving, conga is part of a sensuous repertoire inscribed in the bodily practices of queer/trans collectives as they mediate the violence associated with their visibility while intervening in the public sphere. This bodily negotiation for survival is also a material practice—in the case of the alternative conga, it incorporates flags, chants, streets, objects, and other elements shaping a queer ecology in Cuba.

Trans Engagements

Created in 2001 as a space to promote social awareness, HIV prevention workshops, and family counseling, TransCuba is a Cenesex-sponsored social network of approximately three thousand members across the country.[21] As of 2016, Malu Calabrara has worked with Cenesex and its director Mariela Castro to run the TransCuba network,[22] which organizes a series of social activities for trans intimacy and conviviality at local and regional levels, including weekly meetings, outings, and an annual gala in which all chapters convene. Although TransCuba follows a top-down structure, with Cenesex at its apex, many of the local activities and workshops organized follow the needs of its members. As part of a community-based academic initiative, I traveled to Cuba during the summer of 2017 to collaborate with members of the TransCuba network in Havana and Matanzas and create a digital archive for trans storytelling.[23] In Havana, Nomi Ramírez and Angeline Llorente agreed to form part of this collaboration, as did Sandra Díaz and Vanessa Vega Alfonsi in Matanzas. Due to limited time and resources, we were able to assemble and complete the digital stories only of the two TransCuba members in Havana: Nomi Ramírez and Angeline Llorente. A third digital story was completed with the collaboration of former TransCuba member, Sisi Montiel, an independent trans activist in charge of running the activist network TransFantasía and the Cuban Alliance against HIV/AIDS.[24]

Here, more than centering on discussing the deployment of digital storytelling and digital ethnography, I want to focus on the testimonies of these five trans women in deciding whether to interact with TransCuba, an official network for trans intimacy and space for political trans action. I would like to tune in to a form of "political listening" (Alexandra 43) not only to attend to a collaborative form of knowledge production but also to suggest a critical stance to situate their real-life experiences that bring, as Sisi Montiel puts it, "una sabiduría interna," an internal wisdom, a dynamic force of agency guiding their everyday life, a conga of negotiation, situating the prefix *trans* as a relationality to trans world making.

Originally from Havana, Nomi Ramírez is a TransCuba member who works as an executive assistant at Cenesex's headquarters. A former sex worker, she shares having gone through the many stages any trans woman would usually live through, such as confronting discrimination ("Ha sido una experiencia con todos los matices posibles, desde cosas malas pasando por cosas regulares a cosas buenas por la normalidad de toda la vida de toda chica trans"). She adds that there is a clear pattern of inequality facing trans collectives worldwide ("Creo que realmente hay un patrón de desigualdad que es mundial hacia las personas trans en general"). A sense of hope for Nomi Ramírez means tranquility, peace, and a better future, as she highlights a trans history of marginalization and violence in Cuba:

Esperanza: tranquilidad, paz, un futuro mejor. La esperanza de que, a lo mejor, no en un futuro más inmediato, pero sí en un futuro más a largo plazo, mejoren las condiciones de vida, en especial, quiero que mejoren las de todos, pero en especial para las personas de nuestra comunidad que a través de tanto tiempo hemos sido tan marginadas, tan violentadas, tan olvidadas incluso; especialmente las trans hemos sido muy invisibilizadas.

For Nomi Ramírez, Cenesex has played a pivotal role in the fight for LGBTQ+ recognition, providing her with a sense of hope:

Te digo ahorita y lo mantengo que contamos con el apoyo de esa institución que es el Cenesex. Y que yo te puedo decir que hay un antes y un después y que de verdad es como una luz, un rayo de esperanza; es una guía, es algo que de verdad ayuda en general a todos los miembros de la comunidad LGBT que es el Cenesex. Sí, creo que hay un antes y un después de la labor que realiza esa institución en nuestro país.

Although Cenesex has helped advance a public debate on LGBTQ+ topics, and more notably on trans matters, Ramírez insists on the importance of having a job that ensures her everyday life. As such, her sense of happiness is closely related to her ability to hold an "honorable" job: "Yo soy feliz de estar trabajando [. . .] pero siento que todo ser humano merece la oportunidad de acceder a un trabajo digno, de estudiar, de llevar una vida tranquila para poder tener un mejor futuro, incluso un mejor presente." Her shared story points to the complexities of labor facing trans women in Havana, and in Cuba. According to Nomi Ramírez, a good-paying job is the foundation for a good quality of life, particularly taking into consideration the current cost of living in Cuba amid the collapse of a two-currency economic system. More importantly, she highlights an inevitable reality marking trans bodies in public space: sex work. Although Cuban law does not consider sex work illegal, police officers arbitrarily target trans women working at night when patrolling the streets. On this topic, Angeline Llorente, a trans woman who has resided in Havana since 2011 while being an activist for TransCuba, explains that she likes engaging in "sexo transaccional," or transactional sex, as a means for economic sustenance. She shares her reasons for moving from the province of Granma, in the east, to Havana, as there are more economic opportunities in the capital city:

Soy mujer trans, soy de provincia del país, de la provincia de Granma. Hace seis años vivo en La Habana. Ahora en estos momentos no tengo empleo laboral por cuestiones que he tenido. Soy licenciada en laboratorio clínico y en estos momentos mi trabajo es ejercer la prostitución. Es una experiencia muy fuerte. A la vez, no es fácil, pero bueno, pero me gusta también ejercer la prostitución. Aunque yo tuviese de todo, yo ejercería la prostitución porque me gusta, es una de las cuestiones que siempre me ha gustado.

Llorente moved to Havana for a number of reasons, including a form of discrimination at home that forced her moving out: "Yo vivía con mi familia, pero cuando empecé con los cambios de la transexualidad de mi casa me botó mi abuela. Me dijo que así vestida de mujer no podía estar y ya y decidí venir hacia La Habana a hacer vida porque me habían dicho que en La Habana las muchachas trans tenían más posibilidades, que las personas te aceptaban más." She notes that in the eastern provinces of the island, "existe más el machismo todavía." Once in Havana, she joined Cenesex's medical consultations for three years and at the time was awaiting gender confirmation surgery, a cost-free procedure: "Gracias al Cenesex nosotros podemos tener un cambio de sexo, podemos cambiarnos de nombre. Cualquier problema que tengamos, el Cenesex nos apoya. El Cenesex ha ganado mucho con las Jornadas de la Homofobia, libre de discriminación en los centros de trabajo, en las escuelas."

While Angeline Llorente mentions Cenesex's efforts in fighting trans discrimination in Havana, Sandra Díaz and Vanessa Vega Alfonsi, TransCuba members in the city of Matanzas, are critical of Cenesex's efforts fighting workplace discrimination. In particular, Díaz, a trained dancer, has been turned down from several auditions because her official documents mark her gender as "male":

El Cenesex no me ha dado ningún tipo de solución a este caso; lo he planteado ya varias veces y no me han dado ningún tipo de solución. Solamente me han dicho que yo vaya a lugares donde yo haga la audición y si no me dan respuesta o no me hacen caso, no me prestan atención, yo anoté el nombre de la persona que me atendió, el nombre del hotel, el nombre del jefe de animación y que yo lo llevé para La Habana.

Sandra Díaz has traveled abroad, and her experiences outside Cuba have given her a different perspective about what it means to be a trans woman in

Matanzas, as she mentions, "Cada cual elige su modo de vida en dependencia de lo que tú puedas hacer si tienes un oficio, si tienes una profesión, si tu cabeza te da o no te da, eso depende de la persona," while affirming her agency as an individual: "Yo soy yo. Yo soy Sandra." Having engaged in sex work in the past, her critical view of Cenesex stems not only from her inability to work as a dancer but also from a lack of local services addressing concerns about work, housing, health access, and discrimination:

Aquí mismo en Matanzas tenemos una coordinadora, ok. Es la coordinadora porque ese es el nombre que se le da, porque le dieron ese cargo, pero ahora de momento, yo quiero ir a donde está ella para que ella me ayude a resolver este problema, y ¿a dónde ella va a ir? ¿Dónde está el juez? ¿Dónde está el jurídico? ¿Dónde hay un abogado? Que tú puedas tocar [en la puerta] del presidente aquí del gobierno de la ciudad de Matanzas, a través de él, que él llame a La Habana y diga que sí que el centro me apoya en una carta y que sí soy un transexual, y [que] yo estoy diagnosticada como transexual. Y no hay nada de eso. No tenemos ni siquiera un local para sentarnos todas a hablar nuestros problemas, no solamente de trabajo, de la familia, de las casas, del estudio. No tenemos un local ni siquiera donde podamos nosotras sentarnos a decir "bueno, hay esta situación." Para las enfermedades, porque casi todas estamos diagnosticadas, somos seropositivas.

Although Sandra Díaz actively participates in local TransCuba activities, she and Vanessa Vega Alfonsi along with other trans women get together regularly to air their frustrations. But as Díaz phrases it, "Por mucho que hablemos entre nosotras, no tenemos el poder, ni siquiera verbal, para tú poder avanzar." While Díaz discusses the complexities of everyday survival, Vanessa Vega Alfonsi describes her experiences of discrimination, particularly as they relate to Matanzas's nightlife: "Es un poco difícil porque en la provincia de Matanzas los únicos que no nos golpean mucho, no es menos cierto, es la policía. La policía con nosotros no . . . pero con los heteros en las fiestas [sí nos golpean] . . . y eso es un poco difícil. No hago vida social como tal con los heteros ni de ir a la discoteca con los heteros, simple y llanamente. Lo que tenemos [es] Las Ruinas los fines de semana." Las Ruinas is an LGBTQ+ nightclub housed in the ruins of a nineteenth-century warehouse, on the Matanzas bay. The cost to access the dance club is usually 3 CUC, or 75 pesos. Although Vega Alfonsi sees a grim future for trans women in Matanzas, it is true that they have managed to build their own collectives of care independently to the state's already-limited resources. Their way of organizing does not mimic TransCuba's structures but rather emerges as a shared need to provide support to one another in a spontaneous and unregulated fashion:

Aquí el futuro es negro. Aquí futuro no tenemos ninguna, indiscutiblemente. No tenemos nada. No podemos trabajar. No podemos ir a un hospital a decir, "queremos transformarnos." No tenemos cómo conseguir hormonas, tenemos que automedicarnos para poder lograr una feminización. No tenemos nada. Y yo creo que por el camino que vamos no hay ninguna esperanza, yo no veo ninguna esperanza.

Originally from the countryside, Vega Alfonsi was brought to Matanzas by her mother to become a dancer, but as in the case of Sandra Díaz, she has been unsuccessful in achieving that. Vega Alfonsi describes a specific way of animating trans intimacy, of getting acquitted and of socializing, but also situates *travestismo*, and particularly, putting on makeup and dressing up, as a practice through which a trans identity is accomplished:

Ellas cuando salen, salen siendo gay normal, pajaritas. Entonces, tú las ves porque hacen más afinidad con las trans que con los gays normales, que se visten de varón. Y entonces, empiezan "¡Ay! ¿mañana puedo ir por tu casa? Maquíllame. Déjame ver cómo me veo." Entonces hoy se maquillan, como le pasó a esta. Hoy se maquillan: "Ay sí, sí luzco bien, ¿viste? Ay, mañana voy a dar una vueltecita." Y entonces así sucesivamente ellas empiezan poquito hasta que van cogiendo confianza. "Y sí te ves bien, y sí te ves bien, y sí te ves bien," hasta que ya se quedan en el mundo este de la transexualidad y del travestismo.

Vega Alfonsi's story articulates a *travesti* critique of an essentialist idea of gender by highlighting the material practices shaping an ethics of care (Rizki 151), as well as a performance of gender-based trans intimacy. Although relying on a particular notion of spectacular femininity, a "travesti-pajarita" alliance—that is, an affinity between trans women and effeminate gay men—is materially articulated through an understanding of femininity as a continuum, which powerfully assembles a sense of empathy amid an uncertain future. Vega Alfonsi further adds that whatever she has achieved in life has come at great expense: "Lo poquito que he logrado lo he conseguido con bastante sacrificio. Y entonces, eso me hace sentir triunfadora en la vida porque, como te expliqué, aquí nosotras las trans no tenemos ningún futuro y son muy pocas las que pueden lograr pequeñas cosas por decirlo de alguna manera." As a "triunfadora," a victorious survivor, Vanessa's story recalibrates Cenesex's triumphalist narrative about an unfinished sexual revolution: "Sí ha habido un cambio, pero, en realidad, necesitamos mucho más." Sandra Díaz also revises Cenesex's narrative by revealing the material precarity defining trans life in Matanzas, as she questions the actual impact same-sex marriage legislation would have on any improvement in their living conditions. For Díaz, same-sex marriage is still a social contract based on the accumulation of capital, and one that privileges economically established gay men: "Porque hay familias que a lo mejor tienen la posibilidad de que la pareja tiene una casa y se han comprado cosas y tienen buen trabajo, OK. Pero eso es la minoría. No todos los gays tienen dinero, ni tienen una buena carrera, ni tienen un buen trabajo ni todos trabajan en Varadero, que es el lugar aquí en Matanzas donde se obtiene el dinero."

Back in Havana, a space perceived as an economic silo for trans survival, independent activist and HIV/AIDS community worker Sisi Montiel also maintains a critical view of Cenesex's treatment of trans people and their public exposure. Although Sisi recognizes Cenesex's work in bringing trans issues to light, she notes that there is no open working agenda; that is, trans women's involvement in developing institutional policies alongside revolutionary institutions is not transparent, as it usually involves an ideological negotiation some trans women would rather not engage in. Montiel fathoms trans activism as an everyday practice that promotes trans empowerment through a systematic approach to tackle societal stigmatization and stereotyping on a daily basis, not through a one-day display of diversity, as Cenesex would have it. In accounting for a complexity of experiences, Montiel explains the multiple obstacles facing trans women in Cuba, whose life expectancy averages between forty and fifty years of age:

La transexualidad en Cuba hoy en día se vive con mucho temor, con muchos riesgos. Muchas de las mujeres trans de otras provincias emigran a la capital para tener un mejor nivel de vida económico ejerciendo el trabajo de la prostitución, cosa que solo conlleva a enfermedades, violaciones, detenciones arbitrarias, sanciones policiales. No es aceptable. Somos una comunidad dentro de la comunidad LGBTQ+ que somos muy marginadas, que no somos aceptadas. A pesar de que somos muy rebeldes, somos muy valientes. Ser una mujer trans en Cuba es ser valiente.

According to Montiel's story, a trans woman's life is defined by multiple public risks related to sex work, police harassment and discrimination, double marginalization within LGBTQ+ collectives, limited employment opportunities, and economic hardship in a mostly homophobic and *machista* country. Yet again, as in the case of Vanessa Vega Alfonsi, Montiel underscores the courage that trans women embody as a force shaping their practices of everyday survival. In this sense, Sisi Montiel refers to "una sabiduría interna," an internal wisdom guiding trans people's multiple negotiations: "sabemos que tenemos algo de alguna sabiduría interna que no podemos ejercerla porque nunca la hemos estudiado, eso le pasa a la mayoría de las mujeres trans, tanto a mujeres como hombres trans."

In thinking with the notion of an internal wisdom emerging from trans people's everyday experiences, and specifically of trans women, trans activism in Havana and Matanzas simultaneously includes and transcends a fight for legal rights and recognition. Trans discrimination is multiple, ranging from unequal access to jobs to arbitrary police discrimination and social harassment by heterosexual men and women, passing through a double marginalization within LGBTQ+ collectives, including social stigmatization. The predominance of sex work as a means to achieve economic independence not only defines a trans politics of life and death but also *should* define the design and implementation of labor laws ensuring protection for this type of erotic economy in Cuba. Trans and *travesti* women in Cuba engage in various practices of negotiation that modulate their public exposure and define their relationship with the state and society at large. Thinking with trans women's everyday experiences, a trans relationality emerges as a practice for survival, placing trans activism in Havana and Matanzas as a constant process of engagement and disengagement. A strategic mediation is at the core of a trans wisdom. In tune with a queer conga, as oscillating body movements spontaneously choreographing a sexual formation, many trans women transform Cenesex's vision of activism by doubly and constantly engaging in and disengaging out of a politics of life and death through their bodies, identities, and practices, modulating their public self-exposure. Although Cenesex-driven initiatives, such as TransCuba, certainly promote trans conviviality under the heteronormative sign of Cuban socialism, trans women's everyday practices define their own agential capacity to fight for legal recognition, while triumphantly surviving everyday violence in Cuba.

Queer Havana Nights

A year after the beginning of the Cuban thaw, the warming of Cuba-US relations in December 2014, the gay travel agency ALandChuck.travel announced its "first gay cruise in history" to sail Cuban shores. Departing from Montego Bay, Jamaica, the cruise sailed three times during 2016, on January 15, February 26, and April 8. The eight-day and seven-night cruise visited Santiago de Cuba, María la Gorda, and Cienfuegos, offering a two-day stay in Havana. Operated by Celestyal Cruise Lines, a Greek travel company, the cruise hired on-board event organizers who were gay Cubans, including entertainment managers who had worked for the Cuban Ministry of Tourism (MINTUR) and college graduates from the University of Havana and University of Pinar del Río Law School. These specialists gave travelers an experience "with a gay twist," by leading on-board cultural activities and guided tours in every Cuban port.[25] Often characterized as mysterious and enigmatic, queer culture in Cuba is more a product of a global market wanting to sell a sexualized tropicality than a material reality—that is, the image of a tropical paradise with unlimited sex possibilities for homoerotic desire. Although it is a common misconception to assume that gay tourism before the Cuban thaw did not exist, the reemergence of Cuba in the US imaginary also marked the state's commodification of sexual diversity in the age of global capitalism. The involvement of Cuba's MINTUR in responding to commercial demands for "gay travel specialists" offers a case in point, as it illustrates a state disposition for pursuing a capitalism in drag. The sale of a sexualized tropicality is transforming the precarity defining LGBTQ+ collectives, which become purchasable objects of desire ready for consumption.

In late 2018, John Bolton, then national security adviser for the Trump administration, announced a series of policies to deal with the governments of Cuba, Bolivia, and Venezuela, countries he referred to as "the Troika of Tyranny in this Hemisphere."[26] Whereas the Cuban thaw did not eliminate the embargo on Cuba, the Trump administration's abrupt rollback of diplomatic relations further prolonged a long-standing Cold War framework for US hemispheric policies. In response to Trump's foreign policy toward Cuba, including heightened travel restrictions, Cuba's most famous trans activist and cabaret performer, Imperio, simply said: "Lift the embargo."

The British online newspaper the *Independent* featured Imperio's political message in a news article published a couple of weeks after Bolton's tyrannical characterization of Cuba's socialist government.[27] The article includes a personal interview with Imperio and describes her cabaret performance, "showcasing equality and tolerance three times a week" at a state-run nightclub. Las Vegas, a name alluding to America's Sin City, is located in Vedado, a short walk away from the intersection of San Lázaro and Infanta. As in the case of John Alpert's HBO documentary, this online article highlights Mariela Castro's effort in leading "a rainbow revolution" while connecting economic prosperity with progress in the LGBTQ+ community and constitutional reforms in Cuba. By threading issues of economic trade together with a vision of LGBTQ+ affairs, the featured interview with Imperio echoes the Cuban Revolution's message, labeling the United States as sole actor responsible for the lack of economic reform. The popular transgender drag queen, who is close to Cenesex, also suggests that this absence of economic changes translates into a lack of legislation protecting LGBTQ+ rights on the island. What the article fails to mention is a closer description of the nightlife practices in which young Cubans engage as a means to achieve forms of "economic prosperity" within the complexity of LGBTQ+ politics.

On a typical night, the cabaret Las Vegas opens its doors at around 10 p.m. After passing through a heavy inspection of club bouncers, patrons visit a ticket stand to pay 5 CUC, or 125 pesos, to get in, dance, and party. Las Vegas' outside entrance is usually surrounded by a multitude of attractive young Cuban men who strike up casual conversation with gay strangers. Also known as "pingueros," or male sex workers, young Cuban men gravitate toward Las Vegas looking for a good time and to ensure financial means to provide for their families.[28] Inside the warehouse-looking bar, neon lights mark the lines of a long bar displaying copious amounts of rum, a huge dance floor, tables, chairs, and a large stage, often populated by exotic dancers. Indeed, Imperio is getting ready for the show, while being interviewed by a reporter, a *yuma*, wanting to see beyond a display of sexualized topicality. My queer friends Ulises Quintana de Armas, Norge Espinosa Mendoza, and George Henson joined the host of queer clubgoers, trying to dodge the propositions made by a young escort. On our way to our table, we pay attention to the familiar faces of a crowd entering the bar: some of the young guys from outside, a street bookseller, two gay Canadian retirees, an older Swiss pilot, and a Princeton professor.[29] Everyone has come in to see the cabaret show. The emcee pays tribute to Cenesex's representatives in the crowd. An institutionalized fight for LGBTQ+ legal rights seems to have infiltrated one of the most liberating experiences of queer desire: nightlife. What is not evident, what is ephemeral (echoing José Esteban Muñoz), is but the traces of a once-present queer act, inundating Havana streets. The time of nightlife also blurs the limits containing physical space; the night is also a force of life out in the streets.

The privatization of nightlife—that is, of the queer right to pleasure and leisure—runs counterintuitive to the public defense of same-sex marriage legislation, ambiguously espoused by Mariela Castro's Cenesex. Along with sex work and its demands for legalization, nightlife is a constitutive part of nighttime practices shaping queer/trans intimacy. While leaving Las Vegas, we notice the night draws its indistinct shadows. Shadows of queer ephemera bear witness of a nightly public act. We barely notice them, as we barely noticed the many nights when trans women in Havana were captured and taken into custody by state police while peacefully leaving nightclubs. A couple of days after we met for her interview, Angeline Llorente was detained and taken into custody for two nights for "posing a public threat" while walking the streets at night. The marginalization of trans life dwells in the plane of shadows, coyly emerging as unintelligible zones of queer/trans contact disrupting socialist heteronormativity, as in the alternative conga. The public exposure of queer/trans bodies in Cuba oscillates between visibility and invisibility, legality and illegality, public control and foreign ownership; it is a complicated dance between a sexualized tropicality and a material precarity. The encounters referred to in this article are shadows that attest to the shifting dynamics marking a queer moving, a queer Cuban conga, whose rhythms follow the selfish acts of a pink unicorn blissfully dancing inside a public bathroom.

NOTES

I would like to thank Dr. Tania Lizarazo, associate professor in the Department of Modern Languages, Linguistics, and Intercultural Communication, and faculty member in the Global Studies Program at the University of Maryland, Baltimore, for sharing with me Pedro Lemebel's unicorn chronicles, which map the transgressive character of sexual culture in Latin/x America, as well as to Dr. María A. Gutiérrez Bascón, postdoctoral researcher in the Department of Cultures at the University of Helsinki, for welcoming my contribution to the dossier on twenty-first-century Havana while providing me with insight into the development of this article.

1. In his chronicle "Silvio Rodríguez (o el mal entendido del 'unicornio azul')," the queer Chilean writer Pedro Lemebel writes about a brief encounter he had with Cuban musician Silvio Rodríguez on his first tour to Argentina during the 1980s. Lemebel states to Rodríguez that gay people in Chile have appropriated his song, in particular the image of "the blue unicorn," as a queer symbol that represents a lost and impossible love. The Cuban musician replied in anger and expressed his pity at this reinterpretation of his song. At his concert, as Rodríguez started to play "Unicorn," Lemebel and his friend suddenly left the stadium; they no longer identified with Rodríguez's lost unicorn. They hoped to find their lost unicorns elsewhere, prancing around public bathrooms and city parks. I reimagine Lemebel's unicorn in pink as a poetic image symbolizing queerness.

2. In *Fiesta de diez pesos: Music and Gay Identity in Special Period Cuba* (2014), Moshe Morad examines the role of music in the formation of an underground gay intimacy, known as *ambiente*, in Cuba from 1995 to 2007. In this powerful ethnography, Moshe argues that music shapes the physical, emotional and conceptual contours of a hybrid gay identity during the Special Period. Similarly, I examine an overflow of a queer intimacy in public.

3. In 1961, Cuban state intelligence implemented a campaign targeting citizens accused of being pedophiles, prostitutes or pimps. Known as Operación P, these alleged criminals were arrested and forced into rehabilitation. In *Retrato de familia con Fidel* (1981), Carlos Franqui, former director of the official newspaper *Revolución*, was the first to publish about the incident (Sierra Madero et al. 30).

4. Since 2008, Cenesex has provided free hormonal treatment, gender confirmation surgery, and HIV medication for transgender people.

5. On May 17, 1990, the World Health Organization announced its decision to "declassify homosexuality as a mental disorder." It was not until 2009 that the term *transphobia* was added to the international fight against homophobia. See "International Day against Homophobia, Transphobia and Biphobia," World Health Organization, May 17, 2017, www.who.int/life-course/news/events/intl-day-against-homophobia/en/.

6. "Conga cubana contra la homophobia y la transfobia mañana en La Habana." *Juventud Rebelde*, May 13, 2016, www.juventudrebelde.cu/cuba/2016-05-13/conga-cubana-contra-la-homofobia-y-la-transfobia-manana-en-la-habana.

7. "Cuba, a ritmo de conga contra la homofobia." *The International Lesbian, Gay, Bisexual, Trans and Intersex Association*, May 12, 2014, ilga.org/cuba-a-ritmo-de-conga-contra-la-homofobia.

8. "La actriz Daniela Vega también arrolló en la Conga Cuba contra la Homofobia y la Transfobia (+Fotos)." *Vistar Magazine*, May 14, 2018, vistarmagazine.com/la-actriz-daniela-vega-tambien-arrollo-la-conga-cubana-la-homofobia-la-transfobia-fotos/.

9. All quotes are in reference to a news post from the Cuban Ministry of Public Health's website: "'Educar con límites saludables': 7ma Edición de Las Jornadas de Maternidad y Paternidad. Iguales en derecho y responsabilidades," MINSAP, February 15, 2020, https://salud.msp.gob.cu/educar-con-limites-saludables-7ma-edicion-de-las-jornadas-de-maternidad-y-paternidad-iguales-en-derechos-y-responsabilidades/.

10. Mariela Castro is the daughter of Raúl Castro, first secretary of the Communist Party of Cuba and former president of Cuba, and niece of late Fidel Castro, former prime minister and president of Cuba. She holds an MA in sexuality and a PhD in sociology.

11. According to a Radio Televisión Martí's article on Cenesex, Mariela Castro understands the central role of family dynamics in shaping LGBTQ+ diversity and inclusion. "Cuba: una conga para luchar contra la homofobia," *Radio Televisión Martí*, May 11, 2013, www.radiotelevision marti.com/a/cuba-cenesex-conga-homofobia/22436.html.

12. "Cuba aparca la ley del matrimonio gay," *El País*, December 22, 2018, elpais.com/internacional/2018/12/21/actualidad/1545420601_228519.html.

13. "Cuba Cancels Its Annual Gay Rights Parade, 'Conga against Homophobia,'" *Los Angeles Times*, May 7, 2010, www.latimes.com/world/la-fg-cuba-cancels-gay-rights-parade-20190507-story.html.

14. See Yasmín S. Portales-Machado's article in *Dissent*: "The LGBTIQ March on Havana," *Dissent Magazine*, September 11, 2019, www.dissentmagazine.org/online_articles/the-lgbtiq-march-on-havana.

15. This law is intended to regulate the right to freedom of association recognized to all Cuban citizen under the Constitution. See Flavio Bravo Pardo, "Ley de Asociaciones," *Asamblea Popular del Poder Popular*, December 17, 1985, www.parlamentocubano.gob.cu/index.php/documento/ley-de-asociaciones/.

16. Luz Escobar is an independent journalist for the online news media outlet www.14ymedio.com. This video can be found in her twitter account, @Luz_Cuba: https://twitter.com/Luz_Cuba/status/1127307038340476928.

17. "Al menos tres detenidos en el desfile LGBTI de La Habana," YouTube, uploaded by *El País*, May 13, 2019, www.youtube.com/watch?time_continue=2&v=riZbmT0f6Fs&feature=emb_logo.

18. This is according to the Committee to Protect Journalism in New York City. See "Cuban reporter Iliana Hernández charged with illegally possessing journalistic equipment," Committee to Protect Journalists, January 28, 2020, cpj.org/2020/01/cuban-reporter-iliana-hernandez-charged-with-illeg/.

19. This was posted on May 13, 2019, a couple of days after the clash between LGBTQ+ activists and state police during the Unauthorized Conga. Alberto Roque Guerra, "Sobre el 11M, nuestros derechos y desafíos," Facebook, May 13, 2019, www.facebook.com/alberto.roqueguerra/posts/10216753741228881.

20. Virgilio Piñera's sensual fractality in *La isla en peso* (1941), the queer neobaroque of José Lezama Lima, Severo Sarduy, and Reinaldo Arenas, as well as the literature of Jorge Ángel Pérez, Norge Espinosa, Alberto Abreu, Pedro de Jesús López, Roxana Rojo, Ena Lucía Portela, Achy Obejas, Anna Lidia Vega Serova, Sonia Rivera Valdés, Zoé Valdés, and Wendy Guerra, among many other women and queer/trans writers, point to this playfulness in the representation of queer/trans desire as the basis for intimacy.

21. *TransDebate* is an official blog of the activist network *TransCuba*. See "TransCuba por los derechos sexuales." *TransDebate*, August 15, 2011, www.transcuba.wordpress.com/2011/08/15/por-derechos-sexuales/.

22. Rebecca Sananes, "TransCuba Network: The Activist Network for Trans Rights," Pulitzer Center, May 9, 2016, www.pulitzercenter.org/reporting/transcuba-activist-network-trans-rights.

23. These stories are part of a larger online repository of trans archives, *Queer Utopias* (https://www.queerutopias.org), from Mexico and Cuba funded by University of California's Humanities Institute through the Mellon Public Scholars Fellowship. Featuring the profile of trans activists and cultural workers, this online archive resorts to the community-based practice of digital storytelling, refashioned to imagine a transfeminism that foregrounds its praxis on the affective deployment of vulnerability to foster collaborations that move beyond spaces (e.g., academia, government, popular culture). This transfeminist practice of digital storytelling seeks to democratize the access to practices of knowledge production, while empowering storytellers by insisting on the understanding of lived experience as a strand of embodied knowledge.

24. These organizations, including TransFantasía, form part of a larger network of independent groups of activists known as Macroproyecto Manos. See Mario J. Pentón, "Movimiento alternativo reta hegemonía de Mariela Castro sobre la comunidad LGBTI," *El Nuevo Herald*, June 3, 2017, www.elnuevoherald.com/noticias/mundo/america-latina/cuba-es/article154226054.html. Some of the initiatives are funded by Caribe Afirmativo (https://caribeafirmativo.lgbt/quienes-somos/), a regional NGO that serves as a watchdog for LGBTQ+ rights in the Caribbean.

210 : DAVID TENORIO

25. For more information about this gay cruise, see Ozgur Tore, "First Gay Cuba Cruise in History," *ftnNews*, November 8, 2015, www.ftnnews.com/cruise-travel/28971-first-gay-cuba -cruise-in-history.
26. See John R. Bolton, "Remarks by National Security Advisor Ambassador John R. Bolton on the Administration's Policies in Latin America," White House, November 2, 2018, www.white-house.gov/briefings-statements/remarks-national-security-advisor-ambassador-john-r-bolton-administrations-policies-latin-america/.
27. Chris Riotta's *The Independent* online article features an flashy video capturing trans drag queen Imperio as a LGBTQ+ celebrity in Cuba. See Chris Riotta, "Cuba's Most Famous Transgender Drag Queen Has a Message for Trump: 'Lift the embargo,'" *The Independent*, November 17, 2018, www.independent.co.uk/news/world/americas/cuba-embargo-trump-imperio -drag-queen-transformista-havana-cubana-a8634366.html.
28. In *After Love: Queer Intimacy and Erotic Economies in Post-Soviet Cuba* (Durham, NC: Duke University Press, 2014), the anthropologist Noelle M. Stout examines the multiple negotiations shaping sexual identity in Cuba's erotic economy, networks of transnational capital, threading bodies, queer desires, and economic practices on the island.
29. I'm making reference in specific to Rubén Gallo's *Teoría y práctica de La Habana* (Barcelona: Jus, Libreros y Editores, 2017), a book partially based on his experiences while living in Havana.

REFERENCES

Alexandra, Darcy. "Are We Listening Yet? Participatory Knowledge Production through Media Practice: Encounters of Political Listening." *Participatory Visual and Digital Research in Action*, edited by Aline Gubrium, Krista Harper, and Marty Otañez, Left Coast Press, 2015, pp. 41–55.
Alpert, Jon, director. *Mariela Castro's March: Cuba's LGBT Revolution*. HBO, 2015.
Bejel, Emilio. *Gay Cuban Nation*. Chicago UP, 2001.
Díaz, Sandra. Personal interview. 22 July 2017.
Lemebel, Pedro. *Zanjón de la aguada*. Editorial Planeta Chilena, 2003.
Llorente, Angeline. Personal interview. 11 July 2017.
Miami Sound Machine. "Conga." *Primitive Love*, Sony BMG Music Entertainment, 1985. *Spotify*, open.spotify.com/track/3FdHgoJbH3DXNtGLh56pFu?si=2NlaBcF7QFaS0y12xej59g.
Milstein, Lani. "Toward an Understanding of "Conga santiaguera": Elements of "La conga de Los Hoyos."" *Latin American Music Review*, vol. 34, no. 2, 2013, pp. 223–253, www.jstor.com/ stable/43282555. Accessed 8 Aug. 2020.
Montiel, Sisi. Personal interview. 9 July 2017.
Morad, Moshe. *Fiesta de Diez Pesos: Music and Gay Identity in Special Period Cuba*. Ashgate, 2014.
Moufawad-Paul, J. *Continuity and Rupture: Philosophy in the Maoist Terrain*. John Hunt Publishing, 2016.
Muñoz, José Esteban. "Ephemera as Evidence: Introductory Notes to Queer Acts." *Women & Performance*, vol. 8, no. 2, 1996, pp. 5–16.
———. *Cruising Utopia: The Then and There of Queer Futurity*. New York UP, 2009.
Piñera, Virgilio. *La isla en peso/The Whole Island*. Translated by Mark Weiss, Shearsman Books, 2010.
Ramírez, Nomi. Personal interview. 9 July 2017.
Rizki, Cole. "Latin/x American Trans Studies: Toward a *Travesti*-Trans Analytic." *Transgender Studies Quarterly*, vol. 6, no. 2, 2019, pp. 145–155.

Rodríguez, Silvio. "Unicornio. *Unicornio*, SGAE, 1982. *Spotify*, open.spotify.com/track/0lxu1Pm egx2SELobpAXzz4?si=FbWWEeP9Q5mS5DTZP3s6aw.

Sierra Madero, Abel, et al. ""No sé sabía dónde estaba la verdad y dónde estaba la mentira": Entrevista a Edith García Buchaca, 30 de abril de 2012." *Cuban Studies*, no. 45, 2017, pp. 359–371.

Vega Alfonsi, Vanessa. Personal interview. 22 July 2017.

Wirtz, Kristina. "Mobilizations of Race, Place, and History in Santiago de Cuba's Carnivalesque." *American Anthropologist*, vol. 119, no. 1, 2017, pp. 58–72. *Wiley Online Library*, https://doi .org/10.1111/aman.12817. Accessed 7 Aug. 2020.

Zurbano, Roberto. "Soy un negro más: Zurbano par lui-même." *Afro-Hispanic Review*, vol. 33, no. 1, 2014, pp. 13–60, www.jstor.com/stable/24585165. Accessed 13 Aug. 2020.

MARÍA A. GUTIÉRREZ BASCÓN

Toward a New Cuban Architecture: The Emergence of Private Architectural Studios in Havana (2011–2020)

ABSTRACT

Based on an in-depth analysis of interviews carried out in 2019 and 2020, this article considers the emergence of private studios of architecture in Havana from 2011 to 2020. I open by briefly exploring the contentious relationship that has traditionally existed between architects and the state since the advent of the Cuban Revolution. This fraught engagement functions as the historic backdrop for the configuration of a new Cuban architecture. Next, the analysis frames the recent rise of entrepreneurial architecture in the context of the re-appearance—for the first time in decades—of a key figure for architectural practice: the private client. I then survey six Havana-based offices—H[r]g Arquitectura, Apropia Estudio, Nivel 4 Estudio, Pino Estudio, Órbita XX, and Infraestudio—by charting the diverse architectural sensibilities that they make manifest. I argue that these studios' activity reveals a broad aesthetic and conceptual pluralism. I close the article by outlining some of the shared strategies that these entrepreneurial architects have mobilized to forge new creative spaces beyond state stagnation, which include a tactics of visibility and collectivism. Ultimately, the present article seeks to begin documenting and drawing attention to the value of recent histories of market-driven architecture on the island, in the current context of Cuba's insertion into systems of global capital.

RESUMEN

Basado en el análisis de entrevistas llevadas a cabo en 2019 y 2020, este artículo considera la emergencia de los estudios privados de arquitectura en La Habana en la última década. Abro el artículo con una breve exploración de la relación contenciosa que tradicionalmente ha existido entre los arquitectos y el estado desde el advenimiento de la Revolución cubana. Esta tensa relación funciona como el telón de fondo histórico para la configuración de una nueva arquitectura cubana. Tras esto, el análisis enmarca la reciente eclosión de la arquitectura *cuentapropista* en el contexto de la reaparición —por primera vez en décadas— de una figura clave para la práctica arquitectónica: el cliente privado. Después, trazo un mapa de seis oficinas de arquitectura situadas en La Habana —H[r]g Arquitectura, Apropia Estudio, Nivel 4 Estudio, Pino Estudio, Órbita XX e Infraestudio—, dando cuenta de las diversas sensibilidades arquitectónicas que manifiestan. Concluyo que la actividad de los estudios revela un amplio pluralismo estético y conceptual. Cierro con un repaso breve de algunas estrategias que estos arquitectos independientes han movilizado para fundar nuevos espacios creativos más allá del estancamiento estatal, entre las cuales se ha incluido una táctica de la visibilización y del colectivismo. En última instancia, el presente artículo busca comenzar a documentar y a poner en valor las historias recientes de la arquitectura comercial en la isla, en el contexto actual de la inserción de Cuba en los sistemas del capital global.

Introduction: Architecture and Architects under the Revolution

It is the summer of 2019 in Havana. From a modest house in a peripheral neighborhood of the city, an architect in her seventies reflects on the challenging conditions for architectural practice on the island. "For many years, architecture was sick and locked in a cage," Elena laments.[1] Recalling the prominent names of Cuba's modern movement of the 1940s and 1950s, she continues: "We used to have the Romañaches, the Batistas, the Gutiérrezes, up until the point when someone decided that architecture had to be all about technology, and not about artistic expression."[2] She looks somber, almost disheartened, when she talks about the more recent history and current state of Cuban architecture. All throughout the 1980s and early 1990s, Elena herself saw many of her projects tossed into the drawers of decision makers (*decisores*)—the ones who placed Cuban architecture in a metaphorical prison, according to her own account. *Arquitectura engavetada* (drawer-ed architecture) is what she calls the unrealized projects crafted by her and her colleagues during those relatively barren years.

The origin of the rigid approaches to architecture that Elena alludes to, which typically placed technological or industrialized solutions over aesthetic considerations, can be traced to the early years of the Cuban Revolution. As the new government endeavored to palliate some of the country's most pressing issues, architectural prefabrication became regarded as the most efficient way to deliver housing, schools and hospitals to the population on a massive scale. Heavily influenced by Soviet constructive models, Cuba employed prefabricated systems in the mid-1960s, and more commonly in the 1970s, producing thousands of standardized blocks of concrete across the island. Because the main goal was to resolve Cuba's many building needs, aesthetic issues were generally forced aside while constructive concerns came to the fore.[3] This trend unfortunately resulted in repetitive projects, excessive standardization, and a deficit in expression (Zardoya 22).

In this context, opportunities for creative design were drastically reduced for architects. By 1963, the private practice of architecture was eliminated in Cuba, and the Colegio Nacional de Arquitectos, the professional association of architects, was dissolved in 1967. Most architects then joined teams of builders organized under the centralizing power of the Ministerio de la Construcción. The architectural profession became viewed as a technical occupation rather than an artistic pursuit, and architects largely lost their authority over projects in favor of builders (Coyula "Trinquennium" 36). Only a limited number of renowned figures, such as Fernando Salinas or Antonio Quintana, were offered the opportunity to fully develop their own architectural practice (Deupi 86). For the rest of architects, anonymity became the norm. According to the new socialist notion, architects had to be devoid of personal interests, as collective efforts gained prominence over individual authorship (Zardoya 18). Architect Mario Coyula describes the atmosphere of those years as a "claustrophobic framework" in which "excessive centralization . . . eliminated alternatives and nullified criticism" ("Trinquennium" 37).[4] For Coyula, worse than technological prefabrication was "mental prefabrication" ("Trinquennium" 43), which gave rise to a "static mentality among some decision makers, prejudiced against anything new" ("Trinquennium" 33). The end result was the systematic erosion of the architectural profession as a site for creative expression ("Trinquennium" 37). Although the 1980s provided a welcome respite from some of these tendencies, the renewed creative energies that characterized young architects during those years were not matched by a proper material completion of their designs, as "in the majority of cases, [the projects] remained a plan to be realized on paper only" (Álvarez Tabío "Midair" 156). The following decade, which witnessed the collapse of the Soviet bloc and the onset of an unprecedented economic crisis in Cuba that lasted for well over a decade, did not afford a materially advantageous context for architects to advance some of their aspirations.[5] Even in more recent years, some of the restrictive patterns inherited from previous decades have continued to shape the island's architectural field. For instance, the private practice of architecture is still not legally

FIGURE 1. Alamar housing complex in eastern Havana (1970s–1980s), built with components of the Girón prefabricated system. Photo by the author.

recognized in Cuba. By the same token, merely a handful of selected architects, such as Julia León and José Antonio Choy, have been formally permitted to establish an architectural practice of their own.[6] At least officially, the only existing client—and provider—of architecture continues to be the state.

Toward the Development of a New Architecture:
The Emergence of the Private Client

It is not infrequent that young practitioners who graduate every year from the four schools of architecture in the country struggle to carve fulfilling professional paths.[7] Many of them end up working at stagnant positions at *empresas de proyecto* (state design enterprises) for meager salaries, while their artistic development is curtailed. Architect Hayder Valdivia states that "for younger architects, it is difficult to fully develop all their creative dreams within state firms." For Valdivia, it would be fair to say that state offices could be regarded as mere "blueprint factories" (Valdivia). Scholar María Victoria Zardoya concurs with Valdivia in pointing out the existence of a more vocal, new generation of architects that often complains about the constraining management style of state offices and expresses their wish to practice architecture in an independent setting (Cuadra 434). These practitioners' critical attitude, articulated by a desire to expand architectural practice beyond the orthodoxies of the bureaucratic state apparatus, closely aligns with Elena's mournful critique of architects' loss of centrality in Cuban society after the advent of the revolution.

Undertaken by novel design firms, a notable defiance toward the prolonged monopoly of the state bureaucracy over architectural practice has recently been enabled by the emergence of a key figure: the private client. Crucially, as Raúl Castro's new policies encouraging private initiative were introduced in 2011, a myriad small enterprises started proliferating across the city. The owners of the trendy restaurants and rooftop bars, ice cream parlors and bakeries, art galleries and spas that began to populate Havana soon became the new patrons of architecture. Since the state design offices were unable to provide the architectural services being demanded, the rising class of small entrepreneurs turned to independent architects for their professional assistance in the spatial planning and remodeling of their businesses. These attractive spaces for leisure and consumption promptly became functional to international tourism, but also to a growing middle class of local consumers.[8] In sum, the new entrepreneurial studios of architecture are heavily reliant on an ecosystem of private businesses, whose relative expansion is situated within a changing transnational economic landscape made possible by more relaxed regulations concerning self-employment and other property reforms, including those permitting the sale of houses for the first time in decades. A resolute shift in the US approach to Cuba, which began with the lifting of some of the restrictions on travel and remittances in 2009 and 2011 and ended with the diplomatic rapprochement between the two countries in 2014, decisively contributed to an increase in global investment flows to the island, including diaspora capital.

Nevertheless, the design firms that emerged in the wake of these changes continue to occupy a precarious place within Cuban legal frameworks for private entrepreneurship. Among the 127 occupations recognized as legitimate *cuentapropista* (self-employed) activities before 2021, "architect" was not one of them. In the absence of a specific license for their profession, entrepreneurial architects often operated, prior to 2021, with masonry or interior décor permits. On February 11, 2021, Cuba's Ministry of Labor and Social Security announced a new list of prohibited activities for the private sector, explicitly barring highly qualified professionals such as lawyers, journalists, and architects from operating private businesses related to their professions.[9] At any rate, and in the face of mounting legal constraints, the new studios have surely reinvigorated the practice of architectural design in Cuba within the last decade, while simultaneously transforming the face of the city. Most of the projects taken on by these young architectural firms usually start from a given structure, although some have designed private houses from the ground up as well. As estimated by Valdivia, the number of firms in Havana is around fifty; across the island, the figure rises to a hundred. Largely centralized in Havana, architectural offices are then part of a complex scenario of tensions and contradictions that have a spatial expression in the city's built environment.

Based on in-depth interviews carried out in 2019 and 2020, this article considers the recent emergence of these private firms in Havana by charting the diverse architectural sensibilities that they make manifest. In what follows, I survey six Havana-based offices—H[r]g Arquitectura, Apropia Estudio, Nivel 4 Estudio, Pino Estudio, Órbita XX and Infraestudio—and their differing design practices. While all the studios appear to have an interest in reconstructing a local architecture broadly regarded as suspended in time, their approaches vary significantly. Ranging from an interest in incorporating national historical codes to advancing avant-garde conceptual proposals, while considering questions of sustainability and gender as well, the new entrepreneurial architecture reveals a broad aesthetic and conceptual pluralism. These architects appear to move between an opportunity and a challenge, in an attempt to shape a space between the two: on the one hand, the creative possibilities afforded by a city such as Havana, viewed as a paradoxically privileged urban laboratory where everything needs to be done; on the other hand, the difficulties posed by the still limited legal and material frameworks for private architecture existing on the island today. As a way of engaging with these constraints, some of these offices have strived to reinvent the scope of architectural practice itself—by altogether opting out of calling themselves a "studio" or by expanding their production from buildings to books, furniture and other objects—as if reconstructing an interrupted practice also implied reimagining its limits. I conclude my analysis by briefly outlining some of the shared strategies that these architects have employed in order to forge new creative paths, which have included the mobilization of a tactics of visibility and collectivism, with the organization of public events and exhibitions, and the establishment of an alternative professional association for entrepreneurial architects. Ultimately, the present article seeks to begin documenting and drawing attention to the value of recent histories of market-driven architecture on the island, in the context of Cuba's insertion into systems of global capital.

H[r]g Arquitectura, Apropia Estudio, and Nivel 4 Estudio: The Making and Recycling of Local Architectures

Along with Apropia Estudio and Nivel 4 Estudio, H[r]g Arquitectura is among the private offices with the longest trajectories in Havana. Founded in 2011 by architect Orlando Inclán (Havana, 1976), H[r]g is also one of the largest and most productive firms, having designed around two hundred projects since its inception, and currently employing more than twenty architects and engineers. The studio originated as the executive branch of a previously established organization, Habana[Re]generación, an architectural nonprofit created in 2007 with an eye toward rethinking possible futures for Havana along the lines of sustainable development. Most of the architects and urbanists involved in the founding of Habana[Re]generación work as preservationists at the Office of the Historian, the state agency in charge of the restoration of Old Havana. The name of the collective alludes to, as Inclán explains, "a determination to *regenerate* Havana coming from a *generation* of architects deeply committed to their city." A concern for locating the roots that should guide the future renaissance of the city initially led Habana[Re]generación to research and draw attention to the value of vernacular forms of informal architecture. Among those forms, Inclán highlights the *barbacoa*, an improvised mezzanine built by residents typically using recycled materials to subdivide and rearrange spaces within a given housing unit. In conjunction with low consumption and extended object reuse patterns, these popular practices born out of necessity constitute what Habana[Re]generación has termed "accidental sustainability" (Inclán). As Inclán points out, Havana reached its distinctive sustainable approaches not by design but by circumstance, particularly during the crisis of the 1990s, in which cycling, ride-sharing, and the creative reuse of objects became widespread practices for most Cubans. Brought into architecture, this reuse and recycle framework would translate into the development and repurposing of the existing building stock, as well as in the use of reclaimed components and materials. As an entrepreneurial extension of the research-oriented Habana[Re]generación, what H[r]g Arquitectura proposes to do is bring these publicly relevant concerns around sustainability, in Inclán's words, "into the private sphere," thus gesturing toward a view whereby market relations might be seamlessly incorporated into existing social values around reuse and recycling.

A logic and rhetoric of recycling is indeed mobilized around Malecón 663, the flagship project of H[r]g Arquitectura. Located along Havana's popular seafront promenade, Malecón 663 occupies a three-story building dating back to the early 20th century. It opened its doors in 2017, merging a hostel with a store, restaurant, bar and event venue.[10] The design premise was to re-use a diverse collection of old Cuban furniture put together by the building's owners—a well-known Havana musician and his French wife—giving each of the hostel rooms and common spaces at *Malecón 663* a particular epochal look based on the already available decorative pieces. In room "Mambo n. 5," H[r]g attempts to re-create Cuba's art deco style by incorporating some vintage architectural fixtures to the space (Figure 2). The black high-shine granite staircase becomes a focal point of the room, alluding to the bold angular forms emblematic of art deco. The geometric staircase is mirrored by the zigzag shape of the couch, as well as by other linear decorations in the room, all recreated by interior designer Darío Veranes.[11] The other hostel rooms in Malecón 663 integrate styles inspired by Cuba's eclectic and modern movements. A contemporary touch is incorporated into the common areas of the building by utilizing

FIGURE 2. "Mambo n. 5" room in art deco style, as part of *Malecón 663*. Photo courtesy of Darío Veranes.

FIGURE 3. Upcycled bike wheels and frames as bar stools at *Malecón 663* ground floor, by H[r]g Arquitectura. Photo courtesy of Malecón 663.

current elements, such as a reclaimed iron spiral staircase, and bicycle wheels and frames upcycled as bar stools (Figure 3). The end result of the project is a sumptuously textured assemblage of styles, in which the role of the architect is akin to that of a curator or "recycler" of local material and historical codes.

Apropia Estudio shares with H[r]g Arquitectura a proposal for an architecture that works with what is locally available, as a way of both circumventing material shortages and capitalizing on usually high-quality restorable materials. The studio was founded in 2013 by architects Alejandra Pino (Havana, 1977) and Elisa Alè (Milan, 1971), later joined by architect Hayder Valdivia (Sancti Spíritus, 1973–Havana, 2021). Apropia's name refers to the necessity of constructing an *arquitectura propia*, that is, an architecture made with domestic materials, respecting local codes, and in close connection to contextual demands. Recovering elements such as early twentieth-century cast-iron columns or wooden window frames from the numerous demolition sites across the city has become a common practice at Apropia. As Alè explains, "recycling as much as possible" is one of the studio's goals.[12] For Valdivia, the state of material decline that characterizes Havana can be viewed as an opportunity for architectural design: "Havana has been in disrepair for 60 years; everything needs to be done, so the city has an incredible potential," the architect states. In a context of general decay of Havana's building stock, Valdivia positions entrepreneurial architects' efforts as necessarily preservationist. "It is a self-imposed mission for us," Valdivia asserts, "to recover the architectural values of Havana and, when that is not possible due to necessary demolitions, to build with as much dignity and coherence as possible in relation with our surrounding city."

One of the best exponents of Apropia's attempts at developing coherent insertions within Havana's built environment that also respond to local residents' needs is their *Casa in calle B*, centrally located in El Vedado neighborhood and commissioned by a young musician.[13] By way of building a second floor on top of a single-story eclectic-style house from the early twentieth century, the aim of the project was to add needed multifunctional space to a preexisting structure (Figure 4). A notion that distinguishes Apropia's design for Casa in Calle B is that, instead of advancing feigned historicist claims, the studio inserts a contemporary proposal that contrasts with the eclecticism of the original house. The project thus becomes a design proposition for how new can meet old by adopting a degree of contrast, while preventing the modern addition from overwhelming the historic building. In other words, the divergence between modern and historic is deliberate in *Casa in calle B*, but not overbearing. As for the indoor aspect of the design, the multifunctional style of the top-floor addition is carried into the interiors in the form of a loft aesthetics that maximizes usable space by removing excess walls. The double height ceiling also affords the possibility of installing a mezzanine to create additional floor area, accessed via a metal staircase reminiscent of loft arrangements (Figure 5). In this regard, Valdivia explains that a postindustrial aesthetics is suitable for Havana given

FIGURE 4. *Casa in calle B*, by Apropia Estudio.

FIGURE 5. Interior of *Casa in calle B*, by Apropia Estudio.

the city's prominent industrial heritage. A loft aesthetics is invoked here as a global architectural idiom that can be locally translated and accommodated within the city's heritage and built environment, while simultaneously placing Havana onto a map of global cities.

Formerly known as Trapiche, the studio constituted by architects José A. López (Havana, 1981), Ramón Ramírez (Havana, 1983), Pedro D. Rodríguez (Pinar del Río, 1983) and Héctor E. Sullivan (Havana, 1982) was established in 2008. Meaning "sugar cane press," the studio's previous name evoked the charged imagery around Cuba's former history as a sugar world power, in possible allusion to notions of high productivity and vernacular technologies. The firm is indeed one of the most prolific in the city, with more than forty constructed projects. In 2020, the group changed its name to Nivel 4 Estudio, signaling the desire for a fresher look. In a similar fashion to Apropia Estudio, Nivel 4 architects express concerns for the ways in which today's practitioners might integrate their contemporary designs into a built environment that has not been significantly altered since the advent of the Cuban Revolution. In relation to this issue, Ramírez comments:

Havana is full of paradigms, but these are paradigms from the past. There are no models for the present, and that generates a challenge: how to insert your designs in a city that is stuck in the past, and that has not been able to transition to the present? Unlike other cities in the world, there is no continuous thread that has gradually made Havana evolve into the present.

As a means of solving this challenge, Nivel 4 Estudio looks back at the great Cuban masters of the 1940s and 1950s for creative inspiration. In Ramírez's view, the architecture of the modern movement in Cuba "might have well been designed right in the twenty-first century," due to its way of combining the past with experimental approaches. Themes of national identity and climate adaptation that intensely preoccupied the generation of the 1940s and 1950s thus become key to architects at Nivel 4 Estudio, particularly as an antidote to counter what they see as the detrimental impact of foreign models on Havana's built environment. "We are abandoning our identity by currently importing models from other places that are neither adapted to our climate, nor to our ways, nor to the technologies we have," Rodríguez laments. "The best project is always the one which is specific to a place," he further remarks.

An interest in conversing with modernist national codes can be appreciated in Nivel 4 Estudio's project for a restaurant in Nuevo Vedado neighborhood. Built within the ample courtyard of a mid-1950s residence designed by renowned modernist architect Manuel Gutiérrez, the restaurant Alta Casa opened its doors in 2019. As opposed to Apropia's abovementioned plan for *Casa in calle B*, Nivel 4 chooses to insert their project by analogy with Gutiérrez's midcentury design, rather than by contrast (Figure 6). "In the restaurant we projected, we reinterpreted 1950s Cuban modern architecture by employing analogous materials, by assimilating similar compositional elements such as straight lines and horizontal and vertical planes, and by using exposed structural elements," Ramírez explains. The hope is to solve current architectural needs in a national style. A more liberal adoption of the modernist concern for climate adaptation can be identified in Nivel 4's project Casa en K y 19 (2020), commissioned as a second home by a longtime Cuban émigré.[14] The modular design for this exclusive residence in El Vedado neighborhood projects a bulky front volume forward, producing a bold aesthetic effect (Figure 7). A contrast between light and shade is created through the interplay of volumes, which aids in regulating the impact of direct sunlight and thermal discomfort. Additionally, the ground floor incorporates a fitness center owned by the dweller as a small-scale enterprise. "In this case, we did not produce a mimetic copy of the modernist canon," Ramírez points out. Instead, the architect asserts that the intention was to "leave [their] contemporary trace in El Vedado's skyline," thus renovating the marked 1950s high-rise silhouette of the district while aiming to freely assume some of the lessons of Cuban modernism.

Whether the claim be made to informal building practices (*barbacoa*), to cultivated histories of architecture (eclecticism, art deco, and modernism

FIGURE 6. To the left, *Restaurant Alta Casa*, by Nivel 4 Estudio. Located in the courtyard of a paradigmatic 1950s residence designed by Manuel Gutiérrez (to the right). Photo by Nivel 4 Estudio.

FIGURE 7. *Casa en K y 19*, by Nivel 4 Estudio.

as international styles with a particular Cuban twist), or to possible ways of dialoguing with the city's industrial heritage (loft aesthetics), all the studios examined here appeal to national frames of belonging. In their attempt to develop a locally situated practice, these architects also display various degrees of engagement with their past, revealing an interest in connecting with what has been widely viewed as an interrupted architectural tradition. Binding current design practices with inherited histories of architecture also becomes a way of fending off foreign influences somewhat perceived as pernicious. Valdivia's abovementioned conservationist preoccupation aligns with Rodríguez's concern regarding the introduction of alien architectural models, in possible reference to the investment-driven construction boom of luxury hotels recently taking place in the city.[15] Along similar lines, Inclán states: "we are concerned about what will happen with Havana once we become a prosperous city; that is to say, [there is a risk] that we abandon our awareness around recycling and become a very consumeristic city." These practitioners' cautious positions toward the conceivably damaging impact of abrupt larger-scale investments on the island—and the architectural forms inevitably associated to them— manifest deep-seated anxieties around a potential "Miamization" of Havana, long forewarned by some critics.[16] Paradoxically, the very own capital flows permitting the emergence of small-scale entrepreneurial architecture, if fully unbridled, would leave the city vulnerable to unchecked development, thus radically altering an urban landscape whose architectural values these studios aim to safeguard.

Pino Estudio and Órbita XX: Architecture as a Gendered Practice

In 2017, after a few years as a partner in Apropia Estudio, Alejandra Pino decided to take her own professional path and founded Pino Estudio. Doing architecture in ways that are imbued with emotion and that place quality over quantity, while generating a poetics of affectivity around the crafting of interior spaces, soon became central to the studio's activity. Speaking of her creative process, Pino highlights her emotive, artisanal and decelerated approach to architectural practice:

I am very emotional. I strive for my architecture to have a strong emotional element. If I manage to cause an emotion in you, that is important to me. I also enjoy when things are intimate, so that is why I like for architecture to have a handcrafted component. [At Pino Estudio] we are a bit artisanal and that is why our projects take a bit longer than usual.

This form of narrating architectural design as a process that fundamentally has to do with emotion, interpersonal bonding, and temporal expansion appears to deviate from more traditional—and generally masculine—accounts of the architecture and construction fields as sites devoid from affect. As scholars Torsten Lange and Emily Eliza Scott have indeed noted, architecture is still "a notoriously conservative discipline with roots in the long nineteenth century," which "all too often clings to traditional notions of individual mastery, genius, and autonomy, while also maintaining deeply hierarchical and patriarchal structures" (90). By developing a mode of practice informed by a different temporality and sense of connectivity with the client, Pino seems to be challenging the masculinist notions of accelerated production and self-reliant individuality that have often shaped architectural practice. The architect also resists the hierarchical assumptions that usually assign more prestige and value to big constructions by refusing to situate the commission of larger-scale projects as the final goal of her studio. For Pino, small-scale projects are an end unto themselves: "We do not aspire to get large projects in order to try our best. For me, the most important thing is to do a good job. In the end, we believe that we do not need big opportunities to develop a sound project."[17] Ultimately, the architect weaves a perspective attentive to gender into her attempt to understand the many challenges facing practices of architecture in Cuba today. In Pino's view, a more liberated way of exercising the profession on the island will come about hand in hand with a non-androcentric approach:

Reflecting upon my trajectory with Apropia, which started with Elisa [Alè], and now at Pino Estudio, I have arrived at the idea that we cannot talk about a true emancipation of the architectural profession until we can start rethinking the traditional methods of the field from a feminine perspective. What we were taught was a masculine point of view. It is obvious. There has not been enough time devoted to understand how we, women architects, would have done things expressing ourselves the way we are, without trying to fit into the mold we were given.

When considering her work portfolio at Pino Estudio, the architect cites Lola Café as her most representative project to date (Figure 8). In Pino's account, the femininely-connoted character of her spatial design for the coffeehouse is the result, at least partially, of a relationship of care that she gradually developed with the owner of the space: "I see Lola Café as very feminine; the conception of space is feminine, and I think this has to do with the fact that the owner, who is one of my faithful clients, is also a woman, and that she and I have a beautiful rapport," Pino argues. Similarly, Pino's design for *apartamento Refugio* incorporates her interest in "tender spaces" and "atmospheres."[18] The renovation plan for this centrally located residence embraces smooth curves and desaturated colors to provide a sense of calmness (Figure 9). According to Pino's own description of the project on her social media accounts, the apartment seeks to become "a space of serenity in the midst of Havana's bustling Barrio Chino."[19] Often regarded "as more harmonious, relaxing, or pleasant [. . .] than straight or broken lines" (Gómez-Puerto et al. 1),

FIGURE 8. *Lola Café*, by Pino Estudio.

curvilinear forms have a softening effect on interior compositions. In Pino's design for Apartamento Refugio, curves can be found in the ribbon-like hanging lamp, the soft-edged table and chairs, the oversized mirror, and the wavy floor pattern. The muted shades of blue that embellish both furniture and floors increase the feeling of spaciousness, as cool colors and lighter tones tend to "recede and make spaces feel larger" (Dodsworth 136). The sense of comfort is emphasized with the introduction of a vertical garden, which fully envelops one of the walls while adding a natural quality to the interior arrangement, also promoting temperature control and noise reduction. The floors are an original design coming out of Pino Estudio's 2019 catalog of mosaic tiles, entitled "Sweet 60's: Un diseño sesentón y artesanal." The creation of these unique vintage-inspired tiles is part of a wider strategy to avoid repetition by devising,

FIGURE 9. *Apartamento Refugio*, by Pino Estudio.

in Pino's account, imaginative solutions to the unavailability of certain fixtures in local markets:

[The floor catalog] was not part of a commission by a client, but it was a project that I wanted to develop, because there are almost no materials in Cuba. If you want to produce different designs, it is difficult to make something new out of the same old elements.

This resourceful tactic is applied to the production of furniture as well. For instance, the concrete stools and lamps in Lola Café were generated by the own studio: "since there is no place to buy [this sort of furniture] in Cuba, we gave ourselves the task to produce them," the architect explains. Pino Estudio's creative approach to market shortages operates by expanding the conventional scope of architectural practice toward the material development of decorative elements to be later incorporated into the office's projects. Along the same lines, Pino affirms her conviction that design practice is not exclusively dependent on business incentives: "I like the notion of design for the sake of design. I believe that a true architecture studio should not necessitate direct commissions to function," Pino states.

Similarly, mindful of women's role in architecture—not only as designers but also as clients—Suli Álvarez (Pinar del Río, 1992) founded Órbita XX in 2019. The group was established by Álvarez as a gender-conscious project in architecture and art, after she gained a few years of professional experience as part of H[r]g Arquitectura. The young architect graduated from Universidad Tecnológica de La Habana in 2015, with a thesis that aimed to draw attention not only to the land perimeter of the Bay of Havana, but also to the often overlooked colossal mass of water itself. Challenging the "static simplicity of landed" perspectives (Peters and Steinberg 13) that typically shape critical discourses of the city, Álvarez foregrounds alternative ways of approaching spaces of water in Havana:

Beyond the shoreline, the bay is also a body of water. You have to look at things from other points of view. Why not look at it inversely? To understand water as the "built space," instead of the vacuum. [My question is], when you situate yourself in the middle of the bay, how do you view the rest of the city?

Álvarez's singular take on the Bay of Havana decenters inherited ontologies of space that position the oceanic as an outside to the urban, and that situate land in a hierarchical relation to water. As urban theorist Charity Edwards has noted, "many spatial practitioners typically disregard "wet volumes" (including spaces such as bays, straits, gulfs, gyres, basins, seas, coasts, and tsunamis), maintaining a generalized blindness towards the ocean" (206). Furthermore, Edwards argues that undertheorized spaces—including water bodies—have been "long relegated . . . as feminized or simply surplus to discussions of 'the city'" (215) within established traditions of spatial and urban theory. In contrast with traditional views, what Álvarez seems to be doing for the case of Havana is to attempt to recover the critical potential of a *viewing from the water*, reintroducing wet volumes into our conception of the built environment.

Manifesting an equally unorthodox approach to traditional notions of what an architectural studio should be, Álvarez sought to develop Órbita XX not so much as a conventional office, but as "an atmosphere" or "an orbit." "Órbita XX is not a studio in the same way as the other ones in Havana," the architect asserts. Although the project does involve the design of architectural plans, its focus is considerably widened to include theater production, the curation of exhibitions, and event organization. More significantly, Órbita XX functions as a space of conviviality for women of different generations. The core team is composed of four architects, including Álvarez, and one industrial designer, all born in the 1990s. However, their regular meetings are often expanded to integrate a group of vibrant women in the arts who are in their forties and fifties. It is from this intergenerational exchange that the project derives part of its creative strength. Álvarez notes: "I spend a lot of time with [these women], because they are role models. The fact that they are all independent women is important. They are themselves above all things." Another particularity at the organizational level is that the women architects, artists and entrepreneurs that *orbit* around the project do not gather for the sole purpose of working. Rather, their notions of creative work blur the lines between labor and leisure, threading a personal component into their collective practice. While these artistic and spatial practitioners routinely get together at a kind of office space adjacent to Álvarez's home kitchen in El Cerro neighborhood, their gatherings produce, according to the architect, a "collage of conversations" that do not mirror the conventional meetings she previously experienced while collaborating with other architectural studios:

In the time I worked for H[r]g Arquitectura, I defined for myself a number of things that I did not want to reproduce once I had my own practice. The first one was to not have so many formal meetings, because people usually find them exhausting. Particularly, I think that women function differently. There are other reasons why we women gather, and from there we can create lots of things. . . . [So] we never schedule our gatherings as work meetings. . . . In the end, we work, but without actually working. It is not a traditional way of working. We do not sit at a desk and lean over a blueprint all day. To work stiffly, pencil in hand . . . No, I think that limits creativity.

In its architectural dimension, Órbita XX is ultimately articulated around the goal of providing local women with accessible design and building services. "Our main objective," Álvarez explains, "is to carry out social projects that can help solve women's needs." Therefore, Órbita XX is thought out as a project *by* women, *for* women. As Álvarez argues, the necessity for such a gender-based scheme arises from the fact that most entrepreneurial architecture in Havana is still heavily male-dominated:

Basically, almost all studios are owned by men, and it is usually very complicated for a woman to take a step forward and call a male architect. Women usually turn to male family members when they need architectural services [for these male figures to call an architect]. The relationship flows better from women to women. And for me, that was something that was missing in Havana.

Since the majority of spatial practitioners at Órbita XX have steady incomes from other sources—most of them work as architects at the Office of the

Historian—the project can sustain itself without the need to maximize profit. The economic viability of Órbita XX is grounded in an approximate ratio of one pro bono architectural plan per one remunerated project. For instance, most of the revenue obtained from the design of a commercial spa located in Centro Habana will be dedicated to redesigning, free of charge, a substandard shelter where Yanet,[20] a woman who recently was released from prison for a nonviolent drug offense, is currently living. Highlighting the centrality of subjectivity in spatial practice, and of the ways in which architectural design can potentially support people, Álvarez states: "[Yanet] needs a hand. [This architectural project] just gives her the hope she needs." Most importantly, Órbita XX aims to empower women—particularly from vulnerable groups—to have spatial agency, while intertwining architectural design with social practices of care.

Last, Órbita XX has also been active in challenging the absence of women from accepted architectural historiographies, by underscoring women's historic contribution to the built environment on the island. For that purpose, Álvarez and her team created an Instragram account under the name of Arquitectas.cubanas in June 2020, as a way to collect stories, interviews and creative images related to the participation of women in Cuba's architectural past and present. Álvarez explains that the inspiration for this archival project suddenly came to her one day when she realized that there existed no online site devoted to women architects in Cuba: "I saw [in that absence] an opportunity to do justice and generate a digital archive on the work of Cuban women architects of all times."[21] Mobilizing "the feminist strategy of making visible" as "a critical reaction to that which has been rendered invisible or lacks representation" (Reisinger and Schalk 3), Álvarez and her team have thus started to construct a different kind of archive that uplifts the voices of women in Cuban architecture.

The Conceptual Architecture of Infraestudio

Infraestudio was founded in 2016 by Anadis González (Matanzas, 1994) and Fernando Martirena (Santa Clara, 1992). Inspired by Superstudio—the radical Italian architectural office of the 1960s and 1970s—Infraestudio's very name alludes to González's and Martirena's affinities with a conceptual poetics and avant-garde movements, an affiliation that sets them apart from other design offices in Havana. The prefix *infra*, in its meaning of "beneath" or "inferior," also resonates with the shortcomings these young practitioners detect in the architectural field in Cuba. These weaknesses—absence of juridical backup, scarcity of adequate constructive materials, or insufficient opportunities for students and recent graduates to become acquainted with professional design outside the narrow state sphere—are embraced and turned into a tactical strength, by developing an "infra" practice that emphasizes and expands the conceptual dimensions of architectural design, rather than its functional or constructive ones. "We chose the name Infraestudio," Martirena clarifies, "because we had no legal protection and no previous professional experience, and we did not want to become a traditional studio either; we wanted to create something that, while being *less* than a studio, allowed us to do other things at the same time." For Infraestudio, this means broadening the range of objects that the office produces. Aside from buildings, the studio generates visual art pieces and performances, curatorial projects, and artists' books under Ediciones Infraleves, its independent editorial series. In partial continuity with some of Superstudio's experimental approaches, Infraestudio seeks to decenter the notion of the building as the ultimate object of architecture. This does not amount to, however, completely operating outside the constructive paradigm. On the contrary, Infraestudio has sought to materially realize their designs as part of Havana's built environment. As a result, the young studio has developed several projects for a contemporary art center and various businesses that intervene existing structures in the city, while also designing and building four conceptual houses from scratch. That being said, the architects are adamant to point out their ambiguous relationship with market forces. As Martirena explains, the studio is cautious not to accept all the commissions they receive:

We have taken a path focused on discursive and artistic practices, and we have done a lot of conceptual work. We do not have one piece that means something, but a total oeuvre made of fragments. As such, each of our buildings helps you understand the other ones. Even each of our art pieces helps you understand each building. When you see it as a whole, you realize there is an underlying discourse. That is what we are interested in. So if we started selling ourselves, we would lose our discourse.

Rather than notions of high building productivity, Infraestudio then values the integrity of an artistic practice, articulated by a conceptually cohesive program. In contrast with the popular rationalist motto of "form follows function,"[22] for Infraestudio form follows concept, meaning that the shape of a building does not necessarily have to conform to its intended purpose, but to the concepts that poetically drive the design. A case in point is González's and Martirena's *Grotto House* (2018), a residence commissioned by a local entrepreneur. Planned for a parcel located in a natural reserve in Eastern Havana, Infraestudio's design was based on the piece *Beso* by Cuban conceptual artist Wilfredo Prieto, which consists of two large spherical stones that touch—or *kiss*—each other on a minuscule point. Inspired by this idea of minimal contact—termed *infra-thin* by González and Martirena, following Marcel Duchamp[23]—the architects sketched a house divided into two undulating volumes that barely touch. Separated by a void that functions as an inner courtyard, the volumes in Grotto House simulate a natural cavity between two adjacent rocks.

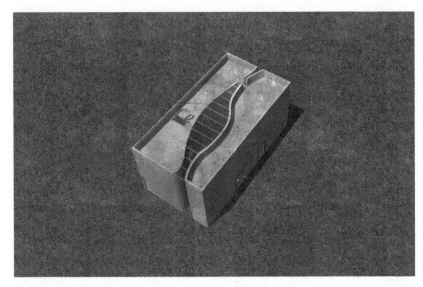

FIGURE 10. Aerial view of *Grotto House*, by Infraestudio.

FIGURE 11. Front view of *Grotto House*, partially covered in vegetation, by Infraestudio.

However, producing a literal copy of a grotto was not the aim. The gesture that underlies the design is only partially mimetic, as mimesis has been sieved through a conceptual filter first. González explains that "the idea was for the house to be as abstract as possible."

With Grotto House, Infraestudio also sought to unsettle traditional notions of domestic comfort. The house clearly separates its public and private domains into the two different volumes that constitute it. To cross from one side to the other, the dweller has to traverse the roofless courtyard. "If it is raining," González clarifies, "when you go from the living room to the bedroom you will get wet." Even if this inconvenience could be easily fixed by placing a glass ceiling to shelter the space, the client of this house "is more comfortable seeing the sky without a piece of glass, even if that means getting wet," Martirena argues. The ambiguity between exterior and interior spaces is also sustained by the absence of a door. The resident enters the house through a three-foot non-gated opening situated between the two volumes. On the opposite side, a five-inch split only lets the light in. Finally, González and Martirena foresee that the passage of time will allow for the rough concrete house to be fully wrapped in vegetation, blending in with the natural landscape as a final act of concealment. The concepts that run through *Grotto House*—new ideas of domestic (dis)comfort, the *infra-thin* as the minimal space that unites and separates elements, the interplay of openness and closeness, or a performative concealment—consistently guide the rest of Infraestudio's architectural and artistic production.

The sculptural quality of Grotto House and its heterodox approach to home design contrasts with Havana's highly regarded modernist residences of the 1940s and 1950s. In fact, González and Martirena are less interested in the purported greatness of midcentury Cuban architecture;[24] they are more interested in generating—in resonance with Valerio Olgiati's proposals for a non-referential architecture[25]—a disruptive aesthetics that disengage from established traditions. In doing so, Infraestudio makes a deliberate claim to artistic genealogies beyond the national canon.

Conclusion: A Diverse Architecture in Search of Legal and Social Recognition

The ample range of design possibilities illustrated by the six studios examined in this article signals a persistent desire to shift away from the relative sense of commercial and aesthetic paralysis that defined the practice of architecture under the Revolution. For Cuban architecture to be (re)constructed after a prolonged period of stasis, Alejandra Pino suggests that both a variety of approaches and a greater degree of autonomy from the state are central: "Cuban architecture needs to liberate itself. It needs to breath. [. . .] Cuban architecture needs freedom because it needs diversity. Diversity is an essential prerequisite for all living systems."[26] Even if entrepreneurial architects at times express ambivalent positions toward market logics, by and large they seem to have welcomed last decade's complex, although timidly favorable (pre-pandemic) economic landscape as a means to usher in a new era of design on the island.

Unlike Elena's projects in the 1980s and 1990s, entrepreneurial architecture of the last decade (2011–2020) was not *engavetada*, that is to say, put away in the drawers of state decision makers—at least not until the ban on private architecture announced by the Ministry of Labor in February 2021. Before this date, the existence of private offices of architecture had not been explicitly challenged by state institutions over the course of the new millennium. In fact, in the years prior to the 2021 prohibition, private architecture seemed to occupy a gray area of *alegalidad*, neither legally regulated nor unambiguously disallowed by the state. During a roundtable discussion in late 2019, architect Islay Martínez (Melena del Sur 1983), cofounder of Estudio Martínez-Becerra in Havana, characterized the pre-2021 legal landscape with a singular blend of uncertainty and hopefulness:

We are like flies that go through a spider web. Thus far, I do not know of anybody that has gotten stuck in it, but it could well happen. Nobody has told us that we cannot cross [the line]. In fact, there are some openings, and one goes across and comes back. [. . .] In our case, we practice without legal protection, since we work with a license that has nothing to do with the practice of architecture, but with interior décor. So far, nobody has come to tell me that I cannot do it.[27]

While acknowledging the perils of juridical informality, Martínez's account brings forward a collective sense of make-do in the presence of a legal framework that, albeit restricting independent architects' operations, also created fissures that allowed them to maneuver. Guided by a moderate sense of optimism, around twenty emerging architectural studios came together in Havana to establish GECA (Grupo de Estudios Cubanos de Arquitectura) on February 4, 2018. GECA was launched as an alternative association of independent architects with the double aim of advocating for a more favorable legal terrain and gaining social visibility for the profession. Since its founding, GECA's executive committee has coordinated a number of collective exhibitions and public events, and has made an active use of social media platforms as a way of engaging with a larger audience.[28]

GECA's most ambitious public event was possibly the Primera Semana de la Arquitectura (March 9–13, 2020), consisting of a series of expert panels and a variety of open studios in which independent architects' workrooms were transformed into short-term exhibition spaces. Due to the health restrictions during the COVID-19 pandemic, the Segunda Semana de la Arquitectura (March 13–19, 2021) was hosted fully online as a number of talks in which the most salient studios explored their recent work and unpacked their approach to design. An intensification of curatorial activity around architectural practice is attested by other collective exhibitions within the last decade: *Señales de vida* (2013), at the Centro de Arte Contemporáneo Wifredo Lam; *Tiempo extra* (2016), at the Fundación Ludwig de Cuba; *Al pan, pan* (2016) and *¿Cómo te lleva la presión?* (2019), both at Galería Taller Gorría; and *E'piritismo cubano* (2019), at Fábrica de Arte Cubano. Ostensibly, these events and exhibitions supported the production of a sense of community among independent architects, and served to turn entrepreneurial architecture into a form of cultural engagement.

The wave of enthusiasm around non-state architecture and its expanding presence in the public arena appeared to wane as Cuba's Ministry of Labor announced its new policies banning architects from participating in the private sector in early 2021. In response to the shift in policy, GECA issued a public statement on their social media pages on February 20, 2021, in which they argued for the urgent "decentralization of architecture" and for the appreciation of small-scale design practices in the constitution of the everyday city. In an effort to remap the contentious relationship that traditionally existed between architects and the Revolution, GECA's executive committee openly engaged state institutions such as the Ministry of Construction (MICONS) as potential partners for negotiation toward a more advantageous legal framework. Nevertheless, a series of meetings between GECA and the head of the MICONS shortly after the announcement of the ban on private architecture did not seem to yield any positive outcomes for entrepreneurial designers. The most impassioned response was penned by Fernando Martirena the same month for a popular media outlet. Summoning the definition of love by French philosopher Jacques Lacan as "giving what you do not have to someone who does not want it," Martirena asserted that independent architects, "despite having been excluded from the new social contract, will keep giving"—in line with Lacan's proposal—"what they do not have to those that do not want it" (Martirena, "Leve aproximación"). Gesturing toward an act of affective commitment with Cuba's built environment, Martirena, as one of the leading young voices of Cuba's independent architectural scene, powerfully contends that the new studios will persist in defying the historic monopoly of the state over architectural practice, beyond imposed material and legal limits. Be that as it may, the new architectural offices have already left a clear mark in the materiality of urban space. Mobilizing a plurality of approaches within the past decade, architects have strengthened a community of practice that points toward new directions in Cuban design, while also making visible a geography of investments that position central areas of the city as enclaves for the emerging local middle classes, in the context of the island's contradictory process of further incorporation into regimes of global capital.

NOTES

I would like to thank the architects who took the time to discuss both their work and the state of the architectural field in Cuba, and who contributed with their views to the writing of this article. Special thanks go to Fernando Martirena, Anadis González, Alejandra Pino, Suli Álvarez, Orlando Inclán, Hayder Valdivia, Elisa Alè, José A. López, Pedro D. Rodríguez, Héctor E. Sullivan, Ramón Ramírez, Daniel Muñoz, Darío Veranes, Gina Rey, Felicia Chateloin, Ayleen Robainas and Nelson Herrera Ysla. I am also indebted to Roberto Zurbano and Gretel Marín for their generous conversation during the initial steps of this research. I thank Dr. David Tenorio at the University of Pittsburgh and my colleagues at the University of Turku for thoroughly reading and commenting on drafts of this article. Finally, I would like to thank the Kone Foundation for their generous financial support to carry out this research.

1. To preserve anonymity, this person's name has been changed.

2. Eugenio Batista (Havana, 1900–Miami, 1992), Mario Romañach (Havana, 1917–Philadelphia, 1984), and Manuel Gutiérrez (Artemisa, 1925–Miami, 2006) were renowned modernist architects, active in Cuba during the 1940s and 1950s. Along with most architects of their generation, they left the island shortly after the triumph of the Revolution in 1959 (Rodríguez vi).

3. This is not to say that industrialized mass-scale construction did not produce its own particular aesthetics. As John A. Loomis has pointed out, standardization was associated to a "'scientific' iconography expressive of a revolutionary socialist identity, more in tune with generalized universalist values than with those of culturally or ethnically specific identity" (117). Similarly, Emma Álvarez-Tabío has argued that the *Girón* prefabricated system, designed by Cuban architects and engineers for the rapid and efficient construction of rural schools, constituted a particular iconography in itself, while also becoming "la imagen alternativa más característica creada por la Revolución" ("Alquimia" 15) (Figure 1).

4. Coyula is referring to what he called the "bitter trinquennium" (*trinquenio amargo*), the dark years in which an excess of political orthodoxy led to a severe control and censorship of the arts, and to the punishment and marginalization of a considerable number of creators. For Coyula, the period approximately lasted from 1967 to 1982 (34).

5. As tourism was embraced as a means of refloating the Cuban economy during the 1990s, most of the architecture produced during the decade had to do with the restoration of historic districts and the development of hotels (Zardoya 28–29).

6. Some of these selected architects have been able to operate legally thanks to the *carnet de artista independiente*, provided by the Sección de Arquitectura at UNEAC (Unión Nacional de Escritores y Artistas de Cuba). The Sección de Arquitectura was created in the 1990s, but up until today, only a small number of these professionals have been included as "artists" within the ranks of UNEAC.

7. A degree in architecture can be obtained in Cuba from four institutions of higher education: Universidad Tecnológica de La Habana "José Antonio Echeverría," Universidad Central "Marta Abreu" de Las Villas, Universidad de Camagüey, and Universidad de Oriente in Santiago de Cuba.

8. As explained by Richard E. Feinberg, these emerging middle classes largely overlap with the private sector, but they also include some public-sector employees within its ranks (43).

9. The changes introduced in February 2021 substituted the restrictive list of allowed activities that previously regulated self-employment with a list of forbidden ones instead. The shift in

policy can be read as attempt by the Cuban government to expand the private sector in the context of a COVID-stricken economy, while also firmly maintaining key sectors like healthcare, communications and architecture beyond the reach of legal entrepreneurship.

10. Previous to being acquired by the current owners, the building had a fully residential use, which raises questions regarding how architectural discourses of material sustainability do not always clearly line up with goals of social sustainability, as projects where recycling is central may become entangled with emerging processes of gentrification.

11. The final look of "Mambo n. 5" room is the result of H[r]g's intervention on the architectural front, and of Darío Veranes's work on the interior design aspects. Veranes designed the stair railing, lamps and 1920s-inspired furniture. In this sense, "Mambo n. 5" constitutes an exception to the other rooms, which were decorated by fully reusing the furniture pieces that were already available.

12. Words pronounced by the architect during a roundtable discussion titled "Interioridades I," which took place in Havana on October 11, 2019. I thank Fernando Martirena for the transcript of the event.

13. Alejandra Pino and Elisa Alè led this project, which received an award at the XI Salón de Arquitectura at the Unión Nacional de Arquitectos e Ingenieros de la Construcción en Cuba (UNAICC) in 2017.

14. In her study on capitalist ventures and solidarity networks in Post-Soviet Cuba, Marina Gold points out that "in practice most of the funds to purchase and renovate houses come from *émigré* Cubans" (136).

15. Several luxury hotels have opened their doors in recent times. The Grand Packard Hotel was inaugurated in Old Havana in 2018, while the controversial Paseo del Prado Hotel started operating in 2019 (Escobar). Other upscale hotels have been planned for the city, including a forty-two-story tower in El Vedado, whose construction has stirred up a debate among local architects (Hernández Busto).

16. In a 2014 article, Coyula warned about a potential future scenario whereby Miami-based Cubans would return to the island to encourage the construction of shopping malls, the unrestricted expansion of suburban sprawl, the privatization of public beaches, and the use of private transport ("¿Cómo será . . . ?" 31–33). In a book published with Joseph Scarpaci and Roberto Segre in 2002, Coyula and his co-authors also alerted the public of foreign investors' attempts to build skyscrapers in El Vedado (351), and celebrated the fact that Havana's seafront had not yet succumbed to a "Miamization" process (352). Cuban-American architect Andrés Duany has also raised similar concerns regarding the possible participation of South Florida exiles in the future planning of Havana (10).

17. Statement offered by the architect during the "Interioridades II" roundtable discussion in Havana, on October 25, 2019. I am grateful to Fernando Martirena for the transcript of the event.

18. Also mentioned by the architect at "Interioridades II."

19. The Instagram post can be accessed at https://www.instagram.com/p/ByIZnpCBK6K/.

20. This person's name has been changed.

21. Álvarez states this in an interview published by the page of Arquitectas Cubanas on Instagram, on Sept. 8, 2020. The post can be accessed at https://www.instagram.com/p/CE2e-ymhP29/.

22. The well-known phrase was originally coined by American architect Louis Sullivan in his 1896 text "The Tall Office Building Artistically Considered."

23. For Duchamp, the "infra-thin" was the minute separation between elements, which constituted a space of possibility. Some examples the artist gave for the "infra-thin" included the warmth of a seat that had just been left, or the separation between the detonation noise of a gun and the apparition of the bullet (Perloff 101).

24. Regarding Cuban modernist architecture, Martirena states the following: "Supposedly,

1950s architecture is the best—an architecture based on climate and identity. These are two topics that are of no interest to us."
25. Swiss architect Valerio Olgiati has proposed a "non-referential architecture"—that is to say, an architecture that is itself meaningful without appealing to external references—as a proper expression for what he deems to be today's "non-referential world," in which no common social ideals have endured (Olgiati and Breitschmid 14).
26. Personal communication with the architect, Aug. 27, 2020.
27. Statement by Martínez at "Interioridades II."
28. As of 2019–2020, GECA's executive committee was composed by Orlando Inclán as president, Hayder Valdivia as vice president, Renán Rodríguez as secretary, Julio Herrera as treasurer, and Fernando Martirena as coordinator of social media and public events. On social media, GECA can be found at /gecacuba (on Facebook), and at /estudios_cubanos_arquitectura (on Instagram).

REFERENCES

Álvarez, Suli. Personal interview. 30 Oct. 2019.
Álvarez-Tabío Albo, Emma. "Cocina al minuto: Acerca de la alquimia, la gula y la improvisación." *Arquitectura / Cuba*, no. 375, 1992, pp. 15–20.
———. "The City in Midair." *Havana Beyond the Ruins: Cultural Mappings After 1989*, edited by Anke Birkenmaier and Esther Whitfield, Duke University Press, 2011, pp. 149–72.
Coyula, Mario. "¿Cómo será La Habana?" *Revista Bimestre Cubana*, vol. 115, no. 40, 2014, pp. 22–33.
———. "The Bitter Trinquennium and the Dystopian City: Autopsy of a Utopia." *Havana Beyond the Ruins: Cultural Mappings After 1989*, edited by Anke Birkenmaier and Esther Whitfield, Duke University Press, 2011, pp. 31–52.
Cuadra, Manuel. *De primera mano: La arquitectura de la Revolución cubana 1959–2018. Entrevistas con sus protagonistas y cronistas*. Kassel University Press, 2019.
Deupi, Victor. "The Profession of Architecture in Cuba Since 1959." *Cuba Facing Forward: Balancing Development and Identity in the Twenty-First Century*, edited by David White et al., Affordable Housing Institute, 2018, pp. 73–103.
Dodsworth, Simon. *The Fundamentals of Interior Design*. AVA, 2009.
Duany, Andrés. "Sólo nos queda La Habana." *La Habana: Arquitectura del siglo XX*, edited by Eduardo Luis Rodríguez, Blume, 1998.
Edwards, Charity. "Of the Urban and the Ocean: Rachel Carson and the Disregard of Wet Volumes." *Field: A Free Journal for Architecture*, vol. 7, no. 1, Nov. 2017, pp. 205–18.
Escobar, Luz. "En el Paseo del Prado surge un hotel de gran lujo que 'estropea el paisaje urbano del Malecón.'" *14ymedio*, 16 Oct. 2019, https://www.14ymedio.com/reportajes/Paseo-Prado-estropea-paisaje-Malecon_0_2748325146.html.
Feinberg, Richard E. *Soft Landing in Cuba? Emerging Entrepreneurs and Middle Classes*. Latin American Initiative. Brookings Institution, Nov. 2013.
Gold, Marina. "Capitalist Ventures or Solidarity Networks? Self-Employment in Post-Soviet Cuba." *Anthropologies of Value: Cultures of Accumulation Across the Global North and South*, edited by Luis Fernando Angosto-Ferrández and Geir Henning Presterudstuen, Pluto, 2016.
Gómez-Puerto, Gerardo, et al. "Preference for Curvature: A Historical and Conceptual Framework." *Frontiers in Human Neuroscience*, vol. 9, no. 712, Jan. 2016, pp. 1–8.
González, Anadis. Personal Interview. 2 Aug. 2019.
Hernández Busto, Ernesto. "Proyecto de megahotel en El Vedado suscita polémica entre arquitec-

tos." *CiberCuba*, 22 June 2020, https://www.cibercuba.com/noticias/2020–06–22-u200807 -e200807-s27061-proyecto-megahotel-vedado-suscita-polemica-arquitectos.

Inclán, Orlando. Personal Interview. 1 Sept. 2019.

Lange, Torsten, and Emily Eliza Scott. "Making Trouble to Stay With: Architecture and Feminist Pedagogies." *Field: A Free Journal for Architecture*, vol. 7, no. 1, Nov. 2017, pp. 89–99.

Loomis, John A. *Revolution of Forms: Cuba's Forgotten Art Schools*. Princeton Architectural Press, 2011.

Martirena, Fernando. "Leve aproximación al Grupo de Estudios Cubanos de Arquitectura: cuando das algo que no tienes a alguien que no lo quiere." *Rialta Magazine*, 24 Feb. 2021, https:// rialta.org/leve-aproximacion-al-grupo-de-estudios-cubanos-de-arquitectura-cuando-das-algo -que-no-tienes-a-alguien-que-no-lo-quiere/.

———. Personal Interview. 2 Aug. 2019.

Olgiati, Valerio, and Markus Breitschmid. *Non-Referential Architecture*. Park Books, 2019.

Perloff, Marjorie. *21st Century Modernism: The "New" Poetics*. Blackwell, 2002.

Peters, Kimberley, and Philip Steinberg. "The Ocean in Excess: Towards A More-than-Wet Ontology." *Dialogues in Human Geography*, vol. 9, no. 3, 2019, pp. 1–15.

Pino, Alejandra. Personal Interview. 27 Aug. 2019.

Ramírez, Ramón. Personal Interview. 23 Aug. 2019, and 5 July 2020.

Reisinger, Karin, and Meike Schalk. "Becoming a Feminist Architect, . . . Visible, Momentous, With." *Field: A Free Journal for Architecture*, vol. 7, no. 1, Nov. 2017, pp. 1–10.

Rodríguez, Eduardo Luis. *The Havana Guide: Modern Architecture 1925–1965*. Princeton Architectural Press, 2000.

Rodríguez, Pedro D. Personal Interview. 23 Aug. 2019.

Scarpaci, Joseph L., et al. *Havana: Two Faces of the Antillean Metropolis*. University of North Carolina Press, 2002.

Valdivia, Hayder. Personal Interview. 22 and 27 Aug. 2019.

Zardoya Loureda, María Victoria. "La Habana." *La arquitectura de la Revolución cubana 1959– 2018: Relatos históricos regionales—Tipologías—Sistemas*, edited by Manuel Cuadra, Kassel University Press, 2018, pp. 9–36.

CARLOS GARCÍA PLEYÁN

El papel de los arquitectos en la rehabilitación de la ciudad consolidada: Hacia un nuevo modelo en la proyección de vivienda social

RESUMEN

El mayor reto social que enfrentan hoy los arquitectos en Cuba es el de la rehabilitación de la ciudad consolidada. Pasó ya la época de los grandes crecimientos urbanos periféricos con sus enormes gastos de suelo y nueva infraestructura. Por otra parte, los derrumbes siguen incrementándose, el patrimonio arquitectónico y urbanístico se va desmoronando y los vacíos urbanos se siguen acumulando. Ello abre una enorme oportunidad para la inserción de nueva vivienda en el tejido urbano existente, pero demanda, también, de un amplio y cuidadoso esfuerzo de proyecto arquitectónico y urbanístico, que tiene poco que ver con la oferta actual de un restringido catálogo de proyectos típicos por parte de las empresas estatales. De la calidad de aquellos proyectos dependerá la supervivencia o no de uno de nuestros patrimonios culturales más valiosos: las ciudades cubanas. ¿Cómo abordar ese enorme desafío? Es imprescindible hallar respuestas tecnológicas, financieras, jurídicas, metodológicas, organizativas e, incluso, institucionales a la altura del problema. Ni las actuales entidades estatales de proyecto, ni arquitectos independientes de forma dispersa pueden enfrentar un reto de tal magnitud. Es vital concebir e implementar un diálogo y una articulación público-privada capaz de ofrecer respuestas económicas, técnicas y de proyecto con la calidad necesaria, pero al mismo tiempo en la magnitud requerida.

ABSTRACT

Rehabilitating the already-consolidated city is the biggest social challenge that architects nowadays face in Cuba. The time of peripheral urban sprawl, with its huge associated costs of land and infrastructure, is long gone. On the other hand, the collapse of buildings continues to escalate, architectural and urban heritage is progressively declining, and vacant spaces keep accumulating throughout the city. All this opens a great opportunity for the insertion of new housing within the existing urban fabric, but it also demands an ample and careful effort when proposing new architectural and urban projects. These projects will have to differ significantly from the limited catalog of standard projects currently provided by state design enterprises. Whether one of our most valuable forms of cultural heritage—Cuban cities—will survive or not will depend on the quality of those projects. How should we approach this massive challenge? It is essential to find technological, financial, juridical, methodological, organizational, and even institutional responses that can rise to the occasion. Neither current state design enterprises nor independent architects in a scattered manner will be able to confront an issue of such proportions. It is vital to conceive and implement a dialogue and a public-private articulation that is able to offer economic, technical, and project-related answers with the necessary standards of quality and, at the same time, in the large scale that is needed.

El problema de la vivienda y la rehabilitación de la ciudad existente

La demanda de trabajo proyectual debiera crecer en los próximos años en forma acelerada. Múltiples razones indican que las principales transformaciones urbanas se desarrollarán en la trama urbana existente, de forma puntual, lo que requerirá de un enorme esfuerzo de diseño arquitectónico y urbanístico, sensible tanto al contexto edificado como a las demandas diferenciadas de la población. ¿Están preparados los arquitectos cubanos para ello? Es cada día más evidente que la intervención en las ciudades cubanas exige de un enfoque innovador en el que la participación de los arquitectos en su rehabilitación debe ser mucho más activa y diferenciada que la ofrecida por las actuales empresas estatales de proyecto. Son diversas las razones que concurren en ese sentido.

En primer lugar, hay que recordar que el problema esencial a afrontar en los próximos años no será el del crecimiento urbano, sino el de la rehabilitación de la ciudad existente. La demanda de nueva vivienda por crecimiento demográfico, por ahora, casi ha llegado a sus límites. La población de las ciudades mayores de cincuenta mil habitantes se halla prácticamente estancada en Cuba desde hace veinticinco años en unos cinco millones. Ello se debe a que el crecimiento natural es casi nulo (natalidad-mortalidad) y la migración campo-ciudad se equilibra con el éxodo al exterior. Por otra parte, tampoco puede crecer la demanda de vivienda por un incremento del número de familias puesto que su tamaño (2.9 personas por familia) es difícil ya que disminuya mucho más. Es por ello que en los próximos diez años las necesidades de nueva vivienda por crecimiento demográfico se han calculado por el Ministerio de la Construcción (MICONS) en solo un 6 por ciento del total requerido (MICONS 5) (ver tabla 1).

En segundo lugar, es un hecho indiscutible que el estado del fondo construido ha ido empeorando gradualmente a lo largo del tiempo debido a la prolongada ausencia de un programa de mantenimiento y conservación. Por una parte, el 35 por ciento de las edificaciones urbanas tienen ya más de medio siglo —52 por ciento en el caso de la capital— (ONEI 398) y, además de vetustas, se trata de inmuebles que han sufrido a menudo fuertes transformaciones y adaptaciones internas (por ejemplo, divisiones, ampliaciones, barbacoas).

TABLA 1. Destino de la vivienda en el Programa constructivo 2019–2028

Destino de las viviendas	Número de viviendas	Porcentaje relativo de viviendas (%)
Cuba		
Crecimiento habitacional	52,000	6
Albergados	45,000	5
Reposición	431,000	46
Subtotal de vivienda nueva a construir	528,000	57
Subtotal de viviendas existentes a rehabilitar	402,000	43
Total de viviendas de nueva construcción y a rehabilitar	930,000	100
La Habana		
Crecimiento habitacional	11,000	6
Albergados	44,000	24
Reposición	46,000	25
Subtotal de vivienda nueva a construir	101,000	55
Subtotal de viviendas existentes a rehabilitar	84,000	45
Total de viviendas de nueva construcción y a rehabilitar	185,000	100

Nota: El número de viviendas ha sido redondeado al millar más próximo.
Fuente: MICONS, *Política de la vivienda en Cuba*, 2018.

Casi trescientas mil familias viven en condiciones habitacionales precarias (ciudadelas y cuarterías), con un considerable hacinamiento. Y por otra parte, las construidas en los últimos sesenta años también adolecen a menudo de serios problemas constructivos que, por ejemplo, han generado filtraciones en más del 48 por ciento del fondo (ONU-Habitat e INV 15). Las dificultades que han existido durante mucho tiempo para adquirir los materiales requeridos para su reparación han incrementado los problemas para su conservación y mantenimiento.

Todo ello configura un panorama donde es manifiesto que en los próximos años las ciudades no debieran ocupar nuevas áreas periféricas, sino que el problema de la vivienda deberá resolverse en su interior, haciendo ciudad sobre la ciudad. Ahora bien, es muy difícil que la intervención en la ciudad consolidada pueda llevarse a cabo de forma masiva con las herramientas y procedimientos actuales, a base de prefabricación pesada y de proyectos típicos. La morfología de la trama urbana, a menudo de tipología medianera, con alta densidad constructiva, requerirá de proyectos específicos para cada parcela en particular (ya se trate de una rehabilitación, una ampliación o de una nueva inserción). Y ello demandará de un esfuerzo de proyecto que no podrá resolverse solo con las empresas estatales, ni cuantitativa ni cualitativamente. Hoy, a lo más que llegan es a un catálogo de proyectos típicos de vivienda, pero no a propuestas específicas para cada ubicación.

Todo esto significa que la demanda de proyectos arquitectónicos y urbanísticos crecerá considerablemente en los próximos años, a no ser que aceptemos el peligro técnico-constructivo y la degradación estética que puede significar la rehabilitación de ciudades (muchas de ellas con patrimonios arquitectónicos y urbanísticos de alto nivel) por esfuerzo propio de sus moradores, sin disponer de proyecto y sin regulación ni control efectivos. Entonces, la pregunta es obvia: ¿está en condiciones el gremio de arquitectos para hacer frente a la enorme demanda que se avecina?

Antecedentes y experiencias

Una mirada retrospectiva revela que de 1953 a 1959 se construyeron unas veinte mil nuevas viviendas urbanas anuales (crecieron de 790 mil a 910 mil en ese periodo), de las cuales unas diez mil tenían proyecto arquitectónico (Segre 125). Tomando en cuenta que en esos años había en Cuba unos ochocientos arquitectos (de los cuales el 90 por ciento trabajaba en la Habana), ello significaría una producción promedio de doce proyectos de vivienda por arquitecto por año. De 1959 a 1963 se construyeron unas doce mil nuevas viviendas urbanas anuales, de las cuales seis mil fueron construidas por el Estado, 4,500 por esfuerzo propio y unas mil quinientas diseñadas por arquitectos privados (Fernández Núñez 106). Parte de ellos había ya emigrado y otros se habían incorporado a las empresas estatales. Ello significa que todavía un número considerable de viviendas (casi un 40 por ciento) seguía construyéndose sin proyecto.

A partir de los años 60, comenzó a incrementarse el papel de la prefabricación pesada y del proyecto típico en la solución del problema de la vivienda. Pero ello no significó que desapareciera la autoconstrucción ni mucho menos. De hecho, el papel de la construcción por medios propios, sin un proyecto producido o avalado por un arquitecto, ha significado una proporción mayoritaria, que ha variado en todo el periodo revolucionario entre un 68 por ciento y un 53 por ciento según el decenio. En total, desde 1959 a la actualidad, se han producido en Cuba 2.7 millones de viviendas y, de ellas, 1.7 millones han sido generadas por esfuerzo propio —un 62 por ciento para todo el periodo (ver tabla 2). Es bueno aclarar que la producción de viviendas no forzosamente equivale a construcción. Una parte de las nuevas viviendas es producto de ampliaciones (tanto horizontales como verticales: "barbacoas", construcciones en azoteas, etc.) y las subsiguientes divisiones. Es obvio que la calidad técnica, estética y funcional de estas operaciones no es siempre la mejor.

Solo en los años 90, cuando la crisis disminuyó drásticamente las posibilidades estatales de construcción de vivienda, el gobierno permitió el surgimiento de propuestas novedosas que pretendían ofrecer una asesoría técnica adecuada a la construcción por esfuerzo propio. Ante las insuficiencias que evidenciaba el programa de vivienda estatal prefabricada, se creó en 1994 una organización no gubernamental, HÁBITAT-CUBA, que propuso un planteamiento

TABLA 2. Producción de viviendas en Cuba por periodos, 1959–2019

Periodo	Fondo habita- cional al inicio del periodo	Producción por esfuerzo estatal al final del periodo	Producción por esfuerzo privado al final del periodo	Total de viviendas producidas al final del periodo	Porcentaje de viviendas por esfuerzo privado (%)	Viviendas producidas por cada 1,000 habitantes al final del periodo
1959–1969	1,560,000	118,000	246,100	364,100	67.6	43
1970–1980	1,905,000	166,100	315,400	481,500	65.5	48
1981–1989	2,363,000	204,100	356,600	560,700	63.6	61
1990–2001	2,900,000	255,200	417,400	672,600	62.1	51
2002–2011	3,534,000	184,700	204,400	389,100	52.5	35
2012–2019	3,886,000	109,900	146,100	256,000	57.1	29
Total	4,110,000	1,038,000	1,685,900	2,723,900	61.9	44

Nota: Se ha estimado una depreciación del fondo de unas doscientas mil viviendas para todo el periodo.
Fuente: Cálculos del autor en base a la estadística censal y los Anuarios estadísticos de la ONEI.

radicalmente distinto. Ya desde la década anterior se había ido conformando un nuevo enfoque, que se haría explícito en la Primera Reunión sobre Política de Vivienda realizada en el año 1991. Este defendía la necesidad de (a) incorporar la rehabilitación y el mantenimiento y no solo priorizar la nueva construcción; (b) ajustar el patrón tecnológico para hacerlo sustentable, lo que cuestionaba la prefabricación pesada como única vía; (c) adaptar la construcción al lugar, al clima y a la familia, evitando la vivienda y el edificio típico; (d) reconocer la necesaria cooperación con el auto esfuerzo desarrollado por la población.

En ese marco conceptual surgió HÁBITAT-CUBA, como una sociedad que funcionaba bajo principios cooperativos. Comenzó organizando el "Programa del Arquitecto de la Comunidad" (PAC) y fue ampliando su acción hacia la experimentación del uso del bambú y la tierra, la rehabilitación y conservación del patrimonio edificado, así como el mejoramiento de los barrios precarios. El PAC tenía la función de atender las necesidades de las familias en cuanto a diseño (mediante un método participativo), asesorías técnicas sobre mante- nimiento y nueva construcción, sobre tecnologías apropiadas y, en general, cualquier servicio que fuera necesario, incluyendo los documentos gráficos obligados para trámites legales. Ello ofrecía solución a unos de los problemas más graves: la producción desde 1959 hasta ese momento de alrededor de un millón de viviendas por esfuerzo propio sin la asistencia técnica adecuada.

Se ha constatado que entre el 60 y el 80 por ciento de las viviendas cons- truidas sufre modificaciones o reformas una o más veces durante su vida útil, tales como ampliaciones, divisiones, resignificación de locales, todo ello con un escaso o nulo asesoramiento técnico que haga posibles las soluciones adecuadas. Los problemas son numerosos y de diverso tipo: deficiencias de iluminación, ventilación y asoleamiento, agudización de problemas funcionales, eliminación total o parcial de las áreas libres por insuficiencia de espacio, deficiencias técnicas como filtraciones, problemas estructurales, conflictos con las viviendas colindantes, soluciones no acordes con el entorno urbano, o violación de las regulaciones urbanísticas o de las ordenanzas de construcción.

A ello se añaden las insuficiencias de los programas docentes de arquitectura. Como escribe la fundadora de HÁBITAT-CUBA, la arquitecta Selma Díaz: "los arquitectos se gradúan en cualquier parte del mundo sin haber visto jamás a un cliente. ¿Es imaginable pensar que un médico se gradúe sin haber visto jamás a un enfermo?" (162).

El programa de los arquitectos de la comunidad se inició con un grupo de arquitectos locales en Holguín en 1994, continuó por la provincia de Cienfuegos y se fue extendiendo rápidamente por todo el país. Bajo esta perspectiva, el profesional se convertía en un agente social importante en la comunidad, vinculaba los resultados de su trabajo al salario que percibía y aumentaba su satisfacción profesional. Eran evidentes, además, los beneficios en las soluciones arquitectónicas y su adecuación al entorno urbano, ya que en la ciudad consolidada no puede haber soluciones tipo porque tampoco existen ni familias, ni lugares tipo.

Se trataba de una organización basada en los principios de una cooperativa de profesionales con las siguientes características:

• Capacitación en diseño participativo antes de comenzar a trabajar con la población.
• Trabajo de cada profesional en una zona concreta de la ciudad, lo que permitía integrar orgánicamente los conceptos y normativas urbanas dentro de las soluciones arquitectónicas.
• Democracia interna: elección de la dirección del grupo territorial por los propios profesionales.
• Vinculación del salario a los resultados obtenidos.
• Control técnico sistemático del grupo territorial sobre el trabajo de cada uno de sus integrantes.

En sus últimas etapas, HÁBITAT-CUBA trabajaba ya también en la escala urbanística llevando adelante experiencias de rehabilitación de manzanas degradadas o reconversión de barrios precarios por medio de un enfoque participativo en el diseño y la gestión de las soluciones urbanas (García Pleyán 209).

A pesar del éxito indudable de la experiencia, en el año 2001 el Instituto Nacional de la Vivienda —en una lamentable regresión a paradigmas anteriores—

consideró que la experiencia ya no era necesaria y, tras haber absorbido a los más de quinientos arquitectos que trabajaban ya en el PAC (y convertirlos prácticamente en inspectores urbanos), disolvió abruptamente la organización. Hasta este momento el PAC no ha podido recuperar los intereses y las prácticas originales que dieron sentido a su creación.

Por otra parte, a finales de los 80 comenzaron a gestarse una serie de proyectos de desarrollo comunitario que fundamentalmente tendían a llenar espacios locales de coordinación y gestión que el Estado no podía satisfacer con eficacia debido a su alto grado de centralización. Entre ellos se destacaron los Talleres de Transformación Integral del Barrio (TTIB), creados en 1988 y conducidos por el Grupo para el Desarrollo Integral de la Capital (GDIC), fundado un año antes, con dos propósitos fundamentales: remediar la fragmentación y sectorialización del crecimiento urbano impulsando su integralidad, así como proponer e impulsar nuevas formas de gobierno en la base para incrementar la participación popular directa en la solución de los problemas que más la afectan (Chappotin Aranguren 105). Así pues, los Talleres constituían equipos técnicos conformados por profesionales residentes en el barrio que, junto con la población, buscaban soluciones locales a los problemas de la comunidad. Estaban integrados por profesionales afines tanto al trabajo social como al constructivo: arquitectos, ingenieros, sociólogos, psicólogos, trabajadores sociales, técnicos en construcción, etc.

Estos equipos multidisciplinarios surgieron en La Habana inicialmente en los barrios con mayores problemas sociales, como Atarés, La Güinera, Pogolotti, Los Pocitos, Alamar o Cayo Hueso. Más tarde se fueron ampliando progresivamente a otros lugares de la ciudad hasta constituir veintiún TTIB, logrando incluso el municipio de Marianao cubrir todos sus Consejos Populares con sus correspondientes Talleres. Estos equipos comenzaron a trabajar en cuatro líneas de acción: mejoramiento de las condiciones materiales de vida, educación urbana de niños y jóvenes, identidad comunitaria y desarrollo de la economía local. Sus dos objetivos principales eran los de generar una participación real de los vecinos en la solución de sus propios problemas involucrándolos en la identificación, ejecución y mantenimiento de sus proyectos, y lograr un cambio de actitud en los actores locales para alcanzar niveles adecuados de integración y cohesión territorial.

La persistencia de altos niveles de centralización en la asignación y gestión de los recursos materiales y financieros hizo que se frustrara un real involucramiento de los gobiernos locales, derivando la actuación de los Talleres hacia temas de educación popular, actividades culturales y de protección medioambiental, salvo en aquellos casos en que se pudo disponer de recursos materiales a partir de proyectos de cooperación internacional. El gobierno de La Habana no admitió la difusión de los talleres al resto de la ciudad con lo que, desafortunadamente, su actuación se fue debilitando con el tiempo.

Situación actual

Como se señalaba al inicio, la compleja situación de la vivienda en las ciudades cubanas se ha ido agudizando cada vez más. En el año 2018, el Ministerio de la Construcción (MICONS), responsable del problema habitacional a partir de la disolución del Instituto Nacional de la Vivienda (INV) en 2014, formuló y presentó a la Asamblea Nacional una "Política de la vivienda en Cuba". En ella se calcula el déficit existente en cerca de un millón de unidades, por lo que se propone un programa constructivo para rehabilitar en diez años unas cuatrocientas mil viviendas y construir otras 530,000 nuevas (MICONS 4). La participación popular que el programa prevé es importante: más de la mitad de la construcción y de la rehabilitación deberá ser asumida por el esfuerzo propio (ver tabla 3). En el caso de La Habana, debido a las características constructivas y urbanísticas de una gran ciudad, la proporción naturalmente disminuye a una cuarta parte pero, de todos modos, ello significa una demanda, solo en la capital, en los próximos diez años, de 4,800 proyectos anuales (casi veinte diarios). ¿Quién va a asumir tal número de proyectos? ¿Cómo se va a asegurar la calidad técnica de esas construcciones y rehabilitaciones? No hay que olvidar, por otra parte, que quedan algo más de tres millones de viviendas (más de medio millón en La Habana) que requieren de acciones de mantenimiento y conservación, si queremos evitar que su depreciación se acelere.

La necesidad de proyectos específicos es ineludible. En primer lugar, no es posible ignorar la diversidad de la demanda. La familia típica de cuatro o cinco habitantes por vivienda, asumida para los cálculos de la vivienda en los

**TABLA 3. Producción de viviendas por esfuerzo propio
en el Programa constructivo 2019–2028**

Tipo de obra	Viviendas por esfuerzo propio	Número total de viviendas (por esfuerzo estatal y propio)	Porcentaje de viviendas por esfuerzo propio (%)
Cuba			
Construcción	300,000	528,000	56.8
Rehabilitación	217,000	402,000	54.0
Total	527,000	930,000	56.7
La Habana			
Construcción	26,000	101,000	25.7
Rehabilitación	22,000	84,000	26.2
Total	48,000	185,000	26.0

Nota: El número de viviendas ha sido redondeado al millar más próximo.
Fuente: MICONS, *Política de la vivienda en Cuba*, 2018.

años 70 y 80, ya no es, ni con mucho, la familia dominante. El promedio de personas por hogar ha pasado a 2.8 en el último censo (ONEI 69) y en este se constataba que las familias unipersonales ya eran el 20 por ciento y las de una o dos personas alcanzaban casi la mitad (ONEI 267). En el 64 por ciento de los hogares no había niños (ONEI 268), mientras que en el 40 por ciento residían personas mayores de sesenta años (ONEI 269). Es decir, se trata de familias pequeñas, a menudo envejecidas, pero además, con recursos económicos más desiguales y con intereses más diversos que en otras épocas (desde viviendas adaptadas para cubrir funciones productivas a viviendas hoteleras para estudiantes o ancianos). No está de más recordar que se trata de datos de 2012 y que estas tendencias demográficas no solo no se han detenido, sino que probablemente se hayan acentuado en el último decenio.

Por otra parte, es difícilmente imaginable enfrentar con proyectos típicos la enorme diversidad de acciones constructivas que demanda el contexto urbano de una ciudad consolidada: rehabilitación de edificios múltiples, reparación de casas individuales, reconversión de viviendas actuales (divisiones y ampliaciones horizontales o verticales), inserción de vivienda nueva en lotes aislados, adaptación de locales diversos —por ejemplo, comercios, oficinas, almacenes— a viviendas o de estas a servicios. Se puede convenir en que este escenario requerirá de una profusa actividad de proyecto arquitectónico y urbanístico que respete y articule los intereses públicos y privados, tomando en cuenta tanto las capacidades económicas y los intereses de las familias con las características del medio ambiente construido y las regulaciones urbanas.

Perspectivas

Son numerosos los retos que plantea esta situación. Se requieren respuestas a desafíos de muy distinto tipo: tecnológicos, financieros, de diseño (arquitectónico y urbanístico), de gestión e, incluso, institucionales. La construcción y rehabilitación privada de la vivienda en el interior de las ciudades demanda de una concepción radicalmente distinta del camino seguido en la actualidad, que privilegia la vivienda nueva aislada, ubicada generalmente en la periferia de las ciudades. O se rehabilita y renueva la ciudad actual, o dentro de unos años habrá que demoler y reconstruir las zonas centrales con la lamentable pérdida de un patrimonio extremadamente valioso. Habrá que encontrar, entonces, respuestas a los siguientes temas e interrogantes:

Adecuación de las soluciones tecnológicas

¿De qué materiales y tecnologías se dispone para la vivienda nueva y para las rehabilitaciones y cuáles serían las más adecuadas? En particular, ¿cuáles para la reparación de edificios? La *Política de la vivienda en Cuba* del MICONS prevé una capacidad constructiva nacional de 59,000 viviendas anuales. Según ese documento, la mayoría de ellas (85 por ciento) se basará en tecnologías inadecuadas para las zonas urbanas: Sandino (30,000 anuales),[1] Petrocasas (15,000) madera y guano (5,000).[2] Solo los sistemas FORSA (5,100)[3] y Gran Panel (4,200) serían adecuados.[4] Pero con ellos no basta. Habrá que prever, asimismo, los materiales, equipos y oficios requeridos por el peso abrumador que debieran tener la conservación y la rehabilitación en las áreas urbanas. ¿Tienen algún papel en la ciudad la previsión de casi ciento cincuenta mil células básicas subsidiadas de 25 metro cuadrados?[5] ¿Cuál debiera ser el papel de la construcción progresiva, estatal o particular, en la ciudad consolidada?[6] ¿Cómo conducirla de forma adecuada?

Diversificación de las soluciones financieras

Hoy día solo existen tres vías para la financiación de la vivienda: el ahorro familiar, los créditos bancarios o los subsidios estatales. Estos últimos se están centrando en el subsidio de pequeñas células básicas más adecuadas a los pueblos y a la parte rural que al tejido de las ciudades grandes. Según el MICONS, el valor de la vivienda está hoy subsidiado entre el 76 y el 82 por ciento, y las acciones constructivas de conservación y rehabilitación lo están en una proporción que va del 81 al 100 por ciento. Según la *Política* tanto el pago de la vivienda como el de las acciones mencionadas ya no será subsidiado por el Estado. ¿Qué opciones tiene, por ejemplo, una pareja joven para acumular el capital necesario para construir o comprar su vivienda? Parece clara la necesidad de flexibilizar los créditos, reintroducir la fórmula del alquiler de vivienda social construida por el Estado o por cooperativas, reexaminar fórmulas hipotecarias que no impliquen el desalojo de la familia, etc.

Diversificación de las opciones de tenencia y gestión

En la actualidad el 88 por ciento del fondo habitacional es de propiedad personal de sus ocupantes. El resto se distribuye en un 4 por ciento de viviendas vinculadas y medios básicos, un 2 por ciento en usufructo, un 3 por ciento en arrendamiento permanente y un 3 por ciento sin titularidad (MICONS 11). Es decir, la abrumadora mayoría se limita a una única solución: la propiedad personal o familiar. ¿Qué impide abrir fórmulas concurrentes como la ya mencionada vivienda social en alquiler, la vivienda en gestión o propiedad cooperativa, las nuevas fórmulas de covivienda (*co-housing*) para jóvenes o parejas mayores?

Aseguramiento de la asesoría técnica a la población

Ya vimos que la ciudad de La Habana requerirá teóricamente cerca de cinco mil proyectos anuales para la construcción y rehabilitación no estatal. Si tomamos en cuenta las ciudades mayores de cincuenta mil habitantes, el programa de vivienda 2019–2028 requerirá asistencia técnica para un total de unas 200,000 viviendas por esfuerzo propio (110,000 nuevas y 90,000 rehabilitaciones). Ello significa una demanda de 20,000 proyectos anuales.

De hecho, no solo requerirán de proyecto arquitectónico, sino que muy a menudo necesitarán de asesoría jurídica o financiera. Este era el objetivo que cubría el Programa del Arquitecto de la Comunidad. Bajo esta u otra fórmula institucional y organizativa será necesario constituir un movimiento capaz de dar una respuesta profesional a tales requerimientos. ¿Se tratará de cooperativas de arquitectos, de organizaciones inspiradas en los bufetes colectivos, de estudios particulares de arquitectura constituidos por arquitectos independientes? Ya grupos como el GECA (Grupo de Estudios Cubanos de Arquitectura) han abierto una reflexión al respecto.[7] Habrá que acordar precios para los proyectos sociales y condiciones de trabajo para el ejercicio de la arquitectura. ¿Cuál podría ser el papel de la Unión Nacional de Ingenieros y Arquitectos de la Construcción de Cuba (UNAICC) en este asunto?[8]

Garantía de las soluciones urbanísticas

No está de más recordar que la ciudad no solo es arquitectura, es también urbanismo; es espacio privado y espacio público, por lo que hay que pensar la vivienda no como un ente aislado sino como un espacio complejo de habitabilidad (hábitat). Es imprescindible conocer cuál es la demanda y la oferta de suelo en la trama urbana existente, ya sea en lotes vacíos o en parcelas construidas reutilizables. Hay que calcular las demandas de urbanización, tanto de servicios primarios como de infraestructura técnica.

Es necesario investigar, evaluar y proponer las distintas opciones en cuanto a estrategias de intervención urbana: ¿Sería conveniente comenzar por las viviendas en peor estado con la consiguiente dispersión de los esfuerzos? ¿Habría que seguir la demanda espontánea de la población, privilegiando con ello las zonas y familias con más recursos económicos? ¿Cuáles serían las escalas adecuadas de intervención: el edificio, la manzana, una zona homogénea, el inicio por las plazas y las vías principales? Cada una de ellas implica una articulación público-privada de distinta dimensión y modalidad. Pretender dar respuesta a problemas tan complejos con recursos tan simples y primitivos como un mero catálogo de proyectos típicos no parece la mejor solución.

Por otra parte, ¿cómo enfrentar el problema de los barrios precarios sin involucrar a la población en la solución de los problemas? No parece conveniente la regularización y rehabilitación de esos barrios sin un adecuado planeamiento comunitario participativo, similar al que llevaban a cabo los mencionados Talleres de Transformación Integral del Barrio. ¿Cómo resolver el problema de las ciudadelas y las cuarterías? ¿Qué hacer con las comunidades de tránsito?

Conclusión

Ninguno de estos graves problemas podrá tener solución con un enfoque rígido o unilateral. Ni con el trabajo estandarizado de las empresas estatales de proyecto, ni con la labor atomizada de arquitectos aislados. Es inevitable encontrar fórmulas organizativas de cooperación público-privada que articulen los esfuerzos y capacidades de los dos. Es difícil hoy cuantificar de qué fuerza técnica se dispone al no existir un registro oficial de arquitectos. Por lo visto, se están graduando desde hace años un mínimo de doscientos estudiantes de arquitectura en las cuatro facultades existentes (aunque habría que restar los emigrados y los que se dedican a otras labores).[9] Parece existir un número de afiliados a la UNAICC de entre 2,500 y 3,000 arquitectos, de los cuales al menos un tercio reside en la capital.[10] Las empresas estatales de proyecto al parecer dispondrían de unos mil arquitectos, pero hay que tener en cuenta también a los que trabajan en el sistema de la Planificación Física (que tiene direcciones en todos los municipios y provincias del país), así como aquellos que laboran en otros organismos que también construyen viviendas y poseen grupos de proyecto, como los Ministerios de la Agricultura, de las Fuerzas Armadas, del Interior y AZCUBA.[11] No hay que olvidar, tampoco, los que trabajan en los órganos locales del Poder Popular, en las Oficinas de los Historiadores y Conservadores de las ciudades patrimoniales, o como arquitectos independientes.

Paradójicamente, es difícil saber el total de arquitectos en ejercicio, pero podría aventurarse una cifra de al menos unos seis mil. Si fueran válidas la cifras de los 20,000 proyectos anuales y una capacidad de doce proyectos por arquitecto al año, el requerimiento de unos 1,700 arquitectos no parece una cifra descabellada.[12] ¿Cuántos de ellos estarían interesados en trabajar en vivienda social? ¿Cuántos estarían dispuestos a asumir el reto proyectual de trabajar a veces con bajos presupuestos, limitaciones de espacio y de materiales? ¿Cuáles serían capaces de asumir el incitante reto de trabajar con clientes de forma participativa? ¿Qué soluciones institucionales y organizativas serían adecuadas para enfrentar el desafío apasionante de responder no solo a las necesidades de vivienda de la población, sino también a la preservación y mejoramiento de las características urbanísticas de nuestras ciudades?

Tal es el reto histórico de los jóvenes arquitectos en Cuba en la actualidad. La solución no puede provenir solo de las instituciones estatales ni de los arquitectos independientes, sino de la capacidad de diálogo que tengan los dos para aunar esfuerzos para enfrentar la situación. Es inadmisible que en el siglo XXI la ciudad que produzcamos se resuma a unos cuantos monótonos barrios periféricos y algunas aisladas obras nuevas o de restauración de arquitectura digna, pero rodeadas por una miríada de acciones constructivas por cuenta propia sin calidad estética ni funcional. En los años 90, en plena crisis, los arquitectos cubanos fueron capaces de concebir dos soluciones útiles para el momento: el Programa del Arquitecto de la Comunidad y los Talleres de Transformación Integral del Barrio. ¿Cuál debe ser la respuesta ahora?

NOTAS

1. Sistema constructivo de origen cubano que utiliza pequeños paneles prefabricados de hormigón fácilmente manejables (de menos de medio metro cuadrado y de unos sesenta y cinco kilos de peso). Fue originalmente concebido para viviendas, aunque también se ha utilizado en la construcción de escuelas, clínicas y otro tipo de construcciones.

2. Las Petrocasas son viviendas rurales construidas con paneles de PVC que se montan localmente. Se han producido en gran cantidad en Venezuela y su tecnología se introdujo en Cuba alrededor del año 2010.

3. Sistema constructivo creado en Colombia en 1995 conformado por moldes metálicos reutilizables (hasta 1,200 veces) en los que se bombea hormigón. El sistema permite disminuir costos y tiempo de construcción de las viviendas.

4. Sistema constructivo que utiliza paneles de hormigón prefabricados. Se ha usado profusamente en Cuba desde los años 70, produciendo barrios de cuatro a seis plantas de gran monotonía formal (la llamada "sopa de bloques").

5. La *Política de la vivienda* prevé una serie de subsidios para "la construcción de células básicas habitacionales a núcleos familiares que estén en disposición de solucionar su problema habitacional por esfuerzo propio" (13). En la página 36 del citado documento se consignan exactamente 145,927 de estas células subsidiadas, a razón de unas 15,000 anuales.

6. Forma de construir por la cual el dueño de una propiedad va haciendo, con los años y de manera progresiva, mejoras y ampliaciones a la vivienda. Se trata de una modalidad ampliamente extendida en América Latina.

7. Agrupación de jóvenes arquitectos cubanos que ejercen la arquitectura de manera independiente (de las empresas estatales de proyecto).

8. La UNAICC sustituyó al antiguo Colegio de Arquitectos de Cuba en el año 1983. Es una organización social profesional autofinanciada. Actualmente tiene unos catorce mil afiliados. Dentro de ella hay una Sociedad de Arquitectura.

9. Las cuatro facultades de arquitectura existentes en el país están vinculadas a las siguientes universidades: Universidad Tecnológica de La Habana "José Antonio Echeverría", Universidad Central "Marta Abreu" de Las Villas, Universidad de Camagüey y Universidad de Oriente en Santiago de Cuba.

10. Datos estimados obtenidos en consultas a diversos profesionales de la Facultad de Arquitectura de la Universidad Tecnológica de La Habana y de la UNAICC.

11. Grupo empresarial azucarero que sustituyó en 2011 al Ministerio del Azúcar (MINAZ). Su función es producir azúcar y sus derivados, así como electricidad con los residuos de la caña. Esta integrado por veinticinco empresas y dos institutos de investigaciones.

12. Evidentemente, el valor de estas consideraciones responde a la calidad de la información disponible, pero el problema en su esencia no varía.

REFERENCIAS

Chappotin Aranguren, Susana. "El Taller de transformación integral: Una alternativa más de desarrollo comunitario en Cuba". *Desarrollo local y descentralización en el contexto cubano*, editado por Roberto Dávalos Domínguez, Universidad de La Habana, 2000.

Díaz Llera, Selma. *Experiencias organizativas de autogestión y ayuda mutua para la vivienda popular.* Centro Cooperativo Sueco, 2004.

Fernández Núñez, José Manuel. *La vivienda en Cuba.* Editorial Arte y Literatura, 1976.

García Pleyán, Carlos. "Diseño urbano participativo en una manzana de Holguín". *La participación: Diálogo y debate en el contexto cubano*, editado por Cecilia Linares Fleites et al., Centro de Investigación y Desarrollo de la Cultura Cubana Juan Marinello, 2004.

Ministerio de la Construcción de la República de Cuba (MICONS). *Política de la vivienda en Cuba.* 2018, https://www.micons.gob.cu/sites/default/files/MICONS/Marco%20Normativo/POLITICA%20GENERAL%20DE%20LA%20VIVIENDA.pdf.

Oficina Nacional de Estadística e Información (ONEI). *Censo de población y viviendas 2012. Informe nacional.* 2014, http://www.onei.gob.cu/sites/default/files/informe_nacional_censo_0.pdf.

ONU-Habitat e Instituto Nacional de la Vivienda (INV). *Perfil de la vivienda en Cuba. Versión ejecutiva.* 2014.

Segre, Roberto. *La vivienda en Cuba en el siglo XX: República y Revolución.* Editorial Concepto.

DOSSIER: VISIONES, ENTUSIASMOS Y DISIDENCIAS DE LA REVOLUCIÓN CUBANA EN LA ESCENA INTELECTUAL LATINOAMERICANA DE LOS AÑOS SESENTA

MARTÍN RIBADERO Y
GRETHEL DOMENECH HERNÁNDEZ

Presentación del Dossier: Visiones, entusiasmos y disidencias de la Revolución cubana en la escena intelectual latinoamericana de los años sesenta

RESUMEN

El objetivo del presente *dossier* es reunir una serie de trabajos en torno al estudio de la relación entre intelectuales y la Revolución cubana durante los años sesenta. A partir del análisis de varias figuras y publicaciones periódicas tanto cubanas como latino-americanas inscritas dentro de la cultura de izquierdas, se busca explorar y profundizar en diversos aspectos como son los debates sobre el concepto de revolución en la isla o las disímiles maneras en que impactó el proceso entre los intelectuales de América Latina. Frente a aquellas miradas centradas únicamente en Cuba y sobre todo en espacios europeo o norteamericano, el *dossier* no solo propone abordar revistas y actores latinoamericanos hasta el momento poco atendidos, sino también experiencias y discursos escasamente analizados como son el viaje revolucionario, el cultivo del género de viaje y la conformación de redes, y posicionamientos de alcance transnacional. El fin que anima a todos los artículos es comprender de forma cabal de qué manera logró estructurarse por parte de los intelectuales, tanto cubanos como latinoamericanos, una profunda adhesión, no exenta de debates y disidencias, a la revolución durante los años sesenta, lo cual permitiría explicar la vigencia que dicho proceso conserva entre quienes se reconocen como parte de esta cultura política.

ABSTRACT

The objective of this dossier is to bring together a series of works around the study of the relationship between intellectuals and the Cuban Revolution during the 1960s. From the analysis of various figures and periodical publications both Cuban and Latin American registered within the left-wing culture, we seek to explore various aspects such as the debates on the concept of revolution on the island or the different ways in which the process impacted among the intellectuals of Latin America. Faced with those views focused solely on Cuba and especially in European or North American spaces, the dossier not only proposes to address magazines and Latin American actors hitherto poorly attended, but also in experiences and discourses poorly analyzed such as the revolutionary journey, the cultivation of travel genre and the formation of transnational networks and positions. All articles in this dossier work to fully understand how Cuban and Latin American intellectuals managed to structure such deep adherence, not without debate and dissent, to the revolution during the 1960s. With this we can explain the validity that process still has among those who recognize themselves as part of this political culture.

Libros, revistas, artículos, cartas, viajes; ideas, conceptos y debates, los intelectuales latinoamericanos han conformado un entramado múltiple de experiencias político-culturales en torno a la Revolución cubana. Para el mundo intelectual y cultural de nuestra región el proceso caribeño fue un evento nodal en la reflexión y definición de su función en cada una de sus sociedades. Quienes tomaron la palabra buscaron, de alguna manera, influir en su derrotero al diseñar una interpretación, elaborar un diagnóstico o precisar su curso a través del debate de ideas o diferentes políticas culturales. Gracias al interés mostrado por parte de la dirigencia revolucionaria, incluso algunos alcanzaron a participar activamente y tener un elevado protagonismo en el ensamblado estatal o en influyentes formaciones culturales cubanas.

Si bien fueron intelectuales cubanos los que dominaron las distintas organizaciones propias del mundo intelectual —desde Casas de las Américas, el ICAIC y la Unión de Escritores y Artistas de Cuba hasta revistas como *Lunes de Revolución* y *Pensamiento Crítico*— no es menos cierto que hombres y mujeres procedentes de distintas capitales culturales de América Latina lograron, con mayor o menor éxito, insertarse en los entresijos del aparto cultural revolucionario o, en su defecto, participar y relacionarse con grupos de la isla, ya sea a través de revistas, círculos de sociabilidad o la correspondencia. Los argentinos Julio Cortázar y David Viñas, el colombiano Gabriel García Márquez, el uruguayo Mario Benedetti, los mexicanos Carlos Fuentes y Octavio Paz, chilenos como José Donoso, el paraguayo Augusto Roa Bastos y el peruano Mario Vargas Llosa, todos parte del denominado *boom* de la literatura latinoamericana, son quizás los casos más notables que evidencian el peso que los escritores no cubanos tuvieron en la revolución y por supuesto en América Latina.

En los últimos años esta historia del *boom* ha recibido la atención del mundo académico dedicado a la historia intelectual y la crítica literaria. Los escritores cubanos y del resto de la región participantes han sido objeto de estudio de distintos investigadores, quienes ofrecen un panorama amplio y complejo de la irradiación generada por la revolución en la vida cultural y literaria de América Latina, en un contexto atravesado por la Guerra Fría, los procesos autoritarios y los efectos de una acelerada modernización cultural. Sin embargo, la relación entre intelectuales latinoamericanos y Cuba no se agota en esos casos como tampoco en el tipo de intervención asumida. Intelectuales como los mexicanos Fernando Benítez, Jaime García Terrés, Enrique Gonzales Pedrero y Laurette Séjourné; los argentinos Jorge Masetti, Alfredo Palacios, Silvio Frondizi y Elías Semán, el uruguayo Carlos María Gutiérrez; el salvadoreño Roque Dalton; el colombiano Camilo Torres Restrepo; los chilenos Enrique Delano, Sergio Aranda y Marta Harnecker; el boliviano Néstor Taboada Terán; brasileños como Theotonio Dos Santos y Vania Bambirra; peruanos como Alberto Flores Galindo y Ricardo Napuri; nicaragüenses como Ernesto Cardenal y el haitiano Gérard Pierre-Charles entre otros. Publicaciones, como las mexicanas *El Espectador* y *Política*; la colombiana *Paz y Socialismo*; las argentinas *Pasado y Presente*, *La Rosa Blindada* e *Izquierda Nacional*; el semanario uruguayo *Marcha* —e incluso cubanas, como la poco estudiada *Pensamiento Crítico*—, conforman solo algunos de los agentes político-culturales que, a pesar de inscripciones socioculturales y tradiciones disímiles, no podrían insertarse sin más en la historia del *boom*, ni tampoco asociarse únicamente con el objetivo de diseñar una específica política literaria.

Un rasgo que define a estos intelectuales, antes que el debate literario, es la elaboración de una serie de impresiones, representaciones e ideas sobre la experiencia cubana con el fin de intervenir en los debates político-ideológicos que se originaban en cada una de sus sociedades. Esta operación de traducción, tal como lo definiera Rafael Rojas, es quizás una de las labores menos atendidas por parte de quienes se han dedicado al estudio del nexo entre intelectuales latinoamericanos y revolución.[1] A partir de la escritura de artículos y libros, viajes a la isla, conferencias y ciclos de debate en universidades, instituciones partidarias y pequeños grupos, quienes se sintieron interpelados por el fenómeno cubano buscaron ejercer, de diferentes maneras, una operación de traducción en cada una de las capitales culturales de América Latina.

La historiografía dedicada a la Revolución cubana ha crecido de manera cuantitativa y cualitativa en las últimas décadas. Entre sus líneas más destacadas, la historia intelectual y de la literatura cubana han logrado convertirse en una zona muy dinámica. Como afirma Michael Bustamante, la expansión de los estudios centrada en escritores, intelectuales y militantes de la isla se ha debido al acceso fluido a diversas fuentes —libros, memorias, correspondencias, revistas— que facilitan la labor de investigadores dedicados el mundo cultural e intelectual en comparación a aquellos interesados en la historia de los trabajadores, la población afrocubana, las mujeres, el estudio de las religiones o de las instituciones estatales.[2] No obstante, los intelectuales externos de la isla y sus ideas, quienes a su vez no formaron parte del *boom*, o el develamiento de los mecanismos concretos a través de los cuales la revolución impactó en muchas familias políticas de la región, han recibido menos atención por parte de la historiografía dedicada a la revolución tanto en Cuba como en Estados Unidos y Europa. Los trabajos de académicos que priorizaron una mirada latinoamericana del fenómeno cubano como Rafael Rojas, Claudia Gilman y

Germán Albuquerque, son un importante aporte aunque, como plantea el *dossier*, aún queda un largo camino por recorrer en cuanto a las problemáticas, ideas, actores y mecanismos de circulación del relato revolucionario tanto en la isla como en el resto del subcontinente.

Bajo estas coordenadas, y en base a una serie de investigaciones en curso, el presente *dossier* reúne una serie de trabajos que buscan ofrecer nuevos aportes sobre la circulación y traducción nocional del hecho cubano realizada por escritores, políticos y periodistas latinoamericanos junto a sus diferentes soportes materiales. Para ello se acudió al estudio de algunas figuras y artefactos culturales poco advertidos aún por la historiografía dedicada a la historia de los intelectuales durante los años sesenta. La idea que guía estas intervenciones es evidenciar las disímiles interpretaciones asignadas a la revolución por parte de familias político-culturales latinoamericanas y aun cubanas (sean marxistas, socialistas, liberales reformistas, nacionalistas revolucionarios, marxistas nacionalistas) con el fin de ampliar y al mismo tiempo precisar el universo de visiones, representaciones, imaginarios y sensibilidades que despertó el proceso caribeño a lo largo de la década del sesenta y parte del setenta.

Por otra parte, los trabajos aquí reunidos plantean la necesidad de reconstruir de manera sistemática un mapa de los intelectuales, de sus redes, trayectorias y emprendimientos, que giraron en torno a la revolución. En los artículos que componen el *dossier* se tiene en cuenta nombres como Alfredo Palacios, Ricardo Masetti, Silvio Frondizi, Jaime García Terrés, Fernando Benítez, René Depestre y Roque Dalton; revistas, como las mexicanas *México en la cultura*, *El Espectador* y *Política*; las cubanas *Lunes de Revolución*, *Cuba Socialista* y *Pensamiento Crítico*; libros de viajes como los de Masetti, Frondizi, Palacios, Carlos Fuentes y García Terrés y; finalmente, el estudio de redes y marcos de sociabilidad existentes en la isla como fuera de ella. Las indagaciones revelan aspectos menos visitados y echan luz sobre los debates en torno a la noción de revolución, sus alcances y límites, así como en las reflexiones enunciadas sobre la función de los intelectuales, tanto en revistas y grupos cubanos como en dos de las más importantes capitales culturales de América Latina: Ciudad de México y Buenos Aires.

El examen de redes, revistas y trayectorias que ocupa a la mayoría de los textos, está animado por el objetivo de reconstruir la trama material que vehiculizó los marcos de participación intelectual. Frente a lo que puede suponerse, y pese a los avances que se registran, todavía el conocimiento de los efectivos mecanismos a través de los cuales se conformaron distintas asociaciones propias del mundo intelectual catalizadas por el hecho cubano no fue casi abordado. A partir de ello, los artículos presentan una parte de ese entramado que, inspirado por el embrujo cubano, nos permiten tener un mejor conocimiento de las sendas concretas y puntos de conexión establecidos entre agentes culturales latinoamericanos y la isla. En este sentido, el enfoque transnacional resulta fundamental en el estudio de la relación entre intelectuales y revolución, y es un marco de análisis que el *dossier* intenta destacar a la hora de trazar una agenda de indagaciones futuras dado el carácter global que adquirió la revolución en sí misma. Como bien han demostrado los autores citados, la labor y tomas de posición emprendida por muchos hombres y mujeres tuvo una naturaleza continental y regional visible en el cultivo de redes, proyectos editoriales, viajes y peregrinajes políticos, a la postre centrales en la modulación de una cultura intelectual transnacional en torno a lo revolucionario y sus distintas acepciones.

El apoyo que recibió el proceso isleño por una buena parte de los intelectuales latinoamericanos y aun cubanos, ha sido una característica marcada por varias investigaciones. No obstante, y como se analiza en el *dossier*, las relaciones entre estos sujetos y la revolución no siempre fue armónica. En varias ocasiones, dudas, reparos, silencios, críticas cuando no disidencias u oposiciones fueron evidentes, incluso durante el tramo de máxima adhesión concitada por el proceso caribeño en la década de 1960. Si bien el contexto de Guerra Fría mermó la fascinación por la revolución en algunos, mientras que radicalizó las posturas a favor en otros, no menos cierto es advertir la multiplicidad de posicionamientos que los intelectuales tuvieron frente al fenómeno cubano en América Latina y en la isla. Aunque el *dossier* no aborda de forma completa la geografía cultural de la región, creemos que los trabajos aquí reunidos son un significativo aporte en el sentido de reconstruir de forma sistemática y compleja esas polémicas y esas tramas materiales que diseñaron un tipo de asociación con la revolución. Todo ello, sin hablar de esa otra gama de intervenciones escasamente exploradas que, a falta de otra palabra, podría ser denominada como "contrarrevolucionaria". Nos referimos a figuras y escritos de familias político-culturales tempranamente opositoras, como fueron ciertos sectores católicos, de las derechas tanto conservadoras como liberales, fuerzas armadas, diplomáticos, empresarios, periodistas y aquellos ubicados en organismos técnicos transnacionales. Esta literatura, de enorme influencia, casi no ha llamado la atención por parte de quienes se dedican al estudio de la revolución o la vida cultural latinoamericana desde una perspectiva de la historia intelectual o cultural, y que sin embargo reclama una profunda indagación dado el poder de presión y persuasión que tuvo a la hora de caracterizar lo que denominaba como el "castrismo" o el "comunismo cubano" en la opinión pública.[3]

El *dossier* inicia con el trabajo del historiador Rafael Rojas, titulado "Tres revistas cubanas: Tres conceptos de Revolución," quien nos propone el análisis de tres revistas —*Lunes de Revolución, Cuba Socialista* y *Pensamiento Crítico*— que captaron, de distintas maneras, el sentido del concepto de Revolución cubana durante los años sesenta e inicios de los setenta. En tiempos en que la isla experimentaba diferentes caminos en la concreción de un programa radical de transformación, estas publicaciones condensaban un sentido específico tanto narrativo como teórico sobre la idea de revolución. En esas batallas intervinieron intelectuales procedentes de disimiles tradiciones político-culturales. El trabajo rastrea y reconstruye esos enfrentamientos dialécticos a través de las revistas mencionadas, brindando al mismo tiempo un panorama detenido del entramado de relaciones y afinidades que permitieron el surgimiento, vigencia y fin de estas significativas publicaciones periódicas cubanas.

A continuación, el ensayo "Cuba revolucionaria en las páginas de tres publicaciones mexicanas" de Elisa Servín examina la narrativa que construyeron varios intelectuales mexicanos en torno a la Revolución cubana. Las figuras seleccionadas para ello se movieron entre la literatura, el periodismo y la política: Fernando Benítez, Carlos Fuentes, Enrique González Pedrero, Víctor Flores Olea y otros. Estos intelectuales recibieron con ferviente entusiasmo el triunfo revolucionario cubano y desde las páginas del suplemento "México en la Cultura" y revistas como *El Espectador* y *Política* se hicieron eco de las transformaciones que vivía la isla. Pero, como bien demuestra Elisa Servín, no fue un mero suceso de divulgación lo que tuvo lugar en la prensa mexicana. La traducción de la Revolución cubana sirvió de motor para renovar a la izquierda nacional y replantear diálogos o rupturas con el propio Estado mexicano. El triunfo del proceso caribeño se convirtió no solo en una victoria latinoamericana, sino también en una posibilidad para muchos intelectuales de cuestionar al marxismo de corte estalinista lo mismo que al oficialismo priista para revitalizar así a la izquierda mexicana.

El efecto magnético que ejerció la revolución también fue visible en el peregrinaje político que emprendieron múltiples figuras del sistema-mundo intelectual. Desde Jean-Paul Sartre, Simone de Beauvoir y Eric Hobsbawm, hasta Waldo Frank, Charles Wright Mills y Susan Sontag, una colorida palestra de escritores, pensadores y académicos se trasladaron a la isla con el fin de experimentar las transformaciones emprendidas en Cuba y al mismo tiempo desplegar un ejercicio de traducción hacia sus respectivas sociedades de origen. En general, los estudios dedicados a analizar este proceso han priorizado actores procedentes de los Estados Unidos y Europa Occidental. En estas investigaciones no solo es escaso el conocimiento respecto a quienes viajaban desde otras partes, como América Latina, sino también las razones y medios desplegados para concretar dicho traslado. El trabajo "La profecía realizada: Viajeros argentinos de izquierda a la revolución cubana" de Martín Ribadero tiene como objetivo aportar al estudio del proceso de peregrinaje político global, a partir de abordar el caso de algunos argentinos como Alfredo Palacios, Jorge Masetti y Silvio Frondizi, con el fin de observar las disimiles maneras que el testimonio de dicha experiencia moldeó el proceso de traducción del fenómeno isleño entre las familias político-culturales argentinas, así como develar los mecanismos específicos empleados en la realización de cada uno de los viajes.

Por su parte, "El intelectual y la revolución. Notas sobre un encuentro de la familia intelectual latinoamericana en 1969" de Grethel Domenech Hernández, nos acerca a uno de los más importantes debates transnacionales de fines de los sesenta publicado bajo el título de "El intelectual y la sociedad," en donde Roberto Fernández Retamar, Edmundo Desnoes, Ambrosio Fornet, René Depestre, Carlos María Gutiérrez y Roque Dalton se dieron cita para discutir sobre el rol del intelectual revolucionario. Tras el triunfo de la revolución se conformó una red intelectual transnacional que tomó como punto de partida el acontecimiento para cuestionar ciertas nociones respecto a la labor de los intelectuales y sus vínculos con la sociedad. En el trabajo, Domenech encuentra que esa red se articuló a través de publicaciones como *Casa de las Américas* y el semanario *Marcha* y en encuentros como el Congreso Cultural de la Habana, en reuniones del comité de colaboración de *Casa* y en diferentes debates, como el que se somete a estudio en este artículo. Aunque las revistas han sido las fuentes privilegiadas para indagar sobre la intelectualidad de los sesenta, las memorias de encuentros y polémicas es otra forma complementaria que nos acercar aún más a tan complejo universo. En ellas se puede tomar el pulso de las discusiones intelectuales y acceder a posicionamientos que, al ser efectuados en un marco menos formal que el de una revista, por ejemplo, nos revelan interesantes zonas de conflicto. En "El intelectual y la sociedad," tal como demuestra la autora, se pueden observar de manera detenida esas discusiones respecto al rol del intelectual durante la revolución y la cuestión del ejercicio crítico.

Finalmente, Juan Alberto Salazar con "La Habana del escritor: Jaime García Terrés y la representación del compromiso intelectual en torno a la Revolución cubana en 1959" examina las propuestas intelectuales de uno de los principales escritores mexicanos de la época, Jaime García Terrés, quien viajó a Cuba inmediatamente posterior al triunfo de enero. Sus impresiones quedaron recogidas en su "Diario de un escritor en La Habana". La experiencia de García Terrés se insertó en los debates sobre el compromiso intelectual que cobraron gran importancia en los años sesenta y fueron centro de polémicas y debates. A través del diario y la labor de Terrés como director de la *Revista de la Universidad de México*, el autor reconstruye el impacto que produjo la Revolución cubana en las reflexiones de Terrés sobre el compromiso intelectual, en una época de debates, de ascenso de la izquierda y de su tránsito ideológico a partir de una revalorización de la tradición de la Revolución mexicana.

En conclusión, y como último objetivo, el *dossier* plantea una serie de cuestiones que buscan alentar una agenda de indagación a futuro a partir de incorporar otros casos y experiencias que, en un punto superior, permitan comprender, por un lado, de qué manera esa relación entre intelectuales y revolución se configuró en el proceso histórico y, por el otro, explicar cómo se confeccionó con el paso del tiempo un sentimiento de pertenencia a la revolución entre algunos y una necesidad de olvido en otros.[4]

NOTAS

1. Rafael Rojas, *Traductores de la utopía: La Revolución cubana y la nueva izquierda de Nueva York*, México, FCE, 2016, pp. 11–37.

2. Michael Bustamante, "Historiar la revolución desde los Estados Unidos," *Temas: Cultura, Ideología, Sociedad*, julio a diciembre 2017, pp. 4–12.

3. Para el caso argentino, Juan Alberto Bozza, "La sombra de la revolución cubana. Anticomunismo y nueva izquierda en la Argentina de los primeros años sesenta," IX Jornadas de Sociología de la Universidad Nacional de La Plata, diciembre 2016, http://www.memoria.fahce.unlp.edu.ar/trab_eventos/ev.8867/ev.8867.pdf.

4. La idea de este *dossier* surgió a partir de la participación de quienes escriben en el Coloquio "¿60 años de qué? Itinerarios de la Resolución Cubana", el cual tuvo lugar los días 23–26 de octubre del 2019 en la Universidad Iberoamericana y en la UAM-Xochimilco de la Ciudad de México.

RAFAEL ROJAS GUTIÉRREZ

Tres revistas cubanas: Tres conceptos de Revolución

RESUMEN

Este ensayo se propone estudiar la forma en que el concepto de revolución se plasmó en tres revistas cubanas de los años 60. Editadas en una perfecta sucesión diacrónica, *Lunes de Revolución* (1959–1961), *Cuba Socialista* (1961–1967) y *Pensamiento Crítico* (1967–1971) son fuentes ineludibles para el estudio de ese proceso de conceptualización. A diferencia de otras publicaciones, como *Casa de las Américas* o *La Gaceta de Cuba*, que por ser más institucionales se volvieron permanentes y se acomodaron a las diversas fases de la ideología del nuevo Estado, estas tres revistas intentaron captar un sentido específico del concepto de Revolución cubana. Su estudio resulta imprescindible para reconstruir la semántica diversa del cambio revolucionario en Cuba, durante los años 60, y su sometimiento, para inicios de la década siguiente, a la hegemonía discursiva del socialismo real. Cada una de aquellas tres revistas formuló su propio sentido narrativo y teórico de la revolución y lo expuso en la esfera pública de la isla con el fin de ofrecer una vía de legitimación simbólica al naciente Estado.

ABSTRACT

This essay analyzes how the concept of revolution was reflected in three Cuban journals of the 1960s. Edited in a perfect diachronic succession, *Lunes de Revolución* (1959–1961), *Cuba Socialista* (1961–1967), and *Pensamiento Crítico* (1967–1971) are unavoidable sources for the study of the process of this conceptualization. Other publications, such as *Casa de las Américas* or *La Gaceta de Cuba*, were linked to institutions, became permanent, and accommodated different phases of the ideology of the new state. The three magazines studied here tried to capture the concept of the Cuban Revolution in their own specific ways. Their study is essential to reconstructing the diverse semantics of revolutionary change in Cuba during the 1960s and exploring how, in the following decade, that variety succumbed to the discursive hegemony of real socialism. Each of these magazines articulated a narrative of the revolution, inserted it in the public sphere, and offered a path to the symbolic legitimization of the nascent state.

Entre 1921 y 1922, Walter Benjamin proyectó una revista titulada *Angelus Novus*, inspirada por el cuadro de Paul Klee que el filósofo asumiría como metáfora de la historia. En la presentación de aquella revista frustrada, Benjamin recordaba, como antecedente, la gran revista romántica *Athenäum* de Berlín, impulsada por los hermanos Schlegel, Novalis, Schelling y Schleiermacher a fines del siglo XVIII. A partir de la experiencia de aquella publicación, el marxista alemán intentaba formular la definición de una revista intelectual. Aunque la publicación estaría dedicada, fundamentalmente, a poesía, literatura y filosofía, Benjamin apuntaba que su práctica fundamental sería la crítica, ya que esta era la única capaz de radiografiar una época: "La verdadera determinación de una revista es manifestar el espíritu de una época. La actualidad de este vale más para ella incluso que su unidad o claridad, y por ende estaría condenada—como el periódico—a la insustancialidad si en ella no se configurara una vida lo bastante poderosa como para salvar aun lo que se vuelve cuestionable porque ella misma lo afirma. En efecto: es injusto que exista una revista cuya actualidad carece de pretensiones históricas".[1] Una revista, agregaba Benjamin, era una publicación "efímera" que captaba la esencia de un momento.[2] En el caso de las revistas producidas en medio de una revolución esa cualidad de acentúa mucho más. Toda revista diseñada para hablar en nombre de una revolución supone una conceptualización propia del proceso de cambio, en un contexto en el que no necesariamente existe un sentido hegemónico del término, dada la multiplicidad de actores involucrados en el mismo. Tres revistas cubanas de los años 60, editadas en una perfecta sucesión diacrónica, *Lunes de Revolución* (1959–1961), *Cuba Socialista* (1961–1967) y *Pensamiento Crítico* (1967–1971), son fuentes ineludibles para el estudio de ese proceso de conceptualización.

A diferencia de otras publicaciones, como *Casa de las Américas* o *La Gaceta de Cuba*, que por ser más institucionales se volvieron permanentes y se acomodaron a todas las fases de la ideología del nuevo Estado, estas tres revistas intentaron captar un sentido específico del concepto de Revolución cubana. Su estudio resulta imprescindible para reconstruir la semántica diversa del cambio revolucionario en Cuba, durante los años 60, y su sometimiento, para inicios de la década siguiente, a la hegemonía discursiva del socialismo real. Cada una de aquellas tres revistas formuló su propio sentido narrativo y teórico de la revolución y lo expuso en la esfera pública de la isla con el fin de ofrecer una vía de legitimación simbólica al nuevo Estado.

La revolución radical

En el primer número del *magazine* cultural *Lunes de Revolución*, fundado y dirigido por Guillermo Cabrera Infante en marzo de 1959, el editorial "Una posición" anunciaba un suplemento de doble carácter generacional y nacional. Decían los editores que la generación intelectual que emergía con la revolución era "la que extendía su cordón umbilical hasta los albores de la pasada dictadura" y que "había sido sometida a un silencio ominoso".[3] Al referirse a las publicaciones culturales previas, de altísima calidad, en el periodo republicano inmediato —*Orígenes, Ciclón, Nuestro Tiempo*—, la dirección de *Lunes* usaba términos curiosos: "hasta ahora todos los medios de expresión habían resultado de vida demasiado breve, demasiado comprometidos, demasiado identificados. En fin, estábamos presos en una cerca de demasiados demasiados".[4]

El triunfo de la revolución, según el editorial, había "roto las barreras" y había "permitido al intelectual, al artista, al escritor integrarse a la vida nacional, de la que estaban alienados".[5] La revolución, decían en una frase muy parecida a las utilizadas por Octavio Paz en *El laberinto de la soledad* (1950), a propósito de la Revolución mexicana, era "una deseada vuelta a nosotros".[6] Comprender ese "nosotros" en términos ideológicos era una forma de desentrañar el sentido de la palabra "revolución" en el campo intelectual de la isla. Para los jóvenes escritores y artistas nucleados en torno a *Lunes de Revolución* ese "nosotros" suponía pluralidad, pero también comunidad.

Desde los primeros números, los referentes históricos de la Revolución cubana, según *Lunes*, estaban claros. En el tercer número, por ejemplo, del 6 de abril de 1959, bajo el título de "Literatura y Revolución", se intentaba una síntesis de la ideología revolucionaria moderna. Allí se traducían y reproducían pasajes de *Los derechos del hombre* de Thomas Paine, un discurso antimonárquico de Saint-Just, un texto del anarquista Piotr Kropotkin, pasajes del *Manifiesto Comunista* de Karl Marx y Friedrich Engels, varios escritos sobre la Revolución rusa —Vladimir Mayakovski, John Reed, Isaac babel, León Trotsky—, sendos ensayos de André Breton y Jean-Paul Sartre sobre la izquierda francesa del siglo XX, algunos testimonios de la guerra civil española —Miguel Hernández, Federico García Lorca, Antonio Ortega, George Bernanos—, dos memorias de revoluciones latinoamericanas aplastadas, una de Miguel Ángel Asturias sobre Guatemala, y otra de Adrián García Hernández sobre Bolivia, y, finalmente, una pequeña antología de escritores y políticos revolucionarios cubanos: José Martí, Nicolás Guillén, Rubén Martínez Villena, Pablo de la Torriente Brau, Guillermo Cabrera Infante; José Antonio Echeverría, Frank País, Carlos Franqui, Fidel Castro. Aquel número, sin embargo, estaba antecedido por un editorial donde se lee: "No somos comunistas. Ninguno: ni la Revolución, ni REVOLUCIÓN, ni 'Lunes de Revolución.' Parecería que no hace falta decirlo ya en Cuba y que a cada uno que exija la aclaración o que sugiera o declare o diga o manifieste o susurre o propale que somos comunistas, decirle: 'Vaya al BRAC (Buró de Represión de Comunistas de la dictadura de Fulgencio Batista) a denunciarlo' o '¿Por qué no se lo comunica a Mariano Faget?' (jefe de aquella institución represiva)".[7]
Y agregaban los editores:

Pero nosotros, los de "Lunes de Revolución," hoy, queremos decir simplemente que no somos comunistas. Para poder decir también que no somos anticomunistas. Somos, eso sí, intelectuales, artistas, escritores de izquierda–tan de izquierda que a veces vemos al comunismo pasar de lado y situarse a la derecha en muchas cuestiones de arte y literatura. Pero eso mismo no nos impide reconocer el formidable aporte hecho por los escritores comunistas a la literatura de revolución —y de decimos "literatura de revolución" porque decir "literatura revolucionaria" implicaría discutir larga, interminablemente sobre la revolución en la literatura, cuando hablamos de la literatura en las revoluciones— en lo que va de siglo y parte del siglo pasado. Tampoco afirmar esto es negar que a partir de cierta fecha —el año 1929, para ser precisos— la posición del intelectual en las esferas oficiales comunistas devino precaria primero y luego tristemente comprometida (y el adverbio tristemente está utilizado en el mismo sentido que se emplearía el adjetivo alegre para la poesía de Mayakovsky.[8]

Estos pasajes, escritos seguramente por Cabrera Infante con el visto bueno de Carlos Franqui, captaban la idea de la revolución de una juventud socialista, crítica del imperialismo y el estalinismo. Ya en el segundo número, del 30 de marzo, se había publicado el ensayo "Imperialismo e industria en América Latina", de Henri Raymond, donde se denunciaba la explotación de los obreros latinoamericanos por el gran capital de Estados Unidos.[9] En el número especial dedicado a la clase obrera, a fines de abril, la visión antiestalinista se hizo visible en estudios como los del marxista francés Henri Lefebvre, quien ya para principios de la década del sesenta apostaba por un marxismo humanista, tan distante del estructuralismo althusseriano como del materialismo soviético. En el número 9, de mayo de 1959, aquella línea de izquierda se consolidó por medio de un tema que se volvería recurrente y, a la vez, emblemático de la posición descolonizadora de *Lunes*: la solidaridad con la liberación nacional de Argelia.[10]

Lunes de Revolución buscó diálogos explícitos con otras izquierdas intelectuales: la francesa, la estadounidense y la latinoamericana. En el número 12, de junio de 1959, la publicación intentaba reconstruir un mapa de la izquierda francesa con semblanzas y perfiles de François Mauriac, Claude Bourdet y Jean-Paul Sartre. A diferencia de Mauriac y Bourdet, que criticaban de manera sistemática el legado estalinista y el modelo soviético, Sartre, sin ser militante del Partido Comunista francés, representaba una posición atractiva para los editores de *Lunes de Revolución*: un existencialista marxista, que, al suscribir el modelo institucional soviético, modulaba sus críticas a Moscú por la importancia de la Unión Soviética para la lucha contra el imperialismo y el colonialismo y por la paz mundial.[11]

Sartre reapareció otras dos veces más en *Lunes*. En el número dedicado a la muerte de Albert Camus, en enero del año sesenta. Al abrir aquel número con la nota necrológica de Sartre sobre Camus, *Lunes* se ponía claramente del lado del primero en la pugna de aquellos dos grades intelectuales franceses de la Guerra Fría. De hecho, en un editorial que antecedía al conocido ensayo de Sartre, *Lunes* reiteraba los tópicos de la izquierda comunista acerca de la "zona de silencio" de Camus sobre la "Argelia ensangrentada" o su "creciente servilismo frente a Estados Unidos".[12] Luego, a raíz de la visita de Sartre a la isla, *Lunes* dedicó otro número al pensador francés, en el que además del ensayo "Ideología y Revolución" y la conversación con los intelectuales cubanos, se publicaron sendos textos de José Álvarez Baragaño y Juan Arcocha. El primero suscribía la tesis de Sartre según la cual la originalidad de la Revolución cubana se debía a su ausencia de ideología previa y el segundo afirmaba que el concepto sartreano de "intelectual comprometido" suponía el "heroísmo del hombre en situación".[13]

A las izquierdas de Estados Unidos, *Lunes* dedicó varias coberturas. Cuando Waldo Frank visitó la isla, en 1959, Alcides Iznaga lo entrevistó para *Lunes* y Heberto Padilla hizo una semblanza del escritor, en las que se defendía la visión humanista del escritor norteamericano sobre la Revolución cubana. En el número 55, del 18 de abril de 1955, *Lunes* propuso una reconstrucción de las impugnaciones literarias del imperialismo y la sociedad de consumo de Estados Unidos dentro de la propia cultura norteamericana: Langston Hughes, Carl Sandburg, Edgar Lee Masters, Robert Bly, Henry Miller, Allen Ginsberg. Y en el número 66 de julio de 1960 publicó un *dossier* sobre "Los negros en USA", encabezado por el ensayo "El negro americano mira hacia Cuba", en el que Richard Gibson, tras asumir las tesis del *Fair Play for Cuba Committee* en Estados Unidos, destacaba una coincidencia de fines entre la Revolución cubana y los movimientos de descolonización de Asia y África, donde, a su juicio, se inscribía la lucha de los negros contra la discriminación en Estados Unidos.[14]

La izquierda latinoamericana y sus tradiciones revolucionarias también tuvieron una presencia constante en *Lunes*. El número 22, del 17 de agosto de 1959, estuvo dedicado a la Revolución guatemalteca de Jacobo Árbenz y a su derrocamiento, en 1954, por un golpe militar de derecha, diseñado por la CIA. La mayoría de las colaboraciones de aquel número corrieron a cargo de Fernando F. Revuelta, pero en un par de entrevistas a Luis Cardoza y Aragón, a cargo de Guillermo Cabrera Infante, y a Miguel Ángel Asturias, ambos escritores eran sumamente críticos con el papel del Partido Comunista guatemalteco durante la revolución de Árbenz y de la llamada "literatura comprometida de izquierda".[15]

Las varias colaboraciones de Carlos Fuentes y, más específicamente, el número 63, de junio de 1960, dedicado a México denotaban la fuerte conexión entre los intelectuales de las revoluciones cubana y mexicana. Había en aquel número intelectuales de muy diverso signo ideológico, Emilio Uranga y Octavio Paz, Alí Chumacero y Agustín Yáñez, Juan Rulfo y Juan José Arreola, pero el núcleo protagónico del mismo era el que concedió las principales entrevistas para la sección de "Los intelectuales mexicanos y la Revolución Cubana":

Carlos Fuentes, Fernando Benítez, Enrique González Pedrero, Víctor Flores Olea y Jorge Portilla. Todos ellos, intelectuales cardenistas que al año siguiente estarían vinculados al Movimiento de Liberación Nacional (MLN).

Es interesante observar que la idea de la Revolución cubana que trasmitían aquellos intelectuales mexicanos no era comunista. Portilla hablaba de una revolución "hispánica", "quijotesca", que completaba los ideales independentistas del siglo XIX; González Pedrero de una revolución "latinoamericana", en la tradición de la mexicana de 1910, que unía las causas de Simón Bolívar, José Martí y Emiliano Zapata; Benítez se quejaba de que a la revolución se le hubiese "colgado el sanbenito de comunista"; Flores Olea decía "en el más profundo sentido del término, la Revolución Cubana es una revolución humanista"; y para Fuentes se trataba de una revolución contra el subdesarrollo: "la máxima lección de la Revolución Cubana es esta: nuestros países sólo podrán alcanzar un desarrollo efectivo a través de la utilización plena y racional de sus recursos propios".[16]

Incluso en los números dedicados a grandes figuras de la cultura comunista como Pablo Neruda y Pablo Picasso, los editores de *Lunes de Revolución* se cuidaron mucho de proyectar una visión favorable de la experiencia soviética. Ninguno de los grandes escritores comunistas cubanos intervino en el homenaje al gran poeta chileno. La visión de Neruda que predominó en el número 88, de diciembre de 1960, fue la del propio grupo de *Lunes*: Virgilio Piñera, Antón Arrufat, Heberto Padilla, Edmundo Desnoes, Pablo Armando Fernández. El homenaje a Picasso, por su lado, a pesar de corresponder al último número del *magazine*, ya clausurado por el gobierno revolucionario, después de la declaración del "carácter socialista" de la revolución, en abril de 1961, incluyó una nota de Juan Marinello, pero preservó la visión de *Lunes* —Guillermo Cabrera Infante, Carlos Franqui, Virgilio Piñera, Oscar Hurtado, Edmundo Desnoes— y hasta le agregó la voz de Lezama Lima con su ensayo "Cautelas de Picasso".[17]

La idea de una revolución radical de izquierda, socialista y anti-imperialista, pero no inscrita en la órbita soviética, se expresó, ante todo, en la lectura de la historia de las ideas políticas cubanas que trasmitió aquel suplemento cultural. *Lunes* consagró un número a las teorías del imperialismo, en el que se reprodujo un pasaje del conocido ensayo de Lenin, pero también la crítica no marxista al imperialismo de clásicos cubanos como Enrique José Varona, Manuel Sanguily y José Martí.[18] Entre las figuras de la historia política y cultural cubana que homenajeó *Lunes* hubo comunistas como Rubén Martínez Villena pero también otros que no lo fueron como el propio Martí, Pablo de la Torriente Brau o José Raúl Capablanca.

Aquella idea de la revolución no solo era sumamente plural desde el punto de vista ideológico, también defendía un margen de autonomía de la cultura, dentro de la defensa mayoritaria de un arte y una literatura comprometida, y afincaba su radicalismo en una demanda de transformación profunda del antiguo régimen. Virgilio Piñera captó, como pocos, aquel concepto de revolución al utilizar la imagen de una "fuerza arrolladora". En su artículo "La Revolución se fortalece", sostenía Piñera, que los beneficios del cambio revolucionario a los trabajadores y los campesinos eran tan concretos, que si cualquiera de los líderes del proceso cubano, "Fidel, Raúl, Camilo, Guevara, Almeida o Ameijeiras", la Revolución seguiría su curso, depurando a la clase dominante de periodo republicano.[19]

La Revolución soviética

A diferencia de *Lunes de Revolución*, que surgió como publicación cuando la Revolución cubana se definía ideológicamente como no comunista, *Cuba socialista* nació como revista mensual tras la reorientación doctrinal de 1961. Desde el primer número en el verano de aquel año, el Consejo de Dirección estuvo integrado por Fidel Castro, Osvaldo Dorticós Torrado, Blas Roca, Carlos Rafael Rodríguez y Fabio Grobart. Aquel comité editorial reunía a las dos principales figuras del gobierno y el Estado, el presidente Dorticós y el primer ministro Castro, y tres de los líderes máximos líderes históricos del Partido Comunista prerrevolucionario: Roca, Rodríguez y Grobart. *Cuba Socialista* era, por tanto, una revista dirigida por la máxima autoridad política e ideológica de la isla.

A pesar de ser una revista de Estado, aquella publicación mensual era también un órgano del campo intelectual. Sus editores eran intelectuales: poco antes de enero de 1959, ninguno de ellos cumplía funciones gubernamentales, todos formaban parte de la oposición pacífica o armada e intervenían en la esfera pública del país. Ahora como funcionarios del nuevo Estado estaban decididos a trazar el nuevo corpus ideológico oficial. Una operación nada fácil, toda vez que los orígenes ideológicos de la revolución misma no eran propiamente comunistas y dentro de la izquierda marxista se abrían múltiples posibilidades para Cuba y América Latina. La izquierda latinoamericana entraba en una fase de diversificación, por lo que el establecimiento de una línea cubana era todo un reto.

Desde los primeros números, los editores subdividieron el objetivo de la publicación en tres funciones: una analítica, otra instructiva y otra más de difusión. A través de la primera, *Cuba Socialista* se proponía someter a la interpretación marxista-leninista los principales problemas de la conducción económica, política y cultural del país. La segunda función suponía instruir o educar teóricamente a los actores dirigentes del país de acuerdo con el enfoque analítico adoptado. Finalmente, el rol de difusión de la revista actuaba en dos sentidos: dar a conocer la experiencia revolucionaria cubana en el mundo y, a la vez, contribuir a asimilar lo mejor del pensamiento socialista mundial, especialmente el desarrollado en la Unión Soviética y Europa del Este.

Aun cuando todos los editores eran partidarios del avance hacia una inscripción de la experiencia cubana en el campo socialista, había diferencias entre ellos en cuanto a las tres funciones. Una diferencia que se manifestó desde los primeros números tenía que ver con las distintas maneras de pensar y narrar el tránsito socialista en Cuba. Editores y colaboradores como Carlos Rafael Rodríguez, Blas Roca o Ernesto "Che" Guevara pensaban que la revolución había pasado de una fase anti-imperialista y agraria a otra propiamente socialista entre 1959 y 1961. Osvaldo Dorticós y el propio Fidel Castro se inclinaban por la tesis de que desde julio de 1953, cuando se produjo el asalto al cuartel Moncada, el núcleo dirigente central de la revolución ya poseía una ideología marxista-leninista.

A partir de los primeros meses de 1962, otras divergencias sutiles aparecieron dentro de la publicación. En marzo de 1962, un incidente en la celebración del aniversario del asalto a Palacio Presidencial por el Directorio Revolucionario el 13 de marzo de 1957, provocó un debate interesante en *Cuba Socialista*. En su intervención en aquella ceremonia en la escalinata de la Universidad de la Habana, Fidel Castro criticó al maestro de ceremonias porque silenció la alusión a Dios en el testamento del mártir estudiantil José Antonio Echeverría.[20] En *Cuba Socialista* se reprodujo el discurso de Castro y una reacción de Blas Roca, en la que es posible leer tensiones controladas entre el liderazgo del viejo partido comunista y la joven dirigencia del Movimiento 26 de Julio.

Según Castro, el escamoteo del catolicismo de Echeverría amenazaba con resquebrajar la "unidad de todos los elementos progresistas y patrióticos, desde el católico sincero, que no tenga nada que ver con el imperialismo ni con el latifundismo hasta el viejo militante marxista".[21] Por ese camino, alertaba Castro, la revolución podría convertirse en una "escuela de domesticados" y pedía a los "responsables" a "hacerse una buena autocrítica".[22] Dado que el líder máximo del partido único en construcción, por entonces en tránsito de las ORI (Organizaciones Revolucionarias Integradas) al PURSC (Partido Unido de la Revolución Socialista) era Aníbal Escalante, viejo militante comunista, Blas Roca decidió emprender aquella autocrítica en *Cuba Socialista*. En su respuesta decía Roca, que "Fidel había lanzado un ataque a fondo al enfoque no marxista, ni dialéctico, ni materialista de los acontecimientos y los personajes históricos".[23]

Roca suscribía las críticas indirectas a Aníbal Escalante al cuestionar no solo la distorsión de las ideas marxistas que suponía pretender la exclusión de los católicos revolucionarios del proceso, sino la incorrecta comprensión de las fases del tránsito socialista. En la fase de destrucción del régimen latifundista y neocolonial era tan necesaria una interpretación incluyente de la historia —en la que pudiera apreciarse al presbítero Félix Varela y al "materialista" Felipe Poey, al "hacendado" Carlos Manuel de Céspedes y al "carretero" Antonio Maceo— como una dirección partidista persuasiva, que no confundiera "dirección" con "imposición" y que diera mayor importancia a la persuasión y al convencimiento de las masas.[24]

Con la destitución de Aníbal Escalante al frente de la construcción del partido único, el núcleo central del viejo comunismo, representado en la dirección de *Cuba Socialista*, afirmó su lealtad a Fidel y Raúl Castro y cedió definitivamente el liderazgo máximo a estos últimos. Pero a cambio de aquel reacomodo, *Cuba Socialista* ganó terreno, especialmente a partir de 1962, para la difusión de las tesis soviéticas sobre Cuba y América Latina. Cada número de la revista aparecía con un largo epígrafe de algún clásico del marxismo-leninismo sobre el principal tema abordado: en el número de abril de 1962, el exergo correspondió a Lenin sobre el papel de la religión en el tránsito socialista. En el siguiente número, de mayo, en plena reestructuración de la dirección del PURSC, le tocó de nuevo a Lenin sobre la "depuración del partido". En esa nueva entrega de *Cuba Socialista*, Severo Aguirre hacía un elogio de la labor de Carlos Rafael Rodríguez al frente del Instituto Nacional de la Reforma Agraria (INRA) y señalaba abiertamente las limitaciones del primer agrarismo revolucionario.[25]

En el número 10 de *Cuba Socialista*, ya realizada aquella "depuración" del partido único, los editores volvían al cauce del proyecto soviético. Allí Jacinto Torras hacía un balance positivo de las que llamaba "relaciones fraternales entre Cuba y la Unión Soviética", desde 1960, y Santiago Cuba se lanzaba abiertamente a un ataque contra el "clero reaccionario" y su vínculo con la contrarrevolución en la isla.[26] Ya para entonces, varios artículos de Blas Roca y Pelegrín Torras sobre América Latina o de Luis Corvalán, específicamente sobre Chile, trasmitían una visión del continente moldeada por los partidos comunistas nacionales. No solo eso, varios autores soviéticos como Yuri Krasin, Vladimir Li, M. Rosental y Mijaíl Strepujov y I. Evenko proyectaron la visión de Moscú sobre diversos temas: desde políticos como el programa del Partido Comunista de la URSS, el sistema electoral soviético o las luchas por la liberación nacional, hasta teóricos como los fundamentos del leninismo, la teoría de Marx del capitalismo contemporáneo o el modelo soviético de planificación económica.

Un interés particular tenía para *Cuba Socialista* la reproducción de aquellos discursos de Nikita Kruschev que trataban la cuestión cubana o latinoamericana. En el número 11, de julio de 1962, se publicaba un discurso del mandatario sobre la "soviético-cubana" en el que se exaltaba la "intrepidez" de Fidel Castro y se proponía un paralelismo entre los inicios de la transición socialista cubana y la época de la guerra civil en la Rusia bolchevique.[27] Kruschev abordaba el tema de las escasez y el desabastecimiento mercantil, que a su juicio se relacionaba con el aumento de la hostilidad del enemigo", y sugería a los cubanos unidad política, pero también aprovechamiento de los avances tecnológicos para enfrentar los problemas económicos de la revolución.[28] No podía suceder que la juventud se frustrara porque después de hacer la revolución y derrotar a Batista, "faltara la carne, el arroz y la leche".[29]

Tan importante era, según el líder soviético, el heroísmo como la industrialización. Una doble perspectiva ideológica y, a la vez, científica del desarrollo socialista que desarrollaron, por su parte, autores como Alfredo Menéndez Cruz para enfrentar las dificultades al despegue de la industria azucarera, o Lionel Soto para aplicar la "instrucción revolucionaria marxista-leninista" a las necesidades de la "planificación, el ahorro y el trabajo productivo".[30] La presencia de Nikita Kruschev en los índices de *Cuba Socialista* a fines de 1962 se acentuó.[31] Sin embargo, después del número de octubre, que coincidió con la "Crisis de los misiles" a fines de ese mes, en el que apareció su alocución sobre los "Problemas candentes del desarrollo del sistema socialista mundial", el mandatario soviético no volvió a figurar más como autor de *Cuba Socialista*.[32]

No quiso decir eso que la revista perdiera su orientación pro soviética, pero sí que su línea editorial abría un flanco de crítica o distanciamiento prudencial con Moscú, provocado por el malestar de la dirigencia revolucionaria con el pacto Kennedy-Kruschev. En el número de noviembre no se aludió a la crisis de los misiles y, junto con un artículo del veterano dirigente comunista César Escalante, en homenaje al 45 aniversario de la Revolución de Octubre, se publicaron sendos ensayos de S. Shkurko y S. Vishniov que alababan el sistema de "remuneración del trabajo", el principio del "interés material" y el liderazgo de la Unión Soviética en la economía mundial.[33] Sin embargo, en el número de diciembre, la crisis de octubre era enfocada desde una perspectiva centralmente cubana a través de la "Respuesta de Cuba al Presidente Kennedy" y un discurso de Fidel Castro, en el que se enfatizaba la resolución del pueblo de la isla a defender la revolución por sí mismo.[34]

A partir de 1963 se observa una mayor dosificación de los autores soviéticos y un aumento de la presencia de firmas cubanas —Osvaldo Dorticós, Armando Hart, Carlos Rafael Rodríguez, Julio Le Riverend, Sergio Aguirre, Mirta Aguirre, Edith García Buchaca, Raúl Cepero Bonilla, Regino Boti— que reflejaban la tensión entre la perspectiva pro soviética y otras más latinoamericanistas y nacionalistas. El Che Guevara, que había publicado un breve texto sobre la política de cuadros en 1962, y que no ocultaba sus críticas al sistema de planificación económica del socialismo real, comenzó a colaborar más asiduamente en *Cuba Socialista*. En febrero de 1963, el número 18 arrancó con el ensayo de Guevara "Contra el burocratismo", aunque seguido de dos autores bien ubicados en la línea del viejo partido comunista: García Buchaca y Soto.[35] Luego, en septiembre del 63, reapareció Guevara en la publicación con un extracto de su manual sobre la guerra de guerrillas.[36]

A partir de 1964, cuando Guevara promueve más abiertamente sus tesis alternativas sobre la dirección de la economía y el tercermundismo de las relaciones internacionales de la isla, *Cuba Socialista* refleja algo de aquella corriente, pero bajo la hegemonía del horizonte pro soviético. De aquel debate se publicaron ensayos de Carlos Rafael Rodríguez, Augusto Martínez Sánchez, Raúl León, Marcelo Fernández Font, Chales Bettelheim, Marcelo Fernández, Luis Álvarez Rom y el propio Guevara.[37] El hecho de que fueran Rodríguez o Roca quienes pertenecían al Consejo de Dirección de la revista, y no Guevara, además de toda la bibliografía favorable al modelo del cálculo económico que se traducía de los soviéticos, hizo que la alternativa del financiamiento presupuestario promovida por el argentino estuviese en minoría. El último artículo de Guevara aparecido en *Cuba Socialista* fue "Posición de Cuba frente a los problemas internacionales", el famoso discurso ante la Asamblea General de la ONU, en diciembre de 1964, que formulaba una estrategia revolucionaria radical en el rol de la isla en el mundo, no compartida por Moscú y buena parte de la vieja dirigencia comunista cubana.

La contradicción entre el guevarismo y el prosovietismo, predominante en *Cuba Socialista*, no solo tenía que ver con la planificación económica o las relaciones internacionales, sino con la política cultural y el compromiso de los intelectuales. En su ensayo "El socialismo y el hombre en Cuba" (1965), Guevara criticó la norma del "realismo socialista" establecida por la burocracia cultural soviética.[38] Sin embargo, en *Cuba Socialista* aparecieron una defensa abierta del realismo socialista, escrita por el teórico soviético Iván Volkov, y varios apuntes que llamaban a una adopción o una crítica condescendiente o relativista de aquella doctrina.[39] Entre 1964 y 1965, la revista reforzó la presencia de enfoques marxista-leninistas sobre la religión, el arte y la ciencia, como los de Kuzin, Shujardin y otros teóricos soviéticos.[40]

A partir del número doble 45–46, correspondiente a los meses de mayo y junio de 1965, que coincidió con la creación del primer Comité Central del Partido Comunista de Cuba, del que ya no formaría parte el Che Guevara, la revista, con un nuevo diseño, aunque el mismo formato, comenzó a dosificar más la presencia de autores soviéticos. Sin embargo, es notable a partir de entonces un mayor interés en la experiencia de otros países del campo socialista como Hungría y Checoslovaquia, China y Mongolia. En el caso chino, luego de varios artículos favorables a la experiencia socialista en ese país, que reflejaban, a su vez, la oposición de Mao al pacto Kennedy-Kruschev, *Cuba Socialista* suscribió la postura adversa del nuevo secretario general del PCUS, Leonid Brezhnev, sobre la revolución cultural.[41]

Si se lee con cuidado la "Respuesta de Fidel Castro a las declaraciones del gobierno chino" en el número 55 de marzo de 1966, se observará que la posición oficial de La Habana no solo compartía las tesis antichina de Moscú, sino que mostraba preocupación por el crecimiento de la corriente maoísta en la izquierda latinoamericana.[42] Tampoco gustaba a la cúpula comunista de la isla, en perfecta sintonía con Moscú, la recuperación de la IV Internacional y el trotskismo dentro del movimiento guerrillero latinoamericano y la Nueva Izquierda occidental. Fidel Castro criticó a los trotskistas en la Conferencia Tricontinental y Blas Roca lo tomó de punto de partida para lanzar una verdadera diatriba contra el trotskismo en *Cuba Socialista*, en la que se presentaba a publicaciones como *The Militant* y *The Newsletter* como medios del imperialismo yanqui.[43]

Entre fines de 1966 y principios de 1967, *Cuba Socialista* mostró claramente las ambivalencias de la posición oficial de Cuba dentro de la Nueva Izquierda. Mientras el Gobierno de Fidel Castro respaldaba las guerrillas latinoamericanas y los movimientos de descolonización y liberación nacional en Asia y África, el núcleo ideológico central del nuevo Partido Comunista era partidario de una lucha anti-imperialista conducida por los partidos comunistas leales al Kremlin. Lionel Soto, un dirigente de clara adscripción soviética, sería el encargado de resumir las tesis centrales de la Tricontinental, así como de ligar la idea del "modelo cubano" o el "camino propio" al socialismo real de la Unión Soviética y Europa del Este.[44]

En febrero de 1967, mientras Mirta Aguirre reseñaba a Engels y B. Kedrov defendía la "dialéctica materialista de las ciencias naturales", los editores anunciaron con parquedad un "receso" en la publicación de *Cuba Socialista*.[45] Es difícil no relacionar el cese de la publicación con las contradicciones a las que se enfrentaba un gobierno que impulsaba guerrillas latinoamericanas, apoyaba al Che Guevara en Bolivia y era percibido como símbolo de la Nueva Izquierda en Occidente, a la vez que mantenía a flote el entendimiento con Moscú. En un año sumamente complejo, que culminaría con la muerte de Guevara en Bolivia, el proceso a la "Microfracción" —un grupo de treinta y cinco militantes comunistas, encabezados por el veterano dirigente Aníbal Escalante, acusados de traición y condenados a largos encarcelamientos— y el arranque de la Ofensiva Revolucionaria, que extendió la propiedad estatal a los medianas y pequeñas empresas de servicio, *Cuba Socialista* cerró sus páginas.

La revolución guevarista

En febrero de 1967, el mismo mes que *Cuba Socialista* entró en receso, comenzó a publicarse en el Departamento de Filosofía de la Universidad de La Habana, la revista *Pensamiento Crítico*. La publicación, dirigida por el filósofo Fernando Martínez Heredia, Director del Departamento de Filosofía de la Universidad de La Habana desde 1966, contó desde los primeros números con otros intelectuales de la nueva generación revolucionaria, como el escritor Jesús Díaz y los filósofos Aurelio Alonso, Thalía Fung y José Bell Lara. La revista, según sus editores, surgía de la "necesidad de información que sobre desarrollo del pensamiento político y social del tiempo presente tiene hoy la Cuba revolucionaria". En la presentación de aquel número de febrero de 1967, agregaban: "hoy todas las fuerzas sociales de nuestro país están en tensión creadora; lo exigen la profundización y la magnitud de las metas de la Revolución". Y concluían: "contribuir a la incorporación plena de la investigación científica de los problemas sociales a esa Revolución es el propósito de esta publicación".[46]

A diferencia de *Lunes de Revolución*, que era un suplemento cultural, y *Cuba Socialista*, que era una publicación centralmente ideológica del nuevo Estado y el nuevo partido, *Pensamiento Crítico* se presentaba como una revista de ciencias sociales, aunque puesta al servicio de la revolución. Su aspiración no era, únicamente, la aplicación de las ciencias sociales al estudio de la Revolución cubana, sino el análisis de los aportes de la experiencia socialista de la isla al "pensamiento político y social del tiempo presente". No localizaban geográficamente aquel "pensamiento", los jóvenes editores, pero el primer número anunciaba una importante inmersión en la realidad latinoamericana. Los autores de aquella primera entrega (Camilo Torres Restrepo, Fabricio Ojeda, Julio del Valle) eran partidarios expresos de la vía guerrillera. Dos de ellos, Torres y Ojeda, de hecho, habían muerto un año antes en la lucha armada de Colombia y Venezuela y eran mencionados por el Che Guevara en su "Mensaje a la Tricontinental".[47]

En aquel mismo número, los editores publicaron un artículo del peruano Ricardo Letts Colmenares, con el pseudónimo de Américo Pumaruma, que cuestionaba la eficacia del modelo guerrillero. Sin embargo, la redacción de la revista antepuso una nota que descalificaba esa posición: la crítica de la vía armada, según *Pensamiento Crítico*, se "apoyaba sobre la memoria de Camilo Torres, Luis de la Puente, Fabricio Ojeda y Turcios Lima, sobre el sacrificio de miles de revolucionarios latinoamericanos".[48] Los editores reaccionaban contra el cuestionamiento concreto del método "fidelista" —plasmado en *La guerra de guerrillas* del Che Guevara— que a juicio de Pumaruma había decidido el fracaso de la guerrilla peruana de Jauja en 1962. Además de una "desnaturalización de la teoría del foco", el artículo, al insistir en la importancia de la teoría, parecía proponer una "guerrilla de gabinete".[49]

En una breve memoria de la revista, que escribió su director, Fernando Martínez, en 1997, se admitía que aquella nota era "dura".[50] Según Martínez, la publicación del texto de Pumaruma se debió a la certeza de que "si nada más existe lo que pensamos nosotros, estamos perdidos", pero aquel nosotros, en La Habana de 1967, era bastante heterogéneo. La tesis de Pumaruma, contraria al tipo de lucha armada que giraba en torno al modelo guevarista, era compartida por sectores del propio Partido Comunista, como pudo constatarse en la respuesta que algunos ideólogos de esa institución dieron al ensayo *¿Revolución en la Revolución?* (1967) de Regis Debray. Para complicar aún más el panorama, dentro de la propia redacción de *Pensamiento Crítico* predominaba una lectura ambivalente de Debray: se le reconocía su aporte teórico a una izquierda que se rebelaba contra la ortodoxia pacifista de los partidos comunistas, pero se le reprochaba que, a diferencia del Che Guevara, no partiese más firmemente de la experiencia cubana.[51]

Las diferencias de los jóvenes marxistas cubanos con Debray eran más prácticas que teóricas y solo emergieron en la publicación luego del arresto del intelectual francés en Camiri, Bolivia, en abril de 1967. Coincidían con la defensa de la lucha armada y la crítica al dogmatismo de los partidos comunistas prosoviéticos, pero temían que la teoría del foco de Debray autonomizara la experiencia guerrillera dentro de América Latina: "mientras que el Che parte de la experiencia de la Revolución Cubana e intenta establecer sobre el plano teórico ciertos principios fundamentales de la guerra de guerrillas, Debray parte del proceso insurreccional de los movimientos actuales del continente, antes de incitar a releer al Che y redescubrir sobre la base de un conocimiento exhaustivo el proceso insurreccional cubano".[52] Dicho de otra manera, lo que inquietaba a los editores de *Pensamiento Crítico* era que la teoría foquista de Debray contribuyera a descubanizar a las guerrillas latinoamericanas.

A pesar de su clarísima orientación guevarista, después del primer número, *Pensamiento Crítico* trató con cuidado el tema de las guerrillas latinoamericanas. Salvo en caso de intervenciones puntuales como la del venezolano Ignacio Urdaneta que reseñó la ruptura del MIR y el grupo de Douglas Bravo con la línea de "paz democrática" del Partido Comunista Venezolano, de entrevistas a guerrilleros peruanos y bolivianos, o del largo ensayo de John William Cooke sobre la potencialidad revolucionaria del peronismo, el tema de la guerrilla no mereció otro *dossier*.[53] La entrega doble de marzo-abril de 1967 se desplazó a la cuestión africana con textos de Amílcar Cabral sobre Guinea, Djuma Mbogo sobre Ruanda, Jean-Paul Sartre sobre el pensamiento político de Patricio Lumumba, Maurice Maschino sobre el "itinerario de la generosidad" de Frantz Fanon y Gerald Chaliand, traductor de *La guerra de guerrillas* de Guevara, sobre el proceso de descolonización norafricana, que conocía muy bien dado su involucramiento en el Frente de Liberación de Palestina.[54] El número siguiente, el cuarto, el tema fue la guerra de Vietnam, con trabajos de Günther Anders, Bernard Couret, Boris Teplinsky, Le Duan y Hamza Alavi. Encabezaba aquel número el "Mensaje a los pueblos del Tercer Mundo" de Bertrand Russell y lo cerraba "Conciencia de clase y partido revolucionario" Michael Löwy, con lo cual el arco teórico de la Nueva Izquierda que se proponía cubrir la revista suponía una defensa de los movimientos de liberación que iba desde el liberalismo progresista occidental hasta el marxismo trotskista latinoamericano.[55]

Ya desde el verano de 1967 se hizo evidente el interés de *Pensamiento Crítico* de avanzar hacia una asimilación del repertorio teórico de la Nueva Izquierda. En el quinto número, de junio de 1967, aparecieron tres figuras básicas del nuevo pensamiento marxista francés: Luis Althusser, André Gorz y Jean-Paul Dollé. Gorz, nacido en Austria, y Dollé, habían estado muy ligados a Sartre y *Les Tempes modernes*, pero para mediados de los años 60 ya habían transitado del existencialismo al comunismo. Althusser aparecía en *Pensamiento Crítico* con un resumen metodológico de sus lecturas de *El Capital*, donde se enfrentaba a dos tendencias, a su juicio, equivocadas, dentro del marxismo: la soviética neohegeliana que reducía el materialismo histórico al dialéctico y la de buena parte de marxismo occidental, dentro de la que citaba a Lukacs y a Gramsci, que hacían lo contrario y reducían la dialéctica al materialismo histórico.[56] Althusser proponía una reconstrucción paralela de ambas partes de la doctrina marxista a través de una hermenéutica de *El Capital*.

La presencia de Althusser en *Pensamiento Crítico* se consolidaba desde aquel número con una generosa reseña de sus tres libros, *Por Marx* y *Leer El Capital I* y *II*, a cargo de Jacques Goldberg. Si Sartre ofrecía el acceso al marxismo desde el existencialismo, como sostenía Gorz, Althusser, dirá Goldberg, hacía la misma operación desde la epistemología estructuralista.[57] La contribución de Dolle a aquel número negociaba la tensión entre la ideología sartreana y la ciencia althusseriana por medio de la síntesis del "humanismo socialista".[58] A tono con las lecturas del propio Guevara, quien desde la selva boliviana seguía de cerca la obra de ambos, *Pensamiento Crítico* abrió las puertas a Sartre y Althusser hasta el verano de 1968, cuando el primero pierde presencia por sus críticas a la invasión soviética a Checoslovaquia, respaldada por Fidel Castro.

También se interesó *Pensamiento Crítico* en otras ramas de la Nueva Izquierda como la estadounidense (Oscar Lewis, Harry Magdoff, Thomas G. Buchanan, Paul Sweezy, Paul Baran), en el partido de los Black Panthers y el movimiento del Black Power (Stokely Carmichael, Huey Newton, H. R Brown, Robert F. Williams), en el marxismo social británico de *New Left Review* (Perry Anderson, Robin Blackburn, Eric Hobsbawm, Ralph Miliband) y en la teoría de la dependencia (André Gunder Frank, Sergio Bagú, Theotonio Dos Santos, Ruy Mario Marini, Vania Bambirra). Pero ninguna otra escuela pesó tanto en la revista como el estructuralismo francés. En el número 10, *Pensamiento Crítico* reprodujo parcialmente la famosa polémica de Louis Althusser, Jorge Semprún y André Daspre sobre arte, ciencia, ideología y humanismo, en *La Nouvelle Critique*, pero con una selección y un enfoque favorables al primero.[59]

En el número siguiente, la revista publicó el brillante ensayo sobre el estructuralismo de *El Capital* de Maurice Godelier.[60] Todavía en 1968 *Pensamiento Crítico* dedicó un número más al estructuralismo francés. En la presentación, luego de citar a Lévi-Strauss, Hjelmslev y Saussure, los editores decían que el estructuralismo "se consolidaba con la coherencia de un método" aplicable a la lingüística, la psicología, le etnología, la antropología, la sociología, la economía, la historia y la filosofía, especialmente, a lo que llamaban "el marxismo", no marxismo-leninismo.[61] En aquel número monográfico sobre el estructuralismo francés, *Pensamiento Crítico* publicó a Jean Cuisenier, Marc

Barbut, Paul Ricoeur, Lucien Sebag y Henri Lefebvre, además de una entrevista de Michel Delahaye y Jacques Rivet a Roland Barthes sobre el cine.[62]

La preferencia por Althusser y el marxismo estructuralista francés obedecía a razones teóricas y políticas. Algunos discípulos del filósofo como Régis Debray y Marta Harnecker, autora del conocido manual *Conceptos elementales del materialismo histórico* (1968), se involucraron directamente en la red de solidaridad con las guerrillas latinoamericanas. Pero, además, Althusser y sus discípulos, especialmente Étienne Balibar, eran de los marxistas franceses que, a la vez que defendían la autonomía intelectual frente a Moscú, proclamaban la necesidad de seguir operando con el concepto de "dictadura del proletariado", y eran críticos resueltos del "eurocomunismo" y la socialdemocracia.[63]

Aquella inmersión teórica y política de *Pensamiento Crítico* en el horizonte de la Nueva Izquierda, cuyas sintonías con el mayo francés del 68 eran evidentes —la revista dedicó su número 25-26 a la revuelta parisina con textos de Raymond Aron, Daniel Cohn Bendit, Jean-Paul Sartre, Roger Garaudy, André Malraux y Ernest Mandel— y produjo una particular conceptualización de la Revolución cubana y latinoamericana. Ya en un número anterior, el 21, la revista se había acercado al 68 por medio de dos ensayos que defendían el espectro de la izquierda radical alemana, a cargo de Giorgio Backhaus y del líder estudiantil Rudi Dutschke, en los que la organización más privilegiada en el análisis era la Federación Estudiantil (SDS) y no la Fracción del Ejército Rojo (RAF), de Andreas Baader y Ulrike Meinhoff.[64] Buena parte de la Escuela de Frankfurt y del pensamiento de izquierda en la Alemania occidental, de Marcuse a Habermas, era vindicado en esos ensayos. En su mensaje a la juventud latinoamericana, Dutschke citaba a Malcolm X y a los Rolling Stones, al Che Guevara y a Frantz Fanon.

Una cuestión que debe enfrentar cualquier estudio sobre *Pensamiento Crítico* es la de la forma en que aquella inscripción en la perspectiva del 68 y la Nueva Izquierda se tradujo en miradas sobre el propio proceso revolucionario cubano. En el sexto número, de julio de 1967, se hizo perceptible una visión histórica del fenómeno cubano que, de acuerdo con la perspectiva guevarista, privilegiaba al Ejército Rebelde y a la lucha armada en la Sierra Maestra como actor y escenario centrales de la revolución insular. En la presentación de aquel número, los editores de *Pensamiento Crítico*, en clara alusión al Partido Socialista Popular prerrevolucionario y, a través de este, a todos los partidos comunistas latinoamericanos pro soviéticos, afirmaban:

Como otros grandes revolucionarios del siglo—los bolcheviques de Lenin—los revolucionarios dirigidos por Fidel Castro tuvieron que luchar contra una poderosa reacción, pero también contra una supuesta "ortodoxia revolucionaria" que marcaba las formas de lucha, de organización revolucionarias, de transformaciones para alcanzar el socialismo… La situación actual de América Latina es la de una crisis que sólo podrá resolverse por una revolución antimperialista que transforme radicalmente las estructuras sociales del continente. Las vanguardias revolucionarias de los pueblos latinoamericanos se reúnen en La Habana, para realizar la unión de las fuerzas para una lucha que forzosamente ha de ser continental.[65]

Se referían a la reunión de la OLAS en La Habana, en el verano de 1967, que Fidel Castro clausuró con un discurso sumamente crítico del papel de la Unión Soviética y el campo socialista de Europa del Este en el Tercer Mundo. Pero la tesis central de aquel número de la revista en 1967 no era coyuntural. Dos años después, en julio de 1969, con el Che Guevara asesinado en Bolivia, las guerrillas latinoamericanas en un momento de repliegue y el Gobierno cubano en medio del relanzamiento de sus vínculos con la Unión Soviética, que siguió al apoyo de La Habana a la invasión soviética de Checoslovaquia, *Pensamiento Crítico* reiteraba la misma visión del proceso revolucionario cubano y su efecto modélico en América Latina. El fenómeno revolucionario de la isla había sido obra exclusiva del Movimiento 26 de Julio y, específicamente, del Ejército Rebelde en la Sierra Maestra.[66] Esta vez, la revista era más proclive al reconocimiento del papel del "llano" o lucha clandestina urbana, por medio de la inclusión de un importante testimonio de Faustino Pérez, pero la tónica del número era la identificación de la Revolución cubana con el ideario del Che Guevara, al que se asimilaban las ideas de Fidel Castro.[67]

Los dos ensayos centrales de aquel *dossier*, el de José Tabares y el de Germán Sánchez, proponían una historia de la Revolución cubana claramente distinta a la de *Lunes de Revolución* y *Cuba Socialista*. El proceso de la isla no era resultado de una izquierda liberal y cosmopolita ni de un movimiento de masas, regido por las leyes del marxismo-leninismo. La cubana era la revolución de un pequeño grupo de jóvenes de clase media, leales a Fidel Castro, que habían llegado al socialismo por la vía del nacionalismo revolucionario radical, delineado desde el asalto al cuartel Moncada y el alegato *La historia me absolverá* en 1953. No había aquí ningún intento de descifrar huellas marxistas o leninistas en la ideología del Movimiento 26 de Julio, como intentarían el presidente Osvaldo Dorticós e historiadores prosoviéticos como Julio Le Riverend, sino, más bien, cierto énfasis en que la vía armada, elegida desde 1953, era también una ruptura con la estrategia de lucha de los partidos comunistas, durante el periodo estalinista.[68]

La vigencia de aquel modelo para la izquierda latinoamericana se reiteraba, en ese mismo número, en los ensayos de Carlos Núñez sobre Bolivia y Regis Debray sobre la guerrilla continental. Recordaba Debray en su texto, que sirvió de prólogo a la edición mexicana de *¿Revolución en la Revolución?* que Guevara acostumbraba decir que "para los revolucionarios cubanos el campo de batalla era el mundo entero".[69] En medio del giro geopolítico del socialismo cubano entre fines de los años 60 y principios de los 70, que implicó el fracaso de la Zafra de los Diez Millones de Cuba al CAME, *Pensamiento Crítico* tomó algunas distancias de sus referentes originarios. Si bien no abandonó nunca la idea guevarista de la revolución, introdujo críticas a Louis Althusser, como la de François George, aunque reivindicó al filósofo estructuralista reproduciendo su conocido ensayo sobre Lenin.[70]

La crisis de la revista se hizo visible entre 1970 y 1971, cuando el ala prosoviética de la dirigencia cubana ganó terreno en la política económica, cultural e internacional de la isla. El Primer Congreso Nacional de Educación y Cultura en 1971, que se manifestó abiertamente contra el "revisionismo de izquierda", creó una plataforma desfavorable para el tipo de izquierda y el tipo de marxismo que defendía *Pensamiento Crítico*.[71] La disolución del equipo editor del Departamento de Filosofía de la Universidad de La Habana y el cierre de la publicación en 1971 marcaron un punto de inflexión en la ideología del Estado cubano, por el cual el concepto de revolución manejado por la ortodoxia marxista-leninista se volvió hegemónico.

Aunque las tres revistas aquí glosadas asumieron una orientación ideológica socialista y colocaron la palabra revolución en el centro de su discurso, solo una ellas, *Cuba Socialista*, logró crear un campo semántico perdurable en las instituciones educativas, culturales e ideológicas de la isla. Como se observa en los documentos programáticos del Primer Congreso del Partido Comunista de Cuba, en 1975, y en la propia Constitución de 1976, la idea de revolución propuesta por *Cuba Socialista* en los sesenta, fue la consagrada en las leyes y normas del nuevo Estado. De acuerdo con aquel relato, la revolución no solo había sido marxista-leninista desde el asalto al cuartel Moncada, sino que sus fuentes doctrinales habían superado, desde un inicio, el campo referencial liberal y humanista de *Lunes de Revolución* y el neomarxista y estructuralista de *Pensamiento Crítico*.

Tras la sovietización del socialismo cubano, aquellos referentes ajenos al marxismo-leninismo soviético, ligados a la ideología de la revolución desde las propias tradiciones liberales, republicanas y nacionalistas de la isla, no fueron totalmente purgados del campo intelectual. Subsistieron en una minoría resistente y alcanzaron cierta resonancia durante la crisis del socialismo real, a fines de los años 80, cuando Fidel Castro lanzó la llamada "Rectificación de errores y tendencias negativas". Sin embargo, en la ideología del Estado y su trasmisión educativa y cultural a la ciudadanía a través de la enseñanza, los medios de comunicación y las organizaciones de masas, se mantuvieron las pautas del concepto soviético de revolución hasta fines del siglo XX.

Los tres conceptos de revolución, con sus diferencias explícitas y sus zonas neutras, ayudan a comprender mejor la pluralidad teórica dentro del primer tramo de la construcción del socialismo cubano, pero también a reinterpretar el rol de Cuba en los debates ideológicos de la Nueva Izquierda latinoamericana de los años 60.[72] Así como no hubo un sentido plenamente hegemónico en la ideología oficial cubana, que unificara semánticamente el uso del concepto de revolución, hasta principios de los años 70, tampoco los diálogos del campo intelectual y las élites políticas de la isla con la izquierda latinoamericana operaron en una misma dirección. Es preciso reconstruir la microfísica de aquellas redes para captar su irreductible conflictividad.

NOTAS

1. Walter Benjamin, *Materiales para un autorretrato*, Buenos Aires, Argentina, FCE, 2017, p. 88.

2. Ibíd., p. 93.

3. "Una posición," *Lunes de Revolución*, no. 1, 23 de marzo de 1959, p. 2.

4. Ibíd.

5. Ibíd.

6. Ibíd.

7. "Una posición. Haciendo lo que es necesario hacer," *Lunes de Revolución*, no. 3, 6 de abril de 1959, p. 3.

8. Ibíd.

9. Henri Raymond, "Imperialismo e industria en América Latina," *Lunes de Revolución*, no. 2, 30 de marzo de 1959, p. 1.

10. "Por la libertad de Argelia," *Lunes de Revolución*, no. 9, 11 de mayo de 1959, p. 6.

11. "Los intelectuales de izquierda en Francia," *Lunes de Revolución*, no. 12, 1 de junio de 1959, pp. 2–3.

12. "Editorial," *Lunes de Revolución*, no. 43, 18 de enero de 1960, p. 2.

13. J. A. Baragaño, "Sobre Jean Paul Sartre," *Lunes de Revolución*, no. 51, 21 de marzo de 1960, pp. 23–27; Juan Arcocha, "Sartre o el heroísmo del hombre en situación," *Lunes de Revolución*, no. 51, 21 de marzo de 1960, pp. 29–35.

14. Richard Gibson, "El americano mira hacia Cuba," *Lunes de Revolución*, no. 66, 4 de julio de 1960, p. 6.

15. Guillermo Cabrera Infante, "La doble caída de Jacobo Árbenz," *Lunes de Revolución*, no. 22, 17 de agosto de 1959, pp. 22–23.

16. "Los intelectuales mexicanos y la Revolución Cubana," *Lunes de Revolución*, no. 63, 13 de junio de 1960, pp. 3–4.

17. José Lezama Lima, "Cautelas de Picasso," *Lunes de Revolución*, no. 129, 6 de noviembre de 1961, p. 28.

18. "Anatomía del imperialismo," *Lunes de Revolución*, no. 81, 17 de octubre de 1960, p. 2.

19. Virgilio Piñera, "La revolución se fortalece," *Lunes de Revolución*, no. 33, 2 de noviembre de 1959, p. 15.

20. Fidel Castro, "Contra el sectarismo y el mecanicismo," *Cuba Socialista*, no. 8, año 2, abril de 1962, pp. 1–2.

21. Ibíd., p. 6.

22. Ibíd., p. 7.

23. Ibíd., p. 8.

24. Ibíd., p. 11.

25. Severo Aguirre, "Ante el tercer aniversario de la Reforma Agraria," *Cuba Socialista*, año 2, no. 9, mayo de 1962, pp. 46–47.

26. Jacinto Torras, "Dos años de relaciones fraternales entre Cuba y la Unión Soviética," *Cuba Socialista*, año 2, no. 10, junio de 1962, pp. 2–6; Santiago Cuba, "El clero reaccionario y la Revolución cubana," *Cuba Socialista*, año 2, no. 10, junio de 1962, pp. 8–29.

27. "Discurso de N. Jruschov en el acto de amistad soviético-cubana," *Cuba Socialista*, año 2, no. 11, julio de 1962, p. 94.

28. Ibíd., p. 93.

29. Ibíd.

30. Alfredo Menéndez Cruz, "Problemas de la industria azucarera," *Cuba Socialista*, año 2, no. 12, agosto de 1962, pp. 1–17; Lionel Soto, "Nuevo desarrollo de la instrucción revolucionaria," *Cuba Socialista*, año 2, no. 12, agosto de 1962, pp. 32–45.

31. Nikita Jruschov, "Problemas de la agricultura en la URSS," *Cuba Socialista*, año 2, no. 13, pp. 51–67.

32. Nikita Jruschov, "Problemas candentes del desarrollo del sistema socialista mundial," *Cuba Socialista*, año 2, no. 14, octubre de 1962, pp. 54–86.

33. Serguei Shkurko, "El principio de interés material y la remuneración del trabajo en la URSS," *Cuba Socialista*, año 2, no. 15, noviembre de 1962, pp. 28–54; S. Vishniov, "La Unión Soviética en la economía mundial," *Cuba Socialista*, año 2, no. 15, noviembre de 1962, pp. 55–79.

34. Fidel Castro, "Un pueblo así es un pueblo invencible," *Cuba Socialista*, año 2, no. 16, diciembre de 1962, pp. 7–32.

35. Ernesto Che Guevara, "Contra el burocratismo," *Cuba Socialista*, año 3, no. 18, febrero de 1963, pp. 1–7.

36. Ernesto Che Guevara, "Guerra de guerrillas: Un método," *Cuba Socialista*, año 3, no. 25, septiembre de 1963, pp. 1–17.

37. Ernesto Che Guevara, "La banca, el crédito y el socialismo," *Cuba Socialista*, año 4, no. 31, marzo de 1964, pp. 23–41; "Posición de Cuba en la Conferencia Mundial de Comercio y Desarrollo," *Cuba Socialista*, año 4, no. 33, mayo de 1964, pp. 1–24; "La planificación socialista, su significado," *Cuba Socialista*, año 4, no. 34, agosto de 1964, pp. 13–24.

38. Ernesto Che Guevara, *El socialismo y el hombre nuevo*, México, Siglo XXI, 1977, p. 13.

39. Iván Volkov, "El realismo socialista," *Cuba Socialista*, año 2, no. 19, marzo de 1963, pp. 83–96; Mirta Aguirre, "Apuntes sobre la literatura y el arte," *Cuba Socialista*, año 3, no. 20, octubre de 1963, pp. 62–82.

40. A Kuzin y S. Shujardin, "La actual revolución científico-técnica," *Cuba Socialista*, año 5, no. 42, febrero de 1965, pp. 87–103.

41. Feng Chong, "Nueva situación en la economía china," *Cuna Socialista*, año 4, no. 40, diciembre de 1964, pp. 101–130.

42. Fidel Castro, "Respuesta a las declaraciones del gobierno chino," *Cuba Socialista*, año 6, no. 55, pp. 2–25.

43. Blas Roca, "Las calumnias trotskistas no pueden manchar a la Revolución cubana," *Cuba Socialista*, año 6, no. 56, abril de 1966, pp. 81–92. Ver también Rafael Acosta de Arriba, "El final del trotskismo organizado en Cuba," Caridad Massón Sena, ed., *Las izquierdas latinoamericanas. Multiplicidad y experiencias durante el siglo XX*, Santiago de Chile, Ariadna Editores, 2017, pp. 229–320.

44. Lionel Soto, "La I Conferencia Tricontinental," *Cuba Socialista*, año 6, no. 58, junio de 1966, pp. 55–80; Lionel Soto, "Lo importante es desarrollemos nuestro camino," *Cuba Socialista*, año 7, enero de 1967, pp. 37–61.

45. "Recesa la publicación de Cuba Socialista," *Cuba Socialista*, año 7, no. 66, febrero de 1967, pp. 2–3.

46. *Pensamiento Crítico*, no. 1, febrero de 1967, p. 3.

47. Camilo Torres, "La violencia y los cambios sociales," *Pensamiento Crítico*, no. 1, febrero de 1967, pp. 4–53; Fabricio Ojeda, "La revolución verdadera, la violencia y el fatalismo geopolítico," *Pensamiento Crítico*, no. 1, febrero de 1967, pp. 54–73.

48. Américo Pumaruma, "Perú: Revolución, insurrección, guerrillas," *Pensamiento Crítico*, no. 1, febrero de 1967, p. 74.

49. Ibíd., pp. 75–76.

50. Fernando Martínez, "A 40 años de *Pensamiento Crítico*," *Crítica y emancipación: Revista Latinoamericana de Ciencias Sociales*, año 1, no. 1, junio de 2008, p. 244. Ver también Fernando Martínez Heredia, *La crítica en tiempo de Revolución*, Santiago de Cuba, Editorial Oriente, 2010, pp. 9–18; Zuleica Romay, "La marcha a contracorriente del pensamiento crítico: Comentarios desde Cuba," *La Tizza*, 8 de marzo de 2017; Germán Sánchez, "*Pensamiento Crítico* ¿Cinco años, cinco décadas o cinco siglos?," *La Tizza*, 8 de marzo de 2017; Néstor Kohan, "*Pensamiento Crítico* y el debate de las ciencias sociales en el seno de la Revolución cubana," *Crítica y teoría en el pensamiento latinoamericano*, Buenos Aires, Clacso, 2006, pp. 389–437.

51. Rachid, "Notas sobre *¿Revolución en la Revolución?*," *Pensamiento Crítico*, no. 4, mayo de 1967, pp. 195–205.

52. Ibíd., p. 201.

53. Ignacio Urdaneta, "Polémica en la Revolución," *Pensamiento Crítico*, no. 7, agosto de 1967, pp. 117–157; "Perú: Una entrevista a dos guerrilleros," *Pensamiento Crítico*, no. 6, julio de 1967, pp. 171–198; Ojarikuj Runa, "Bolivia, análisis de una situación," *Pensamiento Crítico*, no. 6, julio de 1967, pp. 204–220; John William Cooke, "La revolución y el peronismo," Fernando Martínez Heredia, *La crítica en tiempo de Revolución*, Santiago de Cuba, Editorial Oriente, 2010, pp. 86–106.

54. Gerald Chaliand, "Independencia nacional y revolución," *Pensamiento Crítico*, nos. 2–3, abril de 1967, pp. 106–161.

55. Bertrand Russell, "Mensaje a los pueblos del Tercer Mundo," *Pensamiento Crítico*, no. 4, mayo de 1967, pp. 5–9; Michael Löwy, "Conciencia de clase y partido revolucionario," *Pensamiento Crítico*, no. 4, mayo de 1967, pp. 195–206.

56. Louis Althusser, "Materialismo dialéctico y materialismo histórico," *Pensamiento Crítico*, no. 5, junio de 1967, pp. 3–26.

57. André Gorz, "Sartre y Marx," *Pensamiento Crítico*, no. 5, junio de 1967, pp. 77–109; Jacques Goldberg, "Antropología e ideología," *Pensamiento Crítico*, no. 5, junio de 1967, pp. 27–48.

58. Jean-Paul Dolle, "Del izquierdismo al humanismo socialista," pp. 49–76.

59. Louis Althusser y André Daspre, "Dos cartas sobre el conocimiento del arte," *Pensamiento Crítico*, no. 10, noviembre de 1967, pp. 111–121.

60. Maurice Godelier, "Sistema, estructura y contradicción en *El Capital* de Marx," *Pensamiento Crítico*, no. 11, diciembre de 1967, pp. 62–97.

61. "Presentación," *Pensamiento Crítico*, nos. 18–19, julio–agosto, 1968, pp. 3–4.

62. Michel Delahaye y Jacques Rivet, "El futuro del cine: ¿Arte existencial?," *Pensamiento Crítico*, nos. 18–19, julio–agosto, 1968, pp. 123–135.

63. Ver Étienne Balibar, *Sobre la dictadura del proletariado*, Madrid, Siglo XXI, 1977, pp. 11–29.

64. Giorgio Backhaus, "Génesis y características de la izquierda revolucionaria en Alemania," *Pensamiento Crítico*, no. 21, octubre de 1968, pp. 17–66; Rudi Dutschke, "Las contradicciones del capitalismo tardío," *Pensamiento Crítico*, no. 21, octubre de 1968, pp. 67–148.

65. "Presentación," *Pensamiento Crítico*, no. 6, julio de 1967, p. 2.

66. José A. Tabares, "Apuntes para la historia del movimiento revolucionario 26 de Julio," *Pensamiento Crítico*, no. 31, agosto de 1969, pp. 132–144; Germán Sánchez, "El Moncada: Asalto al futuro," *Pensamiento Crítico*, No. 31, agosto de 1969, pp. 99–131.

67. Faustino Pérez, "La sierra y el llano: Eslabones de un mismo combate," *Pensamiento Crítico*, no. 31, agosto de 1969, pp. 67–98.

68. Germán Sánchez, "El Moncada: Asalto al futuro," *Pensamiento Crítico*, no. 31, agosto de 1969, p. 112.

69. Régis Debray, "Nota a ¿*Revolución en la Revolución?*," *Pensamiento Crítico*, no. 31, agosto de 1969, p. 161.

70. François George, "Leer a Althusser," *Pensamiento Crítico*, nos. 34–35, noviembre–diciembre de 1969, pp. 155–189; Louis Althusser, "Lenin y la filosofía," *Pensamiento Crítico*, nos. 34–35, noviembre–diciembre de 1969, pp. 120–153.

71. "Declaración del Primer Congreso Nacional de Educación y Cultura," *Casa de las Américas*, año 11, nos. 65–66, marzo–junio de 1971, pp. 4–19.

72. Germán Albuquerque F., *La trinchera letrada: Intelectuales latinoamericanos y Guerra Fría*, Santiago de Chile, Ariadna Editores, 2017, pp. 81–100.

ELISA SERVÍN

Cuba revolucionaria en las páginas de tres publicaciones mexicanas

RESUMEN

El artículo aborda la narrativa que construyó un grupo de intelectuales mexicanos en torno a la Revolución cubana entre 1959 y 1961 en las páginas del suplemento "México en la cultura" y las revistas *El Espectador* y *Política*. Llevados por el entusiasmo ante las posibilidades que abría la revolución no solo para Cuba, sino para el conjunto de América Latina y su relación con Estados Unidos, Fernando Benítez, Carlos Fuentes, Enrique González Pedrero y Víctor Flores Olea hicieron de la Revolución cubana no solo un ejemplo, sino también un espejo en el que se reflejaba con fuerza el agotamiento de la legitimidad del régimen de la Revolución mexicana. La interpretación que construyó este grupo en su conjunto resultó una pieza fundamental en el complejo proceso de renovación de las izquierdas mexicanas.

ABSTRACT

The article examines the narrative that a group of Mexican intellectuals built around the Cuban Revolution between 1959 and 1961 in the pages of the supplement "México en la Cultura" and the magazines *El Espectador* and *Política*. Carried away by enthusiasm at the possibilities opened by the revolution not only for Cuba but for Latin America as a whole and its relationship with the United States, Fernando Benítez, Carlos Fuentes, Enrique González Pedrero, and Víctor Flores Olea made the Cuban Revolution not only an example but also a mirror that strongly reflected the exhaustion of the legitimacy of the "regime of the Mexican Revolution." The interpretation that this group built as a whole turned out to be a fundamental piece in the complex process of renewal of the Mexican left.

El año 1959 puso a Cuba en el centro del debate público mexicano y latino-americano. El triunfo del movimiento revolucionario en la isla fue recibido con entusiasmo y los foros de la opinión pública, en particular la prensa escrita, dieron cabida a la intensa reflexión que generó desde el primer momento la Revolución cubana. En México los acontecimientos del día a día revolucionario fueron objeto de una intensa discusión política, en una coyuntura en la que la movilización de diversos grupos sociales que venía del año anterior agudizó el cuestionamiento de la legitimidad y los alcances sociales del régimen emanado de la revolución de 1910. La fuerza de los movimientos sindicales, campesinos y estudiantiles que confluyeron en las calles en 1958 había generado ya discusiones y debates entre quienes se asumían de izquierda, en un amplio abanico que iba desde la vertiente más progresista de la política oficial hasta una nueva izquierda intelectual en ascenso, misma que cuestionaba el agotamiento de la Revolución mexicana de 1910, por una parte, y la incapacidad de la vieja izquierda partidaria para entender la coyuntura por otra.

En ese contexto, el proceso revolucionario en Cuba fue un elemento central en los argumentos de quienes se proponían renovar a la izquierda superando los límites del discurso estalinista y del oficialismo autoritario priista. La confluencia de una revolución en ascenso como la cubana frente al anquilosamiento del régimen que se asumía heredero de la Revolución mexicana hizo que la reflexión en torno a Cuba fuera siempre un espejo en el que se reflejaron los límites de la legitimidad del régimen, por una parte, y la necesidad de revitalizar a la izquierda por la otra. En esta reflexión destacó un grupo de intelectuales que, en el camino de impulsar la renovación de la izquierda, fundaron y colaboraron en tres publicaciones que serían lectura fundamental en la primera mitad de los años sesenta. Es el caso de Carlos Fuentes y Fernando Benítez, de Enrique González Pedrero y de Víctor Flores Olea entre otros, quienes escribieron en "México en la cultura", suplemento cultural del diario *Novedades*, así como en las revistas *El Espectador* y *Política*, e hicieron de Cuba un tema central de su colaboración.[1]

El suplemento "México en la Cultura" se publicó semanalmente desde 1949 hasta diciembre de 1961 bajo la dirección del periodista, editor e historiador Fernando Benítez. En el transcurso de la segunda mitad de los años cincuenta el suplemento fue, junto con la *Revista Mexicana de Literatura*, el principal espacio de divulgación y crítica de la nueva oleada de jóvenes intelectuales y creadores artísticos de la llamada Generación del Medio Siglo. Dedicado a la literatura, la poesía, las artes plásticas, el cine y el teatro, en las páginas del suplemento hubo espacio también para una incipiente crítica política que se volvería más evidente a partir de 1958, cuando el gobierno que se decía heredero de la Revolución mexicana reprimió las grandes movilizaciones obreras, campesinas y estudiantiles que tuvieron lugar ese año. A partir de 1959 el suplemento cultural publicó entrevistas y artículos en los que era evidente el apoyo y el entusiasmo que generaba en sus autores el triunfo de la revolución en Cuba.

Ante la creciente necesidad de generar espacios de crítica y análisis político en mayo de 1959 algunos colaboradores asiduos del suplemento como Carlos Fuentes, Jaime García Terrés y Enrique González Pedrero, además de Víctor Flores Olea, Luis Villoro y Francisco López Cámara, fundaron *El Espectador*, publicación mensual a la que algunos consideramos la primera voz de la nueva izquierda mexicana.[2] Influidos por las discusiones que tenían lugar en Europa en torno a la renovación del marxismo y preocupados por la represión que el Gobierno del presidente Adolfo López Mateos ejerció apenas un mes antes en contra del movimiento ferrocarrilero, los editores de esta publicación buscaron ofrecer un espacio de discusión y debate en una coyuntura en la que confluían, por una parte la crítica al autoritarismo del régimen y por la otra, el entusiasmo que generó entre ellos la Revolución cubana.

Un año después, en mayo de 1960, *El Espectador* dejó de publicarse y sus editores se integraron a la naciente revista *Política*, que bajo la dirección de Manuel Marcué Pardiñas sería la principal publicación de análisis y crítica política de la primera mitad de los años sesenta. En *Política* confluyeron todas las vertientes de la izquierda y la Revolución cubana fue un tema central de la revista. Desde el inicio *Política* concentró la opinión que hasta ese momento había encontrado espacio en "México en la cultura" y por un breve lapso de tiempo en *El Espectador*. La fuerza de los acontecimientos, tanto en México como en Cuba había hecho necesario construir más espacios de información, análisis y crítica, así como una alternativa a la gran prensa anticomunista que se alimentaba fundamentalmente de los boletines oficiales y los envíos de las agencias estadounidenses.

La visión que Fernando Benítez, Carlos Fuentes, Enrique González Pedrero y Víctor Flores Olea construyeron en las páginas de "México en la Cultura" y después en *El Espectador* y en *Política* en torno a la Revolución cubana fue fundamental en la narrativa de una incipiente nueva izquierda que vio en la revolución no solo el triunfo de una batalla latinoamericana por la soberanía, la igualdad social y la independencia económica, sino también la posibilidad de renovar al marxismo y revitalizar a la izquierda en una coyuntura determinada por los realineamientos ideológicos de la Guerra Fría. Al utilizar todos los espacios periodísticos a su alcance, este grupo construyó una primera narrativa en torno a Cuba que no escatimó en entusiasmo y solidaridad y que perduró hasta bien entrados los años sesenta.

"México en la cultura"

Hablar de "México en la cultura" es hablar del espacio principal de encuentro y reflexión de intelectuales y creadores artísticos en los años cincuenta. En sus páginas confluyeron consagrados como Alfonso Reyes y Octavio Paz, así como una nueva generación en la que destacaban ya Jaime García Terrés, Gastón García Cantú, Alí Chumacero, Carlos Fuentes o Emmanuel Carballo, y los jóvenes José Emilio Pacheco, Carlos Monsiváis y Elena Poniatowska. El suplemento se fundó en 1949 por iniciativa de Fernando Benítez, periodista, historiador, editor, quien desde sus tiempos como colaborador y después director del diario *El Nacional* en los años treinta y cuarenta había promovido la creación de suplementos culturales en la prensa mexicana. Pensado en su origen como un espacio que diera cabida a la intensa vida cultural que se beneficiaba entre otras cosas del apoyo gubernamental, "México en la cultura" sería escenario de encuentro, crítica y formación en el oficio de escribir para una nueva generación de jóvenes.[3] Como relatara José Emilio Pacheco, quien fue secretario de redacción del suplemento en 1961, en los años cincuenta la vida cultural fluía entre otros lugares "en las oficinas de 'México en la cultura', en el edificio de *Novedades* de Balderas y Morelos [. . .] Mis becas fueron el taller de Arreola, la redacción de 'México en la Cultura' y de la *Revista de la Universidad*. Eso fue incomparable, equivalente a varios doctorados".[4]

Aunque el suplemento se concentró en la literatura y la crítica literaria, las artes plásticas, el cine, el teatro y la música, en la medida en que avanzó la década y la nueva generación de jóvenes escritores y artistas empezaba a señalar su descontento con el anquilosado régimen de la Revolución mexicana en sus páginas apareció también cierta crítica política. Ahí se publicó, por ejemplo, el famoso texto del pintor José Luis Cuevas en el que bajo el título "La cortina de nopal" cuestionaba duramente la hegemonía de la escuela mexicana de pintura y el muralismo nacionalista. El texto generó un intenso debate que muy pronto trascendió de las artes plásticas al ámbito de la discusión política y en el que participó, entre otros, la reconocida crítica de arte Raquel Tibol.[5] Por su parte, en una entrevista concedida a Elena Poniatowska que se publicó en el suplemento en abril de 1958 a raíz de la publicación de *La región más transparente del aire*, Carlos Fuentes expresaba una crítica al mundo literario mexicano "que ha infectado a nuestra literatura de una enfermedad más perniciosa: el miedo a llamar las cosas por su nombre. La literatura mexicana tiene el campeonato mundial del eufemismo. Esta actitud ha conducido, a la postre, al mutismo y a la irresponsabilidad crítica que hoy nos afecta". El país se encontraba inmerso en una coyuntura de sucesión presidencial e intensas movilizaciones sociales y se notaba la ausencia de una crítica intelectual al evidente agotamiento de la revolución de 1910.[6]

Al iniciar 1959 llegaron a México las noticias de lo que ocurría en Cuba. Ya desde 1956 la simpatía y solidaridad de Fernando Benítez con el grupo de rebeldes cubanos dirigidos por Fidel Castro sería manifiesta cuando, como narró Carlos Franqui, Benítez colaboró en la campaña de prensa internacional que el Movimiento 26 de Julio organizó para liberarlos después de ser detenidos en México y fue también el intermediario para que el diario *Excélsior* entrevistara en exclusiva a Fidel en la cárcel, entrevista que sería circulada a nivel internacional por la agencia United Press.[7] En los primeros días de enero de 1959 la joven revolución sería recibida con gran entusiasmo y solidaridad por quienes desde 1956 habían apoyado los intentos insurreccionales del Movimiento 26 de Julio.

La entrada triunfal de los revolucionarios a las calles de La Habana fue reportada por la prensa mexicana con gran interés. Pronto las primeras planas se llenaron con las imágenes de los fusilamientos que se llevaban a cabo todos los días en Cuba. Fernando Benítez y Carlos Fuentes se encontraban en La Habana y participaron en la "Conferencia de Prensa Continental" convocada por Fidel Castro en el Hotel Riviera para contrarrestar la información de las agencias de prensa estadounidenses. Era el primer paso de lo que se conoció como Operación Verdad, que culminó con la creación de la agencia de noticias *Prensa Latina* que nacía con la consigna de trabajar en el ámbito de la opinión pública desde una perspectiva favorable a la revolución.[8]

Muy pronto Fernando Benítez se sumó al esfuerzo que emanó de la "Operación Verdad". El 12 de febrero empezó a publicar en *Novedades* una serie bajo el título "Cuba en el banquillo de los acusados" en la que comparaba las condenas a Cuba con las críticas que habían sufrido los revolucionarios mexicanos en el transcurso de su propia revolución. Un año después sus artículos aparecieron en *La batalla de Cuba*, el primer libro publicado por la naciente editorial Era que contenía también un ensayo de Enrique González Pedrero, en ese momento joven profesor de Ciencias Políticas en la UNAM, llamado "La fisonomía de Cuba".[9] Como señala Luis Hernández Navarro, *La batalla de Cuba* fue "clave en la formación del imaginario social sobre la patria de José Martí en México".[10]

El suplemento cultural también se ocupó de Cuba desde el primer momento. En palabras de José Emilio Pacheco, "la revolución cubana cambió todo".[11] Así, en el número del 25 de enero, se publicó una entrevista realizada por Rosa Castro a González Pedrero, quien se encontraba en la Habana a fines de diciembre de 1958 con su esposa, la escritora cubana Julieta Campos, y pudo presenciar los últimos días del Gobierno de Fulgencio Batista, así como la adhesión popular a los revolucionarios. Para González Pedrero las condenas a los fusilamientos eran parte de una campaña publicitaria que pretendía desorientar a la opinión pública internacional y desprestigiar a la revolución, tratando de compararla con el régimen de Batista. La opinión pública cubana, decía, exigía justicia revolucionaria. Para él no quedaba duda: "existe una identificación plena y rotunda entre la nación cubana y su revolución libertaria. Decir pueblo de Cuba y revolución, en estos momentos, es decir la misma cosa".[12] Meses después González Pedrero sería el primero en publicar un libro en México sobre el tema, *La Revolución cubana*, resultado de una serie de conferencias impartidas en la Escuela Nacional de Ciencias Políticas y Sociales de la UNAM.[13] Carlos Fuentes por su parte, también desde La Habana, argumentó en favor de lo que ocurría en Cuba señalando por qué México debía "comprender y alentar la Revolución cubana. Fidel Castro está haciendo lo que Madero debió hacer: liquidar desde la base la herencia de la dictadura".[14] Este sería un argumento recurrente entre quienes defendían lo que ocurría en ese momento en Cuba. Después de la justicia revolucionaria vendría la tarea de construcción basada en la reforma agraria, la diversificación económica y la libertad civil.

La solidaridad del expresidente Lázaro Cárdenas con la Revolución cubana fue explícita desde 1956 cuando intervino ante el entonces presidente Adolfo Ruiz Cortines para que Fidel, Ernesto *Che* Guevara y Calixto García fueran liberados de la cárcel en México.[15] Poco después el propio Fidel se entrevistó con Cárdenas para agradecerle su intermediación y este dejó constancia en sus *Apuntes* de la simpatía que le despertó "el joven intelectual de temperamento vehemente".[16] En 1958, en combate desde la famosa Sierra Maestra, Fidel mantuvo el contacto con el expresidente mexicano, a quien envió una carta para agradecerle de nuevo su gestión, "gracias a la cual estamos cumpliendo nuestro deber con Cuba".[17]

La gratitud de Fidel Castro hacia el expresidente Cárdenas quedó de manifiesto en el desfile para conmemorar el primer aniversario triunfante del 26 de julio al que Lázaro Cárdenas asistió como invitado. La gratitud de Fidel Castro y el poderoso entrecruzamiento simbólico de la Revolución mexicana y la cubana quedaron de manifiesto en una fotografía clásica en la cual el general Cárdenas aparece junto a Castro en la celebración. Pocos días después, el domingo 2 de agosto, el suplemento publicó una entrevista exclusiva de Poniatowska con el general Cárdenas, realizada a bordo del avión en el que un grupo de colaboradores del suplemento regresaban también de La Habana después de cubrir el evento. En la entrevista Cárdenas expuso algunos de los puntos que serían fundamentales en la primera narrativa sobre la Revolución cubana: se trataba de una revolución popular, producto de la miseria y no del comunismo, a la que había que apoyar por lo pronto en uno de sus primeros objetivos: la reforma agraria. Solo de ahí vendría la posibilidad de mejorar las vidas de los campesinos cubanos. A pregunta expresa de Poniatowska, el expresidente señalaba las semejanzas entre la Revolución cubana y la mexicana: "Ellos están pasando por lo que nosotros pasamos. A nosotros también nos atacaron".[18]

Una semana después el suplemento publicó la crónica de Carlos Fuentes sobre la celebración del 26 de julio que, bajo el título "Las Horas de Cuba", era sin duda la crónica del entusiasmo revolucionario. Al describir a los multitudinarios contingentes campesinos que desfilaban por las calles de La Habana, Fuentes escribía: "Queremos pensar en la entrada de Zapata a México, en el paso de los agraristas por la av. 5 de mayo. Esta mañana en La Habana Zapata encabeza a toda Cuba, a toda Hispanoamérica: es como si nadie hubiese muerto en Chinameca. Esta es la revolución sin traición, sin facciones, sin derrota posible. Esta mañana todo el pueblo cubano apoya su revolución". Fuentes coincidía con lo dicho por Cárdenas y señalaba como objetivo de la revolución el impulsar "la transformación de una estructura económica colonialista y semifeudal en otra de democracia social, producción diversificada e industrialización nacional, cuyo presupuesto y base es la Reforma Agraria". Fuentes, como Cárdenas, destacaba la juventud, la vitalidad y el impulso de los revolucionarios. Y concluía: "Pasa ante mis ojos todo un pueblo, que no es sólo de Cuba. Es de México, es de Hispanoamérica. Nuestra lucha es la misma: esta es la más clara lección de las horas en Cuba".[19]

A lo largo de 1960 "México en la cultura" publicó diversos artículos y notas que, más allá de la narrativa política, dejaban ver el interés por la reflexión intelectual y literaria que generaba la revolución. El 21 de febrero, por ejemplo, en la sección "Autores y libros", se comentaba el libro de Raúl Roa, *En pie*, que contenía el pensamiento político de "este revolucionario cubano". En un recuadro se destacaba una cita del libro a propósito del humanismo que propugnaba la revolución: "Aspira, pues, no a la liberación de una clase sino a la liberación de la humanidad de miedos, prejuicios, miserias, grilletes, oprobios y dogmas. Es la revolución que demandan los tiempos".

El 27 de marzo el suplemento publicó un texto de Alejo Carpentier quien se había integrado como colaborador un mes antes. Carpentier reflexionaba en "La revolución y la novela en Cuba" sobre la inquietud de los escritores cubanos en ese momento por escribir "la" novela sobre la Revolución cubana. Dos semanas después el suplemento publicó en portada como nota principal el texto de Jean-Paul Sartre, "Ideología y revolución", acompañado con una fotografía de Sartre con Fidel visitando la Universidad de La Habana.[20]

En mayo el suplemento publicó una entrevista de José Emilio Pacheco con Arnaldo Orfila Reynal, el editor del Fondo de Cultura Económica, quien entre otras cosas comentaba con entusiasmo los planes y realizaciones que la revolución llevaba a cabo en el plano de la cultura, tales como la transformación de cuarteles en escuelas, o el afán de lectura que le parecía extraordinario: "Una experiencia última de venta de libros populares, bajo la dirección de Alejo Carpentier, ha logrado vender cerca de 300 mil ejemplares de libros cubanos en un par de semanas [. . .] estas nuevas generaciones han asumido la responsabilidad de construir la nueva Cuba y su edificación han de lograrla a pesar de la histérica y malevolente campaña de descrédito que se ha lanzado en contra de la revolución cubana".[21] Quince días después el suplemento publicaba un artículo de Waldo Frank sobre su reciente visita a la isla.[22]

La relación de Carlos Fuentes y Fernando Benítez con el mundo literario cubano redundó en junio de 1960 en la publicación de un número especial del suplemento sobre la cultura que se gestaba al calor de la revolución. Se publicaron poemas, notas sobre la pintura de Wifredo Lam, breves textos de la nueva generación de escritores, un par de columnas sobre música y cine y dos capítulos de la nueva novela de Carpentier, *El siglo de las Luces*.[23] En forma paralela Fuentes acordó con Guillermo Cabrera Infante la publicación de un número especial sobre la nueva literatura mexicana en el suplemento "Lunes de Revolución". En efecto, con fecha 13 de junio, se publicó el número especial con el título *¡Viva Méjico!* cuyo primer artículo, "Los intelectuales mexicanos y la revolución cubana" incluía breves comentarios de Jorge Portilla, Enrique González Pedrero, Fernando Benítez, Carlos Fuentes y Víctor Flores Olea.[24] Ambas ediciones se realizaron en el contexto de la visita que hizo Osvaldo Dorticós a México en la segunda semana de junio.

En 1961 el suplemento publicó algunas notas relativas a Cuba como la entrevista de Emmanuel Carballo a Carpentier en febrero, o la entrevista de Poniatowska con el periodista K. S. Karol en julio.[25] Para entonces los textos de reflexión política se habían trasladado a las páginas de *Política*, la revista fundada por Manuel Marcué Pardiñas en mayo de 1960 que habría de ser la publicación política más importante de los primeros años de los sesenta.

El entusiasmo por la Revolución cubana que Fernando Benítez expresó desde los inicios de 1959 en las páginas de *Novedades* y que continuaba manifestando en sus textos en *Política*, así como la postura pro-Cuba que se leía en el suplemento cultural se encontró cada vez más en abierto contraste con la línea editorial del propio *Novedades*, en realidad el diario más cercano al ala anticomunista y pro empresarial de la prensa mexicana, que era cada vez más crítico del proceso cubano. La contradicción llegó a su límite en diciembre de 1961 cuando Fernando Benítez fue despedido por Ramón Beteta, el director del diario. Con Benítez se iría todo su grupo de colaboradores, "mi equipo, mi glorioso equipo de hermanitos", como los llamaba, quienes le expresaron su solidaridad dejando el suplemento.[26] En la edición del 10 de diciembre, la última que dirigió Benítez, se publicó un texto en portada bajo el título "Al fin de esta jornada", en el que los colaboradores del suplemento despedían a su director.[27] En un pequeño epígrafe escribió Alfonso Reyes: "La vida cultural de México durante estos dos lustros podrá reconstruirse, en sus mejores aspectos, gracias al suplemento de *Novedades*. Cuantos en él pusimos las manos tenemos mucho que agradecerle".[28]

Aunque no se sabe de un hecho en particular que haya motivado la destitución, el propio Benítez y varios de sus colaboradores más cercanos insistieron en atribuir la explicación de su despido a la defensa de la Revolución cubana. De acuerdo, por ejemplo, a José Emilio Pacheco, "La causa no indicada, pero a la vista de todos eran los artículos que Benítez y Carlos Fuentes escribían en la revista *Política* de Manuel Marcué Pardiñas en defensa de la Revolución cubana y muy críticos del régimen del PRI y de Adolfo López Mateos. En un acto insólito que nunca se ha repetido, para las seis de la tarde la redacción entera había renunciado en solidaridad con Benítez".[29]

Dos meses después, en febrero de 1962, inició la publicación de "La cultura en México", la continuación del suplemento cultural que esta vez encontró espacio en las páginas de *Siempre!*, el más importante semanario político de los años cincuenta, dirigido por José Pagés Llergo. La Revolución cubana siguió siendo en tema central en las páginas de este suplemento y ahí se expresaron también buena parte de los debates que sacudieron a los intelectuales latinoamericanos en el transcurso de los años sesenta.

Cuba en *El Espectador*

En paralelo a su colaboración en "México en la cultura", un grupo conformado por Carlos Fuentes, Enrique González Pedrero, Víctor Flores Olea, Jaime García Terrés, Francisco López Cámara y Luis Villoro iniciaron en mayo de 1959 la publicación de una nueva revista mensual, *El Espectador*. La relación entre algunos de ellos venía desde sus tiempos de estudiantes de derecho cuando fundaron la revista *Medio Siglo*. En ella participaron Fuentes, Flores Olea y González Pedrero, quien acababa de regresar de estudiar en París, así como los jóvenes preparatorianos Carlos Monsiváis y José Emilio Pacheco. Serían los tiempos de "las primeras lecturas de los textos marxistas", nunca entendidas, en palabras de Fuentes "como un dogma absoluto o reductor, sino como un método de interpretación de determinados fenómenos de la vida histórica y un llamado a la libertad y a la integración de las posibilidades humanas".[30]

Años después la coyuntura política los llevaría a crear *El Espectador*. El nuevo Gobierno del presidente Adolfo López Mateos mostraba su vertiente autoritaria desde los primeros meses al reprimir con lujo de fuerza al sindicato ferrocarrilero que había emplazado a un paro general para el mes de marzo. El 28 de marzo, a las pocas horas de iniciado el paro, los dirigentes del sindicato encabezados por Demetrio Vallejo y miles de trabajadores y representantes regionales y locales fueron detenidos por policías y soldados, al tiempo que las instalaciones ferrocarrileras en todo el país quedaron en manos del ejército.

La represión contra los ferrocarrileros resultó determinante para el grupo de jóvenes intelectuales. Las posibilidades de democratizar la vida sindical y con ello al régimen se estrellaron en la feroz acometida represora de López Mateos, legitimada con el más burdo anticomunismo. El contraste con lo que ocurría en ese momento en Cuba no podía ser más brutal. El régimen de la Revolución mexicana se agotaba en la represión mientras Cuba se embarcaba en las tareas de la construcción revolucionaria en lo político, lo económico, lo cultural. La intensidad del momento incitó al grupo a publicar *El Espectador*.

En palabras de Flores Olea, con el apoyo de Jesús Silva Herzog, quien en ese momento dirigía *Cuadernos Americanos* y les proporcionó veinticinco mil pesos de financiamiento para publicar dos números, empezaron a reunirse en el café El Carmel de la Zona Rosa: "Ese café era de don Jacobo Glantz, el padre de Margo. Nos sentábamos a planear los números, diseñar y corregir pruebas". Con una dirección rotativa y un tiraje inicial de dos mil ejemplares la revista llegó a vender a través de suscripciones hasta diez mil ejemplares.[31] Sin patrocinadores o publicidad la revista intentó mantener la independencia y vivir solo de venta directa y suscripciones. De acuerdo a otro de sus editores, Enrique González Pedrero, ellos mismos vendían a veces en la calle, voceaban la revista en la Avenida Madero en el centro de la ciudad.[32]

La postura del grupo fue explícita desde la presentación del primer número. En esa coyuntura, señalaban, "la izquierda es inoperante en la vida política de México", aun y cuando "su fuerza natural—la clase obrera"— adquiría una "creciente conciencia". Frente a la exigencia de democracia la izquierda debía trabajar por la unidad, dejar de ser "la izquierda desde arriba" para convertirse en la "izquierda desde abajo [. . .] fundada en el movimiento de independencia sindical". "Pero los editores de EL ESPECTADOR no creen que 'izquierda' y 'sectarismo' sean sinónimos. Una izquierda válida, por definición, es una izquierda abierta, porque reúne a los sectores mayoritarios de una nación. La izquierda, en México, debe ser idéntica a democracia política y a justicia económica".[33]

Para este grupo participar en la discusión pública y sobre todo en la construcción de una nueva izquierda que desde una perspectiva democrática cuestionara la creciente pérdida de legitimidad del régimen de la revolución mexicana era una tarea fundamental. En ese sentido El Espectador se proponía como un espacio de encuentro y discusión para la nueva generación de intelectuales críticos que buscaban darle un sentido político al esfuerzo de renovación que hasta ese momento habían realizado sobre todo en el campo cultural, tal y como era el caso de "México en la Cultura" y la Revista Mexicana de Literatura. En palabras de González Pedrero, asumían que "la política era parte de la cultura, de la cultura de las ideas".[34] O dicho en palabras de Fuentes, "el escritor, el intelectual, no pueden ser ajenos a la lucha por una transformación política que, en última instancia, supone también una transformación cultural".[35] Aunque asumían que la organización política partidaria de la izquierda correspondía a las clases populares, no a los intelectuales, pensaban que como tales les cabía participar en la transformación del país desde la trinchera de la discusión y el debate. Era parte de su responsabilidad histórica.

El otro impulso para editar El Espectador era Cuba. Tal y como lo expresaran en las páginas de "México en la Cultura", para ellos la Revolución cubana representaba en ese momento lo que la Revolución mexicana había sido a principios del siglo XX: la gran posibilidad de conquistar la justicia social a través, sobre todo, de la reforma agraria, de la emancipación económica frente a Estados Unidos y de la independencia política a partir de la construcción de una democracia popular. La figura política que en México había encarnado mejor que nadie esa posibilidad seguía siendo el expresidente Lázaro Cárdenas.

Así quedó de manifiesto en el número 3 de la revista con un artículo sobre la reforma agraria en Cuba, ilustrado con dos fotografías, una de Fidel hablando con un grupo de campesinos con el pie de foto "la solidaridad hispanoamericana ha de demostrarse con actos" y otra de Cárdenas acompañado por tres sonrientes indígenas huicholes y el pie de foto "así hablaba ayer la Revolución Mexicana". Aunque el artículo no tenía firma es muy posible que lo haya escrito Carlos Fuentes se refería a las crecientes dificultades con el Gobierno estadounidense, en este caso a través del embajador Philip W. Bonsal, que estaba generando la Ley de Reforma Agraria publicada el 3 de junio en la Gaceta Oficial de Cuba. El autor del artículo se preguntaba: "¿Se cruzará de brazos América Latina ante el evidente amago contra la Revolución Cubana?" Y daba una respuesta: "*el espectador* piensa que México, como ningún otro país de América, se encuentra en la obligación histórica y moral de pronunciarse abiertamente, oficialmente, a favor de la Reforma Agraria cubana. ¿Qué hubiera dado México porque Hispanoamérica defendiera unitariamente nuestra propia lucha a favor de la justicia agraria? La solidaridad hispanoamericana ha de demostrarse con actos, no en discursos y conmemoraciones". Después de reproducir un largo párrafo del discurso pronunciado por Cárdenas el 1 de septiembre de 1938 a propósito de la reforma agraria en México, el artículo concluía: "Así hablaba ayer la Revolución Mexicana. Así habla hoy la Revolución Cubana. Sólo la ceguera o la mala fe pueden negar que la lucha es la misma".[36]

El siguiente número correspondiente al mes de agosto llevó en portada la foto ya clásica de Lázaro Cárdenas con Fidel Castro en el primer festejo del 26 de julio y que anunciaba el tema: "Cárdenas y la Revolución Latinoamericana". El director en turno de ese ejemplar era González Pedrero quien seguramente escribió el editorial "Un ideario común". En el texto se reafirmaba el interés de quienes editaban *El Espectador* por colaborar en la unificación de la izquierda mexicana, en "la reagrupación de los sectores democráticos y nacionalistas" interesados en avanzar en "el afianzamiento de nuestra independencia económica y política", punto de acuerdo común. Ese interés, señalaba el autor, era también el interés de los países de Hispanoamérica que Lázaro Cárdenas había articulado con claridad en su mensaje desde el Capitolio de La Habana:

El ideario de América Latina es uno solo. Así, cuando Lázaro Cárdenas pugna por la Reforma Agraria no hace sino defender el principio de la repartición justa de la riqueza a la que Cuba, México y todos los pueblos tienen derecho. Cuando Lázaro Cárdenas defiende las instituciones que un pueblo se ha dado libremente está defendiendo la democracia política por la que lucha la izquierda mexicana. Cuando Lázaro Cárdenas cita el Principio de No Intervención está defendiendo la independencia económica contra la agresión imperialista. [. . .] Y, para todos nosotros, el eterno dilema está nuevamente presente. ¿Esperaremos cruzados de brazos a que la tragedia de Guatemala se repita en *lo nacional* y en lo exterior? Es necesaria la unidad interna para impedir el olvido de los principios de la revolución, tanto como precisa el frente unido de solidaridad latinoamericana para defender lo que, en este momento, es cosa de toda América: la Revolución Cubana. Solidaridad y unidad en uno y otro plano que, en definitiva, se complementan. No es posible dudar.[37]

El ejemplar incluía un artículo escrito por Carlos Fuentes, "Carta de La Habana", en donde se encontraba el autor.[38] Fuentes se refería a las declaraciones de Pedro Luis Díaz Lanz, a quien calificaba como "uno de los más oprobiosos traidores de la historia latinoamericana", hechas ante un comité del Senado de Estados Unidos y en las que alertaba sobre la creciente influencia comunista entre quienes conducían la revolución. En el texto Fuentes se proponía aclarar el tema y para ello reproducía algunos párrafos de un artículo publicado por Carlos Franqui, en ese momento director del diario *Revolución*: "Ni los niños creen en Cuba que los principales jefes de las fuerzas armadas sean comunistas. Camilo Cienfuegos, Ameijeiras, Castiñeiras, Guevara, Escalona, Del Valle, Monseni, Hubert, Calixto García, Almeida—¿quién no sabe que son sinceros militantes del Movimiento 26 de Julio?". Y señalaba Fuentes: "para el lector mexicano, poco familiarizado con los nombres de los jefes militares cubanos, habría que proponer un ejemplo. Supongamos que, en 1915, alguien hubiese afirmado que Álvaro Obregón, Plutarco Elías Calles, Salvador Alvarado y Felipe Ángeles eran "agentes del Káiser Guillermo II y convencidos militaristas prusianos [. . .] Esos son los límites del ridículo". En realidad, señalaba Fuentes, detrás de las acusaciones de infiltración comunista se escondía de nuevo el interés de los "círculos conservadores de los Estados Unidos" de no permitir, como había ocurrido en Guatemala en 1954, que "un gobierno democrático lleve a cabo un programa de desarrollo económico nacionalista que, por una parte, independizaría al país y que, por otra parte, necesariamente lesionaría intereses económicos norteamericanos. No, en Cuba no hay infiltración comunista: lo que hay es un programa de independencia económica, visiblemente concretado en la Reforma Agraria".[39]

Una de las preocupaciones centrales de este grupo, tal como lo expresaron en varios artículos, tenía que ver con el papel del intelectual en el ámbito social y político. Para ellos la izquierda intelectual tenía la obligación de contribuir a la unificación de la izquierda, entendida en palabras de Flores Olea "no como la unificación de los 'grupos' o de los intelectuales, sino en la unificación de la *clase trabajadora* revolucionaria [. . .] Lo decisivo es dar vida a una fuerza política de izquierda capaz de actuar en la vida pública de México, capaz de *hacer* historia". Mientras tanto, se preguntaba Flores Olea, "¿Nuestra actual tarea? El análisis, la articulación y expresión sistemática de las necesidades de las clases populares del país. [. . .] Ser cada vez más, *orgánicamente*, los intelectuales del pueblo de México. Participar desde todos los ángulos a la formación de un bloque cultural y social capaz de resolver un día, en la práctica, en la historia, las contradicciones de la actual sociedad mexicana. Y eso trasciende por mucho las polémicas entre 'grupos', entre individuos".[40]

Coincidían en ese sentido con el interés del sociólogo estadounidense C. Wright Mills, autor de *La Élite del Poder y La Imaginación Sociológica*, quien desde fines de los años cincuenta había hecho de los intelectuales uno de los sujetos predilectos de su indagación académica y política. En la primavera de 1960 Mills viajó a México para impartir un seminario en la UNAM y durante su estancia en el país entabló una relación de amistad que terminaría siendo de colaboración con Carlos Fuentes, González Pedrero y su editor en español, Orfila Reynal. En algún momento de su visita Mills sostuvo una conversación-entrevista con el Consejo Editorial de *el espectador* que se publicó en una versión resumida en el ejemplar de abril. Entre los temas destacados durante la conversación abordaron el papel que tenían la izquierda y los intelectuales en los países subdesarrollados, las posibilidades de desarrollo para América Latina en el contexto de la Guerra Fría y la relación con Estados Unidos.[41]

Aunque Cuba no aparecía en el listado de temas era evidente que había sido uno de los ejes de la conversación. Hasta antes de su visita a México Mills no se había interesado en la Revolución cubana, pero el entusiasmo que le transmitieron sus amigos y sus discusiones en la UNAM despertó su curiosidad intelectual por lo que ocurría en la isla. La interpretación de Carlos Fuentes y de González Pedrero, de Pablo González Casanova o del propio Orfila Reynal, sobre las posibilidades de la Revolución en Cuba había sido fundamental para convencer al sociólogo de la importancia que tenía ese proceso en la construcción de una nueva izquierda. Pocos meses después, Mills viajó a Cuba y, como resultado de su visita, publicó *Listen Yankee!*, el libro de bolsillo con el que quiso dirigirse a la opinión pública de su país para que conocieran la revolución más allá del discurso anticomunista que predominaba en la prensa estadounidense. Mills compartía y comunicaba en su libro el entusiasmo por el proceso cubano que le habían transmitido sus amigos en México.[42]

Además de la entrevista con Mills, *el espectador* publicó en abril de 1960 el texto de Jean-Paul Sartre, "Ideología y revolución", acompañado con un par de fotografías de Sartre y Simone de Beauvoir durante su visita a Cuba.[43] El número también incluyó una entrevista que González Pedrero pudo realizar al Che Guevara en La Habana a principios de enero de 1960. Apenas unas semanas antes había sido nombrado director del Banco Nacional de Cuba.[44] Para el Che la revolución era "un movimiento eminentemente agrario que en algunos aspectos puede caracterizarse como antifeudal (. . .) basada esencialmente en el cooperativismo y que tiende a hacer desaparecer de las relaciones económicas entre productor y consumidor al intermediario, con el establecimiento de tiendas populares. La Revolución Cubana ha sido, además, una revolución democrática, nacional, con carácter típicamente latinoamericano".

En 1960 la revolución entraba a su etapa de consolidación con dos tareas fundamentales: la reforma agraria y el inicio del proceso de industrialización. Y sobre el congreso de países subdesarrollados que se llevaría a cabo en La Habana, decía el Che: "El congreso de países sub-industrializados será una gran conquista en favor de la lucha anticolonial. Si las grandes potencias tratan de sembrar la división entre las naciones débiles hasta ahora explotadas, entre otras causas por el aislamiento en el que se han mantenido, debe ser preocupación central de los países insuficientemente desarrollados formar un frente común [. . .] Este bloque común de países sub-industrializados comenzaría con los problemas económicos pero podría, también, jugar un papel de relevancia en los organismos políticos internacionales". Finalmente, ante la pregunta de qué experiencias de la Revolución mexicana podrían ser válidas para Cuba, el Che respondió: "Válidas: la tónica agraria de la Revolución Mexicana (pienso en Zapata y Villa sobre todo). La decisión de defensa del pueblo mexicano. Las medidas de política nacionalista del gobierno de Cárdenas [. . .] a propósito, en Cuba, las inversiones sólo serán aceptadas siempre y cuando se sometan a nuestra legislación, siempre y cuando se 'cubanicen'".

González Pedrero concluía la entrevista con la siguiente reflexión: "Yo hubiese deseado continuar, pero hora y media había sido distraída de la construcción revolucionaria. Cuando bajaba del viejo palacio donde residen las oficinas centrales del Banco Nacional de Cuba, pensaba que la Revolución aún no tiene tiempo de mirarse al espejo, aún no le interesa auto-analizarse y recordaba con insistencia un pequeño letrero situado en la puerta de la dirección de Cultura que decía: 'Durante cincuenta años hemos perdido el tiempo. Sea usted breve'".[45] El último ejemplar de la revista el espectador se publicó con fecha de mayo-junio 1960 y con número doble 9-10. Ya desde fines de 1959, en el número doble 6-7 correspondiente a octubre-noviembre, el Consejo Editorial se refería a las dificultades económicas a las que se enfrentaban por carecer de subsidios en aras de mantener su independencia. Siete meses después los espectadores se despedían con un número de lujo que incluía una crónica de Fernando Benítez bajo el título "Un día con Fidel Castro", la primera parte del discurso pronunciado por el mismo Fidel durante el acto para conmemorar el 1 de mayo en el que abordaba el asunto de la democracia directa, el texto de Simone de Beauvoir, "Cuba: Las posibilidades del hombre", y una reflexión de Carlos Fuentes, "La Lección de Cuba", sobre la concentración del 1 de mayo en la Plaza Cívica de La Habana. Pronto seguirían publicando sus artículos, crónicas y entrevistas en la que habría de ser la publicación más importante de la izquierda en la primera mitad de los años sesenta.

En las páginas de *Política*

En mayo de 1960 *el espectador* dejó de publicarse pues sus editores fueron invitados por Manuel Marcué Pardiñas a integrarse a la nueva revista *Política. Quince días de México y del Mundo* dirigida por él y por Jorge Carrión y que habría de ser la publicación más importante de análisis y crítica política de la primera mitad de los años sesenta. De acuerdo a González Pedrero aceptaron la oferta a cambio de mantener total libertad editorial.[46]

El Ing. Marcué Pardiñas era conocido en los círculos progresistas desde mediados de los años cuarenta cuando editaba la revista trimestral *Problemas Económicos-Agrícolas de México* que, en 1950, ya con apoyo oficial, cedió el paso a la revista-libro trimestral *Problemas Agrícolas e Industriales de México*. Por su parte el periodista y médico Jorge Carrión venía de las filas del Partido Popular encabezado por Vicente Lombardo Toledano, militaba en el Movimiento Mexicano por la Paz y desde 1951 era colaborador cercano de Marcué.[47] Como su nombre lo indica, el objetivo de la publicación era el análisis de los problemas del desarrollo económico del país y contó con la colaboración de académicos, funcionarios e intelectuales de izquierda, algunos de ellos integrantes del Círculo de Estudios Mexicanos.[48] En *Política* confluyeron entonces todas las voces del abanico que formaba en ese momento a la izquierda mexicana y que iban desde el lombardismo gobiernista y el cardenismo renovado hasta los sectores más radicalizados por la ola revolucionaria cubana. Así lo reflejó el Consejo Editorial en el que aparecían nombres representativos de todas las corrientes, desde Vicente Lombardo Toledano y David Alfaro Siqueiros por la izquierda partidaria hasta Víctor Rico Galán que pocos años después se decantaría por la opción insurreccional. Aparecían también los nombres de Fernando Benítez, Carlos Fuentes, Enrique González Pedrero y Víctor Flores Olea.[49]

Desde su nacimiento *Política* hizo público su compromiso con la Revolución cubana.[50] El primer número se publicó el 1 de mayo de 1960 coincidiendo con la celebración en La Habana del Encuentro de Solidaridad con Cuba, realizado en esa fecha emblemática, y al que asistió un grupo de colaboradores de la revista entre quienes se encontraban su director general, Marcué Pardiñas, su director, Jorge Carrión, además de Benítez, Flores Olea, Fuentes, entre otros.[51] Como señala Reynaga Mejía, la imagen fotográfica y la caricatura fueron un elemento esencial de *Política*. Así quedó demostrado desde el primer número en el que se publicó una foto de Marcué y Carrión observando atentos al general Cárdenas firmar una declaración de solidaridad con Cuba a la que se habían adherido diversas personalidades latinoamericanas.[52] Sumándose al compromiso que habían asumido Benítez y Fuentes desde 1959 para informar desde la perspectiva de la revolución, *Política* recibió desde el primero momento los servicios de la agencia cubana de noticias *Prensa Latina*.

Tal como lo habían hecho en "México en la Cultura" y en *el espectador*, Benítez, Fuentes, González Pedrero y Flores Olea llevaron a las páginas de *Política* sus crónicas y análisis sobre el día a día de la revolución en Cuba y sus efectos en la relación con México y con Estados Unidos, sus fervorosas expresiones de solidaridad, su admiración por la figura de Fidel Castro, así como el contraste con lo que ocurría en México, en donde el Gobierno de López Mateos intentaba conciliar los distintos intereses y posturas en relación a Cuba mientras mantenía una respuesta autoritaria frente a la movilización social. Además de insistir en la necesidad de que el Gobierno mexicano se solidarizara sin ambages con los revolucionarios cubanos, no solo por su propio pasado y por estar en sintonía con la opinión mayoritaria, sino por la posibilidad de ser parte de un frente latinoamericano que resistiera las presiones de Estados Unidos, este grupo continuó desarrollando en sus colaboraciones en *Política* el interés por temas que habían expresado ya en las páginas de *el espectador*: las posibilidades de construir una verdadera democracia en México, de avanzar en la justicia social impulsando la reforma agraria, las posibles vías para salir del subdesarrollo y trascender la relación con Estados Unidos desde la defensa de la soberanía nacional, entre otras. Como lo señalaron en distintas colaboraciones, defender a Cuba era defender una opción de desarrollo distinta para México, menos subordinada a los intereses de Estados Unidos, y más comprometida con una verdadera democracia y la solución de los problemas de la desigualdad.

En la medida en que se agudizó el enfrentamiento entre Cuba y Estados Unidos creció también la movilización que llevaba a cabo la izquierda mexicana en apoyo del proceso revolucionario. En particular resultó cada vez más evidente que el expresidente Lázaro Cárdenas se colocaba a la cabeza del movimiento de solidaridad, tal y como se hizo evidente en la convocatoria y la realización después de la Conferencia Latinoamericana por la Soberanía Nacional, la Emancipación Económica y la Paz, que se llevó a cabo en la ciudad de México del 5 al 8 de marzo de 1961 con la presencia de dieciséis delegaciones latinoamericanas, además de representantes de China, la Unión Soviética y varios países africanos. Se trataba del primer esfuerzo de reagrupamiento de una izquierda progresista latinoamericana impulsado por la defensa de la Revolución cubana y los movimientos de liberación nacional, y cuyas actividades fueron dadas a conocer puntillosamente en *Política* en un suplemento especial que incluyó la convocatoria, el temario, las bases de organización y el reglamento.[53]

A propósito de la Conferencia escribió González Pedrero:

Se ha dicho que el objeto de la próxima Conferencia por la Soberanía Nacional es, exclusivamente, la defensa de la Revolución Cubana. Las buenas causas se defienden solas. Los delegados latinoamericanos vendrán a plantear los problemas de sus países, que son comunes a todos, y si cada uno de nosotros sabe defenderse, estará defendiendo a Cuba, al Congo y a Argelia, que no tardará en liberarse. . . Y frente a los que tratan de empequeñecer al Gral. Cárdenas, haciéndonos creer que "ha pasado a la historia", hacemos pública nuestra solidaridad con el hombre que hizo posible un México auténticamente revolucionario. Cárdenas no ha pasado a la historia. Está en ella y sigue haciéndola, y nosotros estamos con él.[54]

Más aún, el propio González Pedrero no dudaría en calificar a la conferencia como el Bandung de América Latina, en referencia a la reunión de 1955.[55]

Ante el vacío que la gran prensa le hizo a la Conferencia el expresidente

Cárdenas decidió hacer un recorrido por los estados del centro del país acompañado de varios delegados extranjeros. Carlos Fuentes y Francisco López Cámara hicieron la crónica de ese viaje en las páginas de *Política*. En algún momento del recorrido, Fuentes preguntó al expresidente: "¿Cuál es la mejor defensa de Cuba? La organización de las fuerzas populares en toda América Latina. Con una fuerza popular organizada, se le puede decir al imperialismo: *no nos toques y no toques a Cuba*. La liberación de los pueblos debe ser obra de los pueblos, y la mejor defensa de Cuba depende del propio pueblo cubano. Mientras más rápidamente diversifique Cuba sus cultivos y se industrialice, más inexpugnable será la Revolución Cubana. No hay mejor ejemplo que el que se da en la propia casa".

Pocas semanas después del viaje, señaló Fuentes,

[. . .] la oportunidad de la Conferencia convocada por Cárdenas fue demostrada [. . .] en abril de 1961, una fuerza de traidores cubanos, armados y alentados por el gobierno de Kennedy desembarcó en Playa Girón y fue derrotada por las fuerzas del pueblo cubano. El 17 de abril de 1961, Lázaro Cárdenas subió al toldo de un automóvil colocado en el centro del Zócalo y habló a los miles de manifestantes que se habían reunido para protestar la invasión de Playa Girón [. . .] la ovación más larga que he escuchado recibió a este hombre que veintitrés años antes, había proclamado la nacionalización del petróleo desde el balcón central de Palacio y ahora, desde el nivel de la calle, defendía la independencia de una pequeña nación amenazada.[56]

El 4 de agosto la Conferencia dio paso a la fundación del Movimiento de Liberación Nacional (MLN), la síntesis del esfuerzo de unificación de la izquierda en aras de impulsar la renovación crítica del legado de la Revolución mexicana en coincidencia con las posibilidades que prometía el proyecto revolucionario cubano. El MLN nacía de la confluencia de entusiasmos y compromisos en un ambiente cargado de apremios solidarios como consecuencia del intento estadounidense por asaltar a la isla en abril. En el programa de la nueva organización destacaba el interés por impulsar una agenda de mayor democracia, justicia social y fortalecimiento de la soberanía económica en México al tiempo que se comprometían a la solidaridad con una Cuba ya declarada socialista.

El compromiso político de los espectadores quedó expresado en la participación de Carlos Fuentes, Enrique González Pedrero y Francisco López Cámara como parte del Comité Nacional del MLN. Por su parte Flores Olea había formado parte de la comisión organizadora. Ahí se enfrascaron también en los debates que atravesaban en ese momento a las diversas corrientes de la izquierda mexicana. Narra Raquel Tibol: "Volví a ver al doctor Jorge Carrión en el muy sencillo local que el Movimiento de Liberación Nacional, constituido en agosto de 1961, tenía en la calle de República del Salvador, el día que polemizó con Carlos Fuentes sobre los principios del movimiento. Ambos eran miembros del primer Comité Nacional Colegiado; pero la preparación, experiencia y sustento teórico en cuestiones políticas era de una diferencia abismal. Los muy numerosos asistentes nos quedamos con la impresión de que, seguramente sin proponérselo previamente, Carlos Fuentes, políticamente de peso liviano, había salido muy castigado por su contrincante de peso completo".[57] Al participar activamente en los trabajos iniciales del MLN este grupo concretó su intención de hacer del intelectual un actor político, con un compromiso por la unificación de la izquierda y a través de ella por la posibilidad de cambiar la realidad del país.

Desde 1961 y hasta que dejó de publicarse en 1967, *Política* fue el foro en el que se expresaron los debates y las distintas posturas políticas que confluyeron en el Movimiento de Liberación Nacional. Poco a poco, sin embargo, los conflictos al interior del MLN y la propia izquierda redundaron en la revista. Las desavenencias se agudizaron al acercarse la sucesión presidencial y con ello el debate en torno al mejor camino para incidir en el proceso electoral que tendría lugar en 1964.

A lo largo de 1963 las fuerzas que confluyeron en el MLN se enfrascaron en una intensa discusión en torno a la posibilidad de sostener una candidatura presidencial independiente. Frente a la postura del Partido Comunista que terminaría por impulsar la formación del Frente Electoral de Pueblo y postular a Ramón Danzós Palomino como candidato independiente, los cardenistas argumentaron su rechazo negándose a dividir un movimiento que desde sus inicios se había proclamado apartidista. En marzo de 1964 Heriberto Jara primero y en junio el expresidente Cárdenas después, dieron su apoyo al candidato presidencial del PRI, el secretario de Gobernación Gustavo Díaz Ordaz, un reconocido anticomunista al que *Política* había criticado en diversos artículos. Esto les valió condenas y críticas en las páginas de *Política*, como el artículo "Implicaciones del voto razonado de Lázaro Cárdenas en Pro de Díaz Ordaz" en el que el autor se preguntaba si "[. . .]¿una personalidad que arrastra a las masas hasta organizarlas en un movimiento con un programa concreto de liberación nacional, de reforma agraria y de sustancial modificación de las injustas estructuras económicas y sociales que prevalecen en el país puede sin previo compromiso claro y público de las fuerzas a las que ahora apoya, y del candidato oficial que las representa, declararse a favor de éste sin menoscabar la responsabilidad adquirida ante aquellas masas por toda una vida de actuación revolucionaria y por ser el promotor principal del programa de liberación?".[58]

A esas alturas la coalición articulada en el MLN y representada en las páginas de *Política* exhibía fracturas difíciles de ocultar. En una carta fechada el 26 de julio de 1964 y que se publicó en la revista el 15 de agosto, Benítez, Flores Olea, Fuentes, González Pedrero y López Cámara se dirigieron a Marcué para pedirle que retirara sus nombres del cuadro de colaboradores de la revista. El argumento central para dejar *Política* era lo que ellos consideraban su creciente sectarismo, dogmatismo e intransigencia. La gota que derramaba el vaso era "una campaña deliberada de provocaciones, injurias y calumnias contra el expresidente Lázaro Cárdenas y contra el Gral. Heriberto Jara". Y concluían su carta señalando: "No cejaremos en nuestro combate limitado pero honesto, por la independencia y el progreso de México, por la completa actualización de la Revolución Mexicana, por el acercamiento de nuestra política exterior al no alineamiento a ninguno de los bandos en pugna, por el eventual desarrollo de una democracia socialista en nuestra patria y también por el derecho a hablar con un lenguaje opuesto al de la enajenación, el sectarismo o la retórica".[59]

En cierto sentido la salida de la revista marcó el fin del esfuerzo compartido por este grupo de intelectuales por incidir como una suerte de colectivo en las tareas de una posible unificación de la izquierda desde un espacio común. Aunque todos siguieron escribiendo y publicando en distintos espacios, la salida de *Política* marcó el fin de un esfuerzo que inició en 1959 en las páginas de "México en la Cultura" y *el espectador*. En los años siguientes la radicalización de las izquierdas y del propio proceso cubano que se afirmaba en el socialismo marxista-leninista, dejó de tener el registro colectivo que construyeron estos autores como un esfuerzo común y un compromiso político compartido por todos.

NOTAS

1. "México en la Cultura" dejó de publicarse en 1961 y el mismo grupo se integró al nuevo suplemento "La Cultura en México" que se publicó a partir de febrero de 1962 en la revista *Siempre!*. Dada la imposibilidad de consultar el segundo suplemento por la contingencia sanitaria no ha sido considerado en este artículo. El uso de minúsculas en el título de la revista *el espectador* era parte del proyecto de sus fundadores. Se usan las mayúsculas por criterios editoriales de *Cuban Studies*.

2. Jaime M. Pensado, *Rebel Mexico: Student Unrest and Authoritarian Political Culture during the Long Sixties*, Stanford University Press, 2013, pp. 139. Eric Zolov, *The Last Good Neighbor: Mexico in the Global Sixties*, Duke University Press, 2020.

3. Víctor Manuel Camposeco, *El suplemento México en la Cultura (1949–1961): Renovación literaria y testimonio crítico*, Consejo Nacional para la Cultura y las Artes, 2015.

4. Armando Ponce, "José Emilio Pacheco: 1958, el año axial," *Proceso*, 4 de febrero de 2014.

5. Camposeco, *El suplemento México en la Cultura (1949–1961)*, p. 106, nota 22. Cuevas acababa su texto señalando: "Quiero en el arte de mi país anchas carreteras que nos lleven al resto del mundo, no pequeños caminos vecinales que conectan sólo aldeas".

6. "México en la cultura," 4 de abril de 1958 (tomado de *Relatos e historias en México*, julio 2012).

7. Carlos Franqui, *Diario de la Revolución cubana*, Barcelona, Ediciones R. Torres, 1976, p. 152. Tomado de Juan Rafael Reynaga Mejía, *La Revolución cubana en México a través de la revista Política: Construcción imaginaria de un discurso para América Latina*, Universidad Autónoma del Estado de México y Universidad Nacional Autónoma de México, 2007.

8. Víctor Manuel Camposeco, "Instantánea de Fernando Benítez," 10 de febrero de 2012, https://revistareplicante.com; Renata Keller, "The Revolution Will Be Teletyped: Cuba's Prensa Latina News Agency and the Cold War Contest over Information," *Journal of Cold War Studies* 21, no. 3, 2019, p. 88.

9. A propósito de la editorial ERA véase a José Carlos Reyes Pérez, "El sueño mayor de hacer libros": ERA. Cultura escrita en español y la difusión de las ciencias sociales a través de una editorial. 1960–1989," tesis de maestría en historia internacional, México, CIDE, 2016.

10. Luis Hernández Navarro, "Las andanzas del marxismo tropical," *La Jornada Semanal*, no. 745, 14 de junio de 2009.

11. Ponce, "José Emilio Pacheco".

12. Rosa Castro, "Entrevista con Enrique González Pedrero" en "México en la cultura," no. 515, 25 de enero de 1959.

13. Enrique González Pedrero, *La Revolución cubana*, México, Escuela Nacional de Ciencias Políticas y Sociales, 1959.

14. "México en la cultura," no. 515, 25 de enero de 1959.

15. Habían sido detenidos en mayo en la ciudad de México por violar las leyes migratorias y proseguir sus actividades contra Batista. Fueron liberados en julio por la intervención directa de Cárdenas ante Ruiz Cortines. Ángel Gutiérrez, "Lázaro Cárdenas y Cuba," en *Desde Diez*, Boletín del Centro de Estudios de la Revolución Mexicana "Lázaro Cárdenas," julio de 1985.

16. Lázaro Cárdenas, *Obras I: Apuntes 1941–1956*, tomo 2, 2ª ed., México, UNAM, 1986, pp. 646–647.

17. Lázaro Cárdenas, *Epistolario de Lázaro Cárdenas*, vol. 2, Siglo Veintiuno, 1974, p. 133.

18. "México en la cultura," no. 542, 2 de agosto de 1959.

19. "México en la cultura," no. 543, 9 de agosto de 1959.

20. "México en la cultura," no. 578, 10 de abril de 1960. Este texto junto con la entrevista con los escritores cubanos y el ensayo "Huracán sobre el Azúcar" se publicó en *Sartre visita a Cuba*, Literatura Ediciones.

21. "México en la cultura," no. 582, 8 de mayo de 1960.

22. "México en la cultura," no. 584, 22 de mayo de 1960.

23. "México en la cultura," no. 587, 12 de junio de 1960.

24. *Lunes de Revolución*, no. 63, 13 de junio de 1960.

25. "México en la cultura," no. 643, 9 de julio de 1961.

26. Elena Poniatowska, "Fernando Benítez, extraordinario promotor de la cultura mexicana," *La Jornada*, 26 de febrero de 2017.

27. Víctor Manuel Camposeco atribuye a Jaime García Terrés la redacción de ese texto. Camposeco, "Instantánea".

28. "México en la Cultura," no. 665, 10 de diciembre de 1961.

29. José Emilio Pacheco, "Carlos Fuentes hace medio siglo," *Proceso*, 20 de mayo de 2012.

30. Carlos Fuentes, "Radiografía de una década: 1953–1963," *Tiempo Mexicano*, Cuadernos de Joaquín Mortiz, México, 1971, 56–57.

31. "*El Espectador*, tribuna juvenil," *El Universal*, 21 de noviembre de 2008.

32. Entrevista de la autora con Enrique González Pedrero, 1 de junio de 2019.

33. *El Espectador*, no. 1, mayo 1959, pp. 2 y 3.

34. Entrevista de la autora con Enrique González Pedrero, 1 de junio de 2019.

35. Fuentes, "Radiografía", p. 64.

36. *El Espectador*, no. 3, julio 1959.

37. Cursivas en el original. *El Espectador*, no. 4, agosto de 1959.

38. En esos días Fuentes también publicó en "México en la cultura" el artículo "Las horas de Cuba," la crónica del festejo del 26 de julio en La Habana. Apareció el 9 de agosto de 1959.

39. *El Espectador*, no. 4, agosto de 1959.

40. *El Espectador*, no. 5, septiembre de 1959

41. *El Espectador*, no. 8, abril de 1960.

42. Elisa Servín, "La experiencia mexicana de Charles Wright Mills," *Historia Mexicana* 69, no. 4, 2020.

43. *El Espectador*, no. 8, abril de 1960. El texto se publicó casi simultáneamente en "México en la Cultura" el 10 de abril lo que indicaba la cercanía de los equipos que editaban ambas publicaciones. En "México en la Cultura" se señalaba que el artículo era un servicio especial de la agencia *Prensa Latina*.

44. Aunque en la publicación aparece la fecha de la entrevista como 8 de enero de 1959 es evidente por el contenido que se realizó en 1960.

45. *El Espectador*, no. 8, abril de 1960.

46. Entrevista de la autora con Enrique González Pedrero, 1 de junio de 2019.

47. Raquel Tibol, "Un testimonio sobre Jorge Carrión", *Proceso*, no. 1515, 13 de noviembre de 2005; Marta Quesada, "Jorge Carrión y la revista *Política*", *La Jornada Semanal*, no. 975, 10 de noviembre de 2013.

48. Miguel Ángel Beltrán Villegas, "El MLN: Historia de un recorrido hacia la unidad (México 1957–1967)," tesis de doctorado en estudios latinoamericanos, UNAM, Medellín, 2000, p. 137. De acuerdo a un informe policiaco Marcué tenía relaciones con el Partido Comunista Mexicano y el Partido Popular de Lombardo Toledano. Renata Keller, *Mexico's Cold War: Cuba, the United States, and the Legacy of the Mexican Revolution*, New York, Cambridge University Press, 2015, p. 57.

49. *Política*, no. 1, 1 de mayo de 1960.

50. Reynaga, *La Revolución cubana en México a través de la revista Política*.; Beatriz Urías Horcasitas, "Alianzas efímeras: Izquierdas y nacionalismo revolucionario en la revista *Política*. Quince días de México y del Mundo (1960–1962)", *Historia Mexicana* 68, no. 3, 2019, pp. 1205–1252.

51. Reynaga, *La Revolución cubana*, p. 105.

52. Ibid., pp. 37–39.

53. *Política*, no. 20, 15 de febrero de 1961. El director de *Política* Jorge Carrión participó en las Comisiones de Trabajo de la Conferencia junto con el ingeniero Jorge L. Tamayo, el licenciado Alonso Aguilar, Antonio Pérez Elías, Rosendo Gómez Lorenzo y Carlos Lagunas (Raquel Tibol, "Un testimonio sobre Jorge Carrión").

54. *Política*, no. 21, 1 de marzo de 1961.

55. Reynaga, *La Revolución cubana*, p. 168.

56. Fuentes publicó después en *Tiempo Mexicano* esos textos. La cita está tomada de ese libro, pp. 105–107.

57. En descargo de Fuentes, la anécdota ejemplifica no solo la confluencia de ideologías y experiencias, sino también de generaciones que se encontraron en el MLN. Frente a militantes de la izquierda partidaria como Carrión o la propia Tibol, Fuentes era un joven escritor sin formación política (Tibol, "Un testimonio sobre Jorge Carrión").

58. *Política*, 15 de junio de 1964, tomado de Beltrán, p. 285.

59. *Política*, no. 104, 15 de agosto de 1964.

MARTÍN RIBADERO

La profecía realizada: Viajeros argentinos de izquierda a la Revolución cubana

RESUMEN

La experiencia de viajar en su modalidad reflexiva y de búsqueda de conocimiento es un atributo de la modernidad. Dentro de esa tradición moderna, el viaje revolucionario, en especial durante el siglo XX, estuvo asociado con la idea de vislumbrar el futuro, el advenimiento de una nueva sociedad. El objetivo del trabajo es estudiar los registros escritos de varios intelectuales argentinos que, encandilados con la originalidad del proceso cubano e identificados con la ascendencia que gozaba allí otro argentino como Ernesto Che Guevara, viajaron a la isla y a la vuelta dejaron sus impresiones sobre lo que entendían, en términos generales, era la realización de una utopía social democrática e igualitarista. Este ejercicio de traducción político-cultural fue realizado por varias figuras entre las que se destacan hombres provenientes de la tradición de las izquierdas como Jorge Masetti, Alfredo Palacios, Silvio Frondizi, Adolfo Gilly y Elías Semán, entre otros. A partir del análisis de testimonios compuestos por un corpus variado el ensayo intenta adentrarse en un aspecto significativo pero poco atendido a la hora de comprender la repercusión global de la Revolución cubana en América Latina: haber sido una experiencia que movilizó recursos simbólicos y materiales y sensibilidades políticas que alteró los ricos y disímiles debates de ideas que en distintas capitales de la región se enfrentaban en la esfera pública.

ABSTRACT

The experience of traveling in its reflective modality and search for knowledge is an attribute of modernity. Within this modern tradition, the revolutionary journey, especially during the twentieth century, was associated with the idea of glimpsing the future, the advent of a new society. The objective of the work is to study the written records of several Argentine intellectuals who, dazzled by the originality of the Cuban process and identified with the ancestry enjoyed by another Argentinian like Ernesto "Che" Guevara, traveled to the island and left their impressions on what they had returned understood, in general terms, shaped the realization of a democratic and egalitarian social utopia. This exercise in political-cultural translation was carried out by several figures, including men from the left, such as Jorge Masetti, Alfredo Palacios, Silvio Frondizi, Adolfo Gilly, Elías Semán, and Juan Carlos Portantiero, among others. From analysis of varied testimonies this essay explores a significant but little attended aspect of understanding the global repercussion of the Cuban Revolution in Latin America: as an experience that mobilized symbolic and material resources and political sensitivities, which altered the rich, dissimilar ideas that different capitals of the region faced in the public sphere.

Viaje y revolución

La experiencia de viajar en su modalidad reflexiva y de búsqueda de conocimiento es un atributo de la modernidad.[1] Dentro de esa tradición, el viaje revolucionario, en especial durante el siglo XX, despuntó como parte de una idea asociada a vislumbrar el futuro, el advenimiento de una nueva sociedad. A partir de la Revolución rusa, intelectuales, cronistas, políticos, expertos y militantes de todo el mundo convirtieron el acto de viajar en una forma de acceder a mundos en radical transformación social y económica.[2]

Esta amalgama entre viaje y revolución tuvo en la Argentina notables protagonistas. Desde Elías Castelnuovo, Aníbal Ponce, Rodolfo Ghioldi, Ezequiel Martínez Estrada, María Rosa Oliver, hasta Carlos Astrada hasta Bernardo Kordon, Leopoldo Marechal, Julio Cortázar, Rodolfo Walsh y Ricardo Piglia, varios fueron los intelectuales que hicieron culto de esta tradición global como parte de la dinámica transnacional que alcanzó la vida cultural nacional durante un importante tramo del siglo pasado.[3] Si bien esta práctica de viaje desde la centuria anterior conformaba un tipo de sociabilidad y búsqueda de distinción por parte de las élites intelectuales argentinas, a partir del octubre ruso un sector dejó de interesarse por el viaje estético al tiempo de elegir otra geografía. En efecto, durante la década de 1920 comenzó a contraponerse una alternativa a la idea de huir de la comarca porteña, asaltada por la inmigración, para refugiarse en los entresijos de salones, museos y palacios de Francia e Inglaterra.[4]

A partir del éxito bolchevique, viajar pasó a convertirse en un momento iniciático y revelador del futuro cuya referencia espacial ahora se hallaba en la periferia de Europa: Rusia. Intelectuales, escritores, pero también trabajadores manuales urbanos y rurales, gracias a las cada vez más firmes redes militantes y partidarias internacionales, afrontaron y registraron estas experiencias en diarios, memorias, cartas y libros. La revolución de signo socialista, finalmente, adquiría un lugar preciso en el mapa y una forma concreta de igualitarismo social en base a la racionalización, planificación y desarrollo de las fuerzas productivas por parte de un país atrasado y periférico similar a la Argentina.[5]

La revolución china de 1949 auspició la siguiente estación del viaje revolucionario en el país y otras zonas de Occidente.[6] La amalgama entre revolución y la tradición milenaria del gigante asiático conformó un aspecto atractivo para mujeres como María Rosa Oliver y hombres como Bernardo Kordon y Carlos Astrada.[7] A pesar de que Cuba rápidamente la reemplazó como la nueva meca revolucionaria, lo mismo que hizo con la revolución boliviana antes, todavía en 1973 Ricardo Piglia, acompañado por Ricardo Nudelman y Rubén Kriscautzky, profesaba un interés político y cultural por el proceso chino, visible en su estancia durante ese año gracias a su militancia en el maoísmo argentino y a las redes internacionales cultivadas por esta franja de la izquierda argentina.[8]

En esta larga saga de pasión revolucionaria, Cuba modificó sustancial-
mente las coordenadas tanto espaciales como ideológicas para los intelectuales
argentinos, en especial de izquierdas. Ya no era Europa o el extremo asiático el
centro mundial de la revolución, con sus diferencias de lenguas, costumbres e
idiosincrasia, sino un territorio cercano y común anclado en América Latina.
La revolución ya no ocurría en otros lados. La Habana, y no Moscú o Pekín,
se convirtió en el eje global. La utopía regeneradora, finalmente, ocurría aquí y
ahora. Para muchos su triunfo revelaba un rasgo de originalidad respecto a similares y anteriores sucesos al combinar liderazgo juvenil, ausencia de partido
tradicional y una flexibilidad ideológica que buscaba, por lo menos durante
los primeros años, atraer simpatías y lograr apoyos diversos, en especial entre
los intelectuales. En la Argentina, hombres y mujeres inscriptos en distintas
tendencias político-ideológicas como peronistas, socialistas, trotskistas, comunistas, nacionalistas, católicos y aún liberales se vieron interpelados por el
proceso cubano, al punto que muchos decidieron viajar a la isla.

El objetivo del trabajo es considerar las experiencias de viajes que intelectuales, militantes y escritores de la izquierda argentina realizaron a Cuba.
La literatura dedicada a analizar este tipo de modalidad cultural, ha afirmado
con agudeza que adentrarse en esta fuente documental puede ser significativa
a la hora de analizar valores, ideas y nociones que los intelectuales enuncia-
ron respecto a aquellas sociedades que experimentaban un fuerte proceso de
transformación social. Estos escritos, se ha resaltado, conformaron un tipo de
mediación a través de la cual se diseminaron a escala global toda una serie de
representaciones y traducciones sobre lo que acontecía en países atravesados
por verdaderos cataclismos como sucedió en la Unión Soviética, China y, para
nuestro interés específico, Cuba.

La pertinencia de proponer una investigación en base a los relatos de viaje
radica en su capacidad por articular un sentido de familiaridad, cercanía y
emoción con juicios y visiones que configuraron las formas en que el proceso
cubano impactó entre los intelectuales argentinos. Asimismo, estos testimonios permiten identificar un tramo particular, un momento de la trayectoria de
quienes decidieron atravesar este tipo de experiencia, al tiempo que identificar
las imágenes y sensibilidades de quienes ejercieron un rol de traductor en sus
respectivas sociedades.[9]

Estos viajes y representaciones sobre la Revolución cubana han sido analizados por algunos investigadores.[10] El estudio más completo y amplio en referencia al viaje revolucionario es el de Paul Hollander. Este autor priorizó
estudiar a intelectuales y militantes procedentes de Estados Unidos y de Europa Occidental, bajo la idea de que estos hallaban en Cuba una alternativa a
sociedades de origen apáticas y estancadas producto del creciente bienestar e
igualdad económica. Sin embargo, si bien su agudeza analítica es destacada en
razón de la repercusión que generó el proceso caribeño entre norteamericanos

y europeos, quienes procedían de sociedades con menores niveles de integración social y marcada desigualdad como América Latina —e incluso regiones como Europa oriental— quedan apartados de este tipo de explicación como también de una necesaria reconstrucción histórica.[11]

Ciertamente, los viajes a la isla fueron asiduos por parte de intelectuales argentinos y del resto de la región, en un contexto de recepción que no descartaba el diseño, tal como afirma Hollander, de un espacio controlado que condicionaba la estancia de los visitantes. A pesar de ello, lejos estaba Cuba, durante los primeros años, de ser un "parque temático" o un "paraíso" de ensueños para la izquierda latinoamericana.[12] Si se revisa detenidamente el testimonio de quienes viajaron, no solo se hallaran distintas visiones sobre su significado, sino también críticas y observaciones, distantes de una mirada complaciente, sea a nivel del proceso en curso como del tipo de política que desplegaba la dirigencia revolucionaria.

Una mirada de conjunto de la literatura académica disponible permite apreciar la ausencia de una indagación histórica sistemática de tales agentes, lo mismo que explicaciones alternativas que den cuenta de los motivos y medios concretos a través de los cuales muchos intelectuales latinoamericanos y específicamente argentinos lograron trasladarse a la isla.[13] Resulta notable, a pesar de parciales aportes, la falta de estudio por parte de la agenda de investigación global dedicada a una de las revoluciones sociales más importantes del siglo XX respecto a los de los efectos que Cuba produjo en las capitales culturales latinoamericanas.[14] En torno a estas coordenada el presente trabajo intenta establecer, en primer lugar, una cartografía de aquellos intelectuales argentinos principalmente de izquierda que se trasladaron a la isla, a partir de reconstruir los motivos y redes que impulsaron o facilitaron concretar dicha experiencia. En segundo término, se analizarán algunos de los testimonios, teniendo en cuenta que el estudio de los relatos de viaje como fuentes documentales requiere indagar en las formas que adquirió este género desde el punto de vista de su estructura narrativa y argumentativa, en el diseño, de una visión de la revolución.[15] Asimismo, interesa conectar esos escritos con los debates y disputas que atravesaba la vida intelectual y política argentina en general y las izquierdas en particular entre fines de los años cincuenta y los primeros de la década del sesenta.

La idea que anima este artículo intenta demostrar que estos relatos conformaron una parte importante del ejercicio de traducción de la Revolución cubana en el espacio argentino durante sus primeros años, en un momento de definición y expansión de la gesta caribeña.[16] Al mismo tiempo, su indagación es un aporte significativo para comprender la trayectoria intelectual de quienes viajaron a la isla, y establecer a partir de estos de qué manera dicha participación influenció en el despliegue de sus carreras y en la reconfiguración de sus identidades y espacios político-culturales. El estudio del viaje revolucionario, en conclusión, forma parte de un capítulo importante de la historia de los intelectuales de las izquierdas de la centuria anterior no demasiado explorado por parte de la historiografía dedicada al análisis de esta cultura política en la Argentina, como tampoco por parte de aquella que eligió priorizar una escala latinoamericana.[17]

Mapa de viaje: Intelectuales argentinos en Cuba

En reiteradas oportunidades se ha señalado el impacto que la gesta cubana tuvo en la Argentina en distintas formaciones y experiencias político-culturales desde 1959 en adelante. La historiografía disponible, en el último tiempo, intentó evidenciar y evaluar su recepción en especial entre algunas formaciones de izquierda, al señalar su falta de crítica de una experiencia marcada por un ambicioso igualitarismo social, pero también, y sobre todo, por una "concentración absoluta del poder" de la dirigencia liderada por Fidel Castro.[18] Estos trabajos han sido llamativamente parciales desde el punto de vista de las fuentes y actores, no solamente asociado al mundo de los intelectuales —priorizando las izquierdas antes que otras culturas políticas—, sino también respecto a otras dimensiones culturales que, solo aquí pueden ser apuntadas, conforman el vasto mundo de los medios de comunicación: la radio, el cine, la televisión y la prensa. Entre todas esas producciones culturales, este artículo ha trabajado —como continuidad de una investigación anterior—,[19] con testimonios publicados entre fines de los años cincuenta y principios de los años sesenta, asociados a lo que se denomina como literatura de viaje, género que no ha suscitado mayor atención por parte de la historia intelectual y de las izquierdas.[20]

Resaltar tal enfoque supone captar la experiencia atravesada por los intelectuales, con el fin de distinguir las actitudes favorables y críticas, valores y aspiraciones, que difundieron en sus respectivos círculos. En un registro complementario, los relatos de viajes conforman una fuente pertinente para distinguir el motivo y tipo de traducción que realizaron de la gesta en la Argentina. En otras palabras: ¿qué motivó el viaje a Cuba? ¿Cuáles fueron las vías, contactos y redes que facilitaron la travesía? ¿Brindó una oportunidad para reconfigurar las carreras de quienes viajaron a la isla? ¿De qué modo? Una propia función de los intelectuales es enunciar y transmitir un tipo de representación, un imaginario, de los hechos y de la experiencia atravesada en sus respectivos espacios de origen. Entonces, ¿cómo eligieron argumentar su visión ideológica sobre un proceso que, en especial durante sus primeros años, cabalgaba entre el nacionalismo revolucionario, el anti-imperialismo y el socialismo de corte marxista-leninista en términos doctrinarios? ¿Todos se detuvieron en figurar o señalar iguales escenas, interlocutores y hechos durante su estadía? ¿De qué manera y sobre qué fundamentaron sus ideas sobre la experiencia cubana?

El corpus de la investigación se conforma de libros y artículos producidos por varias figuras provenientes de la tradición de las izquierdas, y que sin embargo no fueron abordados por parte de la literatura dedicada a estudiar el impacto de Cuba en el país. Estos escritos de viaje se asocian a nombres como Jorge Masetti, Alfredo Palacios, Silvio Frondizi, Ezequiel Martínez Estrada, Adolfo Gilly, Luis Franco, Elías Semán, Juan Carlos Portantiero, Leopoldo Marechal, Marcos Winocur, León Rozitchner, y Enrique Raab, entre otros. A partir del estudio de algunos de estos testimonios como los de Masetti, Palacios, Frondizi, en razón de encontrar en ellos nítidas diferencias, pero también varias similitudes tanto discursivas como de trayectorias, este artículo aborda un aspecto significativo de la repercusión de la Revolución cubana en América Latina. De esta manera, podrá comprenderse con mayor especificidad y riqueza histórica la capacidad de movilización de recursos simbólicos y materiales y sensibilidades políticas que produjo la isla entre los intelectuales argentinos, quienes buscaban ofrecer una particular interpretación del evento al tiempo que reflexionar sobre los problemas comunes que muchos de nuestros países atravesaron desde la mitad del siglo XX en adelante.

El primero: Jorge Masetti y la revolución como conversión

Jóvenes periodistas, escritores, cronistas y dirigentes políticos argentinos concurrieron a la isla del Caribe para ver y tocar la revolución. En esos primeros años, la supuesta "indefinición ideológica", la ausencia de una fuerza política tradicional y la presencia de jóvenes intelectuales y combatientes, hicieron de Cuba un hecho político e ideológico atractivo que parecía testificar el triunfo de la lucha anti-imperialista, democrática e igualitaria que América Latina afrontaba desde su independencia, en un mundo atravesado por la hegemonía norteamericana, la Guerra Fría y la desestructuración de los mundos coloniales en Asia y África.[21]

Muchos escribieron sobre la Cuba revolucionaria sin viajar a la isla. Otros estuvieron allí casi desde su inicio. Incluso antes del triunfo final en enero de 1959. El periodista Jorge Masetti fue uno de ellos. Proveniente de una familia de clase media baja radicada en la localidad de Avellaneda, a las afueras de la ciudad de Buenos Aires, durante su infancia —cursando en un colegio católico— y juventud, Masetti no revelaba especial interés por los asuntos académicos, llegando incluso a abandonar sus estudios medios. Casi bordeando los veinte años, conoció y trabó amistad con otros jóvenes como Rodolfo Walsh y Rogelio García Lupo, a partir de su ingreso a una pequeña agrupación nacionalista denominada Alianza Libertadora Nacionalista. Casi inmediatamente, comenzó con sus primeros trabajos, siendo cadete en un diario afín a esta tendencia ideológica, *El Laborista*. Más tarde, pasó a desempeñarse como cronista en diarios como *La Tribuna* y *La Época*, y a fines de los años cincuenta ya era parte del *staff* de una radio importante de Buenos Aires como era *Radio El Mundo*. Habitué de los círculos de periodistas y escritores que pululaban entre redacciones y distintos espacios de sociabilidad de la bohemia porteña, Masetti forjó una carrera como periodista en el espacio profesional capitalino durante los años del peronismo en el gobierno (1946–1955).

El camino que lo llevó a viajar a Cuba estuvo jalonado por dos hechos periodísticos puntuales, además de los factores biográficos y contextuales reseñados. Tanto el reportaje que publicó el periódico *New York Time* sobre Fidel Castro en febrero de 1957, así como, y sobre todo, el secuestro del corredor de Fórmula 1 durante el Gran Premio de La Habana, el argentino Juan Manuel Fangio en febrero de 1958, tuvieron un gran impacto en el país.[22] A partir de estos sucesos, la revolución emergió con fuerza en la opinión pública nacional y provocó un inusitado interés como noticia global entre los medios de comunicación masivos. Ambos hechos convencieron a Masetti y a la dirección de *Radio El Mundo*, de la conveniencia de realizar un viaje a la isla para entrevistar a los líderes revolucionarios, situación que revelaba cierta ansiedad del periodista por proveerse de un prestigio, a partir de imitar casos exitosos de corresponsales como era por entonces Herbert Matthews, y del grupo empresarial por participar del mercado internacional de noticias. Cabe notar que esta apuesta periodística en relación a la cobertura de la revolución por parte de este medio argentino no fue una excepción en América Latina, si se atiende los casos de mexicanos, uruguayos y ecuatorianos, entre otros.[23]

Gracias a su cercanía con Ricardo Rojo, quien había forjado años antes una fuerte amistad con Ernesto *Che* Guevara en uno de sus viajes, Masetti obtuvo una carta de presentación y el contacto con una organización estudiantil en La Habana, la cual finalmente facilitó su acceso para entrevistar a los jefes revolucionarios en la Sierra Maestra.[24] Una vez arribado a la isla en marzo de 1958, el reportaje a Fidel Castro y Ernesto Guevara se concretó entre algún momento de los de meses abril y mayo. Finalizada su estancia en la isla, y ya de regreso a la Argentina, se dedicó a poner a punto sus escritos para su publicación en formato libro en una pequeña editorial de Buenos Aires llamada Freeland.

El libro, que llevó por título *Los que luchan y los que lloran (El Fidel Castro que yo vi)*, comienza advirtiendo la existencia de una dicotomía en la realidad cubana. Desde su punto de vista, existían "dos Cubas": una "creada para la exportación" y otro "auténtica", que "pugna por ser íntegramente una república". La primera era asociada al poder militar enriquecido y dictatorial liderado por Fulgencio Batista, que solventaba una sociedad ofrecida al consumo extranjero, con sus "carteles de compañías aéreas con bailarines color habano danzando semidesnudos alrededor de una palmera", acondicionado para el turista anglosajón. Esta idea de las dos Cuba —similar a la consideración de las "dos Argentinas" que circulaba entre ciertos círculos intelectuales argentinos, según demostró Carlos Altamirano—, traducía una dicotomía que encontraba al presente dividido entre la explotación económica y la falta de liberad, y otra que se oponía y luchaba "violenta y tenazmente por recuperar lo que había ganado desde su independencia" con el fin de derrocar a Batista.[25]

Masetti, en este cuadro, se presenta a sí mismo como alguien preocupado por la realidad del proceso cubano e interesado por hallar respuesta a la pregunta que desvelaba al mundo en relación a la ideología del movimiento liderado por Fidel Castro. Sin necesariamente tomar partido, a lo largo de todo el libro queda clara su simpatía con el proyecto político que, evaluaba, se identifica en favor de la autodeterminación latinoamericana y contra el asedio de las potencias imperialistas tanto de tinte capitalista como comunista. A diferencia de otros argentinos que viajaron a Cuba durante los primeros años de la década del sesenta —con la excepción de otro periodista argentino como Enrique Raab quien lo hizo en 1973—,[26] es de los pocos que construye o recrea *ex post* una crónica de su estancia en distintos territorios —La Habana, Sierra Maestra, Santiago de Cuba, Bayamo, etc.— y en diálogo con diferentes actores —soldados y líderes del Ejército Rebelde, militantes del 26 de Julio como Humberto Sorí Marín, campesinos, sectores urbanos, incluso el arzobispo de Santiago de Cuba, monseñor Enrique Pérez Serantes—, en un intento de reescenificación de una vida cotidiana en la isla, posible gracias al uso común de la lengua con quienes dialoga o entrevista, y a su condición de argentino que lo emparentaba con el Che Guevara, y por lo tanto lo habilitaba a recorrer con cierta libertad los intrincados senderos de la escenografía revolucionaria de la isla.

A lo largo de casi todo el relato, lo que se narra es la odisea y el esfuerzo realizado para cumplir con el objetivo de entrevistar a Guevara y Castro, en un momento de recrudecimiento de la lucha contra la oposición que emprendiera Batista desde principios de 1958 tanto a nivel de las ciudades como en la sierra.[27] En otro nivel, más allá de lo que las entrevistas aportaron en relación al conocimiento que podría obtener el público argentino, sus páginas permiten apreciar el despliegue de un camino de autotransformación, de un proceso de conversión de periodista en revolucionario, de un extranjero y extraño a un amigo y compañero de armas, cuyo clímax se halla en el relato al describir la huelga general de abril de 1958 y la posterior represión emprendida por el gobierno sobre la población de la sierra: "mecánicamente me alejé y comencé a tomar el nombre de los heridos (. . .) Pero me sentía frío, ridículo, cumpliendo mi misión de periodista. ¡Que hacía yo ahí, con la lapicera en la mano, en lugar de estar apretando el gatillo de una ametralladora!".[28] O también en este otro registro, ya con varias semanas conviviendo con los soldados y días después del fracaso de la huelga general, al afirmar que:

Durante todo el viaje de retorno a La Mesa nos acompañó buen tiempo, salvo en una sola jornada. La mayor parte del trayecto lo hicimos a pie, sintiéndome yo realmente orgulloso cuando el guía que me había proporcionado Fidel, Mario Hidalgo (. . .) me reprochó el que casi no hiciese altos en el camino. Me iba dando cuenta que no solo mi estómago, sino mis piernas también se iban acostumbrando a las montañas de Oriente. Mi barba ya había crecido bastante y había concentrado la cantidad de mugre suficiente como para ser confundido sin posibilidad de equivocación, con un soldado rebelde más (. . .) Poco a poco fui recorriendo los bohíos que había dejado atrás cuando iba en busca de Fidel Castro. Fue una grata sorpresa para mí ser reconocido, y aún el que los guajiros recordasen que me gustaba el café sin azúcar ni guarapo. Para algunos yo ya era decididamente el hermano del Che.[29]

Desde el punto de vista de Masetti, la revolución no solo no era comunista —como reafirma una y otra vez—, sino que antes que ser un hecho que demandase una dilucidación ideológica o una búsqueda de racionalidad política, inserta en algún esquema ideológico, su legitimidad provenía de ser una experiencia de lucha, sufrimiento y resistencia por parte de un pueblo en contra de una dictadura opresora, en donde la oposición violenta emergía como el único camino posible. El cronista, a lo largo de todo su relato, evidencia una constante admiración por un proceso que entreveía "sencillo", "cotidiano", "popular" y "liberador" por parte del movimiento liderado por Castro, el cual decía transformar de manera radical una situación social y política a toda luz insostenible. Y en esa indagación finalmente, el periodista que inició su crónica en búsqueda de la verdad sobre los "barbudos" y sus ideas y planes, expresaba no solo su deseo de formar parte activa en el bando revolucionario, sino también la culpa y vergüenza moral que sentía, ya en camino a Buenos Aires, de ir hacia el "mundo de los que lloran", de dejar atrás a quienes luchan: "Ahí quedaba el ejército de niños y hombres que celebraban a gritos y carcajadas la llegada de un fusil o una ametralladora (. . .) el Che Guevara con su pipa mezclada en la eterna sonrisa; Fidel Castro con su cuerpo enorme y su voz de niño afónico. Y volví a encontrar dentro de mí una extraña, indefendible sensación de que desertaba, de que retornaba al mundo de los que lloran".[30] Masetti regresó a la ciudad de Buenos Aires después de estar dos meses y unas semanas en Cuba. En los días sucesivos ofreció en *Radio El Mundo*, la empresa de medios que lo había enviado a la isla, una crónica extensa de su viaje y de las entrevistas realizadas al Che Guevara y a Fidel Castro. Cuatro meses después publicó su libro y comenzó a dar conferencias en universidades y sindicatos de la Argentina y otros países de América Latina. Incluso se convirtió en un asiduo visitante de la familia de Guevara, por ese entonces instalada definitivamente en la ciudad de Buenos Aires. Tiempo después, una vez triunfante la revolución, volvería a Cuba en calidad de coordinador de un emprendimiento periodístico conocido como *Prensa Latina* y líder de la denominada "Operación Verdad", cuyo objetivo era comunicar todo lo referente a los juicios que el gobierno revolucionario llevaba adelante contra los miembros de la administración de Batista.

Hacia 1960, su reconocimiento como parte activa en la revolución ya no era solo a escala nacional, sino a nivel latinoamericano. Años más tarde, ya alejado de su carrera como profesional de las noticias, moriría en la provincia de Salta al fracasar su intento de crear un foco guerrillero en la Argentina en 1964 bajo el amparo del Che Guevara. Se cerraba así la vida de un hombre que encontró en la revolución la posibilidad de una reconversión de periodista en hombre de acción, y de identificarse con lo que consideraba era una lucha nacionalista y anti-imperialista regional. La isla marcó un antes y después en su trayectoria. La revolución era todo. Le dio todo. Hasta consumirlo.

Alfredo Palacios y el viaje rejuvenecedor.

Hasta donde ha podido constatarse durante todo el año de 1959 no se registran intelectuales o escritores argentinos en Cuba. Recién en los primeros meses del siguiente año, se certifica la presencia de varios. A diferencia de los motivos y mediaciones que llevaron y facilitaron a Ricardo Masetti emprender su viaje, el caso del político y dirigente socialista Alfredo Palacios tal vez deba vincularse a las redes creadas por militantes cubanos exiliados en Buenos Aires años antes, y sobre todo a la política del Gobierno cubano de convocar y atraer a hombres y mujeres de la cultura de izquierda y aun del nacionalismo radical como John William Cooke y Alicia Eguren.[31]

Anticomunista y antiperonista, humanista y demócrata, liberal reformista, hacia fines de la década del cincuenta Palacios era una figura central de un Partido Socialista que intentaba recuperarse del efecto que el nacionalismo popular, representado por Juan Domingo Perón, produjo en el legendario partido, visible en rupturas, expulsiones y abandonos de dirigentes y grupos militantes, a lo que se sumaba la dirección de varios sindicatos. En ese contexto crítico, el viejo dirigente cumplió una función de bisagra, de conector, entre la añeja dirigencia y una nueva generación educada políticamente bajo el impacto del peronismo, la admiración por el creciente poder del movimiento obrero y una acelerada modernización de la vida social y cultural del país.[32]

El viaje de Palacios a Cuba no fue un hecho fortuito, un viaje personal, ni lo hizo en calidad de corresponsal de un diario como Masetti, ni tampoco era la primera vez que incurría en esta práctica.[33] Había sido convidado por la Secretaría de Relaciones Exteriores del Movimiento 26 de Julio, al Primer Encuentro Latinoamericano de Solidaridad con Cuba. Esta invitación, la cual tenía como objetivo ampliar apoyos a nivel regional, fue canalizada a través de las relaciones que un sector del partido —Abel Alexis Latendorf y Juan Carlos Corral— tenían por ese entonces con un grupo de exiliados cubanos miembros del Parido Ortodoxo, Santiago Riera y Disys Guira, quienes habían conformado en Buenos Aires una red de apoyo a la revolución en los años previos al triunfo de enero de 1959.[34]

Palacios arribó a La Habana en mayo de 1960. Estuvo allí un mes. A su regreso dio una serie de conferencias en distintas universidades, publicó un primer texto en la revista mexicana *Cuadernos Americanos*, y finalmente un libro: *Una revolución auténtica. La reforma agraria en Cuba* por la Editorial Palestra. El mismo se dio a conocer en la colección que por ese entonces dirigía Gregorio Selser para esta editorial, quien ya tenía en preparación otros títulos afines como *La revolución cubana* de Fidel Castro y *Anatomía de una revolución*, de Leo Huberman y Paul Sweezy. En esa zaga de interpretaciones ofrecidas, según la editorial, Palacios marcaba una diferencia gracias a su experiencia en asuntos vinculados con la "defensa del valor humano", la "causa de la clase obrera" y la "militancia política".

Desde el título, Palacios consideraba al proceso cubano como una "auténtica revolución". Afirmaba, que el motivo de su viaje había sido demostrar la falacia de las interpretaciones que asociaban la revolución a un "cuartelazo", a un golpe de Estado cuya finalidad era instalar en el poder a dictadores similares a Fulgencio Batista para cercenar derechos y libertades, pero ahora bajo una ideología comunista. Evidenciar lo errado de este diagnóstico avalado por distintos medios estadounidense, a la luz de los efectos de la Reforma Agraria, era la razón por la cual había ido a Cuba, dado que entendía que "si fuera cierto, lo sabe este pueblo a quién jamás he mentido, los denunciaría porque para mí la libertad es el bien supremo".[35] Su intención, proseguía, era demostrar que la experiencia triunfante en 1959 era una auténtica revolución en los términos de su filiación a una tradición anti-imperialista que contactaba con destacadas figuras intelectuales y políticas del panteón cubano como fueron José Martí, Fernando Ortiz y Emilio Roig de Leuchsenring y otras de alcance latinoamericano como Simón Bolívar y los socialistas argentinos Manuel Ugarte y José Ingenieros.

Para Palacios la vida política de Cuba estuvo históricamente jalonada por la lucha contra la anexión española y el dominio económico estadounidense. Esa historia tuvo varios capítulos, siendo el más glorioso el liderado por un grupo de jóvenes quienes, inspirados en Martí y el ortodoxo Eduardo Chibás, decidieron afectar de raíz el nudo del atraso económico nacional y sostén de los gobiernos corruptos y autoritarios anteriores, al promulgar una Reforma Agraria que, por fin, buscaba terminar con el principal escollo para el desarrollo tanto de la isla como de América Latina: el latifundio. Palacios sostenía que Cuba había tomado esta medida apoyada en un marco reconocidamente legal por parte del "mundo libre", alejada de "ideologías extrañas" como la comunista, por lo cual resultaba erróneo asociar esa reforma con las que se emprendieron en Rusia o China.

Una vez trazado ese cuadro histórico —como si la revolución tuviera un punto de fuga en el pasado que había que saturar—, uno de los objetivos del autor era demostrar la inexistencia de la relación de los "barbudos" con el comunismo, tema de central interés durante los momentos finales de la insurrección y los primeros meses del nuevo gobierno en Cuba.[36] Desde su perspectiva, el reformismo que la nueva dirigencia cubana emprendió en diversas áreas sociales —vivienda, educación, recursos naturales, salud—, se asentaba en un "idealismo militante, profundo sentimiento nacional y amor al pueblo", más que en una orientación marcada por la adopción del comunismo de corte soviético. En consecuencia, esas transformaciones no remitían en ningún plano al modelo estalinista o algún paradigma marxista, sino al mejor despertar del pueblo cubano, al humanismo que anidaba en su dirigencia, a la preocupación por el destino del hombre, sus valores y condiciones de vida. Es decir, estas medidas asumían el espíritu de la tradición ética de "nuestra América", cuyo inicio fechaba atrás en el tiempo, hasta remontarse a la experiencia emancipadora argentina liderada por hombres como Mariano Moreno, Bernardino Rivadavia y Bernardo de Monteagudo, también ellos jóvenes ilustrados como eran Castro y Ernesto Guevara. De manera similar a Waldo Frank, otro viajero a la isla y quien es citado en el libro, para Palacios la revolución expresaba el triunfo de una visión filosófica que colocaba al hombre en el centro de todas las acciones políticas. Apelando a Kant y a Spencer, antes que a Marx, el viejo dirigente socialista hallaba en Cuba la realización, finalmente, del valor supremo, el hombre, en un territorio específico de América Latina.[37]

Ahora bien, ¿cómo fundamentaba esta interpretación de la experiencia cubana? Palacios afirmaba haber asumido el rol de "un investigador que recorrió toda la extensión de la república, palmo a palmo, examinándolo todo durante dieciséis horas diarios, sin intervención de acompañantes oficiales". Sin embargo, sus impresiones se basaron principalmente en conversaciones sostenidas, en un pie de igualdad, y casi de manera confesional, con dirigentes políticos y funcionarios de primer nivel pero de ideologías diversas como eran Fidel Castro, el Che Guevara y el ministro de educación, Armando Hart, entre otros. Lejos de cultivar el género de la crónica como hiciera Masetti, el dirigente socialista no solamente creía que la verdad de la revolución emanaba de la palabra de los dirigentes antes que de informes técnicos, lecturas o diálogos sostenidos con otros actores, sino que infería que esos líderes cubanos, formados en esa filosofía humanista de la cual Martí era su primer promotor, no hacían otra cosa que llevar a la práctica de manera conjunta los preceptos éticos que estaban extendidos entre las clases dirigentes latinoamericanas desde fines del siglo XIX.

Palacios, a través de la Revolución cubana, comprobaba, de manera retrospectiva, la realización de ese humanismo reformista de cuño liberal que él mismo profesaba desde hacía décadas. No en vano, esta prédica a la vuelta de Cuba parecía encontrar, después de mucho bregar, un momento de realización cuando en febrero de 1961 ganó unas celebradas elecciones a senador nacional por la ciudad de Buenos Aires. Tiempo después, ese capital político y simbólico cosechado por el Partido Socialista Argentino del cual era parte, se vería dilapidado en razón de la división cada vez más nítida entre quienes defendían al partido como un actor principal para profundizar un cambio político y social en la Argentina posperonista y quienes, como los sectores juveniles, impulsaban la lucha armada en la consecución de una transformación radical, inspirados en las recomendaciones que la dirigencia cubana pregonaba entre la juventud latinoamericana. Dentro del socialismo, un claro ejemplo del poder de encantamiento que el ejemplo cubano y la vía armada tenían sobre jóvenes militantes, provino de Elías Semán quien, un tiempo después que Palacios, también había visitado la isla y publicado sus impresiones en Buenos Aires.[38] En cualquier caso, el viaje de Alfredo Palacios permite observar de qué manera la revolución revitalizó la trayectoria de un viejo dirigente e ideólogo de tradición socialista, liberal y latinoamericanista, identificado con hechos como la Reforma Universitaria de 1918 y figuras como José Ingenieros, Manuel Ugarte y Saúl Taborda. En la Argentina el liberalismo social reformista a principios de los años sesenta, después de décadas de retroceso, parecía renacer de sus cenizas a partir del triunfo de Palacios. Fue, al fin, solo un canto de cisne.

Trotskismo y revolución: Silvio Frondizi en Cuba

Al igual que el socialista Alfredo Palacios, el abogado y militante político trotskista Silvio Frondizi, hermano del presidente de la nación en funciones, Arturo Frondizi, también arribó a Cuba en mayo de 1960 invitado por la Secretaría de Relaciones Exteriores del Movimiento 26 de Julio presidida por Carlos Olivares e impulsado en Buenos Aires por militantes cubanos. A su regreso, y en vista de la multiplicidad de escritos sobre la revolución que circulaban en el espacio argentino —lo cual evidenciaba cómo Cuba se transformó en un punto de identificación político-ideológico de izquierda en el país—, Frondizi decidió divulgar un texto que llevó por título *La Revolución Cubana. Su significación histórica*, resultado de una conferencia que dictó previamente en la Universidad de la República de Montevideo en Uruguay.

Publicado en septiembre de 1960, el libro es una larga interpretación de la Revolución cubana, basada en la idea de que su caso representaba, antes que un fenómeno novedoso, la confirmación de la pertinencia anticipatoria de un modelo teórico que hallaba su fuente en el materialista dialéctico y que el mismo autor había dado cuenta en su anterior trabajo, *La realidad argentina. Ensayo de interpretación sociológica* de 1956. Con la publicación del texto, Frondizi intentaba desmarcarse de aquellos publicados en esos años que, en su consideración y a tono con las nuevas formas de argumentación asociada a las Ciencias Sociales, "más que de tipo científico-sociológico" eran del "tipo literario-descriptivo".[39] Por ese entonces, y como afirma Horacio Tarcus, Frondizi ya había dejado su magisterio como líder interesado en la formación de cuadros teóricos de los integrantes de su pequeño y siempre inestable Movimiento de Izquierda Revolucionaria (MIR), un grupúsculo de los tantos que pululaban en el interior del trotskismo argentino.[40]

Para el autor, la revolución era un claro ejemplo de la vigencia de los postulados marxista-trotskista que asumían la existencia de un desarrollo desigual y combinado del capitalismo mundial y de una explotación de países semicoloniales por parte de las naciones imperialistas y que, impulsados por la competencia, expoliaban zonas periféricas del sistema tal como ocurrió con Cuba. Desde ese ángulo, el proceso isleño evidenciaba una larga cadena de menoscabo que halló un profundo corte en uno de sus eslabone más débiles del sistema global: América Latina. Para Frondizi, esta era una región que recientemente se había integrado al capitalismo de posguerra, a partir de una fuerte penetración del capital norteamericano en la vida económica de sus naciones. Dentro de este cuadro, Cuba era la nación que más sufría esa dominación —desempleo agrario, bajos salarios, recurrentes crisis del sector externo— debido al predominio casi total que ejercían las empresas estadounidenses. Basándose en datos demográficos, económicos y sociales que extrajo de la literatura que consultó durante su estadía —desde el libro de Antonio Núñez Jiménez, *La geografía de Cuba* y el censo nacional de 1953 hasta el informe del Primer Fórum Nacional de Reforma Agraria y las leyes de Reforma Agraria y Fundamental— Frondizi, antes que una crónica como elaboró Masetti o un relato asociado a la cita de autoridad al estilo de Palacios, intentaba elaborar una argumentación solventada en fuentes y estadísticas de las razones de la revolución, el rol de los Estados Unidos, la desigualdad existente, y en especial, la situación de la clase obrera y campesina.

De cara a las tareas que debía emprender para realizar estas transformaciones el gobierno revolucionario, Frondizi consideraba inevitable una inmediata ruptura con todo esquematismo de tipo reformista y el "determinismo y casi fatalismo geopolítico" que afirmaba la imposibilidad del triunfo de "algún movimiento revolucionario en la retaguardia imperialista".[41] A pesar del éxito de la revolución y su amplia legitimidad interna y externa, el autor entreveía la existencia de una "encrucijada" en vista de su continuidad: "(. . .) Es decir, la revolución tiene dos caminos: uno es el de contemporizar con los representantes de la reacción, el imperialismo, la iglesia y la gran burguesía nacional (. . .) El otro camino es el de profundizar la revolución, porque si se quiere sobrevivir no puede detenerse, y no puede hacerlo tanto en el orden interno como en el externo".[42] Si la revolución quería profundizar su lado radical insinuado en sus primeras medidas debía cumplir dos condiciones. Por un lado, frente a una posible reacción imperialista —en el contexto de la puja entre el Gobierno cubano y los Estados Unidos por la cuestión del petróleo—, Cuba para sobrevivir debería establecer una mayor comunión con el resto de América Latina, en una amplia alianza que contemplara la diversidad de fuerzas de izquierdas existentes extracomunistas. De esta manera, la revolución evitaría su aislamiento y al mismo tiempo la tentación de alinearse con la Unión Soviética que, en base a su sensibilidad trotskista, consideraba como parte de un "cerco comunista" a las posibilidades de expansión y un "asqueroso reformismo", en cuanto al tipo de programa que pregonaba afincado en el conocido desarrollo de las fuerzas productivas capitalistas como etapa necesaria para una transformación socialista. Que tal situación sea posible dependía de la "preparación ideológica" que demostrara la nueva dirigencia cubana la cual, observaba, no parecía por el momento asociada a un "contenido auténticamente revolucionario en el sentido socialista de la expresión, sino más bien de tipo pequeño-burgués nacionalista".[43] Para Frondizi, la posibilidad de que Cuba no se alinee con la Unión Soviética y avance en un programa revolucionario socialista obedecía inevitablemente al tipo de ideología que guiaba la acción de la élite revolucionaria. Y es que a todas luces para el trotskista argentino, el proceso isleño distaba bastante de ser una auténtica revolución socialista, no solo por la ausencia en la isla de industrias y de un proletariado urbano, sino porque la ideología que predominaba en el gobierno —sumado a una llamativa visión de Cuba como un país de una poca cultura general— se identificaba con un nacionalismo anti-imperialista pero aún contenido en una perspectiva burguesa. En consecuencia, solo la formación de un verdadero partido de clase de corte obrero y la concentración del poder político en una dirigencia ideológicamente asociada al internacionalismo marxista podría llevar a buen puerto una revolución que, no obstante, hallaba su "significación histórica" en haber dado comienzo a un tiempo histórico marcado por una progresiva "derrota del imperialismo en Latinoamericana y por lo tanto el derrumbe final del capitalismo y la instauración del socialismo".[44]

El viaje de Frondizi a Cuba es uno de los tantos casos de intelectuales en donde la experiencia es codificada en base a un esquema ideológico previo, aunque utilice para ello datos, estadísticas y fuentes diversas. De manera similar a Palacios, aunque a distancia personal y política de su reformismo liberal, una mirada atenta a su escrito revela las diferencias que existían entre los viajeros argentinos en cuanto a las formas a través de las cuales la revolución era interpretada y traducida, a la luz de los debates y tomas de posición asumidas en el interior de la cultura de izquierdas argentinas de principios de los años sesenta. Más precisamente: en Frondizi el traslado a otro país, a otra realidad, pareciera no haber sido un requisito necesario para transformar su visión de la idea de revolución, a pesar de que para ello recurriese a un tipo de argumentación solventada en diversas fuentes y no en una crónica como Masetti o un ejercicio de paráfrasis al modo de Palacios. Sin embargo, si se lo compara con las representaciones por estos últimos ofrecida, es sin duda quien más críticas realizó a la revolución, sobre todo respecto a la injerencia burocratizadora que podría traer una estrecha relación con el comunismo soviético y el bagaje ideológico de la nueva élite cubana. En esta misma línea argumentativa habría que colocar a otro trotskista argentino como Adolfo Gilly y su testimonio de viaje a partir de su estadía en la isla entre 1962 y 1963.[45]

A su regreso a Buenos Aires, Frondizi dejó lentamente de impulsar su agrupación política denominada Movimiento de Izquierda Revolucionaria (MIR), e incluso el internacionalismo socialista, optando por lo que consideraba una solución argentina, nacional y popular de la misma forma que hiciera la izquierda nacional liderada por el trotskista-populista Jorge Abelardo Ramos. Es probable que su viaje, pasado el tiempo, lo haya persuadido de que el éxito de todo movimiento revolucionario en América Latina dependía de una amplitud de fuerzas políticas y sociales, tal como demostró el exitoso el Movimiento 26 de Julio, cuyo punto programático central se afincaba en la idea de liberación nacional antes que en un contenido específico de clase.[46] Pero también, quizás, le propinó otra lección, más personal: ser un dirigente revolucionario implicaba mucho más que un específico saber asociado un conocimiento acabado de la filosofía moderna o de la doctrina marxista y una pertenencia social circunscripta únicamente al contorno de un pulpito de la Universidad de Buenos Aires o las sectas trotskistas. Hacer la revolución para las izquierdas argentinas, a la luz del fenómeno cubano, implicaba ampliar horizontes teóricos y prácticos. Sin embargo, en vista su derrotero posterior, ni siquiera esa mirada matizada de los rígidos esquemas marxistas clásicos respecto a la experiencia política y social latinoamericana evitó que se convirtiera en un "intelectual sin partido", finalmente, en un "hombre solo".[47]

Consideraciones finales

En los casos analizados de los intelectuales argentinos que viajaron a Cuba, y en comparación con otros aquí no abordados como Ezequiel Martínez Estrada, Leopoldo Marechal o Adolfo Gilly, resulta conveniente afirmar la existencia de motivaciones y canales diferentes que impulsaron su traslado a la isla. Mientras que el viaje de Masetti se vinculó inicialmente a una cuestión profesional como periodista (al igual que Enrique Raab en 1973), Palacios, Frondizi, Gilly o incluso en otro marxista como Luis Franco, la política y el debate ideológico conjuraron el interés por describir con sus propios ojos la revolución. En tanto, en escritores no vinculados a las izquierdas como Ezequiel Martínez Estrada, Leopoldo Marechal o incluso David Viñas (del cual lamentablemente no hay registro de esa experiencia) son consideraciones de tipo ideológico-profesional lo que en buena medida motorizó sus traslados, asociados a cumplir actividades como jurado en los distintos concursos literarios que auspiciaba Casas de las Américas.

Pero más allá de estas particularidades, es claro que nunca como entonces los intelectuales argentinos de izquierda, sean estos socialistas, liberales, trotskistas o nacionalista revolucionarios, se movilizaron tanto por una causa internacional. Ni Rusia y China, por no decir España en 1936 o Bolivia en 1952, generaron tanta pregnancia en la definición de una identidad y una trayectoria. Sin embargo, son claras las diferencias entre quienes fueron interpelados por la experiencia cubana. Algunos viajaron por pocos pero cruciales momentos de definición de la situación en la isla y volvieron. Otros, se quedaron hasta sus últimos días de vida, como es el caso de Martínez Estrada. Otros tantos, fueron continuos visitantes interesados por la revolución como experiencia global, pero también como proveedora de un canal, vía el Estado cubano, para elaborar y dictaminar una ambiciosa política literaria transnacional, tal como demuestran los casos de Viñas, Marechal, Martínez Estrada y Julio Cortázar, o, como revelan los casos analizados de Palacios, Masetti y Frondizi para poder participar en la discusión global de las izquierdas y así ganar audibilidad y proveerse de una carrera ya sea como políticos, ideólogos o militantes.

La existencia de una lengua en común, el carácter nacionalista y antiimperialista inicial, la portación de una identidad similar a uno de los líderes de la revolución como el Che Guevara y la amplia política de asimilación que el Gobierno cubano hizo con los intelectuales argentinos, facilitan observar el marcado interés por ver y tocar la revolución. Sin embargo, es por lo menos atendible en base a lo aquí analizado, que una real comprensión de las ideas y las trayectorias de quienes fueron a Cuba durante los años sesenta requiere atender a las particularidades según cada caso. Solo así podrá dimensionarse de manera atenta, sistemática y comprensiva el efecto que la isla tuvo entre argentinos y latinoamericanos, y las razones generales por las cuales la revolución atrajo a tantos intelectuales de nuestra región.

NOTAS

1. Mary Louis Pratt, *Ojos imperiales: Literatura de viajes y transculturación*, Buenos Aires, FCE, 2010.

2. Paul Hollander, *Los peregrinos políticos*, Madrid, Editorial Playor, 1987, pp. 95–196.

3. Ver Silvia Saítta, *Hacia la revolución: Viajeros argentinos de izquierda*, Buenos Aires, FCE, 2007; y el reciente trabajo de Horacio Tarcus (ed.), *Primeros viajeros al país de los soviets: Crónicas porteñas 1920–1934*, Buenos Aires, Dirección General del Libro, Bibliotecas y Promoción de la Lectura, 2018.

4. David Viñas, *Literatura argentina y realidad política*, Buenos Aires, Jorge Álvarez, 1973. Para un avance historiográfico significativo, Leandro Losada (comp.), *Esplendores del centenario: Relatos de la elite argentina desde Europa y Estados Unidos*, Buenos Aires, FCE, 2010.

5. Tarcus, *Primeros viajeros al país de los soviets*.

6. Hollander, *Los peregrinos políticos*, pp. 197–294.

7. Saítta, *Hacia la revolución*, p. 12.

8. Otro momento que cruzó viaje y revolución en los y las intelectuales de América Latina fue la revolución boliviana de 1952, en especial el caso de Alicia Ortiz, tal como demuestra Ximena Espeche, "Tan lejos, tan cerca: Alicia Ortiz y la revolución boliviana de 1952," *Revista Exlibris*, n° 8, 2018.

9. Paul Hollander, *Los peregrinos de La Habana*, Madrid, Editorial Playor, 1986, p. 10.

10. Los estudios sobre Cuba y los intelectuales occidentales, preferentemente europeos y estadounidenses, son el citado de Paul Hollander, a los que habría que sumar a Kepa Artaraz, *Cuba y la nueva izquierda. Una relación que marcó los años 60*, Buenos Aires, Editorial Capital Intelectual, 2011; y Rafael Rojas, *Traductores de la utopía. La Revolución cubana y la nueva izquierda de Nueva York*, México, FCE, 2016, entre otros.

11. Para el caso rumano, consultar el reciente trabajo de Ilinca Ilian, "La Cuba socialista vista por los escritores rumanos (1960–1980), *Revista de Letras*, vol. 57, n° 2, 2017, pp. 73–92.

12. La idea de la Cuba revolucionaria como "parque temático" en Abel Sierra Madero, *Fidel Castro, el comandante playboy: Sexo, revolución y Guerra Fría*, La Habana, Editorial Hypermedia, 2019.

13. Hollander, *Los peregrinos*, pp. 140–211. Hans Magnus Enzenberger, *El interrogatorio en La Habana y otros ensayos*, Barcelona, Anagrama, 2006.

14. Si bien el trabajo de Claudia Gilman es una importante contribución, no menos cierto es que es parcial en cuanto al tipo de intelectual que aborda, principalmente escritores de ficción, las fuentes analizadas y las redes a través de los cuales varios se trasladaron a la isla, además de un mapa al cual cabría agregarle otras zonas nacionales y regionales poco exploradas. Claudia Gilman, *Entre la pluma y el fusil: Debates y dilemas del escritor revolucionario en América Latina*, Buenos Aires, Siglo Veintiuno, 2003.

15. Germán Albuquerque, "El relato de viajes: Hitos y formas en la evolución del género," *Revista de Literatura*, n° 145, pp. 15–34.

16. Respecto al curso de la revolución entre fines de los años cincuenta y la década de 1960, Rafael Rojas, *Historia mínima de la Revolución cubana*, México, El Colegio de México-Turner, 2015.

17. Sobre las izquierdas argentinas, Oscar Terán, *"Nuestros años sesenta": La formación de la nueva izquierda intelectual argentina, 1956–1966*, Buenos Aires, Siglo Veintiuno Editores, 2013. En relación a un enfoque latinoamericano, Carlos Altamirano (dir.), *Historia de los intelectuales en América Latina: Los avatares de la "ciudad letrada" en el siglo XX*, Buenos Aires, Katz, 2010.

18. Ver los trabajos de Terán y Sigal, y en torno a una mirada crítica sobre el vínculo entre la izquierda argentina y Cuba, Claudia Hilb, *Silencio, Cuba: La izquierda democrática frente al régimen de la Revolución cubana*, Buenos Aires, Editorial Edhasa, 2010.

19. Martín Ribadero, *Tiempo de profetas: Ideas, debates y labor cultural de la izquierda nacional de Jorge Abelardo Ramos (1945–1962)*, Buenos Aires, Editorial Universidad Nacional de Quilmes, 2017.

20. Saítta, *Hacia la revolución*, pp. 11–46; Victoria García, "Del Che Guevara a Enrique Raab: Viajeros argentinos a la Revolución cubana," *Castilla. Estudios de Literatura*, vol. 6, 2015, pp. 269–313.

21. Gilman, *Entre la pluma y el fusil*, pp. 35–56.

22. Sobre la repercusión de la Revolución cubana en la prensa masiva argentina y en particular el impacto del secuestro de Fangio, Martín Ribadero, "Cuba 1958: Relatos de revolución," ponencia presentada en Jornada "Los 50s: Variaciones de una década," Centro de Estudios Latinoamericanos, Universidad Nacional de San Martín (CEL-UNSAM), 6 de septiembre de 2019.

23. Es el caso del periodista uruguayo Carlos María Gutiérrez, *En la Sierra Maestra y otros reportajes*, Montevideo, Biblioteca Artigas, 2017.

24. La trayectoria de Jorge Masetti es reconstruida por Hernán Vaca Narvaja, *Masetti: El periodista de la revolución*, Buenos Aires, Editorial Sudamericana, 2018.

25. Jorge Masetti, *Los que luchan y los que lloran (El Fidel Castro que yo vi)*, Buenos Aires, Jorge Álvarez, 1969, p. 10. Sobre la idea de las "dos Argentinas", Carlos Altamirano, *Peronismo y cultura de izquierda*, Buenos Aires, Siglo Veintiuno Editores, 2011, pp. 35–48.

26. Enrique Raab, *Cuba, vida cotidiana y revolución*, Buenos Aires, Ediciones de la Flor, 1973.

27. Rojas, *Historia mínima de la Revolución cubana*, pp. 59–95.

28. Masetti, *Los que luchan y los que lloran*, p. 52.

29. Ibid., p. 55.

30. Ibid., p. 95.

31. Tanto Cooke como Eguren viajaron a la isla en mayo de 1960 por las mismas vías utilizadas por Palacios y también para asistir al Primer Encuentro Latinoamericano de Solidaridad con Cuba. Otro tanto fue el caso del dirigente Fernando Nadra y el escritor y periodista también comunista Alfredo Varela.

32. María Cristina Tortti, *El "viejo" partido socialista y los orígenes de la "nueva" izquierda*, Buenos Aires, Editorial Prometeo, 2009, pp. 59–107.

33. Palacios había sido parte importante de los intelectuales argentinos que viajaron por América Latina pregonando el reformismo universitario durante la década de 1910 y 1920. Pablo Yankelevich, "Las redes intelectuales de la solidaridad latinoamericana: José Ingenieros y Alfredo Palacios," *Revista Mexicana de Sociología*, n° 4, octubre–diciembre de 1996, pp. 127–149. Más recientemente, Juan Suriano, "Alfredo Palacios y la difusión del reformismo universitario y el anti-imperialismo en América Latina," en Martín Bergel (coord.), *Los viajes latinoamericanos de la reforma universitaria*, Rosario, Universidad Nacional de Rosario, 2018, pp. 41–64.

34. Sobre el rol de las y los exiliados cubanos en Buenos Aires a fines de la década de 1950, Manuel Ramírez Chicharro, *Llamadas a las armas. Las mujeres en la Revolución cubana, 1952–1959*, España, Ediciones Doce Calles, 2018, pp. 219 y 224.

35. Alfredo Palacios, *Una revolución auténtica. La reforma agraria en Cuba*, Buenos Aires, Editorial Palestra, p. 38.

36. Rojas, *Historia mínima de la Revolución cubana*, pp. 81 y 96.

37. Palacios, *Una revolución auténtica*, p. 46.

38. Elías Semán, *Cuba Miliciana*, Buenos Aires, Ubu Ediciones, 2019.

39. Silvio Frondizi, *La Revolución cubana: Su significación histórica*, Montevideo, Ediciones Ciencia Política, 1960, p. 49. Sobre el impacto de las Ciencias Sociales en el mundo intelectual y universitarios argentino de fines de los años cincuenta y durante los sesenta, Alejandro Blanco, *Razón y modernidad. Gino Germani y la sociología en la Argentina*, Buenos Aires, Siglo Veintiuno Editores, 2006.

40. Horacio Tarcus, *El marxismo olvidado en la Argentina: Silvio Frondizi y Milcíades Peña*, Buenos Aires, Ediciones El Cielo por Asalto, 1996, pp. 144–160.

41. Frondizi, *La Revolución cubana*, p. 16.

42. Ibid., *La Revolución cubana*, p. 137.

43. Ibid., p. 143.

44. Ibid., p. 167.

45. Adolfo Gilly, *Cuba: Coexistencia o revolución*, Buenos Aires, Monthly Review, 1965.

46. Tarcus, *El marxismo olvidado en la Argentina*, pp. 366–367.

47. Ibid., p. 415.

GRETHEL DOMENECH HERNÁNDEZ

El intelectual y la revolución: Notas sobre un encuentro de la familia intelectual latinoamericana en 1969[1]

RESUMEN

En mayo de 1969 se reunieron en La Habana un grupo de intelectuales entre los que se encontraban Roberto Fernández Retamar, Edmundo Desnoes, Ambrosio Fornet, René Depestre, Carlos María Gutiérrez y Roque Dalton para debatir en torno a la relación entre el intelectual y la revolución. El encuentro dio lugar a una de las discusiones más importantes de la familia intelectual latinoamericana en la década de los sesenta del pasado siglo. Las memorias de este fueron publicadas pocos meses después por Siglo XXI Editores bajo el título *El intelectual y la sociedad*. El presente trabajo busca examinar qué nociones sobre el intelectual revolucionario y latinoamericano se articularon en esta discusión. Al tener en cuenta las memorias de uno de los encuentros más álgidos de ese entonces, es posible analizar la apropiación del hecho revolucionario (tanto cubano como continental) que circuló entre ellos y también es posible llevar a cabo un enfoque transnacional sustentado en la participación de gran parte de la nómina de esta familia en dichas discusiones y en el propio tono transnacional de sus intervenciones.

ABSTRACT

In May 1969, a group of intellectuals met in Havana, including Roberto Fernández Retamar, Edmundo Desnoes, Ambrosio Fornet, René Depestre, Carlos María Gutiérrez, and Roque Dalton, to discuss the relationship between the intellectual and the revolution. The meeting gave rise to one of the most important discussions of the Latin American intellectual family in the 1960s. The memoirs of the same were published a few months later by Siglo XXI Editores under the title *El intelectual y la sociedad*. The present work seeks to examine the notions about the revolutionary and Latin American intellectual articulated in this discussion. Taking into account the proceedings of one of the most critical meetings of the time, it is possible to analyze the appropriation of the revolutionary event (both Cuban and continental) that circulated among them and to carry out a transnational approach based on the participation of this roster in discussions and the transnational tone of their interventions.

Es bien conocido el auge de lecturas, reflexiones y polémicas que tuvieron lugar en los sesenta latinoamericanos del pasado siglo en torno al rol del intelectual en tiempos de revolución. Los debates sobre la condición intelectual en la prensa hicieron eco en toda el área alcanzando un gran protagonismo. Además de su común inscripción progresista, los intelectuales de América Latina compartieron una nueva convicción: la de que podían y debían convertirse en uno de los principales agentes de la transformación radical de la sociedad, especialmente en el Tercer Mundo.[2] El escritor, como bien han señalado Claudia Gilman y Rafael Rojas, se encontró en el centro de este vórtice, como creador, como sujeto revolucionario, como hombre nuevo o como miliciano. Algunos de los modelos o paradigmas intelectuales nombrados fueron Jean-Paul Sartre, Paul Baran, Bertrand Russell y Régis Debray, los cuales se convirtieron en epítomes del rol intelectual.

Tales circunstancias llevaron a que se conformara una amplia red que tuvo como factor aglutinante el debate por el rol del intelectual en el contexto latinoamericano. En este sentido, la investigadora argentina Claudia Gilman en su libro *Entre la pluma y el fusil: Debates y dilemas del escritor revolucionario en América Latina* propone la categoría "familia intelectual latinoamericana" para referirse a la formación de una comunidad que tuvo como elementos unificadores las revistas culturales y los encuentros personales entre críticos y escritores que colaboraban en ellas. El término *familia intelectual* lo retoma Gilman de actores de la época como Jorge Edwards, quien en sus memorias publicadas bajo el título de *Persona non grata* en 1982 expresaba: "Los escritores, sobre todo en América Latina, formamos una especie de familia que se conoce de un país a otro".[3] Además de esta alusión vale recordar también "el título que puso *Primera Plana* a su nota sobre el premio que recibió el novelista venezolano González León: no sólo uso la palabra familia, sino que exageró los rasgos del campo de palabras [. . .] asociado: 'Otro pariente para la familia'".[4]

En las páginas de su libro, Gilman se pregunta "¿cómo se llegó a la conformación de un frente tan poderoso?". Para la autora, este suceso resulta a partir "de las innumerables coincidencias en torno a cuestiones estéticas e ideológicas, uno de los fenómenos más importantes del periodo fue la constitución de un campo intelectual latinoamericano, que atravesó las fronteras de la nacionalidad y que encontró en la Revolución Cubana un horizonte de aperturas y pertenencia".[5] Retomando la interrogante de Gilman y tratando de establecer una incipiente cartografía de esta comunidad se puede decir que las voces de la familia intelectual se articularon alrededor de publicaciones como *Casa de las Américas, Mundo Nuevo, Marcha, Libre* o *Plural*, y durante los sesenta y setenta gestaron y participaron en una serie de congresos que le otorgaron forma a tan disímil grupo.

Esta red se manifestó de forma trasnacional y tuvo sus enclaves lo mismo en el comité de redacción de *Casa de la Américas*, que en los debates que tuvieron lugar en las páginas de *Mundo Nuevo, Libre* o *Plural*. Desde su surgimiento en 1960, *Casa de las Américas*, revista perteneciente a la institución del mismo nombre, se convirtió, tal como sus objetivos lo plantearon, en un foro y espacio de reunión para los escritores y artistas del continente. *Marcha* en Uruguay fue otro de los referentes de esta comunidad intelectual. Con la dirección de Carlos Quijano los vínculos entre las revistas y la intelectualidad revolucionaria se incrementarían a partir de 1959.

Los encuentros y congresos también jugaron un papel fundamental en su conformación.[6] Algunas de sus principales reuniones se dieron alrededor de Casa de las Américas en especial de sus Concursos Literarios, los cuales, a partir de la organización de sus jurados, funcionaron como un enclave anual para el intercambio y diálogos entre los escritores que se iban nucleando en esta red. El certamen permitió la visita a la isla de muchísimos escritores que comenzaron a vincularse a las dinámicas y figuras culturales de ella. El Congreso Cultural de La Habana en 1968 fue otro de sus más importantes momentos, no solo para la familia intelectual latinoamericana, pues sus dimensiones fueron mayores que esta red y contó con la presencia de intelectuales de todo el mundo afiliados a la nueva izquierda. Estas zonas de cierta autonomía, dígase las revistas o encuentros, tuvieron un importante papel en la conformación de esta familia y sirvieron de plataforma en una época en la que la expresión pública se validaba más que nunca en la legitimación intelectual.

Además de dichos enclaves, valdría la pena preguntarse ¿cuál fue la característica esencial de esta red? Sin dudas, su primer rasgo distintivo fue una alineación ideológica con la Revolución cubana y lo que ella representaba o exportaba para el resto de América Latina. Sus integrantes no solo tomaron el proceso cubano como punto de partida, sino que también dispusieron de sus lineamientos como guía intelectual. Para Gilman, Cuba, la "Roma antillana", como la denominó Halperin Donghi, fue el epicentro de la formación de la familia intelectual latinoamericana en los años 60 brindando cierto sentimiento de unidad al mundo letrado.[7] Sin duda alguna La Habana fue el principal centro de reunión y a la vez el enclave simbólico de esta familia.

El peregrinaje a Cuba también fue esencial para la conformación de esta familia.[8] En 1962 Roque Dalton llegó a La Habana tras salir de El Salvador en 1961. Mario Vargas Llosa arribó por vez primera también en 1962 cuando la agencia de Radiodifusión-Televisión Francesa le pidió que se trasladara a la isla a cubrir la Crisis de los Misiles. En 1963 Julio Cortázar acudió para formar parte del jurado de Concurso Literario de Casa de las Américas. La revolución fue un escenario que convocaba y al que se debía llegar para poder establecer una suerte de conversión política.[9]

Por una red de intelectuales revolucionarios

A pesar de ser "familia intelectual latinoamericana" una categoría que nos permite acercarnos al tema desde un enfoque transnacional y encontrar así los ejes

discursivos y problemáticos del universo intelectual latinoamericano de los sesenta, es importante señalar las heterogeneidades dentro de tan variada comunidad. En primer lugar se hace extremadamente complejo trazar la nómina
de este grupo pues no solo estuvo conformado por escritores que integraron
parte del llamado *boom* de la literatura latinoamericana, dígase Julio Cortázar
o Mario Vargas Llosa, sino también por poetas de una marcada militancia política como Roque Dalton y Ernesto Cardenal; críticos literarios como Emir
Rodríguez Monegal, Ángel Rama y Ambrosio Fornet; aquellos escritores que
se vincularon como jefes de las publicaciones como Roberto Fernández Retamar, Rodríguez Monegal y Juan Goytisolo; escritores que no precisamente
formaron parte del *boom*, pero que jugaron un papel fundamental en las discusiones como René Depestre; y por último, los que estuvieron vinculados al
periodismo como Carlos María Gutiérrez y Jorge Ricardo Masetti.[10]

El reto ante tan vasta constelación es que la idea de familia intelectual
latinoamericana resulte reduccionista en su intento de contemplar a tan disimiles sujetos y grupos. Los nombres mencionados con anterioridad son los
casos más emblemáticos, pero no agotan las posibilidades en cada uno de los
campos. Gran parte de los intelectuales, escritores y artistas del continente se
sintieron afectados no solo por el triunfo de la Revolución cubana, sino también por todos los movimientos estudiantiles, políticos, culturales y filosóficos
que emergieron en la década. Su vínculo con redes y participación en congresos o publicaciones no siempre respondió a un intento de crear una comunidad
intelectual revolucionaria.[11]

En términos ideológicos y políticos las ideas de la nueva izquierda pri-
maron en el discurso de la época, no obstante, dentro de esta familia el mapa
de filiaciones o militancias no es tan fácil de cartografiar. La nueva izquierda
de por sí es un término ambiguo que supone una renovación y crítica de los
discursos tradicionales de la izquierda de la primera mitad del siglo XX y que
supuso distintas manifestaciones en los sesenta globales que fueron desde la
New Left Review en Inglaterra, la *Monthly Review* en Estados Unidos hasta las
organizaciones guerrilleras de América Latina. Las distintas formas de asumir
lo que significaba una nueva izquierda guiada por la Revolución cubana se
manifestaron en esta familia intelectual. Varias rupturas y polémicas demuestran estas diferencias ideológicas: la carta abierta a Pablo Neruda en 1966 cri-
ticando la participación del poeta chileno en el Congreso del Pen Club en los
Estados Unidos, la polémica entre Julio Cortázar y José María Arguedas entre
1967 y 1969 o la polémica entre Cortázar y Oscar Collazos en 1969.

Una de las primeras crisis de esta familia fue la aparición en 1966 de la revista *Mundo Nuevo* dirigida por Emir Rodríguez Monegal en París, lo cual supuso una zona de tensión importante y gestó una de las polémicas más importantes de la Guerra Fría cultural latinoamericana. La nueva publicación recibía
capital del Congreso por la Libertad de la Cultura, institución financiada por

la CIA, lo que supuso, para los intelectuales reunidos en *Casa*, una ofensiva imperialista en el terreno cultural. Las discusiones se dieron principalmente en la correspondencia entre Fernández Retamar y Rodríguez Monegal, pero tuvo ecos importantes en las páginas de *Casa* como "New World en español", de Ambrosio Fornet publicado en 1976. La polémica estuvo latente durante los años de existencia de *Mundo Nuevo* (1966–1968) y evidenció significativas rupturas ideológicas del campo intelectual latinoamericano.[12]

Si algo demuestra Rafael Rojas en *La Polis Literaria* es que el *boom* latinoamericano no se puede entender como un fenómeno unificado u homogéneo, dentro de este hubo diferentes posturas en torno a la relación entre literatura y política, o entre literatura y revolución.[13] Esta misma metodología que busca someter a crítica lugares comunes sobre lo que significó el *boom* literario puede aplicarse también a esta familia intelectual. Sin dudas, estamos hablando de una red intelectual que toma a la Revolución cubana como referente y se implica activamente en los debates sobre el rol del intelectual. No obstante, dentro de esta red hubo constantes desplazamiento a posturas más críticas, cercanas o distantes no solo al Gobierno cubano, sino a las propias nociones que se discutían sobre intelectuales y revolución. De ahí la importancia de estudiar los debates para encontrar estas rupturas y conflictos.

Al aproximarnos a relaciones transnacionales tanto intelectuales como de otro tipo es imprescindible el uso de la categoría "redes". Ella permite entender relaciones de tipo regional o global que se tejen mediante conexiones y se van estableciendo entre grupos o sujetos que confeccionan un entramado común en cuanto a discursos, metas, e ideas. El enfoque de redes también ha cobrado gran importancia en la historia de los intelectuales pues permite acercarnos a ellos no como grupo homogéneos, sino como sujetos que ejercen sus discursos y acción en una comunidad y en un espacio público.

De igual forma, la noción de red permite romper con los espacios nacionales y acceder a conexiones y problemáticas que se dieron de forma transnacional. Esta mirada se ha aplicado a temas de la nueva izquierda, los movimientos guerrilleros o los conflictos de la Guerra Fría.[14] Para ello no se trata solo de comparar casos, sino entender, primero, que estos procesos tuvieron lugar de forma transnacional, cobraron vida más allá de fronteras nacionales. Segundo, evitar las miradas reduccionistas que ubican a ciertos problemas como propiedad de ciertas naciones. Tercero, tener en cuenta las semánticas de una época en la que se insistió en términos como revolución latinoamericana, tercermundismo o solidaridad.

La red intelectual latinoamericana referida en estas páginas tuvo una connotación transnacional, no solo porque sus miembros más visibles provenían de diferentes países, sino porque su misma red de publicaciones y de encuentros se gestó a nivel transnacional. Pero, más importante aún, sus debates y reflexiones giraron en torno al rol de un intelectual transnacional que respondió no solo a las necesidades de Cuba, sino a las necesidades y particularidades de un espacio y tiempo latinoamericano. A inicios de los sesenta, la primera postura que se asumió fue la del compromiso como fundamento y regla de pensamiento para el desarrollo artístico y literario. Fue en Cuba donde este debate comenzó a tomar cuerpo y posteriormente sería recepcionado por los intelectuales latinoamericanos que vieron en el triunfo de la revolución un punto de partida para transformar sus realidades.

Lunes de Revolución y *Casa de las Américas* fueron de las revistas cubanas de los 60 que más indagaron en torno a la búsqueda de un modelo de intelectual que simbolizara al máximo la condición de compromiso. La idea fue el fundamento moral que orientó gran parte de las posiciones y trabajos que presentaron asumiendo un papel fundamental en la construcción de la propuesta discursiva de ambas publicaciones. Una de las guías que se siguieron fue la figura de Jean-Paul Sartre y su pensamiento, en especial el relacionado con el rol del intelectual en la sociedad. Sartre se mostraba como el ideal de escritor que realizaba una obra de profunda calidad literaria, a la vez que participaba en los debates políticos y sociales de su época.

Las principales cuestiones que se discutieron en torno al compromiso fueron los límites entre responsabilidad y libertad creadora, compromiso de la obra o compromiso del autor y cómo expresar el hecho revolucionario en el discurso intelectual. En las páginas de *Lunes de Revolución, Casa de las Américas*, con textos de Paul Baran, Jean-Paul Sartre, Roque Dalton o polémicas entre Virgilio Piñera y Nicolás Guillén, Alain Robbe-Grillet y Juan Goytisolo, se expusieron diferentes posturas en torno a la toma de conciencia respecto a la responsabilidad del escritor y del artista. La intención final trataba de forjar un modelo de creador basado en el deber social y reformular así las variantes de participación del intelectual.

En los primeros años de la década, las disputas sobre la responsabilidad social iban más allá de publicar una nota de prensa crítica, manifestar una postura ideológica o convertir la obra en un gesto político, se buscaba alcanzar una reflexión y una autorreflexión sobre el sujeto intelectual y sus nuevas circunstancias. El compromiso no fue entendido como una mera militancia, por lo menos para los colaboradores que se agruparon en estas publicaciones, se pensó como una condición que permeara todas las aristas de la vida pública. Se polemizó cómo el escritor podía asumir una postura política en una coyuntura determinada, pero también se debatió toda una condición, un tránsito hacia un rol intelectual.

Si a partir de 1959 el compromiso había sido el centro de atención en revistas y polémicas, para 1966, aproximadamente, esta condición empezó a declinar y agotarse como una preocupación y más menos en el año 1968 el debate osciló hacia la búsqueda de un intelectual revolucionario.[15] La relación entre escritores o intelectuales y lo revolucionario se fue haciendo cada vez más tensa y comenzaba, de cierta forma, a desmoronarse la idea de revolución como posibilidad infinita. En este sentido, qué condiciones de posibilidad favorecen estos tránsitos o mutaciones que, aunque en apariencia, semánticos, indican toda una serie de cuestiones políticas e ideológicas.

En 1968 el Estado cubano declaró la Ofensiva Revolucionaria con el propósito de eliminar los últimos reductos burgueses de la sociedad, el premio UNEAC de poesía era otorgado a *Fuera de Juego* de Heberto Padilla y el de teatro a Antón Arrufat con *Los siete contra Tebas*, los cuales serían censurados. La invasión a Checoslovaquia era apoyada por Fidel Castro y el Congreso Cultural de La Habana reverenciaba al Che como el paradigma de todo intelectual verdadero. Los escritores latinoamericanos, por otro lado, estaban cada vez más involucrados con el proceso cubano. Mario Vargas Llosa, Roque Dalton, René Depestre, David Viñas, Ángel Rama y Julio Cortázar formaban parte del comité de colaboración de *Casa de las Américas* y mantenían una continua participación en eventos promovidos por la institución del mismo nombre.

El intelectual y la sociedad, 1969

Una de las reuniones más importantes de la familia intelectual latinoamericana fue la que tuvo lugar el 2 de mayo de 1969 en el estudio del pintor cubano Mariano y dio paso al volumen *El intelectual y la sociedad*. El diálogo fue publicado por la revista *Casa de las Américas* en su número 56 del mismo año. En él participaron Roberto Fernández Retamar, Edmundo Desnoes, Ambrosio Fornet, René Depestre, Carlos María Gutiérrez y Roque Dalton. En las siguientes páginas intentaré analizar los debates en torno al intelectual y la revolución que tuvieron lugar en este encuentro. Las intervenciones recogidas en *El intelectual y la sociedad* son una fuente notable para examinar las posturas que se manejaron a fines de los sesenta sobre el rol del intelectual en América Latina. En ellas se puede tomar el pulso de las discusiones intelectuales y acceder a posicionamientos que, al ser efectuados en un marco menos formal que el de una revista, por ejemplo, nos revelan interesantes zonas de conflicto. Para los estudios sobre la intelectualidad latinoamericana en los sesenta, las revistas culturales han sido las fuentes priorizadas llevándose a obviar otras que pueden brindar nuevas luces tales como las memorias de reuniones y encuentros de intelectuales, de ahí la pertinencia de tenerlos en cuenta a la hora de acceder a tan enrevesado universo.

Los participantes que se dieron cita para conversar sobre el intelectual y la sociedad eran figuras centrales del campo intelectual latinoamericano y voces de sus polémicas. Roberto Fernández Retamar había comenzado a dirigir *Casa de las Américas* en 1965 y se mostraba como uno de los exponentes de un intelectual afiliado a la política cultural cubana y sus lineamientos. René Depestre vivía en Cuba desde 1960 y su libro *Por la revolución, por la poesía* fue publicado por el Instituto Cubano del Libro en 1969. Roque Dalton había pasado varios años en Cuba a inicios de los sesenta regresando a El Salvador en 1964 y en 1969 volvía a Cuba para participar en el Premio Casa de las Américas con el poemario *Taberna y otros lugares*. Ambrosio Fornet formó parte de la joven generación que se vinculó de inmediato a la agenda cultural del gobierno revolucionario cubano tras 1959, participó en *Lunes de Revolución, Unión, La Gaceta* y *Casa de las América* convirtiéndose en uno de los principales críticos literarios en la Cuba de los sesenta. Al igual que Fornet, Edmundo Desnoes formaba parte de la constelación de jóvenes escritores cubanos, había sido co-laborador de *Lunes de Revolución* y su narrativa era una de las más prolíficas en los años sesenta. Por último, Carlos María Gutiérrez uno de los fundadores de Prensa Latina y habitual colaborador de *Marcha*, en 1967 publicó su primer libro que tituló *En la Sierra Maestra y otros reportajes*. A pesar de las distintas voces que se unieron en el encuentro es fácil encontrar un nosotros, un lugar de enunciación común entre sus participantes, todos, intelectuales alineados con la idea de lo revolucionario construida desde Cuba.

Como bien anunció Retamar en la primera página, las intervenciones giraron en torno a la relación entre el intelectual y la revolución. Para él, este problema se presentaba en la forma de varias preguntas que igualmente trataron de responder el resto de los participantes: "¿es posible un intelectual fuera de la Revolución? ¿Es posible un intelectual no revolucionario?, ¿es posible pretender establecer normas del trabajo intelectual revolucionario fuera de la revolución?".[16] Además de estas cuestiones que anunciaron el rumbo a seguir, dos interrogantes atravesaron todas las intervenciones: ¿cómo ser un intelectual revolucionario en un país que construye la revolución socialista en el caso cubano?, y ¿cómo ser un intelectual revolucionario en países con movimientos de liberación? La intervención de Retamar expresaba las mutaciones que vivía el concepto de intelectual en esos momentos.

El tránsito de un lenguaje que indagó en el compromiso intelectual a uno que abogó por el intelectual revolucionario es sintomático a partir de esta fecha. No es que de por sí cambiara mucho la intención de la discusión, continuó girando en torno a la función del escritor en la sociedad y de su relación con la política, pero este cambio semántico responde a varias circunstancias que propiciaron una radicalización en los escritores y la asunción de nuevos paradigmas teóricos y discursivos. En 1969 el concepto de intelectual se leía bajo nuevos preceptos y horizontes de expectativas diferentes a los de 1959. En el Congreso Cultural de La Habana se había reverenciado al Che como la figura innegable del intelectual. 1969 era declarado en Cuba *año del esfuerzo decisivo*, el epíteto aludía a un claro llamado al sacrificio nacional. En este contexto el discurso sobre el intelectual adquiría una marcada radicalización política.

Las posiciones de la mayoría de los intelectuales de entonces se debieron también a otra razón: la culpa por no haber participado en la reacción armada

de los cincuenta, no haber sido uno más en las guerrillas del Che o no enca-
bezar los nuevos movimientos de protesta en América Latina. Roque Dalton
comenzaría su exposición permeado por este sentimiento: "al aceptar hablar
sobre estos temas, es confesarnos conscientes de nuestras limitaciones".[17] Más
adelante igualmente expresaría que la revolución "propuso y propone a sus
escritores el 'baño social'", haciendo clara alusión a un sentido de higienización que debían realizar los intelectuales, y como la revolución, en su posición
cuasi supraterrenal y divina les ofrecía esta nueva oportunidad: "Así la Revolución no sólo ha jugado limpio con los escritores y los artistas, sino que les ha
abierto las puertas de la historia [. . .] La falla ha surgido únicamente cuando
el escritor o el artista le ha pedido a la revolución que lo vea a él de manera
excepcional, es decir, que la revolución lo vea a él como él se ve a sí mismo,
lo cual es una ingenuidad imperdonable, una falta de sentido histórico, cuando
no simple mezquindad y mala fe".[18] El fragmento es sumamente ilustrativo de
las representaciones sobre el intelectual compartidas por gran parte de esta red
intelectual latinoamericana a la altura de 1969. En su intervención, el poeta
salvadoreño hacía clara alusión a un proceso de higienización que debían realizar los intelectuales. La revolución, en su posición cuasi supraterrenal y divina
les ofrecía esta nueva oportunidad, era misión del intelectual posicionarse a la
altura del proceso y sus líderes y abandonar sus pretensiones de trascendencia.
La oratoria de Dalton intentaba, en primer lugar, contribuir a la discusión sobre
el rol del intelectual en tiempos de revolución y; en segundo lugar, buscar el
camino ideal que debían seguir los intelectuales latinoamericanos para estar a
la altura que exigían los tiempos.

Más adelante, en la misma intervención, Dalton enunciaba como falla
del escritor o el artista su posición de excepcionalidad, pero en la siguiente
pregunta, medular en su ponencia, pareciera caer en esa misma ingenuidad:
"¿estuvieron los escritores cubanos, los artistas cubanos, como grupo social
y como individuos preparados a nivel histórico para enfrentar fructíferamente
ese encuentro que ya tiene diez años de edad?".[19] Si anteriormente planteaba
como error garrafal que los intelectuales le exigieran a la revolución que los
considerara diferencialmente del resto de la sociedad, resulta, de cierta forma,
incoherente o redundante pedirles a los escritores que hayan estado a la altura
del proceso o que hayan estado preparados a nivel histórico; acaso ¿es posible
estar preparado a nivel histórico? Si los escritores no son un sector exclusivo
entonces ¿por qué estar preparados?

Esta idea de Roque Dalton es recurrente por gran parte de los intelectuales
de la época tanto por cubanos como por latinoamericanos, ¿estuvimos a la
altura del proceso?, es la pregunta que rondó la mayoría de sus posturas. En el
caso de la intelectualidad latinoamericana, Dalton les cuestionaba "¿ha cumplido con sus deberes ante la América Latina en la tarea de manejar, pensar,
elaborar, la experiencia cubana, el conocimiento de Cuba, las proposiciones

de Cuba, las lecciones de Cuba y su Revolución?".[20] En general, los debates intelectuales desde el 59 fueron ubicando al intelectual como un sujeto en
desventaja histórica, el acontecimiento se les había adelantado y ahora ellos
debían transitar lo más rápido posible el camino revolucionario y recobrar el
tiempo perdido.

Podemos notar también una oscilación o constante ambivalencia en sus
posturas que se explica por las mismas complejidades de las relaciones inte-
lectual/revolución e intelectual/sociedad. Anteriormente, en 1962 con un tono
bastante alejado del de 1969, Dalton expresaba: "El poeta es tal porque hace
poesía, es decir porque crea una obra bella. [. . .] Hay que desterrar esa concepción falsa, mecánica y dañina según la cual el poeta comprometido con su
pueblo y con su tiempo es un individuo iracundo o excesivamente dolido que
se pasa la vida diciendo, sin más ni más, que la burguesía es asquerosa, que lo
más bello del mundo es una asamblea sindical y que el socialismo es un jardín
de rosas dóciles bajo un sol especialmente tierno".[21] Sin embargo, qué condiciones hacen que un escritor como Dalton, el cual en 1962 afirmaba que "el
gran poeta de hoy debe tener para construir su obra dos puntos de partida nece-
sarios: el profundo conocimiento de la vida y su propia libertad imaginativa",[22]
en 1969, con un tono arbitrariamente distante a este, se refiera al intelectual
como un sujeto con una "una ingenuidad imperdonable, una falta de sentido
histórico, cuando no simple mezquindad y mala fe". ¿Por qué continuar in-
sistiendo en las fallas del escritor? ¿Por qué hacer ver al intelectual como un
sujeto siempre por debajo de las circunstancias? Este tipo de argumentación es
bien diferente a la de los intelectuales que se aproximaron al acontecimiento
cubano a partir de 1959, es un discurso anti-intelectual y fatalista que insiste
en dibujar al intelectual como un sujeto fracasado frente a las dimensiones de
la revolución.

Claudia Gilman considera que "[e]l paso que va del intelectual comprometido al intelectual revolucionario puede traducirse en términos políticos como
la diferencia entre reformismo y revolución".[23] Para esta autora las exigencias
crecientes de la participación revolucionaria devaluaron la noción de compromiso, bajo la cual una gran parte de los intelectuales encontraron sombra y
protección durante algún tiempo. Aunque las pretensiones revolucionarias au-
mentaron, especialmente en América Latina, el ímpetu de difundir por todos
los países del continente transformaciones sociales y políticas era apremiante
y "el intelectual revolucionario" fue hijo de una radicalización en la acción
intelectual.

Las formas de ser un intelectual eran mucho más extremas para fines de
los sesenta y se habían intensificado nociones como militancia o praxis. Por
citar un ejemplo, de acuerdo a Dalton el problema moral de los intelectuales
solo podría ser resuelto en la práctica revolucionaria o en la militancia revolucionaria: "En la praxis revolucionaria, el intelectual, como categoría histó-

rica incompleta ante el progreso y el ahondamiento de la complejidad social, se realiza como hombre nuevo, como hombre integral: unidad de teoría y de práctica revolucionarias".[24] No obstante, el reclamo de una participación que enarbolara una praxis revolucionaria implicaba una contradicción que ya se había manifestado desde los inicios de la revolución.[25] Al no definirse qué se entendía como "revolucionario" se dejaba abierto un diapasón muy amplio y presto a equívocos en el que la última palabra sobre ello estaría en la voz de los líderes políticos ya reconocidos como tal.

Según Ambrosio Fornet la pregunta lanzada por Retamar al inicio del debate y referente a la imbricación entre lo intelectual y lo revolucionario solo tenía una respuesta: "no, no se puede ser intelectual en una revolución sin ser revolucionario. La afirmación da una pista clara de las nociones ideológicas y conceptuales de la época, revolucionario fue un sustantivo que perteneció a la revolución y no al verbo revolucionar; revolucionario era 'estar aquí con la Revolución'". Este efecto en la transformación del concepto de revolución se hace constar desde los primeros discursos de Fidel Castro y fue una característica fundamental del imaginario cubano posterior a 1959: lo revolucionario es solo la revolución y viceversa.[26]

La asunción del intelectual revolucionario como el intelectual dentro de la revolución se hace notar también en las palabras de René Depestre: "El problema de la responsabilidad del escritor, su derecho a la polémica e, incluso, a la rebelión, adquieren otro contenido, un carácter nuevo, en un país como Cuba, donde el poder político y social, es el principal rebelde, la primera fuente viva de nuestras discusiones, de nuestras rebeliones, en el combate global que sostiene el pueblo cubano para destruir las bases materiales y espirituales del subdesarrollo. En este contexto eminentemente revolucionario, sería ridículo por parte del intelectual el querer ser más polémico y más rebelde que los hombres de acción que han hecho la revolución". Con una posición más cercana al intelectual como creador y no solo como militante, Depestre se lanzaba a dar respuestas a la función del escritor en una sociedad que hace la revolución para salir del subdesarrollo a través de dos niveles diferentes: "puede cooperar con la pedagogía general de la revolución, dando conferencias, escribiendo artículos, siendo profesor pero también habría una responsabilidad estética de hacer obras valiosas que expresen a nivel del arte la marcha de la revolución [. . .] En este contexto eminentemente revolucionario, sería ridículo por parte del intelectual el querer ser más polémico y más rebelde que los hombres de acción que han hecho la revolución".[27] A pesar de defender al intelectual como un creador, Depestre no deja de ubicarlo en desventaja con la vanguardia política que llevó a cabo la revolución, postura muy cercana al *pathos* de culpa mencionado en las páginas anteriores.

En la misma línea discursiva, Carlos María Gutiérrez consideraba que las opciones del intelectual eran mínimas en una época de cambios tan radicales:

"No veo otra salida para nosotros, en este continente y en un proceso revolucionario de este tipo, que el de colaborar, con la máxima eficiencia y la adecuada modestia, en un proceso que no está en nuestras posibilidades dirigir, y del que tampoco podemos ser (por más sacrificios que hayamos cumplidos) sus beneficiarios, del modo que lo puede ser un obrero un campesino".[28]

La mutación hacia una semántica revolucionaria estuvo vinculada a un ambiente en el que cada vez se expandía más la idea de revolución en América Latina. Decenas de organizaciones o focos guerrilleros comenzaron a conformarse a partir de los sesenta por todo el continente. El Movimientos de Liberación Nacional Tupamaros (MLN-T) en Uruguay, el Movimiento de Izquierda Revolucionario chileno (MIR), el Ejército de Liberación Nacional Boliviano (ELN) y El Frente Sandinista de Liberación Nacional (FSLN) en Nicaragua son algunos ejemplos. La mayoría de estos se identificaron como una nueva izquierda que se apartó de las visiones más ortodoxas de la izquierda tradicional que solo reconocía la lucha de clases o la llegada al poder mediante partidos políticos. Los nuevos movimientos comenzaron a tener una identidad propia que recurrió a la lucha armada, a la creación de focos rurales, a establecer redes intelectuales mediante revistas y encuentros y a nuevas lecturas teóricas como las de Ernesto Guevara o Régis Debray. Para Aldo Marchesi, "esta nueva identidad llevó a la conformación de una cultura política transnacional al calor de los diálogos y acercamientos de militantes de la nueva izquierda en la región desde mediados de los sesenta hasta el golpe de estado de 1976 en la Argentina. Esa cultura política estuvo vinculada al resultado de los ensayos de experiencias políticas locales, los movimientos de exilio en la región y la creciente regionalización del autoritarismo".[29]

Además de los grupos de lucha armada, otras propuestas tomaban como centro de acción la solidaridad y un proyecto de tercer mundo. Los más conocidos fueron la Conferencia Tricontinental de los pueblos de África, Asia y América Latina del 3 al 15 de enero de 1966, la cual daría paso a la creación de la Organización de Solidaridad de los Pueblos de África, Asia y América Latina (OSPAAAL). También se realizaron jornadas de solidaridad con Guatemala, día de la solidaridad con el Congo, semanas de solidaridad en contra de la Guerra de Vietnam, etc. En todos se debatieron ideas como el imperialismo, el colonialismo, la guerrilla o los movimientos de liberación. El imaginario intelectual se alimentaba de estas nociones y para el Congreso Cultural de La Habana en 1968 una frase de Julio Cortázar era tomada como referente obligatorio "todo intelectual honesto es un intelectual del Tercer Mundo".[30]

El llamado a lo revolucionario se ejercía así en disímiles frentes y los intelectuales extrapolaron estos discursos a su rol:

Las necesidades de fundamentar realmente esa labor específica son las que imponen al intelectual la obligación (y no lo digo en el sentido moral) de sumirse en la más intensa práctica social que le sea posible, incluida la guerra de guerrillas, la cátedra universitaria, el trabajo agrícola etc. Porque la obra de creación (el poema, el ensayo, la novela) no es anterior a la sociedad ni la trasciende antidialécticamente: es una resultante de la labor de un creador socialmente condicionado. Es esa práctica social en el seno de la revolución (cuyo nivel superior debe ser la militancia partidaria, aunque no se excluyan otros niveles y grados suficientemente eficaces) la única actividad que puede transformar toralmente al intelectual "principalmente burgués," del que partimos, en el cuadro intelectual que la revolución necesita para su construcción socialista y que vendría a ser el principal instrumento de transición entre la cultura de élite y de grupos que heredamos del capitalismo y la cultura íntegramente popular, totalizada.[31]

Un claro ejemplo del tránsito de un intelectual comprometido a uno revolucionario fue el giro en la discusión sobre la libertad de creación. Si a inicios de la década era fundamental declarar qué se entendía por libertad creadora y resguardarla, para la mayor parte de los escritores del debate de 1969 la libertad creadora era un obstáculo e incluso un absurdo. La primera oración de la intervención de Desnoes expresa una idea central en torno a los límites de la libertad de creación y expresión "Yo creo que, para empezar, debemos reconocer que muchos de nosotros hemos sido responsables de haber creado una ilusión, la ilusión de que en Cuba existía una libertad absoluta para expresarse libremente, sin reconocer las exigencias de una sociedad en revolución".[32] Esta aclaración de Desnoes resulta sumamente interesante y nos ubica en la postura de un intelectual que estuvo vinculado a *Lunes de Revolución* y a otros proyectos culturales que abogaron por la libertad de creación. Las exigencias de la sociedad revolucionaria fueron quedando claras desde 1961, la libertad era otro concepto más sujeto a la instancia más importante de la vida: la revolución. Bien continuaría diciendo Desnoes con su lucidez habitual:

La libertad está condicionada por la revolución, no es una libertad individual, caprichosa, que obedece a las ideas o deseos de un individuo, sino a una realidad que nos *abraza* y en la cual participamos. Creo que esto es fundamental. Ahora, esto no consiste en repetir mecánicamente consignas, sino todo lo contrario. Creo que hay que mantener una actitud crítica en la cultura, creo que es una responsabilidad del intelectual mantener una actitud crítica, que no debemos entregar a la burguesía la crítica y darles a ellos el derecho a ejercer la crítica, como dijo en una ocasión Retamar. Nosotros debemos asumir esa obligación y esa responsabilidad.[33]

Para los miembros de este debate la discusión sobre la libertad se mostraba como un rezago del romanticismo inicial tras 1959:

Lo que defendíamos era la libertad de creación, ¿no es así? No voy a decir ahora, eso sería muy cómodo, que toda aquella agitación fue un disparate. De algo sirvió, sin duda. Pero es evidente que no actuábamos como intelectuales revolucionarios, utilizando nuestra propia cabeza para *analizar* nuestros propios problemas: actuábamos por un siniestro reflejo condicionado, cuyo motor histórico—cuya base objetiva, por decirlo así—conocemos muy bien: en lo externo, lo que suele llamarse el fantasma de Stalin; en lo interno, la cordial advertencia del Consejo de Cultura de aquella época, que nos definió como "intelectuales de transición" que muy pronto serían barridos por la "verdadera" intelectualidad revolucionaria.[34]

El debate sobre la libertad creadora estuvo estrechamente relacionado con las discusiones sobre arte y literatura.[35] En la mayoría de los posicionamientos el arte se encontraba en función de la revolución, la mirada se colocaba desde abajo y la creación era aquello que debía llegar a cumplir un rol mítico, pero que nunca lo lograba del todo. No obstante, la revolución fue lo que debió problematizarse, lo que debió debatirse, como bien lo diría Carlos Franqui algún tiempo después en las páginas de *Libre* "el problema es la Revolución no el arte".[36] La intervención de René Depestre se ubica en el mismo rango de la exigencia revolucionaria ya no solo al intelectual, sino también al arte, el cual según él no había explotado todas sus potencialidades, hablando no solo de una responsabilidad ética, sino también de una responsabilidad estética, acercándose a la creación de una forma que los autores anteriores no habían hecho.

La teorización sobre arte y revolución estuvo relacionada también con un aspecto fundamental en los primeros debates sobre el compromiso: la escisión que se produjo entre compromiso del autor y compromiso de la obra. Esta dualidad formuló dos disposiciones fundamentales del campo intelectual latinoamericano de los 60: los escritores que abogaban por una acción social o política como cumplimento de su misión intelectual y los que defendían que la mejor forma de expresar el mentado compromiso era lograr una obra que expresara, desde su renovación estética o de contenido, la realidad revolucionaria. "El problema compromiso de la obra/compromiso del autor supone una tensión permanente, implica un reenvío constante entre los dos extremos cuya estabilidad parece imposible".[37]

Conciencia crítica frente a conciencia revolucionaria

El tema del intelectual como conciencia crítica es otro aspecto fundamental para entender el desplazamiento del compromiso intelectual al intelectual revolucionario y para distinguir otras coordenadas del universo intelectual cubano y latinoamericano de entonces. La dialéctica entre crítica y revolución fue una ecuación pocas veces esbozada e ignorada prácticamente por la mayoría de los intelectuales latinoamericanos.

En el encuentro de mayo de 1969, la noción de crítica de Desnoés, no estaba en consonancia con las seguidas por sus compañeros de debates. El autor de *Memorias del Subdesarrollo* expuso acertadamente la verdadera posibilidad de estar dentro de la revolución y ser un intelectual: "Una vez dentro de la revolución no debemos tenerle miedo a expresar nuestra visión del proceso, nuestras dudas y nuestros deslumbramientos. Porque existe el peligro de que, por oportunismo político, por no entrar en incómodas contradicciones, no luchemos por las cosas que vivimos, sentimos y creemos. Si estás dentro de la revolución, tienes la obligación de contribuir con tu trabajo y tu inteligencia al desarrollo de la sociedad, y la verdad no está en seguir a ninguna autoridad, en plegarse a las consignas, sino en luchar por la encarnación de nuestra visión revolucionaria".[38] Desnoes, consideraba que "en la medida en que seamos más revolucionarios, seremos más críticos",[39] una postura que es difícil encontrar a la altura de 1969 en los intelectuales y muy fácil de hallar en la prensa de los primeros años de la década, en aquel tiempo en que alguien tan radical como José A. Baragaño expresaba que la gran fascinación que ejercía la Cuba revolucionaria en el poeta partía de su constante "vitalismo, su radical ausencia de trabas ideológicas; su libertad con respecto a sí misma". Para Baragaño, la filosofía de la acción revolucionaria hecha realidad creaba el héroe de Nietzsche y el combatiente de Malraux.[40]

Carlos María Gutiérrez entendía que el término de conciencia crítica era un anacronismo y un absurdo que provenía del ámbito burgués y por lo tanto debía ser superado.[41] René Depestre, tal vez el más lúcido en esta discusión junto a Desnoes, le responde a Gutiérrez que la conciencia crítica es una categoría histórica necesaria y a tener en cuenta en cada realidad histórica: "La Revolución es conciencia crítica. Naturalmente, puede dejar de serlo en un momento dado, o bien puede suceder que esta conciencia se adormezca o se atrofie, aun se fetichice en la burocracia o en la violación de su propia legalidad socialista. Esto es otra cosa que no nos incumbe aquí, ya que vivimos una revolución que es la principal conciencia crítica del pueblo".[42]

La negación de una conciencia crítica por parte del intelectual revolucionario estuvo relacionada también con las propias nociones que compartía esta red sobre la revolución. Los intelectuales que participaron en *El intelectual y la sociedad* tomaron como guía la política cultura cubana desde *Palabras a los intelectuales*: "Lo que está claro es que, en una sociedad revolucionaria, el revolucionario se reserva el derecho a la crítica, ¿no? 'El revolucionario critica, debe criticar —ahí estamos de acuerdo—, en nombre de la Revolución y de sus fines, critica como revolucionario a los revolucionarios para servir a los intereses de la revolución'".[43] Una vez más, quedaba el interrogante de quién definía qué era el revolucionario o cuáles eran los intereses de la revolución.

El abandono de la idea de conciencia crítica respondió al propio tránsito de compromiso a revolucionario y demuestra también cómo fue evolucionando la forma de entender el concepto de intelectual por los escritores de la época, concepto extremadamente complicado y polisémico, cargado de diferentes experiencias y expectativas. Según Ambrosio Fornet, al triunfo de la revolución los escritores cubanos entendían por intelectual al "poeta, el novelista, el ensayista, el hombre de cultura que manejaba ideas propias y era capaz de ponerlas en blanco y negro: el escritor, en una palabra".[44] El nuevo intelectual revolucionario debía despojarse de todo rezago burgués, de toda autoconcepción occidental: "El intelectual que se ha politizado al revés, a la europea, siente tarde o temprano la nostalgia de esa función que parece haberle arrebatado el dirigente y el cuadro político. Pero sigue imaginándola como una actividad individual: lleva en el tuétano la idea de que un intelectual, por aislado que esté, por desvinculado de las masas que esté, es la conciencia crítica de la sociedad. Esa idea es inconcebible en una sociedad como la nuestra, en la que hasta un miembro del Partido pierde su autoridad moral desde el momento en que se desliga de las masas".[45] De cierta forma el término había asumido una connotación negativa, no solo por entenderse como un rezago burgués, sino también por los siguientes factores. En primer lugar, la crítica puede convertirse en un arma del enemigo. El intelectual podía convertirse, incluso sin pretenderlo, en una forma de perjudicar la revolución: "si un escritor resuelve escribir un libro de versos donde impugna lo que en la revolución le choca. Este hombre, si quiere hacerlo, tendrá que ir a través de la disciplina impuesta por la construcción socialista, a través de sus organizaciones de masa, para sortear los pantanos ideológicos en que puede caer y que la revolución le ha indicado ya con su carta de ruta".[46] Al respecto, resulta llamativo que en el encuentro no se hiciera alusión a la censura del premio UNEAC de poesía recibido por Heberto Padilla el año anterior.[47] Aunque muchas de las intervenciones se pueden notar atravesadas por esta cuestión, su omisión es más que sugerente, más si se analizaron cuestiones como la crítica del intelectual y la obra revolucionaria.

En segundo lugar, la crítica supone la existencia de un diferente o un contrario que puede estar sujeto a juicio, un otro que se puede interpelar o desglosar, implica una pluralidad de pensamiento e individuos contraria a los propósitos totalizantes del Estado cubano que la redujo a una actitud contrarrevolucionaria o destructiva. Según expresaba Retamar, para esta red la única crítica válida del intelectual revolucionario, o simplemente del revolucionario a secas, era la autocrítica, y la autocrítica colectiva.[48]

La inserción o la posibilidad de una conciencia crítica en el socialismo fueron evadidas en la mayoría de las intervenciones del debate, se daba por sobre entendido que en una sociedad de este tipo la crítica no tenía lugar. En un intento de entablar algún tipo de reflexión al respecto Dalton expresaba: "Creo, y si estas palabras van a aparecer impresas alguna vez yo pediría que se subrayaran suficientemente, que la inserción lógica del intelectual de la revolución esté dentro de esa labor que hay que cubrir para hacer aprehensible el paso de la actividad del constructor del socialismo a la conciencia lúcida sobre sí mismo. Se trata (perdón por la redundancia) de una 'labor colaborativa,' básica para que el proceso actividad-conciencia tenga una oportunidad siempre ascendente en la confrontación con la realidad en transformación".[49]

Tal pareciera que Dalton intentaba encubrir con una narración enrevesada los límites de la crítica en el socialismo.

Los problemas para lograr una definición de intelectual revolucionario contribuyeron también a la intensificación del anti-intelectualismo. Si entendemos por intelectual su acepción más consensuada en los estudios sobre el tema, que lo define como aquel sujeto que debe mantener un discurso y postura que no solo puede responder a una intención de interpretar y entender la realidad, sino que debe responder, ante todo, a una intención transformadora mediante una ética responsable y cuya obra y acción deben tener una repercusión en la esfera pública; la mayoría de estos escritores están, tal vez sin plena conciencia exponiendo un marcado anti-intelectualismo.

Me explico mejor, el tono del debate considera a los intelectuales más que un sujeto necesario en la construcción de realidades revolucionarias, un obstáculo. Para Ambrosio Fornet, por ejemplo, la función del intelectual revolucionario "iba a cumplirla, en la práctica, el dirigente y el cuadro político".[50] Lo anterior supuso una clara anulación de los roles básicos del intelectual que se venían reivindicando desde 1959 en las reflexiones y encuentros de la familia intelectual latinoamericana.

El anti-intelectualismo también se puede notar en la forma en la que Ambrosio Fornet se refería a los intelectuales inmediatamente después del triunfo revolucionario "creíamos que nuestro primer deber como intelectuales era preservar para el futuro y para la cultura nacional lo que solíamos llamar "las conquistas del arte contemporáneo [. . .] lo que defendíamos era la libertad de creación [. . .] éramos vestales de la forma, guardianes subdesarrollados de la Vanguardia".[51] Y, aunque Fornet reconoce que no había que desdeñar esas posturas, afirma que era evidente que no actuaban como intelectuales revolucionarios.

A modo de conclusión

Si nos atenemos a la generalidad de las intervenciones y si asumimos que son una muestra de la opinión de la familia intelectual latinoamericana, la función del intelectual, del intelectual revolucionario, restó mucho de ser una función radical, tuvo más bien un rango reformista de la representación intelectual. Varios factores ilustran esta hipótesis: el abandono de la conciencia crítica como esencia del intelectual, el declive del debate sobre la libertad creadora, la constante alusión al inconveniente que representa el intelectual que exige o cuestiona la revolución, y por último, pero no menos importante, la falta de cuestionamiento sobre la realidad, sobre la sociedad que deseaban construir.

La intención de convertir lo que Dalton llamó "cuestiones concretas": la revolución, el socialismo y el intelectual, en conceptos asimilables y claros no llegó a cumplirse del todo. El rol del intelectual continúo siendo casi una cuestión contemplativa sin llegarse a producir ningún consenso y sin debatirse cuestiones más apremiantes del campo intelectual latinoamericano y cubano. El debate se extendió una y otra vez sobre el intelectual y la revolución, repitiéndose ideas y convirtiendo la discusión en un texto similar a muchos de los manuales soviéticos sobre teoría y praxis. La apuesta constante por la acción política fue mermando poco a poco el fervor intelectual que caracterizó la década del 60. A esto, por supuesto, se le deben sumar las condiciones políticas de Cuba: el desplazamiento hacia un socialismo de corte soviético, la ruptura intelectual después del caso Padilla, las declaraciones del I Congreso de Educación y Cultura y la progresiva eliminación de espacios de debate intelectual contribuyeron a que la isla, principal punto de reunión y faro guía en estas cuestiones, dejara de irradiar posibilidades.

El libro que conformaron estos escritores se tituló *El Intelectual y la Sociedad*, pero más que este binomio lo que les interesaba a los presentes era la relación entre el intelectual y la revolución. La pregunta que más se extraña al respecto es la de ¿cuál es la función del intelectual en la sociedad socialista?, e incluso ¿es posible la existencia del intelectual como lo entendemos desde la modernidad en la sociedad socialista? Preguntas que siguen latentes hasta la actualidad y que llevarían como bien diría Fornet "una descarga" más extensa.

NOTA

Este texto forma parte de la investigación "El intelectual y la revolución: Semánticas de un rol en América Latina (1959-1972)" desarrollada en el doctorado en Historia de la Universidad Iberoamericana, Ciudad de México.

1. Claudia Gilman, *Entre la pluma y el fusil. Debates y dilemas del escritor revolucionario en América Latina*, Buenos Aires, Siglo Veintiuno Editores, 2006, p. 59.

2. Ibid., p. 111.

3. Ibid.

4. Ibid., p. 102.

5. Ya desde 1960 tuvieron lugar importantes momentos que marcaron la dinámica intelectual transnacional de los sesenta, aunque no forman parte precisamente de la gestión de esta familia intelectual vale la pena destacarlos: el Encuentro de Escritores de América en Concepción, Chile en 1960. En 1965 el congreso de la Comunidad Latinoamericana de Escritores en Génova. En 1966 el Primer Congreso Latinoamericano de Escritores en América, Chile. En 1967 Segundo Congreso Latinoamericano de Escritores, México.

6. Gilman, *Entre la pluma y el fusil*, p. 102.

7. Para un mayor análisis del tema del peregrinaje político a Cuba ver los textos: Paul Hollander, *Los peregrinos de la Habana*, Madrid, Playor, 1987; y Henry Eric Hernández, *Mártir, líder y pachanga. El cine de peregrinaje político hacia la Revolución cubana*, Leiden, Almenara, 2017.

8. Sylvia Saítta (selección y prólogo), *Hacia la revolución. Viajeros argentinos de izquierda*, Buenos Aires, Fondo de Cultura Económica, 2007, p. 11.

9. La intención con estos ejemplos no es brindar todos los nombres, sino mencionar a los más activos de cada caso en esta red intelectual.

10. Es importante también identificar otras redes que cobraron especial importancia en los sesenta y que se generaron alrededor de revistas autónomas ligadas al hippismo y la generación *beat* norteamericana *El Corno Emplumado* en México y *Eco Contemporáneo* en Argentina. En Colombia el Movimiento Nadaista desde fines de los cincuenta también asumía diferentes posturas vanguardistas sobre la relación entre el escritor y la sociedad.

11. Para mayor profundización en la polémica de *Mundo Nuevo* consultar los textos: *Política y polémica en América Latina. Las revistas Casa de las Américas y Mundo Nuevo* de Idalia Morejón; y *Mundo Nuevo. Cultura y Guerra Fría en la década del 60* de María Eugenia Mudrovic.

12. Las bifurcaciones no solo se dieron en las formas de pensar lo revolucionario, sino también en la forma de entender al intelectual o escritor. Por un lado, Cortázar y Vargas Llosa defendían la autonomía del creador, por otro Ambrosio Fornet y Óscar Collazos abogaban por el compromiso político y la necesidad de una obra "de la Revolución" para la nueva sociedad. Cómo hacer una literatura estéticamente avanzada y políticamente comprometida fue una de las grandes preguntas que se generaron entre los escritores y críticos literarios del *boom*. La respuesta para unos era una obra políticamente comprometida que expresara el momento histórico que se vivía, tal como lo defendió Casa de las Américas en sus Concursos Literarios. Para otros, como Cortázar, sin seguir una disciplina militante, lo revolucionario tenía una connotación más amplia que cabía en variadas formas y estéticas. *Paradiso,* por ejemplo, alabada por el *boom* pero rechazada por la burocracia cultural cubana, era, para muchos de sus defensores, una "Revolución dentro de la Revolución".

13. Esta ha sido desarrollada por investigadores como Claudia Gilman, Rafael Rojas, Patrick Iber y Aldo Marchesi.

14. Al respecto, ver Leonardo Candiano, "1966: Intelectualidad en disputa. El debate sobre los intelectuales revolucionarios en Casa de las Américas," *Conflicto Social,* n° 19, enero a junio 2018, pp. 36–70.

15. Roberto Fernández Retamar en *El intelectual y la sociedad*, México, Siglo Veintiuno Editores, 1969, p. 8.

16. *El intelectual y la sociedad*, p. 9.

17. *El intelectual y la sociedad*, p. 11.

18. *El intelectual y la sociedad*, pp. 9–10.

19. *El intelectual y la sociedad*, p. 12.

20. Roque Dalton, "Poesía y militancia en América Latina," *Casa de las Américas*, 20–21, 1963, p. 12.

21. Ibid., pp. 13–14.

22. Gilman, *Entre la pluma y el fusil*, p. 160.

23. *El intelectual y la sociedad*, p. 18.

24. El más conocido de los casos son las célebres palabras a los intelectuales de Fidel Castro, pero son ínfimas las muestras de esta indefinición de lo revolucionario o de la definición oportunista de acuerdo a contextos específicos.

25. Recordar las célebres afirmaciones de Fidel Castro en 1961 en sus *Palabras a los intelectuales* "el revolucionario pone algo por encima aun de su propio espíritu creador: pone la Revolución por encima de todo lo demás y el artista más revolucionario sería aquel que estuviera dispuesto a sacrificar hasta su propia vocación artística por la Revolución". Departamento de Versiones Taquigráficas del Gobierno Revolucionario, accedido el 24 de mayo, 2020, http://www .cuba.cu/gobierno/discursos/1961/esp/f300661e.html.

26. *El intelectual y la sociedad*, p. 44.

27. *El intelectual y la sociedad*, p. 75.

28. Aldo Marchesi, *Hacer la revolución. Guerrillas latinoamericanas, de los años sesenta a la caída del Muro*, Buenos Aires, Siglo Veintiuno Editores, 2019, pp. 21–22.

29. *El intelectual y la sociedad*, p. 31.

346 : Grethel Domenech Hernández

30. Roque Dalton, *El intelectual y la sociedad*, p. 16.

31. *El intelectual y la sociedad*, p. 20.

32. Ibid.

33. *El intelectual y la sociedad*, p. 32.

34. Por solo mencionar uno de los ejemplos más notables, un año después, se publicaría por Siglo veintiuno el volumen *Literatura en la Revolución y Revolución en la Literatura*, el cual recogía una polémica sobre el papel del escritor latinoamericano de mano de las voces de Oscar Collazo, Mario Vargas Llosa y Julio Cortázar.

35. "Respuesta de Carlos Franqui," en *Libre: Revista de Crítica Literaria*, edición facsimilar, n° 2, 1971, p. 185.

36. Gilman, *Entre la pluma y el fusil*, p. 147.

37. *El intelectual y la sociedad*, p. 21.

38. *El intelectual y la sociedad*, p. 20.

39. José A. Baragaño, "Una revolución de nuestro tiempo," *Revolución*, 27 de abril de 1959, p. 13.

40. *El intelectual y la sociedad*, p. 57.

41. *El intelectual y la sociedad*, p. 58.

42. Fornet, *El intelectual y la sociedad*, p. 40.

43. *El intelectual y la sociedad*, p. 31.

44. Ibid.

45. Carlos María Gutiérrez, *El intelectual y la sociedad*, p. 59.

46. En 1968 Padilla aún no era un caso y su libro *Fuera de Juego*, a pesar de ser premiado en el certamen de la UNEAC había sido publicado con un *disclaimer* por parte de la institución en el que se acusaba al poeta de diversionismo político. Este suceso no fue diseccionado por la intelectualidad cubana ni latinoamericana, a pesar de que Padilla era un escritor muy renombrado, el suceso no tuvo la recepción crítica que se pudiera haber esperado. No sería hasta 1971 que Padilla provocaría rupturas entre la revolución y los intelectuales de izquierda.

47. Estas palabras de Retamar nos trasladan, a modo de profecía fatal, a dos años después cuando Heberto Padilla fuera obligado a realizar su autocrítica en las instalaciones de la UNEAC frente a gran parte de la intelectualidad cubana de ese entonces.

48. *El intelectual y la sociedad*, p. 15.

49. *El intelectual y la sociedad*, p. 37.

50. *El intelectual y la sociedad*, pp. 32–33.

JUAN ALBERTO SALAZAR REBOLLEDO

La Habana del escritor: Jaime García Terrés y la representación del compromiso intelectual en torno a la Revolución cubana en 1959

RESUMEN

El triunfo de la Revolución cubana en 1959 atrajo a una gran cantidad de intelectuales de distintos países. Los latinoamericanos tuvieron en dicho proceso un especial foco de atención y reflexión a lo largo de los años sesenta y setenta, principalmente. Uno de los primeros en visitar Cuba y expresar sus opiniones al respecto del proceso revolucionario fue el mexicano Jaime García Terrés, director de la *Revista de la Universidad de México*. En marzo de 1959 García Terrés publicó su "Diario de un escritor en La Habana". En este diario es posible observar la construcción de la noción de un cierto tipo de compromiso intelectual a partir de la narración de su visita a la isla revolucionaria. A partir de aquel momento, la revista que dirigía incorporó la reflexión política como uno de sus componentes. Esto era una manera de proyectar una identidad intelectual en aras de posicionar discursos e introducirse a un sector de la vida intelectual latinoamericana, que vivía un acelerado proceso de politización catalizado por la Revolución cubana.

ABSTRACT

The triumph of the Cuban Revolution in 1959 attracted many intellectuals from different countries. Latin American intellectuals received at the time a special focus, which lasted through the 1960s and 1970s. Among them, one of the first to visit Cuba and express his opinions about the revolutionary process was the Mexican Jaime García Terrés, director of the magazine *Revista de la Universidad de México*. In its March 1959 edition, García Terrés published his "Diario de un escritor en La Habana." In this diary of his visit to the revolutionary island, it is possible to observe the construction of a specific kind of intellectual compromise. Afterward, the magazine took on a political line. In this, they projected an intellectual identity to position the magazine in discourses and insert itself into Latin American intellectual life, catalyzed by the Cuban Revolution.

> Me dicen hoy
> que hay una Habana que se perdió
> y en sus aquelarres ellos invocan.
> Me dicen hoy.

La Habana que ahora es puritana
en un tiempo dizque fue un ciclón
que en la mañana era la mecha
y en la noche la explosión.
—Frank Delgado, "La farándula habanera"

En 2010 Frank Delgado lanzó su canción "La farándula habanera" en el disco *Mi mapa* de sello independiente. En esta canción, como en muchas otras desde que comenzó su carrera musical en los años ochenta, Delgado hace nostálgicas alusiones a su ciudad: La Habana, Cuba. Sus referencias poetizadas se pierden entre el ocaso de la utopía y la idealización de los tiempos previos a la Revolución cubana de 1959.

Otra canción del cubano Delgado, homónima al mismo disco, "Mi mapa", plantea la posibilidad de imaginar al espacio desde perspectivas distintas a las cartografías tradicionales: "A veces cuando estoy vencido / me da por consultar tu mapa / y espero que respetes el tratado / sobre náufragos prohibidos, / sobre botellas con cartas". Así, el cantante lleva al terreno de lo personal e íntimo la imaginación sobre la ubicación topológica y trasciende la dimensión meramente geométrica de los mapas.

Esta extrapolación de la cartografía está en sintonía con el planteamiento de Fabienne Bradu, quien reflexiona sobre La Habana representada en la literatura de la cubana Julieta Campos: "La mayoría de las veces, la ciudad está vista desde las otras islas que contiene: desde la casa, el jardín, el cuarto-claustro, desde el recuerdo. Más que una visión, la ciudad es una presencia que se adivina, se reconoce en olores y ruidos, en atmósferas cargadas de su existencia sensual, pero que pocas veces *se ve*".[1]

Este par de aproximaciones literarias y artísticas refieren a un par de cubanos que por un motivo u otro tomaron algún tipo de distancia del proceso revolucionario cubano en distintos momentos. Campos tempranamente —vivía en México desde los cincuenta— y Delgado con su constante crítica oscilante entre la sordidez y la ironía, incómoda desde los ochenta para el régimen cubano.[2] El oxímoron del "enclaustramiento del exilio", presente en Campos, plantea algo que pareciera ser común a algunos de los viajeros extranjeros en la isla, que desde los meses posteriores a la revolución triunfante (enero de 1959) comenzaron a visitarla: la evocación distante, paradójicamente incluso al hacerlo desde el propio territorio habanero. Uno de ellos fue el poeta y funcionario cultural mexicano Jaime García Terrés.

García Terrés, quien podría haber tenido algo de la "farándula habanera" que Frank Delgado recuerda en su canción, visitó La Habana en febrero de 1959, al mes siguiente de que Fidel Castro y sus "barbudos" del Movimiento 26 de Julio entraron a la capital. Es decir, en el tránsito entre "el ciclón", los "aquelarres", la "explosión" y el proceso de puritanismo, como Delgado ha caracterizado al posterior desarrollo de la revolución.

En este trabajo se explora la manera en la que Jaime García Terrés construyó su espacio de experiencia en La Habana revolucionaria, a la luz de reflexiones en torno a sus motivaciones e intenciones para narrar sus vivencias en el "Diario de un escritor en La Habana".[3] A partir de ello, propongo una interpretación sobre su visión del intelectual comprometido, su experiencia personal en La Habana, su autoconcepción como escritor/intelectual, y las implicaciones de publicar un texto con el formato de un diario en un espacio como la *Revista de la Universidad de México*, por cierto, bajo su dirección en aquel momento.[4]

Se parte de la hipótesis de que la Revolución cubana implicó para algunos intelectuales mexicanos la posibilidad de construir una representación escrita de sí mismos como intelectuales comprometidos, con la intención de adquirir notoriedad y ganar posiciones en un momento de politización de la vida cultural latinoamericana.[5] El caso de Jaime García Terrés es elocuente, dado el viraje en sus posturas al respecto de la participación social de los escritores, que venía discutiendo desde principios de los años cincuenta.

Jaime García Terrés: Un joven funcionario

Uno de los componentes más importantes en la carrera de Jaime García Terrés como funcionario fue la temprana construcción de sólidos vínculos con las altas esferas de la cultura mexicana. Esto fue posibilitado, en buena medida, por la privilegiada posición social de su familia.[6] A sus veintitrés años, en 1947, un año después de concluir las materias de la licenciatura en Derecho, Jaime se encontró, al llegar a casa de sus padres, con un viejo amigo de los García Terrés. Se trataba del músico Carlos Chávez, en ese momento director de la institución fundada por él mismo en 1946: el Instituto Nacional de Bellas Artes (INBA). Chávez invitó a Jaime a trabajar con él, primero como Consejero del Instituto y al año siguiente como Subdirector General (1948–1949) y director de la revista *México en el arte*.

Por aquellos años, a finales de noviembre de 1948, el filósofo Pablo González Casanova le escribió a Jaime García Terrés —desde París—. En su carta, González Casanova le preguntaba al funcionario por su tesis de Licenciatura en Derecho, que llevaba por título *La responsabilidad del escritor*. El estudiante doctoral en La Sorbonne lamentaba que García Terrés no pudiera reunirse con él en Europa por tener retrasado su examen de titulación como abogado. Lo que más parecía entusiasmarle a González Casanova era que en París "por más que uno quiera esconderse en la concha burguesa se le echan a uno encima y se la hacen caracol".[7] Por lo que el rito iniciático del intelectual latinoamericano visitando Francia —una tradición al menos desde finales del siglo XIX— parecía tener un corolario en este momento: la posibilidad de adquirir conciencia de clase. Todo esto, en el contexto de la reconstrucción francesa tras la Segunda Guerra Mundial y la fundación de la Cuarta República en mitad de huelgas, elecciones y conflictos políticos internacionales.

Unos meses después de esta premonitoria comunicación transatlántica entre los dos jóvenes intelectuales en formación, Jaime García Terrés recibió de la Embajada Francesa una invitación para ir a estudiar unos meses a París. Tras concluir y hasta publicar su tesis de Licenciado en Derecho, García Terrés aceptó. El joven funcionario dejó su puesto en el INBA y tomó rumbo hacia la capital francesa a principios de 1950, a los veintiséis años.

Por aquellos días de 1950, Celia Chávez acompañó a su padre, el médico Ignacio Chávez —también cercano a los García Terrés—, a recibir el Doctorado Honoris Causa por parte de La Sorbonne.[8] Celia y Jaime se encontraron en París y comenzaron a salir en grupo con el resto del círculo de ella en la ciudad europea. Entre ellos estaba el amigo de la infancia de Celia, Carlos Fuentes, que "como a muchos jóvenes de entonces, les enloqueció la hija del doctor Chávez",[9] así como Octavio Paz —por entonces segundo secretario de la Embajada de México en Francia—, y por supuesto, Pablo González Casanova. Años más tarde, en 1960, ya de vuelta en México, Jaime y Celia contraerían matrimonio.[10]

Durante su estancia, Jaime García Terrés estudió Estética en la Universidad de París y Filosofía Medieval en el Colegio de Francia. Sin embargo, su mayor aprendizaje probablemente haya sido en las noches de bohemia paseando por las calles, los cafés y las *boîtes* parisinas con aquel grupo, que lo acompañaría por el resto de su vida en sus emprendimientos culturales.

García Terrés retomó su trabajo en el INBA a su regreso a México en 1951, ahora como jefe del Departamento Editorial, donde permaneció hasta 1953. Fue en aquel año cuando el rector de la Universidad Nacional Autónoma de México (UNAM), Nabor Carrillo, lo invitó a incorporarse a la universidad como titular de la Dirección General de Difusión Cultural. Con esto comenzó a reformular la propuesta cultural de la institución universitaria, encaminándola hacia la experimentación y la vanguardia artística. Para ello, se valió de las relaciones que había hecho en sus anteriores posiciones y, especialmente, durante su estancia en París. Ello queda claro con la incorporación de varios de aquellos personajes a distintas instancias culturales de la universidad, como el caso de Carlos Fuentes, quien se sumó a la Secretaría de Redacción de la *Revista de la Universidad de México* en noviembre de ese mismo año.

En la *Revista* se conjuntaron la vanguardia artística con la discusión acerca del papel social del intelectual como dos aristas de un mismo asunto: la cultura universitaria atenta a las tendencias culturales contemporáneas. Desde luego, la Revolución cubana fue un catalizador para ambos asuntos a partir de su triunfo en 1959. A la postre, el proyecto de Jaime García Terrés incorporó este tema como uno de los ejes de reflexión de la *Revista*.

García Terrés y el compromiso intelectual en los cincuenta

A la par de sus cargos, Jaime García Terrés mantuvo una constante reflexión sobre las implicaciones de ser intelectual y la manera en que este debía relacionarse con la sociedad. Así lo hizo en uno de sus textos más tempranos, *La responsabilidad del escritor* (1949). El poeta consideraba como una posibilidad que "el escritor influye sobre la sociedad sólo por accidente; que su preocupación no es esa, y que, por consiguiente, no puede vinculársele a una consecuencia no buscada por él".[11] En ese sentido, ponderaba a la literatura como "realización de belleza".[12]

Una vez que se hizo director de la *Revista de la Universidad* —una de sus responsabilidades como titular de la Dirección General de Difusión Cultural de la UNAM—, comenzó a publicar ahí su columna "La feria de los días". En ella retomó la reflexión sobre el escritor y sus compromisos, iniciada en su texto de 1949.

"La feria de los días" era para García Terrés la manera en la que la *Revista* tomaba "una posición ante la marcha de los días".[13] Como parte de las dinámicas verticales de la publicación universitaria, este posicionamiento de la *Revista* en su conjunto era escrito por una sola persona: el director. Pero don Jaime consideraba que esto no implicaba algún tipo de distorsión, pues, aunque "se convirtió en una sección muy personal, no por ello representaba menos la posición de la revista y el equipo que lo hacía".[14]

Resulta difícil situar claramente las experiencias clave —previas a la Revolución cubana— que detonaron las reflexiones de Jaime García Terrés acerca del compromiso intelectual a lo largo de los cincuenta. Aun así, podemos ubicar que en 1954 el médico Ignacio Chávez invitó a García Terrés a unirse al Comité de Amigos de Guatemala en contra del golpe de Estado al presidente Jacobo Árbenz aquel año. Sin embargo, aunque el poeta firmó en los comunicados de dicha organización, su reflexión no se modificó significativamente de lo que pensaba previamente sobre la ponderación del "arte por el arte".

Dos años después de dicho Comité, en septiembre de 1956, García Terrés escribió en "La feria de los días": "la literatura vale, especialmente, como expresión, como creación. Cabe desde luego su enjuiciamiento ideológico, mas este tendrá que ejercitarse fuera del campo de lo literario".[15] A pesar de esto, el poeta tuvo varios vaivenes en sus posicionamientos al respecto. Unos meses antes, en enero de ese mismo año había planteado que "el escritor ha de ser un creador de nuevos caminos, un descubridor de nuevas riquezas, aun cuando para esto deba enfrentarse a la inercia espiritual de los últimos destinatarios de su faena", y "su meta será el estimular antes que complacer".[16] En este punto,

García Terrés consideraba que la producción intelectual podría ser potencial-mente provocadora y estimulante para hallar "nuevos caminos", no necesaria-mente limitados a la creación artística.

Estos planteamientos oscilantes y a ratos contradictorios fueron una cons-tante en las reflexiones tempranas de García Terrés sobre el tema. Los vaivenes se extendieron a lo largo de la década y, en cierta medida, también durante los tempranos años sesenta.

Ya para 1958, en su columna "La feria de los días", García Terrés escri-bió "Más sobre la responsabilidad del escritor", en clara alusión al texto que había escrito casi una década antes, como tesis de licenciatura en Derecho. En él asignaba al escritor en México la misión de luchar contra la mentira, pero puntualizaba los límites para sostenerla: "hay que tener en cuenta, de otro lado, que las únicas revoluciones valederas son las que operan en el espíritu".[17]

El acotado espacio específico en el que podían librarse las batallas inte-lectuales quizá se relacionaba con la incertidumbre de García Terrés sobre sus condiciones de posibilidad. Al respecto, se preguntaba si la participación del escritor "en la cosa pública" era posible al no tener otras "armas sociales" que el lenguaje y el pensamiento. Aunque posteriormente introducía un compro-metedor matiz, si bien un tanto contradictorio: ser "un auténtico escritor, en la cabal faena literaria, ella no excluye una deuda a la sociedad".[18]

En el último mes de 1958 la actividad intelectual reflexiva de García Terrés sobre asuntos políticos tomó un rumbo un tanto imprevisto en el periódico *Excélsior*, otra de las tribunas donde expresaba sus posturas hacia el final de la década. En un balance del año que terminaba, el funcionario afirmaba que si bien el México de 1958 no era ya el México posrevolucionario, "el pueblo mexicano carece aún de la madurez requerida para una plena democracia".[19] Lo cual no le impedía cerrar su columna del último día del año diciendo "vaya aquí un voto de agradecimiento y felicitación al Presidente de la República y al director de PEMEX", a causa de la destitución del superintendente de al-gunas instalaciones petroleras en Poza Rica, Veracruz.[20] Un pronunciamiento que parece un tanto sobredimensionado para los términos en los que García Terrés solía expresarse sobre el acontecer. Sobre todo, este tipo de consignas contradecían un planteamiento que él mismo hacía apenas unos meses antes, al criticar a aquellos intelectuales que establecían "un compromiso personal y directo dentro del mecanismo electoral o en la trama burocrática del gobierno". Características un tanto cercanas a lo que decía ahora en diciembre sobre la "abdicación de la libre dignidad de la inteligencia, y una escueta complicidad contra su eficacia".[21] García Terrés dejaba aquí de lado la crítica al poder para dar lugar a una columna laudatoria del gobierno. Aunque, en realidad fue algo poco usual en sus textos, apuntaba quizá a cierta movilización de capitales políticos y sociales, que más tarde pudieran ayudar a posicionar discursos o proyectos.

Comoquiera, el tránsito entre 1958 y 1959 parecía reorientar sus vaivenes y fijarlos en una postura más concreta. Una autoentrevista inédita no fechada (circa. 1959) deja constancia de ello. A mí me parece que este texto introspectivo, por la forma categórica de sus afirmaciones podría ubicarse precisamente en la sacudida que implicó para García Terrés la Revolución cubana.

La autoentrevista de Jaime García Terrés llevaba por título: "¿Cuáles son sus intereses como escritor?".[22] En ella, comenzaba afirmando que todo escritor es un escritor político, pues "basta que el escritor adopte una actitud, que proponga una imagen del mundo" para que "automáticamente se convierta en un juez—pasivo o activo; explícito o implícito—de la sociedad que ha experimentado". Es decir, insistía ahora en la imposibilidad del intelectual de disociarse con respecto a su medio social de desenvolvimiento y existencia, no apartado por su esfera artística de acción de las implicaciones sociales que ésta tiene.

Al hacer un análisis de la sociedad, García Terrés incorporaba algunas concepciones cercanas a un rudimentario marxismo, al afirmar que: "Nuestras clases superiores resultan, desde el punto de vista humano, tremendamente improductivas: casi lo único que les interesa es ganar dinero y gastarlo sin beneficio real para nadie (No digamos ya para la nación)".[23] Y se lanzaba a la yugular de sus costumbres esnob y timoratas. Más adelante, la sociedad mexicana en su conjunto no parecía salir mucho mejor librada que "las clases superiores": "me parece, por lo que hace a su manera de pensar y conducirse, un conjunto virtual de pequeños burgueses: pequeños burgueses propiamente dichos, pequeños burgueses venidos a más, y aspirantes a pequeños burgueses".[24] Estas afirmaciones sorprenden sobre todo por las lapidarias categorías utilizadas para decir lo que en sus columnas públicas expresaba de manera mesurada, o de plano contradictoria. Sin duda, el que se trate de un texto inédito explica en parte esto. Lo cual no excluye que sea una aproximación a las reflexiones del escritor sobre la realidad en un momento en que se aceleró su proceso de politización y particular compromiso intelectual.

Al referirse a su propio desempeño en Difusión Cultural y la *Revista de la Universidad de México,* García Terrés planteaba que, en cinco años en funciones, es decir hasta 1958-1959, "nadie me ha pedido cuentas de lo que digo o dejo de decir". Así llegaba a una afirmación sobre la sustancial asignatura del intelectual universitario: "combatir siempre por la creación, la palabra y la verdad. Yo a través de ellas tres, por la dignificación del hombre".[25] La efectividad de las armas sociales del escritor que unos años antes cuestionaba —el lenguaje y el pensamiento— era ahora reivindicada como la máxima encomienda para alguien en su posición.

Esto parecía un primer punto de ruptura —o al menos de matices— con la caracterización que uno de los colaboradores de la *Revista de la Universidad*, Juan García Ponce, hizo de ella: "durante el periodo que estuvimos con

Jaime García Terrés, había predominado un criterio antinacionalista, de cultura abierta, dando importancia al arte por encima de su posible contenido social... una revista abierta, descarada y totalmente elitista".[26]

La estructura vertical de la publicación universitaria con García Terrés a la cabeza fue claramente expresada por él mismo. Por lo tanto, esta condición me permite afirmar que la *Revista de la Universidad de México* estaba atravesando a principios de 1959 por un acelerado proceso de politización, vía su director. En ese sentido, la Revolución cubana catalizó su desenvolvimiento y proyección con una fuerza indiscutible.

Diario de un compromiso intelectual construido en La Habana revolucionaria

En noviembre de 1956, ochenta y dos expedicionarios del Movimiento 26 de Julio, comandados por Fidel Castro, zarparon del puerto mexicano de Tuxpan, Veracruz rumbo a Cuba en el yate Granma. Tras un accidentado desembarco se dirigieron a la Sierra Maestra, donde pasaron dos años combatiendo como guerrilleros contra el ejército del entonces presidente cubano Fulgencio Batista, hasta que este último huyó derrotado el 1 de enero de 1959. México fue el primer país del mundo en extender su reconocimiento al nuevo gobierno revolucionario, el 5 de enero de 1959.[27]

Si bien la política oficial operó rápidamente a favor del nuevo gobierno cubano, varios intelectuales mexicanos o asentados en México expresaron sus reservas respecto al triunfo revolucionario en distintos espacios. Por ejemplo, el transterrado español en México, Max Aub escribió en su diario con fecha del 7 de enero de 1959 con una mezcla de dudoso optimismo y sospecha: "Las revoluciones o los sobresaltos hacia la libertad, suceden cuando un grupo está decidido a morir por conseguirla. Los que viven bien—si no a gusto—son incapaces de ella. Verbigracia, hoy, los argelinos, pero no los españoles. Quedan, además, los caudillos románticos—si hay quien los financie—, como Fidel Castro".[28]

En la nota de Max Aub se mezclaban el reclamo hacia la pasividad española y la desconfianza frente a la Revolución cubana. Esto lo llevaba a cuestionar la autonomía financiera y la capacidad organizativa de Castro, a quien le dio el nada halagador adjetivo de "caudillo romántico". Aun así, esta entrada en el diario de Aub es ilustrativa del interés por mirar hacia Cuba por parte de un destacado miembro de la red intelectual en torno de la Dirección de Difusión Cultural de Jaime García Terrés. Un año después, en 1960, Aub comenzaría a dirigir Radio Universidad, otra de las trincheras de la construcción del proyecto cultural universitario de García Terrés.

El propio García Terrés también mostró escepticismo respecto al triunfo de la Revolución cubana. La entrada de los "barbudos" a La Habana no le causó mayor ilusión en un primer momento. En su columna "La feria de los días" de enero de 1959 cuestionaba: "El tirano Batista ha caído. Pero ¿qué es lo que queda en su lugar? ¿Acaso una verdadera democracia? No podemos asegurarlo".[29]

Quizá la falta de certeza sobre lo que podría llegar a ser el nuevo régimen cubano fue lo que le llevó a empacar sus maletas apenas terminó aquel mes de enero de 1959 y abordar un avión con destino a La Habana. La visión de García Terrés sobre la función del intelectual en la sociedad había transitado por varias posiciones a lo largo de la década. En este caso no sería la excepción, y su "Diario de un escritor en La Habana" fue prueba de un nuevo vuelco en su concepción. ¿Cuál es, entonces, La Habana del escritor Jaime García Terrés? Considero que es factible aproximarse a responder esta pregunta a partir del planteamiento de Johann Gustav Droysen de que "lo que tenemos ante nosotros como material histórico es la expresión y la primera prueba de actos de voluntad".[30] Por lo tanto, a través del rastreo e interpretación de dichos "actos de voluntad", expresados en el uso de algunos conceptos, la retórica e incluso el formato mismo del "diario," es posible aproximarse a hablar de las motivaciones y representaciones del compromiso intelectual proyectados por García Terrés en su texto.

Dado que García Terrés estaba a la cabeza de un grupo importante de intelectuales, su viaje —probablemente financiado como viaje de trabajo por la UNAM— fue la punta de lanza para armar un número de la *Revista* que dirigía especialmente dedicado a la Revolución cubana.[31] El que la Universidad apuntalara este tipo de publicaciones —ya que este número de la revista no fue la única en su tipo— avivó un fuerte debate motivado por algunos sectores conservadores de la sociedad mexicana, afines al creciente anticomunismo latinoamericano de la posguerra.

El especial de la *Revista de la Universidad* salió de la imprenta en los primeros días de marzo de 1959. En él se reunieron veintiséis textos dedicados por completo a la Revolución cubana: seis fueron hechos especialmente para la edición y el resto fueron tomados de publicaciones periódicas cubanas, que probablemente García Terrés trajo consigo de su visita a la isla. Otras más eran apreciaciones extranjeras, principalmente estadounidenses y europeas, así como documentos producidos por la propia revolución, discursos de José Martí y de Fidel Castro.

En la portada de la revista, con letras mayúsculas y rojas se anunciaba: "La Revolución Cubana". Debajo, una fotografía de Fidel Castro levantando el puño, con una sonrisa que sostenía un puro y en la otra mano un fusil. Se anunciaban: "testimonios" de Jaime García Terrés, Enrique González Pedrero, Carlos Fuentes y Víctor Trapote, así como "opiniones" de Manuel Cabrera, Leopoldo Zea, Jorge Portilla, Augusto Monterroso y Ernesto Mejía Sánchez (Figura 1).

FIGURA 1. Portada del número de marzo de 1959 de la *Revista de la Universidad de México*, dedicada a la Revolución Cubana. Fuente: Archivo Histórico de la UNAM.

El texto de Jaime García Terrés, que aquí nos ocupa, fue publicado en el formato de diario. Es decir, una reconstrucción de la experiencia vivida, caracterizada por la inmediatez y la incorporación de cierto grado de ficción para llenar vacíos. Una narración basada en el registro cronológico, una "experiencia escrita del tiempo" que agrega la expectativa lectora de "sinceridad" hacia quien escribe y condiciona la recepción del lector,[32] al anclarse en "referentes extraliterarios":[33] es decir, se sustenta en la supuesta veracidad de lo narrado. Por lo que esto se plantea como un punto de partida para comprender la intencionalidad de García Terrés al utilizar este tipo de discurso literario: esperaba que le creyeran y ser un referente de lo que sucedió a partir de lo que vio y lo que vivió. El funcionario universitario buscaba posicionarse como un tipo de intelectual distinto al que hasta entonces había sido: apolítico, en pos de uno comprometido con la sociedad y ya no solo por accidente, que adquiriría nuevamente especial notoriedad en América Latina a partir del triunfo de la Revolución cubana.

Una revisión de los lugares que García Terrés mencionó haber visitado en su estancia de catorce días en La Habana permite hacerse una idea del espacio intelectual construido por el escritor en su relato. Su diario inició el 2 de febrero de 1959 con la afirmación de que "la revolución no está en las calles". De tal manera que el autor lleva la experiencia del proceso revolucionario a una serie de consideraciones abstractas, al ubicarla en "los ánimos, en las conciencias, en los planes para el futuro y en los modos de afrontar el presente".[34] Así, García Terrés parece anunciar y justificar desde el inicio el espacio en donde se ubicarán sus acciones, que como veremos, raramente será "en las calles".

El martes 3 de febrero observó y escuchó a "los bien vestidos parroquianos del restaurante 'La Zaragozana'", "los dependientes de las casas de comercio", "el público del cine", "los meseros de los bares" y una "guapa muchacha que me vende cigarrillos en un expendio de la calle 23".[35] Espacios, que, por el tipo de giro ——y derivado de ubicaciones específicas como la calle 23 del por entonces aburguesado Vedado—, podemos rastrear en alguno de los barrios centrales de La Habana.

Para el día siguiente, miércoles 4 de febrero, García Terrés comenzó una narración de cuatro días en la que la mayoría de sus actividades ——casi todas— se desarrollaron al interior del hotel en el que se hospedaba, el Habana Hilton (Figura 2), uno de los más lujosos de aquellos tiempos en la capital cubana.

Entre conversaciones con intelectuales cubanos como el exdirector del periódico *El Mundo*, Luis Botifoll, familiares y colaboradores de Fidel Castro como su hermana, su chofer, su escolta, sus compañeros de lucha como el mexicano Guillén Celaya o el republicano Alberto Bayo ——quien había entrenado a los guerrilleros en su paso por México—, o bien, funcionarios de alto rango como Alfredo Guevara ——quien presidiría al mes siguiente la fundación del Instituto Cubano de Artes e Industria Cinematográficos (ICAIC)—, García

FIGURA 2. Recuerdos en el archivo personal de Jaime García Terrés de su estancia en el Hotel Habana Hilton en La Habana, Cuba, en febrero de 1959. Fuente: Biblioteca de México, Fondo Jaime García Terrés.

Terrés recorrió detalladamente desde la recepción del hotel el 4 de febrero hasta el piso 25 "ante el panorama nocturno de La Habana, que se admira desde el bar" el 6 de febrero. Resultaría elocuente poder comprobar que el poeta mexicano no hubiera salido de su hotel en ese lapso. Sin embargo, en su narración, hay elementos para afirmar que haya salido o no, aquello que llamó su atención y que consideró como el lugar de un escritor al visitar una ciudad en proceso revolucionario era, en buena medida, dentro de su hotel, con los suyos: sus contrapartes intelectuales, funcionarios, celebridades o bohemios del bar.

El 7 de febrero, García Terrés comenzó el día leyendo el periódico en su hotel, tal como ilustró dicho hábito —no sin un toque irónico— una de las caricaturas de Andrée Burg en la *Revista* (Figura 3) y más tarde salió a dar la vuelta. Llegó al barrio contiguo a su hotel, buscó una banca en el Parque Central e intercambió palabras con personas que se acercaron al sitio donde se sentó.

Al día siguiente, el 8 de febrero, la invitación de una alta funcionaria del gobierno revolucionario le hizo salir de su hotel y su barrio, en fallida búsqueda de Fidel Castro: "llevamos un pase firmado por Celia Sánchez, que nos abrirá todas las puertas".[36] Blasonar dicha condición operaba en dos sentidos:

por un lado, queda claro el interés de García Terrés por hacer un recuento de los dignatarios con los que estableció relaciones, quizá como una manera de recalcar su posición, hablando con sus iguales. Por otro lado, esto permite considerar también que una de las contadas formas de hacer que García Terrés saliera de su hotel era tener la oportunidad de continuar realizando actividades que asumía de escritor, a donde fuera que se dirigiera.

Este planteamiento se apuntala con su anécdota del 10 de febrero, cuando recuerda haberse encontrado con el periodista colombiano Hugo Latorre Cabal quien "no ha resistido la tentación de conocer por sí mismo la realidad cubana", a unas cuadras del Parque Central —de vuelta en el barrio que García Terrés frecuentaba. Juntos fueron a tomar una copa en La Bodeguita del Medio (Figura 4), un sitio popular y famoso por ser una atracción turística desde antes de la revolución, según Peter Moruzzi,[37] pero que Jaime García Terrés consideró: "algo así como una *boîte* genuinamente cubana, frecuentada por personajes de las letras y de la política; no demasiado—y es una inexplicable fortuna—por los turistas".[38]

García Terrés asumía que el hecho de estar en La Habana permitía conocer la realidad del proceso revolucionario de toda la isla, a pesar de que su experiencia se había limitado a unas cuadras de los barrios del centro de la capital y algunos de los veinticinco pisos de su hotel. Por otro lado, en esta disputa entre lo real, lo auténtico y lo genuino, García Terrés comenzó por reafirmarse como algo más que un turista al visitar ese espacio que le correspondía al ser

FIGURA 3. Caricatura de Jaime García Terrés leyendo periódicos en el hotel Habana Hilton, hecha por Andrée Burg para la *Revista de la Universidad*. Fuente: Archivo Histórico de la UNAM.

FIGURA 4. De derecha a izquierda: Jaime García Terrés, el dueño de la Bodeguita del Medio, el cantante y compositor cubano Carlos Puebla y Hugo Latorre Cabal, en 1959. Fuente: Alba C. de Rojo, Jaime García Terrés. Iconografía (México: FCE/El Colegio Nacional/UNAM, 2003), 30.

un personaje de letras. Sin embargo, para validar a la Bodeguita del Medio —que, hay que insistir, era desde entonces uno de los sitios turísticos por antonomasia en La Habana— la equiparó con un bar parisino, una *boîte*. Aludía así a su experiencia de una década antes en París, referente común de los suyos, a quienes estaba dirigiendo su diario y buscando la aprobación de su experiencia personal como lo que un escritor tendría que hacer en La Habana.

Finalmente, también en la Bodeguita, García Terrés tuvo un encuentro con un "Señor Powell", colaborador de un diputado estadounidense, quien lo increpó: "Me pregunta: cómo es posible que el gobierno mexicano ('un gobierno liberal y progresista') tolere 'la campaña pro-dictatorial de algunos periodistas mercenarios'". Es una interrogación que no aguarda respuesta de mi parte. Powell se muestra en verdad indignado, y sigue hablando sin que se le interrumpa".[39]

¿Era este encuentro con Powell una de esas casualidades en las que el escritor intervenía en la sociedad, que García Terrés planteaba en 1949? ¿O se trataba, efectivamente, de un vuelco en la postura del intelectual? Parece difícil ubicarlo por completo en alguna de las dos opciones, pues la inexactitud de su reacción: "interrogación que no aguarda respuesta de mi parte", lejos de exponer una postura clara o una opinión política formada por parte de García Terrés —más allá de la flor que le echa en su texto al gobierno mexicano "liberal y progresista"—, exhibe la superficialidad de la acción. Produjo indignación en el funcionario estadunidense, pero no es posible saber por qué. En la forma, su acción lo aproxima, de algún modo, al modelo del intelectual comprometido con la lucha revolucionaria de la isla, aunque se desconozca su motivación más allá de la "tentación de conocer por sí mismo la realidad cubana".

El 12 de febrero, García Terrés entró al cine a ver documentales de la revolución y se dirigió a buscar a los líderes comunistas cubanos Mirta Aguirre y Carlos Rafael Rodríguez. El 13 compró discos y el 14 transcribió notas sobre el nombramiento de Fidel Castro como primer ministro. Finalmente, el 15 de febrero se despidió de La Habana, recalcando que no habló con Fidel Castro o con otros líderes revolucionarios, aduciendo así haber "logrado una imagen, acaso menos espectacular, pero en todo caso nada oficial, más espontánea, más 'vívida,' del drama cubano".[40] Paradójicamente, tal como se enfatizó a lo largo del análisis de La Habana de García Terrés, la mayor parte de sus interlocutores —en más de una ocasión concertados, no casuales— sí eran dirigentes, intelectuales o personajes estelares de la vida cultural y política cubana y americana.

Así, la reivindicación de la experiencia personal por parte de Jaime García Terrés en su "diario" redactado como "escritor en La Habana" se convirtió en la formulación de una cartografía personal, velada como íntima y sincera por la condicionante de ser un diario. Sin embargo, el encierro de García Terrés en su hotel es aún más elocuente al respecto de su perspectiva sobre el proceso revolucionario desde el bar en el piso 25 del Habana Hilton.

Por momentos, García Terrés parece justificar su propio encierro diciendo que la revolución no está en la calle, exaltando la experiencia al interior del hotel o la autenticidad de espacios cliché como La Bodeguita del Medio. Más allá de lo verdadera o falsa, auténtica o inauténtica que pudiera resultar la experiencia del funcionario universitario, el interés de este trabajo no está puesto en desmentirlo. Lo que se busca es evidenciar las "conexiones entre unos mecanismos de coerción y unos contenidos de conocimiento" —en palabras de Michel Foucault— vertidas en el "diario" a partir de los compromisos, implicaciones y concepciones del escritor.[41] En este sentido, se trata de caracterizar el tipo de intelectual comprometido que García Terrés proyectó de sí mismo en su diario en torno a la Revolución cubana y las experiencias posteriores que esto detonó.

El Espectador: Punto álgido del compromiso intelectual

El Espectador fue una fugaz revista publicada mensualmente entre mayo de 1959 y abril de 1960, expresiva del entusiasmo que despertó la Revolución cubana entre varios intelectuales del círculo cercano a Jaime García Terrés. Esta publicación les permitió expresarse paralelamente en un medio que facilitaba hacer explícitas ciertas consideraciones políticas fuera del ámbito universitario de la *Revista*.

El Espectador era editado por un consejo editorial de dirección rotativa integrado por personajes vinculados a la *Revista de la Universidad de México*: Jaime García Terrés, Carlos Fuentes, Enrique González Pedrero, Francisco López Cámara, Luis Villoro y Víctor Flores Olea. Para el segundo número, en el que Fuentes ocupó el puesto de director en turno, en la carta editorial sin firma, titulada: "El fin y los medios" el grupo se posicionaba ideológicamente:

> *El espectador* se ha presentado como una revista de izquierda. ¿Qué puede significar tal afirmación? En primer lugar, que pretendemos que las páginas de nuestra revista participen en ese debate sobre los principios y problemas que tiene que afrontar la izquierda mexicana. No nos interesa tanto la definición —en abstracto— de la izquierda, como la precisión de los temas, de las ideas, en torno a los que la izquierda pueda devenir factor determinante de la vida política del país. Pero aclaremos: evidentemente no somos fundadores de partidos, ni somos vehículos de ninguna organización política. La organización política, como tal, no es una tarea que nos incumba directamente; ella puede y debe surgir solamente de las clases populares. Y esa labor, de momento, tiene que ver mucho más de cerca con los líderes que con los intelectuales.[42]

Examinar el tránsito de las reflexiones de Jaime García Terrés sobre el compromiso intelectual a la luz de este texto resultaría desconcertante si a la mitad no se colocara la experiencia del poeta observando a la Revolución cubana. Por otro lado, sería importante revisar también las posturas del resto de los integrantes de la red intelectual de la que formaba parte, para comprobar el tránsito conjunto hacia una nueva postura sobre la participación social. Por ahora basta enfatizar que los integrantes de *El Espectador* participaron también en el número de marzo de 1959 de la *Revista de la Universidad* dedicada al proceso en la isla.

La política se convirtió en una de las prioridades de estos intelectuales vinculados también a la revista universitaria, ya que decían en *El Espectador*: "pretendemos ir influyendo en la opinión pública, haciendo que participe en este debate político, que esté alerta de las cuestiones de nuestra vida pública. Tarea tanto más urgente cuanto que la opinión pública, y en particular la opinión sobre política, acusa una indiferencia y un sopor alarmantes, como resultado de los manejos de nuestra 'prensa' tradicional".[43] Así, una vez más denunciaban conjuntamente la opacidad en la actuación de la prensa mexicana, como ya lo habían hecho para justificar la pertinencia de sus textos de marzo de 1959 en la *Revista de la Universidad*, encaminados a desmentir falacias e injurias sobre la Revolución cubana.

Finalmente, apuntaban a hacer un ejercicio de definición del tipo de intelectual que con este grupo buscaban ser, a través de la participación en la opinión pública y la afirmación de sus convicciones de izquierda: "Que un grupo de intelectuales hayamos formado una revista como ésta casi no requiere justificación: queremos ver de frente la realidad del país, entender a nuestros

contemporáneos, preocuparnos por los nuevos estilos de vida, reflejarlos y de-
cirlos... Porque esto es ya un principio de transformación de la realidad. Tal
vez pueda llamársele sentido de responsabilidad histórica".[44]

El tercer número de *El Espectador* fue consecuente con esta declaración al
incorporar un reportaje sin firma sobre la Reforma Agraria en Cuba, que funcionaba como un exhorto a la defensa intelectual y política de la Revolución
cubana, a partir de sus similitudes con la herencia histórica de la Revolución
mexicana: "*El Espectador* piensa que México, como ningún otro país de América, se encuentra en la obligación histórica y moral de pronunciarse abiertamente, oficialmente, a favor de la Reforma Agraria cubana. ¿Qué hubiera dado
México porque Hispanoamérica defendiera unitariamente nuestra propia lucha
a favor de la justicia agraria? La solidaridad hispanoamericana ha de demostrarse con actos, no en discursos y conmemoraciones".[45]

El número, además, coincidía con el mes del primer aniversario del Movimiento 26 de Julio festejado desde el gobierno revolucionario. El expresidente mexicano Lázaro Cárdenas (1934–1940) —quizá el mayor impulsor
del reparto agrario en la posrevolución—, asistió a la conmemoración, por lo
que resulta casi premonitoria la elocuencia del foco gráfico seleccionado para
el artículo, al lado izquierdo del reportaje a ocho columnas, arriba, una fotografía de Fidel Castro rodeado de campesinos con sombreros, con el pie de
foto: "la solidaridad hispanoamericana ha de demostrarse con actos". Y del
lado derecho, una fotografía del General Lázaro Cárdenas: "así hablaba ayer
la Revolución Mexicana" (Figura 5). El reportaje concluía con una frase que
lejos de sepultar a la Revolución mexicana la utilizaba como argumento para
expresar la "obligación histórica de la defensa de Cuba y su Reforma Agraria",
apelando a la de Cárdenas en los años treinta en México: "Así hablaba ayer la
Revolución Mexicana. Así habla hoy la Revolución Cubana. Sólo la ceguera o
la mala fe pueden negar que la lucha es la misma".[46]

Sin embargo, este posicionamiento público no parecía agradar a todos los
personajes cercanos a García Terrés. En una tarjeta enviada desde la Embajada
de México en Francia el 13 de agosto de 1959, Octavio Paz se dirigía sarcásti-
camente al funcionario universitario en los siguientes términos:

"Supongo, Jaime el Libertador, que los furores cívicos y las entrevistas y expediciones
y reuniones no te impedirán, de vez en cuando, pensar en la poesía y, sobre todo, en
escribirla".[47]
Saludos cordiales.
Octavio

Expresiones de desacuerdo como la de Octavio Paz fueron acumulándose.
A los sectores conservadores también les molestaba que se mencionara siquiera a la Revolución cubana, al calor del anticomunismo de la Guerra Fría

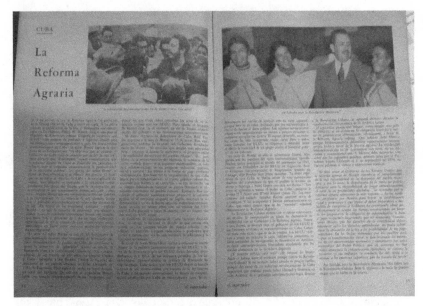

FIGURA 5. El artículo rompía lanzas por la continuidad histórica entre la Revolución mexicana y la cubana. A los herederos —al menos discursivos— de la primera correspondía, ahora, la defensa de la segunda. Fuente: *El Espectador* 1, núm. 3 (julio 1959).

latinoamericana. Si bien desconocemos la respuesta epistolar a Paz por parte de García Terrés, en diciembre de aquel año, el director de la *Revista de la Universidad de México* denunció en su columna "La feria de los días" una campaña "a veces violenta de necia difamación en nuestro perjuicio, tratando de asociarnos a las más inverosímiles conspiraciones".[48] Al respecto, el funcionario defendía la postura de la *Revista*, de pronunciar públicamente sus principios políticos y periodísticos: "lo cual sólo sirvió para confirmar la urgencia y la significación de nuestra actitud; para movernos a continuarla; para seguir reclamando y ejerciendo el derecho de aportar, en la escasa medida de nuestras posibilidades, un contrapeso simbólico a la ola mercenaria de conformismo y mendacidad que embarga a nuestro país".[49]

Con estas afirmaciones, García Terrés redondeaba su proceso de tránsito en la postura sobre las labores de un intelectual. Lo que antes parecía ser solo posible de manera accidental: incidir socialmente, ahora era no solo una posibilidad, sino una obligación y convicción dada su lectura de la situación mexicana. La *Revista de la Universidad* incorporó así la reflexión política como uno de los ejes de la publicación. En ese sentido parecía responder explícitamente al llamado que el escritor estadounidense Charles Wright Mills hacía en el número de octubre de 1959 de la propia *Revista*: "La última oportunidad de los intelectuales".[50]

El artículo era una revisión histórica desde la Ilustración hasta el momento en que Wright Mills escribía, sobre las labores intelectuales. Hacia el final de su texto se preguntaba: "¿dónde se encuentra la *intelligentsia* que está llevando a cabo el gran discurso del Mundo Occidental y cuyo trabajo como intelectuales influya entre los partidos y los públicos y tenga significación para las grandes decisiones de nuestro tiempo?".[51] El llamado retórico del escritor estadounidense era al compromiso con la situación de crisis contemporánea por parte de los intelectuales, asignándoles la labor de buscar respuestas a los problemas que aún no habían sido afrontados. Wright Mills parecía concebir como una necesidad que los "medios de comunicación en masa [estuvieran] abiertos a tales hombres".[52]

En ese sentido, podemos afirmar que la Revolución cubana funcionó como catalizador para la progresiva politización de algunas revistas y otros espacios político-culturales latinoamericanos. De ello dejarían testimonio los textos de la *Revista de la Universidad de México*, pero también aquellos publicados en *Cuadernos Americanos*, *México en la Cultura*, *La Cultura en México*, *Política*, y varias más que tuvieron gran auge entre los años sesenta y setenta, no solo en México, sino a lo largo y ancho de América Latina. En esto cabe considerar las motivaciones de los intelectuales detrás de este tipo de proyectos. Al respecto de lo cual, el análisis de los textos de Jaime García Terrés en torno al compromiso intelectual antes y después de 1959 puede ser expresivo sobre los virajes en las posturas.

Reflexiones finales

Al hablar de las reflexiones intelectuales sobre la Revolución cubana en la *Revista de la Universidad de México*, también estamos hablando de la propia concepción de cultura universitaria en la UNAM. Fue este el momento en el que se afianzó el acceso a estos espacios fundamentalmente a través de la conexión por medio de redes intelectuales como la formulada por García Terrés, construida principalmente sobre relaciones personales. Los intelectuales que participan en estos esquemas suelen trabajar en función de dichos vínculos, lo cual explicaría la elasticidad en algunas de las posturas; y en muchas ocasiones, los vaivenes en su participación pública. Cabría pensar si en la actualidad este modelo continúa vigente. Queda esta como una de las labores pendientes a ser estudiada.

El "Diario de un escritor en La Habana" permite observar el tránsito en la postura de Jaime García Terrés sobre su visión del intelectual comprometido. Su participación en la sociedad posibilitada solamente por accidente, hasta llegar a la autoafirmación como miembro de un proyecto de izquierda, estuvo determinada por la ruptura que la Revolución cubana implicó para el mundo cultural y artístico latinoamericano. La experiencia personal del escritor en La Habana le permitió crear un espacio literario personal e íntimo desde el cual formular su propia y asumida versión del compromiso intelectual a través de su "diario", como un itinerario de su propia transformación.

Más allá de evaluar la autenticidad o impostura de los elementos presentados por García Terrés en su autorrepresentación a partir de su visita a La Habana, me parece que su narración es evidencia de la búsqueda por aproximarse a un círculo específico del mundo cultural latinoamericano. Esta esfera estaba descubriendo —a la vez que construyendo— un nuevo espacio de expresión y discusión cultural, y para ello movilizaba e intercambiaba capitales en una nueva plataforma: la isla de Cuba. De esta manera, la Revolución cubana se convirtió no solamente en un tópico atractivo para ser explorado desde las utopías intelectuales y políticas, sino también una condición de posibilidad para proyectarse como intelectual comprometido en los años sesenta y para algunos, incluso después.

El "ciclón", la "mecha" y la "explosión" de la "Farándula habanera" de Frank Delgado, fueron vividos aún por Jaime García Terrés como un factor de reposicionamiento no solo personal, sino de todo un proyecto cultural, específicamente expresado en la *Revista de la Universidad de México*. A lo largo de dos años, hasta 1961, la revista publicó una gran cantidad de textos alusivos a la Revolución cubana, de diversos autores; frecuentemente enfatizando su compromiso intelectual a través de la defensa del proceso de radicalización en la isla. Este viraje en la publicación solo pudo ser contenido por una agresiva campaña anticomunista que tuvo su mayor auge en 1961. Aquel año fue un nuevo momento para reconsiderar las posturas políticas del director, y por lo tanto, de la *Revista*. Esto llevó a reenfocar las prioridades y espacios de desenvolvimiento, en los que el compromiso intelectual dejó, progresivamente, de estar al centro.

NOTAS

1. Fabienne Bradu, "Julieta Campos: La cartografía del deseo y de la muerte," *Vuelta* (México), julio 1987, núm. 128, 28. En este texto, Bradu discute las implicaciones del estar/no-estar en la isla de la literatura de Campos, su condición de "transterrada" y la posibilidad de plantear un espacio imaginario que se reconstruye en una mezcla de memoria y ficción.

2. "Tengo muchos amigos que tienen un discurso más ligado a la Revolución y son mejor tratados... No he sido nunca mediático, pero el haber estado medio prohibido tiene su encanto". Entrevista de Katheryn Felipe a Frank Delgado, "Frank Delgado: 'Haber estado medio prohibido tiene su encanto'", La Habana, 28 agosto 2017, https://oncubanews.com/cultura/musica/frank-delgado-haber-estado-medio-prohibido-encanto/.

3. Jaime García Terrés, "Diario de un escritor en La Habana," *Revista de la Universidad de*

México, 1959, pp. 3–8. Texto escrito por García Terrés sobre su estancia en La Habana entre el 2 y el 15 de febrero de 1959.

4. El compromiso intelectual fue una discusión especialmente en boga entre los años cincuenta, sesenta y setenta. El italiano Antonio Gramsci desarrolló desde los años veinte y treinta el concepto de intelectual orgánico, es decir aquel que desempeña una función social al señalar las problemáticas propias de una clase social a ser resueltas. Antonio Gramsci, *La formación de los intelectuales*, México, Grijalbo, 1967. En cierta medida, este concepto sirvió como base para los franceses Jean-Paul Sartre y Albert Camus. Patrick Iber plantea que conforme avanzó la Guerra Fría, la noción de compromiso intelectual comenzó a alejar las posturas de Sartre y de Camus. Para el primero, el compromiso llegó a exigir la defensa puntual de una causa, como el comunismo, la Unión Soviética o la Revolución cubana. Para el segundo, "la primera obligación de compromiso del intelectual era con la verdad", pues se oponía a la represión que discursivamente se justificaba por el bien mayor, en este caso, las utopías socialistas. Patrick Iber, *Neither Peace nor Freedom: The Cultural Cold War in Latin America*, Cambridge, Harvard University Press, 2015, "Introduction", Kindle. Sin embargo, para el momento de la Revolución cubana, el pensamiento sartreano era una buena conjugación de la noción gramsciana de intelectual orgánico y los límites de Camus para el compromiso.

5. Un balance general sobre el compromiso intelectual en América Latina en la segunda mitad del siglo XX puede encontrarse en varios textos de Claudia Gilman, especialmente en *Entre la pluma y el fusil: Debates y dilemas del escritor revolucionario en América Latina*, Buenos Aires, Siglo Veintiuno, 2012; y de Rafael Rojas, *La polis literaria*, México, Taurus, 2018. Algunos estudios han abordado la politización intelectual en otras revistas mexicanas como *Política*, es el caso de Juan Rafael Reynaga Mejía, *La Revolución cubana en México a través de la revista Política: Construcción imaginaria de un discurso para América Latina*, México, UAEM/UNAM-CCyDEL, 2007; y Beatriz Urías Horcasitas, "Alianzas efímeras: Izquierdas y nacionalismo revolucionario en la revista Política. Quince días de México y del Mundo (1960–1962)," *Historia Mexicana*, núm. 271, 2019. Finalmente, sobre el diario de García Terrés, Rafael Vargas Escalante escribió una breve semblanza en su libro *De México para América Latina*, México, Grano de Sal, 2019.

6. Los padres de Jaime García Terrés, Trinidad García Aguirre y Elisa Terrés Villaseñor provenían de dos familias de prosapia de finales del siglo XIX. El padre de Trinidad fue el historiador y editor Genaro García y el padre de Elisa fue el médico José Terrés.

7. Carta de Pablo González Casanova a Jaime García Terrés, París, Francia, 13 de noviembre de 1948, archivo personal de Jaime García Terrés y Celia Chávez de García Terrés, Ciudad de México.

8. Entrevista del autor con Celia Chávez, Ciudad de México, 3 de junio de 2019.

9. Carlos Fuentes, "Celia en 1951" en *Celia ¡80 bien bailados!*, México, edición de autor, 2010, p. 11.

10. Entrevista del autor con Celia Chávez, Ciudad de México, 3 de junio de 2019.

11. Jaime García Terrés, *Sobre la responsabilidad del escritor*, México, edición de autor, 1949, p. 25. García Terrés consideraba al escritor como una de las manifestaciones posibles de la labor intelectual, por lo que podemos decir que este autor utilizaba ambas categorías como equiparables.

12. Ibíd., p. 27.

13. Jaime García Terrés y Álvaro Matute, "Los espacios de la literatura," 1985. Biblioteca de México, Ciudad de México, Fondo Reservado/Fondo Jaime García Terrés (a continuación, citado como BM, García Terrés), caja 8, fol. 19.

14. Ibíd., fol. 27.

15. Jaime García Terrés, "La feria de los días," *Revista de la Universidad de México*, 1956, p. 3.

16. Jaime García Terrés, "La feria de los días: Valor dudoso, misión del escritor," *Revista de la Universidad de México*, 1956, p. 3.

17. Jaime García Terrés, "La feria de los días: Más sobre la responsabilidad del escritor," *Revista de la Universidad de México*, 1958, p. 3.

18. Jaime García Terrés, "Los intelectuales y la política," *Excélsior*, 20 de ago. 1958, BM, García Terrés, caja 1, expediente Recortes Jaime 1958 a 1960.

19. "Dos intelectuales hablan de política," *Excélsior*, 5 de diciembre de 1958, BM, García Terrés, caja 1, expediente Recortes Jaime 1958 a 1960.

20. Jaime García Terrés, "El Crepúsculo de los Caciques," *Excélsior*, 31 de diciembre de 1958, BM, García Terrés, caja 1, expediente Recortes Jaime 1958 a 1960.

21. Jaime García Terrés, "Los intelectuales y la política," *Excélsior*, 20 de agosto de 1958, BM, García Terrés, caja 1, expediente Recortes Jaime 1958 a 1960.

22. Jaime García Terrés, "¿Cuáles son sus intereses como escritor?", BM, García Terrés, caja 8, expediente Entrevistas, legajo "¿Cuáles son sus intereses como escritor?".

23. Ibíd., p. 3.

24. Ibíd., p. 3.

25. Ibíd., p. 5.

26. Juan Antonio Rosado y Adolfo Castañón, "Los años cincuenta: Sus obras y ambientes literarios" en *La literatura mexicana del siglo XX*, Manuel Fernández Perera (ed.), México, Fondo de Cultura Económica/CONACULTA/Universidad Veracruzana, 2008, p. 276.

27. Teresa Casuso, *Cuba and Castro*, New York, Random House, 1961, p. 111.

28. Max Aub, *Diarios 1953–1966*, México, CONACULTA, 2002, p. 147.

29. Jaime García Terrés, "La feria de los días: El despotismo y el caos," *Revista de la Universidad de México*, 1959, p. 3.

30. Johann Gustav Droysen, *Histórica: Lecciones sobre la Enciclopedia y metodología de la historia*, Barcelona, Alfa, 1983, p. 184.

31. Se sugiere esta posibilidad a partir de la naturalidad con la que Octavio Paz le escribía constantemente cartas a Jaime García Terrés para que invitara a escritores o artistas extranjeros a la UNAM, con la condición de que se les pagara la estancia en el país con recursos institucionales. Así que, siendo una práctica aparentemente tan cotidiana no resultaría extraño que al director de la *Revista de la Universidad de México* se le tuviera una deferencia equivalente para visitar Cuba en su condición de escritor-cronista. Ver Octavio Paz, *El tráfago del mundo*, México, Fondo de Cultura Económica, 2017.

32. Karmen Ochando Aymeric, "El último silencio (El Diario de campaña de José Martí)" *Guaraguao* 4, no. 11, 2000, p. 48.

33. Maurice Blanchot, *El espacio literario*, Barcelona, Paidós, 1992, p. 23.

34. Jaime García Terrés, "Diario de un escritor en La Habana," *Revista Universidad de México*, 1959, p. 3.

35. Ibíd.

36. Ibíd., p. 6.

37. Peter Moruzzi, *Havana before Castro: When Cuba Was a Tropical Playground*, Layton, Gibbs Smith, 2008, p. 92.

38. García Terrés, "Diario de un escritor en La Habana," p. 7.

39. Ibíd.

40. Ibíd., p. 8.

41. Michel Foucault, "¿Qué es la crítica?," *Daimón, Revista de Filosofía*, no. 11, 1995, p. 13.

42. *El Espectador* (México), junio 1959, p. 3.

43. Ibíd.

44. Ibíd.

45. *El Espectador* (México), julio 1959, p. 15.

46. Ibíd.

47. Tarjeta sin fecha, en sobre de la embajada de México con sello de París, 13 de agosto 8 de 1959, en Paz, *El tráfago del mundo*, 50.

48. Jaime García Terrés, "La feria de los días," *Revista de la Universidad de México*, 1959, p. 3.

49. Ibíd.

50. Charles Wright Mills, "La última oportunidad de los intelectuales," *Revista de la Universidad*, 1959, p. 4.

51. Ibíd., p. 6.

52. Ibíd.

ENRIQUE S. PUMAR, HELENA SOLO-GABRIELE,
AND JOSEPH B. TREASTER

Water and Quality of Life in Contemporary Cuba: Contending Issues and Implications

ABSTRACT

Drawing on field data collected from travelers to and from Cuba, this article examines the levels of potable water contamination in Havana and other municipalities. When respondents were asked to assess the supply of water, they reported that water was available for no more than a few hours a day and that water arrives under low pressure, allowing for contamination that people in our study said made them sick. Our study also found that water concerns varied widely and that water filters are more prevalent in neighborhoods with more recent construction, areas that are also more frequented by foreigners. Working-class neighborhoods, in contrast, rely more often on boiling their drinking water. Our findings refute official data regarding the availability of potable water.

RESUMEN

Basado en datos proporcionados por viajantes a Cuba, este trabajo examina los niveles de contaminación en el agua potable en La Habana y otros municipios. Los participantes de nuestro estudio reportan que solo tienen agua disponible unas horas cada día y que el agua les llega con baja presión, lo cual permite que los niveles de contaminación les afecte su salud. Nuestro estudio también demuestra que los niveles de contaminación son desiguales. En los barrios donde la construcción es más reciente y los turistas residen, los filtros de agua son más abundantes. Sin embargo, en los barrios obreros, las familias hierven el agua con más frecuencia. Nuestras conclusiones cuestionan las estadísticas oficiales sobre el agua potable.

This study focuses on how consumers perceive the availability and quality of drinking water in Cuba. Data is based exclusively on perceptions concerning water quality. We began the study because we believed there was a significant discrepancy between the quality of drinking water in Cuba as reported by the government and that perceived by people who depend on clean, safe water in their daily lives. Our study suggests that the perceived quality of drinking water among Cuban residents and visitors is poor. This contrasts sharply with the Cuban government's reports to international institutions. At the time we collected our data, water was available in some households in Havana and other cities for no more than a few hours a day. Conditions appear to be worse in the countryside. When drinking water arrives through municipal systems, it is under low pressure, allowing for contamination that people in our study said made them sick. Our findings indicate that Cuba needs significant investment in drinking water infrastructure. But the government's data on drinking water conditions—in contrast to our findings—suggests that not much needs to be done.

Cuba has at least one strong incentive to improve its water quality: its important tourism business. Tourist receipts from 1994 to 2020 published by the World Bank show Cuba's dependence on tourism for foreign exchange. Tourists can hardly miss the global warnings about the danger of drinking tap water in Cuba, and that cannot be good for business. Travel websites around the world, including the website of the US State Department, advise travelers to drink only bottled water in Cuba. The State Department adds that diarrhea is common among travelers to Cuba, even among those who stay in the most luxurious hotels. Besides the effects on tourism, another consideration is the impact of poor drinking water on public health.

We found in our study that the means of coping with water concerns varied widely. Our findings suggest that the availability of water filters is more prevalent in neighborhoods with more recent construction which are also more frequented by foreigners. Whereas in working-class neighborhoods, the population relies more often on boiling their water to make it safe for drinking. There is sufficient evidence to suggest that Cuba gave preferential treatment to areas frequented by international tourists. Our respondents found bottled water more readily available in those areas than in other parts of Cuba and they perceived that tourist areas were kept cleaner than their own neighborhoods. An additional sign of stratification is the high cost of bottled water. At the time of our research, respondents estimated the cost of a half-liter bottle of water at between 2 and 5 CUCs or US $2 and $5, a significant portion of the average Cuban worker's salary. (The CUC is a convertible currency not easily available to Cubans.) The government managed pricing seems to be a contradiction in a country that claims aspirations of equality and justice. Tourism is likely to have an increasing impact on Cuba and its estimated 11.1 million people. The government has ambitious plans. By 2018, Cuba was attracting 4.8 million tourists a year, the equivalent of more than 40 percent of its population. The government says that by 2030 it hopes to see 10 million tourists a year. That would be nearly as many visitors as residents.[1]

Cuba is not alone with its shortcomings in drinking water. Dozens of countries struggle to provide water for their people. The World Health Organization says that at least 2 billion of the world's 7.5 billion people routinely drink contaminated water and are often sick. According to the World Health Organization's data, diseases like cholera, typhoid, and hepatitis that spread through water systems and sometimes crop up in Cuba, are far more widespread in other countries. But experts caution that the WHO data may not be entirely reliable. They say that many countries report misleading statistics on their water, disease rates, and other public health issues. "We can urge them to provide full and accurate data," said one former World Health Organization executive. "We try to persuade them that accurate reporting is good for everyone. But in the end, they are sovereign powers." Cuba's shortcomings with drinking water stand out because it has put itself forward as a paragon of public health. It is a leader in some medical specialties and sends teams of doctors on missions to treat people in developing countries.

We recognized, at the outset, that water was a critical global issue and an important issue for Cuba. The United Nations has made the provision of clean drinking water and household sanitation one of its Sustainable Development Goals. The Roman Catholic Church declared in its 2015 *Laudato si'* encyclical that clean, safe drinking water was indispensable for human dignity. Water is mostly regarded as a health and environmental issue. That is a departure point for us. But we also see water as a potentially powerful tool in international relations. We believe our work may be a useful guide to improving daily life in Cuba. And we believe that discussions between American and Cuban diplomats on water quality could be a starting point for talks that could eventually lead to better relations between the two countries.

We know of no study like ours that has attempted to obtain perceptions of water quality from recent travelers to Cuba. Instead of relying on government data or trying to conduct research in Cuba, we collected data in face-to-face interviews at Miami International Airport over two years. This amount of time was necessary to account for the effects of weather variation between the rainy and dry seasons. We chose to work at the airport partly because we believed it would enable us to simulate laboratory conditions insulated from political influence. Moreover, we know of no foreign research team that has managed to secure the necessary authorization to conduct independent field surveys and interviews on Cuban soil. Trying to assess the water quality and its public health impact by interviewing consumers provided us nonpartisan and up-to-date information from people who have personal, daily experience with conditions in Cuba. This strategy follows the same research logic as medical trials in which researchers interview patients rather than scientists.

We found that almost everyone we approached was willing to talk with us about their perceptions of water quality in Cuba. We were most successful with people who were waiting in Miami for Cuba flights to arrive. We were less successful when we tried to talk with those who had just gotten off flights and were eager to see friends and family in Miami. We created a set of questions and trained graduate and undergraduate students to conduct structured field interviews. The students interviewed 514 people and recorded the data in our computer system. We analyzed it and are now publishing the results. We took steps to safeguard the principles of confidentiality and noncoercive data collection from volunteers and our plan was approved by the University of Miami's Institutional Review Board (IRB, #201506914) for research on human subjects. We conducted our interviews in the language of choice of our subjects, and 95 percent chose Spanish. Our conclusions are based on empirical, verifiable evidence.

As is often the case in science, the motivation to jump-start our project came from one unpretentious but profound observation. We heard anecdotally that visitors to Cuba often fell ill after drinking tap water, using ice cubes made from tap water, and eating raw food washed in tap water. We heard of a journalist who checked himself into a hospital in Miami for treatment of gastrointestinal problems after returning from covering President Barack Obama's visit to Cuba in 2016. We found many tourism websites recommending that travelers to Cuba drink only bottled water. One website said: "Tap water is generally unsafe to drink but it is absolutely fine if boiled" (Damecacao.com). Despite all this evidence, the World Health Organization, working with data provided by the government of Cuba, issued a glowing report on drinking water on the island, stating that accessibility to improved water supplies was among the best in the world. By 2015, the agency said, 95 percent of Cubans had access to improved drinking water, up from 93 percent fifteen years earlier. The health agency said that improved drinking water in the country side was a little below the national average, but that in Havana and other cities it was slightly higher than the national average. Our survey showed limitations in the continuity of water available and widespread concern about the quality of the water that was delivered.

Literature Review

Studies of Cuban water tend to fall into four areas of concern. The first examines management of water resources and some of the reforms necessary to optimize water utilization. These studies focus on the formulation and implementation of policy priorities. They often neglect the sociopolitical ecology that contextualizes the efficacy of public policy domains. One valuable illustration of this approach is the examination of water resource management by Marta Rosa Muñoz Campos (2017). She asserted that local water disruptions in Cuba began to show signs of crisis in the 1990s and early 2000s, during the Special Period, or "Período Especial," in which the government took severe economic austerity measures following the cooling of relations with the former Soviet Union and the diminishing of Russian economic and military support. Water scarcity resulted from human-generated activity and geomorphic conditions, she said. Water scarcity persists, she said, despite the government's enactment of a National Environmental Strategy for 2007–2010 and other legislative directives. She said that Cuba should apply national priorities to local conditions. It needed to streamline policy implementation, decentralize state priorities, incorporate more local participation in decision-making, and address poor housing conditions (214). Her study suggested an economic paradox. If Cuba's tourist business keeps growing, demand for clean drinking water is likely to rise. That would put more pressure on the country's water systems. Wanting to protect its tourism income, the government might increase spending on its water system to the benefit of everyone.

The second line of research examines Cuba's capacity to manage demand for drinking water. Cuba has a relatively high average annual rainfall of about 132 centimeters, or 52 inches. But according to a study by Solo-Gabriele and Perez (2015), runoff to the sea is rapid, and Cuba has been unable to capture most of its rainfall for drinking water. Instead, the researchers said, 88 percent of Cuba's drinking water is pumped from the ground. Pumps often leak or otherwise malfunction, they said, and electricity to run the pumps is often interrupted. The pumps need surge suppressors and metering systems to work better: "The water supply system is unstable," Solo-Gabriele and Perez said (383).

These perspectives relate to policy making: namely, the degree of centralization, the need for a more deregulated policy regime, and the need to address the uneconomical, unreliable, and overburdened infrastructure. Others argue that the goals of policy implementation must be considered in a context of human ecology which raises the cost of state action to incalculable levels. In the social sciences, this debate is often referred to as the micro-macro dilemma, where one underlies the central role of agency while the other addresses structural constraints.

The third line of research deals with the concept that to understand the problems associated with clean water, one must consider climate change. In the spring of 2018, the Ministry of Science, Technology, and the Environment (CITMA) announced a national plan with eleven tasks designed to mitigate climate change in Cuba, according to a report on April 12 in *Granma*, the official government newspaper. Task 4 of the plan, called Tarea Vida (Life Task), addressed water and the need to upgrade infrastructure and maintenance. It rolled out new technologies to deal with fluctuations in rainfall in the wet and dry seasons and provided direction on other ways to improve efficiency in water management. Finally, there is the official position. According to government experts, progress has been slow on some of the country's water and environmental goals mainly because of the United States' long-running trade embargo on Cuba. Amnesty International acknowledged in a report in 2009 that the embargo had harmed Cuba, but it said that that did not relieve Cuba of responsibility to respect and protect the human rights and the basic needs of its people.

All these perspectives note deterioration in the delivery of clean drinking water in Cuba. The different perspectives identify different root causes, but all suggest that the problem is serious and requires immediate attention. None of the interpretations documents the impact on daily life in Cuba. Ours does.

Methodological Considerations

The robustness of evidence in science is as good as the reproducibility and transparency of the strategies employed to execute the research processes. We believe our work meets that test. We executed our project in three stages. First, we decided to do face-to-face interviews in Miami. We believed that working in Miami would enable us to create laboratory conditions insulated from political influence. We chose the survey method as a way of developing data for comparison with official statistics. With the survey method, we were able to get insights into how the availability and quality of water affected people's daily routines. Our team developed research questions and structure, secured initial funding, and obtained the approval of the University of Miami's Institutional Review Board, as mentioned earlier. From the start, we wanted to shed new light on an old problem and we wanted to provide an educational experience for students. Hence, we recruited University of Miami students who were bilingual in Spanish and English, trained them in field research and data collection techniques, and sent them out to conduct interviews. Working with students is both a challenge and a splendid opportunity. Coordinating their work in the field required patience and persistence. Their enthusiasm for the project and their drive to reach a meaningful sample size was gratifying to observe.

In the second phase of our work, we field tested our survey questions, amended them, and formulated a data collection strategy. The collection of data took over a year, longer than anticipated. But this process yielded a bonus: as we worked through the year, we were able to get data that reflected the different conditions in the rainy and dry seasons, broadening our perspective. Once we had 514 interviews in hand, we analyzed the data and created a number of academic reports and presentations.[2] Our approach provided a consistent pattern across a diverse population.

All but a few of our 514 interviews were conducted at Miami International Airport between 2015 and 2016. Airport authorities permitted us to conduct our interviews in a passenger terminal where relatives and friends waited for flights arriving from Cuba. We selected flights each week from a published list, using a quota to ensure that we did not oversample a particular destination. Our team interviewed people who were arriving from Cuba and people who had been in Cuba within the year. More than 75 percent of the people we interviewed said they lived in Miami and visited family in Cuba. Our sample was almost evenly divided between men and women. Most were between age thirty and sixty-four. The result was a diverse geographic sample from Pinar de

Rio, Isla de la Juventud, Havana, and Matanzas in the west, through the central provinces of Ciego de Ávila and Camagüey to Holguín, Santiago de Cuba and Guantánamo in the east. The vast majority of respondents (46 percent) lived in or had visited the province of La Habana (see Pumar et al. 2017 for details). In addition, two of our team members visited Cuba during our research, one to conduct a month-long seminar, the other for two days for family reasons. They made personal observations, took photographs and talked with many Cubans in Havana and other parts of Cuba observing up-close the daily struggle of Cuban families to get safe drinking water. Their work transformed our project methodology into a mixed method strategy.

We learned some lessons that may be of value to others. First, sending students to conduct interviews at the airport was time-consuming. One faculty member supervised the students, some of whom became leaders, coordinating the work of others. The students wore name tags identifying them as University of Miami students. We think that helped put our survey subjects at ease. We had some turnover among our student researchers and we spent time training newcomers. Academic calendars and class assignments affected the availability of student researchers. We saved time and effort by storing our data on a digital platform.

One striking discovery in our research was an apparent wariness among some of the people we tried to interview that Cuban government surveillance might extend even to Miami. Despite our assurances that our work was confidential, some people refused to participate in our study, saying that they feared that the government of Cuba might retaliate by refusing to issue them visas for future travel or that it might take other harmful actions.

Each interviewer administered the survey verbally and marked the survey by hand on paper. The interviewer entered data into the online cloud-based database (SurveyMonkey). The data were analyzed as they were collected, using the default tools of the database system. The default tools enabled statistical analyses and various forms of graphic displays. They also enabled text analysis of open-ended responses. Once all data were in hand, they were downloaded into a CSV file and analyzed with Excel. It became apparent that the data needed to be cleaned up. For example, people used several synonyms for Havana: La Habana, Centro Habana, and La Habana Vieja. We grouped the cities and towns by province. In many cases people gave a hometown, but did not say which province it was in. We used chi-square analysis to analyze statistical differences, assuming a 95 percent or higher degree of confidence.

Principal Findings and Implications

We gathered data about sources, access, and health effects of water consumption. We found that bottled water was widely available,[3] but it was too expensive for most Cubans. We found a wide range of prices for a liter of bottled water, but the average cost was 1.2 CUCs; the median cost was 1 CUC, which is equal to US $1. To put the price in perspective, 1 CUC is about 4.5 percent of the monthly salary of an average worker in Cuba. To buy just ten one-liter bottles of water, an average worker would have to spent 45 percent or more of his or her monthly pay. Our respondents told us that a liter of water was sometime available for as little as 0.05 CUC and as high as 4 CUC depending on where the water was purchased.[4] Our respondents said they rarely drank bottled water. Sometimes they drank water directly from the tap. Perhaps one can attribute this risk taking to normal human behavior. But it could be that they thought that bottled water was just not affordable.

Nearly half of our respondents said they had running water for no more than a few hours a day. Most said they stored water in household cisterns. About half of the respondents said the quality of their drinking water was poor, and that they had seen no improvement over the course of a year. Twenty-three percent said the quality of their water had gotten worse; 12 percent had seen an improvement.

According to the World Health Organization, much of the world struggles with unclean drinking water. They have no choice. Clean drinking water is just not available. The result is that more than 840,000 people die every year of diarrhea, more than 360,000 of them children younger than five years old.

Cuba is not among the countries with the most severe health problems related to water. But the water is sufficiently problematic in Cuba that travelers are routinely warned not to drink water from the tap. People living in Cuba are advised to boil their water to avoid illness. Because of the daily disruptions of the water supply in parts of Havana and the rest of Cuba, families store water in cisterns. Water stored in that way, the World Health Organization says, is easily contaminated through the vessel itself and by dipping unsterilized utensils in the cisterns.

Hepatitis A, typhoid, polio, and cholera are some of the diseases that spread through drinking water. Cholera is an acute diarrheal disease that dehydrates and kills. It can easily be treated with antibiotics and rehydration. But too often, people die of cholera. Independent researchers say that cholera is widely underreported. Governments consider the disease stigmatizing. The researchers estimate that nearly one hundred thousand people around the world die from cholera every year.

Cholera is most prevalent in Africa and parts of Asia, the World Health Organization says, but it has been persistent in Haiti in recent years and, to a much lesser extent, in the Dominican Republic. The two countries share the island of Hispaniola, just eighty kilometers (fifty miles) from Cuba across the channel known as the Windward Passage. In 2017, Haiti reported 13,681 cases of cholera and 159 deaths, according to the Pan American Health Organization, a unit of the World Health Organization. The Dominican Republic reported that 122 people came down with cholera in 2017 and four died. Mexico reported one case of cholera in mid-2018. A few cases have been reported in Ecuador in recent years.

The latest reports of cholera in Cuba came in 2015, according to the Pan American Health Organization. That year, the organization said, Cuba reported 65 cases of cholera, but no deaths. Cuba's worst experience with cholera in recent times was in 2012 when it reported 417 cases and three deaths. It reported 181 cases in 2013 and 76 in 2014; no deaths in those years.[5] In our survey, 75 people, or 16.8 percent of respondents, reported hearing of someone in Cuba who had contracted cholera.

Our respondents volunteered that they heard of cases in Cuba of dengue and Zika, two diseases borne by mosquitos that breed in stagnant water. One respondent stated there had been outbreaks of cholera and dengue in the respondent's hometown. The respondent said so many people fell ill that, at one point, extra medical teams were sent to the town to set up temporary hospitals. Reporting about a recent visit to Cardenas, in the province of Matanzas, the informant reports how the shortage of qualified medical personnel and even medicine generated widespread frustrations and complaints about the containment strategies pursued by local officials.

By far most illnesses that respondents reported were gastrointestinal, often accompanied by diarrhea. The respondents said they were sick for up to a few days. We know from World Health Organization findings around the world that sicknesses from waterborne diseases are most likely harmful to Cuba's economy. The illnesses keep people from work and school and increase health-care costs. Cleaning up Cuba's water and reducing illnesses related to contaminated water would be good for Cuba and good for its people, the World Health Organization suggests. It has been campaigning for clean water around the world.

In our Cuba survey, 30 percent of the respondents said they had lost time at work; 26 percent said they had gone to a doctor or nurse and 30 percent said they had been treated in a hospital. Another 30 percent said they had heard of more than one instance of another person getting sick after drinking water. All this is evidence of social disruption, drains on productivity and added costs for running health-care facilities.

We asked respondents what they had observed about the condition of the water in Cuba's bays, rivers, lakes, and beaches. Thirty-three percent recalled seeing garbage, sewage, and other pollution in the rivers; 25 percent reported similar pollution in bays; 11 percent said they had seen pollution in lakes and on beaches. Respondents said they mainly saw garbage and sewage.[6] Thirty-six percent said they smelled foul odors coming from rivers, lakes, bays, and beaches. Table 1 compares pollution levels since the last time the

TABLE 1. A comparison of recreational water quality

	Bays	Rivers	Lakes	Beaches	Respondents
Clean	22.4%	27.9%	16.4%	83.1%	201
	(45)	(56)	(33)	167	
Dirty	56.7%	63.8%	49.6%	53.5%	127
	(72)	(81)	(63)	(58)	
Very dirty	63.6%	52.7%	47.3%	7.3%	55
	(35)	(29)	(26)	(4)	
Do not remember	54.3%	54.3%	68.6%	54.3%	35
	(19)	(19)	(24)	(19)	

respondent had been to Cuba and stratifies the degree of contamination of different waterways.

In responses to open-ended questions, we found anecdotal evidence suggesting that the government maintained places frequented by tourists better than those frequented by average Cubans. A respondent from Miami said that on one visit he spent most of his time in tourist areas and found them cleaner than residential neighborhoods. Another recalled seeing beaches in Playa del Este, a working-class part of Havana, that were "muy sucia," or "very dirty." Yet another observed that tourist hotel beaches were clean while city beaches were dirty: "Las playas de los hotels estaban limpias, las de la ciudad sucias."

Respondents said Cuba's cleanest water was along its beaches. At least half of respondents rated Cuba's freshwater lakes and rivers as dirty or very dirty. The lakes, they said, were in the worst condition. Respondents reported perceived high levels of contamination in Cuba's bays, but they thought that was somewhat understandable considering heavy traffic in commercial shipping in a country heavily dependent on imports. Increased tourism would likely increase pollution of the island's waters, creating a need for more effective regulation of shipping and greater spending for environmental cleanup.

One of the questions in our survey asked visitors who travel to the island frequently to reflect on any changes in water quality. Respondents reported worsening conditions in Cuba's lakes and rivers and improvement along the beaches. They said Cuba's rivers increasingly had become contaminated with garbage and trash. This comparison suggests that contamination of the rivers and lakes is not a recent problem but something that has been building for years. The data in Tables 1 and 2 is consistent with the pattern of careless human activity—and a failure of governmental response–reported earlier in the paper. The worsening trend raises questions about public policy priorities. The rising levels of contamination may seem surprising in a country with

TABLE 2. Comparison of levels of pollution since last visit

	Bays	Rivers	Lakes	Beaches	Respondents
Was cleaner	23.2%	20.3%	10.9%	79.0%	138
	(32)	(28)	(15)	(109)	
Was dirtier	56.1%	69.3%	47.4%	47.4%	114
	(64)	(79)	(54)	(54)	
Smelled better	66.7%	33.3%	44.4%	16.7%	18
	(12)	(6)	(8)	(3)	
Smelled worse	66.7%	61.5%	71.8%	15.4%	39
	(26)	(24)	(28)	(6)	
The water had less garbage	65.2%	34.8%	30.4%	21.7%	23
	(15)	(8)	(7)	(5)	
The water has more garbage	66.7%	68.3%	61.7%	45.0%	60
	(40)	(41)	(37)	(27)	
I do not remember	66.7%	75.0%	77.1%	72.9%	48
	(32)	(36)	(37)	(35)	

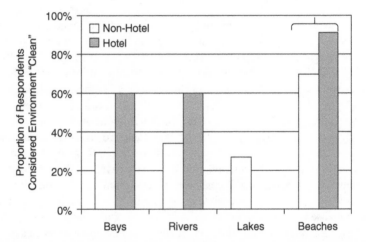

FIGURE 1. Comparison of opinions of those who stayed in hotels versus with families on cleanliness of bays, rivers, lakes and beaches. Dark columns represent respondents who stayed in hotels.

sophisticated public mobilization mechanisms that link the central government with block-by-block neighborhood organizations.

To distinguish between travelers who went to Cuba for family visits and those who went for tourism, we stratified our survey by place of stay: hotel or family home (Figure 1). As expected, drinking water quality was reported to be better in hotels. The perceived improvement in water quality was evident for bays, rivers, and beaches. Among all of the ambient water categories, only the

TABLE 3. Responses to, "Which options could be
beneficial to improve the quality of water."

	Number	*Percentage*
Renovate infrastructure	322	72%
Improve purification systems	259	58%
Renovate water tanks	254	57%
Create community repository tanks	120	27%
Install more municipal water fountains	102	23%
Install more water fountains in buildings	101	22%
Instruction on water quality	84	19%
Instruction on water purification	78	17%
Install more wells	72	16%
Capture and clean more rain water	63	14%

category of beaches was statistically significant (greater than 99% confidence, with 1 degree of freedom) with those staying at a hotel reporting a higher rate of "clean" water quality (91 percent) compared to those not staying at a hotel (70 percent). Seventy-six percent of respondents who stayed in a hotel answered the question for beaches. Fewer (less than 35 percent) answered the question for the other ambient water categories

We asked respondents their opinions on what the government should focus on to improve the quality and availability of drinking water. A majority answered: infrastructure, purification systems and water tanks (Table 3). None of our respondents was an expert in water, engineering, or health care. But all were well acquainted with the rhythms of daily life in Cuba. More than half said improvements in five kinds of infrastructure would be most helpful: water treatment plants, water transmission lines, purification systems, water storage tanks, and aqueducts. About 18 percent said Cubans needed more information on inexpensive ways to make water safe for drinking and how to keep it safe. Besides considering education's role in inculcating civic and social solidarity, perhaps the persistent contamination problem we witnessed in the barrios may be another sign of popular despair and the burdensome transaction cost associated with sanitation.

We asked about mitigation. Again, our respondents are not water experts, but they reported on experiences that may be helpful in improving water quality and availability in Cuba. Respondents said they often experienced a loss of water pressure in their homes. Sometimes there was no water at all, sometimes just a trickle. Based on answers to several of our questions on the availability of water, we extrapolated that water flowed continuously through municipal water lines for perhaps 13 percent of all Cubans. Maintaining steady water pressure in distribution lines is important. When the pressure slackens and when there is no water flowing, bacteria and other foreign material can enter water distribution lines. The respondents associate poor water quality with the deterioration and lack of consistent maintenance of water treatment plants, insufficient plant capacity, and the presence of pollutants in the water. After one visits Cuba, it is relatively easy to realize that this popular assessment is often the subject of casual conversation in informal networks in the streets.

The vast majority of respondents believed that the cause of poor water quality was a lack of maintenance of Cuba's aqueducts (Figure 2). Here is a sampling of responses to questions on water quality, paraphrased by our interviewers:

- Water is not continuous and loses pressure. This makes it necessary to boil water. The treatment the water receives is complete—mechanical, physical, chemical, and biological. But once pressure falls in the pipes, the water becomes contaminated. One respondent said his family had a 1,000-gallon cistern or storage tank in their home that enabled them to have water all the time. Some Havana residents get running water every other day. Some areas receive no piped water at all; these areas receive water by tanker trucks called pipas.
- The sewage system, reservoirs, and cisterns are old and have not received sufficient maintenance or repairs.
- Water drips from the shower and there is little or no water pressure. The water situation is worse during the dry season.
- Pipes are always broken and potable water gets contaminated with waste water. Sometimes people don't have water for three or four days.

Figure 2 shows a breakdown of responses to the question of what the government should focus on to improve the quality and availability of drinking water. Forty-four percent of respondents said they thought Cubans would be willing to buy water purification equipment. Another 11 percent said they would buy the equipment but that they needed the money for other things. There is clearly market demand for water purification equipment. A little more than 79 percent of the respondents said the household device they most wanted was a water purifying filter. Some respondents told us that water filters made in Korea were already being sold in Cuba. But our survey suggests that demand far exceeds supply, and that many Cubans consider the cost of household water filters beyond their means. One respondent told an interviewer that he would like to have bought a water filter. "If I had the money," he said, he would have: "Si tuviera dinero yo lo haría." Similar answers came from 51 percent of our respondents.

Participant Demographics

Considerations regarding the demographic composition and frequency of visits of our participants are relevant for at least one of the implications of our findings, the awareness of the quality of water. We asked respondents for in-

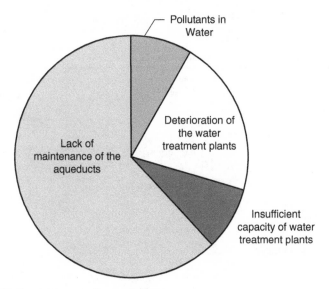

FIGURE 2. Perceived causes of contamination.

formation about themselves, the purpose of their visit to Cuba, and where they spent time. Their responses enabled us to compare water usage around the country. The overwhelming majority of respondents traveled to Cuba for vacations and to visit their families. They were frequent travelers between Miami and Cuba. At least half said they made the trip at least once or twice a year. The overwhelming majority of people visiting Cuba (about 85 percent) said they stayed with family. This finding was important because we believe it provided an accurate glimpse of daily life in Cuba.

Our respondents were evenly split in terms of gender. In terms of place of birth 93 percent reported being born in Cuba. Seven of ten were residents of the United States; 20 percent lived permanently in Cuba. Of those who resided in the United States, the overwhelming majority (76 percent) came from greater Miami. Close to half (44 percent) were between thirty and forty-nine years old; 35 percent were age fifty to sixty-four. More than half (61 percent) identified as Cuban; 35 percent regarded themselves as Cuban American (Table 4). The self-affiliation of ethnic identity is remarkable in that most respondents said they lived permanently in the United States, a sign perhaps of intergenerational segmented assimilation (Portes and Zhou 1993). The average participant in our study was thirty to forty-nine years old, identified as a Cuban man or woman from Miami, and described the United States as home. These people said they typically stayed in Cuba with family. The bulk of our respondents migrated from Cuba after the 1980s, confirming that recent immigrants tend to visit

TABLE 4. Demographics Summary

Demographics (total responses)	Response	Proportion
Gender (467)	Male	49.7%
	Female	50.3%
Age (467)	18–29	11.3%
	30–49	43.5%
	50–64	34.9%
	65+	10.3%
Identity (468)	Cuban	60.9%
	Cuban American	34.8%
	Other	4.3%
Country of birth (468)	Cuba	93.4%
	Other	6.6%
Permanent residence (468)	Cuba	9.6%
	Miami	76.7%
	Cuba and Miami	0.4%
	US but not Miami	12.0%
	Outside US and Cuba	1.3%
Country considered home (456)	Cuba	20.2%
	US	70.6%
	Other	9.2%
Residence during Cuba visit (457)	Family member's house or apartment	91.2%
	Rented apartment from a resident	1.5%
	In a hotel	6.3%
	Other	0.9%
Country visiting (471)	Cuba	84.7%
	US	10.0%
	Transition from Cuba to US to live	5.3%

Cuba more frequently than those who arrived in the states during the 1960s and early 1970s, or what Pedraza (1998) considers the first and second wave of Cuban immigrants to the United States.

Our survey demonstrates a wide gap between data on water quality published by the government of Cuba and the accounts of people with firsthand experience in Cuba. The government's data, published by the World Health Organization along with data provided by the governments of other countries, asserts accessibility of improved water supplies in Cuba is among the highest in the world.

Most of the 514 respondents who live in Cuba or had visited the island within the year told us that municipal water is often available in homes for a few hours a day. When it arrives, they say, it is under low pressure. The result can be contamination of the water. Respondents said they often see garbage and sewage in the country's lakes, bays, and rivers and along the beaches. A visitor who participated in our study had this to say about how the group she was traveling with approached drinking water: "no one in the group drank water from the tap."

Our study suggests that Cuba needs significant investment in infrastructure to consistently provide clean drinking water for its 11.1 million people. The World Health Organization and independent water experts say that investing in safe, clean drinking water leads to improvements in public health and economic benefits. Unclean water causes sickness and sickness leads to lost days at school and at work. Perhaps less tangible but no less meaningful, shortcomings in the quality and availability of water can raise questions for Cubans about the competence of their government. For the first time in sixty years, a president with no family connections to Fidel Castro, the revolutionary founder of modern Cuba, is presiding over the government. As the new president, Miguel Díaz-Canel, has established himself, he has been talking about changes in Cuba. In a 2018 interview with *El País*, the Spanish daily newspaper, he said he was advocating an update of the country's economic and social model—"actualizer el modelo económico y social." He did not go into detail. But this seemed a hopeful development. One way to start the process might be to pledge to truly make Cuba's drinking water and its waterways among the cleanest and healthiest in the world.

We are concerned that if the projected number of tourists materializes, it will further strain Cuba's drinking water system. Before the travel restrictions instituted recently, the number of tourists visiting Cuba annually rose to 4.8 million in 2018, a 50 percent increase from the 3.1 million visitors in 2015. The government says that over the next twenty years, it hopes to increase annual tourist visits to 10 million. That is nearly as many people as now live on the island. The World Travel and Tourism Council, an independent industry group, projected in a report in 2017 that Cuba's revenues from tourism would soon account for 5 percent of gross domestic product. Tourism revenues were 3 percent of Cuba's gross domestic product at the time. The council said it expected investment in tourism to rise to 26 percent of all industrial investment in the next few years (World Travel and Tourism Council 2017). Our study represents an initial response to the work of a scholar in Cuba who has been calling for more decentralization and frequent consultations with local community leaders.[7]

We are puzzled that Cuba has not mobilized forces to deal more effectively with water and other environmental issues, given that it has been so successful in rallying support for so many policy goals. We wonder whether water issues might at some point further galvanize resentment toward the government. It may be worth noting the strong intellectual tradition among political theorists that considers public demonstrations of caring by leaders to be not just a moral obligation but also an opportunity to build public trust. In any society, perceptions of inaction or indifference on the part of the government can easily convert into contagious anomie threatening the state. This is particularly so in regard to human ecology which impinges on daily life. This is one of the conclusions anticipated by Daniel Engster (2007) in his comprehensive treatment of care theory and justice. Already signs of public lassitude are visible in working-class neighborhoods in Havana and in other parts of Cuba.

Perhaps one of the most striking of our findings, at the time we collected our data, was the prespective that the government has not prioritized infrastructure projects to guarantee the safety of Cuba's drinking water. The public health issue of unsafe drinking water only compounds other societal problems like the deterioration of government services and the failure to maintain the country's infrastructure. Anyone who ventures into towns and neighborhoods beyond the paths of tourists sees once elegant buildings practically in ruins. Yet the crumbling buildings are often shared by several families. Visitors see piles of uncollected household garbage on the streets and streets that become shallow rivers after storms. And they see that classes have formed along economic lines. Those at the top are receiving remittances from relatives living in the United States and other countries. Others struggle with meager incomes from work in the small private sector as barbers and mechanics or selling fruit, vegetables, and used clothing in informal markets.

As we have immersed ourselves in water issues in Cuba we have come to think that water could be an excellent subject to bring American and Cuban diplomats together. It is not clear what would enable the United States and Cuba to begin talks on the major issues that separate them. But history has demonstrated that low-level talks on issues like water and border controls have sometimes led to a gradual warming of relationships and movement toward discussions on broader political matters. Water is regarded by many—including the United Nations—as a nonpartisan, humanitarian subject. Perhaps water in Cuba might become a vehicle for reenergizing Cuba's bilateral relations with the United States. President Díaz-Canel acknowledged in his interview with *El País* that relations between Cuba and the United States were in retreat— "retroceso." The reason, he said, from Cuba's perspective, is a sense that the United States had been behaving disrespectfully toward Cuba. That might not change anytime soon. The Trump administration was aggressive toward even some of the United States' best friends.

That doesn't mean that low-level talks on water could not get started. They could begin from a simple base of human need. They could be restricted to technical public health issues and commercial issues related to public health. At the moment, Cuba does not acknowledge that its drinking water and the water in its bays, lakes and rivers and along its shorelines need improvement. Talks would probably have a better chance of starting if neither party had to make concessions. Perhaps a third party—Colombia or Chile or another country in Latin America—might suggest to both sides an opening round to talks on small-scale trade issues with a humanitarian foundation.

Household water filters might offer an inroad. Water filters are widely used around the world in homes with excellent water and in homes with the worst of water. Talking about making water filters available to Cubans would not require any discussion of the overall condition of Cuba's water. Water filters are universally accepted as good for health. Manufacturers and distributors of water filters in the United States would benefit from an opening of the Cuba market. And millions of Cubans would benefit. Successful discussions on water filters could move to household water cisterns and perhaps training by American companies for Cuban families—in person and with videos—on how to treat drinking water and household waste. A next step might be discussions on low-cost ways to make Cuba's water treatment plants more effective. Do they have enough chemicals? Have they tried filtration processes? Does the water distribution system have backup power in case of outages? Eventually, the talks might deal with projects to build new water treatment plants, replace corroded water transmission lines, and extend public water and sewage service throughout the island.

Another possibility for getting talks started might be an initiative from an American company—or even a nongovernmental organization—that specializes in water treatment. One of them might begin exploring ways to begin a conversation. A third country might provide an introduction for a company or a nongovernmental organization to one of Cuba's ambassadors around the world. But engagement might be possible if somehow discussions got underway and the US administration were able to see a business opportunity for American companies that would not undermine the decades-old trade embargo. Any foothold in the slippery terrain between the two countries could develop into a warming in the relationship that could lead to big changes.

The severity of the recent migration crisis has pushed the Biden Administration to restart diplomatic conversations with Cuba. This might be a moment when water could play a role. A first step could be for Cuba and the United States to jointly provide water filters for everyone in the country. It could be presented as a routine measure in keeping with best practices by health experts around the world. It would be a small accomplishment that could warm the atmosphere and lead to progress on more difficult matters.

The incremental approach with an extremely mild initiation is likely to cause little, if any, controversy in the Cuban exile community. Many Cubans living outside Cuba know very well that relatives on the island often struggle to get clean water or any water at all. The humanitarian approach would almost certainly resonate with them. Scholars of neo-functionalist international relations have long made this argument. Ernest Haas (1980, 361), the eminent

Berkeley scholar, wrote about the process of rebuilding relations between adversarial states: "Institutional collaboration can be explored in terms of the interactions of changing knowledge and changing social goals," he said. "It seems axiomatic that parties in conflict will, under conditions of changing the understanding of their desire and of their constraints under which they must act, seek to define an area for joint gains. The definition of joint gains must be based on the goals of the actors on the calculations ('knowledge') that influence the choice of goals."

NOTES

1. For illustrations of our research process, see Newman (2009), Babbie (2016), and Lune, Pumar, and Koppel (2010). For an earlier publication showing our preliminary findings, see Pumar, Solo-Gabriele, and Treaster (2017).

2. Only 21 percent of those interviewed stated they encountered difficulties finding bottle water. Our team member who visited La Habana for an extended period of time in October 2017 found that bottle water was widely available around tourist areas of the city but not so much in other marginalized neighborhoods that are home to average working families. Moreover, he was never offered pure tap water without some sort of treatment during his visit.

3. Someone on our research team paid 3 CUC for a half-liter bottle of water at the Hotel Nacional in the fall 2017.

4. With regard to the inconsistency of government reporting, the Global Health Observatory country report for Cuba from 2002 to 2015 reported only six pieces of data for four health indicators during those years. One of the data sets, the percentage of children suspected of pneumonia taken to a health-care provider, reports data only for 2014. Data for cholera in Cuba was left blank.

5. Walking through the city of Havana, the amount of garbage accumulated at street corners and in public parks is very noticeable, with the exception of areas most frequented by tourists. Many citizens interviewed complained that garbage was not being picked up regularly.

6. See the essay by Marta Rosa Muñoz Campos (2017), a proponent of this recommendation.

7. Our team has exposed this point in more detail in an unpublished paper we presented at the 11th Conference on Cuba and Cuban-American Studies sponsored by Florida International University Cuban Research Institute. See Pumar, Solo-Gabriele, and Treaster (2017).

BIBLIOGRAPHY

Amnesty International. 2009. *The US Embargo against Cuba. It's Impact on Economics and Social Rights.* London: Amnesty International.

Babbie, Earl R. 2016. "The Practice of Social Research." Damecacao.com, http://damecacao.com/cuban-cocktails-dont-drink-water/#Water_Water_Quality.

Engster, Daniel. 2007. *The Heart of Justice: Care Ethics and Political Theory.* New York: Oxford University Press.

Haas, Ernest. 1980. "Why Collaborate? Issue-Linkages and International Regimes. *World Politics* 33: 357–405.

Lune, Howard, Enrique S. Pumar, and Ross Koppel, eds. 2010. *Perspectives in Social Research Methods and Analysis.* Thousand Oaks, CA: Sage.

Muñoz Campos, Marta Rosa. 2017. "Environmental Policy and Management of Water Resources:

Challenges and Perspectives." In *Social Policy and Decentralization in Cuba*, edited by Jorge Domínguez, María del Carmen Zabala Argüelles, Mayra Espira Prieto, and Lorena G. Barbería, 199–220. Cambridge, MA: Harvard University Press.

Newman, Lawrence. 2009. *Social Research Methods: Qualitative and Quantitative Approaches.* 7th ed. New York: Pearson.

Pedraza, Silvia. 1998. "Cuba's Revolution and Exodus." *Journal of the International Institute* 5: https://quod.lib.umich.edu/j/jii/4750978.0005.204?view=text;rgn=main.

Portes, Alejandro, and Min Zhou. 1993. "The Second Generation. Segmented Assimilation and its Variants." *Annals of the American Academy of Political and Social Sciences* 530: 74–96.

Pumar, Enrique S., Helena Solo-Gabriele, and Joseph B. Treaster. 2017. "Drinking Water in Cuba and United States–Cuba Relations: A Neo-Functional Approach." *Cuba in Transition* 27: 1191–1207.

Solo-Gabriele, Helena, and Armando I. Perez. 2008. "Cuba's Water and Wastewater Sectors: Environmental Literature, Institutions, and Economic Issues and Future Work." *Cuba in Transition* 18: 378–389.

World Travel and Tourism Council. 2017. *Travel & Tourism Economic Impact 2017 Cuba.* London: World Travel and Tourism Council.

RESEARCH NOTE

AARON COY MOULTON

Looking Past the Colossus: The Archivo Central del Ministerio de Relaciones Exteriores in Havana and Cuban Foreign Relations during the Cold War

ABSTRACT

This article offers a brief historiographical overview of how the Archivo Central del Ministerio de Relaciones Exteriores (ACMINREX) in Havana has expanded the scholarship of Cuban foreign relations during the Cold War. Beginning with foundational works from John Kirk and Piero Gleijeses, ACMINREX materials were incorporated into multiarchival methodologies exploring Cuban-Canadian and Cuban-African interactions before illuminating inter-American relations in the 1940s and 1950s. Now, the archive's collections appear in multiple works in global Cold War studies examining Cuba's impact. This article concludes with suggestions on the ACMINREX's value for scholars considering further research into Cuban and inter-American foreign relations.

RESUMEN

Este artículo proviene una breve reseña historiográfica sobre cómo el Archivo Central del Ministerio de Relaciones Exteriores (ACMINREX) en la Habana ha ampliado la literatura sobre las relaciones cubanas durante la guerra fría. Empezar con las obras fundamentales de John Kirk y Piero Gleijeses, se incorporaron los materiales del ACMINREX con las metodologías multiarchivas sobre las interacciones cubano-canadienses y cubano-africanos antes de iluminar las relaciones interamericanas de los 1940s y 1950s. En este momento, los colecciones del ACMINREX están fortaleciendo varios trabajos de los estudios de la guerra fría global sobre el impacto cubano. El artículo entonces les ofrece sugerencias sobre el valor del ACMINREX a los interesados en investigar las relaciones exteriores cubanas e interamericanas.

In 1958, Alberto Garcia Navarro was a bit busy as Cuban dictator Fulgencio Batista's ambassador in San José. Pressured by ex-president José Figueres, the Costa Rican government had asked for the removal of Garcia Navarro's military attaché, leaving most consular affairs in the ambassador's hands. It thus fell upon him alone to request visas sending nineteen Cuban exiles out of Costa Rica. Sixteen were supposed to head to what had long been a reliable destination for Batista's opponents, Mexico. That country's chargé d'affaires, though, had grown frustrated with the number of Cubans dumped into the country. He revoked the requests for asylum and declared, "Mexico was no longer willing to receive the human waste that Cuba was throwing out," ominously warning that "the era of [Cuban] asylum in Mexico was coming to an end."[1] All this went far beyond Mexico. Regardless of their current destinations, Cuban exiles were heading to various Caribbean Basin countries, where they would undoubtedly continue networking with various anti-Batista dissidents and Fidel Castro's supporters, so the deportations out of Costa Rica were nothing more than temporary. In fact, Auténtico Manuel Antonio de Varona, Ortodoxo Raúl Chibás, and Castro's sister Juanita all had recently come through to talk with Figueres before heading to Caracas to meet up with Venezuelan president Rómulo Betancourt. Not only were the three about to get at least $10,000 for various anti-Batista plots; others, including Dominican Miguel Ángel Ramírez and Costa Ricans Marcial Aguiluz and Frank Marshall, were supporting conspiracies of their own targeting dictators in Nicaragua and the Dominican Republic.[2] Despite the intrigue and conflicts that spanned the Caribbean Basin detailed in this and other files in the Archivo Central del Ministerio de Relaciones Exteriores in Havana, much of the literature on the Cuban Revolution has kept its eye on issues between Castro and the United States.

The historiography of foreign relations within the Western Hemisphere, called US–Latin American relations by some and inter-American foreign relations by others, has always been a multiarchival one, as Stephen Rabe emphasized in 1989 and again in 2014.[3] Authors of foundational works on US military interventions and economic imperialism from the 1800s into the early 1900s took advantage of myriad resources to highlight both US policies and Latin American reactions.[4] Of course, their expertise in incorporating viewpoints from throughout the Western Hemisphere stood in stark contrast to the available literature on inter-American relations during the international Cold War. Facing Latin American military regimes whose officials, in and out of power, suppressed and even destroyed the documentary record, historians understandably relied heavily on sources slowly making their way through the bureaucracy of the US government's declassification apparatus.[5] Still, scholars adeptly maneuvered to overcome some of these archival challenges by using innovative methods, ranging from oral interviews on the 1965 US military intervention in the Dominican Republic to personal collections on US-sponsored economic development programs to sporadic files on the Argentine military junta's hand in Central America.[6] Thanks to the gradual opening of Latin America–based collections, examinations of the Brazilian military regime, Mexico's then-dominant political party, and Guatemala's dirty war are no longer as reliant on US officials' perspectives. Instead, they are creating a wider vision, more in line with, for example, scholarship of Mexican foreign relations before the 1940s.[7] Nevertheless, in the late 1990s, some experts of Latin American history worried that the long-standing focus on US-based understandings of the Cold War had kept the region on the margins and overlooked local stakes and resulting impacts.[8] New methodologies and collections could hopefully help decenter the history of American foreign relations during the Cold War and refine how scholars understood its ramifications, especially in light of how many people in the Western Hemisphere are still dealing with the repercussions of those years.

In many ways, the study of Cuban foreign relations under Fidel Castro remains caught in this dilemma, perfectly encapsulated in the seemingly never-ending US-imposed embargo on the island and its people that dates back to an era increasingly marbleized. On the one hand, the declassification process in the United States continues to overcome significant hurdles, most recently epitomized in the National Security Archive's efforts to obtain a full account of the Central Intelligence Agency's internal history of the Bay of Pigs debacle.[9] On the other hand, many depositories' persisting refusal to grant Cubans access to even decades-old materials is one of the embargo's aggravating reminders. Meanwhile, research within Cuba faces a unique set of challenges, including acquiring the appropriate visa, identifying the location of materials, and securing the correct permissions to commence any such investigation. Historians have repeatedly navigated through many of these barriers and produced phenomenal works on gender, race, medicine, labor, and more.[10] Such works, though, often center on events within the island, leaving calls for a greater view of Cuban foreign relations in the last half of the twentieth century unanswered.

This article uses Cuba's official foreign relations archive, the Archivo Central del Ministerio de Relaciones Exteriores, or ACMINREX, to highlight some recent successes and lingering difficulties in pursuing this vital need to expand Cuban foreign relations during the Cold War. Located in the Vedado district in Havana, the archive was once located on the coast, until the building fell into the Caribbean Sea. Archivists rescued and restored as many documents as possible—water marks and damage are still visible on many files—and its new building is now located down the road from the Ministerio itself. Though lacking any grand index associated with more familiar depositories, the ACMINREX, thanks to its staff's hospitality, offers some invaluable materials that are already shaping how scholars are reexamining Cuban foreign relations and the Caribbean Basin's international history. In the midst of warnings from Cold War studies experts against any inadvertent overreliance or fetishization of "new" sources, those who have utilized these collections have had to grapple with the archive's limitations while bringing in fresh perspectives and alternative approaches to more familiar collections elsewhere.[11] As a result, examining how ACMINREX collections have contributed to new perspectives of inter-American relations—whether delving into the complexities of Caribbean history before 1959 or exploring the far reach of the Cuban Revolution during the international Cold War—can help scholars, students, and aficionados debating their own methodologies who might like to tap into an overlooked yet interesting depository.

Early Access: On Canada and Africa

Initially, even as the two earliest works took the Cuban Revolution to not just Canada but also Africa, many assumed that only a few privileged scholars could access the ACMINREX's supposedly guarded collections. One of the first appearances of its materials in the scholarly literature certainly aided in magnifying Cuban foreign relations by looking past the United States and gazing upon another North American country. Canada, given the reliance on newspapers and speeches as source material, had long rested on the periphery of more formal examinations of Cuban foreign relations, despite its enduring, though sometimes tumultuous relationship, which originates from its being the only other country in the Western Hemisphere besides Mexico to maintain diplomatic relations with Cuba once the Organization of American States suspended Castro's government. In this vacuum, John M. Kirk soon emerged as the leading authority on Canadian-Cuban bilateral relations. In "Unraveling the Paradox: The Canadian Position on Cuba," Kirk juxtaposes ACMINREX files with those from Canada's Department of External Affairs to illuminate the "examples of cultural faux pas, misunderstandings, and communication that— often despite the best of intentions—simply went awry."[12] Even while digging into the consistencies and contradictions that popped up in Cuban-Canadian foreign relations, he notes the looming influence of the US government in these bilateral affairs, including disagreements over the embargo, humanitarian assistance, and more. As a result of his pairing ACMINREX and Canadian files, Kirk is able to better evaluate Cuban-Canadian relations within a hemispheric context. Of course, much of this success was due to his internationalist history as a translator for prominent Canadian officials and relationships with influential Cuban officials, valuable assets other scholars would attempt to mimic while pursuing their own investigations.

Simultaneously, Piero Gleijeses aimed to outline how Cuba's international reach went far beyond US- or even inter-American relations. He lobbied officials in Havana for access to materials related to Cuban adventurism in Africa from the 1960s into the 1970s. Since "no scholar or writer had had access to the Cuban archives for the post-1959 period" related to such extrahemispheric affairs, it took a couple years and the mediation of revolutionary and leading official Jorge Risquet to clear the path. Years of research including fourteen one-month visits into collections from the ACMINREX alongside the Instituto de Historia de Cuba, the Comité Central del Partido Comunista de Cuba, and the Centro de Información de la Defensa de las Fuerzas Armadas Revolucionarias culminated with the magisterial tome, *Conflicting Missions: Havana, Washington, and Africa, 1959–1976*.[13] In a literature devoted to the confrontations and détentes between the US and Castro governments, Gleijeses uncovers that Cuban officials held a sincere passion to assist African independence efforts, linking their Caribbean island's postcolonial struggles with the turbulent decolonization projects taking place on the other side of the Atlantic Ocean. Although previous scholars had laid the foundation thanks to private collections and Ernesto "Che" Guevara's manuscript on his work in Zaire, Gleijeses's incorporation of official Cuban documents alongside interviews in Cuba and Africa sheds light on another factor uniting Castro's foreign policy and decolonization abroad: a common crusade against antiblack racism, a theme further detailed in his subsequent volume.[14] These revelations both spoke to and inspired new notions regarding how peoples, organizations, and nations once overlooked as part of the Third World were pivotal actors making up a global South who interpreted and defined the stakes of the Cold War on their own terms.

However, Gleijeses stumbled upon a conundrum regarding the ACMINREX collections; the files seemed far less revelatory on Cuban activities in Africa from the 1960s onward as compared to those from other depositories in Havana. This was later confirmed by Jonathan Brown: Castro's coming to power brought a gradual bureaucratic shift where the island's official international affairs would fall more and more under the auspices of the Comité Central del Partido Comunista de Cuba rather than the Ministerio de Relaciones Exteriores, which probably explains a few of those faux pas that Kirk noticed. Consequently, sensitive materials from collections elsewhere overshadowed the handful of reports in the ACMINREX on Cuban officials' activities in Dar es Salaam, aid in Tanzania and the Congo, or perceptions of the economic situation abroad. Scholars celebrated how Gleijeses went above and beyond in making copies of the files he consulted, depositing them with the School of Advanced International Studies at Johns Hopkins University and allowing the Cold War International History Project at the Woodrow Wilson International Center for Scholars to create an accessible online depository to assist others who might not have the opportunity to spend weeks in Havana, yet the resulting electronic dossier had no items from the ACMINREX.[15] Initially, this suggested to many that the archive would be of less value for their own examinations into Cuba's foreign relations. However, Gleijeses's work had an unexpected outcome. Because of his arrival at the ACMINREX and other previously closed archives on the island, some of their staffs initiated new or even created their first declassification procedures to prepare for future visitors.

Before the Cold War: Cuba and the Caribbean Basin

Rather than speaking to the traditional literature on the Cuban Revolution and the Cold War, a plethora of scholarship ended up summoning the ACMINREX's files to recast the agency and influence of actors in the Caribbean Basin in the 1940s and 1950s. Serendipitously, Gleijeses's work inspired new insights into Caribbean foreign relations from Cuban historians. In a true testament to the ACMINREX's declassification efforts laying the groundwork for a wider view of Cuban inter-American relations, this resulting scholarship revolved around the island's local conflicts with Dominican dictator Rafael Trujillo, something slightly unexpected for traditional scholars of US-Cuban relations but not too surprising for those familiar with the rumors and gossip surrounding the tyrant. In *Las relaciones cubano-dominicanas*, Jorge Renato Ibarra Guitart provides a focused examination of Cuban responses to the dictator's foreign policy in the immediate aftermath of the Second World War.[16] In contrast to a literature that had frequently focused on US-Dominican relations, Ibarra Guitart delves into how a Caribbean country dealt with Trujillo's sinister influence bribing the island's labor leaders, pressuring the government to expel Dominican exiles, and having his officials keep a close eye on any plots aiming to topple the despot. In *La expedición de Cayo Confites*, Humberto Vázquez García focuses on one such plot.[17] On the beaches of Cayo Confites in 1947, myriad Dominican exiles supported by Guatemalan president Juan José Arévalo, Venezuelan president Rómulo Betancourt, Cuba's Auténtico political party, and many Cuban students and volunteers—including a young Fidel Castro—organized to invade the Dominican Republic and topple Trujillo's regime. Although relying heavily on reports from US officials stationed throughout the Caribbean Basin, Ibarra Guitart and Vázquez García tapped into ACMINREX materials to incorporate much-needed nuance into how the Auténtico government of Ramón Grau San Martín responded to US and Dominican officials' requests to halt the expedition.

It soon turned out these two works were only the tip of the iceberg regarding what the ACMINREX offers on inter-American relations before 1959.[18] In the first volume of his *La telaraña cubana de Trujillo*, Eliades Acosta Matos reaches back to the 1930s to examine the frequently overlooked conflicts between the Dominican tyrant and Cuba's various governments under Gerardo Machado and Fulgencio Batista, identifying how Cuban officials had long opposed Trujillo's attempts to intervene in their affairs.[19] Following Ibarra Guitart's lead by incorporating more ACMINREX materials, Acosta Matos's second volume hits harder on how the Auténtico governments and Batista in the 1940s and 1950s confronted Trujillo's reach. While reinforcing many of Ibarra Guitart's observations, Acosta Matos unearthed a confidential memorandum where Cuban officials in 1949 summarized the dictator's employment of spies, assassins, and other tools to spread his influence into the island and the rest of the Caribbean as "imperialismo dominicano."[20] A marvelous vista complementing works that long explored the nature of US imperialism over Cuba, the island's officials were paying close attention to a different regime seeking to control their politics, economy, and very people. Borrowing from these Cuban historians of American foreign relations and taking advantage of Ibarra Guitart's invitation to work in Havana in 2013, I combined ACMINREX files with those from other depositories. Not only was my multiarchival methodology able to pinpoint how Trujillo networked with Central American dictators, in a combined opposition to the sentiments of global antifascism that lingered in the region, to undermine democratic governments in the Caribbean Basin in the 1940s and 1950s.[21] My investigations reveal how Batista, following his 1952 military coup, bolstered this counterrevolutionary dynamic by reaching out to and joining those dictators to create an informal coalition whose members aimed to turn back the region's democratic inroads from the mid-1940s.[22] Ultimately, such scholarship illustrated how Trujillo, Batista, and others' power went far beyond their own countries in hopes of manipulating the whole of the Caribbean Basin.

Akin to how Gleijeses's investigations into Cuban-African relations after 1959 fortuitously facilitated insights into Caribbean foreign relations before 1959, this surge ended up invigorating further research into ACMINREX materials and inter-American foreign relations under Castro. This was due, though, in great part to two crucial factors. First, Ibarra Guitart, Vázquez García, Acosta Matos, and my work coincided with the diplomatic negotiations between the administrations of then US president Barack Obama and then Cuban president Raúl Castro that soon resulted in the 2014 temporary thawing of relations and the reopening of embassies. Second, both Acosta Matos and I hit on post-1959 aspects of the island's history that diverged from common US-Cuban narratives. The last chapter of Acosta Matos's second volume follows Trujillo's reactions to Batista's ouster and Castro's taking power.[23] I came upon a handful of reports into the activities of exiles on the island in the late 1950s and early 1960s in what seems to have been a fascinating by-product of Cuban archivists' misplacing some of the more sensitive files while recovering documents during the ACMINREX's collapse into the Caribbean.[24] More importantly, both Acosta Matos and I found documents related to how these exiles networked with Castro's associates to launch unsuccessful expeditions in 1959 against regimes and governments in the Dominican Republic, Haiti, Nicaragua, and Panama, crucial events in inter-American relations and those countries' histories that have at best made passing appearances in histories of the international Cold War and the US government's response to the Cuban Revolution. Coming together, all of this opened the door for a reconsideration of the value of the ACMINREX's collections by scholars interested in the same era as Gleijeses, the Cold War and Castro's government, but a different region, the Western Hemisphere.

The ACMINREX Now: The Cuban Revolution and the Global Cold War

Marvelously, the past years have witnessed an outpouring of scholarship whose use of the ACMINREX continues to connect the Cuban Revolution, once artificially fixed as the mere subject or target of the US-Soviet political rivalry, with hemispheric and international debates and battles that made the Cold War a global conflict. The first work to really explore ACMINREX files and broaden the history of inter-American relations during the Cuban Revolution was Renata Keller's *Mexico's Cold War*.[25] Like many others, Keller had originally approached the ACMINREX in hopes of consulting materials on Cuban-Mexican relations in the 1950s and 1960s but was turned away.[26] Hearing about recent forays into the archive, Keller made a final trip where the ACMINREX staff finally granted her access to invaluable reports from Cuban officials. Although she had already completed pivotal research in Mexican- and US-based collections, the ACMINREX held documents from the Cuban Embassy in Mexico. With this, Keller identifies how the island's officials understood their country's relations with Mexico and domestic events abroad, providing the perfect complement to her examination into how Mexican officials collaborated with the US government and the CIA against Castro's regime. Likewise, Jonathan Brown in *Cuba's Revolutionary World* follows Keller by seeking out additional perspectives into revolutionary intrigues in the early years of the Cuban Revolution, most notably turning up internal debates over the 1959 expeditions and the limits of Cuban adventurism in the Western Hemisphere in the 1960s.[27] Similar to Gleijeses, Brown's examination of the intricacies of Castro's policies proves that other entities such as the Ministerio del Interior ended up playing a greater hand in shaping the country's foreign relations than the Ministerio de Relaciones Exteriores originally had. In the end, both works reaffirmed a central aspect of inter-American foreign relations scholarship: being receptive to new depositories such as the ACMINREX while remaining grounded in a multiarchival methodology to avoid overemphasizing newly available files.

The tome best reflecting the merits of this approach is Hideaki Kami's *Diplomacy Meets Migration*.[28] In a wide-ranging examination of US-Cuban relations during the Cold War, Kami scoured US- and Cuban-based archives for any and every item related to how Cuban and Miami exile and migrant politics shaped high-level bilateral negotiations. It was with this solid foundation that he proceeded to the ACMINREX. There, the staff allowed him to peruse Cuban diplomats' policy papers, diplomatic notes, various planning drafts, and more alongside letters from Cubans living in the United States and records on Cubans waiting to immigrate. What made Kami's research stand out, though, was his accessing memoranda of US and Cuban officials' conversations and meetings in the 1980s that were still unavailable in US-based depositories and consulting records as late as the early 1990s. In fact, the staff even offered their files on anti-Castro sabotage and similar activities which remain an underexplored treasure yet to be thoroughly investigated, especially if connected with similar materials in Britain, France, and elsewhere. Even more revelatory when paired with William M. LeoGrande and Peter Kornbluh's voluminous *Back Channel to Cuba*, Kami's work in the ACMINREX has further uncovered a fraught history that has continued separating the island and the United States.[29]

Multiarchival research with ACMINREX files has not stopped at fleshing out Cuban-US relations but expanded our knowledge of the island's Latin American and global policies after 1959. Regarding Bolivia, Thomas C. Field is currently moving beyond the monolithic place of Guevara's death to dig into Cuba's image in Bolivian nationalism from the late 1960s into the military coup of 1971.[30] Also related to South America, Roberto García Ferreira tracks how Castro's officials in Uruguay sought to nurture their revolutionary prestige in the eyes of leftist organizations while holding onto relationships with sympathetic elites facing intense pressure by local conservative elements.[31] Deeper into the global arena, Eline Van Ommen uses ACMINREX files to supplement her exhaustive work in Western European collections to broaden our understanding of Latin American solidarity movements.[32] Focusing on the Sandinistas' struggles in Nicaragua in the 1970s, Van Ommen traces networks of anti-Somoza resistance from Nicaragua through the Caribbean and across the Atlantic. In a similar historiographical trend placing US, British, and Mexican sources next to ACMINREX files and even personal collections from prominent Cuban officials, Eric Gettig offers a lens into how Cuba engaged with so-called Third World movements.[33] Whether with its abortive Underdeveloped Nations Conference or in the Non-Aligned Movement, many Cubans combined their revolutionary aspirations to bring Latin America closer to Africa and Asia with a defense against US "imperialism." Jumping to the 1990s, Mervyn Bain has incorporated ACMINREX materials to reassess how Castro's regime maneuvered at the end of the Cold War.[34] While much scholarship had simply taken for granted that this pivotal international moment witnessed the loss of the island's ally in the Soviet Union, Bain uncovers that Cuban officials actively pursued various strategies toward Russia in hopes of retaining some semblance of this relationship. Amplifying their individual contributions, the collective result of this energetic output has buttressed a growing body of literature that has only hinted at the reach of the Cuban Revolution's influence.

Despite such successes, there remain some challenges in accessing ACMINREX files, much likely due to what Bain has noted as the archive's lacking a structured or "institutionalized process" for requesting materials.[35] Apparently, there are "Ordinario" and "Extraordinario" collections, with the former readily available for consultation and the latter generally closed off. Multiple scholars have noted that folders and boxes related to crucial events likely understood as sensitive, ranging from the Cuban Missile Crisis to the Guantánamo military base, are either empty or unavailable. Others believe this is the result of an overwhelmed but hardworking staff trying to process, sometimes a bit haphazardly, myriad documents and requests. Following the reception of Keller's *Mexico's Cold War*, the personnel digitized many of their files on Mexico, proving both their willingness to facilitate scholars' requests and their truly brilliant efforts to inspire more research.[36] Regardless, archivists' decisions on what should remain "classified" appear to vacillate when dealing with Cold War 'hot spots,' with the ACMINREX's utility and limitations exemplified in current scholarship on Cuban-Sandinista relations. In her work exploring the relationships and links between the Cuban Revolution and Nicaragua, Emily Snyder focuses on internationalist missions and exchanges over religion, revolutionary identities, and more in following personnel exchanges, convenios between Ministerios de Relaciones Exteriores, and more.[37] Likewise, Mateo Cayetano Jarquín explores the Sandinistas' foreign policies in these same years.[38] However, the two have come upon different materials in the supposedly same folders and collections, further implying that the ACMINREX staff are still constructing their declassification systems. Time will show what these and the "Extraordinario" collections will yield, but Snyder and Jarquín are both following the footsteps of Kirk and Gleijeses by filling in these potential research gaps thanks to their work in Nicaraguan depositories, oral histories, French files, and more, decolonizing what has long been a story of US policy toward Nicaragua and producing something that is a far more American history.

Some of these challenges have actually contributed to historians placing less emphasis on traditional diplomatic mechanisms and examining public, soft, and other forms of "diplomacy." After all, scholars know far too well how those files governments might perceive as irrelevant can be overwhelmingly revelatory and pertinent to our own research. Investigating Mexican solidarity with the Cuban Revolution, Keller found in the ACMINREX a trove of letters from Mexican citizens.[39] What others determined as unimportant products of nonstate actors instead allowed Keller to shed light on how those in one country, debating the legacy of their own revolutionary history, understood and interpreted another revolution. Redirecting the focus to Colombia, Matthew D. Jacobs found in the face of limited sources into Cuba's public diplomacy additional revelations into US public diplomacy.[40] As pro-Castro groups admired events on the Caribbean island, the United States Information Agency and the Kennedy administration aimed to undermine this appeal through an extensive campaign of propaganda. Alternative scholarship through ACMINREX files is not limited to the years after 1959. Most recently, Nicolás Prados offers a brief reexamination of networks of anti-Batista activism scattered through-out the Caribbean Basin deriving from Cuban officials and attaches' reports.[41] Whereas other historians have expended immeasurable energies locating any-thing offering a new glimpse into Castro and the Movimiento 26 de Julio, Prados taps into reports at the ACMINREX and elsewhere and finds Batista's regime anxiously monitoring multiple groups of exiles, dissidents, and more who shared a common enemy in the Cuban dictatorship and lent crucial as-sistance to one another.

Thus, those interested in furthering these new vistas into inter-American and Cuban foreign relations, and perhaps many other topics, might find some-thing of value at the ACMINREX. The first step is to acquire the appropri-ate visa. While individual institutions might offer access, most scholars have gone through the Instituto de Historia de Cuba due to its reputation and long-standing relationship with the ACMINREX, but processing such requests have taken anywhere from some weeks to a couple of days. The archive's official hours currently seem to be 9 to 11:30 a.m. and 1 to 3:30 p.m., three days a week, so a productive research trip should include visits to the numerous other depositories in Havana. Additionally, photography and laptops have been al-lowed since Keller's time there. Most importantly, all who have stopped by have unanimously described the ACMINREX staff as patient, generous, al-ways professional, and beyond civil despite the hurdles and frustrations that come with the bureaucracy and dealing with historians' demands and egos, something for which too many archivists receive too little credit.

Ultimately, one must be prepared for the annoyances and conundrums that come with this research, something experts of inter-American relations have navigated for decades, as Rabe reminds us. Some have characterized the pro-cess as quite difficult and disappointing compared to other archival sites, as seen with items found in a collection or folder not showing up in others' visits or a subsequent trip. As Gleijeses and Bain have described, sensitive topics have been limited and required extraofficial interventions which depend upon one's connections and relationships, especially in light of there not being any formal system for requesting "Extraordinario" collections. Others have simply compared the ACMINREX to other archives dealing with issues related to "na-tional security" where one must be prepared for numerous delays as the staff takes the time to process any item that has a "Classified" or "Sensitive" mark-ing on it, resembling challenges and procedures with Mexican materials at the Acervo Histórico Genaro Estrada, French materials in diplomatic archives at Nantes and La Courneuve, Spanish materials between archives in Madrid and Salamanca, Freedom of Information requests at the National Archives in London, Freedom of Information Act requests at the National Archives in College Park, and plenty other venues. Completing his current examination into the cultural aspects of the neocolonial relationship between the United States and Cuba, Michael Donoghue compares the ACMINREX to diplomatic archives and foreign relations collections elsewhere where files often contain newspapers, periodicals, and more that are not available in traditional depositories but directly informed foreign relations at the time.

No matter the difficulties, the collections at the ACMINREX should continue playing a role in reshaping the literature on Cuban foreign relations. Dovetailing with influential methodological innovations and historiographical trends in inter-American scholarship, these materials have already broadened our understanding of the reaches of Castro's internationalist policies into Africa, the depths of revolutionary aspirations in the Western Hemisphere, and the impact of the Cuban Revolution upon Latin America and other parts of the world according to the very words of its admirers and detractors. Although the US government's policies and embargo remain static at this moment, our very understanding of the history of inter-American and Cuban foreign relations is evolving thanks to scholars' continued efforts in the ACMINREX and elsewhere.

NOTES

My immense gratitude to Jorge Renato Ibarra Guitart, who first invited me to Havana; Belkis Quesada at the Instituto de Historia de Cuba, for handling the laborious bureaucracy that allowed me to even enter the archive in the first place; Eduardo Valido, who guided my first sojourn into ACMINREX's collections; and the various ACMINREX staff who made an unexpected trip immeasurably fascinating. My thanks to Ashley Black, Jonathan Brown, Michael Donoghue, Thomas Field, Roberto García Ferreira, Eric Gettig, Tanya Harmer, Rebecca Herman, Matthew Jacobs, Mateo Cayetano Jarquín, Hideaki Kami, Renata Keller, Randal Sheppard, Emily Snyder, and Eline Van Ommen for sharing not just their research but their time in Vedado more generally. Special thanks to Mike Bustamante and Michelle Chase for offering useful suggestions.

1. Alberto García Navarro a Gonzalo Güello, May 12, 1958, San José, Archivo Central del Ministerio de Relaciones Exteriores (hereafter ACMINREX), *caja* "A Latina/Costa Rica/1950–1961/Ordinario 2," *expediente* "1958."

2. García Navarro a Güello, May 12, 1958.

3. Stephen G. Rabe, "Marching Ahead (Slowly): The Historiography of Inter-American Relations," *Diplomatic History* 13, no. 3 (1989): 297–316; Stephen G. Rabe, "Marching Ahead (Forthrightly): The Historiography of Inter-American Relations," *Passport: The Society for Historians of American Foreign Relations Review* 45, no. 2 (2014): 25–31.

4. For the literature on this era, see T. Ray Shurbutt, ed., *United States–Latin American Relations, 1800–1850: The Formative Generations* (Tuscaloosa: University of Alabama Press., 1991); Thomas M. Leonard, ed., *United States–Latin American Relations, 1850–1903: Establishing a Relationship* (Tuscaloosa: University of Alabama Press, 1999); Mark T. Gilderhus, "US–Latin

American Relations, 1898–1941," in *A Companion to American Foreign Relations*, ed. Robert D. Schulzinger (Malden, MA: Blackwell, 2003), 134–148.

5. For the overarching view of literature in this vein, see Mark T. Gilderhus, "An Emerging Synthesis?: US–Latin American Relations since the Second World War," *Diplomatic History* 16, no. 3 (1992): 429–452.

6. Piero Gleijeses, *La esperanza desgarrada: La rebelión dominicana de 1965 y la invasión norteamericana* (Santo Domingo, DR: Editorial Búho, 2012); Darlene Rivas, *Missionary Capitalist: Nelson Rockefeller in Venezuela* (Chapel Hill: University of North Carolina Press, 2002); Ariel C. Armony, *Argentina, the United States, and the Anti-Communist Crusade in Central America, 1977–1984* (Athens, OH: Center for International Studies and Ohio University Center for International Studies, 1997).

7. Tanya Harmer, *Allende's Chile & the Inter-American Cold War* (Chapel Hill: University of North Carolina Press, 2011); Tanalís Padilla and Louise E. Walker, eds., "Dossier: Spy Reports: Content, Methodology, and Historiography in Mexico's Secret Police Archive," *Journal of Iberian and Latin American Research* 19 (2013); Kirsten Weld, *Paper Cadavers: The Archives of Dictatorship in Guatemala* (Durham, NC: Duke University Press, 2014); Friedrich Katz, *The Secret War in Mexico: Europe, the United States, and the Mexican Revolution* (Chicago: University of Chicago Press, 1981); Jürgen Buchenau, *In the Shadow of the Giant: The Making of Mexico's Central America Policy, 1876–1930* (Tuscaloosa: University of Alabama Press, 1996); Friedrich E. Schuler, *Mexico between Hitler and Roosevelt: Mexican Foreign Relations in the Age of Lázaro Cárdenas, 1934–1940* (Albuquerque: University of New Mexico Press, 1998); Amelia M. Kiddle, *Mexico's Relations with Latin America during the Cárdenas Era* (Albuquerque: University of New Mexico Press, 2016).

8. Greg Grandin, "Off the Beach: The United States, Latin America, and the Cold War," in *A Companion to Post-1945 America*, ed. Jean-Christophe Agnew and Roy Rosenzweig (Malden, MA: Blackwell, 2002), 426–445; Gilbert M. Joseph, "What We Now Know and Should Know: Bringing Latin America More Meaningfully into Cold War Studies," in *In from the Cold: Latin America's New Encounter with the Cold War*, ed. Gilbert M. Joseph and Daniela Spenser (Durham, NC: Duke University Press, 2008), 3–46; Gilbert M. Joseph, "Latin America's Long Cold War: A Century of Revolutionary Process and US Power," in *A Century of Revolution: Insurgent and Counterinsurgent Violence during Latin America's Long Cold War*, ed. Greg Grandin and Gilbert M. Joseph (Durham, NC: Duke University Press, 2010), 397–414.

9. "CIA Releases Controversial Bay of Pigs History," National Security Archive Briefing Book 564, October 13, 2016, https://nsarchive.gwu.edu.

10. Michelle Chase, *Revolution within the Revolution: Women and Gender Politics in Cuba, 1952–1962* (Chapel Hill: University of North Carolina Press, 2015); Devyn Spence Benson, *Antiracism in Cuba: The Unfinished Revolution* (Chapel Hill: University of North Carolina Press, 2016); Jennifer L. Lambe, *Madhouse: Psychiatry and Politics in Cuban History* (Chapel Hill: University of North Carolina Press, 2016); Steve Cushion, *A Hidden History of the Cuban Revolution: How the Working Class Shaped the Guerrillas' Victory* (New York: Monthly Review, 2016).

11. Melvyn P. Leffler, "The Cold War: What Do 'We Now Know'?," *American Historical Review* 104, no. 2 (1999): 501–524; Benjamin R. Young, "Wealth, Access, and Archival Fetishism in the New Cold War History," *History News Network*, June 23, 2019, https://historynewsnetwork.org/article/172318.

12. John M. Kirk, "Unraveling the Paradox: The Canadian Position on Cuba," in *Cuba in the International System: Normalization and Integration*, ed. Archibald R. M. Ritter and John M. Kirk (London: Palgrave Macmillan, 1995), 145–58, at 146.

13. Piero Gleijeses, *Conflicting Missions: Havana, Washington, and Africa, 1959–1976* (Chapel Hill: University of North Carolina Press, 2002), 9.

14. Piero Gleijeses, *Visions of Freedom: Havana, Washington, Pretoria, and the Struggle for Southern Africa, 1976–1991* (Chapel Hill: University of North Carolina Press, 2013).

15. Piero Gleijeses, "Visions of Freedom: New Documents from the Closed Cuban Archives," Cold War International History Project, e-Dossier No. 44, October 16, 2013, https://www.wilson center.org/publication/visions-freedom-new-documents-the-closed-cuban-archives.

16. Jorge Renato Ibarra Guitart, *Las relaciones cubano-dominicanas, su escenario hemisférico (1944–1948)* (Santo Domingo: Archivo General de la Nación, 2011).

17. Humberto Vázquez García, *La expedición de Cayo Confites* (Santiago, DR: Editorial Oriente, 2012). The original version published in Cuba is harder to acquire, but the reprint through the Archivo General de la Nación in Santo Domingo is online.

18. Jorge Macle Cruz, in "Writing the Revolution's History out of Closed Archives?: Cuban Archival Laws and Access to Information," in *The Revolution from Within: Cuba, 1959–1980*, ed. Michael J. Bustamante and Jennifer L. Lambe (Durham: Duke Univ. Press, 2019), 47–66, summarizes the evolution of archival trends in the island where recent laws and procedures expect documents to be transferred to the Archivo Nacional de Cuba. In light of what scholars have been finding predating 1959, it seems ACMINREX materials have not been termed "inactive" and transferred.

19. Eliades Acosta Matos, *La telaraña cubana de Trujillo*, vol. 1 (Santo Domingo: Archivo General de la Nación, 2012).

20. Eliades Acosta Matos, *La telaraña cubana de Trujillo* (Santo Domingo: Archivo General de la Nación, 2012), 2:107–8.

21. Aaron Coy Moulton, "Building Their Own Cold War in Their Own Backyard: The Transnational, International Conflicts in the Greater Caribbean Basin, 1944–1954," *Cold War History* 15, no. 2 (2015): 135–54.

22. Aaron Coy Moulton, "The Dictator's Domino Theory: A Caribbean Basin Anti-Communist Network, 1947–1952," *Intelligence & National Security* 34, no. 7 (2019): 945–61.

23. Acosta Matos, *La telaraña cubana*, vol. 2.

24. Aaron Coy Moulton, "Militant Roots: The Anti-Fascist Left in the Caribbean Basin, 1945–1954," *Estudios Interdisciplinarios de América Latina y el Caribe* 28, no. 2 (2017): 14–29.

25. Renata Keller, *Mexico's Cold War: Cuba, the United States, and the Legacy of the Mexican Revolution* (New York: Cambridge University Press, 2015).

26. Mervyn J. Bain describes a similar frustration in learning in 2010 about ACMINREX materials on Cuban-Russian relations but having to wait until 2014 for access in *Moscow and Havana, 1917 to the Present: An Enduring Friendship in an Ever-Changing Global Context* (Lanham, MD: Lexington, 2018), 35.

27. Jonathan Brown, *Cuba's Revolutionary World* (Cambridge, MA: Harvard University Press, 2017).

28. Hideaki Kami, *Diplomacy Meets Migration: US Relations with Cuba during the Cold War* (New York: Cambridge University Press, 2018).

29. William M. LeoGrande and Peter Kornbluh, *Back Channel to Cuba: The Hidden History of Negotiations between Washington and Havana* (Chapel Hill: University of North Carolina Press, 2014).

30. Thomas C. Field, "Bolivia between Washington, Prague, and Havana: The Limits of Nationalism, 1960–1964," in *Latin America and the Third World*, ed. Thomas C. Field, Stella Krepp, and Vanni Pettiná (Chapel Hill: University of North Carolina Press, 2020), 44–72.

31. Roberto García, "The Cuban Embassy in Uruguay, 1959–1964," *Oxford Research Encyclopedia of Latin American History* (February 2018).

32. Eline Van Ommen, "Isolating Nicaragua's Somoza: Sandinista Diplomacy in Western Europe, 1977–1979," in *Latin America and the Third World*, ed. Thomas C. Field, Stella Krepp, and Vanni Pettiná (Chapel Hill: University of North Carolina Press, 2020), 367–93.

33. Eric Gettig, "Cuba, the United States, and the Uses of the Third World Project, 1959–67," in *Latin America and the Third World*, ed. Thomas C. Field, Stella Krepp, and Vanni Pettiná (Chapel Hill: University of North Carolina Press, 2020), 241–73.

34. Mervyn Bain, "Russo-Cuban Relations in the 1990s," *Diplomacy & Statecraft* 29, no. 2 (2018): 255–73.

35. Bain, *Moscow and Havana*, 35.

36. These digitized files were first used by Ashley Black, "The Politics of Asylum: Stability, Sovereignty, and Mexican Foreign Policy in the Caribbean Basin, 1945–1959" (PhD diss., Stony Brook University, 2018).

37. Emily Snyder, "Internationalizing the Revolutionary Family: Love and Politics in Cuba and Nicaragua, 1979–1990," *Radical History Review* 136 (2020): 50–74.

38. Mateo Cayetano Jarquín, "Red Christmasses: The Sandinistas, Indigenous Rebellion, and the Origins of the Nicaraguan Civil War, 1981–82," *Cold War History* 18, no. 1 (2018): 91–107.

39. Renata Keller, "Fan Mail to Fidel: The Cuban Revolution and Mexican Solidarity," *Mexican Studies/Estudios Mexicanos* 33, no. 1 (2017): 6–31.

40. Matthew D. Jacobs, "Reformists, Revolutionaries, and Kennedy Administration Public Diplomacy in Colombia and Venezuela," *Diplomatic History* 42, no. 5 (2018): 859–85.

41. Nicolás Prados Ortiz de Solórzano, *Cuba in the Caribbean Cold War: Exiles, Revolutionaries and Tyrants, 1952–1959* (Oxford: Palgrave Macmillan, 2020).

PRIMARY SOURCES

EMBAJADOR ERNESTO PINTO
BAZURCO RITTLER

Testimonio: La protección diplomática no admite discriminación

Éxodo masivo hacia la misión diplomática

La Convención de Viena establece que las misiones diplomáticas gozan de extraterritorialidad y los integrantes de una embajada de inmunidad diplomática. Este derecho es respetado en todos los países. Y en alguna forma, en Cuba. Las prerrogativas conllevan asimismo obligaciones. Una de ellas es la de prestar protección a los que acogen a la jurisdicción de un Estado, por ser perseguidos por el gobierno del país al que pertenecen. No todos los diplomáticos cumplen con ello. La tendencia es evitar dificultades, como ser removidos de su puesto o sufrir amenazas.

Si bien la historia más conocida es la llamada "Del Mariel", la migración masiva de Cuba hacia los Estados Unidos, tuvo su episodio de mayor envergadura en el año 1980. Su origen fue una confluencia de factores, que pudieron llegar a resultados concretos —la salida de Cuba de 125 mil personas— gracias a decisiones tomadas en la embajada del Perú en La Habana. Y a complejas negociaciones.

Soy testigo de excepción de todo ello. Estuve a cargo de la Misión Diplomática del Perú en estas difíciles circunstancias. Y soy responsable de las decisiones difíciles —secretas— que se tomaron en aquel entonces.

¿Cuáles fueron estas? En primer lugar, toda decisión y esfuerzo tuvo como propósito cautelar la vida e integridad física de los cubanos. Incluso por encima de los riesgos que asumía mi persona y la de mi familia. Desde este aspecto esencial, opté por dar protección a todas las personas que estaban en peligro. Sin discriminación.

Hay una razón poderosa para hacer hincapié en la no discriminación. Porque en Cuba, los que intentaban extraerse del sistema eran acusado como enemigos, y para justificar esto, se les atribuían la comisión de delitos o faltas de conducta graves. Los llamados "gusanos", los que pensaban de forma distinta o no se dejaban utilizar por la familia Castro, tenían que ser para la dictadura comunista, de cualquier forma, los malos de la sociedad y del sistema socialista.

En ese contexto, para un jurista —que era mi caso— el Derecho de Asilo, no necesariamente debe tener en cuenta la fundamentación legal del Estado

411

perseguidor, sino si los supuestos delitos son también calificados como tales en el Estado que los asila o les brinda protección.

Es el caso de que, dentro de los ingresantes en 1980, antes de la incursión masiva del 4 de abril, se encontraban personas acusadas y con sentencia de conducta deshonrosa. Una señora que había sufrido cárcel, según ella manifestaba, por posar desnuda en revistas, que se vendían clandestinamente. Al ser reclamada por las autoridades cubanas como "delincuente común", por lo que, de acuerdo a los Convenios sobre Asilo, no le alcanzaba la protección diplomática, aduje que el exhibir su cuerpo no era delito en el Perú. La otra persona, era su pareja, acusada de lesbiana. Para mí la opción sexual nunca puede ser motivo de acusación de conducta deshonrosa, menos de discriminación.

Ambas personas siguieron bajo mi protección a pesar de los reiterados pedidos de las autoridades cubanas —que iban hasta las amenazas— para que las entregara.

Resulta también de interés hacer recuerdo de que la primera persona que ingresó a la embajada, después de las 8 de la mañana del día 4 de abril de 1980, es decir minutos después de que fuera retirada la posta, fue un afrocubano. Tuvo —dentro de este clima de incertidumbre— una actitud valiente, y me dijo "espero que muchos seguirán mi ejemplo".

En los que querían abandonar Cuba hubo un número considerable de afrocubanos. En contraste, en el grupo de policías, militares, soplones y elementos de la llamada Seguridad de Estados, que actuaban fuera de la embajada, no pude distinguir a ningún afrocubano.

Instantes después le pregunte al afrocubano que había entrado a la embajada si estaba en su propósito lograr su salida hacia Perú o tal vez a los Estados Unidos. Fue una sorpresa para mí escucharlo decir: "Al Perú o Brasil... en los Estados Unidos siempre seré un ciudadano de segunda categoría".

El asunto no solo era acoger a los ingresantes, y otorgarles permanente protección, así como alimentación, sino mantener en ellos la esperanza viva de que podrían lograr su propósito de salir de Cuba.

Tampoco cabe, en justicia, hacer discriminación entre los que califican para asilo y los que pueden ser considerados como refugiados. Yo otorgué protección, por igual, a los que ingresaron antes del 4 de abril de 1980, como a los que masivamente incursionaron en la sede diplomática después de que se retirara la posta, el 4 de abril.

Asilados: Refugiados o ingresantes

El Derecho es una herramienta del Estado para alcanzar la justicia; es, asimismo, una garantía para la paz y el progreso de una nación. Las dictaduras como el Gobierno cubano ejercen prácticas que usan las normas para reforzar un sistema que permita, a los que tienen ventaja en el mismo, quedarse en el poder.

La dimensión que tomaron estos sucesos, en un contexto político en que la atención hacia el conflicto Este-Oeste tenía mayor vigencia, daba también la posibilidad de diversas interpretaciones. Se decía que convenía, ante todo, mantener buenas relaciones con Castro. Otros pensaban que era preferible apoyar al pueblo frente al gobierno autoritario. Yo sostenía que debía intentarse en las dos cosas, siempre y cuando no se afecte el derecho internacional. Las relaciones con la comunidad internacional serían más importantes que los vínculos con el castrismo.

Para algunos, el caso del ingreso masivo a la embajada del Perú se simplificaba con el calificativo de invasión. Para otros, lo sucedido fue un éxodo masivo hacia el local de la embajada, o sea, la sustracción de un territorio donde existe una jurisdicción para alcanzar protección. Paso previo para abandonar definitivamente ambas jurisdicciones e ingresar a una tercera que sería un país que los acogería definitivamente.

En esa complejidad también se sitúa el asunto de las responsabilidades jurídicas y políticas. Por ejemplo, si se asume que hubo una invasión, entonces se debe, consecuentemente, solicitar una reparación por los daños y perjuicios causados por una acción forzada. Si admitimos que es un éxodo masivo, con consentimiento de los que ejercen jurisdicción al lugar que se ingresa, entonces no hay reclamo contra los causantes.

La confusión se presentó cuando algunos hablaban "de los refugiados" o "los asilados", porque se dieron figuras de naturaleza jurídica distinta en un mismo escenario. La magnitud de los hechos, así como el desenlace político, no permitió su debida diferenciación.

Los sucesos más espectaculares, relacionados con la ocupación de más de diez mil cubanos de la sede diplomática, fueron destacados por la prensa, que dejó en el olvido los temas relacionados con el asilo de los primeros perseguidos que estaban en peligro de muerte. Estos precedieron a lo masivo y fueron el origen del ingreso espectacular de diez mil personas a la embajada y luego del éxodo de ciento veinte mil cubanos de la isla.

Se pueden distinguir dos situaciones jurídicamente diferentes: la de las personas que ingresaron a la embajada antes del 4 de abril de 1980 y la de las que lo hicieron a partir de esa fecha.

Los primeros tuvieron que arriesgar su vida desafiando a la posta cubana. Esta, como se recuerda, no tenía la misión, como equivocadamente se decía, de custodiar la embajada, tal como estamos acostumbrados a ver en los países en que existe libertad para acercarse a las misiones diplomáticas y para salir del país. La función de la posta, que disparaba a matar, era impedir que ciudadanos cubanos abandonaran su país. Es más, el destacamento de postas tenía, en la práctica, el mismo objetivo que otras fuerzas militares que reprimían la salida del territorio cubano. La tropa cubana era estacionada fuera de las misiones diplomáticas sin que interviniera la voluntad del país al que supuestamente protegían.

En la Cuba castrista, y este es quizá el aspecto central del problema, quien ingresaba a una embajada con miras a emigrar del país era tratado como desertor del sistema, y el Gobierno se sentía con el derecho de perseguirlo y castigarlo. Por eso aplicaba la orden de disparar, tanto para detenerlo como para sancionar su conducta, castigo que además tenía el propósito de servir de ejemplo.

Las personas que ingresaron a la embajada en busca de asilo sabían que debían vencer ese obstáculo y se prepararon para ello con un planeamiento previo, como el proteger sus vehículos con sacos de arena. Esto demuestra que actuaban con premeditación y eran conscientes del desafío a una fuerza y del riesgo real de ser alcanzados por las balas. La pena que los esperaba de ser detenidos era extremadamente severa. Exigía, por tanto, de parte de quien había tomado la decisión, una actitud política. Este acto político era perseguido por el Gobierno cubano, que en su legislación contemplaba, incluso, la pena de muerte para los delitos contra la seguridad del Estado.

El Código Penal cubano establecía sanciones drásticas para la salida ilegal sin tipificar exactamente lo que entiende como tal. Incluso el mero intento ya era objeto de drástica sanción. El transponer la "zona rígida" que el Gobierno cubano había establecido de modo unilateral en las proximidades de las sedes diplomáticas de países que respetaban el derecho de asilo era motivo de sanción y persecución. La simple sospecha de un posible ingreso sin autorización cubana a una embajada se interpretaba como delito político. Por esta razón, el deber de protección de una embajada se extendía también a los que solo intentaban el ingreso a la misma, aun cuando no hubieran alcanzado físicamente su propósito.

Esa situación era originada por las normas legales políticamente condicionadas y su aplicación sumamente severa y arbitraria por parte de funcionarios de Cuba. Así, el Código Penal cubano señalaba que resultaban punibles las personas que mostraban conducta peligrosa por haberse apartado de lo que llamaba "moral socialista". En la práctica, significaba que se avalaba la persecución política de quienes, por ejemplo, tenían un sentido ético sobre las libertades que garantizaba el sistema democrático.

Resulta cuestionable, por otro lado, que esta norma y su interpretación obedecieran al orden político de Cuba, singular en el contexto latinoamericano, y a la decisión del Gobierno de Castro de impedir la salida del país y la sustracción al sistema de corte totalitario impuesto.

Para cerrar más el nudo, Cuba había tejido una maraña de obstáculos administrativos que no existían en otros países y que hacían en la práctica casi imposible el viaje al exterior sin el consentimiento expreso de las autoridades. Era así como se exigía, además del pasaporte, un visado especial o autorización de salida. Si esta era denegada por los funcionarios de migración, no cabía apelación. En la práctica, cualquier solicitud podía ser negada con el pretexto de que faltaba tal o cual requisito, ya que los catálogos de exigencias, ingeniosamente, habían sido establecidos de tal modo que podían impedir, legal, pero injustamente, a cualquiera la salida de Cuba.

Se configuraba el caso en que la norma, o sea la ley, no favorecía la justicia, y, por ende, se convertía en un abuso del derecho por parte del Estado cubano, que daba y aplicaba esas disposiciones con clara intencionalidad restrictiva. Se vivía bajo severas restricciones ideológicas que las autoridades calificaban como delitos —como el de peligrosidad, propaganda del enemigo, desacato y otras denominaciones— que solo encontraban su explicación en regímenes en los que cualquier recurso es válido.

Cuba tuvo participación en el afianzamiento de ese derecho y se firmó, en La Habana, en 1928, la Convención sobre Asilo, con lo que se podría decir que el asilo tuvo su primera legitimación oficial precisamente en Cuba. El propio Fidel Castro sacó provecho del amparo que recibió de diplomáticos argentinos, en la capital colombiana, después del Bogotazo; y años más tarde, en México, a mediados de la década de los cincuenta. Ese amparo le dio las posibilidades, después del fracaso del asalto del cuartel Moncada y su prisión en la isla de Pinos, de poder organizar, desde ese país en el que se exiló, la expedición del Granma y, en definitiva, la revolución misma. Castro tenía por eso una deuda con el derecho de asilo.

En América Latina, el asilo cobró gran vigencia. La Convención Interamericana sobre Derechos Humanos, aprobada en San José de Costa Rica en noviembre de 1969, señaló claramente, en su artículo 22, que toda persona tiene derecho a buscar asilo si se siente perseguida por delitos políticos e incluso conexos. Es pues muy amplia la protección que los Estados dieron a las personas. El mismo acuerdo reconoce la obligación de los Estados de América de recibir a los que soliciten asilo. Y con esto cumplió el Perú.

La Constitución Política del Perú, de 1979, aprobada meses antes de los sucesos de la embajada en La Habana, en su artículo 108, hace reconocimiento expreso al derecho de asilo. Ella establece: "El Estado peruano reconoce el asilo político. Acepta la calificación del asilado que otorgue el Gobierno asilante. Si se dispone la expulsión de un asilado político, no se le entrega al país cuyo Gobierno lo persigue". Esta reafirmación del asilo obligaba aún más a los funcionarios diplomáticos peruanos a actuar en respeto a tal derecho.

El ingreso masivo del 4 de abril se asemeja más a la figura del refugio. Pero ambos fundamentalmente tienen el objetivo de proteger. La tergiversación de las normas del derecho y manipulación de la información por parte de las autoridades cubanas se mostró clara e inconfundiblemente con la interpretación antojadiza de lo que era o no uso de la violencia. Así lo expresaron tanto en el curso de las negociaciones como en el comunicado del día 4 de abril de 1980, cuando equivocadamente sostenían que habían hecho uso de fuerza aquellos que ingresaron antes del retiro de la posta, es decir, sin el consentimiento de las autoridades cubanas. En realidad, al que le toca calificar si fue forzado es al que ejerce jurisdicción y es responsable del local al que se ingresa, o sea al Perú.

Es así como actué en el terreno de los hechos, bajo la presunción jurídica de primera urgencia; es decir, dando amparo a los necesitados. Como se comprobó luego, las personas que ingresaron el 4 de abril tenían razones justificadas para que les asistiera protección.

Cabe resaltar que por decisión propia y acción de la diplomacia peruana se le dio primero una protección inicial a la integridad física de todos los ingresantes, y luego una solución humanitaria, sin lesionar los derechos de ninguna persona ni menoscabar los intereses permanentes del país. Sin esta primera protección no se hubiera logrado lo segundo.

En caso de presentarse una duda en la interpretación de alguna de las normas sobre si corresponde asilo o refugio, debe prevalecer la más justa, que es la que protege a la persona. La duda en ningún momento puede ser argumento para negar la protección porque sus efectos serían irreversibles. No hay que olvidar que cuando se devuelve al país de origen a una persona perseguida, entonces se pierde la jurisdicción sobre la misma. Esto se tuvo en cuenta y se practicó en La Habana.

La intensa y tensa negociación con Fidel Castro

En la práctica, ningún asunto importante se resolvía en Cuba sin el conocimiento o consentimiento de Fidel Castro. Hasta ese día, 4 de abril, ningún representante extranjero había logrado tratar un asunto tan crucial para Cuba, con Castro. Este había usado a sus polichinelas, funcionarios de segundo o tercer rango. Con ellos era casi imposible avanzar hacia una solución. Por la simple razón de que nadie de este grupo se atrevía a hacer concesiones. Eso sería un riesgo que no podían asumir. Más bien todos querían ser más castristas que Castro, es decir obstinados en un mal manejo del poder

Por la importancia de los dos encuentros que tuve con Castro el 4 de abril por la noche, los describo en detalle, tal como los expuse en mi testimonio que recoge en sus principales aspectos mi libro *Diplomacia para la Libertad* que público el Congreso de la Republica del Perú. Esta negociación se efectuó bajo una enorme presión, así como con angustiosas expectativas de cerca de diez mil personas que a esa hora ya se encontraban en la embajada, alguna de las cuales —según revelaron después— me encomendaron con sus oraciones.

Las tropas cubanas se pusieron en movimiento. Se acercaron sigilosamente a la misión diplomática y se filtraron entre la oscuridad y los rayos de luna. Luego, rodearon un auto oscuro. Desde ahí me había llegado ese nombre en la voz de una sombra. ¡Fidel!

Se estimuló mi ánimo y rápidamente gané la calle para ir a su encuentro. Mi guardaespaldas, el mayor del ejército peruano —destacado en Cuba—, Casanova, me hacía ver lo arriesgado de mi actitud. No quería escucharlo. Calculaba que Castro podía haber llegado a las inmediaciones de la embajada por dos razones: buscar el diálogo bajo el pretexto de observar *in situ* el estado de las cosas. O para dirigir o disuadir un ataque contra la embajada. No había, por lo tanto, que arriesgarse pasivamente, sino propiciar por cualquier medio el contacto personal que condujera a una conversación que evitara la violencia.

El embate de la masa metálica de un vehículo estuvo a punto de alcanzarme. Con pocos segundos de anticipación, uno de los agentes de Fidel gritó:

—¡Es el jefe de la embajada!

Se escuchó el chirrido de los neumáticos. El auto de Fidel había hecho una maniobra para no atropellarme. Luego, vi alejarse al auto Zil negro y sentí esfumada mi esperanza de un encuentro.

Las voces exaltadas de los que me rodeaban me advirtieron que el automóvil solo había dado media vuelta y se dirigía, por el otro extremo de la berma, a la dirección en la que nos encontrábamos. Crucé rápidamente el jardín de la Quinta Avenida para situarme en el derrotero del coche. Noté que alguien más corría a mi lado e imaginé que era la seguridad de Castro. Miré a mi flanco y vi, asombrado, que era Lilly, mi esposa; muy decidida, me acompañaba en circunstancias tan peligrosas.

Cuando estuve frente al automóvil blindado del Comandante en jefe, que todavía estaba en marcha, calculé una nueva maniobra de su chofer para evadirme. Di un paso más para interponerme. Entonces, el automóvil se vio obligado a detener su marcha. La ventana lateral trasera descendió lentamente y pude ver asomarse el rostro del presidente de Cuba enmarcado en su conocida barba.

—Es hora de que hablemos—dije, mientras me acercaba a la puerta trasera del auto de Fidel.

—Entra, sube al auto. Yo no voy a salir—dijo Castro.

—¿Por qué no?—pregunté. ¿Era posible que Castro tuviera miedo de ingresar a la embajada?

—No quiero ver a todos esos gusanos que están en la embajada—dijo.

Me había pasado el día tratando de localizar al jefe y jerarca de la Revolución cubana y responsable máximo de la situación. Ahora lo tenía delante. Acepté la invitación de Castro de subir a su auto.

Mi esposa Lilly, que tenía experiencia en asuntos internacionales, me había aconsejado que no negociara solo, sin testigos. Ese nuevo encuentro no sería como los anteriores en los que solo conversamos e intercambiamos ideas. Ahora confrontaríamos posiciones y las circunstancias de una situación explosiva a la que se le tenía que buscar una solución urgente. Y había pocas alternativas. Si las tropas cubanas atacaban la embajada, centenares de personas desarmadas morirían. Debía evitar que cualquier acto de violencia ocurriese en el territorio peruano a mi cargo.

De pronto recordé que tenía, en contra de mi costumbre, debajo de la guayabera, el revólver calibre 38 de la Policía Nacional. Atiné a preguntar, sin poder identificar a los que en la oscuridad nos rodeaban, quién estaba encargado de la seguridad de Fidel, porque quería hacer, delante de él, entrega a mi personal del arma que portaba. Vi y escuché un enjambre de armas que rastrillaron y me apuntaron. Luego Castro me mostró su arma, como indicando que yo debía retener la mía. Pero descarté el gesto.

Pausadamente saqué el revólver y, en la penumbra, se lo alcancé al mayor Casanova. Una sensación de alivio pareció surcar el cielo habanero.

Aun cuando Castro siempre portaba su arma al cinto, creí prudente subir a su auto sin revólver. Demostraba, al desarmarme voluntariamente, que mi ánimo era el de buscar una solución no violenta. Apreté la mano de mi esposa. Era una señal de despedida.

Una vez dentro del auto, conducido por un moreno con gorra verde olivo, se inició una rauda marcha seguida por los Alfa Romeo de su escolta. A pesar de mi entusiasmo por la velocidad y el riesgo, no encontré sentido a las maniobras absurdas que hacía el chofer de Castro, solo zigzagueaba por calles casi vacías y oscuras.

El presidente de Cuba, de inmediato, pasando de la cordialidad a un tono más serio, me solicitó mi colaboración.

—Acá hay solo dos caminos—dijo grave—: se está conmigo o en contra de mí. A favor de Cuba o del imperialismo yanqui. Si estás del lado de nosotros, debes firmar una nota autorizando el ingreso de las fuerzas cubanas—dijo Castro.

—No estoy ni del lado de Cuba ni de Estados Unidos—repliqué sin vacilaciones.

—¿Entonces, de quién?—volvió a la carga el jefe de Cuba.

—Del Perú y de mis propias convicciones, que en este caso coinciden plenamente—insistí decidido y claro.

Entonces, tomé la iniciativa de la conversación para establecer mi imparcialidad y neutralidad en los asuntos cubanos.

—Mira, Fidel, estás acostumbrado a atemorizar o a cautivar a la gente. Pero yo no me encuentro ni cautivado ni atemorizado. Lo que tenemos que encontrar es una solución que convenga a los dos países, a corto o mediano plazo. Hoy si es posible.

Luego intenté desviar la conversación hacia un terreno más propicio. Expliqué a Castro que habíamos hecho avances en las negociaciones y que, por lo tanto, me inclinaba a pensar que sería prudente la intervención, en el diálogo, de representantes del Ministerio de Relaciones Exteriores, y señalé concretamente a Alarcón.

En el asiento delantero, al lado de quien manejaba, un sujeto a quien no le había visto el rostro, volteó para decir:

—Tú quieres ganar tiempo con un diálogo diplomático, solo para ventaja tuya. Fidel, dame la orden para arrasar con todos. Saltarán como conejos.

Reconocí a Manuel Piñeiro, al que llamaban Barba Roja; se sabía que había coordinado los movimientos subversivos en Latinoamérica. Ahora su barba lucia rala y descolorida, pero sus ojos revelaban instintos asesinos.

Este, con la ruda actitud de un guerrillero, extrajo su arma. Volvió a mirarnos a todos y contuvo la respiración. Luego, ensayó, con su voz que a veces sonaba femenina, un tono grave.

—Si nos quiere ayudar, entonces que el diplomático firme la nota escrita que nos autoriza el ingreso—embistió Piñeiro.

¿Había Castro perdido el control? ¿Fingía concederle espacio a Piñeiro para dar un golpe de astucia?

Me invadió, en esos instantes, una rebeldía que tuve que contener. Me encontraba frente a un hombre que había adoctrinado a sus lugartenientes a pensar solo en términos de blanco y negro, es decir, sin imaginación para alternativas. Eso era peligroso porque el mismo Fidel Castro se había habituado a ser un protagonista en el escenario internacional. Castro se encontraba presionado por la actitud de Piñeiro, y me pidió que respondiera.

—Yo no me presto para un acto que llevaría a la muerte a cientos de personas, entre ellas, mujeres y niños inocentes—respondí firme y sereno.

Castro no pudo disimular su asombro. Durante muchas décadas estuvo acostumbrado a que nadie contradijera sus propósitos, sus pensamientos eran aceptados como ideología y sus decisiones como órdenes.

A pesar de haber logrado convocar al propio Fidel Castro al diálogo, me encontraba en desventaja y desarmado. Sin embargo, arriesgué aún más y agregué:

—Siempre había pensado que la forma más digna de morir era por la patria y en defensa de las propias convicciones.

Hice una pausa y todos nos miramos.

—Solo puedo colaborar con ustedes en el propósito de la libertad, es entonces importante que me aseguren que nadie morirá ni será tomado preso—concluí.

La pistola pasó, de las manos de Barba Roja, a reposar en el asiento posterior del automóvil Zil, donde se confundió con el negro color del tapiz y la impenetrable oscuridad de la noche.

En saber decidir sobre la vida y la muerte de otros radica el poder

Castro, apoyándose con gestos, interrumpió para decirme:

—La diferencia más importante entre nosotros es que yo sé decidir sobre vida o muerte. Tú no—y le dio énfasis a cada una de las sílabas que componían sus palabras; luego agregó para justificar su dura sentencia—. En la decisión sobre la vida de otras personas radica, en sustancia, el poder—y mientras mesaba su cabellera, agregó—. Y tú no eres capaz de matar ni siquiera en tu propia defensa.

Para mí el mensaje fue claro. Castro había sido informado de que, horas antes, yo no había podido apretar el gatillo para deshacerme de quien, en un intento de secuestro, me amenazó de muerte. No quedó para mí duda de lo bien enterado que estaba Fidel sobre todo lo que ocurría dentro de la embajada. Quizá también el pretendido secuestro pudo haber sido obra de los esbirros dirigidos por el mismo Piñeiro.

El comandante en jefe, que se distanciaba en estatura de aquellos funcionarios que procuraban hacer méritos frente al líder máximo, prosiguió, en tono de diálogo, con una sentencia:

—En el Perú se habla mucho, pero los políticos no hacen nada en concreto. Cambiarán los Gobiernos y ustedes seguirán zigzagueando en su política exterior—dijo mientras dibujaba en el aire unas zetas para remarcar sus palabras.

—Buscamos la democracia—le dije.

—Yo, en cambio, estaré acá firme, en una sola línea, controlando todo—presumió y añadió—. Lo que tú afirmas ahora puede cambiar mañana. Tu país es inestable. Nadie sabe quién va a ser el presidente dentro de seis meses.

—Si en el Perú cambiamos es porque somos más libres—le contesté—. Pero lo importante es ahora resolver. Estoy siempre dispuesto a buscar soluciones, tal como hice cuando vine a negociar el nombramiento del embajador cubano en Lima para restablecer el nivel de relaciones.

Hubo un silencio. Lo aproveché para reiterar:

—Al final de cuentas mi propósito es ayudar a los cubanos.

—Esos que apoyas son todos lumpen—insistió entonces Piñeiro. El revolucionario de tercera línea luchaba por hacer notar su presencia ante el líder máximo.

—La palabra "lumpen" está mal empleada—dije haciendo énfasis en aquel término de origen alemán—. Acá se trata de cubanos, entre ellos profesionales, amas de casa y muchos menores de edad que buscan una alternativa a una revolución desgastada, que lleva veinte años.

—Lumpen—se volvió a escuchar

—Pero ¿no se dan cuenta que también los estoy apoyando a ustedes para resolver un problema grande?

—Si tú no autorizas nuestro ingreso, otro funcionario peruano lo hará por ti—agregó Barba Roja.

—No lo creo. El Perú no saca ningún provecho de esto. Este es un problema entre cubanos; tu Gobierno los persigue. Si no hubiera persecución política en Cuba, no habría motivo para darles asilo ni protección.

Barba Roja hizo un gesto despectivo. No me inmuté. Al contrario, decidí atacarlo para dividir el frente que afrontaba.

Era importante, en esa situación tan apremiante, mantener el nivel de respeto mutuo. Para que funcionara una estrategia de provocación se requerían de dos actores, el provocador y aquel que reaccionase ante una provocación. Yo no estaba dispuesto a caer en el juego que se planteaba.

—Todo está en las manos de Fidel Castro. A ti, Piñeiro, nadie te conoce en el mundo. Fidel, en cambio, está jugando su prestigio internacional. Yo estoy acá para buscar una salida al problema—insistí.

¿Lograría dividir a mis interlocutores? ¿Era mucho lo que estaba arriesgando? El corazón me latía con fuerza. ¿Cuántos miles de personas se habrían doblegado frente a Castro? ¿A cuántas habría mandado a eliminar por no avenirse a sus razones?

El auto se detuvo en la oscuridad de un lugar desconocido.

Fidel y Barba Roja bajaron y caminaron juntos unos metros.

Me quedé sentado en el carro. El chofer me vigilaba.

Castro vestía su usual uniforme verde olivo, de gruesa estructura. Muy abrigado para el clima de Cuba. Posiblemente tenía debajo un chaleco antibalas ya que lo noté rígido en sus movimientos. Irradiaba en la proyección de su sombra bajo la luz de la luna, la figura de un hombre inmenso, mucho más grande que Piñeiro.

Vi cómo conversaban. La sombra de Piñeiro se achicaba aún más y se confundía con la oscuridad.

Mientras los observaba, concluía que era cada vez más evidente que el Gobierno de Castro, enfrentado a su peor crisis, intentaba echar mano del conocido recurso de escenificar un conflicto externo para distraer la atención del interno. De ese modo, lograría cohesionar al pueblo apelando a la causa patriótica para enfrentar el supuesto peligro exterior. Y para ello, el país que ofrecía el menor riesgo de que ese conflicto tuviese consecuencias graves para Cuba era el Perú. Dentro de pocos meses habría un nuevo Gobierno.

Pero, en vez de eso ¿se habrían dado cuenta de que el Perú ofrecía la oportunidad que necesitaba Cuba para solucionar sus problemas internos? Yo estaba seguro de que el Perú —un interlocutor imparcial, neutral— era capaz de salvar a Castro de un problema nacional que comprometía gravemente las relaciones internacionales de Cuba.

Habrían pasado cinco minutos.

Cuando ambos retornaron al vehículo, este arrancó su marcha y nosotros nuestra conversación.

—No se inmiscuya en asuntos internos de Cuba—me advirtió Castro.

—Los derechos humanos, el asilo, son temas de carácter internacional.

—Interesará a otros, no a nosotros en este momento—puntualizó Fidel.

—Recordemos que Cuba suscribió convenios sobre asilo—contesté.

Quise decirle a Fidel el aprecio que tenía por Cuba y su gente. Ese país maravilloso, de inigualable clima, de gente bondadosa, con capacidad de resolver cualquier situación. Poetas, escritores, grandes músicos, apasionados deportistas y extraordinarios médicos habían hecho que Cuba sonase en el mundo.

El auto negro paseaba, con el motor acelerado, por la Quinta Avenida. Providencialmente, se acercaba al parque ubicado entre las calles 26 y 28 de Miramar, donde se alzaba una estatua pequeña de Grocio Prado, un militar peruano que había participado en las luchas por la independencia de Cuba.

Ante una insinuación mía, el coche se detuvo.

—¿Sabes a quién homenajea ese busto?—pregunté a Fidel mientras señalaba la estatua oculta entre el follaje y la oscuridad.

El líder cubano se quedó callado. Entonces le expliqué de quién se trataba.

—¿Cómo me dijiste que se llamaba?—preguntó Fidel enarcando las cejas.

—Grocio Prado.

—Claro que lo recuerdo. Por cierto, fue una gran gesta la del militar peruano que luchó por la independencia de Cuba. Ello ocurrió en abril de... No continuó la frase.

Para no incomodarlo ante una situación en la que habría olvidado un importante aniversario, agregué:

—Muchas cosas han sucedido en abril. Parece que en este mes se levantan todas las ganas. La invasión a la Bahía de Cochinos, el Bogotazo, y ahora el desembalse de frustraciones en la embajada del Perú.

—Coincidencias sin semejanzas—agregó Piñeiro.

Castro lo mandó a callar con un ademán.

Aproveché el silencio para repasar aspectos sobre nuestras buenas relaciones. Argumenté que el Perú siempre había estado al lado de Cuba, incluso antes de haber alcanzado su independencia. El Gobierno peruano propició una acción para que se reconociera el estado de beligerancia y, de ese modo, España perdiera el apoyo internacional necesario para retener su última colonia en América. El peruano Raúl Porras perdió su cargo de ministro de Relaciones Exteriores por oponerse, en la OEA, al aislamiento internacional de Cuba.

—El propio embajador De Habich perdió por ello su carrera, por apoyarnos—intervino Castro.

Entonces me incorpore diciendo:

—Durante los años que trabajé en la delegación peruana ante las Naciones Unidas, yo mismo dediqué horas y esfuerzos a encontrar fórmulas para conciliar intereses a favor de la protección de los Derechos Humanos en Cuba— hice una pausa enfática y continué con voz grave—: intereses permanentes que concuerdan con los de la comunidad internacional. No apoyaría nada que vaya en contra del derecho internacional.

Castro se quedó mirándome, inquisitivo.

Aproveché para continuar:

—Analicemos ahora la situación serenamente, de manera conjunta, de modo que ninguna de las partes pierda, sino que ambos países ganen.

Era su turno y Fidel lo aprovechó:

—El problema no lo originaste tú—asintió apuntándome con su índice—, sino que viene de tiempo atrás.

Se estaba abriendo un ambiente de coincidencias cuando quedó en claro que, para Fidel Castro, el derrocamiento de Velasco Alvarado había sido un duro golpe, sobre todo porque su sucesor, el general Morales Bermúdez, no continuó cultivando las relaciones de cooperación con su Gobierno.

Para Castro, algunos hechos no habían quedado atrás. Se refería al hundimiento de los barcos pesqueros cubanos en el puerto peruano del Callao. También mencionó las supuestas deudas del Perú por la compra o el adelanto de repuestos, suministrados por Cuba a las Fuerzas Armadas peruanas, para los aviones Sukoi, de fabricación soviética, así como para algunos tanques del mismo origen.

Entonces, Piñeiro agregó:

—El capitán Núñez Jiménez, embajador de Cuba en Lima, había anunciado el apoyo de Cuba para acciones militares contra Pinochet. Pero el Perú, o más concretamente, Morales Bermúdez, ignoró ese gesto que habría permitido recuperar los territorios de Arica y Tarapacá arrebatados por Chile en la Guerra del Pacífico.

En esos apremios era conveniente buscar un momentáneo equilibrio de fuerzas, indispensable en una negociación que no debía derivar su curso. Decidí, entonces, mostrarle mi capacidad de administrar información confidencial, lo que era la base del poder en Cuba. Era algo temerario, pero debí tomar el riesgo. Las cosas no podrían ponerse peor de lo que ya estaban.

—A propósito de deudas, Fidel, yo también conozco de algunas cosas que tienes tú ocultas. O que los tuyos te las esconden.

El líder enarcó una ceja y me miró intrigado. Entonces seguí:

—Tus relaciones en Alemania, en áreas tan sensibles como en el entrenamiento de tus servicios de inteligencia.

—No sé de qué hablas—trató de desentenderse.

—¿No te acuerdas de la Lorenz?

Castro calló.

Me refería a Marrita Lorenz, una joven alemana que había sido violada a los siete años durante la invasión de los aliados. Después, habría sido captada por la CIA para eliminar a Fidel. No lo logró, pues Fidel había sido advertido de sus propósitos. Sin embargo, se rumoreaba que había sido amante de Castro y que, incluso, había tenido un hijo con él.

—¿Recuerdas la influencia de la República Democrática Alemana en la conformación de tu eficiente Seguridad del Estado? ¿De la asesoría que recibiste de la organización llamada Stassi y de su director Marcus Wolf? ¿No fue él quien les dio las claves para un servicio de inteligencia eficiente?

Piñeiro me miró con rabia.

Fidel no respondió nada ni hizo gesto alguno. El hecho de que no protestara airadamente o tratara de negarlo mostraba que había tocado un punto sensible.

Como era sabido, no había mayor vergüenza para un comunista, adoctrinado por los soviéticos, que se le descubriera alguna clase de relación con alemanes. Los rusos habían pagado caro su participación en la Segunda Guerra Mundial, con más de veinte millones de muertos. Los comunistas tenían que diferenciarse y distanciarse de todo lo que tuviera olor a hitleriano.

—¿Ya olvidaste el apoyo que les dio Manfred Patche, joven guardaespaldas de Hitler que lo acompañó hasta sus últimas horas en el búnker berlinés?

Me pareció notar que el líder cubano sofocaba una involuntaria expresión de sorpresa.

Fidel alzó la mirada absorta, como si hubiese sido descubierto en medio de una travesura. Había dado en el blanco.

Entonces, luego de una sentida pausa, Castro propuso:

—Podemos llegar a un acuerdo amistoso. Tú nos entregas a unos cuantos que queremos castigar y te quedas con el resto. Todos ganamos.

Rápidamente le contesté:

—O todos perdemos. No se trata de un mercado de trueque. Además, también crearía dificultades a todos, una selección minuciosa retrasaría cualquier solución—precisé.

En ese momento, solo tenía una intención: proteger la vida e integridad de todos los que habían ingresado a la embajada. Ya no tenían tanto interés los aspectos jurídicos que les daban derechos a unos —los que buscaban asilo—, frente a los que penetraron cuando el edificio ya no estaba amenazado por los postas. Todos se habían convertido en sujetos de una decisión política que lograría con Castro. Debía aprovechar la dinámica misma de las circunstancias.

Entonces recordé un escrito de Fidel titulado "Estos son nuestros caminos", que publicó la revista *Cuadernos de Ruedo Ibérico*.

Repetí el fragmento casi de memoria, sin dejar de contemplar a Castro, para no perderme su reacción

—*...que dejemos irse a los que quieren no es sino la confirmación de la* *fe que siempre tuvimos en el pueblo desde el primer momento; esa fe que no ha sido nunca defraudada ni lo será, que nos da la seguridad de que, dejando marchar a los que quieran, salimos ganando...*

Lo vi sonreír al reconocer sus palabras. Luego, Castro, con mirada aprobatoria, preguntó:

—¿Cuál es tu propuesta concreta?

—En este momento hay miles de personas en la embajada, y mañana podrían ser más. Conviene solucionar el problema integralmente. Que todos salgan al extranjero. Una persona fuera del país constituye una fuente de remesas y dinamiza la economía. Un individuo libre consume y produce. En tanto un cubano en la cárcel o muerto no ayuda a nadie.

—Podemos llegar a ese acuerdo—concedió Fidel.

Piñeiro quiso intervenir. Castro le ganó la palabra.

—Pero no basta con que yo los deje ir. Alguien tiene que acogerlos.

—De acuerdo—asentí—, y si nadie muere y cesa la persecución, todos ganan. La salida de familiares les simplificaría a ustedes el deshacerse de los indeseables en Cuba.

—Estudiaré esto último.

Vi nuevamente que Piñeiro, con gestos corporales quiso intervenir, pero Castro le pegó una mirada intimidatoria. Lo estaba fusilando con los ojos.

No sabía qué me dirían luego mis superiores de la Cancillería peruana, pero, en ese momento apremiante, debía llegar a un acuerdo para evitar pérdida de vidas. Sería una solución en la que ambos países saldrían ganando. Cuba consolidaría su situación política interna. El Perú fortalecería su posición internacional de país que sabía hacer respetar las normas generalmente aceptadas.

—Sin embargo—agregó Castro—, creo que las relaciones peruanocubanas deben revisarse en su conjunto. Yo he mencionado lo de los barcos, lo de los repuestos. Solucionemos todo en un paquete.

Se estaba cayendo todo lo acordado. Solo había, entonces, una salida.

Le dije a Castro que esos asuntos no los manejaba yo, ni la propia Cancillería. Eran temas que se veían al más alto nivel, es decir, entre jefes de Estado.

Castro se quedó pensativo. Luego, en tono reflexivo, propuso.

—Se me ocurre que podríamos realizar una reunión con Morales Bermúdez en un tercer país, tal vez... ¿Panamá?

Fidel había recuperado el galope de su verbo por el cauce de encontrar una solución. Intuí su astucia, de encontrarse con el Presidente Peruano en el extranjero. Ahí podía hacerse acompañar él por la gente suya que más lo apoyaría en una solución diplomática.

Le contesté con la mejor presencia de ánimo:

—Con mucho gusto transmitiré de inmediato a mi Cancillería esa buena disposición al diálogo...

—A la Cancillería no, al presidente Morales Bermúdez directamente—

interrumpió Castro—. Las cancillerías ya han cumplido su rol y a partir de ahora el asunto debe tratarse prescindiendo de ellas. Quiero que el general Morales Bermúdez conozca todo lo conversado aquí, y que valore la posibilidad de una reunión a nivel presidencial.

—Entiendo, pero pertenezco a una institución, la Cancillería peruana, en la que se observan reglas. Yo tengo que comunicarme con mi ministro de Relaciones Exteriores, que debe estar al tanto de esta entrevista, no puedo hacerlo directamente con el presidente.

Fidel asintió y luego dijo:

—En este momento yo no tengo funcionarios diplomáticos en Lima, ya que fueron retirados. Propongo que tú mismo lleves mi mensaje a Morales Bermúdez. Eres el único que puede contarle las circunstancias de nuestra conversación y el arreglo al que llegamos.

Fidel estaba esperando una respuesta a su propuesta.

En un chispazo, de esos que hacen encender una idea brillante cuando las circunstancias apremian, le dije:

—Para eso tendría que ausentarme físicamente de la embajada en estas circunstancias tan sensibles. Podría hacerlo si me garantizas que se mantendrá un *statu quo* en la situación de los ingresantes, que no se empleará la fuerza contra esas personas mientras dure mi ausencia. Y que se respete lo acordado, la garantía de salida del país de todos los ingresantes. Acá no hay posibilidades de retroceder.

Algunos latidos de corazón me revelaban esperanza y excitación.

—Pero, comandante, todo está preparado para un ataque—intervino entonces Piñeiro, a quien, evidentemente, le resultaba incómodo que llegáramos a un arreglo.

Entonces me dirigí a Castro:

—Estoy seguro de que Piñeiro, como antiguo revolucionario, ve el asunto desde el punto de vista de la política interna, pero tú, Fidel, coincidirás conmigo en encontrar una solución desde la dimensión internacional.

—Lo que más me preocupa es que se cree una mala imagen de la Revolución.

—¿Por qué?—pregunté.

—Eso de dar asilo a miles de personas acarrearía admitir que hay persecución política en Cuba—enfatizó Castro.

—Tengo la solución—dije, como si se me hubiera escapado un disparo.

—¿Cuál?—insistió Castro.

—No califiquemos a las personas como asilados ni usemos la palabra refugiados. Hablaremos solo de "ingresantes".

—Eso lo dices tú. Pero qué dirá Morales Bermúdez...—dudó Castró, mientras se acariciaba la barba.

—Déjame transmitir la idea a Lima. La consulta cablegráfica no tomará más de media hora, entonces podremos volver a reunirnos.

El presidente cubano paseó la mirada alternadamente por nuestros rostros, el mío y el de Piñeiro. Reflexionó por un segundo, y luego soltó:

—Te garantizo que no habrá empleo de fuerza alguna...por el momento—precisó.

—¿Y la salida de todos?

—Dependerá de las noticias que traigas...de que te autoricen el viaje a Lima, que ya sería una buena señal.

Cuando bajé del auto del curtido guerrillero, tenía la sensación de haber ganado mucho. Estaba seguro de que había evitado un baño de sangre.

¿Logré convencer a Fidel, que llevaba cuarenta años practicando la violencia, de que optara por una solución diplomática? En la práctica, le había demostrado que el poder también radicaba en la capacidad de saber negociar. Sin embargo, no había encontrado la respuesta precisa para el argumento de Castro: "El poder radicaba en la capacidad de decidir sobre la vida de otros".

Cuando retorné a la embajada, los ingresantes me rodearon. Para ellos era como si hubiera hablado con Dios.

Me dieron a entender que Fidel no tenía la culpa de lo que les estaba pasando, y si así fuera, lo perdonarían igual. Les dije que la conversación fue positiva, nada más.

La comunicación telefónica entre la embajada y Lima fue inusualmente rápida. Posiblemente las manos de Fidel estaban detrás de que ello se hiciera posible. Por el télex recibí, diez minutos después, la autorización escrita de la Cancillería peruana para viajar a Lima.

Paralelamente, al teléfono, el embajador Bustamante, secretario general y número dos de la Cancillería —ya habían cambiado al anterior— me aseguró que el lunes a primera hora se gestionaría el envío de pasajes para que, a mediados de la próxima semana, pudiera estar en Lima.

¿No había sido capaz de hacer notar la premura que exigía la situación? ¿No se habían dado cuenta de que ese *statu quo* que tanto esfuerzo me había costado negociar con Castro, a espaldas de Piñeiro, solo se podría mantener por unas horas?

Con voz sonora, como zanjando la cuestión, Bustamante respondió:

—Pero hombre, ¿no te das cuenta de que es Viernes Santo por la noche? Acá en el Perú nadie trabaja. Dile eso a los comunistas de la isla.

Cual lo acordado, a la media hora exacta estaba otra vez en la calle.

Castro apareció nuevamente en su vehículo acorazado, con toda su ruidosa escolta y me invitó a subir al automóvil.

Cuando me disponía a ello, vi que Fidel le hacía señas a Lilly, que se había quedado parada discretamente en la acera. Mientras ella se acercaba, Castro se volvió hacia mí:

—¿Permites que nos acompañe tu compañera?

Hice un ademán para que ella también subiera al auto.

Esta vez, Fidel, Lilly y yo nos sentamos en el asiento trasero, algo estrecho, en tanto que adelante iba, además del chofer, un hombre vestido de traje oscuro, cuya espalda tenía el ancho de un armario, y que, por su contextura, impedía toda visibilidad. Pero la novedad me alimentó el ánimo. ¡Ya no estaba el duro de Piñeiro! Fidel lo había literalmente desembarcado.

La atmósfera ahora era más amigable y el tono conciliador.

—Quiero que sepa, estimada señora—dijo Castro en tono muy cortés—, que yo no tengo nada personal contra ustedes. Es más, creo que su esposo ha desarrollado una excelente labor resguardando los intereses del Perú en La Habana.

Lilly, añadió:

—Y también tuvo presente los intereses de Cuba.

Señaló entonces un letrero de esos que frecuentemente aparecían en las amplias calles de La Habana con frases a favor de la niñez. Este resaltaba una frase de José Martí: "Los niños son la esperanza del mundo".

—Mi preocupación, ahora—dijo Lilly muy convincente—, está en los cientos, quizá miles de niños cubanos que se encuentran en este momento en la embajada. Pese a su inocencia, están amenazados tanto por las tropas apostadas allí, como por el hambre, la inclemencia del clima y otros peligros.

Castro, al escucharla, en esa estrechez en la que estábamos sentados, esbozó una sonrisa nostálgica.

—Siempre es bueno escuchar el consejo de una mujer…—admitió.

La mente de Castro parecía estar ubicada en algún lugar no muy distante del pasado. Tal vez estaba recordando a Celia Sánchez, que ejercía un control equilibrado y muy inteligente de las competencias de cada miembro del gobierno.

Recordé que cuando Celia falleció, el Gobierno de Cuba sufrió un gran vacío. Se habló de graves divergencias entre los hermanos Castro y de una lucha por el poder. La mano dura de Piñeiro, en esos momentos difíciles en el que el gobierno se partía, volvió a tomar preponderancia.

Instantes después, como si se hubiera arrepentido de un momento de debilidad, el comandante en jefe se adelantó en el asiento y dijo:

—Ustedes han vivido demasiado tiempo en los Estados Unidos y seguramente están condicionados a ellos.

¿Estábamos nuevamente retrocediendo? No podía creerlo. Entonces respondí.

—Viví en los Estados Unidos para trabajar en la misión peruana ante las

Naciones Unidas. Siempre he sido imparcial en mi criterio. Y sin duda los Estados Unidos tienen muchas ventajas. Yo si fuera cubano también me iría a vivir ahí. ¿Tu acaso no fuiste a tentar suerte en la Universidad de Yale?

Tras una breve pausa, volvió a la carga, esta vez con un tono aún más reflexivo.

—¿En razón de qué te interesas tanto por los refugiados? ¿Por qué arriesgas tanto?

—Porque yo mismo, siendo un niño, viví algo similar. Tuve que abandonar mi país natal y embarcarme en el buque llamado Rímac hacia el Perú. Escapábamos de las consecuencias nefastas de una guerra.

—Se dice que los hijos de la guerra son los mayores luchadores por la paz y son exageradamente pacifistas—dijo Fidel. Luego agregó—. Pero tú no conoces Cuba. No eres latinoamericano, ni caribeño; eres prusiano.

—Un momento, Fidel. Tú no conoces Europa. Yo nací en Baviera, y ahí somos como los cubanos, mezcla de orgullo y valor, algo así como chocolate con ají.

Castro encendió un habano con una paciente técnica. El comandante en jefe hizo una larga pausa, tras la cual ensayó un nuevo comentario:

—Solo te recuerdo que sería conveniente la entrega del expolicía y otros dos hombres, cuyos nombres luego te diremos.

—¿Los fusilarás?—interrogué.

—Un tribunal revolucionario los juzgará por traición a la patria. Yo no puedo evitar que los manden a fusilar—respondió secamente Castro—. Hay que sacrificar a algunos para satisfacer los requerimientos de la sociedad socialista, que necesita sanciones ejemplares.

No se puede discriminar canjeando la vida de unos por la libertad de otros

En este punto fue enfático, enfrentándome a Castro. Luego agregué:

—En mi concepto, no puede haber justicia social sin justicia humana—repliqué.

Luego aproveché para rechazar su argumento respecto de la capacidad de decidir sobre la vida de otros.

—Tú, Fidel, tomas el camino más fácil, el ya señalado por la naturaleza misma. El matar no es sino adelantarse a un hecho irreversible. Lo difícil y grande es luchar por la vida. Este esfuerzo lo he visto en el ejemplo de mi padre, que era médico. Él, en la Segunda Guerra Mundial, curó a enfermos sin preguntarles su ideología y actuó en su calidad de extranjero como un embajador para la vida. Ese es mi ejemplo y a la vez mi argumento.

—Hay que darle una función socialista a la vida—dijo Castro, poco convencido de lo que él mismo decía.

—El problema migratorio va a ser en los próximos años el más grande desafío para los políticos. Adelántate a esa situación y resuelve el problema para Cuba, ahora mismo, antes de que empeore.

—Problema para los que se quieren ir—interrumpió Fidel.

—Es un problemón tanto para los que se quedan como para los que se van. Insisto en que, si está en juego la vida de una o tres personas, entonces no tendría sentido que sigamos conversando, ni que viaje a Lima. Ya hemos avanzado bastante, Lima está informada. No puedo retroceder a lo acordado anteriormente contigo.

Lilly, mi esposa, me dio, con el codo, un golpecillo entre las costillas, como una señal de aprobación, de apoyo. Estábamos frente a un dictador, esos políticos que sabían administrar temores. Estaba seguro de que demostrándole que mi esposa y yo no nos dejábamos intimidar, ganaríamos.

Era imposible prever cómo reaccionaría Fidel Castro Ruz en circunstancias cruciales. Era Comandante en jefe y mandamás de una isla que había desafiado al mundo. Castro era además un hombre que siempre daría sorpresas.

Un auto que venía en sentido contrario encendió sus faros. Un rayo de luz penetró la oscuridad y conquistó la penumbra que envolvía nuestra conversación.

Afuera, la claridad pálida de una luna plena iluminaba el Malecón del Mar de Camilo.

Después de una pausa más larga que la anterior, Fidel Castro Ruz, con voz clara y calmada, e iluminado por todas las luces, dijo:

—Eres un caso extraño. Fuiste alguien que recibió protección y ahora no desistes en otorgarla a otros. Viaja a Lima, la vida de los ingresantes queda garantizada.

—¿De todos?—pregunte, casi incrédulo.

—Sí, de todos.

Un apretón de manos fue el comienzo de un acuerdo. Se daba inicio al compromiso que salvaría a muchos, y también a los verdaderos intereses de toda la nación cubana, que estaba ganando la paz interna.

—Muchas gracias—contesté, sin dejar de mostrar alivio.

—Ah, ¿quién ganará las elecciones en el Perú?—preguntó el cazurro político.

—Fernando Belaunde Terry—contesté sin mostrar dudas.

—Entonces ganará el Perú—asintió cordialmente.

En esa atmósfera conciliadora, recordé que tenía algo más que tratar con el líder cubano. Ya me había llegado la autorización de viajar a Lima para solucionar los conflictos en una reunión con el presidente Morales Bermúdez. Pero estaba sujeto a la disponibilidad de vuelos y a los trámites administrativos. Las coordinaciones en el Perú podrían tardar unos días.

Entonces, pregunté:

—¿Cuándo sale el próximo vuelo de Cubana de Aviación?

Castro miró a su guardaespaldas, que hasta el momento no había abierto la boca. Este contestó:

—Cuando lo disponga el comandante.

Fidel pareció reflexionar unos segundos.

—Es conveniente que vuelvas lo más pronto posible. Así que mejor nos olvidamos de los vuelos comerciales. Vamos a ver si podemos organizar un vuelo para que viajes mañana mismo temprano y retornes en la noche.

Se confirmaba, una vez más, que las relaciones entre países no pasaban de ser, en síntesis, una expresión de los vínculos entre personas.

El haber logrado entrevistarme con Castro era importante. La negociación, decisiva y su resultado fue lo más conveniente. Estaba muy satisfecho. Le estaba regalando a mi país, así como a los cubanos disidentes una importante victoria.

Convertido en un problema internacional: Consolidar la solución acordada

Había logrado llevar a Fidel Castro a una decisión que salvaría de morir a algunos o quizás a muchos. Mejor aún, de ofrecer una esperanza a aquellos que habían apostado por la libertad.

Un periodista del *New York Times* esa madrugada después de verme bajar con Lilly del auto de Castro, insistía vivamente en obtener la primicia respecto a lo acordado. Yo le dije —con alguna experiencia en el periodismo— que lo importante era mantener la noticia sobre el hecho de que hubo un encuentro, pues de ese modo se aseguraría que el líder máximo ya estaba directamente involucrado en el asunto y por lo tanto sería el responsable de lo que acontecería. No habría duda de que, con esta información, dando la vuelta al mundo, se vería Castro aún más comprometido en una solución, internacionalmente aceptable. Los detalles se sabrían después.

Para mí era un despertar de una pesadilla larga. Abracé efusivamente a Lilly y celebramos nuestra victoria.

La importancia de recordar

Por mi experiencia en este campo, mi formación, así como mis convicciones, fui reiteradamente convocado por instituciones académicas interesadas en derecho internacional. Otras entidades prestigiosas como la Universidad de Miami mostraron especial interés por la trascendencia histórica de las decisiones tomadas. Los efectos sociológicos también son importantes.

El tema de asilo y refugio está recobrando vigencia en la comunidad internacional. Era una oportunidad para que el Perú —que tomó un protagonismo frente a países que concitaban atención en el escenario internacional, como Cuba y los Estados Unidos— pueda tener algo qué enseñar en materia de derechos fundamentales.

Estoy convencido, como embajador y jurista, que actuando así tal cual lo hice en Cuba, se fortaleció el derecho internacional. Sus alcances fueron ampliados luego de darle protección y amparo a las personas antes de que estas fueran calificadas. Es secundario si estas califican bajo el asilo o lo establecido en las pautas para refugiados. Lo prioritario es que sean protegidas.

Esta historia solo estaría completa si se recoge la versión de aquellos que también arriesgaron mucho para lograrla. Las motivaciones de los ingresantes, así como la historia, no estarían completas sin la versión de otros protagonistas. Los que también arriesgaron su vida y muchas cosas para alcanzar la libertad. Como también estaría incompleta la historia si solo se recogiera la versión de los cubanos, tanto la de los favorecidos, como la de los del gobierno. La versión del diplomático de un tercer país, es importante, por ser imparcial y profesionalmente informada.

Eso mismo se lo dije a Carlos Montaner, cuando el productor de Los Ángeles me ofreció hacer una película. En el guion Ernesto Pinto Bazurco salía como el único héroe. Eso me incomoda y me propuse hacer un libro testimonio sobre la importancia de que todos luchemos por la libertad.

El asilo fue utilizado también históricamente en Latinoamérica para alejar a un enemigo sin querer alcanzarlo. Útil esto en política cuando se pretende evitar que el perseguido sea puesto a disposición de la justicia y lo libere de culpa. Y que al ser encarcelado aparezca como preso político.

El asilo forma hoy parte de la tradición diplomática latinoamericana. La preocupación por los asuntos humanitarios se convierte en práctica cotidiana de la política exterior de la mayoría de los países de América. El derecho internacional americano siempre ha prestado deferente atención a este tema.

Lamentablemente años después, en el 2018, el Gobierno del Uruguay, una pequeña república sudamericana donde se firmó una importante convención sobre asilo, negó la protección diplomática al político Alan García Pérez, embarrando así una larga tradición a favor del Derecho Internacional. García Pérez, dos veces presidente democráticamente elegido, y líder del Partido político más antiguo de América, de oposición, sufrió persecución por parte de un Jefe de Estado no elegido, sin que este pudiera lograr que la justicia lo sentencie por delito alguno. A pesar de que no hubo este elemento jurídico indispensable, se le negó toda protección, lo que ocasiono una tragedia

El caso de la Embajada del Perú en La Habana no solo es importante para los del Mariel, sino hizo escuela en situaciones similares que se presentaron en las embajadas de la República Federal alemana en Praga y Budapest, en 1989, luego de la caída del Muro de Berlín.

Poco antes había yo escrito en Suiza una tesis de doctorado sobre el asilo y refugio. Estaba convencido de que Europa necesitaría de experiencias exitosas en esta materia. Europa no podría evitar ser el destino más cotizado por aquellos que sufren persecución en cualquier parte del mundo. Los países que han alcanzado las formas de vida más avanzadas de nuestro tiempo han renunciado a las utopías extremas.

No se han repetido en los últimos cuarenta años casos como este en La Habana. El gobierno cubano, con un tratamiento especial para los diplomáticos, y otras medidas ha podido evitarlo. Por ende, difundir este episodio histórico por entidades académicas es importante y puede enorgullecer a todos los involucrados que actuaron en favor de la libertad.

El Gobierno del Perú, nunca se ocupó por un reconocimiento en la comunidad internacional. Yo fui propuesto para el Premio Nobel de la Paz por iniciativa de la sociedad civil. Así es como recibí el Premio Palmer por iniciativa de entidades estadounidenses convencidas del valor de defender la democracia.

BOOK REVIEWS

Gregory P. Downs, *The Second American Revolution: The Civil War–Era Struggle over Cuba and the Rebirth of the American Republic*. Chapel Hill: University of North Carolina Press, 2019. 232 pp.

Aisha Finch and Fannie Rushing, eds., *Breaking the Chains, Forging the Nation: The Afro-Cuban Fight for Freedom and Equality, 1812–1912*. Baton Rouge: Louisiana State University Press, 2019. 344 pp.

Jesse Hoffnung-Garskof, *Racial Migrations: New York City and the Revolutionary Politics of the Spanish Caribbean*. Princeton, NJ: Princeton University Press, 2019. 408 pp.

There are moments in history that, more so than the patterns of most years or decades, expose both societal fissures and the strength of the ties that prevent societies from ripping apart. We do not yet have the benefit of much hindsight, but 2020 was almost certainly one such moment—for the globe, but possibly for the United States and Cuba in particular. The novel coronavirus wreaked havoc worldwide, reaching pandemic status in March in the United States and Cuba. In late May, police in Minneapolis killed a black man named George Floyd; in late June, police in Guanabacoa killed a black man named Hansel Ernesto Hernández Galiano. In the last months of 2020, the Cuban artists' collective San Isidro went on hunger strike after one of its own was arrested. In late November, members managed to film part of a police raid on the collective's apartment in Old Havana. San Isidro provoked islandwide conversations about freedom of expression and censorship in Cuba, and the Cuban government even agreed to meet with members of the collective. In January 2021, white supremacists stormed the US Capitol in the deluded hope of maintaining Donald Trump's grip on the executive branch; as a result, Trump became the first president in US history to be impeached twice.

Events like these warrant a true reckoning. It's insufficient to ask, "Why did this happen?" without asking "What does it mean that this happened here?" The United States must grapple with the partisan divisions that have led to such an inadequate response to the COVID-19 crisis and an attempted coup d'état; and Cuba must grapple with a new threat to the government's hegemony when faced with an increasingly digitized citizenry. These seem like turning points, moments at which the choices each nation makes could fundamentally change its future trajectory.

The identification of turning points suggests that most moments are not turning points but rather the fulfillment of patterns that have long existed— worth writing about but less consequential than, say, 2020. But what if there are more turning points than we've previously assumed? What if we have overlooked some crucial moments in the formations of the United States and Cuba? The three books reviewed here cover well-worn territory chronologically;

there is no shortage of books about the American Civil War, or a dearth of information on the hundred years between 1812 and 1912 in Cuba. But the contributions of these books extend beyond the periods they cover. By delving into the global politics of the nineteenth century, rooting geographically not just in Cuba but also in Spain, New York City, Florida, and the American South, they show us that the nineteenth century was not just the century that Cuba came into being as a nation. In that century, Spain, the United States and Cuba helped to create one another. *Breaking the Chains, Forging the Nation*, *The Second American Revolution*, and *Racial Migrations* breathe new life into moments that we thought we understood. At the heart of each book is a familiar theme: the place of Africa-descended people in American societies. But these authors have surpassed the familiar to unveil new connections and histories that transform how we think about "in-between" years.

The anthology *Breaking the Chains, Forging the Nation* juxtaposes the José Antonio Aponte conspiracy of 1812 to the racist massacre of black activists and citizens in eastern Cuba in 1912. The contributors ask us to consider the century in between from the perspective of black resistance and rebellion. Between 1812 and 1912, expanded plantation slavery grew Cuba's economy; then Spain abolished slavery on the island; then Cuba became an independent nation. *Breaking the Chains* is critical of histories that leave African-descended actors at the periphery during these pivotal years. Divided into three parts— "Slavery and Resistance in the Era of Aponte," "Black Political Thought and Resistance in the Age of La Escalera," and "Race and Blackness in Postemancipation Cuba"—the anthology's authors challenge traditional periodization of colonial Cuban history.

The first part explores the lived experiences and intellectual contributions of black Cubans on their own terms, not through the lens of white colonial authorities. Manuel Barcia's chapter on the West African roots of rebel leaders brilliantly connects the political and military upheaval among coastal African kingdoms to enslaved activity in Cuba. Postrebellion interrogations of African leaders of slave rebellions show that in dress, language, and relationships, these men and women drew from their war experience on the African continent in their new surroundings. Gloria García locates much more sophisticated methods of resistance than those for which scholars of slavery have previously given their subjects credit. Pushing back against the pervasive notion that most slave resistance was "spontaneous," she reveals that enslaved people engaged in planned, strategic resistance to the worst aspects of their oppression.

Coeditor Aisha Finch's chapter in this part, which conceptualizes the "repeating rebellion" in mid-nineteenth-century Cuba, fully transforms our view of this period. Finch argues that the dozens of rebellions that rocked western Cuba in the 1830s and 1840s were both thematically and literally connected. The subsequent rebellions indicated a growing collective consciousness of power among enslaved people: rebels absorbed the memory of the rebellions that preceded theirs and acted on the basis of that lived knowledge. Michelle Reid-Vasquez's ruminations on women's roles in the 1844 La Escalera conspiracy—during which the colonial government uncovered plans for a regional slave uprising across western Cuba—traces African women's military actions back to the Dahomey kingdom in West Africa and examines the lives of women who lived through La Escalera but were punished for their participation. Both chapters achieve the near impossible in historical studies: they offer possible insight into the motivations and deepest fears and desires of enslaved people. Finch argues that "moments of protest created radical shifts for some of those who participated and propelled others into new acts of resistance" (149). Reid-Vazquez's tracing of the lives of women involved in La Escalera further allows us to see how rebellion changed lives.

Twenty-four years after La Escalera, on the other side of the island, Carlos Manuel de Céspedes called for Cuban independence with the Grito de Yara. In the interim, much had changed, including the island's relationship to the United States. While Southerners had dreamed of adding Cuba as a slave state before the 1860s, by 1868 the United States itself no longer held humans in bondage. Indeed, 1868 was the midst of Reconstruction, during which federal agents restored national authority to the states that had seceded from the Union and engaged in a bloody civil war for four years.

But was it restoration or transformation that those agents and Republican policy makers were after in the late 1860s? Gregory P. Downs's *The Second American Revolution* insists that the result of the "war between the States" was not a restoration of the Union as it had been before Abraham Lincoln's election but a full-throated revolution. The Civil War gave way to an entirely new nation, midwifed by "managerial revolutionaries"—"previously moderate, establishment figures" whom, "as crises worsen . . . act boldly and comprehensively, transformed by time into reluctant but real revolutionaries" (6).

Although it might not have been the intention of Lincoln or his fellow Republicans to create a new nation at the outset of war, create one they did. Lincoln's suspension of habeas corpus, issuing of the Emancipation Proclamation, and establishment of antiracist policies imposed during the military occupation of the South did not restore anything; they created new realities. To understand the Civil War as anything less than transformative and revolutionary, Downs argues, is to fail to understand the possibilities of change in America. Downs's later chapters demonstrate that the revolutionary transformation of America shaped the contours of such change in the Spanish Empire, particularly Cuba. Matthew Karp's 2016 book, *This Vast Southern Empire: Slaveholders at the Helm of American Foreign Policy*, laid out the vision of Southern policy makers who desired a pan-American slave empire.[1] Here, Downs describes the vision of Northern Republicans who desired the opposite: a pan-Atlantic economy based on free labor and the end of slavery. For a moment, it seemed possible: Spain had its own revolution in 1868, and a series of liberal leaders had embraced increased autonomy for their colonies. The last of those even abolished slavery in Puerto Rico in 1873.

Some might argue that these transformations were not revolutionary because they were so easily reversed with the withdrawal of Northern troops from the South and the restoration of white supremacist legal and political power. By the late 1870s, the backlash to Republican Reconstruction known as Redemption was firmly in place in the US South. The rollback paralleled the situation in Spain, where the liberal presidents who served after 1868 found their legacies toppled in the wake of a restorationist coup in 1874. And after ten years of war, in 1878 Spain took Cuba back from the rebels who sought to free it. But Downs argues that we cannot let the reversals of revolutions convince us that revolutions did not happen at all: "The Second American Revolution did not fail; it succeeded, then was overthrown" (50). Downs's cogent analysis of the Civil War—or Second American Revolution, as he prefers—strips away a veneer of inevitability and staidness that the United States has long enjoyed. His work connecting the years after the Civil War to Spain and its empire demonstrate how the very chaos of a United States in the throes of a second revolution opened up the possibilities for such activity elsewhere. The US Civil War and its subsequent reordering of American society influenced revolutionary possibilities in Cuba.

Even as Redemption took hold in the South, ideas about black liberation worldwide proliferated in the United States and the Caribbean. The third part of *Breaking the Chains* delves into postwar revolutionary activity in Cuba, tracing how the independence movements of the nineteenth century shaped the politics of the twentieth. Fannie Rushing's chapter, "Resistance, 'Race,' and Place in Cuba during the Transition of Empires, 1878–1908," traces the evolution of *cabildos de nación*, religious groups based on African ethnicity, into the *sociedades de color* that emerged in the late nineteenth century. The *sociedades* were cornerstones of black political and intellectual life in Cuba, producing thinkers like the journalist Juan Gualberto Gómez and the writer and politician Martín Morúa Delgado. Both men and their contemporaries drew inspiration from black intellectuals and politicians in the United States, where the Civil War had created new possibilities and contributed to fervor around Cuban abolition and liberation in cities like Philadelphia, New York, and Washington, DC.

The post–Civil War United States is the setting for Jesse Hoffnung-Garskof's *Racial Migrations*. Starting with the meetings of the Spanish Caribbean group La Liga on West Third Street in New York City, Hoffnung-Garskof gracefully narrates a period of intense and rapid change across the United

States, Cuba, and Puerto Rico. Founded by the Cuban cigar roller Rafael Serra, La Liga served as a social group and a political education base for Cubans and Puerto Ricans in New York City. On Thursday nights, an exiled Cuban journalist and writer named José Martí joined the mostly African-descended group.

How Martí gained the trust and support of the members of La Liga—trust and support that ultimately launched him into the mythic status he enjoys today—is a central concern of this book. José Martí's legacy has become so venerated as to be meaningless (Lillian Guerra's 2014 monograph on his legacy being an outstanding exception to the rule). But *Racial Migrations* traces the lives of men like Serra (who eventually became a prominent politician in independent Cuba), the Florida-based Bonilla brothers Juan and Gerónimo, and Martí himself, grounding them in the streets of New York and allowing readers to understand how world-changing relationships were forged in person. Hoffnung-Garskof uses the methodologies of microhistory to narrate what Rushing argued explicitly: along the East Coast of the United States, in Havana and San Juan, black men and women spoke to one another about the nations they wanted to live in and then moved those visions into reality.

Hoffnung-Garskof re-creates the lives of Rafael Serra and his wife Gertrudis Heredia, the Puerto Rican native Sotero Figueroa, and the Bonilla brothers, born in Cuba and in Key West. In so doing, he illuminates the Spanish Caribbean diaspora, providing a window into how African-descended Caribbeans made their way in the post–Civil War United States. His discussion of their genealogies also offers up an argument that is bolstered by the chapters in *Breaking the Chains*: the political alliances and movements of black *cubanidad* in the twentieth century came out of the ethnic and racial associations of the nineteenth. Gertrudis Heredia was the granddaughter of *cabildo* leaders in Matanzas. Gertrudis and Rafael were close friends with the widow of Plácido, the poet ultimately executed for his participation in La Escalera conspiracy. Once in New York City, Gertrudis and Rafael played pivotal roles in Cuban independence and black citizenship. The alliances of their youth and early adulthood shaped their cosmopolitan politics.

Racial Migrations does an excellent job of using geography and concrete details of lived experience to make its arguments about political consensus building and the creation of a "race-blind" ideal of Cuban independence. Chapter 3, for example, explores the social world of black Antilleans in New York City, carefully noting how the neighborhoods in which they lived and worked overlapped or were the same as the African American neighborhoods established generations earlier. In Florida, too, black Cubans found common cause with African Americans, taking advantage of Reconstruction-era policies to register as American citizens and helping flip Florida to that party's side. For two young black men to see this was pivotal: "There is strong evidence that the

Bonillas grew up among men who took part in a form of political engagement that was novel for Cuban workers of any color: men who voted in local, state, and federal elections" (72).

Hoffnung-Garskof's microhistorical approach also allows the reader glimpses of women's worlds, which he admits are difficult to access when so many documents are written by men. But Gertrudis Heredia was a midwife. Through birth announcements and certificates, imagining the streets that young Antillean women walked in New York, Hoffnung-Garskof argues that the social networks women created and nurtured were as important to the formation of an Afro-Antillean political force as their male counterparts' actions were. And the world these men and women created in New York city led to the making of a new world, importantly one that took black citizenship seriously, in Cuba.

All three books remind us that it is important to revisit moments in history that we think we understand. Even in well-traveled territory there are paths yet to be uncovered. The less-traveled paths discussed here reaffirm each other, narrating the creation of a new twentieth-century Atlantic World—a new Cuba, a new United States, a new Spain—out of the old cloth of the nineteenth century. When the Bonillas' father, a black Cuban, registered to vote in Florida, when Serra and the Bonillas returned to independent Cuba to join the island's first presidential administration, it must have seemed like these events were without precedent, but they were not. And neither are the events in Cuba and the United States that seem unprecedented today. What seems shocking is made intelligible if we only look closely at the years in between.

ANASA HICKS
Florida State University

NOTE

1. Matthew Karp, *This Vast Southern Empire: Slaveholders at the Helm of American Foreign Policy* (Cambridge, MA: Harvard University Press, 2016).

Helen Yaffe, *We Are Cuba! How a Revolutionary People Have Survived in a Post-Soviet World.* **New Haven, CT: Yale University Press, 2020. 288 pp.**

Helen Yaffe's highly publicized new book revolves around an unsolved question: in the wake of the Soviet Union's collapse and the severe economic crisis that followed, how did Cuba's socialist system survive? This vital query will continue to occupy, and likely confound, historians and researchers for years to come. For while Yaffe covers considerable ground, *We Are Cuba!*—like its title, a favorite new slogan of President Miguel Díaz-Canel—largely echoes the Cuban government's response. This leaves plenty of room for critical interpretations that more thoughtfully thread the needle between sympathetic claims of revolutionary resilience and accounts emphasizing totalitarian staying power alone.

A lecturer of economic and social history at the University of Glasgow, Yaffe organizes her study chronologically and thematically. A first chapter summarizes the results of socialist development strategies in Cuba before 1989. The next provides a brisk discussion of the island's Special Period following the Soviet fall. Yaffe is frank about the crisis's scale. In recounting the Cuban state's efforts to respond by opening the economy to foreign investment and protect subsidized prices of basic goods through a dual-currency system, she acknowledges that such policies left political and psychological "scars" (66). But while critical of outsiders' "cynicism" and "condescension" toward Cuba's socialist project, Yaffe's prose at times betrays an aloofness of her own (5). Thus, she labels those risking their lives to reach the United States aboard rafts in 1994 as Cuba's "most impatient" citizens (57) and calls those engaged in the black market "opportunists" rather than individuals struggling to get by (60). It is here, too, where Yaffe develops a distracting habit that continues throughout the book. Cuba's citizens are a "revolutionary people," she writes, an extension in most respects of their government rather than what they were and are: millions of individuals whose feelings about and responses to their country's challenges are diverse (3).

The middle third of the book pivots to a series of signature projects that, in Yaffe's view, propelled Cuba beyond crisis mode at the turn of the twenty-first century. Having survived predictions that the island would be the next communist domino to fall, the country's authorities moved to reassert their socialist identity (pulling back some economic "necessary evils" from the 1990s) and insert state-run industries into global capital flows, in theory for the benefit of all. With regard to health-care services, the author is on firmest ground. Although she avoids debates about the labor conditions of Cuba's "medical internationalists," Yaffe accurately describes how they became a global calling card of Cuban loyalty to Third Worldist ideals in a neoliberal era while also providing an increasingly significant revenue stream. Investments in a publicly owned biotechnology industry dating to the 1980s have also paid off. Witness Cuba's efforts to develop its own COVID-19 vaccines. That said, Cubans who lived through the "Battle of Ideas" and "Energy Revolution" between 2000 and 2006 may find Yaffe's accounts of these campaigns too fulsome. Many remember their components—especially the ill-considered *maestros emergentes* program—as the last gasp of voluntarist whim under Fidel Castro's mercurial leadership that served to delay, not eliminate, the need for more durable structural reform.

The final third of the book brings readers into the present. Here, Yaffe covers developments, including the rise of Raúl Castro and (later) Miguel

Díaz-Canel into government leadership, the thawing of US-Cuban relations under Obama, and their subsequent refreezing under Trump. Yet although her analysis is comprehensive in some respects, it once again hews closely to many Cuban government axioms while insufficiently addressing, or acknowledging, critical Cuban points of view. For instance, Yaffe takes foreign observers to task for judging "Raúl's reforms" after 2010 a "faltering march toward economic liberalization" when "liberalization," she insists, was not really the goal (205). However, an outsider herself, she overlooks that it was Cuban economists—particularly at the University of Havana—who led the charge in pointing out the limitations of the government's planned "Update of the Social and Economic Model" and the slowness with which authorities implemented many of its agreed-upon terms. Many Cuban economists continue to argue that, notwithstanding the extensive effects of US sanctions and a desire to preserve a commitment to social justice amid rising inequalities, more economic liberalization is the best recipe for saving, not dismantling, core social welfare services on which Cuba's citizens depend (by generating an expanded productive base that can be taxed). Recent moves, beginning in July 2020, to free up more space for the island's private sector—including a pledge to legalize small- and medium-sized private enterprises, not just "self-employment"—suggest that the balancing act between what Yaffe calls "the plan" and "the market" has tipped once again toward the latter (231).

A number of other blind spots are notable in the book. At one point, Yaffe comments briefly on Miami anti-Castro activists' "fiefdom" in the 1960s and beyond, "where dissent against their hard line on Cuba was punished" (179). A reader might share that characterization but also question why she never references the kinds of dissent that have been punished over the years in Cuba itself. Her defense of Cuban "socialism" and "the Revolution" often treat both as abstractions; they appear to be what Cuban authorities say they are as much as fixed concepts. Yaffe benefits throughout from interviews with Cuban government officials and other protagonists of economic policy making, yet she largely takes them at their word—as when former National Assembly president Ricardo Alarcón claims that Cuba's small business owners today do not contribute to the nationalized health services they enjoy. (Of course they do, through progressive taxation on their earnings.) Perhaps most noteworthy, when considering the multiple reasons that might explain the socialist system's survival, Yaffe largely sidesteps migration. From the end of the rafter crisis of 1994 to 2017, Cuba experienced its largest and most sustained wave of out-migration in history, exceeding the total numbers that left the island in the 1960s. With over half a million heading to the United States alone, it seems important to consider the extent to which migration served as a "pressure valve," especially as increased remittance flows helped inject new informal capital into the Cuban economy.

For an author critical of foreigners' economistic takes on the Cuban Revolution's purported "failures"—because they place a capitalistic premium on perennial growth rather than sustainability and equity—ultimately hers is also a quantitative defense of what the Cuban government has achieved on the latter scores. In fact, the sheer volume of statistics employed in the book recalls a piece of video art by José Ángel Toirac from 2005. In *Opus*, the award-winning Cuban artist extracted only the numerical indicators that Fidel Castro cited in a single speech at the height of the Battle of Ideas in 2003 and then compiled a tape of Castro's voice pronouncing the stream of numbers overlaid on each number's written form. The audiovisual collage thus highlighted the disconnect between the performative nature of quantifying detail and many Cubans' perceptions of their everyday struggles at the time.

Yaffe's account, of course, is filled with context surrounding the numbers. And she is right to urge us to take contemporary developments in Cuban society, and in Cuban socialist policy making, seriously. All the same, what her own data-driven approach overlooks are the subjective experiences of a population that has lived in the shadow of one form of crisis or another for decades. At present, Cubans are in the midst of their worst economic recession in thirty years, propelled in part by the Trump administration's cruel sanctions, but not reducible to them either. And many do not have the luxury of feeling so upbeat about present authorities' commitments to "continuity," even as they continue to flirt with reform.

So, too, does Yaffe avoid valid questions about political rights. Either accept the Cuban government's one-party "direct democracy" as the best bulwark for national sovereignty and social equality, she implicitly suggests, or risk shock therapy that will turn Cuba once again into an imperialist playground for a revanchist supporting cast in Miami. But most Cubans this writer knows reject that premise as a false choice. It is possible to oppose the US embargo and defend rights to universal education and health care but also insist on the need for measured market openings and greater political participation and pluralism. After sixty-plus years, Cubans have every right to defend that formula as equally revolutionary.

MICHAEL J. BUSTAMANTE
Florida International University

Rachel Hynson, *Laboring for the State: Women, Family, and Work in Revolutionary Cuba, 1959–1971*. Cambridge: Cambridge University Press, 2020. 332 pp.

A un año del triunfo de la Revolución cubana, el 14 de febrero de 1960, un titular de la *Revista Bohemia* interrogaba: "¿Logrará la Revolución poner fin a las uniones ilegales?"[1] El texto consideraba al concubinato "relaciones silvestres", un "problema", un "atavismo". Asimismo afirmaba que "la Revolución cubana ha dado el primer paso para poner[le] fin" dando "las facilidades económicas y de trámite que son imprescindibles para la unión, para los faltos de recursos y–ay–de cultura".

Seis años después, una mujer rural del oriente del país mostraba que la legitimidad del concubinato persistía, aunque se habían intervenido sus condiciones de posibilidad: "Cuando dos se quieren se van a vivir juntos y es como si estuvieran casados . . . ahora sí están celebrando bodas en el pueblo . . . la Federación [de Mujeres Cubanas] lo organizó . . . Pero es lo mismo, yo hallo que es lo mismo [estar o no casados]".[2]

La conversación entre ambas fuentes delimita un ámbito de transformaciones y disputas relacionadas con la moral y la moral sexual, que tuvieron mucha evidencia en los años siguientes a 1959. Ese es el campo que aborda *Laboring for the State: Women, Family, and Work in Revolutionary Cuba, 1959–1971*, libro de Rachel Hynson publicado en 2019 bajo el sello de Cambridge University Press.

Hynson construye hipótesis y analiza evidencias de las relaciones y prácticas morales impulsadas desde arriba y resistidas desde abajo, y explora la conformación y despliegue —no sin conflictos— del proyecto moral de la Revolución. Por ese camino, halla que el gobierno revolucionario (desde 1961, socialista) produjo un marco de lo virtuoso: el de una "Nueva Familia" que debía verificar la existencia del "Hombre Nuevo" y la "Mujer Nueva" del socialismo. Esa "Nueva Familia" era heterosexual, monógama, nuclear, formalizada por las leyes, donde sus miembros —especialmente los hombres— trabajaban en empleos autorizados estatalmente y las mujeres cedían el control de su reproducción a la gestión médica estatal, incluyendo los partos y abortos hospitalizados. Afirma Hynson que así se buscó transformar —con distintos grados de éxito— el sistema de género previo a 1959.

Laboring for the State muestra, y esa es una de sus virtudes, cómo y en qué sentidos las concepciones de género fueron un frente de lucha tanto para el Estado como para un pueblo que recibió, resistió, transformó y resignificó el proyecto moral de los poderes políticos. Pero la autora va más allá y se pregunta qué dice ese dato de las necesidades productivas, de consenso y de control político del poder institucionalizado, entonces en formación.

Uno de los procesos que explora Hynson es la fuerte campaña de empuje estatal para la formalización de los matrimonios que hubo en los años 60 (capítulo 2). Al mismo tiempo, muestra otros asuntos en juego: el aborto, el uso de anticonceptivos, la hospitalización de los partos y la masificación de los servicios institucionalizados de salud para las familias, las mujeres, los menores (capítulo 1); la prostitución (capítulo 3); y la regulación de la mano de obra masculina y la política para la incorporación de mujeres al trabajo productivo (capítulo 4). Esos cuatro campos fueron intervenidos a través de campañas estatales, y se analizan en el libro con fuentes provenientes de periódicos, revistas, documentos y discursos del gobierno, normas jurídicas e institucionales, e historias orales.

En línea gruesa, *Laboring for the State* afirma que el gobierno revolucionario cubano produjo una ingeniería social que aspiraba a redefinir la familia nuclear y a organizar a la ciudadanía para su servicio al proyecto político, y que el trabajo era central en esa ecuación. La autora también concluye que en ese período el Estado produce una monopolización y cosificación del nuevo sistema moral y que, por esa vía, avanza hacia la afirmación de un poder autoritario.

En su enfoque, la puja gubernamental por la creación de la moral socialista y la Nueva Familia ilustran el biopoder en acción: el ejercicio del poder coercitivo sobre los cuerpos y el trabajo de ciudadanos y ciudadanas, incluyendo su vida reproductiva, sexual, familiar. El lente foucaultiano es fundamental en la lectura de Hynson quien, además, declara afinidad con los enfoques de género y feministas, y la teoría de la hegemonía. La utilización de ese enfoque tiene virtudes: permite analizar la política de control de los cuerpos y advertir dimensiones de la coerción muchas veces desconsideradas. Tiene, también, problemas: puede producir lecturas monolíticas del poder coercitivo, en lugar de advertir las dinámicas entre coerción y consenso que eventualmente aseguran hegemonía y legitimidad al poder político.

Dentro de los estudios cubanos este es un libro pertinente y valioso. Los análisis de los órdenes de género en ese período son escasos, tanto como aquellos que aborden la relación entre proyectos morales, políticos y económicos. Rachel Hynson lo hace.

Al mismo tiempo, *Laboring for the State* se ocupa menos de cuánto esos órdenes morales en juego y conflicto en Cuba, se inscribían en los debates socialistas históricos y contemporáneos a la revolución. Sin embargo, eso es fundamental.

Para 1959, las discusiones sobre la legalización de los matrimonios, el aborto, la prostitución y la participación laboral de las mujeres y hombres ya tenían una larga ruta dentro del socialismo real. Anoto un solo ejemplo, pero hay muchos. El impulso para legalizar el matrimonio se entendía en una clave particular: en la sociedad socialista, el matrimonio podría realizarse como unión libre de amor, y no como una unión fundada en el beneficio y las coacciones materiales, como se entendía que sucedía en el capitalismo. Además, la legalización del matrimonio aseguraría la protección legal de las mujeres y sus hijos dentro de las familias, y sus derechos para con las parejas incluso en situaciones de abandono. Las fuentes históricas cubanas sugieren que al menos una parte de lo que sucedió en esos años, se argumentaba en ese marco. Estaba detrás una concepción moderna de ciudadanía.

De hecho, el socialismo ha sido una de las vías modernizadoras, y ello ha tenido consecuencias para su proyecto moral y social; entre ellas: aspiración al progreso científico y técnico; programas de salud, escuela y alfabetización masivas; abolición del control familiar sobre los matrimonios y fomento de la libre escogencia (por eso, a la vez que se promovían los matrimonios se flexibilizaban los procesos de divorcio); legalización o institucionalización de los abortos. Recordemos, por ejemplo, que fue en la Unión Soviética donde se legalizó el aborto por primera vez, en 1920. Entonces, todo esos asuntos eran centrales para la política socialista y se habían disputado. Sus resultados fueron diversos y dependientes de los distintos contextos y etapas. En línea general, como ha estudiado Maxine Molyneux, en el socialismo real tanto la esfera doméstica como la sexualidad fueron absorbidas por el Estado en forma que incorporaban, pero al mismo tiempo borraban, las implicaciones radicales de la crítica feminista socialista.

El proceso cubano necesita analizarse también con ese lente, porque estuvo muy influenciado por tales conexiones globales. Eso no quiere decir que el proyecto moral de la Revolución cubana en esos años fuera calco del de sus homólogos ideológicos. Pero sí permite comprender la matriz de muchas de las discusiones que, por otra vía, se abordan en *Laboring for the State*.

Estamos, finalmente, frente a un libro muy estimulante que promoverá filiaciones, reflexiones, críticas y, sobre todo, preguntas imprescindibles para comprender la historia y el presente cubanos y, también, la subanalizada relación entre socialismo y patriarcado.

AILYNN TORRES SANTANA

NOTES

1. Leandro Blanco, "¿Logrará la Revolución poner fin a las uniones ilegales?", *Bohemia*, 14 de febrero de 1960, p. 30.
2. Eva Forest, *Los nuevos cubanos (La vida en una Granja del Pueblo)*, Editorial Hiru, Hondarribia, 2007, p. 236.

Devyn Spence Benson, Daisy Rubiera Castillo, and Inés María Martiatu Terry, eds., *Afrocubanas: History, Thought, and Cultural Practices*, **Karina Alma, trans. New York: Rowman and Littlefield International, 2020. 396 pp.**

Nine years ago, editors Daisy Rubiera Castillo and Inés María Martiatu Terry published a collection titled *Afrocubanas* in Havana. The first of its kind, the book brought together essays and primary sources written by black Cuban women who were members of the antiracist organization of the same name. In 2020, editor Devyn Spence Benson and translator Karina Alma made an English-language version of the collection available to a wider audience. Scholars and students of Afro–Latin American and US Afro-Latinx studies who are desperate to find English-language primary and secondary sources authored by Afro-Cuban women now have a resource at hand. The collection is a mandatory reading, alongside *Reyita* (Duke University Press, 2000), for those who wish to explore primary and secondary sources foundational to Afro-Cuban feminisms written by Afro-Cubana historians, journalists, artists, and activists.

The collection is divided into three parts. The first offers historical research. Through an analysis of primary documents "abundant" in regional archives and the press, according to the historian María Cristina Hierrezuelo, the essays center the experiences of black women in nineteenth-century Cuban history (40). While the essays are of varied quality, they provide a first reading of historical sources that provides scholars a model for future research. The authors ask how historical narratives of slavery might be revised if black women were placed at the center rather than at the margins or completely dismissed. Together they argue that Cuban history must be renarrated with black women at its center. At a minimum, black women are the mothers of the national family. Nineteenth-century historical narratives are, at best, incomplete and, at their worst, flawed without a comprehensive understanding of the full humanity of black women, their contributions, sacrifices, and identities. These essays also remind readers that black feminism began with the resistance of female slaves, on the African continent, the slave ships, and the plantations of Cuba.

The second part, titled "Thought," fulfills Rubiera Castillo's call that "Afro-Cubans must be included in the history of ideas and the nation of Cuba, where the contributions of women from their own social group are barely represented" (2). This part includes analytical chapters, essays, and selected newspaper articles written by Afro-Cuban women from the late nineteenth to the early twenty-first century. In publications of primary sources and analytical essays, the authors reflect on Afro-Cuban women's contributions to political thought and debates in the 1880s, to the Partido Independiente de Color in the 1910s, as full members of the revolutionary movement of 1959, and as living examples of the limits of racial equality and inclusion in the postrevolutionary period. The authors are unflinching. They ask and answer the question, Who are we, the black women of Cuba? Each author, however, approaches that question through a different lens. Each meditates on the production of black women authors, their philosophies, their contributions to religious practices, the discursive violence hurled at them as they go through their days. Several essays confront negative stereotypes about black and *mulata* women, stereotypes written into history by white men and reproduced in popular culture. On this topic, Yulexis Almeida Junco's chapter stands out. Authors reach different conclusions on the topic of black women's contributions to Cuban history, popular cultural, and intellectual production. In this way, this part proposes that there is space for heterogeneity within the category of black feminisms, in the plural. The varied experiences of women of color in the nation and their correspondingly varied articulations of black womanhood are not simplified, dismissed, or homogenized. The collection is itself a model of a "room of our own for black Cuban women" that is inclusive of diverse interpretations (181).

Finally, in part 3, "Cultural Practices," authors meticulously document the history of Afro-Cuban artists. Authors provide biographies of poets (Nancy Morejón), professors (Excilia Saldaña), authors (Teresa Cárdenas), composers (Catalina Berroa), filmmakers (Sara Gómez), athletes, and hip-hop artists. The biographies, however, often include interpretations of the subject's body of work as well as the author's self-reflection. Others, like Fátima de la Caridad Patterson, write about their own histories as members of community artistic communities, including popular theater.

With this translation, the editor's goals may have been to rupture silences in the history of Afro-Cuban women—to acknowledge their contributions to the nation, intellectual thought, and popular culture and to do so through the voices and writing of "black Cuban women *themselves*" (xiii). Indeed, here black Cuban women literally write themselves into the historical narrative. Scholars of Cuba, Afro–Latin America, and US Latinx studies now have a resource that enables them to avoid these silences in their own research and writing. The collection is a call to action: to conduct further historical research about black women in Cuban archives; to collect oral histories and interview contemporary Afro-Cuban intellectuals, journalists, and activists; and to choose essays from the collection to include in syllabi.

SOLSIREE DEL MORAL
Amherst College

Anna Clayfield, *The Guerrilla Legacy of the Cuban Revolution.* **Gainesville: University of Florida Press, 2019. 218 pp.**

Anna Clayfield, profesora de estudios hispánicos e latinoamericanos de la Universidad de Chester, Inglaterra, en su libro *The Guerrilla Legacy of the Cuban Revolution*, analizó, en una investigación detallada, cómo el guerrillerismo se perpetuó como una cultura política en los discursos de la Revolución cubana, en la cual la base fundamental era el legado dejado por la guerrilla.

Su investigación mostró, a través del análisis de libros, discursos de líderes políticos (principalmente Fidel Castro, Che Guevara y Raúl Castro), artículos del periódico *Granma* y revistas, como *Bohemia* y *Verde Olivo*, cómo se mantuvo el *ethos* guerrillero en Cuba a lo largo de las décadas, desde los años sesenta hasta la actualidad.

Al investigar las raíces de la guerra de guerrillas, Clayfield se centró en el ataque al cuartel Moncada en 1953 y las acciones del Movimiento 26 de julio que condujeron a la formación del Ejército Rebelde. Sin embargo, se discutió la historia de la guerrilla que derrocó a Batista, dando importancia solo al Movimiento 26 de julio. Otros grupos guerrilleros, como el Directorio Revolucionario, que también actuó especialmente en la guerrilla urbana, no fueron analizados por Clayfield, reafirmando la memoria y la historiografía oficial de la Revolución cubana, que destacó solo el protagonismo del sector de la Sierra Maestra del Movimiento 26 de julio.[1]

Muchos textos del Che Guevara destacaron la importancia de las guerrillas y el enfoque guerrillero como fundamentales para la revolución, como ha demostrado la autora. En "El socialismo y el hombre en Cuba", publicado por Guevara en 1965, Clayfield destacó las referencias a la lucha guerrillera y la necesidad de crear el "hombre nuevo", en el que el desarrollo de la conciencia se produciría a través de estímulos morales y la adhesión al proyecto revolucionario. Sin embargo, la autora no mencionó las críticas a los intelectuales en este texto de Guevara, quienes fueron acusados de no haber participado en la lucha guerrillera y por esta razón habían cometido el "pecado original", y no podían constituir el ejemplo de un "hombre nuevo" defendido por él, lo que creó exclusiones en el medio intelectual cubano.[2]

A lo largo de la década de los sesenta, el discurso guerrillero, según Clayfield, siempre se reforzó en las publicaciones, dando gran legitimidad a los líderes guerrilleros del Movimiento 26 de julio que formaban parte del gobierno. La tradición histórica de la lucha guerrillera en la isla fue muy prominente, en los discursos oficiales hubo una recurrencia de las guerras de independencia, la lucha de los mambises y héroes nacionales como Carlos Manuel de Céspedes, Antonio Maceo, Félix Varela, José Martí, entre otros, que fueron ejemplos de sacrificio y lucha que debería seguir el pueblo cubano.

Los valores, las actitudes y los comportamientos de la guerrilla continuaron siendo alentados en los discursos y publicaciones oficiales de la década de los setenta, años de institucionalización y acercamiento con la Unión Soviética. El papel de las Fuerzas Armadas y la militarización de la sociedad reforzó el código de guerrilla, "coraje, lucha, deber y voluntad", como un comportamiento ideal no solo para el ejército cubano, sino como un modelo para ser imitado por toda la población. Para el gobierno, el pueblo tenía el deber de participar en la defensa de las conquistas revolucionarias, ya sea en el trabajo voluntario de la cosecha del azúcar en 1970, o en la participación de las milicias o de los CDR, los Comités de Defensa de la Revolución, por ejemplo.

452 : *Book Reviews*

Sin embargo, desde mediados de los años setenta hasta mediados de los ochenta, hubo, para Anna Clayfield, una disminución en el discurso guerrillero. El éxodo de Mariel y la amenaza de la invasión de los Estados Unidos a Cuba acentuaron la escalada de la Guerra Fría, y los discursos oficiales fueron envueltos en la mentalidad de cerco e informaron la necesidad de proteger al "primer estado socialista en Occidente". Sin embargo, la muerte de la ex guerrillera Célia Sánchez en 1980, activista de la generación Sierra Maestra, tuvo un importante funeral de Estado con el recuerdo del Che Guevara y Camilo Cienfuegos, héroes guerrilleros que siempre son mencionados en varios discursos. Seis meses después, Haydée Santamaría, otra exguerrillera del Movimiento 26 de julio murió, se suicidó el 26 de julio de 1980, pero, sin embargo, la autora no analizó su muerte.[3]

En 1986, con el "Proceso de rectificación de errores y tendencias negativas", el gobierno cubano, según Clayfield, se alejó de las reformas de la Unión Soviética y reanudó el discurso guerrillero, valorando una vez más a los líderes vinculados a Sierra Maestra a expensas de los vinculados a Moscú. Al cerrar esta década, la autora menciona brevemente la ejecución del general Arnaldo Ochoa en 1989, acusado de corrupción, pero no analiza críticamente su juicio y fusilamiento, junto con otros miembros importantes del gobierno, que ahogó cualquier movimiento reformista en Cuba, como el que ocurrió en la Unión Soviética.[4] Para Clayfield, la ejecución de Ochoa llevó a la necesidad del gobierno por reforzar el discurso guerrillero, para compensar la disminución de credibilidad de la generación de la Sierra Maestra.

The Guerrilla Legacy of Cuban Revolution mostró cómo el guerrillerismo continuó siendo utilizado como un discurso tanto para superar dificultades materiales durante la década de los noventa y el "período especial", como durante los gobiernos de Raúl Castro y Miguel Díaz-Canel, constituyendo un importante arsenal simbólico de propaganda en el discurso oficial de la Revolución cubana.

SÍLVIA CEZAR MISKULIN
Universidad de Mogi das Cruces

NOTAS

1. El Directorio Revolucionario era una organización compuesta principalmente por estudiantes universitarios. Además del Movimiento 26 de Julio y el Directorio Revolucionario, otros grupos participaron en la lucha insurreccional. Ver Rafael Saddi Teixeira, "El ascetismo revolucionario del Movimiento 26 de julio: El sacrificio y el cuerpo en la Revolución Cubana (1952–1958)", tesis doctoral (mimeo), Universidad Federal de Goiás, Facultad de Ciencias Humanas y Filosofía, Goiânia, 2009. https://repositorio.bc.ufg.br/tede/handle/tde/1232.

2. Sílvia Cezar Miskulin, *Los intelectuales cubanos y la política cultural de la Revolución*

(1961–1975), São Paulo: Alameda / Fapesp, 2009, p. 117. Ver también Liliana Martínez Pérez, *Los hijos de Saturno: Intelectuales y revolución en Cuba*, México, FLACSO / Miguel Ángel Porrúa, 2006.

3. La trayectoria de Haydée Santamaría fue analizada por Carolina de Azevedo Müller. Ver Carolina de Azevedo Müller, *Haydée Santamaría y la mitología de una "heroína de la Revolución Cubana"*, trabajo de conclusión del curso para bachillerato y licenciatura en historia. Guarulhos, UNIFESP, 2018.

4. Ver el documental 8-A de Orlando Jiménez Leal de 1992 sobre el proceso y la condena de Arnaldo Ochoa por corrupción y varios otros oficiales, como Tony de la Guardiay Patricio de la Guardia, también acusados y condenados por corrupción y tráfico de drogas.

Megan Feeney, *Hollywood in Havana: US Cinema and Revolutionary Nationalism in Cuba before 1959*. Chicago: University of Chicago Press, 2019. 320 pp.

Megan Feeney's *Hollywood in Havana* is a history of Cuba's engagement with the US film industry during the Republican period (1902–1958). The book argues for the centrality of US films to the development of Cuban notions of democracy, masculinity, and national independence that constituted what she calls "revolutionary Cuban nationalism," which climaxed with the Cuban Revolution, against the government of Fulgencio Batista. Feeney explains how the impact of the US film industry on the island was shaped by the ambiguous approaches of Cuban intellectuals and film critics toward the United States, which they interpreted as a model of both democracy and modernity, as well as a threat to national sovereignty. She shows convincingly how US power was strong but unstable, having unpredictable, counterhegemonic outcomes: US movies Americanized as much as they nationalized. Analyzing the meanings that Cubans made of Hollywood, she demonstrates how Cubans subverted implicit imperialist messages embedded in US movies. Hollywood was a prompt for Cuban intellectuals to criticize US capitalism, exploitation, and domination. Conjunctly, the films were also a source of inspiration and a platform for Cubans to reflect on their national reality, ultimately stirring Cubans to fight for a better country.

The book contributes to the fields of Cuban studies and film studies. It complements recent scholarship that has advanced understandings of the revolutionary culture of the Republican period. It also challenges previous works that have understood Cuba-US cultural relations as a one-way process in which Cubans were passive subjects that mainly imitated US cultural influence. Instead, the book convincingly shows that Cubans metabolized US cultural influence, Cubanized it, and mobilized it for their own ends. It also advances previous understandings of the origins of the Cuban Revolution, focusing on everyday cultural encounters and revealing the connection between film and revolution. In that way, Feeney moves away from more traditional histories that have privileged analyses of Fidel Castro, the armed conflict, or Cuba-US diplomatic relations. Furthermore, the book advances film studies by focusing on sociopolitical trends and film business strategies rather than on individual films. It builds the imbrication of Cuba's political history and the development of US-Cuba film culture into a solid narrative that inserts the films' contents as part of its historical analysis in support of the larger arguments of the book.

Hollywood in Havana offers six chapters organized chronologically. Chapter 1 covers from the arrival of cinema to Cuba in 1897 to the beginnings of the anti-Machado mobilization in 1928. It tracks the growth of US hegemony in Cuba and the simultaneous increasing opposition to Americanization. While Cuban fanzines encouraged the love for US movie stars and their glamour, challenges to US cinematic influence came in many forms: Through Cuban popular music orchestras that provided the soundtrack to the silent movies and could therefore alter its meanings; through the *ruidistas* and the *parlantes* who interrupted the screenings and mocked Hollywood; through strong criticism of films that portrayed Cubans and the Cuban wars of independence in disrespectful ways. Chapter 2 explains the connection between the revolt against the government of President Gerardo Machado and its links to US interests, as well as the emergence of film criticism in Cuba. Several *minoristas* and movie critics conflated movies and politics, using their film reviews as platforms to condemn Machado and US imperialism. As they educated their readers about Hollywood's anti-Hispanic and consumerist messages, they fomented Cuban nationalism and revolution. Chapter 3 traces Cuba's reception of the US Good Neighbor policies during the 1930s through Hollywood films and film business practices in Cuba. Film was a way to assess whether the US was a good neighbor or not. Chapter 4 explores Hollywood's antifascism during World War II and its promotion of freedom-fighting masculinity. Cubans embraced US movie heroes, yet they interpreted them not only as symbols of the fight against the Nazis but also as inspirations to oppose Latin American dictatorships. Chapter 5 looks at the post–World War II era. It connects the Hollywood progressive left's disillusionment with US politics and Cuban's disappointment with the Auténtico rule of corruption and violence. US postwar film noirs were largely critical of US postwar society's greed, corruption, and criminality. Cuban film critics mobilized their criticism to fuel national desires to break with US hegemony. Thus, film noirs fostered Cuban ambivalences about the United States, weakening the bonds of fraternity that had been built during World War II. Finally, chapter 6 focuses on the fight against Batista between 1952 and 1958, explaining how Hollywood and its heroes were an important source of inspiration for the young rebels. Moreover, the chapter explains how the decades-old freedom-fighting masculinity that had been constructed through film criticism moved to the movie theaters, as film cine-clubs became sites for revolutionary clandestine armed action. The epilogue points to changes and continuity on the role of film in Cuban political culture in revolutionary Cuba. The book offers extensive notes, but it does not include a bibliography.

While *Hollywood in Havana* highlights the importance of gender for the construction of revolutionary ideologies of freedom-fighting masculinity, it pays less attention to race. The book could have been a great opportunity to engage in dialogue with the scholarship on Cuba's ideology of racial fraternity, a patriarchal discourse also born out of revolution, to better understand the intersection of race and gender in Cuban revolutionary culture. The reader might also be left wanting to know more about Cuban film productions and their relationship to US cinema and constructions of freedom-fighting masculinity. These points aside, *Hollywood in Havana* is a welcome contribution, thoroughly researched and well argued. It brings a fresh perspective on the origins of the 1959 Cuban Revolution and on the power of film and film criticism to shape the political life of a nation.

CARY AILEEN GARCÍA YERO
Harvard University

Isabel Story, *Soviet Influence on Cuban Culture, 1961–1987: When the Soviets Came to Stay*. Lanham, MD: Lexington Books, 2019. 246 pp.

Isabel Story's *Soviet Influence on Cuban Culture* is a welcome contribution to the fields of Cold War studies and Cuban studies. Only recently have scholars of Latin America begun to decenter the Cold War away from the superpower US-USSR economic and political conflict to explore the cultural links between the Socialist Bloc and the Global South. Within Cuban studies, most scholars have prioritized the analysis of Cuba-US cultural relations over those of Cuba-USSR, even though there were far-reaching art-exchange agreements as early as 1961 between Cuba and the Soviet Bloc. Story advances these historiographies by examining the extent to which the USSR influenced the development of revolutionary culture, focusing on the analysis of theater and visual art production between 1959 and 1986. She argues that Cuban cultural policy constantly responded to the changing needs of the revolutionary process; thus, the island's cultural links to the USSR were flexible and ambiguous. Cubans had varied perceptions of what *Soviet* meant, selectively assimilating some cultural elements from the USSR to develop a distinct form of socialism that was also grounded in Cuba's Caribbean and Latin American roots. Story suggests that Cuba's cultural policy worked to maintain full independence from the USSR and become a beacon of internationalism and anticolonization in the world.

Chapter 1 offers a general account of Cuba-USSR political and economic relations, from the early twentieth century to the dissolution of the USSR in 1991. It joins old debates about the origins of socialism in Cuba, echoing previous arguments that Cuba's turn to socialism in 1961 was not an imposition caused by USSR meddling. Instead, it was a pragmatic solution that enabled the revolutionaries to keep their revolution and its dreams alive.[1] Chapter 2, in turn, analyzes the shifting conceptualizations of socialist realism in the USSR. It argues against misconceptions that associate socialist realism mainly with Stalinist repression. Story explains that the concept was nuanced, malleable, and shaped by shifting Soviet debates about the role of culture in society.

Chapters 3 and 4 focus on Cuban cultural policy: Chapter 3 covers the period 1959–1975 and Chapter 4, the late 1970s and 1980s. Chapter 3 suggests that revolutionary culture was heterodox, inclusive, and characterized by debate until around 1965. The late 1960s and early 1970s saw an increased search for Cuban identity, a consequence of the Cuban state's need for national unity that was accompanied by the increasing institutionalization of culture. The relationship with the USSR was "subsumed by the codes of *cubanía* but within a Marxist-Leninist framework" (p. 67). This chronology is open to debate. Other scholars, such as Rainer Schultz, have argued that the "liberal" moment of the Cuban Revolution closed as early as the summer of 1960. Others situate the revolutionary leaders' drive for unity and the considerable growth of cultural institutions soon after 1959.[2] Story argues that socialist realism was not implemented systemically in Cuba, suggesting that the period known as the Quinquenio Gris (1971–1976) was not a replication of Soviet repressive cultural practice. Instead, she explains that the Quinquenio Gris was a response to the island's increased sense of isolationism, bringing a more bellicose approach to culture that viewed artists as soldiers and art as a weapon of revolution. This controversial question will require further research, given that after 1970 socialist institutionalization expanded under the guidance of Soviet advisers and the island was not experiencing increased isolation during this time. Chapter 4 focuses on the period after 1975, which Story argues was "the most 'Soviet'" moment, particularly in terms of organization and the expectations placed on public culture (p. 195). The revolutionary leadership was working to advance socialist internationalism using national and regional cultural traditions. Simultaneously, policy makers tied cultural development to social and economic progress. They increased the integration of artists into economic production with the goal of achieving cultural unity, excellence, and mass participation. Story points to a gradual move away from Soviet culture after the mid-1980s.

Chapters 5 and 6 focus on theater and visual arts production respectively, contrasting the ways in which both artistic realms developed revolutionary culture. Chapter 5 argues that theater in Cuba, as in the USSR, functioned ambiguously. It was a site of experimentation and dissemination of revolutionary ideals, and also a space of contestation and subversion. Theater could be a powerful tool for democratizing culture, but it was also a potentially destabilizing political force if improperly managed. Therefore, theater was highly monitored and had limited autonomy to push the boundaries of cultural policy. Story's assumption that theater was mostly underdeveloped in prerevolutionary Cuba is debatable. Even though the movie industry overtook theater in the early twentieth century, there was a production scene that included a highly politicized Teatro Bufo and groups such as Teatro Popular. Cuba might not have had a theater academy, but it had a developed theater infrastructure. Moreover, theater was a key area of state cultural policy during the Second Republic, including Raúl Roa's Misiones Culturales, Fulgencio Batista's Teatro—Biblioteca del Pueblo, among other programs that took theater to the rural areas of Cuba.[3]

Unlike theater, Story argues that visual art was more successful at pushing the boundaries of cultural policy through the selective mobilization of different tendencies that allowed for the promotion of Cuban cultural independence and socialist ideals simultaneously. Following the work of Luis Camnitzer, she explains that the photorealism movement was critical of both US hyperrealism and Soviet socialist realism.[4] Visual arts was a site of resistance to Soviet influence and a vehicle for building Cuba's artistic prestige internationally. Finally, chapter 7 provides a summary of the book's content. Overall, the chapters are built more on secondary literature and less on primary source analysis.

Story's book offers a bird's-eye view of the USSR's influence on Cuban cultural policy rather than narrowing in on the ways the Soviets exerted power on the ground. To further expand on her research, Story could explore important questions to unveil Cuba-USSR relations more deeply. For instance, how did the Soviets have an impact on Cuban culture through the relationships between Cubans and Soviet artists working together within cultural institutions? How was socialist realism articulated in everyday creative action? How did Eastern European poster art influence the Cuban poster movement of the 1960s? What intercultural learnings developed through the Cuba–Soviet Bloc theater coproductions of the 1980s? Who were, ultimately, the Soviets who came to stay? Nevertheless, Story's contribution offers a foundation from which to grow future studies of Cuba-USSR cultural relations.

CARY AILEEN GARCÍA YERO
Harvard University

NOTES

1. See James O'Connor, *The Origins of Socialism in Cuba* (Ithaca, NY: Cornell University Press, 1970).

2. See Rainer Schultz, "The Liberal Moment of the Revolution: Cuba's Early Educational

458 : *Book Reviews*

Reforms, 1959–1961," *Cuban Studies 49*, no. 1 (2020): 215–235; D. Benson, *Antiracism in Cuba: The Unfinished Revolution* (Chapel Hill: University of North Carolina Press, 2016); L. Guerra, *Visions of Power in Cuba* (Chapel Hill: University of North Carolina Press, 2012); R. D. Moore, *Music and Revolution* (Berkeley: University of California Press, 2006).

    3. C. A. Yero, "The State within the Arts: A Study of Cuba's Cultural Policy, 1940–1958," *Cuban Studies 47*, no. 1 (2019): 83–110.

    4. L. Camnitzer, *New Art of Cuba* (Austin: University of Texas Press, 1994).

Carmelo Mesa-Lago and Jan Svejnar, *The Cuban Economic Crisis: Its Causes and Possible Policies for a Transition.* **Miami: Václav Havel Program for Human Rights and Diplomacy, Steven J. Green School of International & Public Affairs, and Florida International University. 68 pp.**

Carmelo Mesa-Lago, reconocido experto en temas económicos cubanos se une esta vez a Jan Svejnar, un académico de larga trayectoria en los análisis sobre transición en economías centralmente planificadas, para entregar la monografía *The Cuban Economic Crisis: Its Causes and Possible Policies for a Transition*, que ofrece un análisis vigente sobre el estado actual de la economía cubana, sus causas, y posibles trayectorias futuras para la reforma económica.

    Los autores abarcan tres aspectos fundamentales en este trabajo. Primeramente, se realiza una evaluación de la situación económica de Cuba hacia fines de 2020, cuya conclusión es que se trata de la peor crisis desde el colapso de la Unión Soviética a principios de la década de los noventa, y que se observa una tendencia al agravamiento debido a los efectos de la pandemia de la COVID-19. En segundo lugar, se ofrece un dimensionamiento de las causas principales de este escenario desfavorable, indicándose que concurren cuatro factores fundamentales, el mantenimiento sin transformaciones de fondo del modelo económico de planificación central (interno), junto a otros tres de origen externo, el colapso económico de Venezuela, las sanciones de Estados Unidos bajo la administración de Donald Trump, y los efectos de la epidemia asociados al nuevo coronavirus SARS-CoV-2. La tesis es que se trata de una crisis multicausal que requiere esfuerzo e innovación de parte de la política económica. En tercer lugar, se presenta un recorrido por otras experiencias de transformación y se adelantan tres rutas diferentes para contemplar una reforma más profunda en los años siguientes.

    Este reporte contiene aspectos que vale la pena destacar, fácilmente identificables de trabajos anteriores de Mesa-Lago. En primer lugar, el disgnósitco sobre el estado actual y las causas de la crisis económica en Cuba descansa en un uso profuso de datos para justificar las tesis principales. El lector familiarizado con el tema se puede percatar que es un aporte no menor, dado que la escasez de estadísticas fiables sobre el objeto de estudio, requiere la reconstrucción y elaboración propia de las series correspondientes, y su completamiento demanda un trabajo sistemático. En segundo lugar, es siempre bienvenida la intención de ubicar las ideas principales de la monografía en el marco del debate que tiene lugar en Cuba sobre el tema en cuestión. Ello es fácilmente identificable a partir de la enorme cantidad de referencias a los principales autores de esa discusión, incluyendo a cubanos residentes o no en la isla, y figuras establecidas junto a académicos noveles.

Entre los aspectos más novedosos de la propuesta se encuentran los datos y opiniones referidos al estado de la deuda externa, la relación económica entre Cuba y Venezuela, los emergentes vínculos con Rusia, la pertinencia de recomendaciones de políticas económicas y sociales de organizaciones como la CEPAL, la evaluación concisa de las diferentes estrategias implementadas por economías de planificación central, y la formulación de propuestas concretas para la reforma sobre la base de agrupar los criterios en tres trayectorias posibles que recogen las experiencias de otros países que fueron economías de planificación central.

La lectura de la monografía sobre otras interrogantes que invitan a profundizar en aspectos relevantes. Por ejemplo, aunque se mencionan algunas diferencias respecto a los dos países asiáticos que se presentan como experiencias relevantes (geopolítica, población y extensión superficial, e importancia de la agricultura para las respectivas economías), se dejan de lado otras condicionantes que han sido abordadas por la literatura de la transición para explicar las diferencias en el desempeño económico posterior a las reformas y, especialmente, las opciones de políticas al alcance de los gobiernos. Dos de estas diferencias son especialmente relevantes para Cuba. Por un lado, tanto el éxito económico como las alternativas de políticas en estos países están estrechamente relacionados con el tamaño del sector estatal, incluyendo tanto las empresas estatales como el sector presupuestado. Este último también es un *proxy* de la profundidad de los estados de bienestar. Estos últimos, contrario a las creencias ampliamente difundidas sobre una supuesta mayor gentileza asiática, fueron y todavía son muy rudimentarios en China y Vietnam respecto a los países del centro y este de Europa. Un mayor tamaño del sector estatal obliga a que la restructuración de las empresas públicas tenga que acometerse temprano en la reforma, tanto para corregir las distorsiones en la estructura sectorial, como para evitar desequilibrios macroeconómicos profundos. En este aspecto, Cuba se parece mucho más a Europa del Este, que a China y Vietnam.

En segundo lugar, la invocación al modelo de socialismo de mercado, si bien coincide con aspectos implícitos en las propuestas de numerosos economistas cubanos contemporáneos, debía haber sido analizado con mayor rigor, dada la trayectoria que tiene en los análisis sobre los problemas de las economías centralmente planificadas. Este camino, si bien mejoró parcialmente el desempeño de un país relativamente avanzado como Hungría, también generó sus propias contradicciones. Para un debate de este tipo, hubiese sido bienvenido incorporar un análisis más riguroso de sus implicaciones. Por último, si bien posiblemente se aleja del foco de un estudio de este tipo, conviene integrar plenamente, a la hora de considerar las trayectorias futuras, la relación bidireccional entre reforma y los vínculos con Estados Unidos.

Los aspectos anteriores solo refuerzan la recomendación de su lectura y su añadidura a los mejores ejemplos dentro de la colección de trabajos en estudios económicos cubanos.

RICARDO TORRES PÉREZ
Centro de Estudios de la Economía Cubana, Universidad de La Habana

Ruth Behar, *Everything I Kept / Todo lo que guardé*. Chicago: Swan Isle Press, 2018. 99 pp.

In key moments of her career, the anthropologist Ruth Behar has gifted readers with volumes that refract the essence of a deeply felt inner life. Echoes of earlier works, such as *The Vulnerable Observer* (1996), *An Island Called Home: Returning to Jewish Cuba* (2007), and her young adult novel *Lucky Broken Girl* (2017), resound in this recent collection of poems. Mostly written twenty years earlier, when her impending fortieth birthday produced an intense "pressure of mortality" in her consciousness, Behar's poems find inspiration in the sanctuary of emotional journeys. Committed to collecting and healing the scattered, if vibrant, fragments of a Cuban identity defined as much by her grandparents' immigration to Cuba from Poland and Turkey as by her family's flight from the construction of communism after 1959, Behar invites readers to witness, if not entirely embody, a range of emotions evoked simultaneously in side-by-side translations of her words in Spanish and English. Remarkably precise at times while deliberately divergent at others, the translations stand in conversation with each other, seeking to grasp fine lines of thought, meditation, confession, and action in order to weave them into one coherent, convincing voice.

Crafted in the style of short narratives, Behar's poems have little to do with the seductively lyrical, modernist works of the Cuban poet laureate Dulce María Loynaz, whom Behar credits with awakening her own poetic voice and who generously invited Behar to read manuscripts of her poems aloud to her in the early 1990s when Behar visited Loynaz in her family's decaying Vedado mansion. However, while Loynaz, a recipient of the 1993 Miguel de Cervantes Prize and daughter of the great patriot General Enrique Loynaz del Castillo, may have spurred Behar to write, the quietly cryptic, penetratingly sad poems of *Everything I Kept / Todo lo que guardé* stand on their own. Like all volumes of poetry, the quality of some pieces suffers if extracted from the whole and read on their own. Indeed, within that dynamic lies the beauty of Behar's efforts: no one poem stands alone, often not even from its Spanish- or English-language counterpart. Rather, each meshes with and embodies the inner sanctum of the other.

Some of these poems read like suddenly revived memories: "When we lived in the mountains of Mexico, I would tremble coming out of the shower," declares the poem "Jewels": "You waited for me with two towels you had warmed by pressing them against your chest. They glowed like amber. I wore them like jewels" (65). Others, like the poem "Cuba," subtly indict the sources of hidden traumas whose meaning the child-exile gradually discovers over the course of life: "El día que partimos de Cuba el mar estaba calmado. Yo era una niña. Pensaba que estábamos de fiesta. No lloré. No llevé luto. Nadie me explicó nada. / Llegué a ser esta mujer immune a las palabras tiernas, immune a la belleza alocada de las flores en primavera, immune a tu amor" (88).

Although many of Behar's poems are conversational and some confessional, they all share the elements that poetry must have to feel relevant: honesty, rawness, and a certain unfinished dimension that leaves one hoping for more. *Everything I Kept / Todo lo que guardé* is not a book that consistently reveals the same woman, its author. Rather, it presents a protagonist at odds with her own propensity "to be more in love with things than with life itself," one who nonetheless deeply feels a bond to the rescuing power of intangibles: nature, the world, memory, love, outrage, faith, and God Him- or Herself.

In her introduction, Behar embraces phrases more typical of a nineteenth-century novelist than a twenty-first-century intellectual: "Maybe I should have kept [these poems] under the bed? Instead, I give them to you, dear reader, in the hope that my words might give you a bit of fortitude so you can embark on your own journey and come to understand the things you have kept and carried, long after they have turned to dust" (xv). Perhaps Behar's entreaty will strike some as trite; for those who keep reading, however, and know how this book builds on a lifetime of truth telling, *Everything I Kept / Todo lo que guardé* holds many gifts, easily within reach.

LILLIAN GUERRA

Contributors

Grethel Domenech Hernández es maestra en historia por la Universidad Iberoamericana, CDMX. Es estudiante del doctorado en historia de la misma universidad, y autora del libro *Rehabilitación de la memoria histórica: Lunes de Revolución en el campo intelectual cubano (1959–1961)* (2017).

Carlos García Pleyán es sociólogo cubano y doctor en ciencias técnicas, profesor e investigador titular. Trabajó durante treinta años en el campo del urbanismo y el ordenamiento territorial en el Instituto de Planificación Física y otros organismos, y diez en la Agencia Suiza para el Desarrollo y la Cooperación, COSUDE. Fue profesor en la Universidad Tecnológica de la Habana y la Universidad Politécnica de Cataluña en Barcelona.

María A. Gutiérrez Bascón holds a PhD in Hispanic and Luso-Brazilian studies from the University of Chicago, where she studied post-1990 literary, filmic, and architectural imaginations of the city of Havana. Currently, she is a postdoctoral researcher at the University of Helsinki, where she researches recent urban transformations in Havana.

Joseph R. Hartman is assistant professor of art history and Latinx and Latin American studies at the University of Missouri, Kansas City. Hartman's book, *Dictator's Dreamscape: How Architecture and Vision Built Machado's Cuba and Invented Modern Havana* (2019), focuses on the intersections of architecture, visual culture, and politics in Cuba and the United States insular empire during the twentieth century. Hartman's current work examines the visual and spatial culture of hurricanes in the greater Caribbean.

Ray Hernández-Durán (PhD, University of Chicago, 2005) is professor of art history in the Department of Art at the University of New Mexico in Albuquerque. His primary courses focus on Ibero-American colonial art and architecture with additional specializations in nineteenth-century Latin American art, art of Africa and the African diaspora, and museum studies. His research interests include eighteenth-century painting in New Spain and nineteenth-century Mexican museology and historiography, exemplified by his book, *The Academy of San Carlos and Mexican Art History: Politics, History, and Art in Nineteenth-Century Mexico* (Routledge, 2017).

Aaron Coy Moulton is assistant professor of Latin American history at Stephen F. Austin State University. He has published in Costa Rica, the Dominican Republic, Guatemala, Mexico, and Venezuela with English-language articles earning the Southeastern Council of Latin American Studies Sturgis Leavitt Award and the Conference on Latin American History Antonine Tibesar Prize. His current manuscript, *Caribbean Blood*

Pacts: The Negotiated Cold War against the Guatemalan Revolution, 1944–1954, reveals how Guatemalan exiles, Caribbean Basin dictators, transnational corporations, and British intelligence put into motion what would become the US government's Operation PBSUCCESS, which in 1954 overthrew Guatemala's democratically elected government.

Paul Niell is associate professor in the Department of Art History at Florida State University. He teaches courses in Spanish colonial art history, the visual culture of the African diaspora, and Caribbean cultural landscapes. He is the coeditor, with Stacie G. Widdifield, of *Buen Gusto and Classicism in the Visual Cultures of Latin America, 1780–1910* and the author of *Urban Space as Heritage in Late Colonial Cuba: Classicism and Dissonance on the Plaza de Armas of Havana, 1754–1828*.

Enrique S. Pumar is Fay Boyle University Professor of Sociology at Santa Clara University. His research focuses on inclusive national development and governance and evaluating educational policies. In addition to his academic positions, Dr. Pumar serves on several academic editorial boards and as chair of the Sociology of Development Section of the American Sociological Association. For the past five years he chaired the Department of Sociology. He now heads the Global Migration and Refugee Studies Program at Santa Clara. In 2017, he was a Fulbright Scholar at the Universidad de Valladolid (Spain) and a visiting lecturer at the Instituto de Estudios Ecleciásticos Padre Félix Valera in La Habana (Cuba).

Martín Ribadero es doctor por la Universidad de Buenos Aires y profesor de historia por la misma casa de estudios. Actualmente es investigador y profesor regular en la Universidad Nacional de San Martín. Es autor del libro *Tiempo de profetas. Ideas, debates y labor cultural de la izquierda nacional de Jorge Abelardo Ramos (1945–1962)* (2017) y ha publicado en numerosas revistas académicas de Francia, Alemania, Chile, Uruguay y Argentina.

Fredo Rivera is assistant professor of art history at Grinnell College, where they teach classes on modern and contemporary architecture and urban visual culture, as well as the art of the Americas, with a focus on the Caribbean. They have worked on numerous curatorial and performance projects and is currently project leader for Haitian Art: A Digital Crossroads, a digital humanities project based at Grinnell College Libraries and the Waterloo Center for the Arts. Their current research includes publications on art and architecture in modern Cuba, Haitian art, photography and visual culture, and contemporary Miami.

Rafael Rojas Gutiérrez es licenciado en filosofía por la Universidad de La Habana y doctor en historia por El Colegio de México. Es profesor e investigador del Centro de Estudios Históricos de El Colegio de México y director de la revista *Historia Mexicana*. Es miembro de número de la Academia Mexicana de la Historia. Su último libro es *La epopeya del sentido: Ensayos sobre el concepto de Revolución en México, 1910–1940* (México, Colmex, 2022)

Juan Alberto Salazar Rebolledo es estudiante de maestría en historia en la Universidad Nacional Autónoma de México. El título de su tesis es "Las perspectivas intelectuales mexicanas sobre el triunfo de la Revolución Cubana desde la plataforma universitaria de *Cuadernos Americanos* y la *Revista de la Universidad de México* (1959–1961)." Ha publicado artículos académicos en libros colectivos y en espacios como la *Oxford Research Encyclopedia of Latin American History.*

Elisa Servín es doctora en historia por la Universidad Iberoamericana y profesora en investigadora de la Dirección de Estudios Históricos del INAH. Es autora de los libros *La oposición política: Otra cara del siglo XX mexicano* (2006) y *Del nacionalismo al neoliberalismo, 1940–1994* (2010).

Lee Sessions studies the intersections of natural history, art, and sociopolitical power in the nineteenth-century Caribbean basin. She is currently a Mellon Fellow at the Humanities Institute of the New York Botanical Garden, where she is researching the relationship between botany, state power, and race in Cuba before and after the Spanish-American War. She received her PhD from Yale University and her MA from the Institute of Fine Arts, and she has worked at the Brooklyn Museum and at Lohin Geduld Gallery in New York.

Helena Solo-Gabriele is a professor of environmental engineering at the University of Miami, Coral Gables, Florida. Her research focuses on water quality and evaluating the relationships between the environment and human health. She has served as president of the Association of Cuban American Engineers and of the Association for the Study of the Cuban Economy. In these capacities she has collaborated with colleagues to evaluate water quality issues in Cuba, has contributed to student-led studies that evaluate Cuba's water infrastructure as well as to organizing university-level student competitions that evaluate all aspects of Cuba's infrastructure.

Maile Speakman is a PhD candidate in American studies at Yale University, where she ethnographically researches the social, spatial, economic, and affective impact of US technology platforms in Havana. She has an MA in Latin American studies from Tulane University, where she studied Havana's queer theory networks. She also attended the University of Arts of Cuba (ISA) in 2007.

David Tenorio is assistant professor in the Department of Hispanic Languages and Literatures and a faculty affiliate with the Gender, Sexuality, and Women's Studies Program, the Graduate Program in Cultural Studies, and the Center for Latin American Studies at the University of Pittsburgh. He also served as co-chair of LASA's Sexualities Section and as newsletter editor for the Caribbean Studies Association.

Joseph B. Treaster is a professor, journalist, and author at the University of Miami. He began at the university as the Knight Chair in Cross-Cultural Communication, specializing in the environment. He coordinates the Writing for the Digital Age program. Treaster worked for more than thirty years as a reporter and foreign correspondent for the *New York Times* in New York, Asia, the Middle East, and Latin America and continues to write for the paper. He has worked in more than one hundred countries, covering wars, natural disasters, the environment, human rights, politics, diplomacy, business, and everyday life. Treaster is the author of three books and has written on international issues for *The Atlantic, Harper's, Rolling Stone,* and other national magazines. He contributes to newspapers, academic journals, and online publications (treaster@miami.edu).

Roberto Zurbano Torres es ensayista, crítico cultural y activista contra el racismo. Es miembro de la UNEAC y de El Club del Espendrú; es también investigador en el Centro de Investigaciones Literarias de Casa de las Américas. Fue editor fundador de *Catauro: Revista Cubana de Antropología* y director del Fondo Editorial de Casa de las Américas. Es experto en literaturas afrocaribeñas, músicas alternativas y políticas raciales. Ha sido profesor y conferencista invitado en centros culturales y académicos de Estados Unidos, Canadá, República Dominicana, Brasil, Alemania y Reino Unido. Dos veces ganó el Premio de Periodismo Cultural. Ostenta la Orden por la Cultura Nacional.

On the cover:

I have said many times that Alexis Esquivel Bermúdez (born in Pinar del Río, 1968) is a historian who paints. He is a colleague, a fellow historian. It would take me dozens of pages to explain what he captures in several square inches of canvas. His works frequently address established, sacred historical narratives, contesting them, offering alternative interpretations and visions. At the center of these revisionist approaches, of these historiographical canvases and installations, are concerns over racial justice and inclusion. Esquivel revisits the nation from and through the experiences, dreams, anxieties, and demands of Cubans of African descent. Official histories depict Afro-Cubans as equal members of the national community, but they continue to suffer exclusions and barriers grounded on white supremacy in their daily lives.

Esquivel is a prominent member of the Queloides generation, the group of artists concerned with issues of racism and inclusion that coalesced around the curatorial project of the same name, that he helped create in 1997. As he wrote in the brochure for *Queloides I Parte* (1997), an exhibit that he curated with Omar Pascual Castillo, in collaboration with Julio Moracén, although Cuban art offered many critical perspectives on the country's social and political problems, questions of race received limited attention. When they did, it was through academic discourses centered on cultural questions, through anthropology and folklore: "At no time did they talk about things that you discussed with your family, things that happened in your own street and shaped your everyday life."

These "things" (that *algo*, in Spanish) that was silenced, ignored, or contained, referred to white supremacy, to racial stratification, to structural racism "as a continuing process in the present." But Esquivel's interests are not just denunciatory. He wants to highlight how dominant, official historical narratives perpetuate structures of subordination and to invite critical reassessments of such narratives. His *Carlos Manuel de Céspedes y la libertad de los negros* (Carlos Manuel de Céspedes and the freedom of blacks), originally painted in 1993, remade in 2021 in a much larger format, is a prime example of this revisionist approach. For Cubans, Céspedes is remembered as the "father of the homeland" and as the liberator of slaves. The official narrative conveniently forgets that he was a slave owner who entertained serious doubts about black citizenship and civilization—the very anxieties that Esquivel captures in his painting. Esquivel's Céspedes is a prisoner of his own racist anxieties and insecurities, which render people of African descent inadequate for political participation and citizenship. And that, he tells us, is how the Cuban homeland was created.

On the cover: Alexis Esquivel, *Carlos Manuel de Céspedes y la libertad de los negros*, 1993–2021, acrylic on canvas, 176 x 115 cm.